G000144266

TURKEY: ECONOMIC REFORM AND ACCESSION TO THE EUROPEAN UNION

TURKEY: ECONOMIC REFORM AND ACCESSION TO THE EUROPEAN UNION

Editors

Bernard Hoekman and Sübidey Togan

A copublication of the World Bank and the Centre for Economic Policy Research

© 2005 The International Bank for Reconstruction and Development / The World Bank
1818 H Street, NW
Washington, DC 20433
Telephone 202-473-1000
Internet www.worldbank.org
E-mail feedback@worldbank.org

All rights reserved.
A copublication of the World Bank and the Centre for Economic Policy Research

1   2   3   4   08   07   06   05

The findings, interpretations, and conclusions expressed herein are those of the author(s) and do not necessarily reflect the views of the Board of Executive Directors of the World Bank or the governments they represent.

The World Bank does not guarantee the accuracy of the data included in this work. The boundaries, colors, denominations, and other information shown on any map in this work do not imply any judgment on the part of the World Bank concerning the legal status of any territory or the endorsement or acceptance of such boundaries.

Rights and Permissions

The material in this work is copyrighted. Copying and/or transmitting portions or all of this work without permission may be a violation of applicable law. The World Bank encourages dissemination of its work and will normally grant permission promptly.

For permission to photocopy or reprint any part of this work, please send a request with complete information to the Copyright Clearance Center, Inc., 222 Rosewood Drive, Danvers, MA 01923, USA, telephone 978-750-8400, fax 978-750-4470, www.copyright.com.

All other queries on rights and licenses, including subsidiary rights, should be addressed to the Office of the Publisher, World Bank, 1818 H Street NW, Washington, DC 20433, USA, fax 202-522-2422, e-mail pubrights@worldbank.org.

Cover: Design by Tomoko Hirata. Photographs courtesy of the Ministry of Culture and Tourism of Turkey.

Library of Congress Cataloging-in-Publication Data

Turkey: economic reform and accession to the European Union / edited by Sübidey Togan, Bernard Hoekman.
   p. cm.—(Trade and development series)
  Includes bibliographical references and index.
  ISBN 0-8213-5932-0 (pbk.)
1. Turkey—Economic policy. 2. Turkey—Economic conditions. 3. European Union—Membership. 4. International economic integration. I. Togan, Sübidey. II. Hoekman, Bernard M., 1959- . III. Series.
HC492.T8576 2005
330.9561'04—dc22   2004063747

ISBN 0-8213-5932-0
E-ISBN 0-8213-6084-1
DOI 10.1596/978-0-8213-5932-0

CONTENTS

TABLES

ACKNOWLEDGMENTS

The essays in this volume, with the exception of the last three, were discussed at the conference "Turkey: Towards EU Accession," held May 10–11, 2003, in Ankara, Turkey. Among the participants were economists from Turkey, Britain, Italy, the Netherlands, Central and Eastern European countries, the World Bank, and the Organisation for Economic Cooperation and Development (OECD). The mixed composition of the participants—drawn from various Turkish universities; official agencies in Turkey, including the Ministry of Foreign Affairs, Ministry of Agriculture, Ministry of Environment, Ministry of Labor, General Secretariat for EU Affairs, Undersecretariat of Treasury, Undersecretariat of Foreign Trade, State Planning Organization, Central Bank, Banking Regulatory and Supervisory Agency, Telecommunications Board, and Energy Board; European University Institute; Erasmus University; the World Bank; and the OECD—allowed a wide-ranging discussion of the issues.

The project was supported by the World Bank, European Commission, Robert Schuman Centre for Advanced Studies at the European University Institute, and Bilkent University. We would like to express our appreciation to the sponsors of the project. We are particularly grateful to Ajay Chhibber and James Parks of the World Bank, Giacomo Luciani and Helen Wallace of the Robert Schuman Centre, Hansjörg Kretschmer and Vincent Rey at the European Union Representation of the European Commission to Turkey, and Ali Doğramacı of Bilkent University.

As editors of the volume, we would like to express our gratitude to all the participants in the 2003 conference, including the contributors to this volume and their discussants, for their valuable contributions. We also are grateful to the three referees who provided constructive suggestions for revision of the chapters, to Ines Garcia-Thoumi for helping to find the resources to allow this book to be published, to Rebecca Martin for her assistance in preparing the manuscript, to Thierry Verdier, Riccardo Faini, and Stephen Yeo for their support in co-publishing this volume with CEPR, and to Mary Fisk, Santiago Pombo-Bejarano, and Stephen McGroarty in the Office of the Publisher for their management of the publication process. This volume provides readers with insights into selected aspects of Turkish accession to the European Union, and we hope it will inspire similar studies.

Disclaimer

All opinions expressed in this volume are strictly personal and should not be attributed to any government, official agency, or institution with which authors are or have been affiliated.

Bernard Hoekman and Sübidey Togan

LIST OF CONTRIBUTORS

Erkan Akdemir	Telecommunications Authority of Turkey
İzak Atiyas	Sabancı University, Istanbul
Richard Baldwin	Graduate Institute of International Studies, Geneva, and Centre for Economic Policy and Research (CEPR), London
Erdem Başçı	Central Bank of Turkey
Ahmet Bayener	Ministry of Agriculture and Rural Affairs, Ankara
Alberto Biancardi	Acquirente Unico Spa, Italy
Saadettin Doğan	Undersecreteriat of Foreign Trade, Ankara
Mark Dutz	World Bank
Hasan Ersel	Sabancı University, Istanbul
Harry Flam	Institute for International Economic Studies, Stockholm
Joseph Francois	Erasmus University, Rotterdam, and CEPR
Bernard Hoekman	Groupe d'Economie Mondiale, Institut d'Etudes Politiques, Paris; World Bank; and CEPR
Gareth Locksley	World Bank
Anil Markandya	World Bank
Maria Rita Mazzanti	Italian Electricity and Gas Regulatory Authority
John Nash	World Bank
Hüsamettin Nebioğlu	Undersecretariat of Foreign Trade, Ankara
Şule Özler	University of California at Los Angeles
Ceyla Pazarbaşıoğlu	International Monetary Fund
Erol Taymaz	Middle East Technical University, Ankara
Sübidey Togan	Bilkent University, Ankara
Melek Us	Association of Dairy Beef and Food Manufacturers and Producers in Turkey
Mika Widgrén	Turku School of Economics, Turku, Finland, and CEPR
Kamil Yılmaz	Koç University, Istanbul

ACRONYMS AND ABBREVIATIONS

ACC	agricultural credit cooperatives	IACS	Integrated Administration and Control System
BEPG	Broad Economic Policy Guidelines		
BIPS	border inspection posts	IMF	International Monetary Fund
CAP	Common Agricultural Policy	JAP	joint assessment paper
CCT	Common Customs Tariffs	MARA	Ministry of Agriculture and Rural Affairs
CEE	Central and Eastern European (Countries)		
		M&A	merger and acquisition
CEEP	European Centre of Enterprises with Public Participation	MFN	most-favored nation
		MRA	Mutual Recognition Agreement
CEN	Comité Européen de Normalisation	MRP	Mutual Recognition Principle
CENELEC	Comité Européen de Normalisation Electrotechnique	MTR	mid-term review
		NBI	normalized Banzhaf index
COM	Common Organization of the Market	ncb	national central bank
CPI	consumer price index	OECD	Organisation for Economic Co-operation and Development
CUD	Customs Union Decision		
EAGGF	European Agricultural Guidance and Guarantee Fund	PEP	Preaccession Economic Programme
		PPP	purchasing power parity
ECSC	European Coal and Steel Community	PSBR	public sector borrowing requirements
EEA	European Economic Area	RER	real exchange rate
EFTA	European Free Trade Association	SDR	special drawing rights
EMRA	Energy Market Regulatory Authority	SEE	state economic enterprise
EMU	Economic and Monetary Union	SITC	Standard Identification Trade Classification
ESA	European System of Accounts		
ECB	European Central Bank	SPO	state Planning Organization (Turkey)
ECOFIN	Council for Economic and Financial Affairs		
		SSI	Shapley-Shubik index
EONIA	European Over-Night Index Average	TBT	technical barriers to trade
EPL	employment-protection legislation	TEKEL	Tobacco and Tobacco Products, Salt, and Alcohol Industry
ESCB	European System of Central Banks		
ETUC	European Trade Union Confederation	TFP	total factor productivity
		TL	Turkish lira
EU	European Union	TSE	Turkish Standards Institute
FDI	foreign direct investment	TUBITAK	Turkish Scientific and Technical Research Institute
FTA	free trade agreement		
FX	foreign exchange	TT	Türk Telecom
GATT	General Agreement on Tariffs and Trade	UME	National Metrology Institute
		UNCTAD	United Nations Conference on Trade and Development
GDP	gross domestic product		
GFCF	gross fixed capital formation	UNICE	Union of Industrial and Employers' Confederations of Europe
GNP	gross national product		
HICP	Harmonised Index of Consumer Prices	VAT	value-added system
		WTO	World Trade Organization

OVERVIEW

Turkey first applied for associate membership in the European Union (EU)—then the European Economic Community (EEC)—in 1959. The application resulted in an association agreement in 1963, whereby Turkey and the EU would, in principle, gradually create a customs union by 1995 at the latest. The customs union was seen as a step toward full EU membership at an unspecified future date. The EU unilaterally granted Turkey preferential tariffs and financial assistance, but the process of staged, mutual reductions in tariffs and nontariff barriers was delayed because of the economic and political conditions in Turkey. After pursuing inward-oriented development strategies throughout the 1960s and 1970s, Turkey switched over to a more outward-oriented policy stance in 1980. The opening up of the economy was pursued in part with the aim of integrating the country into the EU.

Turkey applied for full membership in the EU in 1987. The response in 1990 was that accession negotiations could not be undertaken at the time because the EU was engaged in major internal changes, and that matters were further complicated by developments in Eastern Europe and the Soviet Union. However, the EU was prepared to extend and deepen economic relations without explicitly rejecting the possibility of full membership at a future date. Thus the plans for a customs union were revived.

On March 6, 1995, it was agreed at an Association Council meeting in Brussels that a customs union would be created between Turkey and the EU as of January 1, 1996, to be fully phased in by 2001.[1] As a result, Turkey currently imposes no quotas or tariffs on imports of industrial goods from the EU. The associated liberalization for Turkey has been estimated as implying a 7 percent average reduction in tariffs (Harrison, Rutherford, and Tarr 1997). The major exception to free trade is agriculture—neither party liberalized completely. The average tariff rate on imports of agricultural commodities from the EU is 21.4 percent. Agricultural trade is also subject to tariff quotas and price regulation, which have produced a high degree of protection in both the EU and Turkey. Thus, in terms of further liberalization of merchandise trade, accession will primarily have an effect on agriculture.

A major development under the customs union was that Turkey implemented the European Union's Common Customs Tariff on imports of industrial goods from third countries. It has also adopted most of the preferential trade agreements concluded by the EU, as well as other measures covered by the EU's commercial policy (such as antidumping). Turkey has adopted EU competition policies, established a Competition Board, adopted EU rules on protection of intellectual and industrial property rights, set up a Patent Office, and initiated a process of harmonizing technical standards for industrial products and strengthening internal conformity assessment and market surveillance structures.

On December 10–11, 1999, the European Council meeting held in Helsinki produced a breakthrough in Turkey-EU relations. At Helsinki, Turkey was officially recognized as a candidate state for accession, on an equal footing with other candidate states. The result was the creation of a so-called Accession Partnership with the EU, which means that the EU is working together with Turkey to enable it to adopt the *acquis communautaire*, the legal framework of the EU. But, in contrast to other candidate countries, Turkey did not receive a timetable for accession. After the approval of the Accession Partnership by the Council and the adoption of the Framework Regulation on February 26, 2001, the Turkish government announced on March 19, 2001, its own National Program for the adoption of the *acquis communautaire*. Progress toward accession continues along the path set by the National Program.

In late 2004 another milestone was reached with the recommendation of the European Commission that the European Council endorse the launching of formal accession negotiations with Turkey and establish a timetable for accession (European

Commission 2004b). In December 2002, the Copenhagen European Council had concluded that "if the European Council in December 2004, on the basis of a report and a recommendation from the Commission, decides that Turkey fulfills the Copenhagen political criteria, the European Union will open accession negotiations with Turkey without delay." At a December 2004 Council meeting, it was decided to launch negotiations.

Although the process has now been launched, great uncertainties continue to prevail about whether Turkey will be able to achieve its goal of accession to the EU.[2] Some of these uncertainties are economic, and they are the subject of this book. Other uncertainties are more political in nature. Some of these are in the hands of the Turkish government—for example, realization of the EU political and human rights criteria formalized by the European Council in Copenhagen in 1993, and acceptance of restrictions on immigration post-accession.[3] Others are not. Arguably, the greatest uncertainty is whether EU governments and societies are willing to accept a large secular but nonetheless Muslim state as part of the EU. Time will reveal the ultimate outcome. What matters in the short to medium term is the impact that continued progress toward achieving the conditions for membership will have on Turkey. The EU is the focal point for reforms in a large number of policy areas, and the preaccession process, which has been ongoing for several years, is a unique experiment in using international harmonization as a tool in implementing a comprehensive reform strategy.

Much has been achieved by Turkey in recent years, including progress in implementing the customs union—which covers many policy areas, not just trade but also nontariff barriers and competition policies—despite severe macroeconomic shocks and instability. The 1999 European Council decision affirming that Turkey is a candidate for membership was followed by far-reaching constitutional and legislative reforms, ranging from improved civil liberties and human rights to enhanced civilian control of the military. A Department for EU Affairs was set up in 2000 to coordinate all of Turkey's policies related to the preaccession process. A series of constitutional and legislative changes were adopted during 2001–04, some of them major, as well as numerous regulations, decrees, and circulars detailing how these reforms should be implemented. A Reform Monitoring Group, under the chairmanship of the deputy prime minister responsible for human rights, was established to supervise the reforms across the board and to solve practical problems, including bureaucratic inertia and bottlenecks at both the central government and state government levels (European Commission 2004c).

However, clearly much remains to be done on both the macro- and the microeconomic fronts. Accession entails going beyond the customs union for manufactures and integrating the markets for agriculture, services, and factors (labor, investment, and capital flows). Until now, liberalization of trade has been restricted to industrial goods. Because agriculture accounts for about 14 percent of Turkey's gross domestic product (GDP) and services 60 percent, the liberalization of trade to date has thus had limited implications for three-quarters of economic activity. Although this statement is an exaggeration because autonomous reforms have been implemented in these sectors of the economy, joining the EU will require Turkey to adopt and implement the whole body of EU legislation—the *acquis communautaire*—in all areas.

The purpose of this volume is to highlight certain aspects of Turkish accession, with an emphasis on the implications of integrating fully into the single market, adopting the *acquis,* and meeting the Maastricht Treaty criteria for fiscal and monetary policy.[4] The contributors to this volume focus primarily on the impact of accession on Turkey—only two chapters consider the possible impacts on the EU. One reason for this emphasis is that in size Turkey is small relative to the EU as a whole. Turkey's GDP in 2004 was €240 billion compared with the combined GDP of the EU25 of €10.2 trillion.[5] Thus Turkey would account for only 2.3 percent of the EU's total output. Most of the adjustment burden and potential benefits therefore pertain to Turkey. One major exception, however, is related to Turkey's large population: the free movement of workers could have a substantial impact on the EU in both economic and political terms, and the large population of Turkey may also have implications for decision making in a larger EU. The outcome of accession talks on the movement of people is very important not only for the EU but also for

Turkey, because the net benefits of accession will depend on the conditions under which Turkey may accede to the EU.

Although the primary interest in this volume is to assess what accession may mean for Turkey and to gauge how far along Turkey is toward meeting the *acquis,* the Turkish case is also relevant for other countries that may seek to use a strategy of "deep integration" with a large, developed country or common market as a focal point and mechanism for undertaking both trade-related and regulatory reforms. Increasingly, developing countries are negotiating deeper forms of regional integration agreements with high-income trading partners. Even though most of these agreements do not come close to the depth of cooperation entailed by accession to the EU—and in some sectors such as agriculture the accession process is unique in that it implies integration into a common policy involving direct subsidies and managed trade— close study of the implications of seeking to emulate the *acquis* should be of interest to other countries contemplating the design of integration efforts.

The volume is divided into four parts:

- the macroeconomic dimensions of EU accession for Turkey
- sectoral analyses of the effects of integration into the EU (adoption of the *acquis*) for the agriculture, manufacturing, services, and network sectors
- the economic challenges of accession for Turkey's labor market, investment framework, and environmental policy
- an assessment of the net impact for the Turkish economy as a whole of the various changes implied by adoption of the *acquis* in the areas covered by the other parts of the volume, complemented by analyses of the likely implications for the EU in three central areas: European decision making and voting after Turkish accession; international transactions, both trade with and inward migration from Turkey; and the EU budget.

This introduction begins by summarizing the themes and key findings emerging from the chapters that follow. It then briefly discusses the likely impacts of Turkey's accession on the EU, and it concludes with a discussion of lessons for other developing countries that can be drawn from Turkey's efforts to date to bring its policies into alignment with the *acquis.*

Macroeconomic Developments and Prospects

From 1990 to 2000, economic crises began to affect the Turkish economy with growing frequency. Periods of rapid economic expansion alternated with periods of equally rapid decline. Inflation during 1990–2000 fluctuated between 55 and 106 percent, for an average rate of 75 percent. Currently, Turkey is in the midst of a determined campaign to turn around decades of weak performance stemming from pervasive structural rigidities and weak public finances. The past few years have witnessed three major attempts at addressing underlying weaknesses. The first, during 2000, was under the three-year stand-by agreement with the International Monetary Fund (IMF), initiated in December 1999 after a significant drop in output mostly caused by external factors, including the 1999 earthquake. Despite some notable achievements, a worsening current account and a weak banking system led to a liquidity crisis in late 2000. This crisis turned into a full-blown banking crisis in February 2001, in which the government responded by abandoning the crawling peg regime and floating the currency. In May 2001, the IMF increased its assistance under a new stand-by arrangement. Just as the revised program was beginning to show results, the terrorist attacks of September 11 in the United States triggered the reemergence of serious financing problems. In February 2002, the IMF approved a new three-year stand-by credit agreement for Turkey to support the government's economic program. With the implementation of the stabilization program, Turkey envisaged a gradual but steady improvement in its economic conditions. In August 2004, Turkey approached the IMF for what it hoped would be a final three-year stand-by agreement that will serve as an exit program from instability and excessive debt.

The economic stabilization programs proved successful at combating inflation, which fell from 54.7 percent during 2000–01 to 10.6 percent in 2004 because of efforts to maintain fiscal and monetary discipline. According to the Turkish State Planning Organization (SPO), the fiscal deficit during 2001 amounted to 16.4 percent of the gross national product (GNP)—and 20.9 percent of GNP, according to the IMF definition. During 2004, the fiscal deficit was brought back down to 6.2 percent and the government ran a primary surplus of 6.9 percent of GNP. After contracting by 9.5 percent in 2001, real GNP expanded by 7.9 percent in 2002, 5.9 percent in 2003, and 9.9 percent in 2004. The growth was driven by strong productivity gains and by robust private consumption, investment, and exports, and it has not been hindered by cuts in government consumption and investment. The unemployment rate fell from 11.5 percent in the first quarter of 2002 to 10.3 percent in 2004, and the average interest rate on government debt declined from 63.8 percent in 2001 to 25.7 percent during 2004. Ratios of debt to GNP are still high, but they have been falling. The net public debt-to-GNP ratio has decreased from 90.5 percent in 2001 to 63.5 percent in 2004. This decline reflects significant income growth during 2002–04, attainment of sizable primary surpluses over the last three years, and appreciation of the real exchange rate (RER).

Although these are positive developments, it is too early to determine to what extent the rebound reflects a transition to sustainable growth. Substantial risks remain. First, during 2002–04 the RER appreciated to what is arguably an unsustainable level. Although the appreciation of the RER helped to reduce the inflation rate and the debt-to-GDP ratio, it led to a widening current account deficit. The annual deficit in 2004 reached US$15.4 billion,[6] and the current account-deficit-to-GDP ratio increased to 5.1 percent. Because foreign direct investment (FDI) inflows remain weak, the deficit is funded by additional foreign debt, raising concerns about the sustainability of the current account. Second, the public sector debt remains far too high for comfort. Assuming trend economic growth of 5 percent and a primary fiscal surplus of 6.5 percent of GDP, the debt ratio will fall over time as long as real interest rates remain below 15 percent. Currently, the real rates on domestic debt are about 11 percent. But shocks to credibility could easily push them higher and lead to concerns about the sustainability of fiscal policy.[7] A primary fiscal surplus of 6.5 percent remains the minimum

required for safety. Third, the labor force participation rate declined from about 57 percent at the beginning of the 1990s to 48.7 percent in 2004, mainly because of the discouragement of job seekers. The policy of keeping the primary fiscal surplus at 6.5 percent of GDP over the coming years will constrain the use of fiscal policy to drive down the unemployment rate in the economy. But unless employment growth picks up, continually high unemployment and low participation rates could undermine the social and political support for reforms.

As discussed in greater depth by Sübidey Togan and Hasan Ersel in chapter 1, the macroeconomic challenges for Turkey remain substantial. Besides solving the problems summarized in this introduction, during the preaccession period Turkey needs to reduce its annual inflation rate to about 3 percent, keep the debt-to-GDP ratio below 60 percent, and achieve stable growth in real income over time. Unless Turkey's growth performance does improve, its real per capita GDP will never converge with the EU average and the accession of Turkey might create unmanageable stresses. In addition, the authors note that to avoid the risk of speculative attacks on its currency over the coming years, Turkey should continue to follow policies aimed at establishing a sound fiscal framework, a robust banking sector, and sustained price stability. Turkey also must take measures to increase the national savings rate from its rather low level of 22 percent in 2004 (China's savings rate is 44 percent) and reverse the appreciation of the real exchange rate. To attain sustainability of the current account, the real exchange rate has to depreciate gradually over time to its long-run equilibrium level. After accession, Turkey will be expected to join the Exchange Rate Mechanism (ERM II) for at least two years and to meet the Maastricht conditions for monetary and fiscal convergence before a bid for membership in the European Economic and Monetary Union (EMU) is considered. Once admitted to the EMU, Turkey would replace its domestic currency with the euro at an irrevocably fixed exchange rate, confer the bulk of its reserves to the European Central Bank, and be bound by the Stability and Growth Pact. Togan and Ersel argue that for Turkey the problem is not how to stay out of the EMU but, to the contrary, how to reap the net benefits expected of monetary integration by fulfilling the Maastricht criteria as soon as possible. Finally, the authors note that the benefits of integration can only be derived at some cost, and the costs of fulfilling the Maastricht criteria, including the conditions for sustainability of the current account when estimated by expected output losses, could turn out to be quite substantial.

Sectoral Reform Challenges

Achieving and sustaining macroeconomic stability will depend importantly on structural reforms, especially removal and reduction of subsidies and price controls, and the imposition of hard budget constraints on enterprises owned by the public sector. Agriculture has been a heavily distorted sector of the economy, accounting for a significant share of the public sector deficit. The banking sector was at the heart of the 2001 crisis—better regulation and noninterference in lending decisions are needed to reduce the probability of another crisis requiring bailouts or recapitalization of the system. Privatization of state-owned firms is the most direct means of imposing hard budget constraints. These and many other issues are addressed in the sectoral chapters that explore the effects of integration into the EU on agriculture and on the manufacturing, services, and network industries.

Agricultural Markets and Incomes

In chapter 2, Sübidey Togan, Ahmet Bayener, and John Nash study the impact of EU accession on Turkey's agricultural markets and incomes. In Turkey, agriculture accounts for a large share of total output (14 percent) and employment (33 percent). The corresponding figures for the EU15 are 1.7 percent and 4.3 percent. In absolute numbers, Turkey employs about the same number of people in agriculture as the EU15, or more than 7 million. Trade in agricultural products between the EU and Turkey is a relatively small part of their total trade, because it is not part of the customs union and so is subject to duties, quotas, and price regulations. Turkey applies high specific duties to the commodities supported by the EU's Common Agricultural Policy (CAP): cereals and processed cereals, sugar and sugar products, dairy products, and meat. Olive oil is also highly pro-

tected. Turkish exports of vegetables and fruits receive export subsidies. The EU, by contrast, has granted imports from Turkey preferential treatment. Import barriers exist mostly in the form of tariff-quota schemes, in which imports within the quota benefit from preferential treatment. Togan and his colleagues estimate that about 70 percent of imports from Turkey enter the EU duty-free and are not subject to any other import barriers. As a result, most of the adjustment after integration of Turkish agriculture into the CAP will fall on Turkey.

Agricultural support has been important in Turkey, imposing a large burden on taxpayers. In 2003 the total support of agriculture, including the higher prices paid by consumers, was equivalent to 4.4 percent of GDP (OECD 2004a). This figure is much higher than the comparable one for agriculture in the EU—1.3 percent of GDP. These numbers suggest that Turkey's accession to the EU is likely to have important social, distributional, and political effects, unless these transfers are maintained under a common agricultural policy, which is unlikely. Indeed, adoption of CAP-type policies—something Turkey is already in the process of doing—will reduce the overall level of support, even if Turkey becomes eligible for the current CAP levels of financial support.

Since 1993, the CAP has been gradually shifting away from price support to income support, with the result that prices in the EU are now closer (but still above) world market–clearing prices and farmers are compensated by direct income payments. The structure of the CAP is such that it favors the main agricultural products (and farmers) of the original six EU members: Belgium, Germany, France, Italy, Luxembourg, and the Netherlands. Those products are grains, sugar beets, dairy products, and beef. Fruits, vegetables, poultry, and pork—important products of the newer, southern members—receive less or no support. In preparing for the accession of the Central and Eastern European (CEE) countries, the EU decided that farmers from the CEE countries would not be excluded from direct income support payments, but that such payments would be lower: equivalent to 25, 30, and 35 percent of the system prevailing in 2004–06. After 2006, direct payments will be increased gradually in order to achieve parity with the original EU15 in 2013.

Turkish agriculture will confront major reforms in the preaccession period. In Turkey, the most important part of agricultural policy has been price support. State economic enterprises and agricultural sales cooperatives have been commissioned to buy cereals, tobacco, tea, and sugar beet from farmers at prices determined by the government. These prices, which are higher than world market prices, have been protected by import tariffs. The second most important component of Turkey's agricultural policy is the various subsidies, grants, and exemptions lowering the cost of inputs, including capital, fertilizer, seed, pesticides, and water. The output of tobacco, hazelnut, tea, and sugar beet production has been controlled in various ways. Services to farmers, such as research, training, and extension and inspection services, have been provided free or at low cost.

Turkey is implementing significant reforms to move it toward more decoupled and targeted forms of support. Under the government's reform program, output price supports, import tariffs and input subsidies and grants are gradually being replaced by direct payments to farmers based on their holdings of land and animals. Income support has been capped. Privatization of state enterprises in the agricultural sector is also part of the program. The end goal is that Turkey will have an agricultural policy similar to what is now being pursued by the EU in its reforms of the CAP: high intervention prices and protection from the world market will have been replaced by direct income support, lower protection, and prices approaching those on the world market. In chapter 4, Joseph Francois uses a global general equilibrium model to assess the quantitative effects of completion of the customs union by extending its coverage to agriculture. He concludes that despite the importance of the agricultural sector for Turkey, the overall aggregate welfare gain associated with completion of the customs union is limited, although resources will be pulled into agriculture. Commodity-specific impacts are small, with the largest adjustment effects in the more protected sectors, such as grains and meat, and expansion in the sectors that are highly subsidized in the EU, such as sugar.

The Turkish reforms have emerged from the prospect of accession, as well as the need to reduce public expenditure. In the short run they will lead to considerable gains in efficiency. According to Togan and his colleagues, adoption of the CAP will generate substantial changes in the agricultural incomes of producers, the welfare levels of consumers, and the budget revenues of the government. The authors estimate that, in the medium to long term, EU-like policies will lead to a 1.9 percent increase in real household incomes in Turkey. Lower-income households (rural households) will experience an even larger increase in real income. But adoption of the CAP will require substantial adjustments on the part of Turkish farmers. The effect on farmers' incomes will be driven mainly by the amount of CAP-like compensation payments they obtain. Their income will decrease considerably under Agenda 2000 policies without direct payments, but will increase under Agenda 2000 policies with direct payments. The budgetary costs to Turkey of adopting EU-like agricultural policies will depend on whether Turkey receives compensation from the EU budget for introducing these policies. Without compensation, the cost will amount to €3 billion under Agenda 2000 policies with direct payments similar to those applied in the EU and to €1.2 billion if the payments equal only 35 percent of what is granted in the EU member countries.

Manufacturing

In chapter 3, Sübidey Togan, Hüsamettin Nebioğlu, and Saadettin Doğan study the effects of EU integration on the Turkish manufacturing sector. After reviewing developments in the trade in manufactures and in particular the effects of the customs union with the EU, they analyze tariffs and nontariff barriers in trade with the EU and third countries. Because tariffs are now largely a nonissue, they focus more on nontariff barriers, especially technical barriers to trade (product standards). They conclude that challenges lie ahead for both Turkish firms and the government. Both must apply a large number of EU norms. For example, Turkey has adopted all of the 23 new approach directives that require affixing the CE conformity marking, but only 18 of these directives entered into force up to the present time. As a result of these directives, the number of mandatory EU standards decreased from 1,150 in 1999 to less than 500 in 2004 (European Commission 2004c). The Turkish Standards Institute (TSE) is presently concentrating its activities on the transposition of the European and international standards and on achieving full membership in the European Committee for Standardization (CEN) and the European Committee for Electrotechnical Standardization (CENELEC).[8]

Many of the requirements of the *acquis* in this area revolve around accreditation and conformity assessment, in which a large number of government bodies establish criteria as part of regulatory oversight activities and the Turkish Accreditation Agency (TÜRKAK) accredits the inspection service providers. Here a major challenge is for TÜRKAK itself to become accredited and recognized in the EU. Currently, its certifications are not recognized, requiring double accreditation for providers or redundant inspection on entry of goods into the EU. Progress is also needed on the introduction of mutual recognition clauses in national legislation and the acceptance and adoption of simplified procedures for the import of products bearing the CE (Conformité Européene) marking. In 2003 toys, medical devices, and other products bearing the CE marking were entitled to enter the Turkish market freely with no further check on the technical dossiers (European Commission 2004c). Such measures will facilitate trade and reduce costs for traders. Indeed, it has been reported that during the period after the decision was made to accept the CE label, customs authorities sent numerous consignments to the TSE for inspection, arguing that they were not able to assess the risks related to the minimum safety requirements. Numerous studies of the impacts of a customs union have argued that the abolition of such real trade costs is likely to generate significant gains for Turkey. Full implementation of the EU *acquis* on technical barriers to trade, with the accompanying institutional strengthening, will constitute the major change from the status quo in the nonagricultural merchandise trade with the EU.

Market Access and Regulatory Issues

In chapter 4, Joseph Francois complements the analysis of the impacts of extending the customs union to include agriculture by a discussion of the implications of EU accession for regulatory reform in Turkey, focusing in particular on the transportation sector. For this sector, the *acquis* revolves around the EU's common transport policy, which seeks to develop integrated transport systems based on advanced technologies that contribute to environmental and safety objectives; to improve the functioning of the single market in order to promote efficiency and choice; and to improve transport links between the European Union and third countries. The common transport policy places a major emphasis on the strict application of competition rules and state aid disciplines. Challenges range from physical integration to harmonization of infrastructure, vehicle, environmental, and other standards; development of logistics networks; and improvement of border crossings and trade facilitation policies (such as modernization of customs facilities). The EU is concentrating on greater liberalization of rail transport, landing rights/access to airports (allocation of slots), gradual abolition of the queuing system for certain inland waterway markets, and improved application of the rules on work practices in the road haulage sector (European Commission 2004c). An overall goal is a more level playing field through the application of competition principles, including the use of state aid and cross-subsidies.[9]

Railways are a major fiscal burden for the Turkish state. Turkish State Railways (TCDD), manages Turkey's seven largest ports and its railways, locomotive and carriage manufacturers, and repair workshops. During the 1980s and 1990s, rail operation cost the Turkish government more than $10.5 billion in constant 2002 U.S. dollars. As noted by the World Bank's Trade and Transport Facilitation Web page on Turkey,[10] TCDD needs to be restructured, the railway network scaled down, service improved, and prices increased. The *acquis* in this sector requires that TCDD separate out and report on the results of each of its activities (to identify cross-subsidies), and that it end cross-subsidies from ports to rail and from freight to passenger traffic by shifting to a system of direct subsidies for passenger services (motivated by social objectives such as universal service). The much more stringent fiscal discipline associated with implementing the *acquis* will have a beneficial effect on resource allocation and the use of transport services. Existing cross-subsidization of the railways by the ports suggests that port authorities should be subjected to greater scrutiny by regulators and the competition authorities, because in other countries (the threat of) competition by other (new) terminal operators has been shown to be an effective source of market discipline.

Francois explores both the quantitative and qualitative implications of Turkish accession to the EU for the transport sector. He adopts an innovative methodology using data provided by the Organisation for Economic Co-operation and Development (OECD) to determine how far Turkey is from "best practice" as defined by the EU standards for this sector—not just in the regulatory domain but also in terms of "performance." In part, this involves applying numerical estimates of the economy-wide and sector-specific impacts of accession (given the preexistence of the customs union for goods) on the transport sector. This process is complemented by an assessment of the prevailing regulatory regime, using factor analysis (principal components) to identify commonalities across countries and regulations. Francois concludes that there is little support for the claim that accession is exerting significant pressure on Turkey to restructure in view of either general market access conditions or regulatory convergence requirements. Notwithstanding this conclusion, as noted above, Turkey confronts numerous policy changes in adopting the *acquis* in the transport area.

Telecommunications Sector

Chapter 5 by Erkan Akdemir, Erdem Başçı, and Gareth Locksley examines the Turkish telecommunications services from the perspective of EU accession. Turkey is the last OECD country to liberalize its fixed-telephone services. Likewise, its privatization of the public monopoly in fixed lines has been delayed significantly. Yet Turkey, in the medium term, will need to adopt the new set of directives approved and published by the European Parliament and the European Council in 2002. In chapter 5 the authors consider the framework directive, access directive, authorization directive, and universal service directive.

In June 2001, Turkey and the other EU candidate countries signed the eEurope+ Action Plan, by which Turkey committed itself to achieving certain measurable goals in the electronic communications sector. Akdemir and his colleagues provide a detailed comparison of the current Turkish and European statistics and practices in the telecommunications industry. They discuss licensing, price regulation, access regulation, and universal service dimensions. For each dimension, they also describe the main Turkish legislation and its implementation and compare them to those in the EU member and candidate countries. They argue that the main problems facing Turkey are related to the implementation of the new legislation, especially in areas such as access to the network.

Their conclusion was confirmed by the European Commission's 2004 assessment, which found that only limited progress has been achieved in *acquis* alignment to date, despite the fact that the remaining monopoly rights of the state-owned incumbent operator, Türk Telekom, were legally abolished at the end of 2003, including those related to national and international voice telephony and the establishment and operation of telecommunications infrastructure. Thus the market has been open to new entrants since January 2004. However, the authors argue that the (regulatory) measures needed to facilitate market entry are not yet fully in place, including on matters such as numbering, interconnection, conditions of access to the network, and facility sharing, implying that there are still de facto barriers to new entry.

Banking

In chapter 6, Ceyla Pazarbaşıoğlu describes the impact of EU accession on the Turkish banking sector. One of the primary causes of the 2001 currency crisis was the unhealthy structure of the sector, stemming from several factors.[11]

- First, there were problems with state banks. Governments have used these banks for noncommercial objectives such as agricultural support; income redistribution; and industrial, urban, and physical infrastructure development. As a result, the banks faced unrecovered costs from mandates carried out on behalf of the government called "duty losses." The state banks covered their financing needs by borrowing at very high interest rates and at short maturities from the capital markets.
- Second, the banking sector faced problems created by high public sector deficits. As private banks found the financing of public deficits increasingly profitable, government domestic securities as a share of total assets of domestic banks increased considerably, making the banks vulnerable to changes in interest rates. Furthermore, during the 1990s banks began to borrow

funds from abroad and use the funds to buy government bonds.[12] Thus banks also became vulnerable to exchange rate risk.

- Third, in 1994 as part of an effort to prevent an economic collapse following a fear of a bank run, the government introduced full (100 percent) state guarantees for deposits. Before 2001, fear of a renewed banking crisis prevented the authorities from replacing this supposedly temporary measure with a more reasonable deposit insurance scheme.

- Fourth, Turkey lacked competent supervisory authorities, a good regulatory framework, and an effective legal and institutional infrastructure.

Since 1999, Turkey has taken measures to reform the regulatory and institutional framework of its banking sector and restructure the state and private banks. The *acquis* in this area requires, among other things, an independent central bank that, as a primary task, maintains price stability. It also prohibits direct central bank (or public sector bank) financing of the government deficit. Accession entails acceptance of the objectives of the EMU, although compliance with the convergence criteria is not necessarily a precondition. However, because those criteria are indicative of a macroeconomic policy geared to achieving stability, all member states must in due course comply with them on a permanent basis.

In 1999 the Turkish Parliament passed a new banking law, which mandated the creation of an independent Banking Regulation and Supervision Agency (BRSA). The BRSA took over the bank regulatory and supervisory responsibilities previously fulfilled by the Treasury and the Central Bank. For state banks, the Treasury provided floating rate notes to those banks securitizing their "duty losses," and it strengthened their capital base. A law was also introduced prohibiting state banks from running more duty losses—that is, any support provided to the state banks will henceforth have to be budgeted. The state banks were also required to comply fully with all banking regulations. Private banks that had incurred significant losses in the aftermath of the currency crises were either taken over by the Savings Deposit Insurance Fund (SDIF) or asked to strengthen their net worth and balance sheet structure. The capital base of banks under SDIF management was enhanced by the injection of government funds, and measures were taken to facilitate bank mergers and prepare the state banks for privatization.

In addition, the regulation of existing banks was greatly strengthened. Currently, banks are required to maintain an 8 percent capital adequacy standard ratio, on both a consolidated and unconsolidated basis. The maximum open foreign exchange position was reduced from 30 percent to 20 percent. Steps have also been taken to correct flaws such as weak loan loss provisioning and the lenient large exposure and related lending limits. Tighter limits were imposed on both on- and off-balance sheet commitments to related parties, and especially to companies belonging to the same group as a bank. Bank shareholders and managers are now personally liable for the mismanagement and abuse of bank resources. The BRSA requires that banks introduce internationally recognized accounting and auditing standards. All in all, as of 2004 Turkish prudential requirements were in general in conformance with those in the EU for capital adequacy standards, loan classification and provisioning requirements, limits on large exposures, limits on lending to related parties, and requirements for liquidity and market risk management.

The objective of the legislative and regulatory reform has been to bring the regulatory and supervisory regime for the Turkish financial sector up to the level of international practice in line with EU standards. This objective has been achieved to a large extent. Pazarbaşıoğlu argues that Turkey has fulfilled most of the conditions necessary for attaining compliance in the banking sector with the EU integration process. She stresses that the Turkish banking sector will be exposed to certain costs during and after accession in the form of competitive pressures from EU banks that have a strong capital base and risk management skills. However, the Turkish banking system has become more resilient and sounder since the extensive restructuring program and implementation of international standards. This restructuring process came at a large implied fiscal cost estimated to have reached close to one-third of GDP in the initial stages.

A major remaining issue that needs to be solved is the privatization of state banks. In 2003 Turkey decided to privatize the two largest state banks within three years, to withdraw the banking license of another state bank, and to resume the privatization process of another large state bank as soon as market conditions allowed.[13] The data on the Turkish banking sector reveal that in 2004 private domestic banks held about 57.6 percent of the total assets of the banking sector, with the five largest banks accounting for 60 percent of total assets. The share of state banks was 34.6 percent, while that of banks managed by the SDIF was 0.6 percent. Foreign banks' share of total banking assets amounted to 3.5 percent. Thus foreign banks, in terms of their shares of total credits and deposits, remain insignificant in Turkey.

With Turkish accession to the EU, competition in the financial sector will increase as Turkey recognizes the competence of the supervisory authorities of the EU member states and incorporates the principle of home country control in its legislation. According to Claessens, Demirgüç-Kunt, and Huizinga (1998), foreign bank assets as a share of total bank assets over 1988–95 averaged 77 percent in Greece, 31 percent in Spain, 61 percent in Hungary, and 51 percent in the Czech Republic. Thus, with the liberalization of financial markets, the penetration rates of foreign banks in Turkey will increase substantially, causing adjustment costs in the sector. Increased competition will improve the quality and availability of financial services in the domestic market, enable the application of modern banking skills and technology, enhance the country's access to international capital, lower prices for consumers, and lead to a larger variety of financial instruments. Some of the Turkish banks will benefit from larger markets by concentrating on activities in which they have a comparative advantage. Other Turkish banks may be forced to merge with foreign banks or leave the market altogether.

Energy

Chapters 7 and 8 examine Turkey's energy sector. The objectives of the EU's energy policy include improving competitiveness, securing energy supplies, and protecting the environment. The energy *acquis* consists of rules and policies, notably on competition and state aid (including in the coal sector), the internal energy market (for example, opening up of the electricity and gas markets, promotion of renewable energy sources, crisis management, and oil stock security obligations), energy

efficiency, and nuclear energy (European Commission 2004c).

In chapter 7, Izak Atiyas and Mark Dutz describe competition and regulatory reform in the Turkish electricity industry. After reviewing the physical peculiarities of the electricity industry and discussing how those characteristics have shaped the evolution of its industrial organization, Atiyas and Dutz present an overview of regulatory reform in the EU, the key directives, and the recent proposals for amendment advanced by the European Commission. They also identify five main challenges associated with adoption of EU norms in this area: market opening, unbundling, third-party access, public service obligations, and regulation.

Historically, the Turkish electricity sector has been dominated by state-owned enterprises that provide distribution, generation, trading, and transmission services. However, privatization has been widespread for some time. Privately owned firms have entered the industry through build-operate-transfer (BOT) or auto-generator schemes. They account for about 21 percent of electricity generation. In addition, firms have been bidding competitively on build-operate-own (BOO) contracts for electricity generation. Transfer of operating rights contracts (TOORs) have been awarded for eight thermal plants and 14 distribution regions. Privatization of generation assets is envisaged to start in 2006 and to be completed in 2011. All assets in the distribution sector will be divested by mid-2006 (European Commission 2004c).

Many of the benefits of privatization come with the transfer of risk. When private companies bear risk, privatization can be expected to lead to efficiency gains. Under the current regulations in Turkey, the private owners in the electricity sector bear construction and operating cost risks. The private operator signs a long-term power purchase agreement with the state-owned generation enterprise in which the latter commits itself to buy the output of the plant for a period of, say, 20 years at a fixed price in foreign currency. In BOT projects, the price has ranged on average from between $.08 and $.09 per kilowatt-hour for the first five to 10 years of operation. The BOO projects tend to have lower prices. The BOO contract, guaranteed by the Treasury, assures the investor that the project will be profitable irrespective of the future demand for power. As a result, the government retains the commercial risks. Significant problems have arisen with these arrangements. The high-cost electricity purchase agreements have exposed the state providers to significant losses and contingent liabilities. The financial position of these firms is poor partly because of high-cost BOT contracts that involve purchase costs to the Turkish Electricity and Transmission Company (TEAŞ) in excess of the subsequent sales prices to the Turkish Electricity Distribution Company (TEDAŞ) set by the government. The associated subsidies and cross-subsidies will have to be removed as a result of accession.

A new electricity law passed in 2001 provides for the establishment of an independent Energy Market Regulatory Authority (EMRA) to take over regulatory functions from the Ministry of Natural Resources. Standard regulatory functions include tariff setting, market monitoring, and settlement of disputes concerning access. With this law, the government is introducing a market model along EU lines that will transfer most of the task of supplying and distributing electricity and the associated market risks to the private sector, eliminate the need for additional state-guaranteed power purchase agreements, and minimize costs through competitive pressures on producers and distributors, again along the EU model (see chapter 7). The government, then, will largely withdraw from the electricity generation and distribution businesses. Electricity generation companies will sign contracts for power directly with distribution companies without government guarantees. The government's future role will be largely confined to determining sector policy, owning the transmission system, and ensuring that the rules are respected and that prices are determined competitively. The implication is that, once the law is fully implemented, the regulatory and supervisory regime for the electricity sector will have been brought up to the level of international practice in line with EU standards. Although the various BOT and BOO contracts signed in the past imply that the establishment of a competitive environment may take quite a long time, once the system begins to operate Turkey can expect to derive efficiency gains in the sector resulting in price reductions and improvements in the quality of the service.

In chapter 8, Maria Rita Mazzanti and Alberto Biancardi analyze the institutional endowment and regulatory reform in Turkey's natural gas sector. They focus on Turkey's natural gas market and the measures adopted to liberalize the sector and to comply with EU requirements for accession. As in the electricity industry, the main challenge confronting Turkey is to increase competition in the market while dealing with the legacy of past decisions, in this case the long-term take-or-pay contracts signed by Turkey's Petroleum Pipeline Corporation (BOTAŞ). This government-owned company dominates the natural gas sector in Turkey, controlling the pipeline infrastructure for oil and gas transmission, liquefied natural gas (LNG) terminals, and gas distribution. BOTAŞ has monopoly rights on gas imports and exports and on wholesale trading, transmission, and storage activities.

The 2001 natural gas market law (No. 4646) calls for liberalization of the gas market and the creation of a financially sound, stable, and transparent market (Article 1), including the removal of the import monopoly. As noted in World Bank (2004:1), progress in the three years following adoption of the law was slow: "Industry structure remains monolithic, with no separation of functions other than some distribution. Cost transparency, largely due to the existing industry structure, remains deficient. Competition has not developed in the wholesale sector. International investors remain concerned by the delays." The 2001 law requires BOTAŞ to conduct tenders to transfer to other market players its existing contractual obligations on natural gas purchases and sales until its imports fall to 20 percent of annual consumption (the so-called gas release program). Little progress has been made to date on implementing this requirement, and Mazzanti and Biancardi argue that enforcement of measures to limit the market power of the incumbent will be an important determinant of gains to Turkey from reform as well as a requirement for satisfying the *acquis* in this area. Competition in the natural gas industry is impeded by long-term investments and contracts in the upstream activities (gas contracts and infrastructures). Gas tends to be purchased on the basis of long-term contracts with take-or-pay clauses that require the gas purchaser to pay 70–90 percent of the contracted capacity whether it receives the natural gas or not; the reason is that extractors must invest huge amounts mining and transporting the gas and thus confront very high up-front fixed (sunk) costs and almost zero marginal costs.

Breaking up the upstream and downstream (wholesale) monopoly of BOTAŞ is a precondition for the emergence of competition in the sector. Mazzanti and Biancardi note that the targets set by the law for BOTAŞ shares (no more than 20 percent of imports and the wholesale market) are very ambitious, and much more so than the targets set by EU member states. They also argue that the gas release provisions of the law—which have also been used by EU states in introducing competition—could have a beneficial impact, as long as they are designed appropriately.[14]

The Complementary Implications and Challenges of Reform

Although much has been achieved in sector-specific regulation and reform, much remains to be done in some areas, especially energy and transport. Other economic reform challenges are associated as well with accession and realizing gains from the process. Chapters 9–11 consider three important "horizontal" areas: the labor market, (foreign) investment policy, and EU regulations pertaining to the environment. The first two complement the financial (banking) sector as critical determinants of the effects of accession. Labor market regulations will affect the incentives to invest, the costs to workers of layoffs, as well as the overall cost structure of doing business in Turkey. FDI is an important source of knowledge, employment, and competitive pressure on incumbent firms. Finally, environmental regulation has the potential to enhance social welfare by ensuring that firms and consumers confront the appropriate (social) prices of their economic activities, but it also raises the danger of excessively costly regulation that may not be appropriate to Turkey's circumstances and preferences.

In chapter 9, Erol Taymaz and Şule Özler look at the labor market. They argue that one of the most important issues for Turkey in adopting and implementing the EU *acquis* is related to the labor market regulations and employment policies that prevail in the EU. The *acquis* in this area includes EU legislation covering health and safety at work, labor law and working conditions (working hours, part-time work, collective redundancies, worker protection in case of bankruptcy and closure of plants, child labor—minimum working age), gender equality (equal pay and opportunities), and social

inclusion of handicapped people in the workforce. In all of these areas, EU social legislation lays down minimum requirements that must be met by member states.

Adoption of the EU *acquis* will bring radical changes in the functioning of the labor market in Turkey, with vital consequences for firms, workers, and the long-term performance of the economy. The main impact will fall on the informal sector. Taymaz and Özler note that the Turkish labor market is currently quite flexible, because the formal and informal sectors have very different wage-setting mechanisms. The informal sector is largely free from labor regulation and avoids most of the taxes and related charges. Job insecurity is pervasive, and workers receive very few benefits from their employers. By contrast, in the formal sector labor regulations are observed, and taxes and related charges such as social security contributions and payments to various funds are paid. Because the informal sector accounts for some 40 percent of manufacturing jobs, applying EU regulations to this part of the labor market will have major effects.

Taymaz and Özler estimate that when all informal sector firms in the manufacturing sector begin to pay taxes and social security contributions at the same rates applied in the formal sector, the firms affected will lose half of their market shares as their costs rise. As a result, employment in the manufacturing sector will decline by 9 percent, or some 300,000 jobs. As noted by Togan in chapter 12, the effect of this policy change on employment will be even more drastic when one considers its effects on employment in agricultural and services sectors as well. The policy implication is that if a massive increase in unemployment is to be avoided, comprehensive labor market reform will be required that includes both substantial decreases in tax rates on wage income, tax-related charges, and payments to various funds, and reductions in layoff costs. Such measures will also increase the flexibility of the formal market. Such flexibility will benefit the economy overall, because it will remove a disincentive for firms to grow and become part of the formal sector—a step that requires access to the capital markets and banking system, which, in turn, implies becoming subject to taxation. An important corollary not discussed by any of the contributions in this volume is that other policies in the area of taxation and support for the private sector are rendered neutral with respect to the size of firms—in Turkey, as in many other countries, tax and related policies tend to discriminate de facto if not de jure against small firms (Hoekman and Javorcik 2004).

Chapter 10 by Mark Dutz, Melek Us, and Kamil Yılmaz turns to Turkey's FDI challenges. The authors conclude that Turkey would benefit significantly from EU accession, largely because the accession process would help Turkey to overcome its rule-of-law and competition-related constraints to FDI inflows. More rapid and consistent implementation of the rules and regulations that ensure a level playing field for all companies would be assisted by the EU accession process; this process, in turn, would enable Turkey to take full advantage of investment-related benefits.

During the 1980s, Turkey made frequent use of investment and export incentives and also relied heavily on state-owned enterprises. The Turkish public enterprise sector has been and still is very large. The state-owned enterprises have shown, in general, poor economic performance because of the soft-budget constraints they have faced. They are not confronted with the threat of bankruptcy and have benefited from government subsidies in the form of direct transfers, equity injections, and debt consolidation. In recent years, Turkey has eliminated most investment and export incentives, but similar progress could not be achieved for the public enterprises. Although privatization has become a prominent part of the Turkish reforms, it gained momentum only after the 2001 crisis and the associated reforms, because it was recognized that state-owned firms and the related structure of subsidies and soft-budget constraints were a part of the problem underlying the large nonperforming assets of the banks. Turkey recognizes that it will have to stop subsidizing the public enterprises at the prevailing rates, align its state aid policies with those of the EU, apply the same competition policies to all firms whether private or public, and privatize the public enterprises. Greater FDI can play an important role in this transition, as it has in the CEE countries.

In chapter 11, the final major cross-cutting or horizontal issue chapter, Anil Markandya looks at the costs, especially in the public sector, Turkey is likely to incur in meeting the environmental *acquis*. In this area, as in the labor market, the EU *acquis* will probably have major repercussions for Turkey. Joining the EU will require implementing the entire body of EU legislation and standards on environmental protection. This step, in turn, implies substantial investments by the public and private sectors, as well as changes in regulations and supporting institutions. EU policy in this area is based on integration of environmental policy with the sectoral policies of the EU, prevention measures, implementation of the "polluter pays" principle, and measures to address environmental externalities at their source. The *acquis* comprises some 200 legal instruments covering a wide range of areas, including water and air pollution, management of waste and chemical products, biotechnology, radiation protection, and nature conservation.

Markandya breaks down the potential costs of adopting the *acquis* based on three scenarios: a "base case" in which no special reforms are made and the public sector remains much as it is today; a "medium reform" case in which the private sector's share is increased modestly and reforms in pricing proceed to reduce the demand for some of the environmental cleanup services; and a "high reform" case in which the private sector's role is somewhat greater and environmental reforms are implemented with more rigor.

Consider just one representative area subject to environmental regulation in the EU: wastewater collection and treatment. According to the EU urban wastewater directive (91/271/EEC), all urban areas with a total wastewater discharge of 2,000 population equivalent must be connected to the sewer system, and discharges must receive at least secondary treatment except for towns with populations of less than 10,000 and in cases in which such treatment would produce no environmental benefit or would involve excessive cost. Because the majority of the Turkish population lives in municipalities that are not connected to sewer treatment, and because only a very small number of municipalities have wastewater treatment facilities, the implementation costs associated with meeting this EU regulation will be very large indeed. How large will depend in part on negotiations with the EU to determine its interpretation of what is allowed in view of the flexibility provisions embodied in the regulation. But rough estimates of the investment costs of compliance run up to more than $10 billion. Adding the additional operating, maintenance, and replacement costs would further increase this amount.

Wastewater collection and treatment is just one of the relevant directives; others include EU regulations on drinking water, industrial pollution, dangerous chemicals, fuel standards, air quality, and waste management. Markandya estimates that the total investment will run between €28 billion and €49 billion. Although this estimate is very high, he also notes that the costs will be spread over many years—he assumes 17 years. Annual investments would amount to about €2 billion to €3 billion in the high reform (i.e., low-cost) case and €3 billion to €5 billion in the medium reform (i.e., high-cost) case. In the initial years, this investment would amount to 1–1.5 percent of GDP in the low-cost case and 1.5–2.5 percent in the high-cost case. To this one would have to add the extra annual operating costs that will be incurred, which would be in the range of €5 billion to €8 billion. Because Turkey's capital investment spending on environmental areas is about 0.5 percent of GDP, accession will imply an increase of anywhere from a factor of two to four or more. However, many of these investments would probably be made in any event by Turkey, although perhaps not as fast insofar as the EU directives do not correspond to Turkey's priorities at its current stage of development. Important here is the extent to which there is "wiggle room" in the various directives, as well as flexibility on the part of the European Commission in assessing whether achievement of the *acquis* in all of the various areas is a necessary condition for accession.

Also important will be the extent to which funding for some of these investments will be provided by EU member states—although it must be recognized that the money is fungible and that the Turkish government must determine for itself where grants and loans should be allocated for the highest social rate of return. Indeed, determining this allocation and deciding what trade-offs to make will perhaps be one of the greatest challenges confronting successive Turkish governments as the accession process proceeds. In making this determination, the government must compare cost estimates with benefit estimates that evaluate the gains from the implementation of the directives. Undertaking such a cost-benefit analysis is critical. One strong conclusion that emanates from Markandya's chapter, as well as others in this volume, is that such

an analysis is needed to determine where the case for investment is strongest and where it would be better to delay making investments (and negotiate extensions or agree on different sequencing with the European Commission).

Toward an Assessment: Net Effects on Turkey

What will be the net impact on Turkey of all the various policy reforms involved in EU accession? In chapter 12, Sübidey Togan attempts to go beyond the merchandise trade liberalization analysis undertaken by Francois in chapter 4 and quantify the impacts on those areas identified by the chapter authors as requiring the implementation of concrete policy changes. Specifically, Togan considers the welfare effects of integration with the EU associated with policy changes in the agriculture, banking, telecommunications, transportation, electricity, and natural gas sectors. He concludes that a conservative estimate of the resulting net increase in the real income of Turkish households is some 3.6 percent of GDP.[15] Integration with the EU will remove numerous distortions in the price system and improve the business climate for private sector development, which, in turn, will increase the allocative efficiency of the Turkish economy. Because these achievements will make Turkey a better place to invest, investment, including foreign direct investment, can be expected to increase, bringing with it associated employment opportunities. The allocative efficiency gains from integration will be boosted by induced capital formation. But these welfare gains will have a price: the adjustment costs associated with attaining macroeconomic stability, adopting EU labor market rules and regulations, and complying with EU environmental directives.

No assessment of costs and benefits should ignore the opportunity costs associated with the accession strategy. Indeed, one can and should ask what the counterfactual is to accession. Any process of regional integration by definition excludes other options—going it alone or relying more intensively on multilateral approaches as the focal points and anchors for reform. Clearly, the political decision has already been made to pursue the accession path, but that decision does not take away the importance of determining whether alternative strategies might not be superior in economic terms.

It is very difficult, however, to address this question. Virtually everything that is being done and will be done by Turkey could be done unilaterally. Many of the benefits from the reforms undertaken to date were gained autonomously—for example, the steps to exert greater macroeconomic discipline, the measures to strengthen the banking system, and the introduction of greater fiscal discipline for agriculture and state-owned firms. How much the templates provided by the EU model have helped is not possible to determine. Clearly, however, the *prospect* of accession played a role in the pursuit of some of these reforms. The key dimensions of accession as an anchor and focal point for reforms are as follows:

- the availability of the EU "model" to follow and implement
- the prospect of eventual free access to the EU for Turkish workers
- the assistance granted to Turkey by the EU.

Does the EU model (the *acquis*) make sense for Turkey? When it comes to disciplines associated with the single market, we would argue the answer is yes. The agenda here revolves around introducing market disciplines, controlling state aids, and encouraging competition in markets for goods and services. Integrating transport and energy markets also makes good economic sense, as do measures aimed at increasing the contestability of these markets and removing competition-distorting cross-subsidies. This is not to say that the EU model in these areas is perfect—EU trade policy, for example, and the CAP most obviously are not very good examples of efficiency-maximizing policies. But the point is that they are better than the status quo ante prevailing in Turkey, and their adoption therefore improves the expected policy stance in these areas.

Other dimensions of the *acquis* leave room for doubt. Although much of what is being pursued through the EU directives in the social and environmental areas is justifiable and will bring benefits, the costs of implementing regulation in these areas can be high. It is not clear that benefits will always outweigh costs, suggesting that these are areas in which greater care and attention are required to sequence implementation appropriately. As emphasized before, however, the accession process will take a long time, allowing for a more gradual convergence in areas where this is likely to be appropriate in view of Turkey's initial conditions.

In part, the cost-benefit ratio will depend on the extent to which additional grants are made available to Turkey that otherwise would not be forthcoming. Accession implies access to the CAP and Structural Funds, and, as a poor country, Turkey will be a net recipient of such transfers. It is not possible at this point to determine how large this net flow will be. The structure of the present system of EU revenue and expenditure is such that rich member states transfer resources to poorer members. Because Turkey is poor relative to the EU25 (even though the difference will be smaller than it was before the accession of the 10 new members), accession will clearly have budgetary effects for the EU if the current criteria are maintained for transfers among EU members. Allocations are determined in part by voting power (in turn, a function of population and size of the economy) as well as relative poverty, and so there is a possibility that the rules of the game will be changed before Turkey accedes in order to manage the fiscal and redistributive repercussions of its accession. In addition, it is projected that by 2020 Turkey's population will be larger than that of any other EU25 member. This projection may raise concerns about the decision-making procedures of the EU, as well as worries about possible immigration effects.

Effects of Turkey's Accession on the EU

The effects of Turkey's accession on the EU will depend importantly on what accession will entail for EU transfers to Turkey, EU governance (decision making), and trade and factor flows, especially migration.[16] Because the trade in goods, services, and capital has already been either covered by the customs union or addressed unilaterally by both parties in terms of bilateral flows, the effects on the EU in these dimensions are likely to be limited in the sense that they will have already occurred at the time of any accession decision. In any event, the aggregate impacts on intra-EU trade will be small. Production and trade in agricultural goods will be affected by accession, but the major effects will be in Turkey, not in the EU, because import barriers are relatively low for Turkish agricultural exports.

Decision Making

In chapter 13, Richard Baldwin and Mika Widgrén evaluate the impact of Turkey's membership on EU voting. They analyze the EU's decision-making efficiency (its capacity to act, as measured by the probability of proposals passing a vote) and the distribution of power in the EU's leading decision-making body, the Council of Ministers. They also compare two alternative Council voting rules: those accepted in the Treaty of Nice and implemented by the accession treaty of the 10 new entrants in 2004 and the rules laid down in the draft Constitutional Treaty (CT). The latter are conditional on the ongoing ratification process.

Baldwin and Widgrén conclude that, in terms of capacity to act, the enlargement will likely have relatively little impact, as long as the CT voting rules come into effect. In particular, Turkey's membership will have only a negligible effect on the EU's capacity to act—in large part because moving from 27 members (the EU25 plus Bulgaria and Romania) to 29 (Turkey and Croatia) does not change much. The answer, however, is quite different if the CT is rejected and the Nice Treaty rules remain in place. Under the Nice Treaty voting rules, the enlargement would substantially lower the EU's ability to act. These findings confirm earlier conclusions by the authors that an enlarged EU cannot function well under the Nice Treaty rules. They also suggest that if the CT is rejected, the Nice Treaty voting rules must be reformed before further enlargement takes place.

As for the distribution of power, they find that Turkish accession will have a big impact. Under both the Nice Treaty and CT rules, Turkey would be the second most powerful member of an EU29. Under the CT rules, Turkey would be substantially more powerful than countries such as Britain and Italy; under the Nice Treaty rules the power differences among the countries with a population of more than 50 million would be small. This situation suggests that the acceptability of the Constitutional Treaty and the probability of Turkey's membership may well be negatively affected.

Migration and the EU Budget

Turkey is likely to have a population larger than Germany's 82 million by 2020, if not earlier. Turkey is poor by European standards—PPP (purchasing power parity)-adjusted per capita income is roughly $7,000—and income disparities within the country are great. The population in the southeast has less than half the average national income, and the large rural population is generally much poorer than the urban population. As discussed by Harry Flam in chapter 14, these facts have implications for both the EU budget and for emigration from Turkey.

If the existing rules for contributions to and receipts from the EU budget remain unchanged—including the Common Agricultural Policy—Flam estimates that Turkey would receive a net transfer of €12 billion from the EU, corresponding to about 14 percent of the present EU budget. The overall net contribution to the 10 new entrants in 2004 and Turkey is projected to correspond to about 60 percent of the present budget. Flam concludes from this that it is unlikely that current rules will remain unchanged in the face of such large increases in net transfers from richer to poorer countries.

As noted earlier, the major trade impacts of Turkish accession on the EU are likely to be in the movement of labor. The decision to emigrate depends on a variety of factors, but real wage differentials are clearly important, as are social networks, culture, language, and geographic distance.[17] It will take decades for Turkey to attain an income level comparable with that of the EU15, implying that income differentials will be a strong incentive for migration from Turkey to the EU. The prospect of large-scale immigration from Turkey (as well as from new members and other candidate countries) is a source of considerable concern among the EU15. This was a major factor in the French decision to subject approval of Turkish accession to a referendum. Fears that immigrants will depress wages, boost unemployment, and cause social friction and political upheavals prevail in many EU member states. Clearly, free migration will not be allowed immediately upon full membership. For the 2004 new EU members, the length of the transition period was seven years, as it was for Greece, Portugal, and Spain. For Turkey, the period may be longer, and it may be subject to longer-term controls. However, because accession is unlikely to occur before 2012, this is an issue that would only come into play in 2020. By that time, Turkey should have converged more toward the average income levels of the EU25, reducing migratory pressures.

As noted by Flam, the strength of the incentive to move and the total number of people who might move are also a function of how rapidly wages rise in Turkey. As workers leave and the supply of workers declines in Turkey, wages will go up. Conversely, immigration will have a depressing effect on wages in the EU—albeit much smaller because the EU labor market is much bigger. The net impact on the Turkish economy will be determined by the extent to which capital owners are affected in Turkey, the impact of the loss of (qualified) workers on Turkish GDP, the extent to which earnings in the EU are remitted, and the magnitude and impact of reverse movements as people of Turkish origin relocate upon retirement and repatriate capital. Much also will depend on the skill levels of the people who move. Unskilled migrants are more likely to be complementary to more skilled nationals in the host economy because they will allow the latter to increase their productivity and thus their real wages.

Whatever the specific impacts, overall welfare will increase as a result of migration, but there will be a redistribution of income. Turkish GDP will decline, and the EU's GDP will rise. EU firms (capital owners) and more highly skilled workers are likely to benefit from the increased supply of less-skilled workers. Turkish migrants will gain from the move, and less-skilled EU workers will lose. The overall welfare increase will stem from a more efficient allocation of labor; Turkish laborers become more efficient when they move to European countries, and the optimal allocation is achieved when the marginal productivity of labor is equalized across EU members.

Flam concludes that the Turkish immigrant population in Germany may rise by some 60 percent by 2030. About 3 million people of Turkish origin are presently in the EU, the overwhelming majority in Germany, which implies a total movement of some 1.8 million Turks.[18] Although this is a highly speculative exercise—as stressed by Flam, much depends on the parameters assumed in the model—these numbers are manageable in view of the current overall EU25 population of 450 million. However, Flam's projections assume no restrictions are placed on migration—a strong assumption.

What such immigration will imply for wages and employment in the receiving countries is even more speculative. While those who have investigated the impacts of immigration suggest that it is likely to be limited, it should be noted that in contrast to the debates between the proponents and opponents of trade integration (where there is significant disagreement about the impact of greater trade on labor market outcomes), there is agreement that immigration will have much greater impacts than expanded trade between poor and rich countries. One reason is that migrants will seek employment in all sectors, not just tradables.[19]

Implications for Other Developing Countries

The requirements for accession to the EU provide a ready-made template, if a constantly evolving and expanding one, for countries seeking to implement far-reaching structural reform programs. What is the relevance of the Turkish experience? What lessons can be drawn for other countries with a starting point similar to that of Turkey that will not be able to accede because they are not part of Europe?

A first lesson is that the prospect of accession is not a panacea. What matters are the autonomous decisions on economic policy made by governments. Although Turkey's accession to the EU was already under discussion in the 1960s, very little progress was made in converging toward EU norms until the early 1990s. A related lesson is that much of what is associated with accession can be pursued by countries that will not be able, or may not desire, to accede. The EU *acquis* is a public good in the sense that any country can avail itself of that body of legislation and regulation. What matters is implementation, which, in turn, requires commitment and the relevant institutions to apply the standards. The regular monitoring and interaction between the European Commission and the partner government, facilitated by the provision of technical and financial assistance, can help to maintain progress. However, accession does not have to be part of the equation for countries to obtain such assistance—a very similar structure is available in the form of the association and economic partnership agreements that many countries have signed with the EU.

Such agreements can have major potential downsides if they involve asymmetric liberalization of trade in favor of the EU, while keeping barriers to imports from the rest of the world at high levels. For this reason, the standard policy advice to governments implementing such discriminatory trade agreements is to pursue a parallel strategy of lowering most-favored-nation protection rates as well (Schiff and Winters 2003). Turkey, because it formed a customs union with the EU, has adopted the common external tariff, which tends to imply a low average level of protection, at least for manufactures.[20] Assuming the problem of trade diversion is addressed through the adoption of low, and ideally uniform, levels of external protection, the EU model of regulatory principles has much to offer countries that are similar to Turkey—that is, emerging markets that have extensive state involvement in the economy, limited competition in service markets, and weak banking systems. A process of "conversion à la carte" is, by definition, not feasible when it comes to accession, but it *is* possible in the context of partnership agreements. Indeed, this option was made explicit by the EU in its 2004 European Neighborhood Policy, which offers partner countries that do not have the prospect of accession the opportunity to adopt parts of the *acquis* and through this harmonization share the benefits associated with the relevant elements of the EU's Internal Market. The challenge for partner countries is to determine where such approximation-cum-harmonization will be beneficial and where not. The Turkish case and its experience offer valuable guidance on what part of the "EU package" would be beneficial to adopt and emulate (with assistance from the EU in the context of such agreements) and which parts are best left on the shelf for the future.

The Turkish experience—as well as those of the CEE countries that acceded to the EU—reveals clearly that trade policy is important, in that the liberalization of trade with the EU led to significant improvements in productivity and trade performance, but that in itself is not sufficient. In an environment characterized by limited, if any, competition in the key network services industries—energy, telecom, transport—a weak financial sector, and limited fiscal discipline (and thus extensive cross-subsidization and transfers), trade liberalization needs to be complemented by measures to harden budget constraints and to enact pro-competitive regulation. The limited stock of inward FDI—a phenomenon that also characterizes neighboring countries in the Middle East and is in striking contrast to the situation in CEE countries—is indicative: foreign investors either perceive the attractiveness of locating in Turkey to be limited or perceive the barriers to FDI to be prohibitive. In practice, the answer is likely to be a mix of these two

factors. A long history of macroeconomic instability and high-cost services will lower the interest of an investor, especially in light of the fact that the Central and Eastern European countries offer an alternative location. Administrative barriers to FDI (including red tape) have also been high in the past. Finally, slow progress on privatization helps to explain low FDI.

A similar situation prevails in neighboring countries, although with one major difference: most Arab countries have experienced macroeconomic stability. Administrative barriers to FDI, monopoly provision of services, state-owned enterprises, and slow privatization all reflect political decisions. It is an open question to what extent trade agreements that do *not* involve the prospect of accession could assist countries that want to pursue an investment and services liberalization agenda, although the Turkish experience suggests that even in a context of possible accession, progress on this overall agenda can be slow. However, the deepening of accession efforts in the future will, by necessity, imply that much of the "behind the border" reform agenda must be implemented for accession to become feasible. This may or may not be true for association agreements that include services and investment policies. Much tends to be made of the fact that bilateral and regional trade agreements are increasingly covering these areas, but there is little experience with actual implementation. In principle, again, reforms in this area can and should be implemented unilaterally. Trade agreements may help by allowing gradual commitments to be made in a more credible manner, but much depends on the substance of the reforms. A key requirement (precondition) for the network services industries and the financial sector is appropriate regulation to ensure efficiency, to guard against systemic risks, and to achieve social or equity objectives (e.g., universal service obligations). These are complex areas. Much can be learned from the experience of other countries—such as in the natural gas sector (see chapter 8 by Mazzanti and Biancardi)—but what matters first and foremost is clear objectives. Also important is the establishment of an effective, general competition authority and mechanisms to assess the impacts and effects of reforms.[21] Indeed, an important policy decision is to what extent a country should rely on general competition law to discipline the behavior of enterprises, including dominant firms in the network services industries, as opposed to sector-specific regulatory bodies.

Conclusion

To join the EU, Turkey will have to attain macroeconomic stability, adopt the EU's Common Agricultural Policy, and liberalize its services and network services industries. Integration will be beneficial for Turkey, because it will remove many distortions in the price system, boosting the allocative efficiency in the economy and, in turn, making the country a more attractive place to invest. With accession, Turkey will also be eligible for EU Structural Funds, with the resulting increase in infrastructural investments further contributing to prospects for economic growth. In addition, Turkey will reap benefits from monetary integration, as well as from migration of Turkish labor to the EU. However, the welfare gains derived by Turkey from integration will have a price: the adjustment costs associated with attaining macroeconomic stability, adopting the CAP, liberalizing services and the network industries, and complying with EU environmental directives.

According to the European Commission (2004a), 71 percent of the Turkish population supports EU membership. This high percentage of support can be explained in part by the economic benefits that Turkey expects to derive from membership. Equally important is the recognition in Turkey that the system of governance of a rule-based society, as in the EU with its many institutions, may provide better prospects for meeting the demands of various groups in society.[22] Support for EU membership also stems from the process of Westernization and from geostrategic considerations.[23]

Turkish accession will also affect the welfare of current members of the EU. Welfare will increase because of the further specialization, reflected in trade, capital, and labor flows, as well as the likely growth effects of integration. The empirical research on the economic effects of immigration indicates fairly small and on the whole positive effects.[24] There will also be political gains for the EU. Turkey is a large and fast-expanding market. It is, in fact, the largest market in its neighborhood and has a GDP that amounts to 55 percent of that of Russia. Located at the crossroads of Europe,

Eurasia, and the Middle East, Turkey has the potential to act as a major link between these markets. With harmonization of commercial legislation, EU companies will be able to use Turkey as a joint investment and export base for the Middle East and Eurasia. Istanbul is already emerging as a base for transnational corporations operating in the Caucasus and Central Asia. Finally, Turkish membership could help to secure stability and security in the Balkans and Caucasus, thereby increasing EU energy security.

Although the potential net gains for Turkey and the EU members are significant, Turkey faces major challenges in implementing the *acquis*. Major challenges also must be overcome in realizing the potential gains associated with increased labor flows from Turkey—even if they will probably be relatively small compared with the size of the EU labor force. The same is true of decision making and management of the net annual budgetary cost of Turkish membership to the EU. The Baldwin-Widgrén analysis in chapter 13 points to the importance of passage of the EU Constitutional Treaty and the acceptance by existing members of a significant role for Turkey in decision making. Estimates reported by Flam in chapter 14 and in Togan (2004) suggest that budgetary costs will be quite high unless the rules on the CAP and Structural Funds are changed—constituting yet another challenge that will have to be negotiated successfully before accession.

Notes

1. Decision No. 1/95 of the EC-Turkey Association Council of December 22, 1995, on implementing the final phase of the customs union (96/142/EC).

2. "By [their] very nature, [accession negotiations are] an open-ended process whose outcome cannot be guaranteed beforehand" (European Commission 2004b: 10).

3. The Copenhagen criteria for membership were established in preparation for the eastern enlargement and cover political and human rights as well as economic criteria. Membership criteria include "stability of institutions guaranteeing democracy, the rule of law, human rights and respect for and protection of minorities." As noted by many observers, such as Flam (2003), Turkey confronts serious problems in meeting the political and human rights criteria: they imply placing the military under political control and ridding it of its power in the judicial system, and they have direct implications for recognizing individual and collective cultural rights for minorities (i.e., the Kurds). In its recommendation to launch accession negotiations, the Commission argued that in "order to guarantee the sustainability and irreversibility of the political reform process, the EU should continue to monitor progress of the political reforms

closely, on the basis of an Accession Partnership setting out priorities for the reform process. The Commission will, following the analysis in the Regular Report, propose to revise the Accession Partnership in spring 2005. On this basis, a general review of the way in which political reforms are consolidated and broadened will take place on a yearly basis starting from the end of 2005. The pace of the reforms will determine the progress in negotiations. In line with the Treaty on European Union and the Constitution for Europe the Commission will recommend the suspension of negotiations in the case of a serious and persistent breach of the principles of liberty, democracy, respect for human rights and fundamental freedoms and the rule of law on which the Union is founded. The Council should be able to decide on such recommendation by a qualified majority." See European Commission (2004c, 6).

4. The European Commission reports on Turkey provide an extensive list of actions taken by the government (European Commission 2004b, 2004c).

5. In this volume, EU15 refers to the 15 members of the EU prior to the 2004 enlargement in which 10 more countries became members, creating the EU25. The 15 original member countries were Austria, Belgium, Denmark, Finland, France, Germany, Greece, Ireland, Italy, Luxembourg, the Netherlands, Portugal, Spain, Sweden, and the United Kingdom. Those added during the enlargement were Cyprus, Czech Republic, Estonia, Hungary, Latvia, Lithuania, Malta, Poland, Slovak Republic, and Slovenia.

6. All dollar amounts are U.S. dollars unless otherwise indicated.

7. The short maturity of debt stock and the large share of foreign currency–linked securities imply particularly high rates of rollover on domestic and international markets, increasing the vulnerability to interest rate and currency rate shocks.

8. The major standards-setting bodies in the EU are CEN, CENELEC, and the European Telecommunication Standards Institute (ETSI).

9. The competition authorities have an important role to play. The Turkish Competition Authority has taken action in the transport sector, such as investigating a price-fixing cartel in Black Sea maritime shipping (see OECD 2004b).

10. See http://inweb18.worldbank.org/ECA/Transport.NSF/Countries/Turkey? Opendocument.

11. The ratio of nonperforming loans to gross loans of the banking system in Turkey reached about 22 percent in 2001. The situation improved during 2002 due to acceleration of out-of-court settlements and voluntary debt restructuring arrangements.

12. The average excess return on Turkish government bonds over the London Interbank Offered Rate, or LIBOR (both measured in U.S. dollars), amounted to only 4 percent over the period 1990–93, but was 22.9 percent over the period 1995–November 2000. In chapter 6, Pazarbaşıoğlu argues that the fiscal cost of the 2001 financial crisis has initially amounted to €50 billion (some 34 percent of GDP). If Turkey had adopted the legislative, regulatory, and institutional framework of the EU banking system at the beginning of the 1990s and had enforced these rules, then the cost of the crisis would have been much smaller.

13. The state banks to be privatized within three years are Ziraat Bank and Halk Bank. The government has withdrawn the banking license of Emlakbank, and it will resume the privatization process of Vakifbank as soon as market conditions allow.

14. See World Bank (2004) for an in-depth discussion of the challenges in and policy options for introducing greater competition into the Turkish natural gas market, including an analysis of the sector's strengths and weaknesses.

15. This is equivalent to about a 2.8 percent increase in real GDP.

16. The 2004 European Commission recommendation states: "The negotiations will be complex and reflect . . . the need for provisions facilitating the harmonious integration of Turkey into the EU. The application in Turkey of the common agricultural policy and the cohesion policy are two examples. The rules regarding the free movement of persons are a third. It is likely that there will be, as in previous enlargement rounds, a need for substantial and specific arrangements and in some areas long transition periods. In the case of free movement of persons permanent safeguards can be considered. . . . The EU will need to prepare itself because . . . the Union's capacity to absorb new members, while maintaining the momentum of European integration, is also an important consideration in the general interest of both the Union and the candidate countries. . . . In any event, the EU will need to define its financial perspective for the period from 2014 before the financial implications of certain negotiating chapters can be tackled" (European Commission 2004b: 7–8).

17. For a survey, see Ghatak, Levine, and Wheatley Price (1996).

18. Flam obtains a number of 1.3 million for Germany, based on an initial Turkish-origin population there of 2.2 million. The number in the text takes into account the additional 800,000 Turks in the rest of the EU as of 2002.

19. Borjas, Freeman, and Katz (1992, 1997) found that unskilled immigrants, particularly from Mexico, increased the ratio of unskilled to skilled workers in the United States by some 20 percent, whereas trade flows were found to have increased the (implicit) ratio by only 4 percent. Freeman (2004) notes that industries that export still hire a sizable number of unskilled workers, while import-competing industries have large numbers of skilled workers. He also observes that the evidence that immigration has a larger impact on the ratio of skilled to unskilled workers does not necessarily mean that large wage impacts are associated with immigration. Even large-scale inflows of workers into specific locations are not found to have big effects on wages (Borjas, Freeman, and Katz, 1996).

20. In principle, any country can choose to adopt the common external tariff of the EU, so that even if a customs union is not on the table any country with a free trade agreement with the EU could emulate the Turkish solution in this dimension. But better than adopting the idiosyncrasies of the EU political economy of protection would be to move toward a system of low and uniform tariffs.

21. The Turkish experience, like that elsewhere in the world, illustrates the need for a competition authority. The Black Sea maritime case of restrictive business practices (see note 10) is a case in point.

22. This may explain the support provided to EU membership by followers of the Islamist political parties as well as by representatives of different minority groups.

23. During the Tanzimat period (1839–77), Westernizing reforms were responsible for the adoption of a series of Western law codes, creation of a judicial organization with secular law courts, introduction of French-style provincial administration (1864), and use of the so-called millet system, which made it possible for the Christian minorities to have their own religious autonomous administration with representative councils. These liberal reforms culminated in the declaration of a constitution and the convocation of a parliament in 1876–77. The process of reforms continued after the national War of Independence of 1919–23. Under Mustafa Kemal Atatürk's leadership, the newly founded Republic of Turkey carried out an extensive and

comprehensive program of modernization and secularization. Atatürk believed that total Westernization of the country was an absolute precondition for Turkey's becoming a member of the Western family of nations. He succeeded in forging a modern nation out of a failing empire and a traditional community, based on the model of the Western countries. Turkey's aspiration to membership in the EU stems from the process of modernization and Westernization, the roots of which may be traced to Atatürk's reforms designed to establish a secular order in a country with a predominantly Muslim population. The Turkish elite consider membership in the EU a natural, desirable, and inevitable step in this process. Furthermore, Turkey realizes that it sits strategically at the edge of three regions of conflict—the Balkans, the Middle East, and the Caucasus. Because of the complexity of its security, Turkey seeks to cultivate stability in order to minimize the potential for conflict. For Turkey, EU membership can help to secure this stability and contain conflict, particularly in the Balkans. Furthermore, the EU and Turkey have a mutual interest in preventing and containing any instability that could arise in the Commonwealth of Independent States (CIS) region.

24. In addition to chapter 14 by Flam, see the studies by Zimmerman (1995), Haisken-De New and Zimmerman (1996), Winter-Ebmer and Zimmerman (1998), and Storesletten (2000).

References

Boeri, T., and H. Brucker. 2000. *The Impact of Eastern Enlargement on Employment and Labour Markets in the EU Member States: Final Report.* Berlin: European Integration Consortium.

Borjas, G. 1995. "The Economic Benefits from Immigration." *Journal of Economic Perspectives* 9: 3–22.

Borjas, George, Richard B. Freeman, and Lawrence F. Katz. 1992. "On the Labor Market Effects of Immigration and Trade." In *Immigration and the Work Force: Economic Consequences for the United States and Source Areas,* ed. G. Borjas and R. Freeman. Chicago: University of Chicago Press for National Bureau of Economic Research.

———. 1996. "Searching for the Effect of Immigration on the Labor Market." *American Economic Review* 86: 246–51.

———. 1997. "How Much Do Immigration and Trade Affect Labor Market Outcomes?" Brookings Papers on Economic Activity, 1–90.

Claessens, S., A. Demirgüç-Kunt, and H. Huizinga. 1998. "How Does Foreign Entry Affect the Domestic Banking Market?" Working Paper, World Bank, Washington, DC.

European Commission. 2004a. "Euro Barometer 2004," Public Opinion in the Candidate Countries, Brussels.

———. 2004b. "Recommendation of the European Commission on Turkey's Progress towards Accession." COM(2004) 656 final, Brussels.

———. 2004c. "Regular Report on Turkey's Progress towards Accession—2004." COM(2004) 656 final, Brussels.

Flam, Harry. 2003. "Turkey and the EU: Politics and Economics of Accession." CESifo Working Paper 893, March. http://www.cesifo.de.

Freeman, Richard. 2004. "Trade Wars: The Exaggerated Impact of Trade in Economic Debate." *World Economy.*

Ghatak, S., P. Levine, and S. Wheatley Price. 1996. "Migration Theories and Evidence: An Assessment." *Journal of Economic Surveys* 159–98.

Haisken-De New, J., and K. F. Zimmerman. 1996. "Wage and Mobility Effects of Trade and Migration." CEPR Discussion Paper No. 1318, Centre for Economic Policy Research, London.

Harrison, G. W., T. F. Rutherford, and D. G. Tarr. 1997. "Economic Implications for Turkey of a Customs Union with the European Union." *European Economic Review* 41: 861–70.

Hoekman, B., and Beata Smarzynska Javorcik. 2004. "Policies Facilitating Firm Adjustment to Globalization." *Oxford Review of Economic Policy* 20 (3): 457–73.

OECD (Organisation for Economic Co-operation and Development). 2001. *Market Effects of Crop Support Policies.* Paris: OECD.

———. 2004a. *OECD Agricultural Policies 2004.* Paris: OECD.

———. 2004b. "Anticompetitive Practices in the Maritime Transport Industry in Turkey." COM/DAFFE/TD(2004)63, September.

Schiff, Maurice, and L. Alan Winters. 2003. *Regional Integration and Development.* Washington, DC: World Bank and Oxford University Press.

Storesletten, K. 2000. "Sustaining Fiscal Policy through Immigration." *Journal of Political Economy* 108: 300–23.

Togan, S. 2004. "Turkey: Toward EU Accession." *World Economy* 27: 1013–45.

Winter-Ebmer, R., and K. F. Zimmerman. 1998. "East-West Trade and Migration: The Austro-German Case." IZA Discussion Paper No. 2. http://www.iza.org.

World Bank. 2004. "Turkey: Gas Sector Strategy Note," Report No. 30030-TR. Washington, DC, September.

Zimmerman, K. F. 1995. "Tackling the European Migration Problem." *Journal of Economic Perspectives* 9: 45–62.

PART I

MACROECONOMIC POLICIES FOR EU ACCESSION

MACROECONOMIC POLICIES FOR TURKEY'S ACCESSION TO THE EU

Sübidey Togan and Hasan Ersel

This chapter investigates the macroeconomic policies appropriate for Turkey both before and after its accession to the European Union (EU).[1] The first section of the chapter considers the recent macroeconomic developments in Turkey, and the second examines the macroeconomic policy framework for EU membership. The third section analyzes the macroeconomic challenges faced by Turkey, emphasizing the issues related to inflation, fiscal policy, public debt, sustainability of current account, and exchange rate regimes. The final section offers conclusions.

Macroeconomic Developments in Turkey

Over the past decade, economic crises began to affect the Turkish economy with increasing frequency. Periods of economic expansion alternated with periods of equally rapid decline. Although inflation during the period 1990–2000 fluctuated between 54.9 percent and 106.3 percent, the average inflation rate amounted to 75.2 percent. Currently, Turkey is in the midst of a determined campaign to turn around decades of weak performance stemming from pervasive structural rigidities and weak public finances. The past few years have witnessed three major attempts at addressing underlying weaknesses. The first was during 2000 under the three-year standby agreement initiated in December 1999 after a significant drop in output caused by mostly external factors, including the earthquake.

Despite some notable achievements, a worsening current account and a fragile banking system led in late 2000 to a liquidity crisis that turned into a full-blown banking crisis in February 2001. In response, the government decided to abandon the crawling peg regime and floated the currency. In May 2001, the International Monetary Fund (IMF) increased its assistance to Turkey under a new standby arrangement. But just as the revised program was beginning to show results, the terrorist events of September 11, 2001, in the United States triggered the reemergence of serious financing problems. In February 2002, the IMF approved a new three-year standby credit for Turkey to support the government's economic program. With the implementation of the stabilization program, Turkey envisages a gradual but steady improvement in its economic conditions. In August 2004 Turkey approached the IMF for a final three-year standby agreement—an exit program from instability and excessive debt.

Monetary Developments and Inflation

During the past two decades, Turkey has experienced high and variable inflation. There is strong evidence that, in the medium and long term, a close correlation exists between the rate of growth of monetary aggregates and inflation. This correlation appears in figure 1.1 between the monthly series of annual consumer price index (CPI) inflation and the monthly series of the annual growth rate of base money over the period January 1987–September 2004.

**FIGURE 1.1   Inflation and the Growth Rate of Reserve Money:
January 1987–September 2004**

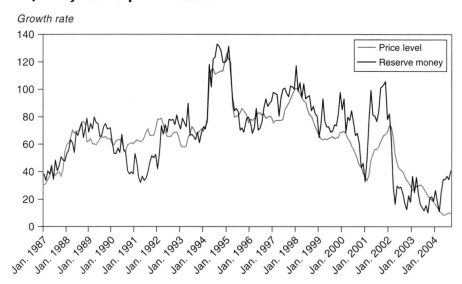

Source: Central Bank of Turkey.

**FIGURE 1.2   Inflation and the Rate of Depreciation of the Turkish Lira:
January 1987–September 2004**

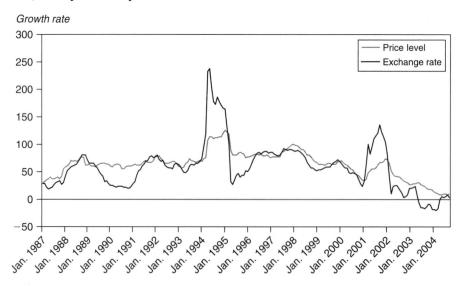

Source: Central Bank of Turkey.

A close relation also exists between the annual inflation rate and the annual rate of change in the exchange rate on a monthly basis over the same period (see figure 1.2).[2]

Recent empirical studies of Turkish inflation have drawn attention to a set of factors that affect inflation in Turkey.[3] Besides the obvious relation between the aggregate demand and supply, public sector deficits and exchange rate developments seem to be the major factors affecting the rate of inflation.

In equation 1.1, the relation between total demand and supply is proxied by the output gap. Almost all researchers agree that, besides the output gap, public sector deficits play a significant role in explaining inflation in Turkey. We model the effect of public sector deficits on inflation through two variables. The first variable is the noninterest expenditures. In contrast to interest expenditures, this portion of the public expenditures is determined by the government and is the major factor behind the changes in public sector deficits. The

TABLE 1.1   Estimated Inflation (Monthly)

	Coefficient	t-Statistic
Constant	0.01	1.872
Public price (d log(p_{public}))	0.31	14.35
Exchange rate (d log(E) + d log($E(-1)$))	0.04	2.753
Output gap (OG)	0.033	2.567
Noninterest expenditures ($NIEXP$)	0.012	1.822
Base money (d log ($M(-1)$) + d log($M(-2)$))	0.025	1.963
CPI inflation (d log($CPI(-12)$))	0.192	4.282
Dummy	−0.016	−6.072
AR(1)	0.463	6.364
R-squared: 0.802		
Adjusted R-squared: 0.792		
Durbin Watson statistic: 1.884		

Note: The dependent variable was d log(CPI), and the estimation period was January 1990–November 2003. The diagnostic tests for this regression indicate that there is no evidence of deviation from normality, autocorrelation, and heteroscedasticity.
Source: The authors.

second variable is the public sector component of the wholesale price index. The movement of this variable is almost totally determined by administrative decisions. Adjustments in these prices, regardless of their relation with public sector deficits, have an impact on inflation. Because most of the goods and services produced by the public sector are used as inputs, changes in these prices have an impact on private sector costs. Yet as these changes are publicly announced, they have a signaling effect. In this sense, the role of public sector prices is very similar to that of the exchange rate. The third variable influencing inflation in the equation is the exchange rate, which affects the prices of imported commodities. Fourth, in this equation the effect of monetary expansion on inflation is captured by movements in the base money. Thus one can now estimate Turkish inflation by using monthly data to solve

(1.1) $\mathrm{d}\log(CPI) =$
$\beta_0 + \beta_1 \mathrm{d}\log(p_{public}) + \beta_2 (\mathrm{d}\log(E)$
$+ \mathrm{d}\log(E(-1))) + \beta_3 OG(-1)$
$+ \beta_4 NIEXP + \beta_5 (\mathrm{d}\log(M(-1))$
$+ \mathrm{d}\log(M(-2))) + \beta_6 \mathrm{d}\log(CPI(-12))$
$+ \beta_6 Dummy$

where CPI denotes the consumer price index, p_{public} the public sector component of the wholesale price index, E the Turkish lira/U.S. dollar exchange rate, OG the output gap measured by the difference of

the monthly industrial production index from its trend, $NIEXP$ the moving average of the consolidated budget noninterest expenditures over the past 12 months, M the base money supply, and *Dummy* the dummy variable taking the value of 1 during the summer months of June, July, and August of each year and 0 otherwise. When we checked all the variables used in the estimation for unit roots, we learned that the series as used in the equation are all stationary. The results of the estimation are presented in table 1.1.

To deal with the problem of identifying the long-run determinants of inflation, we carried out the Johansen cointegration test with the variables that were significant in the short-term inflation equation and that were found to be $I(1)$—that is, CPI, $NIEXP$, M, p_{public}, and E.[4] The significant cointegration equation found among four of these variables can be expressed as

(1.2) $CPI = -2.234 + 0.000357\,M$
$+ 0.279695\,p_{public} + 0.000315\,E$

As one would expect from economic theory, base money and exchange rate play an important role in explaining inflation in the long run. By contrast, the presence of the public sector component of the wholesale price index reflects an invariant characteristic of policymaking in Turkey. The rather popular political instrument used to achieve short-term objectives seems to have had a strong inflationary impact in the long run.

Real Exchange Rate and Current Account

Until the end of the 1970s, Turkey followed a fixed and multiple exchange rate policy while experiencing relatively high inflation rates. The policy led to a loss of competitiveness and eventually to the foreign exchange crisis of the late 1970s. The gross national product (GNP) shrank by 0.5 percent in 1979 and by 2.8 percent in 1980. With the stabilization measures of 1980, Turkey devalued its lira by 100 percent and eliminated the multiple exchange rate system, except for imports of fertilizers and fertilizer inputs. After May 1981, the exchange rate was adjusted daily against major currencies to maintain the competitiveness of Turkish exports. Multiple currency practices were phased out during the first two years of the 1980 stabilization program, and the government pursued a policy of depreciating the real exchange rate (RER)—on average by about 6 percent annually over the period 1980–88.[5]

In January 1984, domestic commercial banks were allowed to engage in foreign exchange operations within certain limits, and restrictions on foreign travel and investment from abroad were eased and simplified. Determination of the exchange rate was further liberalized by permitting banks to set their own rates within a specified band around the central bank rate. In August 1988, major reform was introduced, and a system in which the market set foreign exchange rates was adopted. In 1989 foreign exchange operations and international capital movements were liberalized entirely.[6]

A drawback of the RER depreciation policy pursued during the 1980s was the decline in real wages, measured in terms of foreign currency.[7] By the second half of the 1980s, popular support for the government had begun to fall off. In the local elections of March 1989, the governing political party suffered heavy losses. To increase political support, the government conceded substantial pay increases during collective bargaining in the public sector. Pressure then built up in the private sector to arrive at similarly high wage settlements, real wages began to increase, and the RER started to appreciate.

According to the government, the appreciation of the RER after 1989 stemmed from market forces. During the 1990s, Turkey's public finances deteriorated considerably. The large public sector deficits were financed by borrowing from the market at very high real interest rates. Significant capital flowed into the country because it was offering not only high real interest rates but also the prospect of steady real appreciation of the exchange rate. Thus the government's implicit commitment to the RER appreciation insured the private sector, domestic and foreign, against currency risk. It encouraged capital inflows from abroad and lending to the public sector, giving rise to the phenomenon of large, arbitrage-related, short-term capital inflows.

The policy pursued during the first half of the 1990s was not sustainable. By 1993 the current-account-deficit-to-GDP (gross domestic product) ratio had reached 3.6 percent. In 1994 the country faced balance of payments crises from which the GDP shrank by 5.5 percent. But with the introduction of stabilization measures, the trend in the RER reversed. The RER depreciated by 64 percent during January 1994 and April 1994. The country had to reverse its economic policies, however, because of the relatively weak coalition governments. The RER began to appreciate again after April 1994, and by September 1995 it had appreciated by about 23.5 percent.

Between 1995 and 1997, the economy went through a boom period of above-trend growth, only to find itself badly hit in 1998 by the Russian crisis. In August 1999, a severe earthquake hit the Marmara area of Turkey, and another large shock hit the Bolu area in November 1999. Because of these shocks, real GDP shrank by 4.7 percent in 1999. At the end of that year, Turkey embarked on an ambitious stabilization program. Central to the program has been the policy of using a predetermined exchange rate path as a nominal anchor for reducing inflationary expectations.

During 2000, the RER appreciated considerably, which aggravated further the current account deficits, leading to concerns about the sustainability of the exchange rate regime. The current-account-deficit-to-GDP ratio reached 4.9 percent in 2000. This episode ended with a severe currency crisis in February 2001. There was a serious run on the Turkish lira (TL), interest rates skyrocketed, and foreign exchange reserves began to decline rapidly. The government decided to abandon the crawling peg regime and to float the currency. The exchange rate then depreciated sharply.

On May 15, 2001, the IMF increased its assistance under a new standby arrangement. This program aimed to strengthen the balance of public finances in a way that would prevent deterioration in the future. During 2001, Turkey introduced a set of structural reforms. But the terrorist attacks of September 11, 2001, threatened the progress of the reforms. Turkey responded with a strengthened medium-term program intended to clean up the banking sector, consolidate fiscal adjustments, and achieve disinflation, and in February 2002 the IMF approved a three-year standby credit for Turkey to support the government's economic program. During 2001, the GNP contracted by 9.5 percent, and the loss in employment was put at more than 1 million.[8] Toward the end of 2001, the RER began to appreciate again. With the appreciation of the RER, considerable economic recovery was observed during 2002–04.

Figure 1.3 shows developments in the current account-to-GDP ratio over the period 1975–2003. Currency crises arose in the late 1970s, 1994, and 2001. The figure indicates that the probability of a balance of payments crisis increases in Turkey as the current-account-deficit-to-GDP ratio increases above the critical level of 5 percent.[9] By October 2004, the annual current account deficit had reached $14.17 billion, and the current-account-deficit-to-GDP ratio had increased to about 5 percent by the third quarter of 2004.

FIGURE 1.3   Current-Account-to-GDP Ratio, 1975–2004

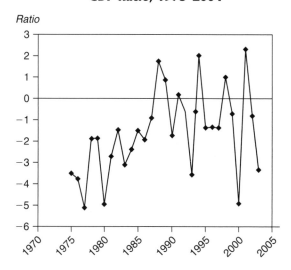

Source: Central Bank of Turkey.

FIGURE 1.4   Real Exchange Rate, 1980–2004

Note: An increase in the real exchange rate indicates its depreciation.
Source: The authors.

Figure 1.4 shows the time path of the RER over the past two decades, and it reveals four episodes of RER developments. After the foreign exchange crisis of the late 1970s, the RER began to depreciate sharply in response to the stabilization measures of 1980. It continued to depreciate until 1988, when it began to appreciate—that is, until 1994, when the country was faced with another currency crisis. In 1994 the RER depreciated sharply, but it appreciated again from April 1994 to February 2001, when the country was faced with yet another currency crisis. After the sharp depreciation of the RER from February 2001 to April 2001, it began to appreciate, especially after October 2001. It appreciated until March 2004 by about 36.3 percent. During March 2004 and May 2004, the RER depreciated by about 11 percent, and thereafter it stayed relatively constant until October 2004.

Fiscal Developments

Table 1.2 shows the structure of the revenues and expenditures of the public sector from 1998 to 2002. The public sector consists of the central government, revolving funds, social security institutions, extrabudgetary funds, local governments, and state economic enterprises (SEEs). The table reveals that, on average, during 1998–2002 revenues made up 29.24 percent of GNP, expenditures 42.4 percent

TABLE 1.2 Structure of Revenues, Expenditures, and Public Sector Borrowing Requirements (PSBR), 1998–2002

	Share of Total Revenue					Share of Total Expenditure							
	Taxes	Nontax Income	Factor Income	Social Funds	Privatization Revenues	Current Expenditures	Investment Expenditures	Interest Payments	Other Transfers	Stock Changes Fund	Revenue/GNP	Expenditure/GNP	PSBR/GNP
1998	80.62	4.94	19.93	−9.27	3.78	31.63	19.43	35.88	9.89	3.16	25.56	34.99	9.42
1999	87.01	5.93	18.60	−11.84	0.31	32.45	16.17	37.21	10.82	3.35	25.57	41.09	15.52
2000	82.51	7.37	11.41	−6.30	5.00	29.19	16.34	41.30	11.07	2.10	30.45	42.23	11.78
2001	81.64	6.63	16.31	−7.34	2.76	26.41	11.21	49.31	9.80	3.27	33.26	49.65	16.39
2002	76.60	9.74	23.38	−10.24	0.53	28.74	14.21	44.66	10.82	1.57	31.38	44.06	12.68
Average	81.67	6.92	17.93	−9.00	2.48	29.68	15.47	41.67	10.48	2.69	29.24	42.40	13.16

Source: Turkish State Planning Organization.

of GNP, and public sector borrowing requirements (PSBR) 13.16 percent of GNP. Taxes are the main source of revenues, forming about 81.67 percent of the total; indirect taxes make up about 70 percent of tax revenue. Although factor incomes generated by the profits of SEEs have constituted, on average, 17.93 percent of total revenues, the social funds have not generated revenue; they have been subsidized from the budget. On the expenditures side, current expenditures and investments constitute, on average, 29.68 percent and 15.47 percent of total expenditures, respectively. The most important expenditure item during the period 1998–2002 was the interest payments—on average, they were 41.67 percent of total expenditures.

Public Sector Borrowing Requirements and Public Debt   During the 1990s, the PSBR amounted on average to 12 percent of GNP. The high deficit incurred during the period was financed by borrowing from the market at very high real interest rates, as shown in figure 1.5.[10] Table 1.3 reveals that between the end of 1995 and the end of 2001 Turkey's debt stock more than doubled in terms of the debt-to-GDP ratio and reached 95 percent at the end of 2001. In 2002 the debt stock shrank somewhat, but it remained at almost twice its level in 1995. By 2002

FIGURE 1.5   Real Interest Rate, January 1990–October 2003

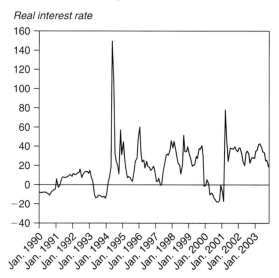

Note: Some data are missing in this figure because auctions could not be held during the indicated months.
Source: The authors.

external and foreign exchange (FX) indexed debt had reached 59.4 percent of total debt.

The evolution of public debt is best explained by decomposing the annual change in debt into various components as shown in table 1.3. Concentrating on developments during the past two years, the World Bank (2003) notes that the debt-to-GNP ratio in 2001 alone rose by 37.6 percent. Although the country ran a primary surplus of 5.5 percent of its GNP with the introduction of the IMF stabilization program, three factors mainly contributed to the increase in the debt-to-GNP ratio: (1) the high interest rates prevailing in the country; (2) depreciation of the real exchange rate, leading to increases in the ratio of FX-denominated debt to GNP; and (3) the costs of the banking crisis. In response to the banking crisis, the government issued new bonds in order to recapitalize failing banks. The bonds issued for this purpose amounted to 20 percent of GNP (table 1.3). In 2002 the debt picture improved, but this time it stemmed mainly from the real appreciation of the real exchange rate.

The PSBR-to-GNP and debt-to-GNP ratios given earlier are based on data from Turkey's State Planning Organization (SPO). Two other sets of data on the PSBR-to-GNP ratio, and thus on the debt-to-GNP ratio in Turkey, are also available—the first from the IMF and the second from the EU, consistent with the European System of Accounts 1995 (ESA 95) codes. The differences among the three sets of data are mainly attributable to the large duty losses. During the 1990s, the state banks faced unrecovered costs from duties carried out on behalf of the government, and they covered their financing needs from markets by borrowing at very high interest rates and at short maturities. The direct subsidies given through the state banks to farmers and small business were not shown in the government budget figures of the SPO; instead, they were shown on state banks' balance sheets as performing assets accruing interest income. The PSBR-to-GNP ratios of the SPO do not reflect the subsidy components given through the state banks, whereas the figures estimated by the IMF and EU do. A close look at the data in table 1.4 will reveal that the public sector, according to the IMF definition, ran a deficit equal to 18.9 percent in 2000, 21.1 percent in 2001, 12.1 percent in 2002, and 10 percent in 2003. As a result, the net debt-to-GNP ratio, according to the IMF definition, increased

TABLE 1.3 Debt and Fiscal Sustainability, 1994–2002

	1994	1995	1996	1997	1998	1999	2000	2001	2002
Stock of public debt (% of GNP)									
Domestic debt	14.0	12.2	20.5	20.4	24.4	40.9	39.1	57.2	47.7
FX-denominated/indexed							2.7	20.4	15.3
Floating rate								28.6	20.5
External debt	30.7	29.1	26.0	22.5	19.3	20.1	18.3	37.7	32.1
External + FX-denominated/indexed	30.7	29.1	26.0	22.5	19.3	20.1	21.0	58.1	47.4
Total debt	44.7	41.3	46.5	42.9	43.7	61.0	57.4	95.0	79.8
Public debt dynamics (% of GNP)									
Change in debt		−3.4	5.2	−3.6	0.8	17.3	−3.6	37.6	−15.2
Debt-creating items									
Interest payments		7.3	10.0	11.0	16.2	22.1	21.9	23.5	16.3
Debt-reducing items									
Primary balance		2.7	−1.2	−2.1	0.9	−2.0	2.7	5.5	3.9
Growth effect		1.7	1.5	2.0	0.9	−1.8	2.4	−3.9	4.8
Inflation effect		6.5	5.3	9.2	8.8	8.7	13.8	13.0	11.2
Revaluation effect		4.4	1.9	1.6	2.5	−1.2	3.8	−13.2	10.1
Seigniorage		3.0	2.4	2.9	2.4	3.2	1.8	1.4	1.5
Other		0.0	0.0	0.1	0.5	0.1	1.6	−18.1	−1.8
Privatization		0.0	0.0	0.1	0.5	0.1	1.6	1.9	0.1
Cost of financial sector bailout		0.0	0.0	0.0	0.0	0.0	0.0	−20.0	−1.9

Source: World Bank 2003.

TABLE 1.4   Ratios of Public Sector Borrowing Requirements (PSBR) and of Debt to GNP and GDP, 2000–03

	PSBR/GNP		PSBR/GDP	Debt/GNP		Debt/GDP
	SPO	IMF	EU	SPO	IMF	EU
2000	11.8	18.9	9.8	57.5	57.4	65.4
2001	16.4	21.1	15.9	91.0	93.9	102.6
2002	12.8	12.1	13.6	78.7	79.2	89.5
2003	9.4	10.0	10.1	70.5	70.9	80.2

Note: The debt/GNP figures of the IMF refer to the net debt of the public sector as a ratio of centered GNP, where centered GNP is defined as the sum of quarterly GNP in the last two quarters of the year and in the first two quarters of the next year. The debt/GDP figures of the EU refer to the ratio of the gross debt of the public sector to GDP.

Sources: IMF 2004; Turkish State Planning Organization (SPO) 2004; http://www.treasury.gov.tr.

from 57.4 percent in 2000 to 93.9 percent in 2001, and then decreased to 79.2 percent in 2002 and to 70.9 percent in 2003. Public debt, according to the IMF definition, is a net debt that is measured in percent of centered GNP, defined as the sum of quarterly GNP in the last two quarters of the year and in the first two quarters of the following year.[11] By contrast, the EU measures the debt in gross terms. Thus total gross public debt, according to the EU definition, decreased from 102.6 percent of GDP in 2001 to 89.5 percent in 2002 and 80.2 percent in 2003.

Structure of Taxes   Because taxes constituted about 80.25 percent of total revenues during 2000–02, this section will consider the tax burden in Turkey, compare the composition of tax revenues in Turkey with that of tax revenues in the EU, and compare the main features of personal, corporate, and value added tax (VAT) systems in Turkey and the EU.

Turkey is an upper-middle-income country, whose per capita income falls at the lower end of those of this group of countries. A comparison of the central government tax revenues of Turkey with those of other countries reveals that Turkey has a relatively high tax burden in its per capita income group (see World Bank 2003). When compared with those of lower-middle-income countries, Turkey's tax burden is markedly above the revenue average of 13.6 percent of the lower-income group. It is also significantly above the average of 21.3 percent for all upper-middle-income countries. In fact,

TABLE 1.5   Total Tax Revenue as Percentage of GDP, 1998–2000

	1998	1999	2000
Austria	44.3	44.1	43.7
Belgium	45.8	45.4	45.6
Denmark	50.1	51.2	48.8
Finland	46.1	46.8	46.9
France	45.1	45.7	45.3
Germany	37.1	37.8	37.9
Greece	35.6	36.9	37.8
Ireland	31.7	31.3	31.1
Italy	42.5	43.3	42.0
Luxembourg	39.8	40.9	41.7
Netherlands	40.0	41.2	41.4
Portugal	33.3	34.1	34.5
Spain	34.0	35.0	35.2
Sweden	51.6	52.0	54.2
United Kingdom	36.9	36.4	37.4
Turkey	28.4	31.3	33.4

Source: OECD 2003.

it is comparable with that of Ireland (see table 1.5), but it is still below the tax/GDP figures in the member countries of the EU.[12]

Table 1.6, which shows the composition of tax revenues in Turkey and the EU, reveals that EU countries obtain a significantly larger percentage of tax revenues from social security and payroll taxes (32.7 percent) compared with Turkey (14.3 percent). In Turkey, the share of taxes on goods and services (35.7 percent) is higher than the similar share in the EU (28.8 percent).

TABLE 1.6   Revenue from Major Taxes as a Percentage of Total Tax Revenue, 1998

	Personal Income	Corporate Income	Social Security and Other Payroll	Property	Goods and Services	General Consumption Taxes
Austria	22.5	4.8	40.3	1.3	27.9	18.7
Belgium	30.7	8.5	31.5	3.2	24.9	15.3
Denmark	51.6	5.6	3.9	3.6	33.2	19.6
Finland	32.3	9.0	25.2	2.4	30.7	18.5
France	17.4	5.9	39.5	7.3	26.6	17.5
Germany	25.0	4.4	40.4	2.4	27.4	17.9
Greece (1997)	13.2	6.4	32.3	3.8	41.0	22.6
Ireland	30.9	10.7	13.8	5.2	38.7	22.2
Italy	25.0	7.0	29.5	4.8	27.4	14.2
Luxembourg	18.8	19.7	25.6	8.4	26.1	13.7
Netherlands	15.2	10.6	39.9	4.9	27.7	16.9
Portugal	17.1	11.6	25.5	2.9	41.3	23.3
Spain	20.8	7.3	35.2	6.0	29.4	16.6
Sweden	35.0	5.7	33.5	3.7	21.6	13.6
United Kingdom	27.5	11.0	17.6	10.7	32.6	18.1
EU	23.9	7.1	32.7	5.4	28.8	17.2
Turkey	27.0	5.8	14.3	2.8	35.7	30.0

Source: Noord and Heady 2001.

Table 1.7 compares for 2002 the personal tax, corporate tax, and VAT systems of Turkey and the EU countries. The table reveals that the average income tax and social security contribution rate on gross labor income in Turkey amounts to 43.2 percent, whereas the same tax rate is 25.8 percent in Ireland and 29.7 percent in the United Kingdom. The corporate income tax in Turkey is 44.1 percent, whereas it is 16 percent in Ireland and 30 percent in United Kingdom. By contrast, the VAT rate in Turkey is 18 percent, whereas it is 15 percent in Luxembourg and 16 percent in Germany and Spain. According to the table, tax rates are in general very high in Turkey. With such high tax rates, Turkey should have achieved a much higher total-tax-to-GNP ratio than the 31.8 percent achieved in 1999. Currently, the country has a large share of employment declared to be at the minimum wage because of attempts by both employees and employers to reduce their tax burden, and it has relatively large employment in the informal sector. As a result, Turkey's tax base is rather narrow.

Employment and Growth

Table 1.8, which shows developments in the labor market for 2001–03, reveals that Turkey, with a population of 70.7 million and a labor force participation rate of 48.3 percent in 2003, has created jobs for about 21 million people. During 2003, 33.9 percent of the labor force was employed in agriculture, 18.2 percent in industry, and 47.9 percent in services. The unemployment rate was 10.5 percent. The average unemployment rate during 1990–2000 was 7.6 percent, but it increased considerably with the financial crisis of 2001.

These figures indicate that Turkey must create jobs for its unemployed workers, as well as for those entering the labor force for the first time at the average rate of 900,000 persons a year. In addition, Turkey has to increase the labor force participation rate from its current low level of 48.3 percent to the levels that prevailed at the beginning of the 1990s. At that time, the labor force participation rate was 56.5 percent. By contrast, the comparable level in the EU was about 63 percent. Job creation, then, is a major challenge that Turkey must meet over time.

The Turkish labor market is extremely flexible because of the country's formidable informal sector, whose wage-setting mechanism is quite different from that of the formal sector. The informal sector is largely free from most types of labor regulation, and it does not pay most taxes and related charges. Activities in this sector rely largely on the provision

TABLE 1.7   Personal Tax, Corporate Tax, and VAT System: Turkey and EU Countries, 2002

	Marginal Income Tax and Social Security Contribution Rate on Gross Labor Income	Average Income Tax and Social Security Contribution Rate on Gross Labor Income	Corporate Income Tax Rate	Standard VAT Rate
Austria	55.3	44.7	34.0	20.0
Belgium	66.7	55.6	40.2	21.0
Denmark	50.4	44.2	30.0	25.0
Finland	57.4	45.9	29.0	22.0
France	53.0	48.3	—	19.6
Germany	63.9	50.7	38.9	16.0
Greece	44.1	36.0	—	18.0
Ireland	33.9	25.8	16.0	21.0
Italy	54.5	46.2	—	20.0
Luxembourg	47.9	34.2	30.4	15.0
Netherlands	51.0	42.3	34.5	19.0
Portugal	39.4	32.5	33.0	19.0
Spain	45.5	37.9	35.0	16.0
Sweden	50.4	48.6	28.0	25.0
United Kingdom	39.2	29.7	30.0	17.5
Turkey	45.6	43.2	44.1	18.0

— Not available.

Note: The first two columns report marginal and average personal income tax and social security contribution rates for a single person without dependents at 100 percent of the average production wage. The corporate income tax rate for Turkey refers to the total effective tax burden of a nonpublicly owned company. In the case of a publicly owned company, the tax burden goes down to 36.7 percent.

Source: OECD tax database (http://www.oecd.org).

TABLE 1.8   Labor Market Indicators: Turkey, 2001–03

	2001	2002	2003
Population (thousands)	68,610	69,626	70,712
Population 15 and over (thousands)	47,158	48,041	48,912
Labor force (thousands)	23,491	23,818	23,640
Participation ratio (%)	49.8	49.6	48.3
Civilian employment (thousands)	21,524	21,354	21,147
Unemployment (thousands)	1,967	2,464	2,493
Unemployment rate (%)	8.4	10.3	10.5
Employment by sector (thousands)			
Agriculture	8,089	7,458	7,165
Industry	3,774	3,954	3,847
Services	9,661	9,942	10,135
Sectoral distribution of employment (%)			
Agriculture	37.6	34.9	33.9
Industry	17.5	18.5	18.2
Services	44.9	46.6	47.9

Source: Treasury statistics, 1980–2003.

of labor without formal employment contracts. Job insecurity is pervasive, and workers receive very few benefits from their employers. Because wages in the informal sector are determined by demand and supply conditions, the informal sector itself is flexible. By contrast, the formal sector observes labor regulations, and it pays all taxes and related charges such as social security contributions and payments to various funds. Thus, this sector is not as flexible as the informal sector. Until now, Turkey has successfully solved the unemployment problem by means of its large informal sector.[13] Indeed, over time this sector has grown considerably through the lax enforcement of tax, social security, and labor laws. But the current system of formal and informal sectors, with the informal sector accounting for about 60 percent of total employment, does not seem to be sustainable in the long run.[14]

As for the growth of GDP, over the period 1950–2002, GDP increased at an average annual rate of 4.9 percent.[15] However, over the same period the average growth rate declined. The growth rate of GDP was 7.1 percent during 1950–59, 5.4 percent during 1960–69, 4.7 percent during 1970–79, 4.1 percent during 1980–89, and 3.6 percent over the period 1990–2002. Besides experiencing decreasing average growth rates of real income, Turkey has recently faced greater economic volatility, because economic crises have begun to affect the Turkish economy with increasing frequency. As noted earlier, during the last decade periods of economic expansion have alternated with periods of equally rapid decline.

Macroeconomic Policy Framework for EU Membership

Upon accession, Turkey, according to Article 122 of the treaty establishing the European Community (hereafter known as the "Treaty"), will be treated as a "Member State with a derogation" until it fulfills the convergence criteria.[16] The Central and Eastern European (CEE) countries, when signing the accession treaty, have accepted the goal of monetary union as part of the *acquis communautaire,* the entire body of legislation of the European Communities and Union. To become members of the European Economic and Monetary Union (EMU), the CEE countries must fulfill the convergence criteria, which involve conditions on price stability,

interest rate convergence, budget deficits, government debt, and exchange rate stability.[17]

Macroeconomic Policy Framework for EMU Members

On January 1, 1999, 11 of the 15 member countries of the EU entered the third and final stage of the process leading to the formation of the EMU. At that time, the exchange rates among the currencies of the participating countries were irrevocably fixed in relation to the new single currency, the euro, and the newly formed European Central Bank (ECB) had taken over responsibility for monetary policy in the Euro Area. Individual member countries of the EMU therefore no longer have control over either monetary policy or exchange rate policy; they have surrendered their sovereignty in monetary and exchange rate policy to the supranational authority, the ECB.

Monetary Policy   The European System of Central Banks (ESCB) is composed of the European Central Bank and the national central banks (NCBs) of all 15 EU member states.[18] Because not all members joined the monetary union from the outset, the term *Eurosystem* was adopted to describe the ECB and the NCBs of the 11 member states that have adopted the euro. All decisions related to the Eurosystem are made by the decision-making bodies of the ECB, the Executive Board, and the Governing Council. The Executive Board comprises the president and the vice president of the ECB and four other members. It implements monetary policy in accordance with the guidelines and decisions laid down by the Governing Council. The Governing Council comprises the members of the Executive Board and the governors of the NCBs participating in the Euro Area. It is the primary decision-making body of the ECB.

The Treaty specifies that the main task of the Eurosystem is to deliver price stability (Article 105). According to Article 107 of the Treaty, the Eurosystem is solely responsible for the Euro Area's single monetary policy, and it is to pursue the goal of price stability free from political pressure by EU institutions, interest groups, or individuals. The Treaty does not precisely define price stability. The Eurosystem interprets it as a year-to-year increase in the Harmonised Index of Consumer Prices (HICP) for the Euro Area of below 2 percent (European Central Bank 2003b), which is to be maintained over the medium term. The phrase "below 2 percent" delineates the upper bound for the rate of measured inflation in the HICP.

To achieve price stability, the Eurosystem uses two pillars. The first pillar is what the Eurosystem calls "economic analysis." It consists of a broadly based assessment of the outlook for price developments and the risks to price stability in the Euro Area as a whole. The assessment concentrates on the medium impact of the current conditions of inflation. The second pillar is an assessment of the evolution of monetary aggregates (M3) and credit. It analyzes the longer-run impact of monetary aggregates on inflation. The two perspectives offer complementary analytical frameworks to support the Governing Council's overall assessment of risks to price stability. The inflation forecast is published twice a year. If the forecast exceeds the target (i.e., the 2 percent definition of price stability), the presumption under an inflation targeting strategy is that monetary policy will be tightened. Although the Eurosystem's strategy resembles inflation targeting, the Eurosystem does not want to give the appearance that it acts mechanically.

In conducting monetary policy, the Eurosystem uses mainly short-term interest rates and focuses on the overnight rate EONIA (European Over-Night Index Average, a weighted average of overnight lending transactions in the Euro Area's interbank market). Control over EONIA is achieved in two ways. First, the Eurosystem has two facilities at its disposal: a marginal lending facility and a deposit facility. These facilities operate under overnight maturity and are available to counterparties at their own initiative. They are administered on a decentralized basis, with their features harmonized across the Eurosystem. Overnight liquidity is provided at a prespecified interest rate against eligible collateral. In normal circumstances, the interest rate on the marginal lending facility defines the ceiling for EONIA in the market. Similarly, the deposit facility defines the floor for overnight market rates. All financial institutions fulfilling the general eligibility criteria may access this facility. Access is granted through the NCB in the country in which the financial institution is established and on all days that the national payment and securities settlement systems are operational.

The second way in which control is exercised over EONIA is ECB auctions, usually weekly, with a maturity of two weeks at a rate the ECB chooses. These auctions, called refinancing operations, provide the liquidity needed by the banking system, and the chosen interest rate serves as a guide for EONIA. Transactions related to weekly tenders are conducted by the NCBs in the form of standard (fixed-rate or variable-rate) tenders. The NCBs are responsible for collecting the tender offers and transmitting them to the ECB. They also inform credit institutions about the results of the tenders and arrange the settlement aspects—that is, receiving the collateral and providing the liquidity. Both the ECB and the NCBs conduct longer-term refinancing operations monthly, with a maturity of three months. These operations provide the financial sector with additional longer-term liquidity. In addition, the NCBs may carry out structural open-market operations. The Governing Council can authorize fine-tuning, outright transactions of securities, foreign exchange swaps, and the collection of deposits to be conducted, in exceptional circumstances, by the ECB itself.

Although in conducting monetary policy the Eurosystem uses mainly short-term interest rates, it is the long-term interest rate that affects the economy. Indeed, households and firms borrow for relatively long periods. Thus central banks control the short maturity, while it is the long maturity that really matters. Yet these banks do influence the long-term rates by being clear about their longer-run aims and intentions.

Overall, the Eurosystem constitutionally enjoys considerable independence, both in defining its objectives and in deciding how to conduct monetary policy. The ECB is accountable to the European Parliament.

Fiscal Policy   The Euro Area does not have a central fiscal authority.[19] There is a budget for the EU as a whole, but it is relatively small. Spending amounts to only a little over 1 percent of GDP, devoted mostly to common agricultural policy and the structural funds, and deficit financing is prohibited. Thus, budgetary decisions in the Euro Area will remain almost exclusively the province of member states, albeit subject to surveillance by the EU as a whole in the context of the requirements set out in the Maastricht Treaty and subsequently the Stability and Growth Pact.

For countries seeking to qualify for EMU membership and those already members, the Maastricht Treaty and the SGP established certain targets on the size of debt and deficits and other obligations. For countries already in the EMU, the targets were intended to achieve and maintain "sound" budgetary positions and to avoid harsh penalties. Article 104 of the Treaty establishes that "member states shall avoid excessive government deficits" and that compliance with budgetary discipline will be judged on the basis of two criteria:

(a) whether the ratio of the planned or actual government deficit to gross domestic product exceeds a reference value, unless either the ratio has declined substantially and continuously and reached a level that comes close to the reference value, or, alternatively, the excess over the reference value is only exceptional and temporary and the ratio remains close to the reference value

(b) whether the ratio of government debt to gross domestic product exceeds a reference value, unless the ratio is sufficiently diminishing and approaching the reference value at a satisfactory pace.

As is well known, these two reference values were set at 3 percent and 60 percent, respectively.

The SGP was designed to provide concreteness to several provisions of the Treaty on economic policies in the EU. It consists of a resolution of the European Council and of two regulations (No. 1466/97 and No. 1467/97) of the Council for Economic and Financial Affairs (ECOFIN).[20] The resolution reaffirms the commitment to fiscal discipline and introduces the notion that the "medium-term budgetary objective of positions close to balance or in surplus" should be respected by member states in order to "allow all Member States to deal with normal cyclical fluctuations while keeping the government deficit within the reference value of 3 percent of GDP." The medium term is understood to represent about three years.

Regulation No. 1466/97 clarifies the procedures to be followed in implementing the surveillance of the Stability and Growth Pact, as envisioned in general terms in Article 99 of the Treaty. In particular, it establishes, first, that member states must every year submit an update to the stability program that contains a medium-term objective for the budgetary position, as well as a description of the assumptions and of the main economic policy measures the country intends to take to achieve the targets; and, second, that the European Council, on a recommendation from the Commission, must deliver an opinion on each program and its yearly updates and, if deemed necessary, a recommendation. Three types of recommendations are possible. First, the Council could issue a recommendation that the program be adjusted if deemed deficient in some respect. Second, if after approving the program the Council identifies a "significant divergence of the budgetary position from the medium-term budgetary objective, or the adjustment path towards it," the Commission can issue a recommendation (early warning) in accordance with Article 103(4). Third, if the divergence persists, the Council can issue a recommendation to take corrective action, and can make the recommendation public.

Regulation No. 1467/97 first tries to make more precise the notion of "exceptional and temporary" excess of the deficit over the 3 percent of GDP threshold, as introduced by Article 104 of the Treaty. Article 2(1) of the regulation specifies that an "exceptional and temporary" excess of the deficit is allowed "when resulting from an unusual event outside the control of the Member State concerned and which has a major impact on the financial position of the general government or when resulting from a severe economic downturn." Articles 2(2) and 2(3) further specify that a deficit will be considered exceptional "if there is an annual fall of real GDP of at least 2 percent" or if a member state can argue successfully that the circumstances are "exceptional," based on "the abruptness of the downturn or on the accumulated loss of output relative to past trends." The regulation then clarifies the "excessive deficit procedure" set out in Article 104 of the Treaty, including the imposition of fines.

Countries found exceeding the 3 percent of GDP limit must take corrective action "as quickly as possible after [its] emergence." The timing of the policy decisions and the rhythm at which the Commission, which monitors the process, prepares its reports imply that a country can run deficits in excess of 3 percent of GDP for two years in a row without incurring sanctions. If a country fails to take corrective action and to bring its deficit below 3 percent of GDP by the deadline set by the

Council, it is sanctioned. The sanction takes the form of a nonremunerated deposit. The deposit starts at 0.2 percent of GDP and rises by 1/10th of the excess deficit, up to a maximum of 0.5 percent of GDP. Deposits are imposed each year until the excessive deficit is corrected. If the excess is not corrected within two years, the deposit is converted into a fine; otherwise, it is returned.[21]

Exchange Rate Policy The exchange rate of the euro in relation to other currencies such as the dollar and the yen is determined by the market, although market misalignments and excessive exchange rate fluctuations are corrected through a combination of economic policy dialogue, the occasional use of interventions, and verbal exchange rate management.

Macroeconomic Policy Framework
for Accession Countries

Based on the Treaty, three distinct phases for the adoption of the EMU *acquis* by accession countries can be identified: (1) the preaccession period, (2) the period from accession to the adoption of the euro, and (3) the Euro Area phase, after adopting the euro.[22]

Preaccession Phase During the preaccession phase, accession countries carry out the economic reforms and policies needed to fulfill the Copenhagen economic criteria, which are the existence of a market economy and the capacity to cope with competitive pressure and market forces within the EU.[23] In this context, countries have to establish functioning property rights, competition, free price formation, and a well-developed financial sector. If a country is to be able to cope with international competition and if capital is to be channeled smoothly within a country, it is of paramount importance that the domestic banking and financial sector are efficient. Such efficiency requires a high degree of financial intermediation, liquid capital markets, banks with a sufficient capital base, a functioning system of banking and securities supervision, and a sound payments system. In addition, the accession countries must adopt the EMU legislation in order to acquire the status of "Member State with a derogation," which they need to adopt the euro (Article 122). According to

Italianer (2002), the requirements of the legislation are

- Completion of the orderly liberalization of capital movements (Article 56)
- Prohibition of any direct public sector financing by the central bank (Article 101)
- Prohibition of privileged access of the public sector to financial institutions (Article 102)
- Alignment of the national central bank statutes with the Treaty, including the independence of the monetary authorities (Articles 108 and 109).

The first requirement—that capital movements be completely liberalized—underpins the efficient allocation of resources in the internal market.[24] The second and third requirements are related to central bank economic independence, which rests on the condition that operating procedures not be restricted by government policies. Traditionally, the greatest threat to central bank economic independence is pressures to monetize the fiscal deficit. As a result of the second and third requirements, the central bank is prohibited from having primary dealings with the fiscal authorities. Essentially, this prohibition means no automatic overdraft facility for treasuries and no central bank purchases of debt directly from the government. The prohibition of privileged access complements the prohibition of central bank financing, imposes market discipline in public sector borrowing, reinforces freedom of capital movements, and gets rid of the distortions in the allocation of financial resources toward the public sector. The two requirements force the market to establish the relevant price, thereby making concessionary finance more difficult, and they make transactions more visible, thereby making the monitoring of central bank performance much easier. The fourth requirement related to central bank independence prepares the national central bank for its future assignment of seeking price stability, and it reinforces fiscal discipline.

Policy coordination in the preaccession phase between the EU and the accession country is achieved through (1) preparation of an annual Preaccession Economic Programme (PEP) by the accession country, (2) annual evaluation of the PEP by the European Commission, (3) a fiscal notification system, (4) a report on the macroeconomic and financial sector stability developments in candidate countries, (5) macroeconomic forecasts by the

Commission, (6) meetings between the ECB and candidate countries aimed at bringing financial and payment systems in line with those in the Eurosystem, and (7) the Commission's regular reports on progress toward accession.

The PEP concentrates on the economic reforms needed for EU accession, and the PEP procedure offers an opportunity to develop the institutional and analytical capacity necessary to participate in the EMU upon accession, particularly in the areas of economic analysis and medium-term policy planning. The PEP consists of four parts: (1) a review of recent economic developments, (2) a detailed macroeconomic framework, (3) a discussion of public finance issues, and (4) an outline of the structural reform agenda. It places special emphasis on public finance by presenting the medium-term fiscal objectives in terms of the general government deficit, the primary balance, and the public indebtedness. Moreover, the candidate countries specify and explain the factors underpinning their choice of objectives, and the programs undertaken to achieve the objectives should demonstrate the feasibility of the government's fiscal objectives by means of a projection of the main fiscal aggregates. Shortly after submission of the PEP, the Commission evaluates the program. The evaluation does not make an assessment of whether a country has made progress toward meeting the Copenhagen criteria—this is provided on an annual basis by the Commission's regular report on progress toward accession. Yet the accession countries report to the Commission through the fiscal notification system the debt and deficit figures calculated in accordance with the EU methodology based on the ESA 95 system of national accounts. These notifications use the same format as the fiscal notifications provided by member states in the framework of the excessive deficit procedure (see European Commission 2002).

From Accession to Adoption of the Euro Phase

Upon accession, the new member state will have the status of "Member State with a derogation" granted in the accession treaty. It will have to show adherence to the aim of economic and monetary union and compliance with the relevant parts of Title VII of the European Commission Treaty and the other EMU *acquis*. These parts are

- Treatment of exchange rate policy as a matter of common interest and, eventually, participation in the exchange rate mechanism (Article 124)

- Treatment of economic policies as a matter of common concern and coordination of economic policies between the member states through participation in Community procedures (Articles 98 and 99)
- Avoidance of excessive government deficits and adherence to the relevant provisions of the SGP (Article 104)
- Further adaptation of the national central bank's statutes with a view toward integration into the European System of Central Banks (Article 109)
- Progress toward achieving a high degree of sustainable convergence (Article 121).

With accession, the common macroeconomic policy framework becomes more constraining, with a strong reinforcement of fiscal discipline and the integration of other economic policies. Budgetary policy and outcomes become subject to the excessive deficit procedure and the nonpunitive parts of the SGP. The Maastricht Treaty specifies that these countries will have to make progress toward fulfillment of the Maastricht criteria, and, under the conditions of the SGP, they will have to endeavor to avoid excessive deficits. Furthermore, the exchange rate policy becomes a matter of common interest. This development means that, to protect the smooth functioning of the single market, competitive devaluations are not allowed. Thus, new member states must avoid policies leading to excessive fluctuations of the exchange rate. Participation in the ERM II is expected sometime after accession. Such participation implies setting the central rate to the euro and the fluctuation bands within ±15 percent by mutual agreement.

Because the economic policies of the accession countries become a matter of common concern, these policies will be subject to policy coordination and multilateral surveillance procedures. Shortly after accession, the new member states will be required to submit a full notification of government debt, deficit, and associated data. New member states also will have to prepare convergence programs, which will set out their budgetary strategies for the coming years, in particular with respect to the medium-term objective of reaching a budgetary position "close to balance or surplus." The European Council will examine the programs, and, based on the Commission's recommendation, will adopt an opinion on each of the programs.

In addition to the convergence programs, economic and fiscal policy coordination and surveillance in the EU are achieved through the Broad Economic Policy Guidelines (BEPG). These guidelines, which are prepared on an annual basis, present the member states' consensus opinion on macroeconomic and other structural economic policies in the medium term. Each year, the European Commission reviews in its annual economic report the implementation of the guidelines by the member states.[25]

Participation in the Euro Area will be the ultimate goal for each new member state. A favorable decision is made when the conditions for adoption of the single currency are met, after determining whether a new member state has achieved a high degree of sustainable convergence. Prior to accession, there is no requirement that the EU assess progress made on convergence criteria, or that candidates for accession meet the criteria. As it was for the present member states, adoption of the euro occurs when a high degree of sustainable convergence has been demonstrated within the internal market.

Euro Area Phase   The adoption of the euro will add two key elements to the macroeconomic framework of "Member States with a derogation." One is the single stability-oriented monetary policy and the ensuing single exchange rate policy. The second is implementation of the sanction provisions of the SGP, by which member states surpassing the 3 percent ceiling in their deficit will be subjected to substantial fines. The aim is to allow the ECB to conduct an independent monetary policy supported by prudent national fiscal policies, which are subjected to the SGP and policy coordination. The Treaty does not specify any mandatory timetable for fulfillment of the conditions for introduction of the euro. In other words, although the economic policies of the new member states will have to pursue a high degree of sustainable convergence, the speed at which this should happen is left undetermined by EU legislation.

Prospects for Central and Eastern European Countries   The Central and Eastern European countries that acceded to the EU on May 1, 2004, will have to coordinate their economic and fiscal policies with the Community in the ECOFIN Council. They must submit annual convergence programs, and restrictions on capital movements

will no longer be permitted. The EU expects each of the acceding countries to join the ERM II—that is, to agree to an exchange rate arrangement between the euro and each country's currency. This phase will last at least two years. The test period for the exchange rate criterion will probably be from May 1, 2004, to April 30, 2006. It is crucial that a country avoid devaluation within the two-year test period, because that country would fail the exchange rate criterion.

During the second half of 2006, the convergence test will probably be conducted by the ECB and the European Commission. The decision on acceptance into the EMU will be made by ECOFIN on the basis of a proposal of the European Commission and after consultation with the European Parliament and after a discussion in the European Council. The examination of the budget and of government debt will likely be based on the data for 2005 or the latest available figures. In January 1, 2007, the euro will probably be adopted as national currency. The central bank governor of each new EMU country then becomes a member of the Governing Council, the main decision-making body of the ECB.[26]

The Macroeconomic Challenges Facing Turkey

Turkey realizes that, in the long run, price stability and fiscal discipline create the best conditions for sustained, robust economic growth, but currently the situation is problematic. The data in table 1.9 show the EMU convergence criteria for Turkey and the Central and Eastern European countries. The table reveals that the CEE countries are about to satisfy the criteria, but that Turkey is far from satisfying the conditions. In 2003 the inflation rate in Turkey was 25.3 percent, compared with a reference value of 2.7 percent for the EU; the budget deficit as a percentage of GDP was 8.8 percent, compared with a reference value of 3 percent for the EU; the debt-to-GDP ratio was 80.2 percent, compared with a reference value of 60 percent for the EU; and interest rates were 28.5 percent, compared with a reference value of 6.2 percent for the EU.[27]

The challenge facing Turkey is how to move from the current state of affairs to one in which the Maastricht criteria will be satisfied. The main issues are reducing the inflation rate to about 3 percent over time and reducing the debt-to-GDP ratio to 60 percent over time, while attaining sustainability

TABLE 1.9 European Economic and Monetary Union Convergence Criteria, 2000–03

	Inflation Rate (%)				Budget Deficit (% of GDP)				Government Debt (% of GDP)				Interest Rates, 10Y Bonds (last)	Exchange Rate against Parity (max, 2Y)	Currency Regime
	2000	2001	2002	2003	2000	2001	2002	2003	2000	2001	2002	2003			
Czech Rep.	3.9	4.7	1.8	0.1	−4.0	−3.2	−4.6	−6.6	29.2	29.0	22.4	37.6	5.1	−5.0	Managed float (EUR)
Estonia	4.0	5.8	3.6	1.3	−0.7	1.1	1.2	2.4	6.6	6.2	5.4	5.1	2.3	−0.4	Currency board (EUR)
Hungary	9.8	9.2	5.3	4.7	−3.5	−5.0	−9.6	−5.7	56.1	51.5	50.4	58.6	8.4	−9.3	Target zone (EUR)
Latvia	2.7	2.5	1.8	2.9	−2.8	−1.9	−2.7	−1.6	10.0	12.2	13.9	16.3	7.4	−9.9	Peg (SDR)
Lithuania	1.0	1.3	0.3	−1.2	−2.8	−1.4	−2.8	−1.7	28.3	29.0	25.0	23.6	6.4	0.2	Currency board (EUR)
Poland	10.1	5.5	1.9	0.7	−2.7	−6.3	−5.4	−4.5	43.8	38.0	48.0	51.0	7.3	−17.2	Float
Slovakia	12.0	7.3	3.3	8.5	−6.8	−7.2	−1.9	−3.6	32.9	42.7	32.0	42.8	5.1	−6.3	Managed float (EUR)
Slovenia	8.9	8.5	7.5	5.6	−1.4	−1.3	−1.1	−1.4	25.1	25.4	32.2	26.8	4.0	−4.3	Managed float (EUR)
Bulgaria	10.1	7.9	5.8	2.3	−1.1	−1.0	0.2	0.0	83.8	72.5	60.9	53.7	5.4	−0.8	Currency board (EUR)
Romania	45.7	34.5	22.5	15.3	−4.1	−3.7	−1.7	−2.3	29.2	31.2	25.7	26.2	17.3	−19.2	Managed float (US$)
Turkey	54.9	54.4	45.0	25.3	−6.1	−29.8	−12.6	−8.8	65.4	102.6	89.5	80.2	28.5	16.3	Float
Reference value	2.8	3.3	3.0	2.7	−3.0	−3.0	−3.0	−3.0	60.0	60.0	60.0	60.0	6.2	+/− 15%	

Note: Parity refers to the last three-year average exchange rate against the euro. In the case of Turkey, the interest rate is the annual compound interest rate obtained in the auction of treasury bills and government bonds during November 2004. SDR = special drawing rights.

Sources: Deutsche Bank Research, EU Enlargement Monitor, April 2002, and EU Monitor, September 2004; State Planning Organization 2004; Central Bank of Turkey (http://www.tcmb.gov.tr).

of the current account and decreasing the unemployment rate in the economy.

Inflation

As of November 2004, the annual inflation rate in Turkey was 9.8 percent, and the government was aiming to reduce the inflation rate to 8 percent in 2005. To satisfy the Maastricht criteria on inflation, Turkey must reduce the inflation rate further, to 3 percent. The annual inflation rate in Turkey has been reduced in recent years through strict implementation of the IMF economic program, which calls for controlling the growth of base money. Another factor leading to a lower inflation rate has been the decrease in the cost of imported goods, achieved as a result of real appreciation of the Turkish lira. But reducing the inflation rate over time through real appreciation of the currency is not sustainable in the long run, because the real appreciation of the currency will lead to problems of sustainability of the current account. Current account sustainability in Turkey as of December 2004 requires that the real exchange rate be depreciated to its long-run equilibrium level.[28] Yet reducing the inflation rate by reducing the public sector component of the wholesale price level, p_{public}, is also not sustainable, because this policy will lead to increases in the ratio of the public sector borrowing requirement to GDP, leading, in turn, to problems related to the sustainability of fiscal policy. Thus p_{public} should be increased at least at the same rate as the inflation rate in the economy. The only policy option for reducing the rate of inflation is therefore to control the growth rate of base money.

To reduce the inflation rate from its current level of 9.8 percent to around 3 percent, Turkey will probably go through a disinflation period. But disinflation in general entails costs, and the most commonly used measure of the costs of disinflation is the "sacrifice ratio," which can be defined as the number of percentage points of lost output associated with a policy-induced 1 percent reduction in inflation. Following Ball (1994), we identify disinflation episodes as the time range within which trend inflation falls substantially and define trend inflation as a centered five-quarter moving average of the actual inflation rate.[29] During the time period between the first quarter of 1987 and the third quarter of 2003, we identify in Turkey two disinflation episodes. The first episode starts at the fourth quarter of 1994 and ends during the fourth quarter of 1996. The second episode starts at the first quarter of 1998 and ends during the first quarter of 2001. The trend inflation rate decreases by 29.62 percent during the first episode and by 43.05 percent during the second episode. We assume that output is at its potential level at the start of the disinflation episode. For potential output and output gap projections, we consider the estimates provided by the Turkish State Planning Organization (SPO).[30] They have estimated the potential output using the linear method, the Hodrick-Prescott method, and the production function method (see State Planning Organization 2003). The sacrifice ratio is then calculated by the formula

$$(1.3) \quad SR = \left[\sum_{t=S}^{Z+4} (y_t - y_t^*) \right] \bigg/ (\pi_t - \pi_{t-1})$$

where y_t stands for the natural logarithm of real output, y_t^* for the natural logarithm of potential output, π_{t-1} for the trend inflation rate at the beginning of the episode, π_t for the trend inflation rate at the end of the episode, and the disinflation episode starts at period S and ends at period Z. The calculations are presented in table 1.10. In the table,

TABLE 1.10   Estimates of the Sacrifice Ratio

Episode	HP Filter	Production Function	Linear Method
April 1994–April 1997	0.000	0.000	−0.013
April 1994–April 1996	0.005	0.006	−0.003
January 1998–January 2002	−0.001	−0.001	−0.001
January 1998–January 2001	0.005	0.005	0.007

Source: The authors.

the first line of each episode denotes the estimate of the sacrifice ratio obtained under the assumption that output returns to its potential level four quarters after the end of an episode, as in Ball (1994). By contrast, the second line of each episode denotes the estimate of the sacrifice ratio obtained under the assumption that output returns to its potential level right at the end of the episode.

The table reveals that the estimates of the sacrifice ratio in Turkey are not very much different from zero,[31] which indicates, in turn, that disinflation in Turkey will entail relatively little output cost. The result probably stems from the extreme flexibility of the Turkish labor market.[32] But the output costs of disinflation will increase as the Turkish labor market becomes less flexible.[33] Thus it would be advisable for Turkey to follow the disinflationary policies as long as the labor market is flexible.

Public Debt and Fiscal Policy

To analyze the issues associated with reducing the debt-to-GDP ratio from 80.2 percent in 2003 to 60 percent over time, we consider the government budget constraint represented by

$$(1.4) \quad \begin{aligned} G_t - T_t + i_t B_{t-1} + i^* E_t B_{t-1}^* + FSB_t \\ = (B_t - B_{t-1}) + E_t(B_t^* - B_{t-1}^*) \\ + M_t - M_{t-1} + PRIV_t \end{aligned}$$

where G refers to government expenditures excluding the interest payments, T government revenues, B the TL-denominated debt stock of the public sector, B^* the FX-denominated debt stock of the public sector, i the nominal interest rate on the TL-denominated government debt, i^* the interest rate on the FX-denominated government debt, E the exchange rate, FSB the public expenditure for the financial sector bailout, M the monetary base, and $PRIV$ privatization revenues. Let $Y_t = p_t$, y_t be the nominal GDP, p the GDP deflator, and y real GDP. Denoting the primary-surplus-to-GDP ratio by $ps_t = (T_t - G_t)/Y_t$, the TL-denominated debt-to-GDP ratio by $b_t = (B_t/Y_t)$, the FX-denominated-debt-to-GDP ratio by $b_t^* = (E_t B_t^*)/Y_t$, the privatization-revenues-to-GDP ratio by $priv_t = (PRIV_t/Y_t)$, the financial-sector-bailout-to-GDP ratio by $fsb_t = (FSB_t/Y_t)$, the domestic rate of inflation by π, the foreign rate of inflation by π^*, the growth rate of real GDP by g,

the real rate of interest by r, the foreign real interest rate by r^*, the real exchange rate by q, the rate of depreciation of the real exchange rate by η, and the velocity of money by V, we get the equation determining the time path of the total-debt-to-GDP ratio $d_t = b_t + b_t^*$:

$$(1.5) \quad \begin{aligned} d_t = {}& - ps_t + \frac{(1+r)}{(1+g)} b_{t-1} \\ & + \frac{(1+r^*)(1+\eta)}{(1+g)} b_{t-1}^* \\ & - \frac{1}{V} \left[\frac{g + \pi + \pi g}{(1+\pi)(1+g)} \right] \\ & - priv_t + fsb_t \end{aligned}$$

The equation shows that debt-to-GDP ratio decreases with increases in the primary-surplus-to-GDP ratio ps, the growth rate of real GDP g, the privatization-revenues-to-GDP ratio $priv$, and the seigniorage-revenues-to-GDP ratio, defined as $\frac{1}{V} \left[\frac{g+\pi+\pi g}{(1+\pi)(1+g)} \right]$. By contrast, the debt-to-GDP ratio increases with increases in the real domestic interest rate r, the real foreign interest rate r^*, the rate of depreciation of the real exchange rate η, and the financial-sector-bailout-to-GDP ratio fsb.

Over 2000–03, seigniorage and privatization revenues were running at about 1.3 and 1.7 percent of GDP, respectively. The crucial parameters determining the time path of the debt-to-GDP ratio turn out to be the primary-surplus-to-GDP ratio, the domestic and foreign real rates of interest, and the rate of real exchange rate depreciation. Turkey is committed to the primary surplus target of 6.5 percent of GNP over the next few years. In 2004 the domestic real interest rate was running at about 12 percent and the foreign real interest rate at about 8 percent (see OECD 2002 and IMF 2004). Finally, it is noteworthy that Turkey, after appreciating the real exchange rate by 13 percent in 2002, appreciated the real exchange rate by a further 23.8 percent in 2003. All these factors have contributed to reducing the debt-to-GDP ratio. But even under these favorable circumstances, it will take quite a long time to reduce the debt-to-GDP ratio from its level of 80.2 percent in 2003 to 60 percent and below. Here three issues deserve careful analysis.

First, the real appreciation of the exchange rate contributed substantially to the reduction in the debt-to-GDP ratio during 2002 and 2003. But this policy is not sustainable in the long run, because the real appreciation of the currency will lead to problems of sustainability in the current account, as explained later in this chapter in some detail.

Second, EU accession will entail costs for Turkey that must be identified and financed. These costs will include the social consequences of economic restructuring, such as those in the agriculture sector, where restructuring presents particular problems for small farmers. The process of adopting the *acquis communautaire* entails, among other things, comprehensive structural reforms of the public administration and the productive sectors, as well as extensive investment in human resources and the environment. From a budgetary perspective, the fiscal costs of EU accession in the other accession countries have been estimated to be over 3 percent of GNP annually. Turkey would also face significant fiscal costs—costs that would have to be financed in the context of continuing fiscal adjustment.[34] This situation implies either a reduction in the primary-surplus-to-GDP ratio by the same amount or further increases in the revenues of the public sector.

Third, to reduce the debt-to-GDP ratio from its level of 80.2 percent in 2003 to 60 percent over time, Turkey, even in the face of the higher costs of EU accession, must stick to the primary surplus target of at least 6.5 percent of GNP over the next few years. Any downward deviation from the target will postpone achievement of the 60 percent debt-to-GDP ratio. Achievement of the primary surplus target of at least 6.5 percent of GNP over time requires that Turkey increase its tax revenue by broadening its tax base. In this context, Turkey could introduce, like Russia and Ukraine, a flat tax on income at a relatively low rate. The introduction of such a flat tax at a low rate would improve tax compliance and efficiency,[35] and it would increase the tax base and thus the tax revenue, as long as the necessary steps are taken simultaneously to modernize the tax administration and improve tax compliance.[36] Such measures also will help to decrease the share of the informal sector in the economy.

Finally, the government's desire to achieve a primary surplus target of at least 6.5 percent of GNP over the next few years will constrain its use of fiscal policy for decreasing the unemployment rate in

the economy, which was 9.5 percent during the third quarter of 2004. That constraint may have serious political implications, unless the country tries to broaden its tax base, reduce the tax burden of economic units in the formal sector, and improve tax compliance in the country.

Sustainability of Current Account

The basic presumption of our approach is that the current account is sustainable. If not, Turkey could face an exchange rate collapse or an external debt default, which, in turn, would imply a reduction in real income and employment, deviating from the long-run growth path. Starting from the notion that under current account sustainability the country must satisfy its lifetime budget constraint, we contend that the current policies are sustainable if continuation of the current government policy stance and private sector behavior into the future does not entail a drastic policy shift or lead to a currency or balance of payments crisis.

Here we emphasize the points stressed earlier by considering the balance of payments relation, which can be written as

$$(1.6) \qquad TB_t^\$ - i^* D_{t-1} + FDI_t + D_t - D_{t-1} \\ - \Delta R_t = 0$$

where $TB^\$$ denotes the noninterest current account (NICA), i^* the foreign rate of interest, D the stock of foreign debt, FDI the net foreign direct investment, R the foreign exchange reserves of the country, and ΔR_t the change in reserves. Also, $(TB_t^\$ - i^* D_{t-1}) = Current\ Account_t$ and $(FDI_t + D_t - D_{t-1}) = Capital\ Account_t$. All variables are measured in terms of foreign currency. If $d_t = \frac{E_t D_t}{p_t y_t}$ is the foreign-debt-to-GDP ratio, $tb_t = \frac{E_t TB_t^\$}{p_t y_t}$ the noninterest-current-account-to-GDP ratio, $fdi_t = \frac{FDI_t E_t}{p_t y_t}$ the FDI-to-GDP ratio, and $\Delta r_t = \frac{(\Delta R_t) E_t}{p_t y_t}$ the change-in-reserves-to-GDP ratio, the equation determining the time path of d_t can be written as

$$(1.7) \qquad d_t = -tb_t + \frac{(1 + r^*)(1 + \eta)}{1 + g} d_{t-1} \\ - fdi_t + \Delta r_t$$

where r^* denotes the foreign real rate of interest and η the rate of depreciation of the RER. The equation reveals that the external-debt-to-GDP ratio decreases with increases in the noninterest-current-account-to-GDP ratio tb, the FDI-to-GDP ratio *fdi*, and the growth rate of GDP *g*. By contrast, the debt-to-GDP ratio increases with increases in the foreign real interest rate r^*, rate of depreciation of the RER η, and changes in the reserves-to-GDP ratio Δr.

Following the approach of von Hagen and Harden (1994), we solve this expression forward for *n* periods and obtain

$$(1.8) \qquad d_t = \Gamma_t \delta_{t,n} d_{t+n} + \Gamma_t \sum_{i=1}^{n} \delta_{t,i} A_{t+i}$$

where

$$\delta_{t,k} \prod_{i=1}^{k} \frac{1 + g_i}{(1 + r_i^*)(1 + \eta_i)}$$

and

$$A_t = tb_t + fdi_t - \Delta r_r.$$

Here, $\delta_{t,k}$ can be interpreted as the "k-periods ahead" discount factor used to calculate the present value of assets and liabilities in period $t + k$ for period *t*. $\Gamma_t x_{t+k}$ denotes the period *t* expectation of the variable *x* in period $t + k$. The equation shows that current-debt-to-GDP ratio equals the expected discounted present value of foreign debt outstanding in period $t + n$ relative to GDP, plus the sum of all discounted A_t's between period *t* and period $t + n$. Theoretically, the intertemporal budget constraint requires that $\lim \Gamma_t \delta_{t,n} d_{t+n} \leq 0$ as *n* becomes very large, so that foreign debt remains bounded relative to GDP. If the intertemporal budget constraint were violated, private investors would realize that the government's liabilities would eventually exceed its revenue-raising capabilities. As a result, the price of the debt of the country would fall to zero, and the country would see itself barred from international capital markets.

To translate the intertemporal budget constraint into a practically more relevant requirement, we consider the above relation for a limited period of time n^* and add the condition that the discounted-debt-to-GDP ratio at the end of period $t + n^*$ should not exceed the debt-to-GDP ratio at time *t*. We use actual data on d_t, tb_t, and fdi_t for any year during the time period 1984–2003. For each year *t* of the time period, we estimate the expected discounted present value at time *t* of foreign debt outstanding in period $t + n^*$ relative to GDP, plus the sum of all discounted A_t's between period *t* and period $t + n^*$. As for the government policy stance and the private sector behavior over the period *t* to

$t + n^*$, we assume that the values of tb_{t+i} and fdi_{t+i} for $i = 1, \ldots, n^*$ will remain unchanged at their initial values of tb_t and fdi_t. Thus we assume that the government, private sector, and rest of the world will not change the policies they pursue in period *t* over the time period $t + 1$ and $t + n^*$.

A look at Turkey's annual GDP growth rate over the period 1980–2003 reveals that the average growth rate of GDP amounted to 4.1 percent during 1980–1989 and to 3.7 percent during 1990–2003. Thus for the growth rate of GDP over the time period *t* to $t + n^*$ we take the figure of 4 percent. By contrast, the foreign real interest rate is to equal 8 percent. Finally, we assume in the following calculations that $\Delta r = 0$ for each year of the period *t* to $t + n^*$ and that over the same period η equals zero.

Following the approach of von Hagen and Harden (1994), the current account is not sustainable if

$$(1.9) \qquad S(n^*) = d_t - \Gamma_t \delta_{t,n} d_{t+n}$$
$$= \Gamma_t \sum_{i=1}^{n} \delta_{t,i} A_{t+i} < 0.$$

This is a rather mild sustainability condition. Here d_t denotes the actual debt-to-GDP ratio in period *t*, and $A_{t+i} = (tb_t + fdi_t)$ for $i = 1, \ldots, n^*$. The result of the calculations for $n^* = 10$, $n^* = 20$, and $n^* = 25$ are shown in table 1.11.

The table reveals that during 1993 the current account was unsustainable in the sense that the actual debt-to-GDP ratio in 1993 fell short of the expected discounted present value of foreign debt outstanding in period 2003 relative to GDP by 14.03 percent when $n^* = 10$ and that the actual debt-to-GDP ratio in 1993 fell short of the expected discounted present value of foreign debt outstanding in period 2018 relative to GDP by 27.26 percent when $n^* = 25$. This finding indicates that the current account needed adjustment in the NICA-to-GDP and FDI-to-GDP ratios. During 1994, Turkey increased the NICA-to-GDP ratio considerably, but there was not much change in the FDI-to-GDP ratio. The table indicates that the policy was successful; the sustainability measure was positive thereafter. The warning signals for the 2001 currency crisis were evident in the negative figures of the sustainability measure for the year 2000. The situation improved after the crisis, when the sustainability measure increased and became positive at the end of 2001. Although the current account was sustainable in 2001 and 2002, the system was not sustainable again in 2003.

TABLE 1.11   Current Account Sustainability Measures, 1984–2003
(values of S (n^*), percent)

	10 Years	20 Years	25 Years
1984	1.55	2.61	3.00
1985	6.53	11.01	12.69
1986	4.85	8.18	9.43
1987	12.30	20.73	23.89
1988	39.31	66.27	76.38
1989	29.16	49.15	56.65
1990	2.20	3.71	4.28
1991	19.12	32.23	37.15
1992	11.54	19.46	22.43
1993	−14.03	−23.65	−27.26
1994	36.46	61.45	70.83
1995	3.00	5.06	5.83
1996	1.74	2.93	3.38
1997	3.06	5.16	5.95
1998	21.57	36.37	41.91
1999	9.89	16.67	19.21
2000	−25.41	−42.83	−49.36
2001	58.32	98.31	113.31
2002	12.70	21.40	24.67
2003	−8.79	−14.81	−17.07

Source: The authors.

A look at the sustainability measure for 2003 with $n^* = 25$ reveals that the actual-debt-to-GDP ratio in 2003 fell short of the expected discounted present value of foreign debt outstanding in the period 2028 by 17.07 percent. The system is not sustainable. The sustainability of the current account requires that the value of the sustainability measure be increased so that it becomes positive. This goal can be achieved either through an increase in the NICA-to-GDP ratio tb_t or through an increase in the FDI-to-GDP ratio fdi_t during each year of the period 2004–28 or through a combination of increases in both the NICA-to-GDP and FDI-to-GDP ratios during the same time period. During 2003, the actual value of $A_t = (tb_t + fdi_t)$ was −1.08 percent. For Turkey to achieve the minimal condition for external sustainability, the value of A_t during each time period of the interval 2004–29 would have to be 0 percent. Thus Turkey has to increase the sum of its noninterest-current-account-to-GDP ratio and its FDI-to-GDP ratio during each period of the interval 2004–29 by at least 1.08 percent. Supposing that fdi_t during the time period 2004–28 remains constant at its 2003

level of 0.03 percent, we next turn to the study of the determinants of noninterest-current-account-to-GDP ratio.[37]

Using quarterly data from 1988 (first quarter) to 2003 (second quarter) we note that one of the main determinants of this ratio is the RER. A second factor that strongly affects the NICA-to-GDP ratio is the aggregate demand for domestic goods and services, consisting of total consumption plus investment demand in the home country as well as the rest of the world. As the aggregate domestic demand for goods and services in the home country increases, it triggers imports, and, other things being equal, the NICA-to-GDP ratio is expected to decline. Similarly, as aggregate domestic demand for goods and services increases in the rest of the world, it triggers imports of the foreign country, and, other things being equal, the NICA-to-GDP ratio in the home country is expected to increase.

To explain the developments in the NICA, the following equation is estimated:

$$(1.10) \quad (NICA/GDP)$$
$$= \beta_0 + \beta_1 \, d\log(ADD)$$
$$+ \beta_2 \, d\log(ADDF) + \beta_3 \, RER + \beta_4 DQ3$$
$$+ \beta_5 \, D1999 + \beta_6 \, D93ST + \beta_7 \, D2000$$

where $d\log(ADD)$ denotes the annual growth rate of real aggregate domestic demand in the home country; $d\log(ADDF)$ the annual growth rate of real aggregate domestic demand in the rest of the world; $DQ3$ the third-quarter seasonal dummy; $D1999$ the recession and earthquake dummy for the year 1999, taking the value of 1 for the second, third, and fourth quarters of 1999 and 0 otherwise; $D93ST$ the structural break dummy in 1993, taking the value of 1 after 1993 and 0 otherwise; and $D2000$ the exchange rate–based stabilization measures, taking the value of 1 for all quarters of 2000 and 0 otherwise. The $D93ST$ dummy refers to the structural break in Turkey's balance of payments that took place after the liberalization of the capital account in 1990. Because economic agents respond with lag to such decisions, a series of tests were conducted to identify the structural break resulting from this decision. All of the variables used in the estimation were checked for unit roots, and it was learned that the series are all stationary. Because of the simultaneity problems faced in the model, we use instrumental variable techniques to estimate the parameters.[38] The results of the estimation are presented in table 1.12.

TABLE 1.12   Results for Quarterly Instrumental Variable Regression of Ratio of Noninerest Current Account (NICA) to GDP

Variable	Coefficient	t-Statistic
C	−2.56863	−1.41186
d log (aggregate domestic demand, home country)	−29.89038	−12.12362
d log (aggregate domestic demand, foreign country)	38.84045	1.95129
Real exchange rate	0.03719	1.97118
DQ3	1.84541	4.52182
D1999	−3.82977	−4.34096
D93ST	−0.91545	−2.34142
D2000	−2.72463	−3.18816
R-squared	0.82106	
Adjusted R-squared	0.79787	
Durbin-Watson statistic	2.14602	

Source: The authors.

The coefficients of the variables are all statistically significant, and all have the expected signs. An increase in the growth rate of aggregate domestic demand in the home country reduces the NICA-to-GDP ratio; an increase in the growth rate of aggregate domestic demand in the rest of the world increases that ratio. The ratio increases as the RER depreciates. The coefficient of the structural change dummy is negative, which indicates that liberalization of the capital account had a negative impact on the NICA-to-GDP ratio, as expected.

The above considerations reveal that the NICA-to-GDP ratio can be increased by decreasing aggregate demand for domestic goods and services and/or by depreciating the RER. Decreasing the aggregate demand for goods and services requires that the country aims for a more ambitious fiscal objective than the constant primary surplus of 6.5 percent of GDP. But this will be very painful after so many failed stabilization attempts. The alternative is to depreciate the RER and keep the RER at its "long-run equilibrium level" over time.[39]

To determine the extent of depreciation in the RER, we consider the regression equation reported in table 1-12. But, this equation yields rather high levels of required rates of depreciation of the RER for alternative specifications of the sustainability condition. We therefore consider a different approach in order to determine the extent of the required rate of depreciation of the RER for achieving current account sustainability. We consider the elasticity of the ratio of noninterest-current account-to-GDP with respect to

the RER, $\theta = \left(\frac{d\ NICA/GDP}{d\ RER} \frac{RER}{NICA/GDP} \right)$. Then starting from initial trade balance we derive that

$$\theta = (\eta_{im} + \eta_{exp} - 1),$$

where η_{im} and η_{exp} denote the import and export elasticities with respect to the RER. Estimates based on estimated Turkish import and export functions range quite widely. Here we consider the estimates of Tansel and Togan (1987) who determine the export price elasticity as 0.933 and import price elasticity as 0.472. Thus, $\theta = 0.405$. Considering the ratio of exports to GDP of 19.6 percent, the parameter values imply that a reduction of the ratio of noninterest-current account-to-GDP of 1 percent requires a depreciation of the RER by 12.6 percent. Thus sustainability of the current account following the approach of von Hagen and Harden (1994) requires that the RER at the end of 2003 be depreciated by 13.6 percent.

An alternative specification of the sustainability condition requires that the ratio of the stock of foreign liabilities to GDP stay constant over time at its initial value in time period 2003. In that case, the equation determining the time path of the debt-to-GDP ratio d can be solved for the equilibrium value of the sum of tb and fdi, under the assumption that $\Delta r = 0$, as

$$(1.11) \quad (tb + fdi) = -\left[\frac{(g - r^* - \eta - r^*\eta)}{(1 + g)} \right] d$$

Assuming that η equals 0 and setting the values of $g = 0.04$, $r^* = 0.08$, and $d = 0.612$ of the year

2003, the equilibrium value of $(tb + fdi)$ is determined to be 2.354 percent. Because in 2003 the actual value of $(tb_t + fdi_t)$ equaled -1.08 percent, Turkey must increase the sum of its noninterest-current-account-to-GDP and FDI-to-GDP ratios over time by 3.4 percent. Suppose again that fdi_t over time stays constant at its 2003 level of 0.03 percent. Then the increase in tb_t, and thus in A_t over time, can be achieved by depreciating the RER by about 42.8 percent and maintaining it at about that level over time.

Finally, following the suggestion of Reinhart, Rogoff, and Savastano (2003), we consider cases in which the country tries to decrease its ratio of stock of foreign liabilities to GDP from its initial value of 0.612 to 0.5 and 0.4 over a period of 10 years. In those cases, Turkey has to increase the sum of its noninterest-current-account-to-GDP ratio and its FDI-to-GDP ratio over time by 4.3 and 5.2 percent, respectively. This change, under the assumption that fdi_t over time stays constant at its 2003 level, requires that the RER be depreciated by 54.2 percent and 65.5 percent, respectively.

Consider now the issue of increasing the FDI-to-GDP ratio. A striking feature of foreign direct investment flows to Turkey is that the level is too low compared with that of FDI flows to developing countries with similar levels of GDP per capita. In particular, the FDI flows to Central and Eastern European countries are much larger than those to Turkey. However, in terms of population, Turkey's is larger than that of Poland, the Czech Republic, and Hungary combined. In terms of GDP, Turkey's economy is four times larger than that of the Czech Republic or Hungary, and one-quarter larger than that of Poland in 2000. In terms of gross fixed capital formation, Turkey's investments during 2000 were three to four times larger than those of the Czech Republic and Hungary and roughly a sixth larger than those of Poland. In terms of average annual inflows of FDI during the 1990s, Turkey attracted inflows valued at US$800 million, which is roughly one-fifth of the US$4.1 billion in FDI inflows to Poland and significantly lower than the inflows to the Czech Republic and Hungary, each of which attracted about US$2.1 billion per year.

An explanation of the factors determining the FDI flows must begin with a definition of the investment climate in the country. It is the policy, institutional, and behavioral environment, present and expected, that influences the perceived returns and risks associated with investment in terms of both quantity and productivity of investment flows. Investment climate thus defined depends on a wide array of factors that can be grouped under the headings of (1) macroeconomic and trade policies, (2) infrastructure, and (3) governance and institutions.

Although Turkey had an open trade regime over the past two decades, it was unable to attract large FDI inflows. One of the main culprits behind this failure was the uncertain macroeconomic environment, which, along with the uncertainties stemming from domestic politics and the ensuing high real interest rates, produced a very erratic growth performance. Throughout the past two decades, Turkey put on hold many decisions that could help foreign investors cope with high inflation. One of the critical measures that Turkey did not introduce was the inflation accounting framework in the context of the highly inflationary environment. Infrastructure-related factors were at play as well. Although the quantity and quality of Turkey's broadly defined infrastructure—including its geographic and demographic endowments and its physical and financial infrastructure—help to position Turkey as a potentially powerful magnet for FDI inflows, these factors were ineffective in Turkey's effort to increase those flows. The main bottlenecks, as emphasized by Dutz, Us, and Yılmaz in chapter 10 of this volume, seem to have been insufficient respect for the rule of law and weak competition in local markets, reinforced by an uneven application of bureaucratic red tape. To attract higher levels of FDI flows in the future, Turkey must therefore not only improve its macroeconomic environment, but also increase respect for the rule of law, increase competition in local markets, and reduce the bureaucratic red tape.

Once Turkey is able to attract higher levels of FDI into the country, it does not need to depreciate its RER by as much as before in order to attain sustainability in its current account. With increases in the FDI-to-GDP ratios, the calculated required rates of depreciation of the RER decreases. When the net FDI-to-GDP ratio increases by 1.08 percent to 1.11 percent of GDP while the non-interest-current-account-to-GDP ratio stays constant at its 2003 value of -1.11 percent, then the system becomes sustainable under the approach of von

Hagen and Harden (1994) with no change in the RER. For increases in net FDI-to-GDP ratio below 1.08 percent, the required rate of depreciation of the RER will be positive but less than 13.6 percent. In the second case when sustainability requires that debt-to-GDP ratio stays constant over time the system becomes sustainable with no change in RER when the net FDI-to-GDP ratio increases by 3.4 percent while the non-interest-current-account-to-GDP ratio stays again at its 2003 value of -1.11 percent. In this case for increases in net FDI-to-GDP ratio below 3.4 percent, the required rate of depreciation of the RER will again be positive but less than 42.8 percent. Finally, under the third approach when sustainability requires that debt-to-GDP ratio decreases over a period of 10 years from its initial value of 0.612 to 0.4, the system becomes sustainable with no change in RER when the net FDI-to-GDP ratio increases by 5.2 percent while the non-interest-current-account-to-GDP ratio stays at its 2003 value of -1.11 percent. For increases in net FDI-to-GDP ratio below 5.2 percent, the required rate of depreciation of the RER again be positive but less than 65.5 percent.

Employment and Growth

As emphasized earlier in this chapter, the unemployment rate in 2003 was high in Turkey. The employment challenge facing the country is to create jobs for those unemployed, to create new jobs for those entering the labor force for the first time at an average rate of 900 thousand persons per year, and to increase the labor force participation rate from its low level of 48.3 percent.

To solve the unemployment problem over time, Turkey has to preserve the flexibility of the labor market and achieve a relatively high but sustainable growth rate of GDP over the next decades. Turkey can no longer sustain the flexibility of the labor market through the lax enforcement of laws on taxation and social security, because such enforcement tends to create different problems for Turkish society.[40] Instead, the country has to attack the root of the problem, which is the large wedge between labor costs and workers' disposable income because of the high labor taxes. Such a high tax wedge raises labor costs, discourages work in the formal economy, and contributes to high nonemployment in the working-age population. The challenge facing Turkey is to reduce the high labor taxes without increasing the fiscal deficits. The country has to introduce tax reforms that will aim to lower the personal income and social security taxes, while broadening the tax base through, for example, the introduction of a relatively low flat tax and simultaneously modernizing the tax administration.

Achieving a relatively high but sustainable growth rate of GDP is also a challenge for Turkey. According to a recent study by Togan (2003), the problem can be analyzed in terms of the growth of productivity and the growth of employment.[41] Noting that Turkey achieved annual productivity growth of 3.12 percent over the period 1950–99, Togan emphasizes that the percentage contribution of the three sources of growth to productivity growth were (1) 38.1 percent from growth in the amount of capital per worker in the economy (capital deepening), (2) 25.15 percent from improvements in labor quality, and (3) 36.75 percent from total factor productivity (TFP) growth.[42] Thus if Turkey wants to achieve higher growth rates of GDP than the 3.6 percent a year achieved over the period 1990–2002, it has to increase, on the one hand, the productivity growth rate—through capital deepening, improvements in labor quality, and increases in the growth rate of the TFP—and, on the other hand, the growth rate of employment.[43]

Togan (2003) points out that Turkey, to increase the amount of capital per worker, has to increase not only its investment ratio but also its domestic savings rate, because too much reliance on foreign savings over considerably long periods of time may lead to problems of solvency and sustainability of the current account. In addition, Turkey has to increase its investment in human capital formation. It must increase not only the proportion of the adult population with primary, secondary, and higher education, but also the quality of education at each of these levels. Turkey also must increase TFP growth. Because the sources of TFP growth are better technology, better organization, specialization, and innovations on the shop floor, Turkey has to increase the channels of acquiring knowledge, as well as the competitive pressure in the economies under consideration. Besides creating the knowledge itself through strict enforcement of intellectual property rights, Turkey can adopt the knowledge created by others, mainly through international trade, FDI, and licensing. Finally, various economists have shown that trade liberalization affects productivity change positively.[44] TFP growth also depends on the macroeconomic policies followed.

To elaborate statistically the relationship between the TFP and trade and macroeconomic policies, we follow the approach of Burnside and Dollar (2000) in which

$$(1.12) \quad TFP = \alpha_0 + \alpha_1 \, INFLATION \\ + \alpha_2 \, OPEN \\ + \alpha_3 \, BUDGET \, SURPLUS$$

where *INFLATION* refers to the rate of inflation measured by the GDP deflator, *OPEN* to the trade indicator, and *BUDGET SURPLUS* to the ratio of budget surplus to GDP. In the equation, the second term indicates the effect of instability in macro policies. It is hypothesized that instability in macroeconomic policies negatively influences the TFP and that its coefficient should therefore be negative. The third term refers to trade policies measured by the ratio of exports and imports to GDP. The coefficient would be positive if trade liberalization contributes to increases in the TFP. Finally, it is hypothesized that a budget surplus positively influences the TFP. Insolvent debt paths characterized by large budget deficits will require monetization of debts and thus inflation, leading to instability in the economy. Uncertainty from instability reduces both the willingness and the capability of economic units to take a long-term view toward increasing efficiency, which eventually decreases the TFP. Furthermore, falling budget deficits will lead to greater private use of private savings, leading to increases in the TFP.

Based on annual data for 1951–99, the estimation yields

$$(1.13) \quad TFP = 0.593 - 0.0713 \, INFLATION \\ (0.477) \quad (-2.741) \\ + 0.2454 \, OPEN \\ (2.693) \\ + 0.6832 \, BUDGET \, SURPLUS \\ (1.996)$$

$n = 49$ (1951–99); $R^2 = 0.311$; DW = 2.2686.

The variables have the expected signs. Instability in macroeconomic policies proxied by the inflation rate negatively influences the TFP. Yet trade liberalization and budget surplus positively affect the TFP.

The factors just mentioned determine productivity and its growth rate, which, in turn, influence the growth rate of GDP. However, for a given level of productivity growth, GDP growth depends positively on the growth rate of employment, and the level of employment in the economy is determined largely by the flexibility in labor markets. Increases in labor market flexibility increase employment and reduce the unemployment rate in the economy. Thus, GDP increases until labor is fully employed with increases in labor market flexibility.

In summary, to increase the growth rate of its GDP, Turkey must (1) increase not only its investment ratio but also its domestic savings rate, (2) increase its investment in human capital formation, (3) follow outward-oriented and prudent macroeconomic policies, and (4) increase the flexibility in the labor market. The pursuit of these policies, however, should not jeopardize the sustainability of fiscal policy or the sustainability of the current account.

Exchange Rate Policy

As for an appropriate exchange rate regime, the Maastricht criteria do put restrictions on the permissible exchange rate regime after accession. Floating within a band or target zone measuring no more than 15 percent from a euro central rate, with intervention at or within margins of the band, is permissible. Even without adopting a formal target zone, the country could manage to maintain its exchange rate within 15 percent of some euro central rate. Definitely permissible under the Maastricht exchange rate criterion are a conventional fixed exchange rate regime and a currency board with the euro. Furthermore, any of the previous regimes could be combined with the adoption of the euro as a parallel currency. Under such a scheme, the euro would be joint legal tender with the domestic currency. However, full, unilateral euroization, with the abolition of the domestic currency, is not compatible with the Maastricht criteria for joining the EMU. The argument is that, once the domestic currency has been abolished, the Council of Ministers can no longer determine the conversion rate at which the candidate EMU member's currency eventually joins the EMU.

Before we turn to the question of what the exchange rate arrangement for Turkey ought to be during the preaccession period, a quick glance at current practice by the 10 new members and candidate countries is useful. Table 1.9 characterizes the current exchange rate regime of each of these countries. Among the 10 CEE countries, Bulgaria, Estonia and Lithuania have currency boards with respect to the euro; Latvia has a fixed exchange rate regime with a peg against the special drawing rights (SDR); Hungary has a target zone with a central rate fixed against the euro and a 15 percent fluctuation band on either side; the Czech Republic, Slovakia, Slovenia, and Romania have managed float; Poland has floating currency.

The countries under consideration had opted during the early 1990s for different exchange rate regimes. Although most of them chose some kind of fixed exchange rate arrangements, others such as Slovenia opted for more flexible solutions. Since then, most of these countries have moved toward more flexible exchange rate arrangments. For example, Poland now has fully flexible exchange rates. Meanwhile, in all of these countries except Romania inflation is under control, and as of 2003 five countries satisfied the Maastricht condition on inflation (the Czech Republic, Estonia, Lithuania, Poland, and Bulgaria). All of these countries are interested in adopting the euro as early as possible. According to Nuti (2002), the benefits of early adoption of the euro include greater exchange rate certainty, greater policy credibility, lower transaction costs, lower interest rates, greater macroeconomic stability, and greater economic integration through both trade and investment. The costs of euroization are loss of seigniorage, loss of a lender of last resort, and, more generally, loss of monetary policy.

According to the optimum currency area literature of Mundell (1961) and McKinnon (1963), the costs will exceed the benefits of joining the currency area as long as the country exhibits a high degree of nominal rigidity in domestic prices and costs, a relatively large size in terms of GDP and low degree of openness to trade in real goods and services, a high incidence of asymmetric (nation-specific) shocks as opposed to symmetric shocks, a less diversified structure of production and demand, a low degree of real factor mobility across national boundaries, and an absence of significant international (and supranational) fiscal tax transfer mechanisms. Consider the case of asymmetric shocks and assume that the monetary policy of the Eurosystem does not take into account the business cycle in the accession country. Also assume that a shock calls for depreciation of the accession country's real exchange rate. Under these assump-

tions, the Eurosystem's monetary policy will not change, and real depreciation will call for a lower price level in the accession country. Thus if prices and wages are downward inflexible in the accession country, higher unemployment or capacity utilization may result—a situation that might be avoided if the accession country conducted its own monetary policy and devalued it currency in nominal terms. Yet as long as the accession country conducts a large share of its trade with countries in the Euro Area, the likelihood of the country being hit hard by an external shock originating from a country or region outside the EU is rather small. A high degree of real factor mobility can be an effective substitute for nominal exchange rate adjustments in the face of sysmmetric shocks. Real factors, whose mobility matters, are labor and physical capital. Finally, the existence of international (and supranational) fiscal tax transfer mechanisms with serious redistributive powers spanning the member countries of the currency area will ensure compensation of the loss of the exchange rate instrument if the accession country were to give up monetary autonomy.

The optimum currency area literature emphasizes that during the period in which the conditions just stated are not satisfied, it is advisable for the accession country to adopt a flexible exchange rate regime. Clearly, any individual CEE country should have doubts about the net advantage of giving up national monetary independence. The migration of workers is not free, and all the candidate countries are relatively small compared with the Euro Area, with the exception of Poland and Romania, and then only in terms of population. The candidate countries are all very open to the EU, and the diversification of exports to the EU is growing. As for the instruments to absorb asymmetric shocks in the absence of independent monetary and exchange rate policies, the picture for the CEEs does not look worse than that for the existing EMU members.[45] Maurel (2002) notes that one cannot assess ex ante the optimal currency area criteria, because the mere fact of entering a monetary union also influences the way in which those criteria are satisfied. Corricelli (2002) emphasizes that the 10 candidate countries would incur relatively small losses from asymmetric shocks and that the CEE countries do qualify to join the EMU.

Buiter and Grafe (2002) point out that only two exchange rate regimes are sustainable in the long run. These are the free-floating exchange rate and a symmetric monetary union, which is defined to be a monetary union with a monetary authority that satisfies the following conditions: (1) its mandate spans the entire monetary union, (2) it acts as lender of last resort on the same terms in every union member state, (3) seigniorage is shared fairly among all union member states, and (4) it is accountable to the legitimate political representatives of the citizens of the whole union. To join a monetary union with a fixed exchange rate, a country must resolve its fiscal problems, attain price stability, achieve a sound banking sector, and ensure its current account is sustainable. Until these conditions are satisfied, Turkey should avoid adopting a fixed exchange rate regime. Currency board arrangements and euroization should not be alternatives for Turkey.[46] Because participation in the EMU is a must for Turkey, it will ultimately be part of a symmetric monetary union.[47] But during the period before accession, Turkey could pursue an exchange rate policy with central bank interventions aimed at attaining the long-run equilibrium value of the RER. In the terminology of the IMF's "Exchange Arrangements and Exchange Restrictions Annual Report," we thus refer to "Crawling Band" with a +/− 10 percent width.[48] The country could pursue this policy until it resolves its fiscal problems, attains price stability, and achieves sound banking sector and sustainability in the current account.

Conclusion

The criteria for accession to the EMU include a ceiling for the permissable rate of inflation one year prior to accession and a constraint on the permitted variations of the nominal exchange rate— membership in the ERM for a two-year period prior to accession while observing the normal fluctuation limits of the ERM. This constraint means that Turkey would be free to choose the exchange rate regime until accession. During this period, the risk of speculative attacks on the Turkish currency will be unavoidable, unless Turkey establishes a sound fiscal framework, achieves a sound banking sector, and ensures that its real exchange rate equals its long-run equilibrium level. In addition, Turkey should pursue a policy of maintaining the real exchange rate at around its long-run equilibrium level. By contrast, a look at fiscal issues reveals that Turkey, to reduce its debt-to-GDP ratio from its 2003 level of 80.2 percent to 60 percent over time, must stick to the primary surplus target of at least 6.5 percent of GNP, even in the face of the increased costs of EU accession for a considerable period of time. Any downward deviation from the target will postpone achievement of the 60 percent debt-to-GDP ratio. The primary surplus target of at least 6.5 should be achieved within the context of a fiscal reform that will broaden the tax base by reducing the tax burden substantially on both labor and capital.

Notes

1. The authors thank Juergen von Hagen and seminar participants at the Center for European Integration Studies (ZEI) in Bonn for their useful comments. They are particularly in debt to anonymous referees, whose comments helped them to correct several errors in an earlier draft. Sübidey Togan thanks ZEI for its hospitality and the Alexander von Humboldt Stiftung for financial support while this paper was written.

2. The value of the correlation coefficient between the monthly series of annual CPI inflation and the monthly series of the annual growth rate of base money is 0.7572, and that between the monthly series of annual CPI inflation and the monthly series of the annual rate of change in the exchange rate is 0.7698.

3. See, for example, Metin (1995, 1998), Lim and Papi (1997), and Kibritçioğlu (2002).

4. The output gap, which has been found to be stationary, and the dummy variable have been included in the Johansen cointegration test as exogenous variables.

5. Anyone constructing real exchange rate indices is faced with choosing the price index, the currency basket, weights, and a mathematical formula. In formulating the RER, we use the CPI, because these data are available on a monthly basis for a large number of countries. For the currency basket, we consider countries that are major competitors of Turkey in world markets, as well as major suppliers of imported commodities to Turkey. These countries are the following: Western Europe: Belgium, France, Germany, Greece, Italy, the Netherlands, Portugal, Spain, Switzerland, and the United Kingdom; America: Brazil, Canada, Mexico, and the United States; Middle East and North Africa: Egypt, Iran, Syria, Tunisia; Central and Eastern European and Commonwealth of Independent States countries: Czech Republic, Hungary, Poland, Russia; Asia: China, Indonesia, Japan, Republic of Korea, Malaysia, Taiwan (China), Thailand. To determine the weights of different countries, we use the approach developed by Zanello and Desruelle (1997), in which overall trade weights are derived by combining the bilateral import weights with the double export weights, using the relative size of Turkish imports and exports in overall Turkish trade to average both sets of weights. In formal terms, the import weight can be expressed as $w_i^m = (M_i/M)$, the export weight as

$$w_i^x = \left(\frac{X_i}{X} \right) \left(\frac{y_i}{y_i + \sum_h X_h^i} \right)$$

$$+ \sum_{k \neq i} \left(\frac{X_i^k}{X} \right) \left(\frac{X_i^k}{y_k + \sum_h X_h^k} \right)$$

and the overall weight as

$$w_i = \left(\frac{M}{X+M} \right) w_i^m + \left(\frac{X}{X+M} \right) w_i^x$$

where M_i denotes Turkish imports from country i, M the total value of Turkish imports, X_i Turkish exports to country i, X the total value of Turkish exports, y_i the value of domestic manufacturing production for the home market of country i, and X_i^k exports of country k to country i. The formula used to estimate the RER is

$$RER = \prod \left[\frac{CPI_i / E_i}{CPI / E} \right]^{w_i}$$

where $\prod$ stands for the product sign, i for the index that runs over the country's trade partners, E_i for the exchange rate defined as domestic currency per unit of U.S. dollar of country i, E for the Turkish lira/U.S. dollar exchange rate, and w_i for the competitiveness weight attached by Turkey to country i, calculated using the method of Zanello and Desruelle (1997).

6. Turkey opened the capital account in 1989 before it had taken measures to upgrade banking and financial market supervision and regulation, adopt international auditing and accounting standards, strengthen corporate governance and shareholder rights, and modernize bankruptcy and insolvency procedures. The 1994 and 2001 crises occurred while the country was facing large fiscal deficits, public debts, and high inflation rates. Problems of competitiveness led to substantial current account deficits. In addition, the currency and maturity mismatches on the balance sheets of the banks had left the authorities with little leeway for using either interest rate or exchange rate adjustments to restore balance without undermining the stability of the banking sector. Finally, there was an excessive dependence on short-term foreign borrowing to finance the current account deficits. These weaknesses contributed substantially to the balance of payments crisis of 1994 and 2001.

7. Let $p^* E/p$ be the RER where p^* denotes the gross domestic product (GDP) deflator in the foreign country, E the exchange rate, and p the GDP deflator in the home country, and let $py = wL + rK$ be the nominal GDP where y stands for real GDP, w the nominal wage rate, L total employment, r the return on capital, and K the stock of capital. Expressing the capital income in this equation as $rK = \lambda (wL)$, where λ stands for the profit margin, the RER can be written as

$$\frac{E p^*}{p} = \frac{\left(y / L \right) E w^* (1 + \lambda^*)}{\left(y^* / L^* \right) (1 + \lambda) w} \quad -$$

where (y/L) denotes labor productivity in the home country, (y^*/L^*) labor productivity in the foreign country, λ^* the profit rate in the foreign country, and w^* the wage rate in the foreign country. Thus for given values of productivities and profit rates in the two countries, depreciation of the RER leads to a decrease in wages measured in foreign currency (w/E).

8. The severity of the 2001 crisis when compared with the effect of the previous foreign exchange crisis is explained by the fact that by 2001 Turkey had a high level of "liability dollarization," with high public and private foreign debt denominated in foreign currencies, and a high share of foreign currency–denominated bank deposits. The sharp depreciation caused a large increase in both the gross and the net indebtedness of the economy, which more than offset the positive effect of depreciation on the demand for exports.

9. In addition to the size of the current account deficits, the quality of the sources of financing the deficit is important. A high percentage of short-term debt increases the probability that sudden capital outflows will lead to a crisis. It is recognized that foreign direct investment (FDI) is by far the surest form of external financing. But FDI flows into Turkey have been rather low. Thus external sustainability is an important issue for Turkey.

10. Real interest rate is defined as

$$r_1 = \left[\left\{ \frac{1 + \left(\frac{i_t}{100} \right)}{1 + \left(\frac{\pi_t}{100} \right)} \right\} - 1 \right] * 100$$

where i_t denotes the annual rate of interest on government bonds and treasury bills, attained as the weighted average rate in auctions during the month t weighted by total sales during the month, and π_t denotes the expected annual rate of inflation at time t over the period t to $t + 12$. In the calculations of the real interest rate, we set the expected annual rate of inflation at time t over the period t to $t + 12$ equal to the actual annual rate of inflation over the period t to $t + 12$. The average level of real interest rates over the period February 1994 to October 2003 was 25.5 percent.

11. Net debt figures are from IMF (2004), measured in percent of centered GNP, defined as the sum of quarterly GNP in the last two quarters of the year and in the first two quarters of the following year, in line with the IMF definition.

12. Consideration of total tax revenues, including social security contributions, reveals that total tax receipts in Turkey amounted in 1999 to 31.3 percent of GDP, compared with general government receipts of 40.7 percent in EU countries. According to Noord and Heady (2001), the unweighted average of total tax revenue as a percent of GDP in the EU is 42.1 percent, and the GDP weighted average is 40.7 percent.

13. Other factors contributing to the country's relatively low unemployment rate are labor migration from the country and the achievement of relatively high growth rates of GDP over time.

14. Various methods can be used to estimate the size of the informal sector in the labor market.

Castells and Portes (1989) define informal employment as the sum of unpaid family workers, domestic servants, and the self-employed, minus professionals and technicians.

An alternative approach to determining the size of the informal sector considers the coverage of workers by social security institutions (Assaad 1997). Workers are divided into two groups: those who are covered by a social security program and those who are not. The covered workers are considered to be part of the formal sector and uncovered workers to be part of the informal sector.

A third approach to determining the size of the informal sector is provided by Bulutay (1999). He considers the data provided by Turkish Household Labour Force Survey Results on "employed persons by size of workplace and status in employment." As he defines the informal sector, it consists of (1) the self-employed, (2) unpaid family workers, (3) employers who employ two or three workers, and (4) regular and casual employees in private sector work places that employ one to three workers.

In his estimation of informal employment, Togan (1997) defines employment in the informal sector as the sum of employment in the agricultural sector and in the private, nonagricultural informal sector. He determines employment in the private, nonagricultural informal sector by deducting from regular and casual employers in the nonagricultural sector (reported by the State Institute of Statistics) the number of registered wage earners reported by the Ministry of Labor.

A fifth estimation method used to determine the size of the informal sector considers the share of subcontracting activity in the economy.

Calculations by each of these methods reveals that, on average, informal labor makes up about 60 percent of total employment in Turkey.

15. The growth rate of GDP at time period t is calculated as $[GDP(t) - GDP(t-1)]*100/GDP(t-1)$. The average annual growth rate over the time period under consideration is then the average of these growth rates over the indicated time period.

16. According to Italianer (2002), there are two formal reasons a new member state has this status. First, the procedures foreseen in Article 121(1) for assessment of the conditions for adoption of the euro cannot be applied before accession. Second, one of these conditions cannot possibly be met upon accession, because it requires participation in the Exchange Rate Mechanism (ERM II), which is not open to nonmembers. More important, the economic rationale for the construction of the EMU presupposes participation in the internal market before adoption of the euro. The free movement of goods, the freedom to provide services, the free movement of persons, and full liberalization of capital movements are expected to be accomplished before adoption of the euro, except for negotiated transition periods in a limited number of areas.

17. Price stability requires that, over a period of one year before the examination, a country's inflation rate not exceed the average rate of the three best-performing EU member states in price stability by more than 1.5 percentage points. Interest rate convergence requires that the average long-term interest rate not exceed that of the three EU countries with the best inflation performance by more than two percentage points. The budget deficit criterion requires that the ratio of general government deficit to GDP not exceed 3 percent. The government debt criterion requires that the ratio of general government debt to GDP not exceed 60 percent. Finally, the exchange rate stability criterion requires that the country observe the normal fluctuation margins of the ERM II for at least two years without devaluing. In the ERM II, the euro is the anchor currency. Although the standard fluctuation band for the exchange rates of the partner countries is ±15 percent around the central rate, narrower bands are possible.

18. This section is largely based on Mottiar (1999).

19. This section is based mainly on the work of Gali and Perotti (2003).

20. ECOFIN, a formation of the Council of the European Union, is made up of the ministers responsible for economic affairs and finance in the EU countries.

21. In late 2003, France, Portugal, and Germany faced excessive deficit proceedings after violating the 3 percent limit for three years in a row. In January 2004, this situation culminated in the European Commission taking legal action against the council of finance ministers over the latter's decision to suspend the SGP. These events have led to substantial public debate on the effectiveness of the SGP for ensuring fiscal discipline, and on the wider issue of the optimal institutional structure for fiscal policy within the EU. See, for example, Fatas and others (2003).

22. This section draws heavily on European Commission (1998), European Parliament (1999), and Italianer (2002).

23. At the Copenhagen summit of June 1993, the EU member states agreed that "accession will take place as soon as an associated country is able to assume the obligations of membership by satisfying the economic and political conditions required. Membership requires that the candidate country has achieved stability of institutions guaranteeing democracy, the rule of law, human rights and respect for and protection of minorities, the existence of a functioning market economy as well as the capacity to cope with competitive pressure and market force within the Union. Membership presupposes the candidate's ability to take on the obligations of membership including adherence to the aims of political, economic and monetary union" (European Council 1993). These criteria have from then on been referred to as the Copenhagen criteria.

24. With the entry into force of the Treaty on European Union on November 1, 1993, the principle of full freedom of capital movements was incorporated into the treaty. As of January 1, 1994, which corresponds to the start of the second stage of the economic and monetary union, Articles 73a–73g of the Treaty on European Union introduced new arrangements for capital movements. Article 73a states that as of January 1, 1994, Articles 67–73 of the Treaty of Rome no longer apply and are replaced by Articles 73b–73g of the Maastricht Treaty. Article 73b introduces the principle of full freedom of capital movements and payments, both between member states and between member states and third countries. This article is directly applicable. Article 73c introduces the possibility of maintaining certain existing restrictions vis-à-vis third countries. Article 73d sets out the areas in which member states can maintain information, prudential supervision, and taxation requirements without capital movements being hindered. Article 73e provides for the derogations adopted prior to the entry into force of the Treaty on European Union to be maintained for a transitional period. Article 73f provides for the possibility of taking safeguard measures if movements of capital to or from third countries cause serious difficulties for the operation of the economic and monetary union. Article 73g allows the European Community or a member state to take measures on movements of capital to or from third countries for security or foreign policy reasons.

25. In addition, member states participating in the Euro Area have to prepare yearly stability programs that will report on the medium-term budgetary objectives and on measures the member states intend to take toward fiscal convergence.

26. On voting modalities in the Governing Council after enlargement, see European Central Bank (2003a).

27. The figures for the government-deficit-to-GDP ratio and the debt-to-GDP ratio were obtained from State Planning Organization (2004). These figures have been harmonized with the deficit and debt definitions of the EU.

28. Consideration of current account sustainability in Turkey reveals that under perfect capital mobility there will always be an unavoidable risk of speculative attacks on the Turkish currency, unless the country resolves its fiscal problems, attains price stability, achieves a sound banking sector, and brings its real exchange rate equal to the RER's long-run equilibrium level. Currently, Turkey is trying hard to satisfy the first three conditions, but its RER is, as emphasized later in this chapter, overvalued.

29. Ball (1994) defines trend inflation as a centered ninequarter moving average of the actual inflation rate. In our calculations, we start with the monthly consumer price index series and determine the quarterly CPI series as the average of the three monthly CPI series. Thereafter, we determine the annual quarterly inflation rate as $(p(t) - p(t-4))100/p(t-4)$, where $p(t)$ denotes the CPI value during quarter t. The trend inflation is then defined as the average of inflation rates between $(t-2)$ and $(t+2)$.

30. We are grateful to Zafer Mustafaoglu of the SPO for providing the estimates of potential output and output gap projections.

31. Similar results were obtained by Yavuz and Çetinkaya (2002).

32. As emphasized earlier, the reason for this flexibility lies in the existence of a formidable informal sector, whose wage-setting mechanism is quite different from that of the formal sector.

33. As Turkey begins to enforce the labor, tax, and social security laws within the economy, labor market flexibility will decrease, unless the country decreases the tax and social security contribution rates substantially and changes the labor law accordingly.

34. For estimates of the costs of EU accession for Turkey, see in this volume chapter 2 on agriculture, chapter 9 on labor markets, and chapter 11 on the environment.

35. A flat tax on income of 13 percent was introduced in Russia in 2001. The income tax revenue growth then outstripped the rates of economic growth and inflation in both 2001 and 2002. The flat tax has also boosted the share of total tax revenue held by the personal income tax. After the adoption and success of the flat tax in Russia, Serbia, Slovakia, and Ukraine adopted it, and other countries are in the process of adopting it as well.

36. If tax rates are reduced and the tax system is simplified but taxes cannot be effectively enforced in the private sector, the country may find itself facing major revenue shortfalls.

37. During 2003, inward and outward FDI flows amounted to 0.23899 percent and 0.20990 percent of GDP, respectively. Thus the net FDI inflow was 0.0290946 percent of GDP.

38. To deal with the simultaneity problem in a simple way, a four-quarter lagged value of RER is used as the instrumental variable.

39. The literature basically includes two approaches to determining the long-run equilibrium value of the RER. According to Williamson (1994) and Wren-Lewis and Driver (1998), the fundamental equilibrium exchange rate (FEER) is the real exchange rate that would exist when the economy is at full employment (internal balance) and in current account equilibrium (external balance). Thus the FEER is the RER that will bring the current account into equality with the "sustainable" capital account, where home and foreign aggregate outputs are set at their full employment values. By contrast, the model of a behavioral equilibrium exchange rate (BEER) by Clark and MacDonald (1998) analyzes the actual behavior of the RER using econometric techniques, where the reduced form equation is estimated with assumed longer-term fundamentals and short-term variables using cointegration analysis. MacDonald and Stein (1999) and Hinkle and Montiel (1999) consider productivity and net foreign assets as fundamental variables. Other variables identified in the literature include real interest differentials, measures of openness of trade and the exchange system, and size of fiscal balance. Finally, Stein and Allen (1995) distinguish between medium- and long-term factors influencing the RER. The approach developed in this chapter can be considered an extension of the FEER approach. The latter approach requires that the NICA-to-GDP ratio be sustainable.

40. The economic units may begin to assume they can avoid the rule of law.

41. Productivity is defined as GDP measured at constant prices, Q, divided by employment, L—that is, Q/L.

42. Letting Q stand for GDP, K for capital, L for labor, and H for the index of labor quality, total factor productivity, using the Cobb-Douglas production function, is defined as $Q/[K^\alpha(HL)^{(1-\alpha)}]$, where α denotes the output elasticity with respect to capital.

43. Symbolically, the relations can be expressed by the equations

$$\dot{q} = \dot{A} + \alpha\dot{k} + (1-\alpha)\dot{H}$$

and

$$\dot{Q} = \dot{q} + \dot{L}$$

where $\dot{Q}$ denotes the growth rate of output, $\dot{q}$ the growth rate of labor productivity, $\dot{A}$ the growth rate of technical progress, $\dot{k}$ the growth rate of the capital-to-labor ratio, $\dot{H}$ the growth rate of labor quality, $\dot{L}$ the growth rate of employment, and α the output elasticity with respect to capital.

44. See, for example, Özler and Yılmaz (2003). Yet many economists argue to the contrary. They maintain that if trade liberalization reduces the domestic market shares of domestic producers, the incentives of those producers to invest in superior technologies might decrease as protection is lifted. Furthermore, they stress that liberalization of trade under asymmetric information in markets may prove fragile for developing economies.

45. On the similarity of business cycles of countries in the Euro Area and the accession countries, see European Forecasting Network (2003).

46. Before the collapse of its currency regime in 2001, Turkey did have a regime very close to the currency board. But the system failed, because Turkey had neither a sound fiscal framework nor a sound banking sector and had not attained price stability. Furthermore, it did not have a graceful exit strategy.

47. The European Monetary Union is such a symmetric monetary union that has strict conditions on fiscal policy. The budgetary decisions by member countries are subject to surveillance by the EMU as a whole in the context of the requirements set out in the Maastricht Treaty and subsequently the Stability and Growth Pact.

48. "Crawling pegs" refers to pegs with central parity periodically adjusted in fixed amounts at a preannounced rate or in response to changes in selected quantitative indicators. "Crawling band" refers to crawling pegs combined with bands larger than ±1 percent. "Managed Floating with no Preannounced Path for the Exchange Rate" refers to regimes in which the monetary authority intervenes in the foreign exchange market without precommitment to a preannounced path for the exchange rate. Finally, "Independent Floating" refers to regimes in which the exchange rate is market-determined, with any foreign exchange intervention aimed only at preventing excessive volatility in the exchange rate movement. For a system of classification of exchange rate regimes different from that of the IMF, see Reinhart and Rogoff (2002).

References

Assaad, R. 1997. "Explaining Informality: The Determinants of Compliance with Labor Market Regulations in Egypt." Paper presented at the Economic Research Forum Fourth Annual Conference, Beirut, Lebanon, September 7–9.

Ball, L. 1994. "What Determines the Sacrifice Ratio?" In *Monetary Policy*, ed. N. G. Mankiw. Chicago: University of Chicago.

Buiter, W. H., and C. Grafe. 2002. "Anchor, Float or Abandon Ship: Exchange Rate Regimes for Accession Countries." Discussion Paper No. 3184, Centre for Economic Policy Research, London.

Bulutay, T. 1999. "Giriş: Türkiye'de Azörgütlü Kesim." State Institute of Statistics, Ankara.

Burnside, C., and D. Dollar. 2000. "Aid, Policies and Growth." *American Economic Review* 90: 847–68.

Castells, M., and A. Portes. 1989. "World Underneath: The Origins, Dynamics, and Effects of the Informal Economy. In *The Informal Economy*, ed. A. Portes, M. Castells, and L. A. Benton. Baltimore: Johns Hopkins University Press.

Clark, P., and R. MacDonald. 1998. "Exchange Rates and Economic Fundamentals: A Methodological Comparison of

BEERs and FEERs." Working Paper 98/67, International Monetary Fund, Washington, DC.

Corricelli, F. 2002. "Exchange Rate Policy during Transition to the European Monetary Union: The Option of Euroization." *Economics of Transition* 10 (2): 405–17.

European Central Bank. 2003a. "The Adjustment of Voting Modalities in the Governing Council." *European Central Bank Monthly Bulletin* (May): 73–83.

———. 2003b. "Editorial." *European Central Bank Monthly Bulletin* (May): 8.

European Commission. 1998. "Reports on Progress towards Accession by each of the Candidate Countries." Composite paper, Brussels: EC.

———. 2002. "Enlargement Paper 13." Brussels.

European Council. 1993. "Conclusions of the Presiding." European Council meeting, Copenhagen, June 21–22, SN 180/1/93 REV 1.

European Forecasting Network. 2003. "EFN Report on the Euro Area Outlook: Autumn 2003." http://www.efn.uni-bocconi.it.

European Parliament. 1999. "EMU and Enlargement: A Review of Policy Issues." Directorate General for Research Working Paper, Economic Affairs Series ECON 117, European Parliament, Luxembourg.

Fatas, A., J. von Hagen, A. Hughes Hallet, R. Strauch, and A. Sibert. 2003. "Stability and Growth in Europe: Towards a Better Pact." In *Monitoring European Integration 13*. London: Centre for Economic Policy Research.

Gali, J., and R. Perotti. 2003. "Fiscal Policy and Monetary Integration in Europe." Discussion Paper No. 3933, Centre for Economic Policy Research, London.

Hinkle, L., and P. Montiel. 1999. *Exchange Rate Misalignments: Concepts and Measurements for Developing Countries.* Washington, DC: World Bank.

IMF (International Monetary Fund). 2004. Various issues. *Exchange Arrangements and Exchange Restrictions Annual Report.* Washington, DC: IMF.

———. 2004. Turkey: "Seventh Review under the Stand-By Arrangement, and Requests for Waiver of Applicability and Nonobservance of Performance Criteria, Rephasing of Purchases, and Extension of Arrangement." Staff report, Washington, DC.

Italianer, A. 2002. "The Macroeconomic Policy Framework for EU Membership and Euro Area Participation—The Role of Budget Policy." Paper presented at Conference on "EU Accession—Developing Fiscal Policy Frameworks for Sustainable Growth, Brussels, May 13–14.

Kibritçioğlu, A. 2002. "Causes of Inflation in Turkey: A Literature Survey with Special Reference to Theories of Inflation." In *Inflation and Disinflation in Turkey*, ed. A. Kibritçioğlu, L. Rittenberg, and F. Selçuk. Aldershot, UK, and Burlington, VT: Ashgate.

Lim, C. H., and L. Papi. 1997. "An Econometric Analysis of the Determinants of Inflation in Turkey." Working Paper No. WP/97/170, International Monetary Fund, Washington, DC.

MacDonald, R., and J. Stein. 1999. *Equilibrium Exchange Rates.* Boston: Kluwer Academics.

Maurel, M. 2002. "On the Way of EMU Enlargement towards CEECs: What Is the Appropriate Exchange Rate Regime?" Discussion Paper No. 3409, Centre for Economic Policy Research, London.

McKinnon, R. I. 1963. "Optimum Currency Areas." *American Economic Review* 717–25.

Metin, K. 1995. "An Integrated Analysis of Turkish Inflation." *Oxford Bulletin of Economics and Statistics* 57: 513–31.

———. 1998. "The Relationship between Inflation and the Budget Deficit in Turkey." *Journal of Business, Economics and Statistics* 16: 412–22.

Mottiar, R. 1999. "Monetary Policy in the Euro Area: The Role of National Central Banks." *Central Bank of Ireland Quarterly Bulletin* (winter): 57–69.

Mundel, R. A. 1961. "A Theory of Optimum Currency Areas." *American Economic Review* 657–75.

Noord, P. van den, and C. Heady. 2001. "Surveillance of Tax Policies: A Synthesis of Findings in Economic Surveys." Economics Department Working Paper No. 303, Organisation for Economic Co-operation and Development, Paris.

Nuti, D. M. 2002. "Costs and Benefits of Unilateral Euroization in Central Eastern Europe." *Economics of Transition* 10: 419–44.

OECD (Organisation for Economic Co-operation and Development). 2002. *OECD Economic Surveys: Turkey.* Paris: OECD.

Özler, Ş., and K. Yılmaz. 2003. "Does Foreign Ownership Matter for Survival and Growth? Dynamics of Competition and Foreign Direct Investment." Paper presented at the 10th Annual Conference of the Economic Research Forum for the Arab Countries, Iran and Turkey, Marrakesh, December 16–18.

Reinhart, C., K. S. Rogoff, and M. Savastano. 2003. "Debt Intolerance." Brookings Papers on Economic Activity, 1–74.

State Planning Organization. 2003. *Pre-Accession Economic Programme 2003.* Ankara: SPO.

———. 2004. *Pre-Accession Economic Programme 2004.* Ankara: SPO.

Stein, J., and P. Allen. 1995. *Fundamental Determinants of Exchange Rates.* Oxford: Clarendon Press.

Tansel, A., and S. Togan. 1987. "Price and Income Effects in Turkish Foreign Trade." *Weltwirtschaftliches Archiv* 123: 521–34.

Togan, S. 1997. "Türkiye'de İşgücü Piyasasında Esneklik." In *Türk İşgücü Piyasası ile İlgili Temel Gelişmeler*, ed. T. Bulutay. Ankara: State Institute of Statistics.

———. 2003. "Labor Market Flexibility in Turkey." In *Competitiveness in the Middle Eastern and North African Countries*, ed. S. Togan and H. Kheir-El-Din. ERF Research Report Series. Cairo: Economic Research Forum for the Arab Countries, Iran and Turkey.

Undersecretariat of the Treasury. 2003. *Kamu Borç Yönetimi Raporu.* Ankara: Hazine Müsteşarlığı.

von Hagen, J., and I. J. Harden. 1994. "National Budget Process and Fiscal Performance." *European Economy. Reports and Studies 3. Towards Greater Fiscal Discipline.* 311–93. European Commission: Directorate General for Economic and Financial Affairs.

Williamson, J. 1994. *Estimating Equilibrium Exchange Rates.* Washington, DC: Institute for International Economics.

World Bank. 2003. *Turkey Country Economic Memorandum: Toward Macroeconomic Stability and Sustained Growth.* Report No. 26301-TU. Washington, DC: World Bank.

Wren-Lewis, S., and R. Driver. 1998. *Real Exchange Rates for the Year 2000.* Washington, DC: Institute for International Economics.

Yavuz, D., and A. Çetinkaya. 2002. "Calculation of Output-Inflation Sacrifice Ratio: The Case of Turkey." Working Paper No. 11, Central Bank of Turkey, Ankara.

Zanello, A., and D. Desruelle. 1997. "A Primer on the IMF's Information Notice System." IMF Working Paper WA/97/71. Washington, DC: International Monetary Fund.

PART II

AGRICULTURE, MANUFACTURING, SERVICES, AND NETWORK INDUSTRIES

ANALYSIS OF THE IMPACT OF EU ENLARGEMENT ON THE AGRICULTURAL MARKETS AND INCOMES OF TURKEY

Sübidey Togan, Ahmet Bayener, and John Nash

Integration into the European Union (EU) is one of Turkey's central foreign policy priorities.[1] As a part of this integration, Turkey will have to adopt an agricultural policy and institutional framework compatible with the EU's Common Agricultural Policy (CAP) and accept the full body of the legislation and policies on agriculture in the EU as it exists on the date of accession. For Turkey, the adoption of EU-like agricultural policies will constitute a significant modification of current policies, and such policies will have enormous implications for the incomes of both farmers and the wider population.

The purpose of this chapter is to explore these issues of EU enlargement to Turkey. The chapter is organized as follows. The first section reviews the agricultural situation in Turkey. The second and third sections consider the agricultural policies in Turkey and in the EU, respectively, as they are now and as they may evolve in line with changes recently proposed formally by the European Commission (the administrative arm of the EU government). The impact of introducing the CAP is analyzed in the fourth section using a partial equilibrium model of the agricultural sector. The fifth section discusses issues related to institutional development. Conclusions are presented in the final section.

Agricultural Situation

Agriculture is an important part of the Turkish economy; it contributes about 12 percent to the gross domestic product (GDP), while the corresponding figure for the EU15 is 1.7 percent.[2] Although the Turkish GDP grew at 4 percent per year over the period 1980–2003, the growth rate of agriculture was only 1.1 percent per year, and it fluctuated widely over the period. As a result, the sector shrank as a share of the economy, from 25 percent in 1980 to 12 percent in 2003. The sector still accounts for a very large share of employment, although this share has also fallen considerably. Between 1980 and 2003, the number of people employed in agriculture fluctuated between 7.2 million and 9.2 million, but because of a steady increase in employment in other sectors, agriculture's share in civilian employment dropped from 54.2 percent in 1980 to 33.9 percent in 2003.

Turkey has a total land area of 78 million hectares (see table 2.1 for land use in Turkey). The total agricultural area of 39 million hectares consists of arable land (24 million hectares), the area used for permanent crops (2.5 million hectares), and permanent meadows and pastures (12.7 million hectares). Fallow land makes up more than 20 percent of total arable cropland. In addition, Turkey has slightly more than 20 million hectares of forested land. The total irrigated area is about 4.5 million hectares, or 19 percent of total arable area. It is estimated that the country can potentially irrigate about 8.5 million hectares.

Turkey's agricultural land, exposed to both maritime and continental weather conditions, tolerates

TABLE 2.1   Land Use in Turkey, 1995 and 2000

	1995 (thousand hectares)	Percentage Distribution	2000 (thousand hectares)	Percentage Distribution
Arable land	24,373	31.5	23,826	30.8
Area sown	18,464	23.8	18,207	23.5
Vegetable gardens	785	1.0	793	1.0
Fallow land	5,124	6.6	4,826	6.2
Permanent crops	2,461	3.2	2,553	3.3
Vineyards	565	0.7	535	0.7
Orchards	1,340	1.7	1,418	1.8
Olive groves	556	0.7	600	0.8
Permanent meadows and pastures	12,659	16.3	12,671	16.4
Total agricultural land	39,493	51.0	39,050	50.4
Forests and woodland	20,199	26.1	20,703	26.7
Other land	17,271	22.3	17,210	22.2
Total land area	76,963	99.3	76,963	99.3
Total area	77,482	100	77,482	100

Source: Food and Agriculture Organization Statistical Database.

TABLE 2.2   Value of Agricultural Production: Turkey, 2000

Product	Value (US$ millions)	Percentage Distribution
Crops	28,163	68.48
Livestock	10,600	25.77
Forestry	1,101	2.68
Fishing	1,246	3.03
Total	41,129	100.00

Source: Turkish State Planning Organization.

a wide range of crops. Climate and geography also have an important bearing on the location and type of animal husbandry carried out in Turkey. According to table 2.2, which shows the value of agricultural production during 2000, crops account for 69 percent of production value, livestock products for 26 percent, forestry for 3 percent, and fishing products for 3 percent.

In Turkey, the family-owned farm is the basic unit of agricultural production, and family members provide most of the farm labor. The number and size of holdings are inferred from agricultural censuses, which are conducted every 10 years on the basis of small sample surveys. The picture that emerges from these censuses is that of a large number of small farms. The 2001 census revealed that 83.4 percent of farms had less than 10 hectares of land. The average size of farm holdings was 6.1 hectares (see table 2.3).[3]

An examination of Turkey's foreign trade in the agricultural commodities HS (Harmonized System) 01–24, HS 41.01–41.03, HS 51.01–51.03, and HS 52.01–52.03 reveals that over the period 1999–2001 the average annual agricultural exports amounted to US$4.06 billion, or about 14.2 percent of total exports.[4] Turkey's agricultural exports to the EU of $1.8 billion made up about 12 percent of its total exports to the EU. By contrast, Turkey's total agricultural imports amounted on average to $2.7 billion, or about 6.2 percent of total imports. Agricultural imports from the EU, valued at $0.7 billion, made up about 3.2 percent of Turkey's total imports from the EU.

Table 2.4 shows that the three agricultural commodities with the highest shares of total agricultural exports were edible fruits and citrus fruits, 28.5 percent; foods made of vegetables, fruits, and other plants, 13.0 percent; and processed tobacco and substitutes, 12.2 percent. The three agricultural commodities with the highest shares of exports to the EU, of total agricultural exports to the EU, were edible fruits and citrus fruits; foods made of vegetables, fruits, and other plants; and processed tobacco

TABLE 2.3   Agricultural Holdings and Land Engaged in Crop Production, Turkey

Size of Holdings (decares)	Holdings		Total Area		Average Size of Farm Holdings (decares)
	Number	Percent	Decares	Percent	
Less than 5	177,893	5.89	481,605	0.26	3
5–9	290,327	9.61	1,951,672	1.06	7
10–19	539,507	17.86	7,374,515	4.00	14
20–49	950,539	31.46	29,523,341	16.02	31
50–99	559,999	18.54	38,123,216	20.68	68
100–199	327,330	10.83	43,881,626	23.81	134
200–499	153,688	5.09	42,076,313	22.83	274
500–999	17,431	0.58	11,218,554	6.09	644
1,000–2,499	4,198	0.14	5,476,930	2.97	1,305
2,500–4,999	222	0.01	695,541	0.38	3,133
5,000 +	56	0.00	3,526,174	1.91	62,967
Total	3,021,190	100	184,329,487	100	61

Note: The figures on the number of holdings and area are from the 2001 census.
Source: Turkish State Institute of Statistics.

and substitutes. Yet the three agricultural commodities with the highest shares of exports to the EU, of total sectoral exports, were other animal products, 95.3 percent; products made from meat, fish, and crustacea, 83.9; and plants and floriculture products, 76.1. Overall, exports of agricultural commodities to the EU formed 44.3 percent of all of Turkey's agricultural exports.

As for imports of agricultural commodities, the three commodities with the highest shares of total agricultural imports were cotton, 19.0 percent; animal or vegetable oils and fats, 13.6 percent; and cereals, 12.0 percent. The three agricultural commodities with the highest shares of imports from the EU, of total agricultural imports from the EU, were cotton, hides and skin, and animal or vegetable oils and fats. Finally, the three agricultural commodities with the highest shares of imports from the EU, of total sectoral imports, were plants and floriculture products, 89.4 percent; cereal products, wheat flour, and pastries, 89.3 percent; and vegetable lacquers, resins, and balsams, 86.4 percent. Overall, imports of agricultural commodities from the EU made up 25.7 percent of all agricultural imports.

Table 2.4 further reveals that Turkey is a net exporter of commodities such as edible fruits and citrus fruits; foods made of vegetables, fruits, and other plants; and sugar and sweets. It is a net importer of commodities such as cotton and oilseeds, various seeds and fruits, and industrial plants. By contrast, in its trade with the EU, Turkey is a net exporter of edible fruits and citrus fruits; foods made of vegetables, fruits, and other plants; and processed tobacco and substitutes. It is a net importer of hides and skin, cotton, and various foods.

Agricultural Policies in Turkey

The main objectives of agricultural policies in Turkey are set out in the government's five-year development plans. These objectives are to (1) ensure adequate levels of nutrition, (2) increase yield and output, (3) reduce the vulnerability of production to adverse weather conditions, (4) raise levels of self-sufficiency, (5) provide adequate, stable incomes for those working in the agricultural sector, (6) increase exports, and (7) develop rural areas. In pursuit of these objectives, the government has implemented various measures. In the crops sector, government interventions have primarily taken the form of price supports, augmented by high tariffs. In the livestock sector, quantitative restrictions and tariffs have been the main mechanism used to support prices. In addition, farmers were given input subsidies and credits to improve

TABLE 2.4 Exports and Imports of Agricultural Commodities: Turkey, 1999–2001

Harmonized System (HS) Code Description	Exports Average, 1999–2001 (US$ thousands)	Exports Percentage Distribution	Exports to EU, Average 1999–2001 (US$ thousands)	Exports from EU as a Share of Total Exports	Imports Average, 1999–2001 (US$ thousands)	Imports Percentage Distribution	Imports from EU, Average 1999–2001 (US$ thousands)	Imports from EU as a Share of Total Imports	Net Exports, Average 1999–2001 (US$ thousands)	Net Exports in Trade with EU, Average 1999–2001 (US$ thousands)
Live animals and animal products										
01 Live animals	19,159	0.47	1,471	7.68	26,326	0.98	15,467	58.75	−7,168	−13,996
02 Meat and edible offal	13,916	0.34	708	5.09	418	0.02	64	15.41	13,498	643
03 Fish and sea products	54,154	1.33	38,532	71.15	22,508	0.83	12,378	54.99	31,647	26,154
04 Milk and dairy products; eggs; honey	35,301	0.87	6,316	17.89	30,824	1.14	20,828	67.57	4,477	−14,512
05 Other animal products	36,423	0.90	34,701	95.27	18,860	0.70	2,516	13.34	17,563	32,185
Vegetable products										
06 Plants and floriculture products	15,262	0.38	11,613	76.09	16,203	0.60	14,490	89.43	−941	−2,877
07 Vegetables, plants, roots, tubers	304,529	7.50	100,117	32.88	75,451	2.80	6,605	8.75	229,079	93,512
08 Edible fruits; citrus fruits	1,159,461	28.54	743,676	64.14	57,082	2.12	6,103	10.69	1,102,379	737,573
09 Coffee, tea, spices	58,123	1.43	22,574	38.84	27,450	1.02	3,135	11.42	30,673	19,439
10 Cereals	203,561	5.01	33,582	16.50	323,726	12.00	57,506	17.76	−120,165	−23,923
11 Products of the milling industry	82,013	2.02	26,202	31.95	5,175	0.19	4,431	85.61	76,838	21,772
12 Oilseeds, various seeds/fruits; industrial plants	52,430	1.29	28,351	54.07	233,454	8.66	31,223	13.37	−181,024	−2,872
13 Vegetable lacquers, resins, balsams	1,341	0.03	145	10.84	14,110	0.52	12,194	86.42	−12,770	−12,049
14 Vegetable plaiting materials	16,471	0.41	10,819	65.68	2,695	0.10	62	2.28	13,776	10,757

Animal or vegetable oils and fats									
15 Animal or vegetable oils and fats	241,189	5.94	81,999	34.00	366,550	13.59	74,579	20.35	−125,361	7,419
Foodstuffs, beverages, tobacco									
16 Products made from meat, fish, crustacea	34,964	0.86	29,342	83.92	830	0.03	369	44.43	34,134	28,973
17 Sugar and sweets	258,178	6.36	25,237	9.77	14,019	0.52	9,125	65.09	244,158	16,112
18 Cocoa and cocoa products	81,023	1.99	12,256	15.13	68,351	2.53	22,007	32.20	12,672	−9,751
19 Cereal products, wheat flour, pastries	116,732	2.87	13,538	11.60	30,841	1.14	27,544	89.31	85,891	−14,006
20 Foods made of vegetables, fruits, and other plants	528,298	13.00	352,375	66.70	17,542	0.65	12,057	68.73	510,757	340,319
21 Various foods	93,845	2.31	11,226	11.96	101,011	3.75	81,416	80.60	−7,165	−70,190
22 Alcoholic and nonalcoholic beverages	38,877	0.96	18,984	48.83	14,331	0.53	12,365	86.28	24,546	6,619
23 Residues of food industry; fodders	13,271	0.33	357	2.69	167,152	6.20	17,820	10.66	−153,881	−17,463
24 Processed tobacco and substitutes	496,247	12.22	145,360	29.29	308,653	11.45	11,652	3.77	187,594	133,708
Hides, wool, and cotton									
4101–4103 Hides and skin	21,519	0.53	209	0.97	199,473	7.40	106,243	53.26	−177,954	−106,035
5101–5103 Wool and animal hair	6,553	0.16	3,255	49.67	42,362	1.57	1,905	4.50	−35,809	1,350
5201–5203 Cotton	79,630	1.96	46,330	58.18	511,392	18.96	129,916	25.40	−431,762	−83,586
Total	4,062,470	100.00	1,799,277	44.29	2,696,790	100.00	694,001	25.73	1,365,680	1,105,276

Source: The authors.

yields and income and to counterbalance the implicit protection given to domestic input industries through border measures. Finally, administrative controls have been applied to the production of a few important crops.

Output Price Supports, Input Subsidies, and Supply Control Measures

Output price supports, input subsidies, and supply control measures are three important components of agricultural support policies. *Government price supports* for most major crops (such as grains, oilseeds, cotton, sugar beet, tobacco, hazelnut, and tea) have in the past been announced by decree each year, but this practice is changing because of the reform program discussed later in this section on agricultural policies. Related state-owned enterprises (SOEs) and agricultural sales cooperative unions (ASCUs) were commissioned to buy at the announced floor prices. Crops could also be sold to independent buyers. For some crops, a system of "deficiency payments" or premiums was introduced in 1993 in place of floor prices. The High Planning Council announced a target price for those crops as well as an intervention price, and the target price moved in parallel with the world prices. Farmers selling their crop to ASCUs or commodity exchanges received the difference between the price obtained and the target price in the form of a payment directly from the state-owned Turkish Bank of Agriculture. The payment was then reimbursed by the Treasury. The deficiency payments were implemented for sunflower seed, soybean, cotton, and olive oil. Tea growers were also fully compensated for the costs incurred in implementing the strict pruning requirements to control supply. Direct payments were, until recently, only a minor part of the agricultural support system. The main types of direct payments were natural disaster relief, the return on sugar beet pulp, deficiency payments for oilseeds and cotton, and incentive premiums for milk and meat.

Input subsidies are a second important component of agricultural support policies. The most important have been the credit, fertilizer, and irrigation subsidies. Short-term and investment credit for agriculture has long been subsidized by the government at interest rates well below inflation and commercial rates. The result is that interest rates on

loans from the Turkish Bank of Agriculture have been significantly negative in real terms. In addition, the unpaid loans of the ASCUs have been routinely covered as "duty losses" of the Treasury.

The domestic manufacturers and consumers of fertilizers have received subsidies since 1961. The subsidy was set until recently as a percentage of market price, with the percentage varying considerably over the years. In 1996 and 1997, the subsidy was about 40–50 percent of the market price, depending on the type of fertilizer. In November 1997, the government decided to fix the fertilizer subsidy at a nominal amount of Turkish lira (TL) per kilogram. This shift in policy has reduced the fertilizer subsidy substantially in real terms, and inflation has eroded its value.

Agriculture has also received substantial subsidies through irrigation projects. The Turkish government has been investing heavily in irrigation, financing the associated capital investments largely through the budget. Farmers have paid no fee for the resource value of water they have used for irrigation, whether privately extracted or supplied by a public scheme, even though farmers who grew crops on irrigated land did contribute to the cost of operating and maintaining the infrastructure. But even in this situation the bulk of operating and maintenance costs were financed through budget allocations.

Supply control measures, the third component of Turkish agricultural policies, have been used to control the fiscal cost of support policies. Tobacco, hazelnuts, and tea have been under area or production control. Sugar beet output has been indirectly controlled to some extent by the state-owned sugar company (Şeker) through contracts with growers. Tobacco farmers have received payments to compensate for the area controls, and tea producers to compensate for lost production from pruning.

Agricultural producers have also received general services either free or at subsidized prices. The measures taken to improve the production basis of agriculture were mainly research, training and extension services, inspection, pest and disease control, and land improvements (including capital investments in small-scale irrigation works). In addition, only the large farms are required to pay income tax. In all transactions related to agriculture, a 5 percent sales tax is applied at the point of sale. Consumers have not benefited from subsidies directly. They are protected indirectly through price controls, market intervention, and a lower value-added tax on food.

Agricultural Trade Policy

Table 2.5 shows the applied most-favored-nation (MFN) tariff rates for the major agricultural commodity groups during 2002. The table reveals that the agricultural sector is highly protected in Turkey. The three sectors with highest simple average tariff rates applied to imports from third countries are the products made from meat, fish, and crustacea (HS 16) with a tariff rate of 132.70 percent; meat and edible offal (HS 02), 116.52 percent; and milk and dairy products (HS 04), 105.20 percent. The three sectors with the highest weighted average tariff rates applied to imports from third countries are products made from meat, fish, and crustacea (HS 16) with a tariff rate of 124.08 percent; sugar and sweets (HS 17), 124.08 percent; and edible fruits and citrus fruits (HS 08), 120.17 percent. The table also reveals that Turkey, upon becoming a member of the EU, could have to change its tariff schedule on agricultural commodities substantially. To align its tariff schedule with the current EU schedule, Turkey would have to increase its tariffs on cereals; processed tobacco and substitutes; residues of the food industry and fodders; alcoholic and nonalcoholic beverages; vegetable lacquers, resins, and balsams; cotton; and vegetable plaiting materials. In all other categories, Turkey would have to decrease its tariff rates.

As for the market access conditions for agricultural commodities imported from the EU, the preferential regime applied by Turkey to imports of agricultural products originating in the EU is determined by Decision No. 1/98 of the EC–Turkey Association Council of 1998. Under this decision, Turkey must grant a large number of commodities duty-free access to the Turkish market up to the quota limits specified in the decision. A look at the quota levels and trade data for the agricultural commodities specified in Decision No. 1/98 of the EC–Turkey Association Council reveals that for most of the commodities the quota limits have been exceeded. Thus "out of quota" tariff rates are, in general, applicable to imports of these commodities from the EU. Consideration of the "out of quota" tariff rates for these commodities, together

with the MFN tariff rates shown in table 2.5 for the other agricultural commodities, reveals that the three sectors with the highest simple average tariff rates are meat and edible offal (HS 02), with a tariff rate of 116.52 percent; milk and dairy products (HS 04), 99.60 percent; and products made from meat, fish, and crustacea (HS 16), 76.90 percent. The three sectors with the highest weighted average tariff rates applied on imports from the EU are edible fruits and citrus fruits (HS 08) with a tariff of 120.17; milk and dairy products (HS 04), 101.79; and meat and edible offal (HS 02), 71.40 percent.

The preferential regime applied by the EU to imports of agricultural products originating in Turkey is determined by Decisions No. 1/72, 1/80, and 1/98 of the EC–Turkey Association Councils of 1972, 1980, and 1998, respectively. Under these decisions, almost all of the agricultural commodities originating in Turkey are imported by the European Community free from ad valorem duties, and the EU applies tariff quotas only for a relatively small number of commodities (see chapter annex tables 2.17 and 2.18). These tables reveal that those commodities made up about 30 percent of Turkish exports to the EU during 1999. In addition, the EU applies an entry price system for about 30 fruits and vegetables such as tomatoes, artichokes, courgettes, tangerines, lemons, and apples. For these commodities, specific duties are applied as long as the value of consignment falls below the entry price. These commodities, shown in annex table 2.19, made up about 4.8 percent of Turkish agricultural exports to the EU during 1999.

Finally, a sanitary ban on the import of livestock and meat products has remained in place. Export subsidies, applied to a number of products and limited to a maximum of between 10 percent and 20 percent of the export values and between 29 percent and 100 percent of the quantities exported, have continued for processed fruits and vegetables, fruit juices, olive oil, potatoes, apples, poultry meat, and eggs.

The considerations just described reveal that substantial border measures still affect trade between the EU and Turkey and that the external tariffs applied by the EU and Turkey to third countries' imports differ significantly. Completion of the customs union between the EU and Turkey to cover agricultural products implies the abolition of all border measures and the adoption of the EU external

TABLE 2.5 Most-Favored-Nation Tariff Rates of EU and Turkey, 2002

HS Code	Description	Number of Tariff Lines	Tariff Rates Applied by Turkey to Imports from EU (simple)	Tariff Rates Applied by Turkey to Imports from EU (weighted)	Tariff Rates Applied by EU to Imports from Third Countries (simple)	Tariff Rates Applied by Turkey to Imports from Third Countries (simple)	Tariff Rates Applied by EU to Imports from Third Countries (weighted)	Tariff Rates Applied by Turkey to Imports from Third Countries (weighted)
Live animals and animal products								
01	Live animals	27	27.85	1.72	19.72	27.85	56.69	1.72
02	Meat and edible offal	10	116.52	71.40	55.89	116.52	68.55	71.40
03	Fish and sea products	89	38.90	19.61	11.39	78.30	11.61	37.60
04	Milk and dairy products; eggs; honey	72	99.60	101.79	55.16	105.20	69.17	103.22
05	Other animal products	30	2.50	7.00	0.35	2.80	0.11	7.09
Vegetable products								
06	Plants and floriculture products	37	17.90	7.49	9.25	18.50	12.90	8.46
07	Vegetables, plants, roots, tubers	78	22.20	20.44	13.30	22.30	13.80	20.44
08	Edible fruits; citrus fruits	93	48.10	120.17	8.56	48.10	12.15	120.17
09	Coffee, tea, spices	45	37.70	46.13	6.11	38.00	4.32	47.27
10	Cereals	39	25.60	16.97	66.35	25.70	79.15	16.97
11	Products of the milling industry	40	36.30	28.86	35.87	36.70	44.47	29.65
12	Oilseeds, various seeds/fruits; industrial plants	88	16.40	5.29	3.65	17.20	0.98	5.55
13	Vegetable lacquers, resins, balsams	29	1.40	1.54	2.88	2.60	2.76	2.06
14	Vegetable plaiting materials	14	0.00	0.00	0.10	0.00	0.01	0.00

Animal or vegetable oils and fats

15	Animal or vegetable oils and fats	107	18.10	17.74	15.49	20.20	22.90	17.86

Foodstuffs, beverages, tobacco

16	Products made from meat, fish, crustacea	39	76.90	65.27	21.32	132.70	22.79	124.08
17	Sugar and sweets	53	58.90	63.18	22.79	79.70	48.46	124.08
18	Cocoa and cocoa products	24	38.60	22.38	7.12	99.30	3.06	51.11
19	Cereal products, wheat floor, pastries	66	58.20	54.45	26.05	83.90	22.88	78.96
20	Foods made of vegetables, fruits, and other plants	173	58.50	62.41	25.47	60.80	27.59	73.92
21	Various foods	54	25.20	28.64	13.42	42.02	15.89	42.37
22	Alcoholic and nonalcoholic beverages	41	11.90	2.01	22.52	17.04	13.87	6.27
23	Residues of food industry; fodders	49	6.30	1.12	18.03	7.81	26.96	2.84
24	Processed tobacco and substitutes	17	14.70	0.22	51.55	33.78	51.01	23.98

Hides, wool and cotton

4101–4103	Hides and skin	44	0.00	0.00	0.00	0.00	0.00	0.00
5101–5103	Wool and animal hair	36	0.00	0.00	0.00	0.00	0.00	0.00
5201–5203	Cotton	15	0.00	0.00	0.18	0.00	0.01	0.00

Source: The authors.

tariff applied to third countries.[5] As a result, the prices of agricultural products for which border measures still exist would become much closer in the EU and Turkey, with the remaining differences due to quality and to transportation and marketing costs. Such a development would, however, require that the parties harmonize their agricultural price policies.

Agricultural Reform Implementation Project

The overly generous system of agricultural support policies pursued until the late 1990s was fiscally expensive and unsustainable, and they encouraged waste and abuse (World Bank 2000). They did not provide a cost-effective way for addressing policy objectives such as alleviation of rural poverty and regional development, and the "duty loss" system of administration burdened the Treasury with enormous debts. There were other problems as well. Support and administered prices were announced only after key production decisions had been made, and payments were delayed by intervention agencies. These problems confirm the difficulties inherent in trying to administer outcomes in a dynamic, complex market. Neither the overall demand-supply balance nor the equilibrium in the very complex intertemporal, spatial, and quality dimensions could be achieved. The Turkish government recently tried to replicate the market by establishing more quality-differentiated prices. But success in duplicating the price flexibility of freely functioning commodities market was limited.

In the late 1990s, Turkey decided to reform its agricultural policies. Beginning in late 1999, with support from the International Monetary Fund (IMF) and the World Bank, the government developed the Agricultural Reform Implementation Project (ARIP) to phase out current production- and input-oriented support and replace it with area-based income support payments during the 2001–04 period. ARIP was intended to achieve following:

- To phase out the unsustainable and distortionary system of subsidies for fertilizer—credit and price supports that disproportionately benefited large farmers, placed a regressive tax on consumers, and cost about $5 billion a year. ARIP was determined to link domestic prices to world prices.

- To privatize most state enterprises in agriculture and to turn the agricultural sales cooperative unions (ASCU) into true private sector unions of producer-owned cooperatives in order to reduce government involvement in the marketing and processing of agricultural products.
- To introduce a unified national program of direct income support (DIS). These reforms are intended to increase the efficiency of the agricultural sector and thereby help Turkey meet the preconditions for accession to the EU.

Implementation of ARIP began in 2000 with a pilot program of income support payments applied to four regions. An important part of the pilot program was preparation of a farm registry and testing of the eligibility conditions. All agricultural land users received $50 per hectare of agricultural land, up to a maximum of 20 hectares per farmer. The program was extended nationwide in 2001–02. Table 2.6 shows the intervention prices and direct payments for selected commodities over the period 1998–2002. The table reveals how the government has tried to compensate for the drop in intervention prices with increases in direct payments.

The intention of direct income support is not to fully compensate every farmer for income lost by removal of the old subsidy system, but rather to cushion the blow and continue to provide adequate support to the agricultural sector in an incentive-neutral way. Within the existing legal framework, the DIS payments should be usable as collateral, thereby giving farmers enhanced access to credit. Payments under the DIS system will be ongoing but should become more explicitly targeted or merged with the general social safety net system. Thus DIS allows the government to disengage from its current support mechanism in a politically acceptable and humane way. The government is also easing the transition for growers of certain crops that were grossly overproduced (i.e., tobacco and hazelnut) by making onetime payments to farmers to cover their cost of switching to alternative activities. This program is distinct from, and in addition to, DIS.

After the policy change, the fertilizer subsidy decreased from 31 percent in 1999 to almost 20 percent by the end of 2000, and it was phased out in 2002. By 2002, credit subsidies channeled through Ziraat Bank, as well as most other input subsidies, were also phased out. In addition, price supports for grains

TABLE 2.6   Agricultural Supports: Turkey, 1998–2002
(US$ millions)

	1998	1999	2000	2001	2002
Market price support					
Cereals	425.8	356.7	183.0	27.8	0.0
Tobacco	276.9	146.6	81.8	43.3	26.7
Sugar beet	245.2	141.6	70.5	40.1	0.0
Payments based on inputs used					
Fertilizer	476.7	238.6	153.4	60.5	0.0
Pesticides	33.0	24.7	19.2	14.7	0.0
Seed	6.6	3.4	4.6	0.8	0.0
Development of animal husbandry	0.0	0.0	19.2	31.9	50.1[a]
Incentive premiums					
Milk	31.5	25.6	19.2	9.8	0.0
Compensation payment					
Tea	13.8	7.1	25.2	22.1	26.7
Natural disaster relief	29.7	37.2	22.4	0.0	0.0
Credit subsidy	1,663.2	1,675.3	562.7	274.8	0.0
Deficiency payments	0.0	265.8	298.2	280.5	145.1
Direct income support	0.0	0.0	0.0	68.1	1,159.0
Total	3,202.4	2,922.6	1,459.6	874.4	1,357.5

a. The figure includes the milk premium.
Source: Turkish Ministry of Agriculture and Rural Affairs.

were reduced, with the aim of eliminating the supports completely by 2002. Even though grain support prices were not announced by a decree by the government in 2002, the Turkish Grain Board (TMO) announced its purchasing prices based on production, its stocks, and expected market conditions.

Estimates of Support in Agriculture

Agricultural production in Turkey is protected. According to the official estimates of the Organisation for Economic Co-operation and Development (OECD), total transfers from consumers and taxpayers to agricultural producers, as measured by the producer support estimate (PSE), amounted to a peak of $9.955 billion in 1998 (almost 25 percent of producers' receipts) and fell slightly to $6.8 billion (21 percent) in 2000. As a result of the reform efforts, the PSE decreased to $2.251 billion (10 percent) in 2001, but increased to $6.1 billion (23 percent) in 2002. According to the OECD (2003a), market price support remained the most important type of support, for a share of 69 percent of total support to producers in 2001 and 75 percent in

2002. Payments based on input use are the other category of support to producers. This category as a share of total support decreased from 22 percent in 1999 to 8 percent in 2001, and further to 2 percent in 2002. By contrast, the total transfers to the agricultural sector measured by the total support estimate (TSE) amounted to $13.84 billion in 1998 (6.9 percent of GDP) and $12.1 billion in 1999 (6.6 percent of GDP). The TSE decreased to $5.4 billion (3.6 percent of GDP) in 2001, but increased again to $7.7 billion (4.1 percent of GDP) in 2002. At the same time, the corresponding figures for all OECD countries fell from 1.39 percent of GDP in 1998 and 1999 to 1.2 percent in 2002. The TSE for the EU fell from 1.52 percent of GDP in 1999 to 1.3 percent in 2002. Over the same period, the PSE in the EU, as a percentage of producers' receipts, fell from 43 percent to 36 percent.

The Common Agricultural Policy of the EU

The Common Agricultural Policy (CAP) of the European Union, which was set up against the backdrop of the food shortages and rations that followed World War II, had five founding aims: (1) higher productivity, (2) a fair standard of living for farmers, (3) stable markets, (4) regular food supplies, and (5) reasonable prices for consumers. It was based on the principles of a single market in farm products with common prices and the free movement of agricultural goods within the community, preference for community members, and shared costs. Its main mechanisms were support prices set above world price levels and the use of import taxes, nontariff barriers to imports, and export subsidies to maintain the higher internal prices. As production responded to higher prices, surpluses became chronic and increasingly expensive. As a result, the CAP has been subjected to various reforms. In particular, production has been artificially constrained by mechanisms such as milk quotas and compulsory set-asides for arable crops; prices have been cut, and producers have normally been given direct payments in compensation; and more emphasis has been put on rural development and encouraging farmers to look to markets and diversified forms of income to reduce their dependence on subsidies.

The CAP is financed by the European Agricultural Guidance and Guarantee Fund (EAGGF), which is an integral part of the EU's budget. In the 2003 EU budget of €99.69 billion, appropriations for the EAGGF accounted for about €44.78 billion. In addition to budget costs, the CAP imposes a cost on EU consumers through higher food costs. The additional cost to consumers varies according to movements in world prices, but in 2003 it was estimated by the OECD at about €55.5 billion.

In the EU, like in Turkey, it eventually became clear that price supports, import tariffs and nontariff barriers, export subsidies, and the other government interventions required by the CAP were creating unsustainable pressures on the EU budget and friction in international trade relations. Furthermore, they were not achieving the social objectives of environmental preservation and equity. The EU therefore embarked on a far-reaching reform program for CAP that is still under way. The reform began with the McSharry reforms of 1992 and was accelerated with the Agenda 2000 agreement, which was approved at the Berlin Council in March 1999. The underlying principle of the reform was the same as that of ARIP: to minimize the government's

role in setting prices and allow prices to be closely linked to world prices, while compensating farmers for income losses with area-based direct payments that would not be linked to output or input use. Under the Agenda 2000 agreement, some intervention prices were set at levels so low that they would be binding only in years of very low world prices, and other intervention prices were reduced greatly, with producers compensated by direct income support payments. The agreement represented a significant shift from price supports to direct payments, and it helped to reduce the economic distortions of the CAP. It will go some way toward helping agriculture to meet the challenges of further trade liberalization and enable the formulation of an integrated EU rural development policy that shifts the emphasis from production support to environmental and rural economy measures in the future. But, as described in the rest of this section, further reforms also are under way.

Common Organization of Market

Within the CAP framework, the Common Organization of Market (COM) is the basic instrument used to manage agricultural production and to stabilize markets in accord with the declared objectives of the CAP. COMs, which were introduced gradually, now cover most EU agricultural products, accounting for 90 percent of the final agricultural output of the European Community. The essential features of the current CAP under Agenda 2000 reform is summarized in the following sections (see Europarl 2002 and Csaki and others 2002).

COM for Cereals   In the past, at the core of the COM for cereals was a state intervention system based on guaranteed prices, but after the 1993/94 marketing year, compensation payments per hectare became the main mechanism.[6] The intervention price was set at a very low level to serve as only a safety net in years of extremely low world prices. It was €101.31 per metric ton from the 2001/02 marketing year, and it would decline further, to a little over €90 per metric ton under the CAP Mid-term Review proposals described later in this chapter. This intervention price applies to a predefined "standard quality" that meets the regulations on moisture content and specific weight.

Direct area payments to cereal producers, set in euros per metric ton, were introduced to compensate farmers for reductions in price supports. To receive such compensation, farmers must withdraw 10 percent of their land from production. Small farmers with a total output of less than 92 metric tons are exempt from set-aside as a compulsory requirement to receive compensation payments. For the 2001/02 marketing year, these direct payments were fixed at €63 per metric ton of the historical yield. For durum wheat, the supplementary direct area–based income payment per hectare amounts to €344.5 in traditional areas (traditional durum wheat aid) and €138.9 in other areas (well-established durum wheat aid).

To apply for direct area payments, each member state must draw up a *regionalization plan* by taking into account specific factors that influence yields such as soil fertility. The area concerned must not exceed the region's "base area"—that is, the average number of hectares in the region allocated to growing crops or set aside within the context of the public assistance scheme in 1989, 1990, and 1991.[7] If the total eligible claims exceed the base area, then all claims are reduced proportionately. Article 9 of Council Regulation No. 1251/1999 states that the base areas of future member states will be established by the European Commission. Finally, aid for the production of "traditional durum wheat" is limited to certain regions that are mentioned in Annex II to Council Regulation No. 1251/1999, and per member state a maximum area that may be eligible for the "traditional durum wheat aid" is fixed in Annex III of that regulation.[8]

According to Article 3 of Council Regulation No. 1252/1999, the historical reference yield for cereals should be the average of the median three years of the five-year period 1986/87–1990/91.[9] For maize, a specific yield can be set, possibly distinguishing between irrigated and nonirrigated areas. In the areas thus defined, per hectare payments are calculated by multiplying the basic amount per metric ton by the historical average cereal yield for the area. Article 7 of Council Regulation No. 1252/1999 states that applications for payments may not be made for land that on December 31, 1991, was under permanent pasture, permanent crops, or trees, or was used for nonagricultural purposes.[10]

As for import duties, export taxes, and export refunds, under commitments to the World Trade Organization (WTO), the EU can levy an import duty on cereal imports from third countries, which is payable by the European Community importer. Within the limit of the agreement, the duty cannot exceed the intervention price, increased by 55 percent less the representative CIF (cost, insurance, freight) price. Under these rules, the EU is allowed to vary the tariffs for cereals over time.

COM for Oilseeds   The McSharry reforms removed the system of institutional prices for oilseeds (i.e., rapeseed, sunflowers, and soybeans), but since the 1993/94 marketing year their producers also qualify for compensatory payments.[11] These payments are aligned with the one applicable for cereals (€63 per metric ton of reference yield since 2002). The area grown with oilseeds is taken into account in determining the individual farmer's set-aside obligation as described under the regulations for cereals. As a prerequisite for the imposition of specific oilseed production provisions, production area constraints for the member countries have been implemented under the Blair House agreement. This agreement includes a system of reduced aids for regions where the predetermined agricultural area is exceeded. For nonedible oilseeds for industrial use, specific regulations apply and require that set-aside areas, for example, be planted with several oil-bearing crops for industrial purposes. Currently, there is no regulatory levy on imports, and the Common Customs Tariff rates apply.

COM for Sugar Beet   The EU sugar market is highly protected.[12] Besides protection at the border, the CAP on sugar is implemented through a marketing quota system. Sugar beet quotas are allocated to and administered through sugar refineries on the basis of equity shares. The intervention price for refined beet sugar is set, since the 1998/99 marketing year, at €631.9 per metric ton for white sugar and €523.7 per metric ton for raw sugar in order to guarantee a basic price for sugar beet of €47.67 per metric ton. Intervention is provided for limited quantities corresponding to a production quota for which there is an almost total guarantee (quota A) and a quota with a partially guaranteed price (quota B). For net importers, quota A equals net production, and quota B equals 10 percent of quota A. For net exporters, quota A equals that part of net production consumed domestically, and quota B equals net exports. The EU insists that the total of quotas A and B should not exceed internal consumption plus the quantity that can be exported within the limits of the WTO commitments. Furthermore, the COM is based on a system of sugar and isoglucose production levies to cover the cost of storage and production refunds for the manufacture of certain chemical products. The regulations are complemented with import tariffs and warrants of export refunds. Agricultural areas planted with sugar beets are not eligible for compensatory area payments and are not subject to set-aside obligations.

COM for Fruits and Vegetables

In late July 1996, the European Council reached a political agreement to reform the fresh and processed fruit and vegetable sector.[13] The reform was intended to improve the organization of supply by strengthening producer organizations (POs), tightening up the criteria for recognizing POs, and setting up an operation fund co-financed by the EU for promotion and quality campaigns and the cessation of farming operations that are not covered by European Community compensation schemes, which, with this reform, will provide on-retributive compensation—that is, they will not encourage production. Based on the first year's experience, some rules were modified in 2001 to simplify the regime, to make it more flexible, and to increase producer responsibility.

EU-wide aid schemes are in place to assist producer organizations supplying tomatoes, peaches, pears, and citrus fruits. This aid is granted for the fresh produce delivered during prescribed periods. Aid is paid to recognized producer organizations, which then pay out to the growers. Delivery to approved processors is based on contracts specifying the quantities they cover, the price, and the schedule of supply. These contracts require the processor to process the products delivered. The minimum characteristics of the raw material supplied for processing and the minimum quality requirements for the finished products are defined. Annual EU thresholds have been established to limit the total volume of aid, and there are penalties for overrunning thresholds. Aid per hectare is available to growers of grapes for use as dried muscatel grapes, sultanas, and currants, within a maximum guaranteed area. Contracts must be concluded between the producer or producer organizations

and processors. The aid level is fixed per hectare of specialized area harvested, on the basis of the average yield per hectare of the area concerned.

COM for the Wine-Growing Sector

The common market organization for wine (Council Regulation No. 1493/1999) aims to maintain a balance between supply and demand in the European Community market, thereby giving producers a chance to bring production into line with market developments and to allow the sector to become competitive. This goal is pursued by financing the restructuring of a large portion of the present vineyards, and it should give rise to products in demand at home and abroad. The Common Customs Tariff rates apply to imports of wine into the European Community. To prevent imports from having adverse effects, and subject to compliance with the rules of the WTO, an additional import duty may be imposed.

COM for Milk and Dairy Products

The market for milk and dairy products is one of the most important (about 18 percent of the total value of agricultural production) and most regulated markets in the EU.[14] The current market regime comprises the target price for milk (2000–05, €309.80 per metric ton), intervention price for butter (2000–05, €3282.00 per metric ton), intervention price for skimmed milk powder (2000–05, €2,055.20 per metric ton), a producer quota system, support of prices by the imposition of tariffs on dairy products, warrant of export subsidies, the guaranteed purchase and storage of butter and skimmed milk powder through intervention agencies, and a milk quota system introduced in 1984 (117.49 million metric tons, EU total). Farmers who exceed this reference amount of their quota are subject to a payable levy. Since 1998, milk quotas have been transferable from one individual to another within one EU member state through sale, lease, or inheritance. Also related to these measures are a public intervention scheme, private storage, production aids for using milk in animal feedstuffs and processing milk into casein, special measures to reduce stocks, and some aids for reducing or ceasing production. Import levies and export refunds are also applied.

From 2005 on, intervention prices for butter and skimmed milk powder will be reduced by 15 percent in three equal steps of 5 percent each. In the final stages of reform, they will amount to €2,789.70 per metric ton and €1,746.90 per metric ton, respectively. According to the EU's impact analyses, these changes will put the intervention price after 2007 below the expected world price levels. Benefits for farmers will be provided by three complementary measures: (1) increasing available milk quotas by 1.5 percent in three equal steps over three years in parallel with the price reductions starting in 2005, (2) retaining a crop premium for silage cereals, and (3) implementing a new yearly payment for dairy cows. The payment for dairy cows is to be paid on a flat rate basis per metric ton of the quota held in the 1999/2000 marketing year and amounting to €17.24 per metric ton in the final stages of reform.

On June 26, 2003, EU farm ministers adopted a fundamental reform of the CAP. With the reform, the intervention price for butter will be reduced by 25 percent over four years, which is an additional price cut of 10 percent compared with that of Agenda 2000 reforms.

COM for Beef and Veal   In 1999 the beef support "regime" was altered significantly as part of the Agenda 2000 CAP reform process; the practice of EU-subsidized purchases of surplus beef from the market (intervention buying) was reduced to a minimal "safety net." In return for this reduction in market price support, farmers received direct aid in the form of premiums based on the number of cattle they held in a reference period.

Direct aid includes various types of direct farmer support measures (Council Regulation [EC] No. 1254/1999 and Commission Regulation [EC] No. 2342/1999). They are designed to compensate for the reductions in the intervention price (slaughtering premium and the special beef premium), support the incomes of producers who are specialized in beef production (suckler cow premium), encourage producers to undertake extensive farming (extensification payment), assist producers in less favored areas or in member states highly specialized in beef production (additional suckler cow premium), balance the market throughout the year (deseasonalization premium), and permit member states to support specific production systems (national expenditure envelopes).

The intervention price was set for the 2001/02 marketing year at €3,013 per metric ton of carcass weight (for R3 classification) and was replaced in July 2002 by a basic price for storage, fixed at €2,224 per metric ton. The payment for private storage is granted when the average Community market price level is less than 103 percent of the basic price. As of July 2002, producers also could benefit from a safety net intervention system. When the average market price for bulls or steers in a member state falls to less than €1,560 per metric ton of carcass weight, the EU buys beef into intervention stores.

Since 2002, steer and bull premiums have been set at €150 and €210 per head, and the premium for suckler cows at €200 per year. Although the bull premium is paid once a lifetime for bulls older than nine months or at a minimum carcass weight of 185 kilograms, the steer premiums are paid twice a lifetime, at the age of 9 months and after 21 months. The suckler cow premium is granted per calendar year and per holding within the limits of regional ceilings for not more than 90 animals. These premiums are granted provided that the stocking density on the holding is not more than two livestock units per unit of forage area used for these animals. In addition to these premiums, a slaughter premium applicable at slaughter or export to a third country of €80 has been introduced for bulls, steers, suckler cows, and heifers over the age of eight months, and of €50 for calves more than one and less than seven months in age (with an upper limit of 160 kilograms).[15] The slaughter premium is paid directly to the farmer, provided that the eligible animals have been held for a minimum period of two months. Extensive production (stocking density less than 1.4 livestock units per hectare) may qualify for an additional payment of €100 per premium granted.[16]

The reform of the CAP agreed to in June 2003 changes the way the EU supports its farm sector. In January 1, 2005, a single-payment scheme replaced most of the direct aid payments currently offered to farmers, and it is not linked to what a farmer produces. The amount of the payment is calculated on the basis of the direct aids a farmer received in a reference period (2000–02). Member states may delay implementation of this scheme up to 2007, but by 2007, at the latest, all member states must have at least introduced the scheme. Full decoupling is the general principle from 2005 onward. However, member states may decide to partially implement the single-payment scheme and grant additional payment to the beef producers by way of choosing from the options for partial decoupling of direct payments. Under such partial decoupling, member states may opt to keep up to 100 percent of the slaughter premium for calves. However, member states may also opt to keep up to 100 percent of the suckler cow premium and up to 40 percent of the slaughter premium for calves coupled. Alternatively, they could keep up to 100 percent of the slaughter premium coupled or, instead, up to 75 percent of the special male premium.

The relatively high internal price supports are complemented by measures affecting imports of beef and veal to the EU and by refunds on EU exports to third countries. A basic import tariff (less than 20 percent for most beef products) and an additional variable levy (ranging from 180 to 390 percent) are imposed. Exports are subsidized, and the refunds are set by the European Commission, depending on world market conditions, the present and anticipated condition of the EU market, and the competitive environment in third-country markets. Under the WTO Uruguay Round agreement, these levels are to be reduced in the future.

COM for Ovine Meat   This COM comprises a safety net intervention system and a direct payment for ewes of €21 (€16.8 for female goats and for ewes kept for milk production) per head and year since 2002.[17] Each member state has an upper limit on the number of animals eligible for direct payment for ewes.

The reform of the CAP agreed to in June 2003 means that this simplified premium system will be incorporated into a new support structure. Full decoupling will be the general principle from 2005 onward. However, member states may decide to maintain a proportion of direct aids to farmers in their existing forms, notably where the states believe agricultural markets may be disturbed or production may be abandoned because of the move to the single-payment scheme. Fifty percent of the sheep and goat premiums under the 2001 system can continue to be granted as coupled payments.

Future Evolution of the CAP

Although the Agenda 2000 reforms made the CAP much more efficient, it is recognized that the budgetary pressures of accession and international trade obligations will require further reform in the same direction.

Reforms from the Mid-term Review and Future Directions   In June 2003, the EU endorsed a series of additional reforms that had been proposed in the

Mid-term Review of the CAP in January. The thrust of the reforms is to continue to reduce the reliance of the CAP on market-distorting measures such as price supports and to channel more of the support given to farmers through payments linked to environmental, food safety, general rural development, and animal welfare objectives (i.e., to receive direct income payments, farmers would have to comply with the conditions tied to these objectives). The catchphrase for this refocusing of the mechanisms of support is "support for producers, not for production." The reform program is supposed to be budget-neutral.

The key elements of the reforms are as follows:[18]

- Most support will take the form of a single decoupled farm payment for EU farmers, independent from production, with member states allowed to maintain limited coupled elements (up to 25 percent of the value of current payments) to avoid abandonment of production.
- This payment will be linked to the respect for environmental, food safety, animal and plant health, and animal welfare standards, as well as to the requirement to keep all farmland in good agricultural and environmental condition ("cross-compliance").
- There will be a strengthened rural development policy with more EU money and new measures to promote the environment, quality, and animal welfare and to help farmers meet EU production standards starting in 2005.
- Direct payments for bigger farms will be reduced ("modulation") to finance the new rural development policy.
- A mechanism will be implemented for financial discipline to ensure that the farm budget fixed until 2013 is not exceeded.
- Specific revisions to the market policy of the CAP include:
  — Making asymmetric price cuts in the milk sector, with the intervention price for butter reduced, as noted earlier, by 25 percent over four years. For skimmed milk powder, a 15 percent reduction over three years, as agreed on in Agenda 2000, is retained.
  — Reducing the monthly increments in the cereals sector by half while maintaining the current intervention price.
  — Implementing reforms in the rice, durum wheat, nuts, starch potatoes, and dried fodder sectors.

According to the Mid-term Review, the reforms have the following objectives:

- First, *enhance the competitiveness* of EU agriculture by setting intervention as a real safety net measure, allowing EU producers to respond to market signals (i.e., world prices), while protecting them from extreme price fluctuations. The reforms as adopted by the member states did not go as far as was proposed in the Mid-term Review, which had included further reduction in the support price for cereals, but they still represented progress toward this goal.
- Second, *promote market-oriented, sustainable agriculture* by completing the shift from product to producer support with the introduction of a decoupled system of payments per farm, based on historical references and conditional upon cross-compliance to environmental, animal welfare, and food quality criteria. Again, the Mid-term Review proposal was more ambitious than the program actually adopted, because it will allow member states to pay up to 25 percent of support (or more for durum wheat and certain kinds of beef payments) as coupled payments if necessary to avoid abandonment of production. It is expected, however, that few states will use this exception.
- Third, *strengthen rural development* by transferring funds from the first pillar (payments to producers) to the second pillar (funding to promote rural development) of the CAP. This transfer process is known as "dynamic modulation." Payments under the second pillar will be increased to 30 percent of the CAP budget from its current 10 percent. Because small farmers will be exempt from modulation, it would affect 25 percent of farmers, who now receive about 80 percent of the direct payments. Funds saved by "modulation" will be redistributed to the member states based on several criteria, and the southern states are expected to be the net gainers. The reform will also expand the scope of the currently available instruments for rural development to promote food quality, meet higher standards, and foster animal welfare.

Although this reform process is being driven largely by the internal needs of the EU—particularly the need to simplify the CAP and control the potentially explosive budgetary implications that accession of the Central and Eastern European countries would have for an unreformed CAP—the reforms would have other salutary effects outside the EU. Most important, they will reduce the need to rely on export subsidies to dispose of surplus production, and they will provide an alternative way to support farmers' incomes without high domestic prices. Thus the reforms will increase the EU's flexibility to agree in the Doha negotiations to phase out export subsidies and increase market access (i.e., to reduce tariffs and nontariff barriers). This point is important, because the EU is almost alone in its position—maintained throughout the WTO's Cancun ministerial meeting in September 2003—that export subsidies should not be phased out (only reduced) under the Doha Round agreement. Most other WTO members interpret the Doha Declaration's wording that export subsidies would be reduced "with a view to eliminating" them as meaning that the eventual agreement will require that these subsidies eventually be totally eliminated.

Although the magnitudes have not been estimated definitively, the reform process would also lead to some direct improvements in international market conditions for developing country (and other) producers. The European Commission's simulations estimate that by 2009–10 EU exports of cereals will fall by 3.8 percent and exports of beef by 60 percent. Eurocare estimates that the EU will become a net importer of beef. Other simulations indicate an effect on world cereal prices of 2 percent or less, although, because it would entail a move from a very trade-distorting mechanism of support to one with relatively small trade-distorting effects,[19] there is some reason to think that the impact may be more substantial.

Beyond the Mid-term Review The adoption of the proposals in the Mid-term Review would essentially decouple payments from production in the grain and oilseed markets and partially decouple them in beef, but some important sectors are not touched by the reforms, including sugar and tobacco. The same motivations for reform are present in these sectors, and other pressures will be operating to ensure that these sectors also are eventually reformed, using much the same model used for grains and oilseeds. One of these motivations is the Doha negotiations. As noted, the EU will be under tremendous pressure to agree to the elimination of export subsidies. Another very important motivation—especially for sugar—is the "Everything but Arms" (EBA) initiative. Under the EBA, the EU has eliminated tariff and nontariff barriers[20] to the imports of all products from the developing countries. For most products, this system has been in effect since 2001, but for rice, bananas, and sugar there are phase-in periods. For sugar, the phase-in period is until 2009, but after 2009 sugar will enter the EU duty- and quota-free from developing countries, clearly ending the sugar regime under the CAP. Before the regime ends, sugar prices in the EU will have to fall to something much closer to world prices, and producers may have to be brought under the direct payment system. The EU is also currently negotiating Economic Partnership Agreements with many other developing countries. Although it is not clear what form these agreements will take, the basic intention is that essentially they will be reciprocal free trade agreements. Such agreements will put even more pressure on the CAP to complete the transition to a regime of very low import barriers for products that can be produced in developing countries and a regime in which farmers are compensated for income losses by decoupled direct payments.

In September 2003, the European Commission tabled its proposal for reforms in the cotton, tobacco, sugar, and olive oil sectors. The main features of the proposals are the following:

- *Tobacco.* The production-coupled premium on tobacco would be completely eliminated, with most of it rolled into the decoupled single-farm payment and the rest put into a fund for restructuring tobacco-producing areas.
- *Olives.* The current system of production-linked payments would be eliminated. For farms under 0.3 hectares, coupled payments would be eliminated and replaced with only single-farm payments. For large farms, 60 percent of their coupled payments would be converted into single-farm payments. The rest of the budget that would have funded the coupled payments for these farms would be converted into payments based on hectares or number of trees to ensure the permanence of olive trees in marginal areas or low-output olive groves. This measure may act as a production incentive, but it is intended to be an environmental measure.

- *Cotton.* Sixty percent of the current coupled payments would be converted into single-farm payments. The other 40 percent would be retained as an area-based payment, based on cotton hectarage. Thus this 40 percent would remain fully coupled, though based on area rather than production. The new area payment would be given for a maximum number of hectares, but administered in the same way as current blue box measures, with area ceilings set on a regional basis and any excess in the region resulting in a reduction in payments to all farmers in the region.[21] This situation implies that the measure may not be very effective in controlling the area planted, because farmers have little incentive to stay below the ceiling.
- *Sugar.* There is no specific proposal but rather two options: (1) relatively small changes in the current system, or (2) radical reform, with domestic prices lowered to world market levels and direct support payments increased in compensation. In view of the pressures facing the CAP sugar regime, it seems likely that something close to the second option will have to be adopted.

Impact of Introducing the Common Agricultural Policy in Turkey

This section employs a partial equilibrium model of the Turkish agricultural sector to simulate the effects of introducing the CAP.[22] The model provides information about the likely impact of the CAP on farmers' and consumers' incomes and its budgetary implications. Because the CAP has been a "moving target," the model does not incorporate the most recent reforms, but rather uses the Agenda 2000 scenario. Subsequent reforms have been of the same variety as those in the Agenda 2000 program, but they have moved further in reducing support prices and distributing support as decoupled payments. These later reforms could then be generally expected to result in lower domestic producer and consumer prices than those produced by Agenda 2000 reforms, but with higher direct payments.

The model considers 11 major agricultural products: wheat, barley, maize, sunflower, sugar beet, potato, grapes, milk, beef, poultry, and ovine meat. Table 2.7 shows the base period results for the major

TABLE 2.7 Base Period Results of Model for Major Activities

	Actual Price (thousand TL per metric ton)	Border Equivalent Price (thousand TL per metric ton)	Quantity Produced (thousand metric tons)	GOV (billions of TL)	GOV Share (percent)	VA, Inclusive Direct Payments (billions of TL)	VA Share (percent)
Wheat	97,325	73,412	15,866.67	1,544,223.37	18.10	781,454.26	16.16
Barley	80,765	56,850	6,189.17	499,868.64	5.86	284,464.38	5.88
Maize	90,000	64,475	2,152.33	193,709.97	2.27	74,848.48	1.55
Sunflower	292,692	141,069	816.67	260,259.67	3.05	205,825.27	4.26
Sugar beet	36,612	20,585	16,807.79	618,223.98	7.25	543,851.74	11.25
Potato	132,444	100,017	5,081.33	672,992.07	7.89	595,596.29	12.32
Grapes	280,139	222,260	3,250.67	910,638.60	10.67	847,373.01	17.52
Milk	167,041	97,945	7,466.33	1,450,093.01	16.99	682,852.63	14.12
Beef	2,153,528	1,085,793	444.67	1,086,378.40	12.73	326,386.03	6.75
Poultry	748,350	469,748	725.00	542,553.75	6.36	180,598.86	3.73
Sheep	2,244,433	1,762,319	237.67	753,628.09	8.83	312,353.42	6.46

	Intermediate Inputs, Actual Price (thousand TL per metric ton)	Intermediate Inputs, Border Price Equivalent (thousand TL per metric ton)	VA, Actual Price (thousand TL per metric ton)	VA, Border Price Equivalent (thousand TL per metric ton)	NPR (percent)	EPR (percent)	NPR on Tradable Inputs (percent)
Wheat	48,074	45,462	49,251	27,949	32.57	76.22	5.74
Barley	34,803	32,153	45,962	24,697	42.07	86.10	8.24
Maize	55,224	52,335	34,776	12,140	39.59	186.45	5.52
Sunflower	66,654	59,687	252,031	81,381	107.48	209.69	11.67
Sugar beet	4,425	4,243	32,357	16,342	77.86	98.00	4.29
Potato	15,231	13,486	117,213	86,531	32.42	35.46	12.94
Grapes	19,462	19,684	260,677	202,576	26.04	28.68	-1.13
Milk	102,760	76,925	91,458	47,712	70.55	91.69	33.59
Beef	1,709,127	1,301,899	734,001	83,372	98.34	780.39	31.28
Poultry	499,248	382,865	249,102	86,882	59.31	186.71	30.40
Sheep	1,856,693	1,370,015	1,314,248	1,350,414	27.36	-2.68	35.52

Note: Gross output value (GOV) comprises the output value from main products and, if applicable, from by-products. Consequently, value added (VA) is calculated on the basis of these gross output values. All variables are measured in terms of 2000 prices. TL = Turkish liras; NPR = nominal protection rate; EPR = effective protection rate.

Source: The authors.

activities carried out under the agricultural policies followed during 2000.[23] From the table it follows that wheat, milk, and beef are the most important commodities considered, because these commodities have the highest shares of total gross output. But the order changes to grapes, wheat, and milk when we consider the value added shares, and to grapes, wheat, and potato when we consider the value added shares measured at border price equivalents.[24] The table reveals that crop products constitute 68.93 percent of total value added generated by the 11 commodities and that animal products account for 31.07 percent of the total value added.

Impact on Producers

The domestic prices of the commodities shown in table 2.7 diverge considerably from the border price equivalents. Examination of the profile of nominal protection rates (NPRs)[25] reveals the height of protection in agriculture in Turkey observed earlier in table 2.5 for aggregates such as cereals and oilseeds. Table 2.7 shows a similar picture for the 11 commodities analyzed. The NPRs of these commodities are all positive, and NPR exceeds 100 percent for sunflower. Indeed, the NPRs lie between 50 percent and 100 percent for beef, sugar beet, milk, and poultry, and are between 20 percent and 50 percent for barley, maize, wheat, potato, sheep, and grapes. To examine the effects of agricultural policies on farmers' incomes, we consider first the NPRs of purchased intermediary inputs to agriculture. Consider, for example, wheat production. Although the cost of intermediate inputs per metric ton of wheat amounts to TL 48.074 million, the cost of intermediate inputs evaluated at border price equivalents amount to TL 45.463 million. Thus, the intermediate inputs are taxed on average by 5.74 percent. Among the inputs, the most important cost positions are fertilizers (28.2 percent), seeds (25 percent), and fuel (21.4 percent). A comparison of the domestic prices of each of these inputs with their border price equivalents reveals an implicit taxation of 32.6 percent for seed and subsidization of 3.4 percent for fertilizers.

Farmers' income is determined by the difference between input costs and revenues originating from the sale of agricultural produce, and by any non-price-related monetary transfers to farmers (e.g., per hectare payments for crops or per head payments for

livestock). Agricultural policies with an impact on input prices, output prices, or other direct monetary transfers translate into changes in the value added, defined as the difference between the value of gross output and the value of intermediate inputs, or, in terms of factor payments, the return to land, labor, and owned capital. This effect is computed using the effective protection rate (EPR).[26] Table 2.7 displays the value added of the analyzed activities at domestic prices in relation to value added at border price equivalents. As expected, the levels of effective protection are more pronounced than those of nominal protection. The incomes of producers of crop and livestock products are all implicitly subsidized under the agricultural policies followed during 2000 except for the incomes of producers of sheep. The extent of relative subsidization measured by the EPR is highest for beef, and this measure decreases for sunflower, poultry, maize, sugar beet, milk, barley, wheat, potato, and grape production. Sheep production has a negative EPR, with an absolute value less than 100, indicating the comparative advantage of the country in the production of sheep.

Alternative Agricultural Policy Options for Turkey

We assume that, as a new entrant, Turkey will have to adjust to the EU and accept its legislation and policies. Accession negotiations will therefore focus on how long Turkey will have to adopt the EU legislation and how it will do so. However, agricultural policy in the EU is also evolving beyond the changes introduced under the McSharry reforms and Agenda 2000. Because it is not easy to anticipate what EU agricultural policies will be at the time of Turkey's accession, we use a simulation approach to analyze the potential impacts, using the following scenarios:

- Scenario A1: partial adoption of Agenda 2000 without direct payments
- Scenario A2: complete adoption of Agenda 2000, including direct payments equal to those currently applied in the EU
- Scenario B: adoption of the European Commission proposal similar to that given CEE countries, including direct payments at a level of 35 percent of payments granted in the EU member countries
- Scenario C: free trade with direct payments.

Simulation results for Scenario A1 are presented in table 2.8a. When Turkey adopts Agenda 2000 without direct payments, domestic prices decrease substantially for all commodities except grapes, milk, and poultry. For example, the price of wheat decreases from TL 97,325,000 per metric ton in the base case scenario to TL 73,412,000 per metric ton. Similarly, the prices of barley, maize, sunflower, sugar beet, potatoes, beef, and sheep fall significantly. With the decrease in output prices, the gross output value decreases for all commodities under consideration except poultry and milk. Similar considerations hold for the value added; it decreases for all commodities except grapes, milk, poultry, and sheep. Relative to the base case scenario, the largest decreases occur for sunflower, beef, and wheat. Finally, the share of crop products in total value added generated by the 11 commodities decreases from 68.93 percent in the base case scenario to 62.66 percent in Scenario A1.

In Scenario A2 Turkey adopts Agenda 2000 in full and introduces direct payments to agricultural producers equal to those applied in the EU (table 2.8b). Because prices are basically the same as in Scenario A1, only those activities to which the direct payment schemes apply will be affected. Among the production activities considered are wheat, barley, maize, sunflower, milk, beef, and sheep. As a result of the direct payments, the value added relative to the base period increases as shown in table 2.8b by 71.42 percent for barley, 57.72 percent for beef, and 48.06 percent for sheep. For sunflower, the decline in value added in Scenario A2 (Agenda 2000 with direct payments) is smaller than that in Scenario A1 (Agenda 2000 with no direct payments). For wheat, barley, maize, and beef, the decline in value added turns into increases in value added. Whereas wheat production declines by 41.78 percent in Scenario A1, it increases in Scenario A2 by 38.62 percent relative to the base run. Similar considerations apply for barley, maize, and beef. The increase in milk production goes up from 24.47 percent in Scenario A1 to 45.82 percent in Scenario A2, and the increase in sheep production goes up from 6.28 percent in Scenario A1 to 48.06 percent in Scenario A2. As for the share of crop products generated by the 11 commodities, in total value added, it decreases from 68.93 percent in the base case to 62.32 percent in Scenario A2.

Table 2.9a displays the results of Scenario B. In this scenario, direct payments are introduced, but, following the EU proposals for Central and Eastern European countries, on a level of 35 percent of direct payments granted to agricultural producers in the EU. The final results of the introduction of the CAP will depend on the positions taken by the government of Turkey and the European Commission. Because the negotiations have not yet started, we analyze only the effects of the introduction of direct payments at the rate of 35 percent of EU levels.[27] Table 2.10 shows the positions taken in agricultural negotiations between the Slovak Republic and the European Commission. The table reveals that the main issues in the agricultural negotiations will be the shares of compensation payments for crops and livestock as a percentage of the EU direct payments, the level of reference yield for crop compensation payments, the level of quotas for sugar and milk, slaughter premiums, suckler cow premiums, and ewe ceilings.

In Scenario B, the value added generated in the production of wheat, barley, maize, sunflower, milk, beef, and sheep decreases considerably compared with the value added generated in Scenario A2. The change in value added compared with the base case becomes negative for wheat, maize, and beef production, indicating the extreme vulnerability of the sectors to changes in direct payments. The share of crop products in total value added generated by the 11 commodities decreases now from 68.93 percent in the base case to 62.52 percent in Scenario B.

Table 2.9b presents the results of Scenario C— removal of current trade interventions but with direct payments as under Agenda 2000. In the free trade scenario with direct payments, the value added increases compared with the base case for wheat, barley, beef, and sheep production. For all other commodities, the value added decreases. The share of crop products of total value added generated by the 11 commodities remains almost unchanged.

Effects of Policies on Producers' Incomes in the Medium Term: Adjusting for Supply Response Effects

The discussion so far has been based on the assumption that the output levels for all analyzed activities remain constant (i.e., the assumption of totally inelastic supply). This is a simplifying

TABLE 2.8a Simulation Results for Partial Adoption of Agenda 2000 without Direct Payments (Scenario A1)

	Domestic Price (thousand TL per metric ton)	NPR, Main Outputs (percent)	Quantity Produced (thousand metric tons)	GOV (billions of TL)	GOV Change Relative to Base Run (percent)	NPR, Intermediary Inputs (percent)	VA (billions of TL)	VA Share (percent)	EPR (percent)	VA Change Relative to Base Run (percent)
Wheat	73,412	0.00	15,867	1,164,796	-24.57	-1.60	455,001	10.17	2.60	-41.78
Barley	74,155	30.44	6,189	458,955	-8.18	5.56	248,900	5.56	62.84	-12.50
Maize	76,283	18.31	2,152	164,187	-15.24	1.97	49,326	1.10	88.78	-34.10
Sunflower	141,069	0.00	817	115,206	-55.73	-2.70	67,777	1.52	1.98	-67.07
Sugar beet	26,867	30.52	16,808	451,569	-26.96	0.98	379,559	8.48	38.19	-30.21
Potato	100,017	0.00	5,081	508,220	-24.48	-3.14	441,846	9.88	0.49	-25.81
Grapes	376,586	69.43	3,251	1,224,157	34.43	-1.13	1,160,892	25.95	76.29	37.00
Milk	180,301	84.08	7,466	1,512,916	4.33	15.43	849,966	19.00	138.60	24.47
Beef	1,614,137	48.66	445	846,529	-22.08	15.97	175,193	3.92	372.56	-46.32
Poultry	888,077	89.05	725	643,856	18.67	19.13	313,190	7.00	397.21	73.42
Sheep	2,055,348	16.63	238	708,689	-5.96	15.69	331,980	7.42	3.44	6.28

TABLE 2.8b Simulation Results for Adoption of Agenda 2000 with Direct Payments (Scenario A2)

	Domestic Price (thousand TL per metric ton)	Quantity Produced (thousand metric tons)	Direct Payments (billions of TL)	GOV (billions of TL)	GOV Change Relative to Base Run (percent)	VA (billions of TL)	VA Share (percent)	EPR (percent)	VA Change Relative to Base Run (percent)
Wheat	73,412	15,867	628,217	1,793,013	16.11	1,083,218	17.85	144.26	38.62
Barley	74,155	6,189	238,716	697,671	39.57	487,616	8.04	219.01	71.42
Maize	76,283	2,152	41,339	205,526	6.10	90,665	1.49	246.98	21.13
Sunflower	141,069	817	70,112	185,318	-28.80	137,889	2.27	107.47	-33.01
Sugar beet	26,867	16,808	0	451,569	-26.96	379,559	6.26	38.19	-30.21
Potato	100,017	5,081	0	508,220	-24.48	441,846	7.28	0.49	-25.81
Grapes	376,586	3,251	0	1,224,157	34.43	1,160,892	19.13	76.29	37.00
Milk	180,301	7,466	145,791	1,658,707	14.39	995,757	16.41	179.52	45.82
Beef	1,614,137	445	339,577	1,186,106	9.18	514,770	8.48	1288.54	57.72
Poultry	888,077	725	0	643,856	18.67	313,190	5.16	397.21	73.42
Sheep	2,055,348	238	130,488	839,176	11.35	462,468	7.62	44.09	48.06

Note: All variables are measured in terms of 2000 prices. TL = Turkish liras; NPR = nominal protection rate; GOV = gross output value; VA = value added; EPR = effective protection rate.

Source: The authors.

TABLE 2.9a Simulation Results for Adoption of Agenda 2000 with Direct Payments at 35 Percent (Scenario 2B)

	Border Equivalent Price (thousand TL per metric ton)	NPR Main Outputs (percent)	Domestic Price (thousand TL per metric ton)	Quantity Produced (thousand metric tons)	Direct Payments (billions of TL)	GOV (billions of TL)	GOV Change Relative to Base Run (percent)	NPR Intermediary Inputs (percent)	VA (billions of TL)	VA Share (percent)	EPR (percent)	VA Change Relative to Base Run (percent)
Wheat	73,412	0.00	73,412	15,867	219,876	1,384,672	-10.33	-1.60	674,877	13.41	52.18	-13.64
Barley	56,850	30.44	74,155	6,189	83,550	542,506	8.53	5.56	332,451	6.61	117.50	16.87
Maize	64,475	18.31	76,283	2,152	14,469	178,656	-7.77	1.97	63,794	1.27	144.15	-14.77
Sunflower	141,069	0.00	141,069	817	24,539	139,745	-46.31	-2.70	92,316	1.83	38.90	-55.15
Sugar beet	20,585	30.52	26,867	16,808	0	451,569	-26.96	0.98	379,559	7.54	38.19	-30.21
Potato	100,017	0.00	100,017	5,081	0	508,220	-24.48	-3.14	441,846	8.78	0.49	-25.81
Grapes	222,260	69.43	376,586	3,251	0	1,224,157	34.43	-1.13	1,160,892	23.07	76.29	37.00
Milk	97,945	84.08	180,301	7,466	51,027	1,563,943	7.85	15.43	900,993	17.91	152.92	31.95
Beef	1,085,793	48.66	1,614,137	445	118,852	965,381	-11.14	15.97	294,045	5.84	693.16	-9.91
Poultry	469,748	89.05	888,077	725	0	643,856	18.67	19.13	313,190	6.22	397.21	73.42
Sheep	1,762,319	16.63	2,055,348	238	45,671	754,360	0.10	15.69	377,651	7.51	17.67	20.90

TABLE 2.9b Simulation Results for Adoption of Free Trade with Direct Payments (Scenario 2C)

	Domestic Price (thousand TL per metric ton)	Quantity Produced (thousand metric tons)	Direct Payments (billions of TL)	GOV (billions of TL)	GOV Change Relative to Base Run (percent)	VA (billions of TL)	VA Share (percent)	EPR (percent)	VA Change Relative to Base Run (percent)
Wheat	73,412	15,867	628,217	1,793,013	16.11	1,071,679	24.17	141.66	37.14
Barley	56,850	6,189	238,716	590,568	18.14	391,569	8.83	156.17	37.65
Maize	64,475	2,152	41,339	180,111	-7.02	67,468	1.52	158.21	-9.86
Sunflower	141,069	817	70,112	185,318	-28.80	136,573	3.08	105.49	-33.65
Sugar beet	20,585	16,808	0	345,981	-44.04	274,666	6.20	0.00	-49.50
Potato	100,017	5,081	0	508,220	-24.48	439,691	9.92	0.00	-26.18
Grapes	222,260	3,251	0	722,494	-20.66	658,508	14.85	0.00	-22.29
Milk	97,945	7,466	145,791	1,076,369	-25.77	502,024	11.32	40.93	-26.48
Beef	1,085,793	445	339,577	955,562	-12.04	376,650	8.50	915.98	15.40
Poultry	469,748	725	0	340,567	-37.23	62,990	1.42	0.00	-65.12
Sheep	1,762,319	238	130,488	777,044	3.11	451,437	10.18	40.66	44.53

Note: All variables are measured in terms of 2000 prices. TL = Turkish liras; NPR = nominal protection rate; GOV = gross output value; VA = value added; EPR = effective protection rate.
Source: The authors.

TABLE 2.10   Selected Positions in Agricultural Negotiation between the Slovak Republic and European Commission (EC)

	EC Proposal	Slovak Proposal
Share of compensation payments for crops and livestock (% of EU)[a]	35	100
Reference yield for crop compensation payments (cereal metric ton per hectare)[b]	4.16	4.99
Sugar quota—type A (metric tons)[c]	189,800	190,000
Sugar quota—type B (metric tons)[c]	19,000	45,000
Milk quota (metric tons)	946,150	1,235,000
Slaughter premium—adults (head)[d]	204,062	260,000
Slaughter premium—calves (head)[d]	62,841	60,000
Suckler cow premium (head)[d]	39,708	50,000
Ewe ceilings (head)[d]	219,360	370,000

a. As percent of payments granted to farmers in EU member countries.

b. Reference yield used in calculation of compensatory payments for crops.

c. Sugar beets used to produce sugar up to the A quota secure a higher price (about €46.72 per metric ton in 2000). Sugar beets used to produce sugar above the A quota and up to the B quota secure a slightly lower price (about €32.42 per metric ton in 2000). Sugar production exceeding the sum of both quotas has to be exported at world market prices (i.e., without export refunds). It is known as C sugar.

d. Number of head eligible for compensation payments.

Source: Csaki and others 2002.

assumption, but one that presumably captures the essence of short-run effects. However, after some time producers would begin to adjust to the new price situation, readjusting the output mix and the overall level of resource intensity. The medium- to long-term supply response in the model is determined by the elasticities of supply.[28]

When supply effects are taken into consideration, modeling the impact of introducing the CAP with direct payments becomes tricky for the following reason: the direct payments are made per hectare currently planted, with the amount per hectare computed by multiplying a basic per metric ton payment amount by a historical regional yield for the 1986–91 baseline period. The payments are not based on the individual farmer's current levels of production (yield). For this reason, the direct payment should not affect the farmer's cultivation decisions,[29] but it does affect the farmer's decision on how many hectares to plant. Under Agenda 2000, these payments were originally crop-specific for large farmers (the "professional farmer" scheme) and non-crop-specific for small farmers (the "small producer" scheme). However, even for

large farmers, under Agenda 2000 the payments per hectare for cereals and oilseeds have been progressively aligned, and by the end of the Agenda 2000 period they will be virtually equal.[30] Thus the payments will not affect whether a large farmer chooses to plant, say, wheat or sunflower, or the farmer's decision on how much seed or fertilizer to use. They will, however, affect the amount of arable land in cultivation. In this sense, the direct payments do have an impact on agricultural production, but they do not have as much of an effect on incentives to plant individual crops as would additional income from higher prices for the products. This factor makes it difficult to model the payments' effects. In the simulations, we first treat the payments as if they do *not* come from higher prices. The resulting supply response should then be regarded as a lower bound (Case I).[31] In Case I, the payments do not produce any supply response, but they do increase value added. Next, we treat the payments as if they come from higher prices and thus generate an increase in production. The resulting supply response should be regarded as an upper bound (Case II).

We adjust the medium-run supply elasticities, e_i, to capture the difference in the ratio of value added to price. In particular, the adjusted elasticities, ε_i, are calculated (as emphasized by Valdes 1973) by multiplying the unadjusted elasticities with the ratio of value added to product price so that $\varepsilon = e_i v_i$, where v_i is the ratio of the per unit value added at base run prices to the base period price. The supply response is then computed by applying the relation

$$(2.1) \qquad \frac{\Delta q_j}{q_j} = \varepsilon \left(\frac{VA_{jA2}}{VA_{jBase}} - 1 \right)$$

where q_j indicates the quantity of product j, VA_{jA2} the value added generated in the production of commodity j in Scenario A2 (Agenda 2000 with direct payments), and VA_{jBase} the value added generated in the production of commodity j in the base case. Here we first incorporate the direct payments under Agenda 2000 as part of the value added; thereafter we abstract from considering direct payment as part of value added.

Table 2.11 shows the effects of the alignment to Agenda 2000 under alternative elasticities of supply. For each commodity, the first column shows the results under the assumed medium-run supply elasticities and the second column the results under the assumption of a completely inelastic supply response. The table reveals that output quantities under the Agenda 2000 scenarios decrease, on average, by 3.7 percent for Scenario A1 and increase by 2.5 percent for Scenario A2 under Case II. As expected, the introduction of direct payments gives incentives to increase the output relative to the case in Scenario A1.

Furthermore, the changes in total value added in the simulations with a supply response are larger than under a totally inelastic response. Similarly, Case II results in higher changes in total value added compared with Case I. Consider, for example, wheat production. Whereas total value added generated in wheat production increases by 38.62 percent in Scenario A2 (Agenda 2000 with direct payments) under the inelastic response assumption and Case II, the increase goes up to 46.20 percent under the elastic supply assumption and Case II. By contrast, under elastic supply the value added under Case I increases by only 30.41 percent. Under free trade with direct payments (Scenario C) and Case II, value added generated in wheat production goes up by 37.14 percent

under inelastic supply and by 44.36 percent under the elastic supply assumption. Note that in Scenario C, the value added increases despite the lower prices for wheat, barley, beef, and sheep. As a result, the quantity produced increases under elastic supply and Case II—5.26 percent for wheat, 4.50 percent for barley, 1.78 percent for beef, and 15.64 percent for sheep production. In all other cases, the quantity produced decreases by 0.53 percent for maize, 4.64 percent for sunflower, 14.87 percent for sugar beet, 21.78 percent for potato, 2.07 percent for grapes, 17.11 percent for milk, and 40.75 percent for poultry.

Impact on Consumers

Changes in agricultural output prices also have an impact on consumers through food prices. Lower food prices lead to a decrease in consumer spending on food. A consumer with a fixed, nominal disposable income (i.e., a fixed amount of money available for consumption) is able to increase his or her overall consumption of total goods and services by a percentage derived from multiplying the absolute value of the percentage decrease in food expenditure by the share that food expenditure makes up of total consumption. This increase in the consumer's ability to purchase goods and services is equivalent to an increase in his or her real income. The relative increase in real consumer incomes is highest for households with low disposable incomes, because poor households allocate a higher share of expenditures to food products. In the medium to long term, consumers will adjust to the new set of relative prices, moving away from the consumption of foods that have become relatively more expensive as a result of the policy changes. The medium- to long-term impact on income, therefore, is expected to be more moderate than the short-run impact. The exact amount will be determined by the price elasticity of demand for each product, which regulates the extent of consumers' adjustments to changes in food prices.

To trace the effects of changes in output prices on consumers, we start with the information on expenditure given in table 2.12 and annex table 2.20 for the average consumer and for the average consumer in urban and rural areas, respectively. Consider a commodity such as bread. Annex table 2.20 reveals that for the average consumer the

TABLE 2.11 Simulation Results for Alignment to Agenda 2000 under Positive Supply Response

(percent change relative to 2000 base run)

	Wheat		Barley		Maize		Sunflower		Sugar Beet		Potato		Grapes		Milk		Beef		Poultry		Sheep	
	Elastic	Inelastic	Elastic	Inelastic	Elastic	Inelastic	Elastic	Inelastic	Elastic	Inelastic	Elastic	Inelastic	Elastic	Inelastic	Elastic	Inelastic	Elastic	Inelastic	Elastic	Inelastic	Elastic	Inelastic
Scenario A1																						
Alignment, excluding direct compensatory payments																						
Price change	−24.57	−24.57	−8.18	−8.18	−15.24	−15.24	−51.80	−51.80	−26.62	−26.62	−24.48	−24.48	34.43	34.43	7.94	7.94	−25.05	−25.05	18.67	18.67	−8.42	−8.42
Quantity change	−5.92	0.00	−1.49	0.00	−1.84	0.00	−9.24	0.00	−9.08	0.00	−21.48	0.00	3.44	0.00	15.81	0.00	−5.37	0.00	45.94	0.00	2.21	0.00
GOV change	−29.04	−24.57	−9.56	−8.18	−16.80	−15.24	−59.82	−55.73	−33.59	−26.96	−40.70	−24.48	39.06	34.43	20.83	4.33	−26.26	−22.08	73.19	18.67	−3.89	−5.96
Total VA change	−45.22	−41.78	−13.81	−12.50	−35.31	−34.10	−70.11	−67.07	−36.54	−30.21	−41.75	−25.81	41.72	37.00	44.15	24.47	−49.21	−46.32	153.09	73.42	8.63	6.28
Scenario A2(a)																						
Complete alignment, including direct compensatory payments (Case I)																						
Price change	−24.57	−24.57	−8.18	−8.18	−15.24	−15.24	−51.80	−51.80	−26.62	−26.62	−24.48	−24.48	34.43	34.43	7.94	7.94	−25.05	−25.05	18.67	18.67	−8.42	−8.42
Quantity change	−5.92	0.00	−1.49	0.00	−1.84	0.00	−9.24	0.00	−9.08	0.00	−21.48	0.00	3.44	0.00	15.81	0.00	−5.37	0.00	45.94	0.00	2.21	0.00
GOV change	9.24	16.11	37.49	39.57	4.14	6.10	−35.37	−28.80	−33.59	−26.96	−40.70	−24.48	39.06	34.43	32.47	14.39	3.32	9.18	73.19	18.67	13.81	11.35
Total VA change	30.41	38.62	68.85	71.42	18.90	21.13	−39.20	−33.01	−36.54	−30.21	−41.75	−25.81	41.72	37.00	68.88	45.82	49.25	57.72	153.09	73.42	51.33	48.06
Scenario A2(b)																						
Complete alignment, including direct compensatory payments (Case II)																						
Price change	−24.57	−24.57	−8.18	−8.18	−15.24	−15.24	−51.80	−51.80	−26.62	−26.62	−24.48	−24.48	34.43	34.43	7.94	7.94	−25.05	−25.05	18.67	18.67	−8.42	−8.42
Quantity change	5.47	0.00	8.53	0.00	1.14	0.00	−4.55	0.00	−9.08	0.00	−21.48	0.00	3.44	0.00	29.60	0.00	6.69	0.00	45.94	0.00	16.88	0.00
GOV change	22.46	16.11	51.48	39.57	7.31	6.10	−32.03	−28.80	−33.59	−26.96	−40.70	−24.48	39.06	34.43	48.25	14.39	16.48	9.18	73.19	18.67	30.15	11.35
Per unit VA change	38.62	38.62	71.42	71.42	21.13	21.13	−33.01	−33.01	−30.21	−30.21	−25.81	−25.81	37.00	37.00	45.82	45.82	57.72	57.72	73.42	73.42	48.06	48.06
Total VA change	46.20	38.62	86.05	71.42	22.52	21.13	−36.05	−33.01	−36.54	−30.21	−41.75	−25.81	41.72	37.00	88.99	45.82	68.27	57.72	153.09	73.42	73.06	48.06
Scenario C(a)																						
Free trade with direct payments (Case I)																						
Price change	−24.57	−24.57	−29.61	−29.61	−28.36	−28.36	−51.80	−51.80	−43.78	−43.78	−24.48	−24.48	−20.66	−20.66	−41.36	−41.36	−49.58	−49.58	−37.23	−37.23	−21.48	−21.48
Quantity change	−6.13	0.00	−5.53	0.00	−3.52	0.00	−9.33	0.00	−14.87	0.00	−21.78	0.00	−2.07	0.00	−30.90	0.00	−10.27	0.00	−40.75	0.00	0.97	0.00
GOV change	9.00	16.11	11.61	18.14	−10.29	−7.02	−35.44	−28.80	−52.36	−44.04	−40.93	−24.48	−22.31	−20.66	−48.71	−25.77	−21.08	−12.04	−62.81	−37.23	4.10	3.11
Total VA change	28.73	37.14	30.04	37.65	−13.03	−9.86	−39.84	−33.65	−57.01	−49.50	−42.25	−26.18	−23.90	−22.29	−49.20	−26.48	3.55	15.40	−79.34	−65.12	45.92	44.53
Scenario C(b)																						
Free trade with direct payments (Case II)																						
Price change	−24.57	−24.57	−29.61	−29.61	−28.36	−28.36	−51.80	−51.80	−43.78	−43.78	−24.48	−24.48	−20.66	−20.66	−41.36	−41.36	−49.58	−49.58	−37.23	−37.23	−21.48	−21.48
Quantity change	5.26	0.00	4.50	0.00	−0.53	0.00	−4.64	0.00	−14.87	0.00	−21.78	0.00	−2.07	0.00	−17.11	0.00	1.78	0.00	−40.75	0.00	15.64	0.00
GOV change	22.22	16.11	23.46	18.14	−7.52	−7.02	−32.10	−28.80	−52.36	−44.04	−40.93	−24.48	−22.31	−20.66	−38.47	−25.77	−10.47	−12.04	−62.81	−37.23	19.24	3.11
Total VA change	44.36	37.14	43.84	37.65	−10.34	−9.86	−36.72	−33.65	−57.01	−49.50	−42.25	−26.18	−23.90	−22.29	−39.06	−26.48	17.46	15.40	−79.34	−65.12	67.14	44.53

Note: GOV = gross output value; VA = value added.

Source: The authors.

TABLE 2.12   Structure of Household Expenditures
(1994 prices, Turkish liras)

	Average	Rural	Urban
Total expenses per household	111,044,759	66,698,941	167,764,049
Food, beverages, and tobacco per household	39,552,432	30,202,155	51,511,644
Food and nonalcoholic beverages per household	36,457,528	28,287,252	46,907,494
Expenditure shares (% of total expenditure)			
Cereals and pasta	7.24	9.54	6.07
Meat and meat products	5.18	5.69	4.92
Milk, dairy products, and eggs	4.61	5.84	3.99
Fat	3.00	4.76	2.10
Fruit, fresh or dried	7.82	9.65	6.89
Sugar and sugar products	1.95	3.07	1.38
Other food and nonalcoholic beverages	3.03	3.86	2.61
Alcoholic beverages	0.34	0.30	0.36
Tobacco	2.45	2.57	2.39
Total food, beverages, and tobacco	35.62	45.28	30.70

Source: Turkish State Institute of Statistics.

expenditure share for bread is 3.5371 percent. Next, we consider the value share of the primary commodity in bread, wheat. Multiplying the expenditure on bread with this share, we obtain the value of the analyzed primary commodity (wheat) in the bread expenditure. Considering the price relation $p_i = p_i^*(1 + NPR_i)$, where p_i denotes the domestic price, p_i^* the Agenda 2000 price of wheat, and NPR_i the nominal protection rate on wheat, we obtain the relation $p_i^* = \frac{p_i}{1 + NPR_i}$. We then normalize the domestic price so that $p_i = 1$ for wheat in the base case. By means of the NPR, we determine the foreign price of wheat. Then, by multiplying the expenditure on bread in the form of wheat with the foreign price, we can determine the value of the primary commodity (wheat) evaluated at foreign prices in the bread expenditure. By adding the value of the contents of bread other than wheat, we arrive at the value of bread evaluated at Agenda 2000 prices. Based on the expenditure of the average income group on bread evaluated at base year prices and the expenditure on bread evaluated at Agenda 2000 prices, we determine the effect of Agenda 2000 on the bread expenditure in percentage terms. Once we conduct similar calculations for all the commodities under consideration, we obtain the expenditure on food, beverages, and tobacco evaluated at Agenda 2000 prices. If E stands for total expenditure, F for food expenditure in the base case, and F^* for food expenditure evaluated at Agenda 2000 prices, F^* can be defined as $E^* = F^* + (E - F)$. The effect on consumer welfare is then calculated as $(E - E^*)100/E^*$.[32]

Table 2.13 summarizes the main results of the simulations. For each scenario, we estimated the impact of changes in food prices on, first, the nominal expenditure (change of food expenditure relative to the base period food expenditure) and second, consumers' real income (reduction in purchasing power of nominal income induced by changes in the expenditure on food). The table reveals that, on average, the price changes under the Agenda 2000 scenario (Scenarios A and B) produce a 5.91 percent decrease in the expenditure on food, beverages, and tobacco. As for the expenditure on food and nonalcoholic beverages only, consumers would have to spend 6.41 percent less than under the current base period market conditions. In the Agenda 2000 scenario, the greatest decreases in expenditure occur in the groups fat (30.53 percent), sugar and sugar products (13.44 percent), and meat and meat products (9.48 percent). Because of the significant price changes in the main agricultural products of the Agenda 2000 scenario (compared with the prevailing prices in Turkey), decreases in expenditure were recorded for all food product

TABLE 2.13   Simulation of Scenario Effects on Real Income, Selected Household Types

Reference Scenario (removal of all divergences)	Inelastic Demand			Own Price Elasticities		
	Average	Rural	Urban	Average	Rural	Urban
Change in real income	5.50	8.09	4.23	3.91	5.97	2.89
Change in nominal expenditure (%)						
Food, beverages, and tobacco	−14.64	−16.53	−13.23	−10.56	−12.45	−9.14
Food, and nonalcoholic beverages	−15.88	−17.64	−14.52	−11.45	−13.29	−10.03
Cereals and pasta	−13.21	−18.41	−9.06	−12.04	−16.90	−8.16
Meat and meat products	−29.12	−27.79	−29.90	−13.20	−12.63	−13.54
Fish and fish products	0.00	0.00	0.00	0.00	0.00	0.00
Milk, dairy products, and eggs	−25.85	−26.44	−25.40	−18.75	−19.14	−19.82
Fat	−37.10	−37.11	−37.10	−29.16	−28.56	−29.86
Fruits, fresh and dried	0.00	0.00	0.00	0.00	0.00	0.00
Vegetables and potatoes	−2.54	−3.01	−2.15	−2.34	−2.78	−1.98
Sugar and sugar products	−22.10	−24.39	−19.51	−20.68	−22.82	−18.24
Other food and nonalcoholic beverages	0.00	0.00	0.00	0.00	0.00	0.00
Alcoholic beverages	−1.08	−1.09	−1.08	−0.87	−0.88	−0.87
Tobacco products	0.00	0.00	0.00	0.00	0.00	0.00

Agenda 2000 Scenario	Inelastic Demand			Own Price Elasticities		
	Average	Rural	Urban	Average	Rural	Urban
Change in real income	2.15	3.43	1.51	1.87	3.03	1.28
Change in nominal expenditure (%)						
Food, beverages, and tobacco	−5.91	−7.32	−4.85	−5.14	−6.49	−4.13
Food, and nonalcoholic beverages	−6.41	−7.82	−5.33	−5.58	−6.93	−4.53
Cereals and pasta	−8.03	−11.19	−5.51	−7.22	−10.11	−4.91
Meat and meat products	−9.48	−9.44	−9.50	−5.20	−4.86	−5.41
Fish and fish products	0.00	0.00	0.00	0.00	0.00	0.00
Milk, dairy products, and eggs	4.96	5.07	4.88	2.87	2.92	2.83
Fat	−30.53	−29.36	−31.88	−27.96	−27.14	−28.91
Fruits, fresh and dried	0.00	0.00	0.00	0.00	0.00	0.00
Vegetables and potatoes	−2.54	−3.01	−2.15	−2.34	−2.78	−1.98
Sugar and sugar products	−13.44	−14.83	−11.86	−12.44	−13.73	−10.98
Other food and nonalcoholic beverages	0.00	0.00	0.00	0.00	0.00	0.00
Alcoholic beverages	−0.12	−0.14	−0.11	−0.10	−0.11	−0.09
Tobacco products	0.00	0.00	0.00	0.00	0.00	0.00

Source: The authors.

groups under the assumptions of Scenarios A and B except for milk and dairy products. Scenario C (free trade with direct payments) also induces a decrease in consumers' expenditure on food, beverages, and tobacco of about 14.64 percent. Expenditures for almost all product groups will be reduced.

The results in table 2.13 of the simulated introduction of EU-type agricultural policies in Turkey reveal an increase in consumers' real income of 2.15 percent as an impact of food price changes on average households. The increase is more pronounced in the lower-income group, the rural sector. Because food makes up a higher share of their total expenditures and because their food consumption basket has a different mix, lower-income households experience a more significant change in real income than the average of all groups. The immediate introduction of Agenda 2000 in Turkey would increase the real incomes of the households with the lowest incomes by 3.43 percent, which is significantly higher than the increase of 1.51 percent for households with the highest income—that is, the urban sector.

Columns 4–6 of table 2.13 present the results of the simulation of changes in consumers' real income and in nominal expenditures under the elastic demand assumption.[33] As expected, the effects of the "elastic" scenarios are substantially lower than those of the "inelastic" scenarios. Under the Agenda 2000 scenario, real income increases in the elastic variant are 1.87 percent instead of 2.15 percent in the inelastic demand. The pattern of impacts on the different groups of households under the elastic variant is principally the same as just described.

Impact on the State Budget

In addition to the implications for farmers' incomes and for consumers, the implementation of EU policies would have wide budgetary implications. The most important budgetary effects are the direct effects on internal price support measures (e.g., intervention purchases and border measures) and those stemming from direct income transfers.

When estimating the effects of the policy changes on tariff revenues and export refunds, we assume that before accession Turkey will adopt the EU-like agricultural policies on its own and will not receive any compensation from the EU budget for doing so. Under this assumption, we suppose that any subsidies to agriculture resulting from adoption of the EU-like agricultural policies will have to be financed from the Turkish Treasury.[34] Later, we relax this assumption by considering the case in which Turkey would receive compensation from the EU budget for introducing the EU-like agricultural policies. It should be noted that the total trade-related budgetary effects under Scenarios A1, A2, and B are similar, because the level of domestic support prices is the same for all scenarios under consideration.

The trade-related budgetary implications of adopting EU-like agricultural policies are analyzed by multiplying the net traded quantity by the difference between the base period domestic price and the Agenda 2000 price. Whenever the base period domestic price exceeds the Agenda 2000 price, the product determines the loss in tariff revenue for imported commodities such as sunflower. For exported commodities, the product can be considered the decrease in export subsidies, as long as the base period domestic price exceeds the Agenda 2000 price, such as for wheat. Finally, for poultry the Agenda 2000 price exceeds the base period domestic price. Because poultry is an imported commodity, the product is considered to be an increase in tariff revenue.

Table 2.14 shows that after adoption of the Agenda 2000 policies Turkey will incur a net trade-related revenue loss of €226 million. In the longer term, the losses could become even greater as producers and consumers adjust to the new price levels. These results account only for expenditure on the commodities analyzed in this study. Thus they are likely to underestimate the true trade-related budgetary effects of an implementation of CAP-type market regimes in Turkey.

The budgetary effects of direct income transfers can be determined for each agricultural commodity such as wheat, barley, maize, and beef. For wheat, direct income support can be determined from the relation [direct payments (euros/metric ton)] * [exchange rate (lira/euro)] * [historical grain yield for the EU compensatory area payments (metric tons/hectare)] * [quantity of wheat produced (metric tons)]/[actual yield in 2000 per hectare (metric tons/hectare)]. The direct income support for other commodities can be similarly determined. A close look at the figures in table 2.14 reveals that direct payments to agriculture will amount to €2.772 billion under Scenarios A1 and A2 and to €970 million under Scenario B.

Overall, the budgetary costs to Turkey of adopting EU-like agricultural policies when uncompensated by the EU budget for introducing those policies will be €2.998 billion under Scenario A policies and €1.196 billion under Scenario B policies.

After accession to the EU, Turkey will be eligible for payments under the EU's Structural Funds and Cohesion Fund. But after accession, Turkey will also have to contribute to the EU budget in the form of VAT-based and GNP-based contributions. The VAT-based contribution is determined by the relation 0.008522 * 0.55 * GDP, where the value of 0.008522 denotes the proportion used in calculation of the VAT-based contribution, and the parameter value of 0.55 is derived from the relation that the VAT base may not exceed 55 percent of national GDP.

TABLE 2.14   Trade-Related Budget Effects and Direct Payments under Agenda 2000

		Net Exports, 1999–2001 Average (metric tons)	Trade-Related Effects on Budget (billions of TL)	Agenda 2000 Direct Payments (billions of TL)	
				Scenario A	Scenario B
Wheat	EX	617,845	16,729	628,217	219,876
Barley	EX	160,508	1,061	238,716	83,550
Maize	IM	−881,072	−12,085	41,339	14,469
Sunflower	IM	−394,310	−66,002	70,112	24,539
Sugar beet	IM	−31,675	−309	0	0
Potato	EX	91,237	3,467	0	0
Grapes	EX	470,095	−45,339	0	0
Milk	IM	−146,669	1,945	145,791	51,027
Beef	IM	−69,392	−37,429	339,577	118,852
Poultry	IM	−374	52	0	0
Sheep	EX	42,162	7,972	130,488	45,671
Total			−129,939	1,594,239	557,984
Total (€ millions)			−226	2,772	970
Total budgetary cost (€ millions):					
Scenario A			2,998		
Scenario B			1,196		

Note: Because of the prevailing sanitary ban by Turkey on imports of livestock and meat products, the 1990–96 average of net exports for beef, sheep, and poultry is used. TL = Turkish liras; EX = export; IM = import.

Source: The authors.

Table 2.15 shows that Turkey's VAT-based contribution will amount to €1.023 billion. The GNP-based contribution is determined by the relation 34.46 ∗ (exchange rate) ∗ (share of Turkish GDP in EU GDP), where 34.46 denotes the amount measured in terms of billions of euros that must be met by the EU budget requirement by the GNP-based contribution.[35] From table 2.15, we note that Turkey's GNP-based contribution will be €878 million.

After accession, Turkey will receive from the EU budget direct income support payments, trade-related net subsidies, payments under the Structural Funds and Cohesion Fund. The direct income support will amount to €2.772 billion in Scenarios A1 and A2 and to €970 million in Scenario B. Trade-related net subsidies, consisting of subsidies on exports minus tariff revenues on imports, are determined by multiplying the net traded quantity (exports minus imports) from third countries by the difference between the Agenda 2000 price and the border price. Basing the calculations on the average 1999–2001 net trade figures with third

countries, trade-related net subsidies from the EU will be €23 million. The payments under the Structural Funds that Turkey may receive from the EU after accession can be calculated, assuming that Turkey falls under Objective 1 of the Structural Funds.[36] According to the European Commission (2002), per capita payments under Objective 1 currently amount to €217 per inhabitant per year. Therefore, assuming Objective 1 applies to Turkey, the country would receive about €14.6 billion— that is, about 6.75 percent of the 2000 GDP. Turkey's potential gains from the Cohesion Fund have been estimated on the basis of the payments granted to Greece, Ireland, Portugal, and Spain. Cohesion Fund payments are granted to countries with a per capita GNP of less than 90 percent of the EU average. The total amount to be spent in 2002 was about €45 per inhabitant. If Turkey receives equal payments, it could expect to receive about €3 billion.

The calculations just presented are optimistic, because, according to EU rules, transfers from the

TABLE 2.15   Contributions to and Revenues from EU Budget

		Turkish Liras (billions)	Euros (millions)
Contributions to EU budget			
VAT-based contribution		588,682	1,023
GNP-based contribution		505,112	878
Total contribution		1,093,793	1,902
Revenues from EU budget			
Direct payments to agriculture	Scenario A	1,594,239	2,772
Direct payments to agriculture	Scenario B	557,984	970
Trade-related budgetary effects		13,473	23
Structural Funds		8,421,079	14,641
Cohesion Fund		1,746,307	3,036
Total revenue	Scenario A	11,775,099	20,472
Total revenue	Scenario B	10,738,843	18,670
Net revenue from EU budget			
Unrestricted	Scenario A	10,681,305	18,570
Unrestricted	Scenario B	9,645,050	16,768
Structural operations (restricted)	Agenda 2000	4,983,338	8,664
Restricted	Scenario A	5,497,258	9,557
Restricted	Scenario B	4,461,002	7,755

Source: The authors.

Structural Funds and Cohesion Fund cannot exceed 4 percent of GDP. Thus this requirement places an upper bound on the amount that Turkey can receive from the EU under these funds. For Turkey, this requirement is binding, and therefore the payments under the Structural Funds and Cohesion Fund cannot exceed €8.664 billion. The total annual net revenue that Turkey can receive from the EU under accession will therefore be about €9.557 billion under Scenario A and €7.755 billion under Scenario B.

Furthermore, an assessment of Turkey's potential gains from the Structural Funds must bear in mind that funding of projects under the priority objectives are subject to a co-financing mechanism. The amount just estimated therefore constitutes the EU's share of project funding and must be complemented by funds from the national budget. The EU's contribution to structural funding is subject to two ceilings. The first is a maximum of 75 percent of the total eligible cost and, as general rule, is at least 50 percent of the eligible public expenditure for measures carried out in the regions covered by Objective 1. When the regions are located in a member state covered by the Cohesion Fund, the European Community contribution may rise, in exceptional cases, to a maximum of 80 percent of the total eligible cost. The second ceiling is a maximum of 50 percent of the total eligible cost and, as a general rule, is at least 25 percent of the eligible public expenditure for measures carried out in areas covered by Objectives 2 and 3. Assuming that Turkey will qualify for assistance under Objective 1 and the Cohesion Fund, and assuming an EU participation rate (on average) of 75 percent, the EU's contribution of €8.664 billion would have to be accompanied by a Turkish co-financing share of about €2.9 billion from the national budget.

Welfare Effects

The situation just described reveals that, in Turkey, integration into the EU will lead to substantial changes in the agricultural incomes of producers, the welfare levels of the consumers, and the budget revenues of the government. On the effects of integration into the EU, we have five observations.

TABLE 2.16   Impact of Changes in Agricultural Policies on Agricultural Incomes

	Gross Agricultural Output (billions of TL)	Value Added Inclusive Direct Payments (billions of TL)
Base run with current policies	8,532,570	4,835,604
Agenda 2000 without direct payments	7,799,080	4,473,629
Agenda 2000 with direct payments	9,393,319	6,067,868
Agenda 2000 with 35 percent direct payments	8,357,064	5,031,613
Free trade with direct payments	7,475,246	4,433,256

Note: All variables are measured in terms of 2000 prices. TL = Turkish liras.
Source: The authors.

First, the impact on farmers' incomes of the introduction of EU-type agricultural policies (Scenarios A1, A2, B, and C) will be driven mainly by the amount of CAP-like compensation payments granted to the farmers (see table 2.16), and the impact will be greater in the medium to long term as farmers adjust to the new policies. The largest reduction in farmers' incomes is produced by Agenda 2000 policies without direct payments (Scenario A1). From the point of view of the farmers, the best alternative among the various EU policies considered is the Agenda 2000 scenario with direct payments given at the EU levels.

Second, the impact will not be uniformly distributed across all agricultural products; some farmers will gain and others will lose from the reforms as a result of changes in relative rates of protection.

Third, EU-type agricultural policies will reduce agricultural prices substantially in Turkey, leading to lower food prices. In the short term, food expenditures are projected to fall by as much as 5.91 percent compared with the current base period conditions. In the medium to long term, EU-like changes in agricultural policies (Scenarios A1, A2, and B) would induce a 5.14 percent average drop in food expenditures. Expenditures are projected to fall for the major food product groups, with the largest decreases projected for fat products (30.53 percent), sugar and sugar products (13.44 percent), and meat and meat products (9.48 percent).

Fourth, because Turkish households spend on average about 36 percent of their disposable income on food and beverages, policy reforms that affect food prices will undoubtedly affect consumers' real income. In fact, the model estimates that, in the medium to long term, EU-like policies (Scenarios A1, A2, and B) will lead to a 1.87 percent increase in real household incomes in Turkey. This impact is higher (2.15 percent) in the short term, before consumers can adjust to the higher prices for some food products. Therefore, although farmers as a group could lose from the new policies, depending on the amount of direct payments, the population as a whole stands to gain from the introduction of these policies. Furthermore, because food makes up a higher share of their total expenditures and their food consumption basket has different mixes, lower-income households (i.e., rural households) experience a more significant increase in real income.

Fifth, the budgetary costs to Turkey of adopting EU-like agricultural policies (when Turkey will not receive any compensation from the EU budget for introducing these policies) will amount to €2.998 billion under Scenario A policies and to €1.196 billion under Scenario B policies. Yet after the EU accession, Turkey will be a net recipient of funds from the EU; it can expect to receive from the EU €9.557 billion in net transfers under Scenario A and €7.755 billion in net transfers under Scenario B.[37]

Institutional Development and EU Accession

The institutional and human capital enhancements implied by EU membership require significant effort and investment during the preaccession period. Not only is the alignment of legislation necessary; Turkey also must develop the judicial and administrative capacity to implement and enforce the *acquis communautaire*. In preparation for joining the EU and adopting regulations and policies of the EU, Turkey will have to strengthen some institutions and create others. This section first outlines Turkey's key institutions for agriculture in the context of implementation of the *acquis* and, in particular, the mechanisms to operate the CAP. The section then briefly discusses Turkey's status and ability to adopt and implement the *acquis*.

Implementing Agencies for Agricultural Policies

The Ministry of Agriculture and Rural Affairs (MARA), Ministry of Industry and Trade, Turkish Bank of Agriculture, and Treasury are the main organizations responsible for the formulation and implementation of agricultural policy in Turkey. The main task of MARA is to assist in the elaboration and implementation of agricultural policies, particularly services such as research and development, quarantine and inspection, rural development, and small-scale irrigation works.

MARA also carries out commercial functions through the Turkish Grain Board (TMO), an affiliated state economic enterprise. For more than six decades, the TMO has functioned as a buffer stock agency in order to stabilize the grain prices received by producers and paid by consumers. The board announces the purchase prices, which are later re-determined based on market conditions. The TMO uses its stock capacity to regulate the market, so that prices in the bread and pasta industries are stabilized, and so producers and consumers do not face high price fluctuations (MARA 2002). Under the Agricultural Reform Implementation Project, the prices of the TMO will be increasingly linked to the world price (with a margin equal to the tariff) in order to allow state procurement to function only as a "buyer of last resort," which is now the case in the EU. The TMO also declares a sales price for grain no less than either (1) the TMO's purchase price plus the storage cost up to the date of sale, including imputed interest charges on stocks, or (2) the tariff-inclusive import parity price for grain of equivalent quality as of the time the grain is sold. Prices increase in general to take into account the depreciation of the Turkish lira. This system discourages wheat buyers from letting the TMO incur all of the storage costs and then buying the grain at

a subsidized price later in the year, which has been the case in the past. TMO's new purchase and sales pricing policies have been very successful in eliminating its deficit (TMO 2002).

The Turkish Bank of Agriculture is, as explained early in this chapter, the principal supplier of agricultural credit for crop and livestock production. It was the channel through which the bulk of the credit was extended to farmers through the agricultural credit cooperatives (ACCs) and the agricultural sales cooperatives unions (ASCUs). Virtually all of these loans carried negative real interest rates, with losses covered by the Treasury. The ACCs provided short- and medium-term credit in the form of a limited cash payment (up to 25 percent of the total loan) plus production inputs (e.g., seed, fertilizer, feed, and machinery.). The ACC system was a retail network of the Turkish Bank of Agriculture for the distribution of subsidized credit in kind to small farmers, with some independence from the government since 1995. It was the only source of production credit for smallholder farmers. Because almost all of the financial requirements were provided by the Turkish Bank of Agriculture, the cost-effectiveness of the ACCs was never a concern. Recently, the Turkish Bank of Agriculture was commercialized (about 500 branches were closed in rural areas), and the credit subsidy was eliminated. Since then, an alternative arrangement for providing small farmers with credit has not yet been established.

In the past, the ASCUs operated under the control of the Ministry of Industry and Trade. They were authorized to set prices for members' commodities and to implement support purchases from producers on behalf of the state. They also were authorized to set up facilities such as warehouses and primary processing and packing plants and to market commodities in accordance with wholesale and retail market practices. Today, within the framework of the Agricultural Reform Implementation Project (ARIP), financial aid is granted to assist the restructuring and transformation of ASCUs into genuine cooperative organizations—that is, independent, financially autonomous, self-managed cooperatives that sell and process members' production.

Financial aid is also provided for improving public services to facilitate reform implementation. Regulations are in place to control water and soil pollution and to protect wetlands. National and regional plans distribute information on ways to combat desertification and reduce discharges of nutrients. The government plays a large role in investment in infrastructure, especially irrigation works.

Status of Implementation of the Acquis in Agriculture

This section examines Turkey's status and ability to assume the obligations of EU membership.

Adoption of the Common Market Organizations

The markets policy is the most important instrument of the CAP. As noted earlier, it places products or a group of products under a particular regime, the Common Organization of the Market (COM), so that common rules govern production and trade. The CAP is seeking to gradually reduce institutional prices toward the world market levels, while consolidating direct aid as the basic support mechanism for European Community farming. The *acquis* requires that the intervention agencies be capable of carrying out tasks such as regular market and price monitoring, buying-in, public storage, and sales and stock control in premises that meet Community standards. Furthermore, the *acquis* specifies precise rules for producer organizations, which must be fulfilled if such an organization is to benefit from Community support. Finally, the COMs require specific administrative structures for operation of the Community supply-management instruments such as production quotas in the sugar, dairy, and starch sectors.

During late 1990s, Turkey, with the introduction of ARIP, completely reformed its prevailing output price support and input subsidy policies. The ASCUs were restructured, and the TMO was downsized. The TMO will preserve the assets needed to carry out a minimum level of purchases and storage and will liquidate the rest of its assets.

In addition, a process of privatizing the agricultural state economic enterprises has begun. The sugar law adopted on April 19, 2001, opens the market to competition, reduces state interference, and aims to maintain stable and self-sufficient sugar production. The state-owned sugar company will operate on a commercial basis, and sugar mills will be transferred to the Privatization Agency. In addition, a sugar board was established. The sugar law aims to maintain the demand and supply balance through a system of production quotas like that used in the EU. In the tobacco sector, the Turkish Parliament adopted a new law restructuring the Directorate General for the Tobacco and Tobacco Products, Salt and Alcohol Industry (TEKEL). The law converts TEKEL from a monopoly to a commercial enterprise that will operate under free-market conditions. Parliament also adopted new regulations on tobacco, tobacco products, and alcoholic beverages. The processing facilities of TEKEL are to be privatized. In January 2002, a tobacco law was adopted that aimed to end state-subsidized tobacco purchases as of 2002 and to introduce auction sales, individual purchasing contracts between producers and buyers, and liberalization of the market.

In this restructuring, some firms were liquidated, such as the Turkish Agricultural Supply Corporation, the state firm responsible for input supply. Although the achievements described are considerable, Turkey, according to the European Commission (2004), lags behind in adopting the EU's common market organizations.

Implementation of the Integrated Administration and Control System of Payments

According to the *acquis,* the administrative structures and systems needed for handling the CAP expenditure under the Guarantee Section of the European Agricultural Guarantee and Guidance Fund must meet certain requirements. In particular, the paying agencies must be accredited and must offer sufficient guarantees that the admissibility of claims and compliance with European Community rules are checked before payment is authorized and that the payments effected are correctly and fully recorded in accounts. To help combat fraud and ensure that the direct payments scheme is effectively applied, the EU introduced the Integrated Administration and Control System. Farmers wishing to claim direct payments must complete detailed IACS forms, which are designed to ensure that only eligible land is entered into the scheme and that only one claim is made on any individual piece of land. According to the *acquis,* the IACS must have a computerized database, an alphanumeric identification system for agricultural parcels, and a system for identifying and recording animals.

Turkey realizes that direct income support is at the heart of ARIP and that registration of farmers is a critical part of the DIS program. Two approaches have been used to build an adequate registry of farmers in Turkey. The first approach is based on the existing land registry records (cadastre), and the second is based on certificates of farmers. Land registry was used where it exists, but it was complemented by farmer certificates. In addition, MARA developed a farm registry system in collaboration with related organizations. The database of this system includes information on the number of farmers, their demographic characteristics and assets, the number and the size of land parcels, and land use. This information is more accurate than formal statistics, and to access it, all provinces and districts are provided an online connection to the MARA Registration Center. The 2.6 million farmers registered hold a total of 16.4 million hectares of land, of which 16.3 million hectares are eligible for direct income support. The number of parcels registered is 15.5 million. In 2001, direct payments of about TL 500 trillion were made, paid in two installments. DIS continued in 2002 with a payment of TL 135 million ($85) per hectare of land up to 50 hectares. Transition payments to help farmers divert from hazelnut and tobacco increased in 2002 to $0.2 million, and transition payments were to be granted until 2004. In addition to the farmer registry, a Geographic Information System (GIS) and Remote Sensing Department was established within MARA to classify and map agricultural land, estimate production and production capacity for various products, and create a database for land use planning purposes.

These are considerable achievements. Yet, according to the European Commission (2004), Turkey has achieved little progress in introducing an IACS for payments. This situation is particularly serious because the data required for IACS are not easily available. It requires a uniform, centralized database that would allow payments control at the central level, and an integrated system of on-the-spot controls needs to be developed. According to EU legislation, the individual member states are obliged to control areas that have at least 5 percent of applicants for payments. Fifty percent of the requested area must be verified—one part on-site and one part perhaps from aerial photography. The

registration system in Turkey developed under the DIS is certainly a start on an IACS. It includes a very comprehensive audit and financial management system that is in line with the kind of control system mentioned earlier.

By the end of 2004, all EU member states will be required to use a land register and parcel identification control system based on GIS analysis of digital images. Turkey could adopt this system from the outset. Over time, GIS maps of the whole territory of Turkey should be prepared. Such a system will derive the basic data from the cadastre map of the Turkish territory, which needs to be digitized. The cadastre data will then be superimposed with ortho-photomaps, which will allow identification of the exact borders of cultivated agricultural land and of less favored areas. The processed ortho-photomaps, along with other relevant cadastre data (on disadvantaged areas, protected areas, environmentally sensitive areas, and so forth), will be given to an institution in charge of the data processing, and the result is expected to be an entirely new register of land use. Because introduction of the IACS and establishment of an agency to disburse direct payments and other subsidies to farmers are prerequisites for the functioning of the CAP, it appears that Turkey must extend the present system in order to develop the land register and parcel identification control system like those of the EU and establish the associated payment agency.

Food Safety and Quality Standards   Food safety issues in the EU are spread over food, veterinary, phytosanitary, and animal nutrition legislation. Food legislation includes general rules for hygiene and control, food labeling, food additives, food packaging, and genetically modified foods. Veterinary legislation addresses animal health, animal welfare, animal identification and registration, internal market control systems, external border controls, and public health requirements for establishments in relation to animal products. Phytosanitary legislation includes plant health (harmful organisms, pesticides), seeds and propagating material, and plant hygiene. Finally, animal feed legislation includes the safety of feed materials and additives, labeling, contaminants in feed, controls, and inspections.

The *acquis* requires that each member state have appropriate administrative structures to inspect and control the implementation of all food legislation. In particular, the various hygiene control officials must be trained in inspection and in the Hazard Analysis and Critical Control Point (HACCP) system. Food operators must implement HACCP, and laboratories used in hygiene and foodstuff analysis must comply with the European Community system on accreditation, method of sampling, and analysis.[38] In the realm of plant and animal health and nutrition, the *acquis* requires that appropriate inspection arrangements be available at the site of origin, that nondiscriminatory checks be performed during transport and at the destination point, and that satisfactory testing arrangements be available.

A recent white paper on food safety stated that the commission is determined to set the highest standards of food safety (see European Commission 2000). The white paper proposes the following: (1) establishment of an independent European Food Authority with responsibility for independent scientific advice on all aspects of food safety, operation of rapid alert systems, and communication of risks; (2) an improved legislative framework covering all aspects of food products "from farm to table"; (3) greater harmonization of national control systems; and (4) dialogue with consumers and other stakeholders. According to the white paper, imported foodstuffs and animal feed should meet health requirements at least equivalent to those set by the European Community for its own products. The white paper on food safety also states that it is essential that the EU candidate countries implement the basic principles of the treaty establishing the European Community, pass food safety legislation, and put in place control systems equivalent to those in place within the European Community. Similar considerations will certainly apply to Turkey. Because the EU will not take any risks that might lead to lower food safety standards or affect EU consumers, it is of prime importance that Turkey comply with the EU's *acquis* on food safety.

In Turkey, food legislation has been updated continually since 1985. The harmonization of "Good Agricultural Practices" has been completed, and the regulation on agricultural quarantine has been in force, and regularly strengthened, since 1991.[39] A food act was passed in 1995, according to which all stages of food production are targeted for inspection. Turkey has formally adopted a number of typical elements of food safety regulations and control systems by adopting some of the EU rules and regulations. In particular, Turkey has started to set up the Rapid Alert System for Food and Feed, and has revised the regulation on the Establishment and Duties of Province Control Laboratories. Accreditation has been initiated for some of the laboratories involved in the ring test organized by the Food Analysis Performance Assessment Scheme and Turkish Scientific and Technical Council. Fifteen provincial laboratories have been brought up to EU standards. The Plant Health Regulations, which are the Turkish equivalent of the basic Council Directive 2000/29/EC, dating back to 1991, were amended in 2003. HACCP control instructions have been prepared to improve food processing. In the veterinary area, Turkey amended the Law on Animal Health and Surveillance in 2004, creating the legal bases for banning the administration of certain substances to animals and imposing sanctions in this regard. It has also upgraded the control performance of the veterinary service, including the implementation of residue monitoring plans.[40]

Trade and Border Control   Implementation of the CAP requires the establishment of effective customs control for trade with third countries. Because Turkey's borders will become EU borders at the point of accession, Turkey will have to protect its long borders and ensure, for example, an adequate veterinary infrastructure to manage livestock inspection and control disease. Thus Turkey needs to assess the current conditions and to design technical specifications for construction of other veterinary and phytosanitary border crossings along its future EU border.

EU controls on third-country imports require that a system of border inspection posts (BIPs) be completed to EU standards at external borders with third countries. Currently, some 283 EU BIPs are operated by national authorities. Most of these are at ports and airports; others are at road or rail links located, in particular, on the eastern borders of the EU.

The accession of Turkey will extend the EU's eastern frontier with Georgia, Armenia, Iran, Iraq, and Syria. Veterinary checks on imports at the BIPs include documentary, identity, and physical checks of the animals or animal products. After these checks at the first border crossing into the EU, animals and products can in principle circulate freely in the internal market. It is therefore essential that BIP facilities and procedures are adequate to maintain animal and public health safety. Setting up border inspection posts for veterinary and other controls in the new member states requires that buildings, equipment, and staff be in place to carry out the required border checks. EU legislation sets out minimum standards for BIP facilities, depending on the types of products to be checked.

Conclusion

Accession to the EU implies some major changes, both in the incentive structure for agricultural production and in the institutions of the sector. This chapter modeled and quantified the probable changes in the incentive structure and examined their implications for the structure of production, value added in primary agriculture, and welfare of producers and consumers. It also investigated qualitatively what changes will be needed in major institutions by comparing those existing currently in Turkey with those of the EU's Common Agricultural Policy.

The results of any modeling exercise should be taken with a grain of salt, and that is even truer of those in this chapter. One reason is that the CAP is a moving target undergoing fundamental reforms. The general direction of the reform program is clear, but how far it will have gone by the time of Turkey's accession is not. It is quite possible—some would argue likely—that the price structure in the EU will in another 5–10 years be very close to that prevailing in world markets, but this development depends on some future political decisions, and so is by no means certain. Clearly, however, prices will be much lower than they are at present. Because of the uncertainties, this chapter modeled several different scenarios, but all results should be interpreted as indicative of general orders of magnitude rather than as precise numerical forecasts. If the model were run using the scenario of the recently adopted reform program that is an extension of Agenda 2000, Turkey's producers and consumers would face lower prices. Turkish consumers would gain even more than they would under the Agenda 2000 scenario, and producers would lose more in price supports but would receive substantially higher direct payments.

One important difference between Turkey and the accession countries of Central and Eastern Europe is that in most of the latter, agricultural prices were lower than those in the EU at the time those countries began accession negotiations. In Turkey, the converse is true, which implies that the prices for many major agricultural products in Turkey will have to be reduced at some point between now and accession. As quantified in this chapter, such a reduction would be of great benefit to Turkish consumers, especially the poor. It would, however, require adjustments on the part of Turkish farmers. Under its current reform program, ARIP, Turkey has made a good start in this adjustment process. The way in which it has done this—by partially compensating farmers by means of an incentive-neutral, WTO-compatible direct income support system—is fully consistent with the mechanisms of the CAP. By bringing agricultural prices in Turkey more in line with world prices, the reforms will begin to make Turkish agriculture more efficient. This improvement, in turn, would help Turkey to meet one of the EU's primary criteria for accession countries—that its producers be able to compete in the unified market that follows from membership. Of course, an important lesson from other reform-minded countries is that to realize the benefits of the reform program in increased competitiveness, producers must be supported by having the appropriate infrastructure and services, as well as continued sectoral and economy-wide reforms.

As for institutions, Turkey has made a good start in some areas, but it still has a long way to go in others. The DIS system in Turkey lays the foundation for a system to administer direct payments under the CAP, and the financial management system of the DIS should be a good basis on which to build the Integrated Administrative and Control System of payments. But some improvements will clearly be needed. For example, the system will have to be based on GIS analysis of digital images, implying that GIS maps will have to be prepared for all of Turkey. Food safety and quality standards will have to be improved, as will veterinary border posts. But with a good investment program and support from the EU and international community, Turkey should find it feasible to complete the improvements in the period leading up to accession.

TABLE 2.17 Arrangements Applicable to European Community Importation of Agricultural Products, Other than Fruits and Vegetables Originating in Turkey

HS	Description	1999 Turkish Exports to EU (US$)	Tariff Rates Applied by EU on Imports from Third Countries	Ad Valorem Duty on Imports from Turkey		Specific Duty on Imports from Turkey		Over-Quota Duty on Imports from Turkey
				Ad Valorem Duty	Tariff Quota (metric tons)	In-Quota Duty	Tariff Quota (metric tons)	
0204	Meat of sheep or goat	123,880	78.10–157.20	0	—	0	200	
020725	Frozen turkeys	—	20.85				1,000	
02072510		—				ECU/t 170		
02072590		—				ECU/t 186		
020727	Frozen cuts of turkeys	—	27.64					
02072730		—				ECU/t 134		
02072740		—				ECU/t 93		
02072750		—				ECU/t 339		
02072760		—				ECU/t 127		
02072770		—				ECU/t 230		
040690	Cheese	338	67.76				1,500	ECU 67.19/100 kg
04069029		804,042				0		
04069031		—						
04069050		—						
04069086		—						
04069087		—						
04069088		—						
0811								
08111011	Frozen strawberries	125,928	25.27	0	—	0		
08112011	Frozen raspberries	—	19.89	0	—	0	100	
08119019	Other fruits, frozen	1,122	18.93	0	—	0		
10020000	Rye	—	103.90			Reduction according to Article 3(4)		
1107	Malt	1,538						
110710			50.40			Reduction of ECU/t 6.57		
11072000			29.30			Reduction of ECU/t 6.57		

CN code	Description						
1509							
15091010	Olive oil	—	81.30			10% reduction	
15091090		121,068,014	81.30			10% reduction	
15099000			69.90			5% reduction	
151000	Other olive oil	—					
15100010		2,201,779	79.20			10% reduction	
15100090			79.20			5% reduction	
2002	Prepared tomatoes						
200210		3,622,783	16.80	0	8,000		
20029011		485,353	16.80	0			
20029019		78,337	16.80				
2002	Prepared tomatoes						
20029031		12,924,543	16.80	0	30,000 t		
20029039		4,760,473	16.80	0			
20029091		5,718,862	16.80	0			
20029099		256,187	16.80				
2007							
20079130	Prep. of citrus fruit, with sugar	—	32.50	0	—	0	100
20079939	Other preparations with sugar	1,000,696	39.26	0	—	0	100
200850	Apricot pulp	481,445	25.39	0	600		
ex 20085092		27,604	25.39	0			
ex 20085094							
2204	Wine						
220410	Sparkling wine	32,099	9.80			0	—
220421	Other wine, 2 liters or less	4,196,588	8.70			0	—
220429	Other	2,224,958	17.70			0	—
220600	Other fermented beverages	2,358	8.51			0	—
ex 2007	Undenatured ethyl alcohol	—	28.00–39.26			0	—
200900	Vinegar and substitutes	—				0	—

Note: ECU/t = European currency unit per metric ton.

Source: Decision 1/98 of the EC-Turkey Association Council of February 25, 1998.

TABLE 2.18 Arrangements Applicable to European Community Importation of Fruits and Vegetables Originating in Turkey

HS		1999 Turkish Exports to EU (US$)	Tariff Rates Applied by EU on Imports from Third Countries	Time Period	Tariff Rates Applied by EU on Imports from Turkey during Specified Time Periods	Tariff Quota (metric tons)
ex 070190	Potatoes	805,142	13.85	January 1–March 31	0	—
070310	Onions	444,377	11.20			—
ex 07031011				February 15–May 15	0	—
ex 07031019				February 15–May 15	0	—
ex 07031011				May 16–February 14	0	2,000
ex 07031019				May 16–February 14	0	2,000
070820	Beans	460,017	13.37			—
ex 07082020				November 1–April 30	0	—
ex 07082095				November 1–April 30	0	—
ex 07089000				July 1–April 30	0	—
070930	Aubergines	1,546,945	14.90			—
ex 070930				January 15–April 30	0	—
ex 070930				May 1–January 14	0	1,000
070940	Stick celery	8,598	14.90			—
ex 07094000				January 1–April 30	0	—
070990	Fresh or chilled vegetables NES	179,561	13.08			—
07099071	Courgettes			December 1–end of February	0	—
ex 07099073	Courgettes			December 1–end of February	0	—
ex 07099079	Courgettes			December 1–end of February	0	—
070990	Fresh or chilled vegetables NES					500
ex 07099073	Courgettes			March 1–November 30	0	—
07099075	Courgettes			March 1–November 30	0	—
07099077	Courgettes			March 1–November 30	0	—
ex 07099079	Courgettes			March 1–November 30	0	—

HS code	Description	Quantity	Duty	Period		
ex 07099090	Pumpkins and courges			December 1–end of February	0	—
ex 07099090	Other wild onion			February 15–May 15	0	—
080221-22	Fresh or dried hazelnuts	354,662,275	3.70			
08022100					3	—
08022200					3	—
080610	Fresh table grapes	21,850,312	16.10			
08061021				Nov. 15–April 30, June 18–July 31	0	—
ex 08061029				Nov. 15–April 30, June 18–July 31	0	—
08061030				Nov. 15–April 30, June 18–July 31	0	—
ex 08061040				Nov. 15–April 30, June 18–July 31	0	—
ex 08061050				Nov. 15–April 30, June 18–July 31	0	—
08061061				Nov. 15–April 30, June 18–July 31	0	—
08061069				Nov. 15–April 30, June 18–July 31	0	—
080711	Watermelon	784,893				
ex 08071100				April 1–June 15	0	—
ex 08071100				June 16–March 31	0	14,000
080719	Melons	1,437,680				
ex 08071900				November 1–May 31	0	—
080940	Plums	1,278,413				
ex 08094010				May 1–June 15	0	—
ex 08094020				May 1–June 15	0	—

Note: NES = not elsewhere classified.

Source: Decision 1/98 of the EC-Turkey Association Council of February 25, 1998.

TABLE 2.19 Agricultural Products for Which EU Entry Price System Applies

HS	Description	1999 Turkish Exports to EU (US$)
07020000	Tomatoes	2,306,800
07070005	Cucumbers	1,303,757
07091000	Artichokes	9,307
07099070	Courgettes	1,417,562
08051030	Oranges	5,191,270
08051050	Oranges	174,027
08052010	Clementine	439,670
08052030	Satsumas	69,803
08052050	Mandarins	—
08052070	Tangerines	—
08052090	Citrus hybrids	8,010,676
08053010	Lemons	13,367,259
08061010	Grapes	21,834,061
08081000	Apples	—
08081050	Apples—Granny Smith	1,735
08081090	Other Apples	5,350
08082010	Pears	—
08082050	Other pears	1,520,560
08091000	Apicots	674,115
08092005	Sour cherries	189,787
08092095	Table cherries	37,176,175
08093010	Peaches	—
08093090	Other peaches	310,744
08094005	Plums	1,270,287
20096011	Fruit juices	—
20096019	Fruit juices—grapes	410,950
20096051	Fruit juices—grapes	271,163
20096059	Fruit juices—grapes	768
22043092	Wine of fresh grapes	—
22043094	Wine of fresh grapes	—
22043096	Wine of fresh grapes	—
22043098	Wine of fresh grapes	16,965
Total		95,972,791

Source: Turkish State Institute of Statistics.

TABLE 2.20 Structure of Household Expenditures
(1994 prices, Turkish liras)

	Average	Rural	Urban
Total expenses per household	111,044,759	66,698,941	167,764,049
Food, beverages, and tobacco per household	39,552,432	30,202,155	51,511,644
Food and nonalcoholic beverages per household	36,457,528	28,287,252	46,907,494
Expenditure shares (% of total expenditure)			
Cereals and pasta			
Rice	0.7659	1.1584	0.5663
Flour	1.6416	3.9502	0.4677
Bread	3.5371	2.6741	3.9759
Bread and bread products			
Pasta	0.3113	0.5020	0.2144
Other bread products	0.4088	0.7150	0.2532
Confectionary products			
Rolls (fancy cake)	0.2885	0.1857	0.3408
Rolls (ordinary)	0.0634	0.0730	0.0585
Rolls (durable)	0.2251	0.2840	0.1952
Meat and meat products			
Meat			
Pork			
Veal	1.5659	1.2013	1.7513
Beef	0.5351	0.8484	0.3758
Sheep, lamb, and goat	1.5581	2.1953	1.2341
Poultry	0.7116	0.6450	0.7454
Subproducts and edible offal	0.1471	0.1772	0.1318
Smoked products	0.2997	0.2515	0.3243
Canned meat products			
Fish and fish products			
Fresh and frozen fish	0.3588	0.3698	0.3532
Processed fish			
Other water animals	0.0011	0.0016	0.0008
Fish ready-to-cook and fish dishes			
Milk, dairy products, and eggs			
Milk			
Fresh milk	1.0733	1.2479	0.9845
Dry (powder) and condensed milk	0.8019	1.2451	0.5765
Dairy products			
Cheese and curd	1.9321	2.4456	1.6710
Ice cream	0.0758	0.0290	0.0996
Other dairy products	0.0205	0.0395	0.0109
Eggs	0.7103	0.8310	0.6489
Fat			
Vegetable fat			
Vegetable oil	1.6869	2.6487	1.1977
Margarine	0.7650	1.0891	0.6001
Animal fat			
Dairy butter	0.5337	0.9984	0.2974
Lard/fat	0.0117	0.0193	0.0078

TABLE 2.20   (Continued)

	Average	Rural	Urban
Fruit, fresh or dried			
Fresh fruit			
Fresh fruits, temperate zones	2.2800	2.4176	2.2101
Fresh fruits, tropical zones	0.1158	0.0812	0.1333
Dried fruit and nuts	0.4174	0.4317	0.4101
Fruit, canned			
Frozen fruit	0.0068	0.0084	0.0060
Bottled fruit			
Jam, marmalade, and jelly	0.2569	0.3638	0.2026
Fruit juices, syrups, and nectars	0.0845	0.0528	0.1006
Vegetables and potatoes			
Fresh vegetables and mushrooms	3.0108	3.6075	2.7073
Dried vegetables	1.0826	1.7756	0.7302
Frozen vegetables	0.0587	0.0962	0.0396
Potatoes			
Potatoes	0.5085	0.8146	0.3529
Potato products	0.0013	0.0007	0.0017
Sugar and sugar products			
Sugar	1.3920	2.4582	0.8498
Sugar products—nonchocolate	0.2004	0.2435	0.1785
Chocolate products	0.1588	0.0993	0.1891
Honey	0.1953	0.2680	0.1583
Other food and nonalcoholic beverages	3.0312	3.8650	2.6072
Coffee, tea and cocoa			
Coffee—all sorts	0.0840	0.0541	0.0991
Tea, including dried herb and others	1.0452	1.7319	0.6961
Cocoa	0.0067	0.0058	0.0071
Other food	1.5310	1.8555	1.3659
Soft drinks			
Fizzy soft drinks	0.3415	0.2098	0.4085
Mineral water	0.0228	0.0078	0.0305
Alcoholic beverages			
Spirits	0.2095	0.1852	0.2218
Wine	0.0151	0.0121	0.0166
Beer	0.1132	0.1017	0.1190
Tobacco			
Cigarettes	2.4142	2.4970	2.3721
Tobacco products	0.0352	0.0749	0.0150

Source: Turkish State Institute of Statistics.

Notes

1. The authors are grateful to Mr. Antonio Nucifora for his assistance and advice on the model used in this paper to quantitatively estimate the effects of adopting the Common Agricultural Policy of the European Union.

2. EU15 refers to the 15 members of the EU prior to the 2004 enlargement in which 10 more countries joined the EU. The 15 countries are Austria, Belgium, Denmark, Finland, France, Germany, Greece, Ireland, Italy, Luxembourg, the Netherlands, Portugal, Spain, Sweden, and the United Kingdom.

3. The last agricultural census was carried out in 2001, but the results of this census are still not available. The large number of multiparcel agricultural land holdings, the landless peasants in some parts of eastern Turkey, and the feudal structures in eastern and southeastern Anatolia are three of the major problems in Turkish agriculture. The land fragmentation is in part a consequence of the inheritance provisions of the 1926 Civil Code, which is patterned after the Swiss Civil Code. To attack the problem of landless peasants, the government has pursued various agrarian reforms since the formation of the Republic, but more work needs to be done. Finally, the local lord's hegemony in eastern and southeastern Turkey is a peculiarity of the Turkish agricultural setting.

4. All dollar amounts are U.S. dollars unless otherwise indicated.

5. A review of the tariff binding commitments of Turkey and the EU under the World Trade Organization (WTO) on agricultural products reveals that by 2004 Turkey's tariff bindings will all be almost above the EU final bound levels under the Uruguay Round agreement, which will be further reduced by the ongoing Doha Round negotiations. Thus, under the accession process, Turkey will have to conform to the lower EU levels.

6. For the COM on cereals, see Council Regulations (EC) No. 1251/1999 and No. 1253/1999.

7. See Article 2 of Council Regulation No. 1251/1999. In the Central and Eastern European (CEE) countries, the arable base area for each accession country has been determined by taking the average for the years 1997, 1998, and 1999.

8. In the CEE countries, aid for durum wheat applies to the durum wheat used to produce pasta. The glassiness of the variety grown should be higher than 73 percent. Furthermore, durum wheat must have been grown for a minimum of some 20 years to qualify for aid. Finally, aid is contingent on the area under durum wheat production constituting at least 2 percent of the total area under cereal production.

9. For CEE countries, the reference yields have been determined as the average of the median three years of the period 1994/95–1998/99. The reference yields have been set at 4.26 metric tons per hectare for Hungary, 2.96 tons per hectare for Poland, and 4.16 tons per hectare for Slovakia.

10. For CEE countries, the date is December 31, 2000.

11. The regulations that apply to sunflower seed are governed by Council Regulation (EC) No. 1251/1999 amending Regulation No. 3405/93.

12. Sugar beets are governed by Council Regulation (EC) No. 1260/2001.

13. Fruits and vegetables, including grapes, are governed by Regulation (EC) No. 2699/2000 amending Council Regulation (EC) No. 2200/1996, No. 2201/1996, and No. 2202/1996.

14. Milk and dairy products are governed by Council Regulation (EC) No. 1255/1999 on the COM for milk and dairy products. Also applicable is Council Regulation (EC) No. 1256/1999 amending Regulation (EEC) No. 3950/1992 establishing an additional levy in the milk and milk products sector.

15. Ceilings have been established per member state on the basis of slaughterings and exports registered in 1995. Where the national ceiling is exceeded, the premiums are reduced proportionately.

16. In particular, member states may choose between two formulas for granting additional extensification premiums on suckler cows and special beef payments: (1) a simple supplement of €100 per premium where the stocking intensity is less than 1.4 livestock units per hectare; or (2) as of 2002, €40 where the stocking intensity is between 1.8 and 1.4 livestock units per hectare and €80 if less than 1.4 livestock units per hectare.

17. Ovine meat is governed by Regulation (EC) No. 2529/2001.

18. More information on the reforms is available at http://europa.eu.int/comm/agriculture/mtr/index_en.htm.

19. Even decoupled payments involve some distortion as they are currently administered. But, according to an analysis by the OECD, this distortion is very small. See OECD (2001) and Dewbre, Anton, and Thompson (2001).

20. This elimination of barriers does not include food safety, sanitary, and phytosanitary requirements, and it is subject to rules of origin.

21. In WTO terminology, subsidies in general are identified by "boxes" given the colors of traffic lights: green (permitted), amber (slow down—that is, will be reduced), and red (forbidden). The Uruguay Round agreement on agriculture has no red box, although domestic support exceeding the reduction commitment levels in the amber box is prohibited. A blue box refers to an amber box with conditions designed to reduce distortions. Subsidies that are tied to programs that limit production are included in the blue box.

22. For a discussion of the modeling methodology, see Csaki and others (2002).

23. The policies have been projected using the 2000 price and cost situation, because complete data for later periods were not available at the time of preparation of this chapter.

24. The exchange rates used in the study for 2000 were TL 624,325 to the U.S. dollar and TL 575,179.98 to the euro.

25. Given the domestic price of commodity i, p_i, and its border equivalent price, p_i^*, the nominal protection rate (NPR) is defined as

$$NPR_i = \left(\frac{P_i}{P_i^*} - 1 \right) * 100$$

26. The effective protection rate (EPR) is computed on the basis of the ratio of value added in the production of i measured at domestic prices (VA_i) over such value added at border prices (VA_i^*) and is shown by

$$EPR_i = \left(\frac{VA_i}{VA_i^*} - 1 \right) * 100$$

$EPR > 0$ implies direct protection of domestic producers of the commodity; $EPR < 0$ implies underlying disincentives to domestic producers of the commodity; and $EPR = 0$ implies a neutral structure of net incentives.

27. We do not consider the effects of the imposition of quotas on sugar and milk production by the EU.

28. The assumed output supply elasticities, taken largely from Koç, Uzunlu, and Bayaner (2001), are 0.28 for wheat, 0.21 for barley, 0.14 for maize, 0.16 for sunflower, 0.34 for sugar beet, 0.94 for potato, 0.10 for grapes, 1.18 for milk, 0.34 for beef, 1.88 for poultry, and 0.60 for sheep.

29. This is why these kinds of payments are classified under WTO rules as "green box"—that is, payments that minimally distort trade.

30. For a description of the direct payments and an estimate of their effects, see OECD (2003b).

31. In Case I, there is a negative supply response to the drop in prices due to the alignment with Agenda 2000 prices (except grapes, the price of which increases), and no compensating increase in price or production from the direct payments. In Case II, the negative effect of alignment with Agenda 2000 prices is offset by the direct payments.

32. Note that this approach determines the equivalent variation in consumer income. Alternatively, one could determine the change in consumer surplus.

33. The assumed price elasticities of demand, taken largely from Koç, Uzunlu, and Bayaner (2001), are 0.12 for bread and pasta, 0.81 for beef, 0.7 for sheep meat, 1.23 for poultry, 0.5 for milk, 0.3 for dairy products, 0.2 for fat, and 1.09 for butter.

34. This assumption helps to highlight the impact of EU-like agricultural policies on the state budget.

35. Note that the EU budget must be balanced during each fiscal year. So this value of 34.46 will change from year to year by the requirements of the budget during that year.

36. Structural Funds allow the EU to grant financial assistance to resolve structural economic and social objectives. Objective 1 of the Structural Funds is the main priority of the EU's cohesion policy. The EU aims to narrow the gap between the development levels of the various regions. "Objective 1 regions" refers to areas lagging behind in their development and in which GDP is below 75 percent of the European Community average. Objective 2 of the Structural Funds aims to revitalize all areas facing structural difficulties, whether industrial, rural, urban, or dependent on fisheries. Objective 3 covers the entire EU territory outside of areas covered by Objective 1 and serves as a reference framework for all measures to promote human resources in the member states. It takes account of the title on employment in the Treaty of Amsterdam and the new European strategy for employment.

37. For alternative quantitative analyses of the effects of adopting the CAP, see Çakmak and Kasnakoğlu (2001); Çağatay, Saunders, and Amor (2001); Grethe (2004); and Oskam and others (2004). Whereas Çakmak and Kasnakoğlu (2001) study the impact of the CAP on producers, consumers, and foreign trade, Çağatay, Saunders, and Amor (2001) concentrate only on the effects on producers and foreign trade. Both papers abstract from consideration of the impact on the state budget. According to Çakmak and Kasnakoğlu (2001), adoption of Agenda 2000 policies with direct payments equal to those currently applied in the EU will lead to reductions in producers' welfare, which is contrary to our results summarized in table 2.16. The comprehensive study by Oskam and others (2004) analyzes the likely consequences for Turkey's agricultural and agrifood sectors should it become an EU member in 2015.

38. HACCP is a system that establishes process control through identification of the production points most critical to controlling and monitoring the production process. It involves seven principles. First, analyze hazards. Potential hazards associated with a food and measures to control those hazards are identified. The hazard could be biological such as a microbe, chemical such as a toxin, or physical such as ground glass or metal fragments. Second, identify critical control points. These are points in a food's production—from its raw state through processing and shipping to consumption by the consumer—at which the potential hazard can be controlled or eliminated. Examples are cooking, cooling, packaging, and metal detection. Third, establish preventive measures with critical limits for each control point. For a cooked food, for example, this might include setting the minimum cooking temperature and time required to ensure the elimination of any harmful microbes. Fourth, establish procedures to monitor the critical control points. Such procedures might include determining how and by whom cooking time and temperature should be monitored. Fifth, establish the corrective actions to be taken when monitoring shows that a critical limit has not been met—for example, reprocessing or disposing of food if the minimum cooking temperature is not met. Sixth, establish procedures to verify that the system is working properly—for example, testing time and temperature recording devices to verify that a cooking unit is working properly. Seventh, establish effective recordkeeping to document the HACCP system. This documentation would include records of hazards and their control methods, the monitoring of safety requirements, and action taken to correct potential problems. Each of these principles must be backed by sound scientific knowledge—for example, published microbiological studies on time and temperature factors for controlling food-borne pathogens.

39. "Good Agricultural Practices" refers to applying available knowledge to use of the natural resource base in a sustainable way for the production of safe, healthy food and nonfood agricultural products in a humane manner, while achieving economic viability and social stability.

40. See chapter 10 of Oskam and others (2004) for a discussion of animal and plant health issues in Turkey.

References

Çağatay, S., C. Saunders, and R. Amor. 2001. "The Impact on the Agricultural Sector of the Potential Extension of the Customs Union Agreement to Cover Agricultural Commodities." Unpublished paper, Lincoln University, New Zealand.

Çakmak, E. H., and H. Kasnakoğlu. 2001. "Tarım Sektöründe Türkiye ve Avrupa Birliği Etkileşimi: Türkiye'nin AB'ye Üyeliğinin Analizi" [The Turkey–European Union Interaction in Agricultural Sector: Analysis of Turkey's of EU Membership]. Working Paper, Agricultural Economics Research Institute, Ministry of Agriculture and Rural Affairs, Ankara.

Csaki. C., A. Nucifora, Z. Lerman, T. Herzfeld, and G. Blaas. 2002. *Food and Agriculture in the Slovak Republic: The Challenges of EU Accession.* Washington, DC: World Bank.

Dewbre, J. H., J. Anton, and W. Thompson. 2001. "The Transfer Efficiency and Trade Effects of Direct Payments." *American Journal of Agricultural Economics* 83: 1204–15.

Europarl. 2002. "European Parliament Fact Sheets." http://www.europarl.eu.int/factsheets/default.htm.

European Commission. 2000. "White Paper on Food Safety." COM (1999) 719 final. Brussels: EC.

———. 2002. "Regional Policy Interim Report." http://www.europa.eu.int/comm/regional_policy/sources/docoffc/official/reports/pdf/interim1/report_en.pdf.

———. 2004. "2004 Regular Report on Turkey's Progress Towards Accession." COM (2004) 656 final. Brussels: EC.

Grethe, H. 2004. "Turkey's Accession to the EU: What Will the Common Agricultural Policy Cost?" Humboldt University Working Paper 70/2004. Berlin.

Koç, A., V. Uzunlu, and A. Bayaner. 2001. "Türkiye'de Tarımsal Ürün Projeksiyonları 2000–2010" [Forecasts for Agricultural Products in Turkey for the Period 2000–2010]. Agricultural Economics Research Institute, Ankara.

MARA (Ministry of Agriculture and Rural Affairs). 2002. "Data files." Research Planning and Coordination Council, MARA, Ankara.

OECD (Organisation for Economic Co-operation and Development). 2001. "Market Effects of Crop Support Policies." OCED, Paris.

————. 2003a. "Agricultural Policies in OECD Countries: Monitoring and Evaluation."OECD, Paris.

————. 2003b. "Risk Related Non-price Effects of the CAP Arable Crop Regime: Results from an FADN Sample." AGR/CA/APM(2002)14/REV1, Directorate for Food, Agriculture, and Fisheries, February 27.

Oskam, A., A. Burrell, T. Temel, S. van Berkum, N. Lonworth, and I. M. Vilchez. 2004. "Turkey in the European Union: Consequences for Agriculture, Food, Rural Areas and Structural Policy." Wageningen University, Wageningen.

TMO (Turkish Grain Board). 2002. TMO files. http://www.tmo.gov.tr.

Valdes, A. 1973. "Trade Policy and İts Effects on the External Agricultural Trade in Chile, 1945–1965. *American Journal of Agricultural Economics* 55: 154–64.

World Bank. 2000. "Turkey Country Economic Memorandum: Structural Reforms for Sustainable Growth." Report No. 20657-TU, World Bank, Washington, DC.

3

INTEGRATION AND THE MANUFACTURING INDUSTRY

Sübidey Togan, Hüsamettin Nebioğlu, and Saadettin Doğan

This chapter studies the effects of European Union (EU) integration on the manufacturing sector.[1] The first section describes the main developments in Turkey's trade regime and trade performance, and the second examines the structure of protectionism. Market access issues emphasizing contingent protectionism and the issues related to technical barriers to trade are the subjects of the third and fourth sections. The fifth section analyzes conditions of competition, and the final section offers conclusions.

Main Developments in Turkey's Trade Regime

In 1994 Turkey signed the agreement establishing the World Trade Organization (WTO), and a customs union was created between Turkey and the EU as of January 1, 1996. According to the Customs Union Decision (CUD) of 1995, all industrial goods, except products of the European Coal and Steel Community (ECSC), that comply with the European Community norms could circulate freely between Turkey and the EU as of January 1, 1996. For ECSC products, Turkey signed a free trade agreement (FTA) with the EU in July 1996, and as a result, ECSC products have received duty-free treatment between the parties since 1999.[2]

The Customs Union Decision required Turkey to implement the European Community's Common Customs Tariffs (CCTs) on imports of industrial goods from third countries as of January 1, 1996, to adopt by 2001 all of the preferential trade agreements the EU has concluded over time, and to implement on the commercial policy side measures similar to those of the European Community's commercial policy. Adhering to the stipulations of the Customs Union Decision, Turkey maintained rates of protection above those specified in the CCT for certain "sensitive" products until 2001. In order to adopt EU's preferential trade agreements, Turkey signed FTAs with the European Free Trade Association countries, Israel, and the Central and Eastern European (CEE) countries. FTAs are being discussed with the Mediterranean countries. As for export subsidies, Turkey joined the Tokyo Round Agreement on Subsidies and Countervailing Duties of the General Agreement on Tariffs and Trade (GATT), agreeing to eliminate export subsidies by 1989. Recently, Turkey eliminated most of the export incentives that were introduced during the 1970s and 1980s. Within this context, GATT legal subsidies such as research and development subsidies and subsidies to facilitate the adaptation of plants to new environmental regulations were introduced in 1995.

Basic data on Turkey's merchandise trade are shown in table 3.1. The table reveals that in 2003 Turkish merchandise exports amounted to US$47.2 billion and merchandise imports to $69.3 billion.[3] Exports to the EU15 made up 49.7 percent of total exports, and imports from the EU made up 42.8 percent of total imports.[4] The table further

TABLE 3.1 Exports and Imports, Turkey, 1990–2003

SITC	Commodity	Total Exports, 2003 (US$ millions)	Percentage Distribution, Total Exports	Annual Growth Rate of Exports, 1990–2003 (percent)	Exports to the EU, 2003 (US$ millions)	Percentage Distribution, Exports to EU	Share of Exports to EU of Sectoral Exports	Annual Growth Rate of Exports to EU, 1990–2003 (percent)
	Agricultural products							
0 + 1 + 4 + 22	Food	4,735	10.03	2.01	1,949	8.31	41.17	2.32
2 – 22 – 27 – 28	Agricultural raw materials	522	1.11	2.56	220	0.94	42.24	0.41
	Mining products							
27 + 28	Ores and other minerals	572	1.21	4.23	246	1.05	42.95	2.56
3	Fuels	980	2.08	7.93	211	0.90	21.53	–0.31
68	Nonferrous metals	457	0.97	8.64	222	0.94	48.45	9.03
	Manufactures							
67	Iron and steel	3,342	7.08	5.12	939	4.00	28.09	16.52
	Chemicals							
51	Organic chemicals	171	0.36	1.53	107	0.46	62.55	4.28
57 + 58	Plastics	545	1.15	9.20	112	0.48	20.50	5.40
52	Inorganic chemicals	230	0.49	5.99	80	0.34	34.68	5.38
54	Pharmaceuticals	220	0.47	10.28	72	0.31	32.64	17.99
53 + 55 + 56 + 59	Other chemicals	726	1.54	10.19	65	0.28	8.97	4.00
6 – 65 – 67 – 68	Other semimanufactures	4,143	8.77	12.52	1,645	7.01	39.70	12.21
	Machinery and transport equipment							
71 – 713	Power generating machinery	246	0.52	24.80	85	0.36	34.47	22.77
72 + 73 + 74	Other nonelectrical machinery	1,566	3.32	18.16	537	2.29	34.29	17.73
75 + 76 + 776	Office machines and telecommunications equipment	1,978	4.19	17.99	1,569	6.68	79.30	17.27
77 – 776 – 7783	Electrical machinery and apparatus	2,076	4.40	16.83	999	4.26	48.14	14.64
78 – 785 – 786 + 7132 + 7783	Automotive products	4,928	10.44	24.42	3,139	13.38	63.70	29.30
79 + 785 + 786 + 7131 + 7133 + 7138 + 7139	Other transport equipment	1,542	3.27	20.70	853	3.63	55.31	23.07
65	Textiles	5,262	11.14	10.14	2,340	9.97	44.48	7.50
84	Clothing	9,962	21.10	7.21	7,079	30.17	71.07	5.94
8 – 84 – 86 – 891	Other consumer goods	2,675	5.67	16.37	954	4.06	35.66	12.44
9 + 891	*Other products*	335	0.71	30.17	44	0.19	13.02	16.10
	Total	47,211	100	9.01	23,466	100	49.70	8.56

SITC	Commodity	Total Imports, 2003 (US$ million)	Percentage Distribution, Total Imports	Annual Growth Rate of Imports, 1990–2003 (percent)	Imports from EU, 2003 (US$ million)	Percentage Distribution, Imports from EU	Share of Imports from EU of Sectoral Imports	Annual Growth Rate, Imports from EU, 1990–2003 (percent)
	Agricultural products							
0 + 1 + 4 + 22	Food	2,789	4.03	3.29	548	1.85	19.65	1.70
2 – 22 – 27 – 28	Agricultural raw materials	2,471	3.57	6.42	894	3.01	36.19	6.76
	Mining products							
27 + 28	Ores and other minerals	2,262	3.26	4.58	670	2.26	29.61	–0.05
3	Fuels	11,575	16.71	8.06	460	1.55	3.97	7.71
68	Nonferrous metals	1,411	2.04	9.55	308	1.04	21.80	4.23
	Manufactures							
67	Iron and steel	3,282	4.74	5.46	1,232	4.15	37.53	1.91
	Chemicals							
51	Organic chemicals	2,102	3.03	7.39	1,059	3.57	50.39	6.83
57 + 58	Plastics	2,837	4.09	12.80	1,645	5.54	58.00	11.57
52	Inorganic chemicals	543	0.78	2.82	178	0.60	32.78	0.99
54	Pharmaceuticals	2,302	3.32	17.09	1,546	5.21	67.14	17.05
53 + 55 + 56 + 59	Other chemicals	2,643	3.82	7.00	1,560	5.26	59.03	7.65
6 – 65 – 67 – 68	Other semimanufactures	3,489	5.04	8.27	2,245	7.56	64.33	7.66
	Machinery and transport equipment							
71 – 713	Power generating machinery	758	1.09	12.52	382	1.29	50.34	12.44
72 + 73 + 74	Other nonelectrical machinery	7,250	10.46	5.21	4,607	15.52	63.54	4.18
75 + 76 + 776	Office machines and telecommunications equipment	4,166	6.01	10.95	1,618	5.45	38.83	12.15
77 – 776 – 7783	Electrical machinery and apparatus	2,065	2.98	6.82	1,175	3.96	56.93	5.75
78 – 785 – 786 + 7132 + 7783	Automotive products	6,209	8.96	11.67	5,150	17.35	82.95	13.91
79 + 785 + 786 + 7131 + 7133 + 7138 + 7139	Other transport equipment	1,012	1.46	1.80	711	2.40	70.29	4.88
65	Textiles	3,441	4.97	13.03	1,185	3.99	34.43	13.49
84	Clothing	422	0.61	24.93	204	0.69	48.26	21.68
8 – 84 – 86 – 891	Other consumer goods	3,540	5.11	10.07	1,910	6.44	53.96	9.27
9 + 891	*Other products*	2,714	3.92	27.10	391	1.32	14.42	18.75
	Total	69,283	100	8.27	29,678	100	42.84	8.06

Note: SITC = Standard International Trade Classification.
Source: The authors.

89

reveals that the three export commodities with the highest shares of total exports were clothing, 21.1 percent; textiles, 11.1 percent; and automotive products, 10.4 percent. The three import commodities with the highest shares of total imports were fuels, 16.7 percent; other nonelectrical machinery, 10.5 percent; and automotive products, 9 percent. Similarly, the three export commodities with the highest shares of exports to the EU were clothing, 30.2 percent; automotive products, 13.4 percent; and textiles, 10 percent. The three commodities with the highest shares of imports from the EU were automotive products, 17.4 percent; other nonelectrical machinery, 15.5 percent; and other semi-manufactures, 7.6 percent.

During the period 1990–2003, Turkey's total exports grew at an annual rate of 9 percent and total imports at a rate of 8.3 percent. The export commodities with the highest annual growth rates were other products, 30.2 percent; power generating machinery, 24.8 percent; and automotive products, 24.4 percent. The import commodities with the highest growth rates were other products, 27.1 percent, clothing, 24.9 percent; and pharmaceuticals, 17.1 percent. Similarly, the export commodities to the EU with the highest growth rates were automotive products, 29.3 percent; other transport equipment, 23.1 percent; and power generating machinery, 22.8 percent. The imported commodities from the EU with the highest growth rates were clothing, 21.7 percent; other products, 18.8 percent; and pharmaceuticals, 17.1 percent.

A look at the EU's share of total sectoral exports reveals that the highest shares of exports to the EU are held by office machines and telecommunications equipment, 79.3 percent; clothing, 71.1 percent; and automotive products, 63.7 percent. Among the sectors considered, other chemicals, other products, and plastics have the lowest shares. The three sectors with the highest EU shares of sectoral imports are automotive products, 83 percent; other transport equipment, 70.3 percent; and pharmaceuticals, 67.1 percent. Among the sectors considered, fuels, other products, and food have the lowest EU shares of sectoral imports.

Table 3.2 shows similar information for the EU. It reveals that in 2001 the EU's merchandise exports amounted to ECU (European currency unit) 982.6 billion and merchandise imports were ECU 1,028 billion. Exports to Turkey made up 2 percent

of total EU exports, and imports from Turkey were also 2 percent of total EU imports. The table further reveals that the three export commodities with the highest shares of total EU exports were other nonelectrical machinery, 12.1 percent; other consumer goods, 10.3 percent; and automotive products, 10 percent. The three import commodities with the highest shares of total EU imports were office machines and telecommunications equipment, 14.3 percent; fuels, 14.1 percent; and other consumer goods, 10.3 percent. During the period 1990–2001, total EU exports grew at an annual rate of 8.2 percent and total imports at the rate of 7.5 percent. The export commodities with the highest growth rates were office machines and telecommunications equipment, 15.4 percent; pharmaceuticals, 14.2 percent; and organic chemicals, 11 percent. The three import commodities with the highest growth rates were pharmaceuticals, 12.4 percent; electrical machinery and apparatus, 12.1 percent; and office machines and telecommunications equipment, 11.8 percent. Examination of Turkey's share of total sectoral EU exports reveals that the highest shares of exports to Turkey are held by ores and other minerals, 5.7 percent; plastics, 5 percent; and agricultural raw materials, 4.6 percent. Among the sectors considered, food, clothing, and fuels have the lowest shares of exports to Turkey. The three sectors with the highest shares of imports from Turkey of sectoral EU imports are textiles, 11.7 percent; clothing, 11.2 percent; and iron and steel, 6.4 percent. Among the sectors considered, fuels, pharmaceuticals, and other chemicals have the lowest shares of imports from Turkey of sectoral EU imports.

As noted earlier, as of January 1, 1996, Turkey and the EU entered a customs union. Table 3.3 shows the evolution of Turkish trade with the EU over the period 1990–2003. The data reveal that with the formation of the customs union, the share of imports from the EU of total imports went up from 47.2 in 1995 to 53 percent in 1996, but then began to decrease, reaching 45.4 percent in 2003. Comparison of the growth rate of Turkish imports from the EU prior to formation of the customs union with that observed after formation of the customs union shows that the average growth rate of imports from the EU has even declined, from 9.1 percent during 1990–95 to 1.5 percent during 1996–2003. On the other hand, annual average

TABLE 3.2 Exports and Imports, EU, 1990–2001

SITC	Commodity	Total Exports, 2001 (thousands of ECU)	Percentage Distribution	Annual Growth Rate of Exports, 1990–2001 (percent)	Exports to Turkey, 2001 (thousands of ECU)	Share of Exports to Turkey of Sectoral Exports, 2001	Total Imports, 2001 (thousands of ECU)	Percentage Distribution	Annual Growth Rate of Imports, 1990–2001 (percent)	Imports from Turkey 2001 (thousands of ECU)	Share of Imports from Turkey in Sectoral Imports, 2001
	Agricultural products										
0 + 1 + 4 + 22	Food	54,042,390	5.50	4.80	378,968	0.70	66,571,904	6.48	4.52	2,094,348	3.15
2 – 22 – 27 – 28	Agricultural raw materials	10,740,870	1.09	7.48	491,794	4.58	23,074,732	2.24	1.14	228,864	0.99
	Mining products										
27 + 28	Ores and other minerals	4,860,506	0.49	5.76	275,558	5.67	17,659,307	1.72	5.50	270,064	1.53
3	Fuels	23,892,389	2.43	7.25	311,131	1.30	144,980,806	14.10	5.81	246,383	0.17
68	Nonferrous metals	11,936,772	1.21	6.99	197,170	1.65	23,351,448	2.27	6.51	239,103	1.02
	Manufactures										
67	Iron and steel	19,976,063	2.03	2.97	667,511	3.34	14,075,992	1.37	4.47	905,075	6.43
	Chemicals										
51	Organic chemicals	33,838,441	3.44	11.04	676,813	2.00	20,696,334	2.01	9.25	89,717	0.43
57 + 58	Plastics	20,724,369	2.11	7.67	1,027,062	4.96	10,758,582	1.05	4.68	114,084	1.06
52	Inorganic chemicals	5,388,087	0.55	4.72	81,981	1.52	6,264,051	0.61	7.71	128,624	2.05
54	Pharmaceuticals	43,908,279	4.47	14.16	915,569	2.09	22,620,592	2.20	12.37	42,924	0.19
53 + 55 + 56 + 59	Other chemicals	38,460,679	3.91	7.48	1,229,805	3.20	17,193,103	1.67	7.44	44,913	0.26
6 – 65 – 67 – 68	Other semimanufactures	87,731,435	8.93	8.24	1,509,193	1.72	68,710,081	6.68	5.46	1,509,363	2.20
	Machinery and transport equipment										
71 – 713	Power generating machinery	34,903,182	3.55	9.54	595,281	1.71	24,777,213	2.41	11.57	92,876	0.37
72 + 73 + 74	Other nonelectrical machinery	118,584,299	12.07	6.77	2,719,502	2.29	53,724,194	5.23	6.99	404,780	0.75
75 + 76 + 776	Office machines and telecommunications equipment	96,408,088	9.81	15.37	1,909,617	1.98	146,734,704	14.27	11.75	1,005,984	0.69
77 – 776 – 7783	Electrical machinery and apparatus	50,751,415	5.17	10.10	896,479	1.77	47,678,281	4.64	12.06	845,547	1.77
78 – 785 – 786 + 7132 + 7783	Automotive products	97,777,703	9.95	9.16	1,920,099	1.96	50,701,618	4.93	8.21	1,892,016	3.73

TABLE 3.2 (Continued)

SITC	Commodity	Total Exports, 2001 (thousands of ECU)	Percentage Distribution	Annual Growth Rate of Exports, 1990–2001 (percent)	Exports to Turkey, 2001 (thousands of ECU)	Share of Exports to Turkey of Sectoral Exports, 2001	Total Imports, 2001 (thousands of ECU)	Percentage Distribution	Annual Growth Rate of Imports, 1990–2001 (percent)	Imports from Turkey 2001 (thousands of ECU)	Share of Imports from Turkey in Sectoral Imports, 2001
79 + 785 + 786 + 7131 + 7133 + 7138 + 7139	Other transport equipment	63,162,827	6.43	10.38	972,860	1.54	56,327,638	5.48	10.78	706,280	1.25
65	Textiles	24,739,564	2.52	6.07	978,099	3.95	19,178,029	1.87	5.02	2,242,208	11.69
84	Clothing	17,559,440	1.79	4.29	218,928	1.25	53,910,204	5.24	8.05	6,060,245	11.24
8 – 84 – 86 – 891	Other consumer goods	101,086,773	10.29	7.32	1,443,680	1.43	106,259,111	10.34	8.11	867,501	0.82
9 + 891	*Other products*	22,106,890	2.25	2.54	398,968	1.80	32,781,100	3.19	2.83	124,630	0.38
	Total	982,580,462	100	8.23	19,816,069	2.02	1,028,029,024	100	7.48	20,155,528	1.96

Note: SITC = Standard International Trade Classification; ECU = European currency unit.

Sources: Data provided by Eurostat; the authors.

TABLE 3.3 Trade with EU, 1990–2003

	Total Imports (US$ millions)	Imports from EU (US$ millions)	Growth Rate of Total Imports (percent)	Growth Rate of Imports from EU (percent)	Share of Imports from EU of Total Imports	Total Exports (US$ millions)	Exports to EU (US$ millions)	Growth Rate of Total Exports (percent)	Growth Rate of Exports to EU (percent)	Share of Exports to EU of Total Exports	Trade Balance with EU (US$ millions)	Real Exchange Rate
1990	22,302	9,898	—	—	44.38	12,959	7,177	—	—	55.38	–2,721	99.67
1991	21,047	9,987	–5.63	0.90	47.45	13,594	7,348	4.90	2.38	54.05	–2,639	96.66
1992	22,870	10,656	8.66	6.70	46.59	14,719	7,937	8.28	8.02	53.92	–2,719	100.94
1993	29,429	13,875	28.68	30.21	47.15	15,348	7,599	4.27	–4.26	49.51	–6,276	91.59
1994	23,270	10,915	–20.93	–21.33	46.91	18,105	8,635	17.96	13.63	47.69	–2,280	124.35
1995	35,708	16,861	53.45	54.48	47.22	21,636	11,078	19.50	28.29	51.20	–5,783	116.72
1996	43,627	23,138	22.18	37.23	53.04	23,224	11,549	7.34	4.25	49.73	–11,589	116.67
1997	48,559	24,870	11.30	7.49	51.22	26,261	12,248	13.08	6.05	46.64	–12,622	110.32
1998	45,921	24,075	–5.43	–3.20	52.43	26,974	13,498	2.72	10.21	50.04	–10,577	100.42
1999	40,687	21,417	–11.40	–11.04	52.64	26,589	14,349	–1.43	6.30	53.97	–7,068	94.30
2000	54,509	26,610	33.97	24.25	48.82	27,775	14,510	4.46	1.12	52.24	–12,100	85.17
2001	41,399	18,280	–24.05	–31.30	44.16	31,334	16,118	12.81	11.08	51.44	–2,162	106.33
2002	51,554	23,321	24.53	27.57	45.24	36,059	18,459	15.08	14.52	51.19	–4,863	96.11
2003	69,340	31,496	34.50	35.05	45.42	47,253	24,350	31.04	31.92	51.53	–7,146	88.23
Average 1990–95			8.31	9.13	46.62			9.90	7.46	51.96		
Average 1996–2003			4.20	1.46	50.38			8.39	9.30	50.68		

— Not available.

Note: An increase in the real exchange rate (RER) indicates depreciation of the RER.

Source: State Planning Organization (http://www.dpt.gov.tr); the authors.

growth rate of Turkish exports to the EU, which was 7.5 percent prior to formation of the customs union, increased to 9.3 percent over the period 1996–2003. Similarly, the share of exports to the EU of total exports increased from 51.2 percent in 1995 to 54 percent in 1999, but thereafter the share declined to 51.5 percent in 2003. Finally, table 3.3 reveals as well that Turkey has run a trade deficit with the EU during every year of the period 1996–2003 and that the deficit has been substantial by any standard. It reached $12.6 billion in 1997 and $7.1 billion in 2003.

These findings reveal that the formation of the customs union between Turkey and the EU did not lead initially to considerable increases in trade with the EU. Substantial increases in trade with the EU were achieved only during the period 2002–03. The reasons vary. First, the formation of the customs union did not lead to considerable reductions in trade barriers on the EU side, because the EU had abolished the nominal tariff rates on imports of industrial goods from Turkey on September 1, 1971, long before the formation of the customs union. But at that time certain exceptions were made. The European Community had retained the right to charge import duties on some oil products over a fixed quota and to implement a phased reduction of duties on imports of particular textile products. Moreover, the trade in products within the province of the ECSC have been protected by the Community through the application of nontariff barriers and, in particular, antidumping measures. With the formation of the customs union, quotas applied by the EU were abolished, but the EU retained the right to impose antidumping duties.

Second, not until 2003 did Turkey incorporate into its internal legal order the European Community instruments related to removal of technical barriers to trade that would allow Turkish industrial products to enter into free circulation in the EU.

Third, during the 1990s economic crises began to affect Turkey with increasing frequency. Periods of economic expansion alternated with periods of equally rapid decline. After a year of severe recession in 1994 when the gross national product (GNP) shrank by 6.1 percent, the economy went through a boom period of above-trend growth between 1995 and 1997. Then, in 1998, the economy was badly hit by the Russian crisis. In August 1999, the Marmara area of Turkey was hit by a severe earthquake, which was followed by a further large shock in the Bolu area in November 1999. As a result of these shocks, real GNP shrank by 6.1 percent in 1999. At the end of 1999, Turkey embarked upon a stabilization program, but a severe banking crisis arose in November 2000. Developments in February 2001 led to a total loss of confidence in the government's stabilization program and a serious run on the Turkish lira. With the floating of its currency, the country faced its severest economic crisis. The loss of income and wealth and the associated social and political stresses were unprecedented. As a result of these developments, the country saw substantial decreases in import demand during 1994, 1999, and 2001.

Fourth, with the substantial reductions in trade barriers on the Turkish side during 1996, the increase in imports was inevitable, so long as it was not accompanied by a real devaluation of the Turkish lira. As table 3.3 reveals, there was no change in the real exchange rate during 1996, and it then began to appreciate until the currency crisis of 2001. The real appreciation of the Turkish lira stimulated the import growth and hampered the growth of exports, leading to higher trade balance deficits. Also during the period 2001–03, the euro appreciated against the U.S. dollar, leading to increases in the dollar value of EU exports, which was then reflected in the higher dollar trade values of Turkish imports from the EU and of exports to the EU.

Table 3.4 shows the commodity composition of Turkish exports to the EU and imports from the EU, as well as the shares of Turkish exports to the EU of total EU imports and the shares of Turkish imports from the EU of total EU exports over the period 1995–2001. The table reveals that in absolute terms Turkey achieved large increases in exports for clothing, automotive products, textiles, other semimanufactures, office machines and telecommunications equipment, and iron and steel. For these commodities, Turkey experienced considerable increases in the shares of its exports to the EU of total EU imports. As for Turkish imports, again in absolute terms, large increases in imports were observed for chemicals, office machines and telecommunications equipment, automotive products, and other consumer goods. For those commodities, the shares of Turkish imports from the EU of total EU exports also increased.

TABLE 3.4 Effects of Customs Union between Turkey and EU, 1995–2001
(thousands of ECU)

SITC	Commodity	Turkish Exports to EU						
		1995	1996	1997	1998	1999	2000	2001
	Agricultural products							
0 + 1 + 4 + 22	Food	1,488,476	1,551,769	1,812,357	1,780,063	1,907,213	1,841,607	2,094,348
2 − 22 − 27 − 28	Agricultural raw materials	179,233	205,765	216,488	210,663	213,382	213,457	228,864
	Mining products							
27 + 28	Ores and other minerals	221,117	212,143	237,159	239,314	243,109	322,824	270,064
3	Fuels	128,412	122,060	125,193	81,415	127,553	191,871	246,383
68	Nonferrous metals	86,544	97,097	99,635	157,722	152,601	216,471	239,103
	Manufactures							
67	Iron and steel	294,209	229,501	371,900	545,231	592,639	791,231	905,075
5	Chemicals	237,583	198,285	258,291	274,909	297,999	386,476	420,262
6 − 65 − 67 − 68	Other semimanufactures	572,754	638,208	776,036	879,443	979,327	1,234,435	1,509,363
	Machinery and transport equipment							
71 − 713	Power generating machinery	31,551	48,097	73,328	81,867	86,265	89,163	92,876
72 + 73 + 74	Other nonelectrical machinery	106,447	129,455	175,601	211,566	261,858	330,166	404,780
75 + 76 + 776	Office machines and telecommunications equipment	167,685	214,597	388,026	688,309	671,934	936,482	1,005,984
77 − 776 − 7783	Electrical machinery and apparatus	301,881	386,368	449,078	574,577	614,099	714,463	845,547
78 − 785 − 786 + 7132 + 7783	Automotive products	270,766	357,760	301,337	389,917	995,122	1,212,181	1,892,016
79 + 785 + 786 + 7131 + 7133 + 7138 + 7139	Other transport equipment	391,498	625,377	485,647	670,554	665,531	675,812	706,280
65	Textiles	1,013,714	1,110,291	1,440,550	1,663,269	1,774,158	2,041,595	2,242,208
84	Clothing	3,434,992	3,636,313	4,175,655	4,632,190	4,808,707	5,576,756	6,060,245
8 − 84 − 86 − 891	Other consumer goods	271,714	347,685	403,340	442,251	582,351	679,154	867,501
9 + 891	*Other products*	45,150	48,420	54,352	75,862	69,906	74,247	124,630
	Total	9,243,725	10,159,191	11,843,971	13,599,124	15,043,754	17,528,392	20,155,528

TABLE 3.4 (Continued)

SITC	Commodity	Turkish Imports from EU						
		1995	1996	1997	1998	1999	2000	2001
	Agricultural products							
0 + 1 + 4 + 22	Food	615,174	607,284	632,062	605,447	501,142	579,811	378,968
2 − 22 − 27 − 28	Agricultural raw materials	393,666	459,321	589,606	447,182	379,080	533,469	491,794
	Mining products							
27 + 28	Ores and other minerals	487,556	528,444	462,002	269,811	152,588	261,142	275,558
3	Fuels	119,124	227,392	264,755	271,988	387,760	763,082	311,131
68	Nonferrous metals	183,778	228,589	260,355	224,136	180,355	253,115	197,170
	Manufactures							
67	Iron and steel	586,834	694,789	845,798	641,451	479,250	880,515	667,511
5	Chemicals	2,043,193	2,441,128	3,184,322	3,213,593	3,465,937	4,569,685	3,931,231
6 − 65 − 67 − 68	Other semimanufactures	978,841	1,339,036	1,568,580	1,567,096	1,400,645	1,912,605	1,509,193
	Machinery and transport equipment							
71 − 713	Power generating machinery	178,837	252,654	393,062	555,062	442,280	545,555	595,281
72 + 73 + 74	Other nonelectrical machinery	2,372,464	3,786,516	3,994,368	3,678,348	2,596,553	3,538,331	2,719,502
75 + 76 + 776	Office machines and telecommunications equipment	765,742	1,023,595	1,523,088	1,995,757	2,799,791	4,055,137	1,909,617
77 − 776 − 7783	Electrical machinery and apparatus	546,930	769,613	1,065,654	1,226,264	1,059,906	1,300,772	896,479
78 − 785 − 786 + 7132 + 7783	Automotive products	1,237,308	1,909,360	3,201,332	2,866,472	2,304,918	5,568,748	1,920,099
79 + 785 + 786 + 7131 + 7133 + 7138 + 7139	Other transport equipment	690,618	1,214,031	968,872	941,586	946,855	1,032,438	972,860
65	Textiles	584,726	786,038	997,564	946,855	859,326	1,063,715	978,099
84	Clothing	64,034	122,894	171,487	205,098	174,845	248,766	218,928
8 − 84 − 86 − 891	Other consumer goods	808,246	1,041,430	1,324,120	1,391,441	1,331,107	1,750,501	1,443,680
9 + 891	Other products	690,158	514,377	185,256	447,875	406,893	567,749	398,968
	Total	13,347,228	17,946,494	21,632,282	21,495,462	19,869,232	29,425,136	19,816,069

Share of Imports from Turkey of EU Imports

SITC	Commodity	1995	1996	1997	1998	1999	2000	2001
	Agricultural Products							
0 + 1 + 4 + 22	Food	2.955	2.948	3.225	3.075	3.327	2.966	3.146
2 − 22 − 27 − 28	Agricultural raw materials	0.871	1.151	1.067	1.058	1.099	0.850	0.992
	Mining products							
27 + 28	Ores and other minerals	1.767	1.718	1.597	1.650	1.778	1.798	1.529
3	Fuels	0.198	0.155	0.147	0.132	0.163	0.129	0.170
68	Nonferrous metals	0.531	0.719	0.586	0.885	0.889	0.855	1.024
	Manufactures							
67	Iron and steel	2.942	2.754	4.000	4.424	5.813	5.454	6.430
5	Chemicals	0.552	0.447	0.501	0.495	0.506	0.542	0.542
6 − 65 − 67 − 68	Other semimanufactures	1.490	1.578	1.688	1.816	1.827	1.861	2.197
	Machinery and transport equipment							
71 − 713	Power generating machinery	0.349	0.438	0.529	0.497	0.439	0.360	0.375
72 + 73 + 74	Other nonelectrical machinery	0.371	0.413	0.500	0.529	0.605	0.618	0.753
75 + 76 + 776	Office machines and telecommunications equipment	0.245	0.290	0.440	0.681	0.584	0.581	0.686
77 − 776 − 7783	Electrical machinery and apparatus	1.251	1.530	1.491	1.736	1.632	1.392	1.773
78 − 785 − 786 + 7132 + 7783	Automotive products	1.278	1.555	1.024	1.073	2.309	2.506	3.732
79 + 785 + 786 + 7131 + 7133 + 7138 + 7139	Other transport equipment	1.797	2.549	1.458	1.665	1.407	1.219	1.254
65	Textiles	7.796	8.397	9.287	10.134	11.041	10.800	11.692
84	Clothing	11.049	10.863	10.768	11.306	10.999	10.878	11.241
8 − 84 − 86 − 891	Other consumer goods	0.487	0.580	0.578	0.589	0.702	0.662	0.816
9 + 891	*Other products*	0.282	0.284	0.300	0.332	0.310	0.217	0.380
	Total	1.695	1.749	1.761	1.914	1.929	1.696	1.961

TABLE 3.4 (Continued)

| SITC | Commodity | Share of Exports to Turkey of EU Exports | | | | | | |
		1995	1996	1997	1998	1999	2000	2001
	Agricultural Products							
0 + 1 + 4 + 22	Food	1.488	1.399	1.296	1.286	1.078	1.101	0.701
2 − 22 − 27 − 28	Agricultural raw materials	4.901	5.835	6.835	5.484	4.259	4.812	4.579
	Mining products							
27 + 28	Ores and other minerals	14.852	15.620	10.797	8.375	4.228	5.376	5.669
3	Fuels	0.893	1.469	1.544	1.941	2.337	2.564	1.302
68	Nonferrous metals	2.635	3.061	3.021	2.716	2.190	2.122	1.652
	Manufactures							
67	Iron and steel	3.532	3.959	4.475	3.625	3.204	4.515	3.342
5	Chemicals	2.781	3.081	3.414	3.349	3.250	3.529	2.762
6 − 65 − 67 − 68	Other semimanufactures	1.764	2.225	2.327	2.339	1.998	2.247	1.720
	Machinery and transport equipment							
71 − 713	Power generating machinery	1.139	1.427	1.815	2.232	1.723	1.808	1.706
72 + 73 + 74	Other nonelectrical machinery	2.889	4.141	3.951	3.663	2.744	3.225	2.293
75 + 76 + 776	Office machines and telecommunications equipment	1.825	2.169	2.550	3.143	3.913	4.014	1.981
77 − 776 − 7783	Electrical machinery and apparatus	1.945	2.417	2.899	3.228	2.715	2.700	1.766
78 − 785 − 786 + 7132 + 7783	Automotive products	2.339	3.306	4.764	4.075	3.220	6.166	1.964
79 + 785 + 786 + 7131 + 7133 + 7138 + 7139	Other transport equipment	1.966	3.280	2.153	1.945	1.918	1.729	1.540
65	Textiles	3.480	4.376	4.947	4.667	4.269	4.532	3.954
84	Clothing	0.561	0.953	1.235	1.450	1.275	1.565	1.247
8 − 84 − 86 − 891	Other consumer goods	1.354	1.611	1.781	1.865	1.701	1.833	1.428
9 + 891	*Other products*	6.328	3.878	1.296	2.557	1.965	2.486	1.805
	Total	2.328	2.866	3.000	2.931	2.614	3.126	2.017

Note: For abbreviations, see table 3.2

Source: Data provided by Eurostat; the authors.

Structure of Protection

To study the structure of applied tariffs, we consider tariff and tariff-like charges on imports in trade with the EU, with countries with whom the EU has free trade agreements, and with third countries. In each case, we use the 12-digit Harmonized Commodity Description and Coding System (HS) data on customs duties and the mass housing fund tax.[5] Let t_c^i denote the rate of customs duty on commodity i and t_{is} the ad valorem equivalent of the mass housing fund tax rate. The relation between domestic prices and foreign prices is written as $p_i = (1 + t_c^i + t_{is}) E p_i^\$$, where p_i denotes the domestic price of commodity i, $p_i^\$$ the foreign price of commodity i, and E the nominal exchange rate. To calculate the ad valorem equivalent of the mass housing duty, we let M_i denote the CIF (cost, insurance, freight) value of the import of commodity i measured in Turkish liras; m_i the quantity of the import of commodity i measured in units (the U.S. dollar–denominated housing fund tax is reported); $FUND_1^i$ the U.S. dollar–denominated mass housing fund tax rate on commodity i; $FUND_2^i$ the ad valorem housing fund tax rate on commodity i; and E the exchange rate (Turkish lira per U.S. dollar).

The base of the customs duty is the CIF price. Therefore, this duty is calculated as $t_c^i M_i$. The mass housing fund tax levy is usually specific. For those taxes, the ad valorem equivalents of the specific rates must be calculated. Given the foreign price of the commodity, $p_j^\$ = \frac{M_i}{m_i E}$, the Turkish lira equivalent of the U.S. dollar–denominated levy is calculated as $FUND_1^i m_i E = (M_i(FUND_1^i / p_i^\$))$. The ad valorem mass housing fund tax rate is given by $FUND_2^i M_i$. The sum total of all the above taxes and surcharges is denoted by

$$(3.1) \quad t_i = \left(t_c^i + \left(FUND_1^i / p_i^\$ \right) + FUND_2^i \right)$$

Next we consider the tradable sectors in the 1996 input-output table. The average applied tariff in sector j is then calculated as

$$(3.2) \quad applied\,tariff_j = \sum_{i=1}^{k} t_i^j \left(M_i^j / M^j \right)$$

where t_i^j denotes the applied tariff rate on commodity i of sector j, M_i^j the import of commodity i into sector j, M^j total imports of sector j, and k the number of commodities in sector j ($j = 1, \ldots, 68$).

Table 3.5 shows the nominal and effective protection rates for the 68 tradable sectors of the 1996 input-output table prepared by Turkey's State Institute of Statistics. The table reveals that the weighted average nominal protection rate (NPR) during 2002 in trade with the EU is 1.95 percent; in trade with Romania, a representative country among the economies with which Turkey has free trade agreements, 1.76 percent; and in trade with third countries, 5.3 percent. By contrast, the weighted average effective protection rate (EPR) is 11.24 percent.[6]

Table 3.6 shows the frequency distribution of the NPRs and EPRs. Forty-eight out of 68 sectors have zero NPRs in trade with the EU and in trade with the countries with which Turkey has FTAs. In trade with the EU, five sectors have NPRs larger than 50 percent, and seven sectors have NPRs of between 10 percent and 50 percent. Similar considerations apply for NPRs in trade with countries with which Turkey has FTAs. The NPRs in trade with third countries are larger than 50 percent in seven sectors, between 10 percent and 50 percent in 10 sectors, and positive but less than 5 percent in 38 sectors. Concomitant with the relatively low NPRs are the low EPRs. Six sectors have EPRs above 50 percent, and six sectors have EPRs between 10 percent and 50 percent. In 20 sectors the EPRs are negative but larger than -100. The EPR is less than -100 in only one sector.

Table 3.5 shows that NPRs in trade with the EU and with countries with which Turkey has FTAs are all zero for industrial commodities and positive for agricultural and processed agricultural commodities. For trade with third countries, the average NPRs are high for food products, 11.1 percent for iron and steel, 10.92 percent for wearing apparel, 10.28 percent for footwear, 7.01 percent for textiles, and 6.74 percent for plastics. The most protected sectors measured in terms of EPRs are the manufacture of sugar; manufacture of bakery products; processing and preserving of fruits and vegetables; growing of fruits, nuts, beverage and spice crops; and manufacture of cocoa, chocolate, sugar confectionary, and other food products. The sectors indicating a clear-cut comparative advantage include the manufacture of textiles; casting of metals; manufacture of fabricated metal products; manufacture of furniture; manufacture of office, accounting,

TABLE 3.5   Nominal and Effective Protection Rates, 2002
(percent)

I-O Code	Sector	NPR, EU	NPR, EU with FTAs	NPR, Other	EPR
01	Growing of cereals and other crops NEC	8.83	8.84	8.84	9.93
02	Growing of vegetables, horticultural specialties, and nursery products	14.37	16.00	16.00	17.74
03	Growing of fruit, nuts, beverage and spice crops	74.23	70.49	78.46	82.18
04	Farming of animals	2.33	2.29	2.74	−2.60
05	Agricultural and animal husbandry service activities, except veterinary activities	21.82	26.35	26.35	48.50
06	Forestry, logging, and related service activities	0.22	0.28	0.28	0.08
07	Fishing	30.10	12.80	56.06	50.42
08	Mining of coal and lignite	0.00	0.00	0.00	−0.17
09	Extraction of crude petroleum and natural gas	0.00	0.00	0.00	−0.17
10	Mining of metal ores	0.00	0.00	0.77	0.05
11	Quarrying of stone, sand and clay	0.00	0.00	0.00	−0.27
12	Mining and quarrying NEC	0.00	0.00	0.02	−0.16
13	Production, processing, and preserving of meat and meat products	1.51	1.52	1.52	−1.52
14	Processing and preserving of fish and fish products	14.25	9.48	28.48	19.92
15	Processing and preserving of fruit, and vegetables	55.54	46.79	65.09	90.68
16	Manufacture of vegetable and animal oils and fats	13.82	9.37	14.59	18.24
17	Manufacture of dairy products	107.61	107.46	109.49	a
18	Manufacture of grain mill products, starches, and starch products	21.71	17.12	24.78	46.99
19	Manufacture of prepared animal feeds	6.36	6.36	6.57	−0.08
20	Manufacture of bakery products	83.23	8.72	109.61	b
21	Manufacture of sugar	78.49	78.49	78.49	b
22	Manufacture of cocoa, chocolate, sugar confectionery and other food products NEC	34.64	12.16	55.61	54.49
23	Manufacture of alcoholic beverages	2.73	2.90	4.03	0.86
24	Manufacture of soft drinks; production of mineral waters	0.11	0.01	9.03	−5.47
25	Manufacture of tobacco products	2.01	17.29	17.29	11.37
26	Manufacture of textiles	0.00	0.01	7.01	−2.95
27	Manufacture of other textiles	0.00	0.00	3.02	−0.07
28	Manufacture of knitted and crocheted fabrics and articles	0.00	0.00	10.25	3.70
29	Manufacture of wearing apparel, except fur apparel	0.00	0.00	10.92	7.01
30	Dressing and dyeing of fur; manufacture of articles of fur	0.00	0.00	2.05	0.62
31	Tanning and dressing of leather; manuf. of luggage, handbags, saddlery, and harnesses	0.00	0.00	1.17	−0.85
32	Manufacture of footwear	0.00	0.00	10.28	8.87
33	Sawmilling and planing of wood	0.00	0.00	0.71	−0.41
34	Manufacture of wood and of products of wood and cork	0.00	0.00	4.95	3.23
35	Manufacture of paper and paper products	0.00	0.00	1.49	0.18
36	Publishing	0.00	0.00	1.53	0.55
37	Printing and service activities related to printing	0.00	0.00	2.18	0.88

TABLE 3.5 (Continued)

I-O Code	Sector	NPR, EU	NPR, EU with FTAs	NPR, Other	EPR
38	Manufacture of coke, refined petroleum products	0.00	0.00	2.91	1.96
39	Manufacture of basic chemicals, plastics in primary forms and synthetics rubber	0.01	0.01	6.31	2.79
40	Manufacture of fertilizers and nitrogen compounds	0.00	0.00	6.49	4.00
41	Manufacture of pesticides, other agrochemicals and paints, and varnishes	0.00	0.00	6.00	2.92
42	Manufacture of pharmaceuticals, medicinal chemicals, and botanical products	0.00	0.00	0.97	0.12
43	Manufacture of cleaning materials, cosmetics, and other chemicals and manmade fibers	0.01	0.02	4.29	1.07
44	Manufacture of rubber products	0.00	0.00	3.61	1.38
45	Manufacture of plastic products	0.00	0.00	6.74	3.30
46	Manufacture of glass and glass products	0.00	0.00	4.90	2.32
47	Manufacture of ceramic products	0.00	0.00	4.76	2.63
48	Manufacture of cement, lime, and plaster-related articles of these items	0.00	0.00	1.94	0.87
49	Cutting and finishing of stone and man. of other nonmetallic mineral products NEC	0.00	0.00	1.21	0.40
50	Manufacture of basic iron and steel	0.00	0.00	11.10	6.23
51	Manufacture of basic precious and nonferrous metals	0.00	0.00	3.40	1.54
52	Casting of metals	0.00	0.00	0.00	−1.89
53	Manufacture of fabricated metal products, tanks, reservoirs, and steam generators	0.00	0.00	2.29	−0.87
54	Manufacture of other fabricated metal products; metalworking service activities	0.00	0.00	2.55	−0.06
55	Manufacture of general-purpose machinery	0.00	0.00	2.53	0.16
56	Manufacture of special-purpose machinery	0.00	0.00	1.65	−0.06
57	Manufacture of domestic appliances NEC	0.00	0.00	2.55	0.61
58	Manufacture of office, accounting, and computing machinery	0.00	0.00	0.06	−0.35
59	Manufacture of electrical machinery and apparatus NEC	0.00	0.00	2.77	0.58
60	Manufacture of radio, television, and communication equipment and apparatus	0.00	0.00	2.95	1.25
61	Manufacture of medical, precision and optical instruments, watches, and clocks	0.00	0.00	1.81	0.32
62	Manufacture of motor vehicles, trailers, and semitrailers	0.00	0.00	4.33	1.71
63	Building and repairing of ships, pleasure and sporting boats	0.00	0.00	0.25	−0.22
64	Manufacture of railway and tramway locomotives and rolling stock	0.00	0.00	1.69	0.48
65	Manufacture of aircraft and spacecraft	0.00	0.00	0.00	−0.02
66	Manufacture of transport equipment NEC	0.00	0.00	4.03	1.60
67	Manufacture of furniture	0.00	0.00	1.14	−0.66
68	Manufacturing NEC	0.00	0.00	3.29	1.36
Average		1.95	1.76	5.30	11.24

Note: I-O = input-output table; NPR = nominal protection rate; FTA = free trade agreement; EPR = effective protection rate; NEC = not elsewhere classified.

a. Less than −100.

b. More than 100.

Source: Turkish State Institute of Statistics; the authors.

TABLE 3.6   Frequency Distribution of Protection Rates, 2002
(percent)

	NPR, EU	NPR, EU with FTAs	NPR, Other	EPR
> 50.00	5	3	7	6
10.01–50.00	7	7	10	6
5.01–10.00	2	5	8	4
0.01–5.00	6	5	38	31
0	48	48	5	0
−0.01–100.00	0	0	0	20
< −100.00	0	0	0	1
Total	68	68	68	68

Note: For abbreviations, see table 3.5.
Source: The authors.

TABLE 3.7   Nominal and Effective Protection Rates, 2002
(percent)

	NPR, EU	NPR, EU with FTAs	NPR, Other	EPR
Commodity groups				
Primary commodities	18.23	18.06	20.21	25.57
Mining and energy	0.00	0.00	0.08	−0.17
Manufacturing	3.07	2.07	6.11	4.50
Trade categories				
Export industries	11.64	10.06	22.26	21.54
Export- and import-competing industries	0.53	0.36	5.89	1.81
Import-competing industries	3.90	3.90	5.73	3.82
Non-import-competing industries	24.62	20.12	28.72	27.03

Note: For abbreviations, see table 3.5.
Source: The authors.

and computing machinery; manufacture of basic precious and nonferrous metals; manufacture of basic iron and steel; and mining products.[7]

Now we move from the structure of protection at the industry level to a more aggregate level. Table 3.7 presents the NPR and EPR for broad industry groups. In the upper part of this table, industries have been classified into three industry groups. In the lower part, they have been divided into four trade categories: export, export and import competing, import competing, and non-import competing.[8]

Calculations presented in the upper part of table 3.7 reveal that primary commodities receive the most protection, contrary to the tendency for protection to escalate from the lower to higher stages of fabrication. The lower part of the table shows that the most protected sectors are the export industries and the non-import-competing industries.

Contingent Protectionism

Article 36 of the Customs Union Decision of 1995 specifies that as long as a particular practice is incompatible with the competition rules of the customs union as specified in Articles 30–32 of the decision and "in the absence of such rules if such practice causes or threatens to cause serious prejudice to the interest of the other Party or material injury to its domestic industry," the European Community or Turkey may take the appropriate measures. Article 42 allows antidumping actions as long as Turkey fails to implement effectively the competition rules of the customs union and other relevant parts of the *acquis communautaire*. In such cases, Article 47 of the Additional Protocol signed in 1970 between Turkey and the European Community remains in force. According to the article, the Association Council, if it finds dumping, will address recommendations to the persons with whom such practices originate. The injured party may take suitable measures if the Council has made no decision within three months and if the dumping practices continue. In the event a party needs an immediate action, it may introduce an interim protection measure such as antidumping duties for a limited duration. But the Council may recommend the abolition of those interim measures. Finally, Article 61, which addresses safeguards, states that safeguard measures specified in Article 60 of the Additional Protocol will remain valid. According to Article 60, the Community or Turkey may take the necessary protective measures if serious disturbances occur in a sector of the economy of the Community or Turkey or if they prejudice the external financial stability of one or more member states or Turkey, or if difficulties arise that adversely affect the economic situation in a region of the Community or Turkey.

Table 3.8 shows the products that were subject to definitive antidumping and antisubsidy measures by both parties at the end of 1995 and those subject to antidumping and antisubsidy investigations during the period 1996–2002. The table reveals that at the end of 1995, eight products exported from Turkey were subject to definitive antidumping and antisubsidy measures by the EU. Ad valorem duties were imposed in five cases, a duty and "undertakings" were imposed in one case, and in the remaining cases undertakings were imposed. In undertakings, the Turkish firms must commit themselves to raising the export prices in the European Community market to agreed-on levels or to restrict the quantities exported to the Community to agreed-

on levels. These products were cotton yarn, polyester fibers and yarns, semifinished products of alloy steel, and asbestos cement pipes. After 1996, the EU opened new investigations involving Turkish exports of cotton fabrics, bed linen, iron and steel products, paracetamol, color television receivers, and hallow sections. By contrast, at the end of 1995 Turkey had imposed duties on three commodities: benzoic acids, printing and writing papers, and polyester. After 1996, Turkey opened two new investigations involving imports of ball bearings and polyvinyl chloride from the EU and imposed antidumping duties in the case of the latter.

Both the EU and Turkey have been active users of contingent protection measures, but the EU even more so. The results indicate that the formation of the customs union does not grant protection from antidumping by the European Community. The EU has continued to protect its sensitive sectors through contingent protection measures and has protected the sectors most where Turkish penetration measured by the share of Turkish exports of EU imports was highest (see table 3.2). With Turkey's accession to the EU, the contingent protection measures will no longer be available to both parties.

Technical Barriers to Trade

Technical barriers to trade are said to exist as long as the EU and Turkey impose different technical regulations as conditions for the entry, sale, and use of commodities; as long as the two parties have different legal regulations on health, safety, and environmental protection; and as long as the parties have different procedures for testing and certification to ensure conformity to existing regulations or standards.[9] The different country requirements for the entry, sale, and use of commodities can be imposed by governments in the form of technical regulations and by nongovernmental organizations in the form of standards. Technical regulations that relate to either technical specifications or testing or certification requirements are mandatory, and the product must comply with the specifications to which it is subjected. However, standards are voluntary, not legally binding, and arise from the desire of producers or consumers to improve the information in commercial transactions and to ensure compatibility between products.

TABLE 3.8 Products Subject to Antidumping Investigations, 1996–2002

Commodity	OJ Reference	Measure
Investigations by EU		
Definitive antidumping and antisubsidy measures in force as of December 31, 1995		
Cotton yarn	L82, 27.03.1992 and L289, 24.11.1993	Duties
Cotton yarn	L182, 27.07.1994	Duties
Polyester fibers and yarns	L272, 28.09.1991	Undertakings (countervailing)
Polyester yarns (man-made staple fibers)	L88, 3.04.1992	Duties
Polyester yarns (POY and PTY)	L347, 16.12.1988	Duties
Semifinished products of alloy steel	L182, 2.07.1992	Duties and undertakings
Synthetic textile fibers of polyester	L306, 22.10.1992	Duties
Asbestos cement pipes	L209, 31.07.1991	Undertakings
New investigations after January 1, 1996		
Cotton fabrics, unbleached	C50, 21.02.1996	Provisional duty imposed, but no definite measure imposed
Cotton fabrics, unbleached	L295, 20.11.1996	Provisional duty imposed
Cotton fabrics	L42, 20.02.1996	Terminated without the imposition of measures
Bed linen	L171, 07.05.1996	Terminated without the imposition of measures
Cotton fabrics, unbleached	C210, 11.07.1997	Terminated without the imposition of measures
Steel wire rod	C144, 22.05.1999	Terminated without the imposition of measures
Steel ropes and cables	C127, 05.05.2000	Duties
Paracetamol	C134, 13.05.2000	Terminated without the imposition of measures
Colour television receivers	C202, 15.07.2000	Terminated without the imposition of measures
Welded tubes and pipes, of iron and nonalloy steel	C183, 29.06.2001	Duties
Flat rolled products of iron and nonalloy steel	C364, 20.12.2001	Pending
Steel ropes and cables	L34, 03.02.2001 and L211, 04.08.2001	Undertakings
Hallow sections	C249, 16.10.2002	Pending
Investigations by Turkey		
Definitive antidumping and antisubsidy measures in force as of December 31, 1995		
Benzoic acids	14.08.1991	Duties
Printing and writing papers	20.05.1992	Duties
Polyester ELYAF	08.01.1993	Duties
New investigations after January 1, 1996		
Ball bearings	26.12.1998	Terminated without the imposition of measures
Polyvinyl chloride	02.11.2001	Duties

Note: OJ = *Official Journal* of the EU.
Sources: Undersecretariat of Foreign Trade and various issues of the reports of the Commission on Anti-Dumping and Anti-Subsidy Activities.

Technical barriers have two aspects: (1) the content of the norms (regulations and standards), and (2) the testing procedures needed to demonstrate that a product complies with the norm. The technical barriers to trade (TBTs) thus come in two basic forms, content-of-norm TBTs and testing TBTs. In either case, the costs of the product design adaptations, reorganization of production systems, and multiple testing and certification needed by exporters can be high. These costs are both upfront and onetime—for example, learning about the regulation and bringing the product into conformity—and ongoing, such as periodic testing. TBTs are said to distort trade when they raise the costs of foreign firms relative to those of domestic firms. As emphasized by Baldwin (2001), liberalization requires closing the gap between the costs of the foreign and domestic firms. The two main dimensions to such a step are content of norms and conformity assessment. Liberalization of the content of norms involves making product norms more cosmopolitan and thus narrowing the cost advantage of domestic firms. Liberalization of the second involves lowering the excess costs that foreign firms face in demonstrating the compliance of their goods to accepted norms. The European Commission (1998) has pointed out that the removal of technical barriers to trade will lead to four types of benefits: (1) economies of scale; (2) rationalization of products or production, increased efficiency, and price reductions as a result of increased competition; (3) restructuring of industry (e.g., plant closures, mergers, reorganization, relocation) to gain comparative advantage; and (4) innovation, stimulated by the dynamics of the single market.

The EU Approach to Technical Barriers to Trade

The basic objective of the EU policy and approaches to removing technical barriers to trade is to achieve free trade within the European Community. Currently, this policy has two approaches: enforcement of the Mutual Recognition Principle (MRP) and harmonization of technical regulations.

Mutual Recognition Principle Mutual recognition refers to the principles enshrined in the Treaty Establishing the European Economic Community (Treaty of Rome), interpreted by the European Court of Justice, as set out in the 1979 Cassis de Dijon judgment. In this ruling, the court stated that Germany could prohibit imports of a French beverage (cassis de Dijon) only if it could invoke mandatory requirements such as public health, protection of the environment, and fairness of commercial transactions. In other words, the court introduced a very wide definition of Article 28 (ex 30) of the Treaty of Rome, which prohibits quantitative restrictions on imports between member states and "all measures having equivalent results." As a result of this ruling, the European Commission stated that a product lawfully produced and marketed in one member state shall be admitted to other member states for sale, except in cases of mandatory requirements (the Mutual Recognition Principle). Thus, the basic EU approach under the MRP has been to promote the idea that products manufactured and tested in accordance with a partner country's regulations could offer levels of protection equivalent to those provided by corresponding domestic rules and procedures. Mutual recognition, in other words, reflects the existence of ex ante trust between the trading partners.

The European Commission (1998) divides the traded products into regulated and nonregulated commodities. The regulated products are those whose commercialization is governed by the regulations of member states, and the nonregulated products are those for which no regulations have an impact on commercialization. The regulated products are further divided into commodities under the harmonized sphere and those under the nonharmonized sphere. Products under the harmonized sphere are covered by European rules for the harmonization of regulations and mandatory specifications. Commodities under the nonharmonized sphere are governed by national rules. The MRP is considered the first line of defense against technical barriers in the regulated nonharmonized sphere.

The principal examples of success of the MRP are those regulations that are new and have been notified to the European Community under the 83/189 procedures, but then they have been negotiated away or had specific mutual recognition clauses inserted into the regulations.[10] Any problem in implementation of the MRP is harder to identify, because it relies on complaints from firms or trade associations.

In its relations with third countries, the European Community has advocated the use of mutual recognition agreements (MRAs) in many regional or bilateral forums. These agreements are based on the mutual acceptance of test reports, certificates, and marks of conformity issued by conformity assessment bodies of one of the parties to the agreement, in conformity with the legislation of the other party. Such agreements were signed with Australia, Canada, Israel, Japan, New Zealand, Switzerland, and the United States. The European Community also negotiated protocols to the Europe Agreements on Conformity Assessment and Acceptance of Industrial Products (PECAs) with some of the then-candidate countries. PECAs represent recognition of the progress made in adopting and implementing the relevant Community legislation on industrial products and in creating the necessary administrative infrastructure. The agreements cover a wide range of sectors, from medical devices to pressure vessels and electrical equipment.

In 1992 the European Economic Area (EEA) Agreement was signed between the European Free Trade Association (EFTA) countries and the EU. In extending the EU Single Market to the EFTA countries, the EU felt that ongoing and effective surveillance and enforcement were essential. Accordingly, the EFTA Court of Justice and the EFTA Surveillance Authority were established in 1992. Through the EEA Agreement, the EFTA countries Iceland, Lichtenstein, and Norway participate fully in the EU internal market and thus in the establishment of common product requirements and methods of conformity assessment. Outside the areas covered by EEA legislation related to product requirements, EEA states are permitted to introduce national product requirements, if it can be proved that such requirements are needed to meet public health, environmental, safety, and other social considerations. To ensure transparency, the EEA states are required to notify the EFTA Surveillance Authority and the European Commission of all draft national technical rules for products. Finally, the EEA Agreement forces the EFTA countries to accept future European Council directives on the Single Market without formal participation into the formation of these new laws.

In summary, MRAs seek to facilitate trade while safeguarding the health, safety, and environmental objectives of each party. Each party is free to set its health, consumer protection, environmental, or other regulations at whatever level it deems necessary, as long as they comply with international obligations. These obligations require that each side have full confidence that the certification process on the other side can wholly satisfy its requirements.

Harmonization of National Regulations and Standards   The EU legislation on harmonizing technical specifications has followed two distinct approaches, the old approach and the new approach. The old approach was based on the idea that the EU would become a unified economic area functioning like a single national economy. It dealt with the content-of-standards issue using negotiated harmonization, and it sought adoption of a single standard that laid out in detail technical regulations for single products or groups of products. The regulations were implemented by the directives of the European Council, and the designated bodies in EU nations performed the conformity assessments. Technical regulations were harmonized using the old approach for products such as chemicals, motor vehicles, pharmaceuticals, and foodstuffs. Under this approach, the Council issued directives such as Directive 70/220/EEC on the harmonization of the member states' laws related to the measures to be taken against air pollution caused by gases from positive-ignition engines of motor vehicles. The directive detailed EU specifications applying to the related products and their testing requirements. Under the old approach, European standards institutions such as CEN (Comité Européen de Normalisation) and CENELEC (Comité Européen de Normalisation Electrotechnique) were not mandated to draw up supplementary technical specifications. But over time, the need was recognized to reduce the intervention of the public authorities prior to a product being placed on the market. So the "new approach" was adopted and applied to products that have "similar characteristics" and that have been subject to a widespread divergence of technical regulations in EU countries.

Under the new approach, only "essential requirements" are indicated. This approach gives manufacturers greater freedom on how they satisfy those requirements by dispensing with the "old" type of exhaustively detailed directives. Directives under the new approach provide for more flexibility by using the support of the established standardization bodies—CEN, CENELEC, and the national standards bodies. The standardization work is easier to update and involves greater participation from industry.

Under the new approach, the European Council issues a directive that lays down "essential requirements"—the 1989 machinery directive is one example. So far, 23 directives have been adopted on the basis of this approach. Examples of product sectors regulated in accordance with the new approach are toys, machines, construction products, medical equipment, telecommunications terminal equipment, and recreational craft. Once a new approach directive has been issued, member states must conform their national laws and regulations to it. The European Commission is empowered to determine whether the national measures are equivalent to the essential requirements. The Council refers the task of formulating detailed standards meeting the essential requirements to CEN, CENELEC, and the European Telecommunications Standards Institute.

Conformity Assessment and Market Surveillance

To ensure that products meet the requirements laid down in the new approach directives, special conformity assessment procedures have been established. They describe the controls to which products must be subjected before they are considered compatible with the essential requirements and thus placed on the internal market. The extent of the controls a product must undergo varies according to the risk attached to use of the product. Requirements may range from a declaration by the manufacturer stating that certain standards have been applied, to extensive testing and certification by independent, third-party conformity assessment bodies (notified bodies). In 1993 Council Decision 93/465/EEC was adopted in connection with the new approach directives. It provides an overview of all the conformity assessment procedures available under the directives, divided up into modules and grouped by category of risk.

For products regulated by the new approach directives, a CE (Conformité Européne) marking confirms conformity with the essential requirements of the directives and is required for a product to be placed on the internal market. The CE marking indicates not only that the product has been manufactured in conformity with the requirements of the directive, but also that the manufacturer has followed all the prescribed procedures for conformity assessment. It ensures free access to all of the EU. Meanwhile, the manufacturer or its local representative is required to keep all necessary technical documentation as proof for the relevant authorities that the requirements have been satisfied.[11]

The final stage of implementation of the new approach system consists of market surveillance procedures that develop a common approach to enforcement. Market surveillance consists of the control that the relevant authorities in the member states are required to carry out to ensure that the criteria for CE marking have been satisfied—after the products have been placed on the market. The control is intended to prevent misuse of the CE marking, to protect consumers, and to secure a level playing field for producers. Basically, market surveillance is carried out in the form of random inspections to ensure that the technical documentation as required by the directive is available, but it also may include examination of the documentation or the product itself.

Coverage of EC Technical Regulations

Table 3.9 provides crude estimates of the sectoral value added covered under the old approach and the new approach. A large proportion of European Community value added in manufacturing has been covered by the Community's technical regulations policy: 33 percent by the old approach directives and 42 percent by the new approach directives, with each approach dominating different sectors. Finally, columns four and five show the share that each sector holds in intra-EC trade and world trade. The table reveals that sectors dominated by the old approach represent 29 percent of EC value added, 26 percent of intra-EC trade, and 17 percent of EC imports from the rest of the world. Sectors dominated by the new approach represent 33 percent of EC value added, 43.5 percent of intra-EC trade, and 56 percent of EC imports from the rest of the world.

Turkish Policies and Approaches

With the formation of the EU-Turkey customs union, Turkey has removed all customs duties and equivalent charges as well as quantitative restrictions

TABLE 3.9 EC Technical Regulation Directives and European Community (EC) Imports, 1995

ISIC	Manufacturing Sector	Coverage of EC Technical Regulations (percent of sectoral value added)			Import Structure (percent)	
		Old Approach	New Approach	Total	Intra-EC Imports	World
200	Mining	96	0	96	0.4	2.4
311–312	Agribusiness	100	0	100	5.8	3.8
313	Beverages and sugar	63	37	100	3.2	1.1
321	Textiles	0	59	59	3.6	4.2
322	Clothing	0	77	77	2.3	5.6
323	Leather goods	0	0	0	0.4	1.0
331	Wood and wood products	0	100	100	1.9	2.2
341	Paper and paper products	63	0	63	4.7	2.5
351–352	Chemicals	22	76	98	14.7	9.2
353	Petroleum refineris	100	0	100	1.5	1.6
354	Petroleum and coal products	0	100	100	0.8	8.5
355	Rubber and rubber products	54	0	54	3.7	2.1
361	Pottery, china, etc.	0	79	79	0.3	0.6
369	Nonmetallic products	11	55	66	1.9	1.0
371	Iron and steel	0	24	24	6.9	7.1
381	Metal products	0	43	43	3.1	2.2
382	Machinery	0	93	93	14.0	16.5
383	Electrical and electronic goods	18	82	100	10.0	13.5
384	Transport equipment	74	19	93	15.6	8.3
	Other manufactured goods	0	62	62	5.3	6.7
	All sectors	33	42	75	100.0	100.0

Note: Coverage of EC technical regulation is measured in percentage value added. ISIC = International Standard Industrial Classification.
Source: Messerlin 2001.

on industrial products.[12] Thus industrial products move freely between the EU and Turkey—with the exception of contingent protection measures and technical legislation. According to Decision 1/95 of the EC-Turkey Association Council establishing the customs union, Turkey must harmonize its technical legislation with that of the EU. Decision 2/97 of the Association Council listed the areas in which Turkey must align its legislation. This work should have been finalized before the end of 2000, but, unfortunately, it was not completed until the beginning of 2005. According to Annex II of Decision 2/97, Turkey was supposed to incorporate into its internal legal order 324 instruments that correspond to various European Economic Community or European Community regulations and directives. Currently, Turkey has incorporated into its legal order only 203 of these 324 instruments. In the

meantime, the number of instruments that Turkey has to incorporate into its legal order has increased to 560, and Turkey has incorporated 276 of them. Thus, progress has been rather slow.

Turkey also must establish the so-called *quality infrastructure*, a generic term encompassing the operators and operation of standardization, testing, certification, inspection, accreditation, and metrology (industrial, scientific, and legal). In the EU, national quality infrastructures that function according to the same principles and obey the same rules are a critical element of the free circulation of goods in the Single Market. Turkey, as a member of a customs union with the EU and as a candidate country, has to align its national quality infrastructure to the European one. Products manufactured in a future EU member state must satisfy the same requirements prevailing in the EU, and conformity to these requirements must be demonstrated in the same "harmonized" way and according to the same principles.

Recently, Turkey has taken major steps to align with the *acquis*. Law 4703 on the Preparation and Implementation of Technical Legislation on Products, which entered into force in January 2002, has been supplemented by secondary legislation. This framework law provides the legal basis for harmonization with the EC legislation. It defines the principles for product safety and for implementation of the old and new approach directives, including the conditions for placing products on the market; the obligations of the producers and distributors, conformity assessment bodies, and notified bodies; market surveillance and inspection; withdrawal of products from the market; and notification procedures.[13] The legislation on market surveillance, use and affixing of the CE conformity mark, working principles and procedures for the conformity assessment bodies and notified bodies, and notification procedures between Turkey and the EU for technical regulations and standards which apply to non-harmonized regulated area entered into force during 2002.[14] Furthermore, Turkey has adopted all of the 23 new approach directives that require affixing the CE conformity marking, and 18 of the directives entered into force up to the present time. They cover commodities and product groups such as low-voltage equipment, toys, simple pressure vessels, construction products, electromagnetic compatibility, gas appliances, personal protective equipment, machinery, medical devices, nonautomatic weighing instruments, telecommunications terminal equipment, hot water boilers, civil explosives, lifts, and recreational crafts.

Overall, then, Turkey has advanced the harmonization of its technical legislation both on a sectoral (vertical) basis and at a horizontal level. It is in the process of establishing the necessary structures on conformity assessment and market surveillance. By now Turkey has the legal basis on which accreditation could be based. In order to assign the notified bodies that would deal with the certification of products, the ministries have established the criteria for the selection of such bodies for the products covered by certain new approach directives. Although in Europe, as in Turkey, accreditation is not mandatory to be appointed as a notified body, since the Turkish Ministries did not feel adequately

prepared to select notified bodies, they made accreditation one of the criteria for their selection by signing protocols with the Turkish National Accreditation Body, TURKAK.[15] However the fact that TURKAK has been a member of European Accreditation Agency since 2003 and yet has not signed any multilateral agreement with the European partners makes its accreditation non-functional. Thus, even though TURKAK has given accreditation to potential notified bodies, this accreditation is meaningless in the eyes of national accreditation bodies of the EU.

Because of this the market is also reluctant to use TURKAK, because TURKAK accreditation is not accepted within the EU. This situation presents Turkish conformity assessment bodies with a disadvantage. The relatively large Turkish firms wishing to obtain CE marking for products exported to the EU market usually contact local subsidiaries of European notified bodies that use their European laboratories for testing. But for other Turkish companies this process seems to be expensive and slow. The small and medium-size enterprises (SMEs) that export products find it particularly difficult to pay the high costs. In Turkey, marking and certification parallel to the EU system are implemented only in the automotive sector, which is subject to the old approach directives. Istanbul Technical University (ITU) does automotive testing under the authorization of the Ministry of Industry and Trade, and it performs acoustic, emissions, and other tests. The Turkish Standards Institute (TSE),[16] Tofaş-Fiat, and Ford-Otosan also have engine and emissions test facilities; Seger has an audible warning devices laboratory; Tam-Test is implementing testing and certification in the case of agricultural tractors; Fren Teknik has test facilities for brakes and Brisa has a pneumatic tires laboratory. Turkey is implementing all relevant automotive EC directives via these facilities.[17] Crash tests, electromagnetic compatibility (EMC), and other tests on complete cars are largely conducted abroad; as of May 2003 the National Metrology Institute (UME) was able to run the EMC tests on vehicles.[18]

Other than for the automotive sector, as of 2005 Turkey is suffering from a lack of certification bodies (see European Committee for Standardization 2003). To make its conformity assessment compatible with that in the EU, Turkey has opened up the certification, testing, and calibration market to other Turkish actors. However, Turkish firms are reluctant to enter the market for conformity assessment bodies as long as uncertainties prevail regarding the acceptance of notified bodies by the European Commission. Some of the Turkish firms in cooperation with the notified bodies in the EU have entered the Turkish market. Over time competition will ensure lower costs for conformity assessment. The expense, time, and unpredictability incurred in obtaining approvals can then be reduced by having products evaluated in Turkey once the Turkish notified bodies are accepted by the European Commission and joint ventures with notified bodies in the EU increase. These savings can be particularly important where rejection of products in the EU can create delays and necessitate additional shipping or other costs. In addition, the SMEs can benefit from procedures in which all testing and certification steps are carried out locally at lower costs. Turkish firms, and in particular the SMEs, can then be expected to increase their competitiveness in the EU market

Although, in principle, standards are voluntary in Turkey, in the absence of a proper market surveillance system the technical ministries and the Undersecretariat of Foreign Trade have turned the standardization regime and licensing before production into a mandatory regime in order to protect the market and the consumers. This pre-market control system gives the TSE a great deal power. According to the European Committee for Standardization (2003), the TSE has misused its power in several cases of imports and has created technical barriers to trade. The TSE asked for the technical files of the imported products when they entered the Turkish market, and the processing of the files took an usually long time. There are also cases in which products bearing the CE marking were asked for further inspection. Yet the Turkish internal market is regulated largely through mandatory standards and marking issued by the TSE. Since 2004 products covered by directives on toy safety, medical devices, active implantible medical devices, low voltage electrical equipment, electromagnetic compatibility and machinery are not subject to mandatory controls when imported and used in the internal market. But products covered by the remaining 12 new approach directives are subject to mandatory controls.

In Turkey, 500 standards are mandatory for the domestic market as well as for imports. For all of these the TSE occupies a monopoly position, and for 500 of them TSE certification is mandatory. For these mandatory standards, manufacturers mostly need first a TSE certificate and then a Ministry of Industry and Trade license to put the products on the market.

The system in use in Europe, for those areas under the new approach directives, is in-market control. Under this system, the responsibility for placing a product on the market is left to the producer, so long as it is certified that the product satisfies the minimum requirements set under the directives. Market surveillance, the safeguard of the system, is the responsibility of public authorities. The market surveillance authorities carry out their operations in an impartial and nondiscriminatory way. They shall have the power, competence, and resources to regularly visit commercial, industrial, and storage facilities; to regularly visit, if appropriate, workplaces and other premises where products are put into service' to organize random and spot checks; to take samples of products and subject them to examination and testing, and to require all necessary information. Through this system, measures are taken in the EU to ensure that products meet the requirements of the applicable directives, that action is taken to bring noncompliant products into compliance, and that sanctions are applied when necessary. Member states are free to choose the type of sanction they are going to use. The only requirement is that the penalties be effective, proportionate, and dissuasive.

Technical Barriers and Trade between the EU and Turkey

To determine those sectors and products in which technical regulations are important for Turkish exporters, we used data produced by a study undertaken by the European Commission (1998). This study provides information, at the three-digit level of the NACE (Nomenclature Générale des Activités Économiques dans les Communautés Européennes) classification, about whether trade is affected by technical regulations and the dominant approach used by the European Commission to remove such barriers in the EU.[19] It classifies the technical regulations as follows: those in which barriers are overcome using mutual recognition, old approach, new approach, and those in which there are no technical barriers.

TABLE 3.10   Trade Coverage of Technical Regulations and of Different Approaches to Their Removal, 1990–2001
(percent)

	Old Approach	Mutual Recognition	New Approach	Subject to Technical Barriers	No Technical Barriers
Manufacturing Imports of EU					
1990	24.507	28.463	29.869	82.838	17.162
1991	23.662	29.839	29.187	82.689	17.311
1992	23.550	29.692	29.165	82.407	17.593
1993	21.970	30.615	28.662	81.248	18.752
1994	21.925	29.543	30.041	81.508	18.492
1995	19.078	30.497	31.459	81.034	18.966
1996	18.593	31.266	31.331	81.189	18.811
1997	18.700	32.269	30.435	81.404	18.596
1998	18.795	32.990	30.632	82.418	17.582
1999	18.663	33.245	30.627	82.535	17.465
2000	17.407	31.318	33.835	82.560	17.440
2001	18.108	31.602	32.538	82.248	17.752
Manufacturing Exports of Turkey to EU					
1990	8.815	63.561	14.911	87.287	12.713
1991	9.436	66.096	10.349	85.881	14.119
1992	8.735	66.411	10.694	85.840	14.160
1993	7.334	68.648	9.470	85.452	14.548
1994	9.048	64.839	10.607	84.494	15.506
1995	10.029	61.501	12.685	84.215	15.785
1996	10.143	61.589	12.267	83.998	16.002
1997	10.096	58.503	13.465	82.064	17.936
1998	12.474	56.552	13.042	82.069	17.931
1999	16.432	52.961	13.545	82.939	17.061
2000	17.634	50.762	14.332	82.728	17.272
2001	20.707	47.358	14.887	82.951	17.049

Note: The variables show the percentages of different approaches to the removal of technical barriers to trade in total manufacturing imports for the EU and in Turkish manufacturing exports to the EU.
Source: The authors.

Table 3.10 shows the overall trade coverage of technical regulations and of the different approaches to their removal in the EU and to their application to Turkish exports to the EU. Here we aggregated, following the approach of Breton, Sheehy, and Vancauteren (2001), the value of manufacturing imports across the four-digit Standard Identification Trade Classification (SITC) categories, which are subject to old approach directives, new approach directives, mutual recognition, and a residual.[20] We then identified the proportion of total imports value in sectors subject to old approach directives, new approach directives, mutual recognition, and a residual.

The table demonstrates that a very high proportion of EU manufacturing imports and of Turkish manufacturing exports to the EU are subject to technical barriers. The average value of the proportion over the period 1990–2001 is 82.0 percent for the EU and 84.2 percent for Turkey. In the EU, sectors subject to old approach directives make up on average 20.4 percent; mutual recognition and new approach directives, 31 percent each; and sectors subject to no technical barriers, 18.0 percent. For Turkish exports to the EU, the average values of the shares are 11.7 percent for old approach products; 60.0 percent, mutual recognition; 12.5 percent, new approach products; and 15.8 percent, sectors subject to no technical barriers. Sectors with no significant technical barriers to trade include nonferrous metals, footwear, and sawing and processing of wood. Old approach products include mainly motor vehicles and parts, and new approach products include sectors specified earlier, such as machinery.

Developments in the proportions of sectors subject to technical barriers over the period 1990–2001 reveal that the proportion of manufacturing imports subject to technical barriers has been relatively stable in the EU and that for Turkish exports to the EU declined from 87.3 percent in 1990 to 82.9 percent in 2001. In the EU, the proportion of sectors subject to mutual recognition and new approach directives has increased slightly over time, and the proportion of sectors subject to old approach directives has correspondingly declined. As for Turkish exports to the EU, the proportion of sectors subject to the new approach has been relatively constant. As the share of sectors subject to the old approach has increased, a corresponding decline appears in the share of sectors subject to mutual recognition.

We now turn to consideration of the index values of revealed comparative advantage (RCA) defined as

$$(3.3) \quad RCA_i = \ln\left[\frac{(X_i/X)}{(M_i^{EU}/M^{EU})}\right]$$

where X_i denotes Turkish exports of commodity i to the EU, X the total value of Turkish manufacturing exports to EU, M_i^{EU} the total EU imports of commodity i, and M^{EU} the total value of EU imports. Equation 3.3 considers the share of commodity i exports to the EU of total Turkish exports to the EU relative to the share of commodity i imports by the EU to total EU imports. If this ratio is greater than 1, the natural logarithm of the variable will be positive. In that case, the country is said to have a comparative advantage in producing that product, and the higher the value, the more competitive the product. Using the index of revealed comparative advantage, it is possible to determine in which product categories Turkey has the greatest comparative advantage. Table 3.11 shows the nine sectors with the highest RCA values by the different EU approaches to technical barriers to trade. The table reveals that the highest RCA values are attained in the sectors with no technical barriers. Turkey seems

also to be quite an efficient producer of goods from the sectors under mutual recognition as well as from the new approach sectors. Thus if trade between Turkey and the EU is constrained by technical barriers to trade, then with the accession of Turkey, competition in the EU for these products may intensify.

This analysis reveals that, for Turkey, sectors subject to technical regulations in the EU account for considerable shares of Turkish exports to the EU. The calculations demonstrate that accession will affect the exports of Turkish old and new approach products to the EU, and that Turkey has a comparative advantage in sectors subject to new approach directives. Therefore, it is of utmost importance that Turkey establish the quality infrastructure needed, encompassing the operators and operation of standardization, testing, certification, inspection, accreditation, and metrology. The Turkish quality infrastructure has to function according to EU principles and obey the same rules as in the EU. Only then will Turkey be able to participate in the free circulation of goods in the enlarged Single Market.

Conditions of Competition

Over the past few decades, Turkey has used intensively three tools of industrial policy: investment incentives, export incentives, and a policy of state-owned enterprises. In using these measures, the government has tried to obtain a preferred allocation of resources. The purpose of the investment incentive scheme has been to increase investment and overcome the barriers imposed by capital market imperfections to entry into industry. But investment incentives in Turkey have also been a barrier to competition. Through the incentive system, established firms have obtained cost advantages that have helped them to consolidate their market position. Entrants, competing with scarce fiscal resources, have been at a disadvantage relative to well-informed incumbents. The credit incentives, which were supposed to promote entry, have often turned into instruments that have reinforced the position of large incumbents. Furthermore, the government, with its large share of the banking system, has also directly controlled the allocation of credit, and credit from public banks has often been extended on the basis of political considerations. Overall,

TABLE 3.11 Sectors with Highest RCA Values in Each Category

SITC		RCA, 1999–2001	Turkish Exports to EU, 1999–2001 Average (thousands of ECU)
Old approach			
7831	Public transport-type passenger motor vehicles	3.2198	181,834
5238	Other metallic salts, peroxysalts of inorganic, acids	2.9270	65,203
7611	Television receivers, color, whether or not combined	2.2189	725,383
5323	Synthetic inorganic tanning matter; preparations	1.4908	895
5237	Percarbonates; commercial ammonium carbonate	1.3940	26,140
7139	Parts, NES, for the engines of 7132, 7133 and 7138	1.1439	217,582
5234	Polysulphides, dithionites, sulphites, sulphates	0.8834	5,148
5233	Hypochlorites; chlorites; chlorates; bromates; iodates	0.8047	1,190
8986	Magnetic tapes, recorded	0.7545	4,692
Mutual recognition			
6534	Fabrics, woven, < 85% synthetic staple fibers, mixed	3.1060	101,494
8462	Panty hose, socks, and other hosiery, knitted or crocheted	2.5733	285,684
6542	Fabrics, woven, > 85% wool or fine animal hair	2.4675	29,022
8454	T-shirts, singlets and other vests, knitted or crocheted	2.4476	984,273
6529	Other woven fabrics of cotton	2.4372	4,265
8442	Suits, ensem., dresses, skirts, trousers, knitted, women	2.3862	349,327
6513	Cotton yarn, other than sewing thread	2.3166	235,351
6524	Other woven fabrics > 85% cotton, weight > 200 g/m^2	2.2850	85,496
6536	Fabrics, woven, > 85% artificial staple fiber (excluding pile)	2.2635	21,646
New approach			
7753	Dishwashing machines of the household type	3.4565	11,569
6624	Nonrefractory ceramic bricks and similar products	2.7997	117,996
6762	Rods (excluding 6761), iron, steel, hot-rolled, hot-drawn	2.6528	188,512
6761	Bar and rods, hot-rolled, irregular wound coils, iron, steel	2.4310	114,585
6612	Hydraulic cements, whether or not colored, clinkers	2.4192	160,431
8121	Boilers (excluding 711), radiators, etc., not electrical	2.2241	83,012
6794	Other tubes, pipes, and hollow profiles of iron, steel	2.1659	132,205
7752	Household-type refrigerators and food freezers	2.0630	152,836
6652	Glassware for domestic use (excluding 66511, 66592, 66593)	1.8532	105,440
No technical barriers			
7753	Dishwashing machines of the household type	3.4565	11,569
6581	Sacks and bags of textile materials, for packing goods	2.8222	109,778
6579	Special products of textile materials	2.5383	39,282
6564	Tulles and other net fabrics; lace, in the piece	2.5145	10,051
8122	Ceramic sinks and similar sanitary fixtures	2.3625	58,256
6584	Bed, table, toilet, and kitchen linen	2.3485	471,456
6112	Composition leather, basis of leather, slabs, sheets	2.0423	1,380
6931	Stranded wire, ropes, slings, and the like, of metal	1.9921	44,441
6252	Other knitted or crocheted fabrics, noncoated, etc.	1.7149	70,236

Note: RCA = revealed comparative advantage; SITC = Standard International Trade Classification; NEC = not elsewhere classified.

Source: The authors.

established firms benefit from the investment incentive schemes such as investment allowances, but new entrants do not, because to benefit from devices such as investment allowances, they must show positive profits in their income statements first.

In Turkey, the investment incentive scheme has been used while no specific competition legislation or competition policy has been enforced in the country. To promote competition within the country, Turkey eliminated quantitative restrictions in foreign trade during the 1980s and substantially decreased the levels of nominal and effective protection rates. With the formation of the customs union with the EU, all of the tariff barriers on imports of industrial commodities from the EU were completely eliminated, as noted earlier.

On the export side, over the 1980s Turkey used various export incentive measures. But in 1985 it agreed to eliminate export subsidies by 1989. After 1989, Turkey eliminated most of the export incentives, introduced GATT legal subsidies, and reduced substantially the nominal and effective export subsidy rates. The reduction in the nominal and effective protection and subsidy rates was not sufficient, however, to ensure proper functioning of markets in Turkey. During the 1950s, a similar situation in Europe had led to the adoption of competition policies aimed at ensuring effective competition, allocating resources efficiently, and creating the best possible climate for fostering innovation and technical progress.

In June 1989, Turkey adopted the law titled On the Prevention of Unfair Competition in Importation, containing both antidumping and antisubsidy provisions. Turkey adopted its competition policy during December 1994 with the Law on the Protection of Competition. The key provisions of the competition law are based on the EU's competition law: agreements, decisions, and concerted practices in constraint of competition; abuse of dominant position; and mergers and acquisitions. The statute contains not only rules on forbidden practices and provisions against the abuse of a dominant market position, but also regulations on acquisitions and mergers. The Competition Authority responsible for the implementation and enforcement of the prohibitions set out in the law opened its doors in October 1997. As indicated by OECD (2002) competition policy, institutions in Turkey are in place and active, but competition policy is not fully integrated into the general policy framework for regulation. Turkey's competition law has no rule equivalent to Article 86 of the Treaty Establishing the European Community to govern the permissible operations of monopolies providing public services. Nevertheless, special rules limit competition in some sectors such as the financial sector, tobacco industry, mineral products, agriculture, and postal services. In addition, Turkey has to control its anticompetitive state aid policy.[21]

It could be said, then, that Turkey has achieved considerable progress in the fields of investment and export incentives, but it has not achieved similar progress in dealing with public enterprises. Although privatization has become a prominent part of the Turkish structural adjustment program, since 1983 privatization has not gained momentum.

Table 3.12 presents basic data on Turkey's manufacturing sector for 2000. The data are taken from two surveys, "Annual Manufacturing Industry Statistics" and "Small Manufacturing Industry Statistics," published by the State Institute of Statistics. The first survey covers all firms in the public sector and private firms employing 10 or more employees. The second survey covers all private firms employing less than 10 employees. The table reveals that the sectors with the highest shares of total value added of the manufacturing sector were petroleum and coal, 12.49 percent; textiles, 12.29 percent; food processing, 11.45 percent; and chemicals, 9.71 percent. The sectors with the highest shares of total manufacturing employment were textiles, 18.56 percent; food processing, 15.41 percent; wearing apparel and footwear, 9.62 percent; and metal products, 7.98 percent. The sixth column of the table gives the share of 1998 public sector value added of the total value added of the corresponding manufacturing subsector. From the table, it follows that the average share of public sector value added of the total manufacturing industry value added was 18.91 percent. Petroleum and coal had the highest share with 89.83 percent, followed by the tobacco industry with 78.25 percent, and the beverages industry with 50.58 percent.

The seventh and eighth columns of table 3.12 indicate exposure to international trade. Column seven provides a measure of competitiveness on the domestic market measured by the rate of import penetration. If Q, X, and M stand, respectively, for

TABLE 3.12   Characteristics of Turkish Manufacturing Industries, 2000

ISIC	Sector	Value Added (US$ millions) (1)	Share of Sector of Total Manuf. Value Added (2)	Employment (3)	Share of Sector of Total Manuf. Employment (4)	Public Sector Value Added (US$ millions) (5)	Share of Public Sector of Total Sectoral Value Added (6)	Import Penetration (percent) (7)	Export Ratio (percent) (8)	Rate of Exposure to International Competition (percent) (9)
311 + 312	Food processing	4,687.9	11.45	255,437	15.41	609.8	13.01	7.47	9.44	16.20
313	Beverages	908.2	2.22	11,194	0.68	459.4	50.58	0.77	1.98	2.74
314	Tobacco	1,063.8	2.60	18,951	1.14	832.4	78.25	1.97	5.28	7.15
321	Textiles	5,030.6	12.29	307,689	18.56	56.0	1.11	17.31	39.88	50.29
322 + 324	Wearing apparel and footwear	1,533.9	3.75	159,561	9.62	19.1	1.25	30.70	86.35	90.54
323	Fur and leather products	110.8	0.27	10,358	0.62	0.0	0.00	50.93	38.19	69.67
331	Wood and cork products	526.7	1.29	67,688	4.08	0.0	0.01	12.03	3.99	15.54
332	Furniture and fixtures	449.2	1.10	72,072	4.35	0.0	0.01	53.63	44.26	74.16
34	Paper and products	1,314.5	3.21	56,459	3.41	111.5	8.48	27.49	5.30	31.33
351 + 352	Chemicals	3,977.7	9.71	59,537	3.59	287.9	7.24	49.13	13.66	56.08
353 + 354	Petroleum and coal	5,112.4	12.49	9,882	0.60	4,592.3	89.83	17.08	2.34	19.02
355 + 356	Rubber and plastic products	1,574.5	3.85	60,577	3.65	4.3	0.27	9.01	8.90	17.11
36	Nonmetallic minerals	2,712.5	6.62	92,160	5.56	23.1	0.85	9.01	20.84	27.98
37	Basic metals	2,216.0	5.41	65,729	3.96	454.8	20.52	40.04	27.04	56.25
381	Metal products	1,946.2	4.75	132,276	7.98	50.2	2.58	15.95	11.20	25.36
382	Machinery	1,822.5	4.45	100,594	6.07	96.5	5.29	63.39	18.98	70.34
383	Electrical machinery	2,218.8	5.42	68,616	4.14	44.4	2.00	62.00	38.25	76.53
384	Transport equipment	3,218.6	7.86	84,358	5.09	82.0	2.55	48.87	25.22	61.76
385	Professional and sci. measuring equip.	251.1	0.61	11,327	0.68	12.0	4.80	69.28	11.23	72.73
39	Other manufacturing industries	271.9	0.66	13,647	0.82	5.9	2.16	56.67	61.23	83.20
3	Manufacturing	40,947.8	100.00	1,658,112	100.00	7,741.6	18.91	33.10	21.78	47.67

Note: ISIC = International Standard Industrial Classification.

Source: Annual manufacturing industry statistics and small manufacturing industry statistics provided by Turkish State Institute of Statistics.

sectoral output, exports, and imports, the domestic demand D will be equal to $D = Q - X + M$, and the rate of import penetration will equal $[M * 100 / D]$. A low level of penetration does not necessarily mean that there are barriers to entry. The table reveals that the professional and scientific measuring equipment sector had the highest import penetration with 69.28 percent, followed by the machinery sector with 63.39 percent and electrical machinery with 62.00 percent. Column eight of table 3.12 gives the export ratio, defined as $[X * 100 / Q]$. From the table, it follows that the wearing apparel and footwear sector had the highest export ratio at 86.35 percent, followed by other manufacturing industries at 61.23 percent, furniture and fixtures at 44.26 percent, and textiles at 39.88 percent. Finally, column nine gives the rate of exposure to international competition, defined as $[(export\ ratio) + [1 - (export\ ratio/100)] * import\ penetration]$. The construction of this indicator rests on the idea that the exported share of production is 100 percent exposed and that the share sold on the domestic market is exposed in the same proportion as the penetration of the market. The table reveals that the wearing apparel and footwear sector had the highest exposure to international competition with an index value of 90.54 percent, followed by the other manufacturing industries sector with an index value of 83.20 percent and the electrical machinery sector with an index value of 76.53 percent.

Defining the markup by the relation

$$(3.4) \qquad \lambda = \frac{(value\ added - labor\ cost)}{labor\ cost}$$

we note from the first two columns of table 3.13 that the markup calculated for three-digit International Standard Industrial Classification (ISIC) sectors in Turkey are much higher than the markup in Belgium, a small open economy considered to be the benchmark country in the analysis. The data in this table were obtained from the "Annual Manufacturing Industry Statistics" of the State Institute of Statistics for the period 1999–2000 for the Turkish economy, and from the OECD STAN Database for Belgium for the period 1997–99. The table shows that the markups in all other sectors in Turkey exceed those in Belgium, and that the average markup in Turkey relative to that in Belgium, $[(1 + \lambda)/(1 + \lambda')]$, is highest in the sectors coke, refined petroleum products, and nuclear fuel

FIGURE 3.1   Average Value of Markups for Manufacturing, 1980–2000

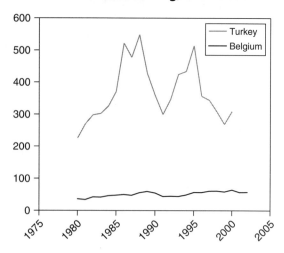

(ISIC 353 + 354); other manufacturing (ISIC 39); and wood and products of wood (ISIC 331). The lowest average markups in Turkey relative to those in Belgium, $[(1 + \lambda)/(1 + \lambda')]$, are found in the sectors paper and paper products (ISIC 341); leather, leather products, and footwear (ISIC 323 + 324); and nonferrous metals (ISIC 372). Figure 3.1 plots the average value of the markup for the manufacturing industry over the period 1980–2000. On the other hand, defining the markup as

$$(3.5) \qquad \lambda = \frac{(output - labor\ cost - material\ cost)}{(labor\ cost + material\ cost)}$$

we note from the last two columns of table 3.13 that the markups in Turkey exceed those in Belgium except in the sectors electrical and optical equipment (ISIC 383 + 385); iron and steel (ISIC 371); and publishing, printing, and reproduction of recorded media (ISIC 342). The average markup in Turkey relative to that in Belgium, $[(1 + \lambda)/(1 + \lambda')]$, is now highest in the sectors tobacco products (ISIC 314); other nonmetallic mineral products (ISIC 36); and coke, refined petroleum products, and nuclear fuel (ISIC 353 + 354). The results are striking. They indicate the lack of competition in the Turkish manufacturing sector.

To further illustrate the arguments about the conditions of competition in the Turkish manufacturing sector, we consider in table 3.14 the four-firm concentration ratios. The table reveals that the concentration ratios are relatively high and that the most concentrated sectors are the manufacture of coke coal and briquettes (ISIC 3542), manufacture of sporting and athletic goods (ISIC 3903),

TABLE 3.13   Average Markups, Turkey and Belgium
(percent)

ISIC	Commodity	Markup I		Markup II	
		Turkey, 1999–2000	Belgium, 1997–1999	Turkey, 1999–2000	Belgium, 1997–1999
31	Food and beverages and tobacco				
311 + 312 + 313	Food products and beverages	347.52	80.03	46.49	29.66
314	Tobacco products	362.79	100.54	74.76	19.78
32	Textiles, apparel, and leather				
321	Textiles	268.62	53.29	52.69	37.66
322	Wearing apparel, dressing, and dyeing of fur	252.56	45.01	45.73	26.52
323 + 324	Leather, leather products, and footwear	211.08	55.45	49.84	47.96
33	Wood products				
331	Wood and products of wood and cork	427.71	51.09	59.09	39.72
332	Furniture; manufacturing NEC	381.65	45.59	66.02	43.22
34	Paper, paper products				
341	Paper and paper products	215.81	71.33	57.24	47.09
342	Publishing, printing, and reproduction of recorded media	312.06	60.19	54.77	61.46
35	Chemical products				
353 + 354	Coke, refined petroleum products, and nuclear fuel	1,628.89	174.81	52.48	14.53
351 + 352 − 3522	Chemicals, excluding pharmaceuticals	384.18	80.80	67.88	43.63
3522	Pharmaceuticals	404.26	115.64	107.81	76.67
355 + 356	Rubber and plastics products	312.54	66.59	66.74	42.76
36	Nonmetallic minerals				
36	Other nonmetallic mineral products	387.83	60.35	109.65	56.55
37	Basic metals				
371	Iron and steel	202.95	37.78	34.65	38.63
372	Nonferrous metals	196.86	44.10	30.97	19.69
38	Fabricated metal				
381	Fabricated metal products, except machinery and equipment	290.62	42.38	74.69	49.58
382	Machinery and equipment NEC	239.35	50.04	62.49	54.58
383 + 385	Electrical and optical equipment	274.18	39.49	55.84	59.07
384	Transport equipment	274.78	36.18	47.63	24.37
39	Other manufacturing				
39	Manufacturing NEC	479.38	51.03	49.40	37.72

Note: ISIC = International Standard Industrial Classification; NEC = not elsewhere classified.

Sources: OECD STAN Database and annual manufacturing industry statistics provided by the Turkish State Institute of Statistics.

manufacture of aircraft (ISIC 3845), manufacture of watches and clocks (ISIC 3853), tire and tube industries (ISIC 3551), and petroleum refineries (ISIC 3530). The most competitive sectors are manufacture of wearing apparel (ISIC 3222); spinning, weaving, and finishing textiles (ISIC 3211); manufacture of plastic products (ISIC 3560); and knitting mills (ISIC 3213).

In summary, with the formation of the EU-Turkey customs union Turkish industries became subject to greater competition. But markups and concentration ratios are still high compared with those in benchmark countries such as Belgium.[22] It seems that Turkey has to complete the harmonization of technical regulations, privatize its public enterprises, liberalize entry and exit into

TABLE 3.14 Concentration of Domestic Activity, 1997–2000
(four-firm concentration ratios)

ISIC Rev 2	Commodity	1997	1998	1999	2000
3111	Slaughtering, preparing, and preserving meat	34.15	29.64	32.45	31.13
3112	Manufacture of dairy products	51.54	50.25	51.55	49.57
3113	Canning and preserving of fruits and vegetables	19.08	17.34	16.16	18.90
3114	Canning, preserving, and processing of fish and crustacea	91.72	89.85	81.40	84.98
3115	Manufacture of vegetable and animal oils and fats	46.66	42.28	43.25	43.92
3116	Grain mill products	17.01	17.97	25.46	24.30
3117	Manufacture of bakery products	29.52	30.37	31.30	34.81
3118	Sugar factories and refineries	39.14	33.43	35.94	31.62
3119	Manufacture of cocoa, chocolate and sugar confectionery	58.61	49.26	51.03	53.03
3121	Manufacture of food products NEC	25.47	28.75	21.88	24.94
3122	Manufacture of prepared animal feeds	22.66	26.41	27.40	28.95
3131	Distilling, rectifying, and blending spirits	60.97	66.08	71.99	74.50
3132	Wine industries	74.24	74.21	80.89	75.16
3133	Malt liquors and malt	74.56	80.12	69.04	76.49
3134	Soft drinks and carbonated waters industries	63.17	64.82	60.90	66.06
3140	Tobacco manufactures	54.81	58.92	57.64	70.82
3211	Spinning, weaving, and finishing textiles	9.90	7.68	9.44	11.08
3212	Manufacture of madeup textile goods, except wearing apparel	21.74	22.99	24.71	25.32
3213	Knitting mills	14.93	12.20	22.89	13.95
3214	Manufacture of carpets and rugs	43.34	41.66	43.84	39.65
3215	Cordage, rope, and twine industries	82.12	88.77	70.69	95.91
3219	Manufacture of textiles NEC	67.88	65.07	66.28	65.04
3221	Manufacture of fur and leather products	23.98	23.95	22.03	24.89
3222	Manufacture of wearing apparel, except fur and leather	12.03	7.45	8.79	9.21
3231	Tanneries and leather finishing	21.42	30.47	19.40	19.42
3233	Manufacture of products of leather and leather substitutes	58.23	68.77	57.75	61.04
3240	Manufacture of footwear, except vulc. or molded rubber	34.04	32.18	38.43	28.27
3311	Sawmills, planing, and other wood mills	37.98	34.23	38.27	35.16
3312	Manufacture of wooden and cane containers and small cane ware	61.99	47.05	64.11	51.02
3319	Manufacture of wood and cork products NEC	67.83	60.53	63.29	60.22
3320	Manufacture of furniture and fixtures, except primarily of metal	45.99	44.06	44.37	49.66
3411	Manufacture of pulp, paper, and paperboard	55.42	42.42	39.29	38.82
3412	Manufacture of containers and boxes of paper and paperboard	24.46	25.52	27.95	26.09
3419	Manufacture of pulp, paper, and paperboard articles	45.79	41.45	56.87	47.00
3421	Printing, publishing, and allied industries	63.28	40.42	50.08	45.55
3511	Manufacture of basic industrial chemicals, except fertilizers	47.00	53.20	54.64	67.81
3512	Manufacture of fertilizers and pesticides	56.58	54.43	55.28	54.65
3513	Manufacture of synthetic resins, plastic materials	92.64	88.30	90.34	86.91
3521	Manufacture of paints, varnishes, and laquers	49.15	45.49	39.82	38.84
3522	Manufacture of drugs and medicines	31.28	31.59	29.74	33.37
3523	Manufacture of soap and cleaning preparations, perfumes	62.17	66.35	71.32	63.36
3529	Manufacture of chemical products NEC	37.67	44.02	44.98	43.68
3530	Petroleum refineries	97.81	97.86	97.51	97.39

TABLE 3.14   (Continued)

ISIC Rev 2	Commodity	1997	1998	1999	2000
3541	Manufacture of asphalt paving and roofing materials	88.54	73.54	72.19	92.33
3542	Manufacture of coke coal and briquettes	100.00	100.00	100.00	100.00
3543	Compounded and blended lubricating oils and grease	87.51	85.54	79.22	88.25
3544	Liquid petroleum gas tubing	88.96	84.60	87.49	84.17
3551	Tire and tube industries	97.88	98.03	98.24	99.08
3559	Manufacture of rubber products NEC	28.85	22.80	25.84	23.66
3560	Manufacture of plastic products NEC	18.01	16.38	16.48	14.41
3610	Manufacture of pottery, china, and earthenware	74.71	58.05	60.97	69.81
3620	Manufacture of glass and glass products	43.64	40.68	42.21	39.51
3691	Manufacture of structural clay products	47.09	43.91	41.59	42.78
3692	Manufacture of cement, lime, and plaster	31.23	29.52	33.68	34.95
3699	Manufacture of nonmetallic mineral products	27.70	26.82	25.89	20.08
3710	Iron and steel basic industries	32.29	31.76	36.69	32.91
3720	Nonferrous metal basic industries	40.27	42.40	44.92	49.06
3811	Manufacture of cutlery, hand tools, and general hardware	28.72	33.58	20.19	24.52
3812	Manufacture of furniture and fixtures, primarily of metal	49.40	43.18	45.58	40.87
3813	Manufacture of structural metal products	23.59	24.04	24.80	24.41
3819	Manufacture of fabricated metal products	26.31	25.96	27.67	23.85
3821	Manufacture of engines and turbines	92.31	88.68	86.78	92.53
3822	Manufacture of agricultural machinery and equipment	81.46	81.59	79.93	80.73
3823	Manufacture of metal and wood working machinery	46.89	45.84	37.63	35.70
3824	Manufacture of special industrial machinery and equipment	26.99	26.61	21.65	21.16
3825	Manufacture of office, computing, and accounting machinery	75.13	86.06	82.19	90.88
3829	Machinery and equipment, except electrical	51.73	49.54	54.52	48.10
3831	Manufacture of electrical industrial machinery and apparatus	58.63	56.01	57.51	53.22
3832	Manufacture of radio, television, and communication equipment	75.40	69.75	64.74	62.37
3833	Manufacture of electrical appliances and housewares	48.54	51.99	51.95	45.45
3839	Manufacture of electrical apparatus and supplies	27.08	24.94	29.73	26.14
3841	Ship building and repairing	50.28	46.01	48.48	52.18
3842	Manufacture of railroad equipment	98.04	98.78	96.62	94.21
3843	Manufacture of motor vehicles	40.81	40.60	46.44	47.32
3844	Manufacture of motorcycles and bicycles	78.79	77.45	80.31	76.12
3845	Manufacture of aircraft	100.00	100.00	100.00	99.78
3849	Manufacture of transport equipment NEC	94.08	95.81	94.22	100.00
3851	Controlling equipment NEC	34.87	43.34	36.34	55.93
3852	Manufacture of photographic and optical goods	62.06	76.78	81.98	84.30
3853	Manufacture of watches and clocks	100.00	100.00	100.00	98.73
3854	Other	79.65	81.46	65.87	65.64
3901	Manufacture of jewelery and related articles	48.80	46.02	47.12	53.39
3902	Manufacture of musical instruments	100.00	100.00	—	—
3903	Manufacture of sporting and athletic goods	100.00	100.00	100.00	100.00
3909	Manufacturing industries NEC	31.38	32.74	39.74	45.58

— Not available.

Note: For abbreviations, see table 3.13.

Source: Turkish State Institute of Statistics.

various sectors of the economy, and impose hard budget constraints on all public and private enterprises. Further integration with the EU will then remove the distortions in the price system, which, in turn, will boost the allocative efficiency in the economy.

Conclusion

Although customs duties and equivalent charges, as well as quantitative restrictions on industrial products, were eliminated with the formation of the customs union in 1996 between Turkey and the EU, the free movement of industrial products between the parties could not be established until 2003. The two remaining issues are contingent protectionism and technical barriers to trade. Article 44 of the Customs Union Decision allows the EU to impose antidumping measures until Turkey implements effectively the competition rules and the rules on the intellectual, industrial, and commercial property rights of the customs union. Similar considerations apply for Turkey. Since 1996, both parties have been active users of these measures.

On another front, under Decision 2/97 of the Association Council, Turkey had to incorporate into its internal legal order, before the end of 2000, 324 instruments corresponding to various European Economic Community and European Community regulations and directives on technical legislation. But the work has still not been completed. In addition, Turkey has to align its national quality infrastructure to the European one. Products manufactured in Turkey must satisfy the same requirements as those prevailing in the EU, and the demonstration of conformity to these requirements must be done in the same "harmonized" way and according to the same principles as in the EU. Recently, Turkey has taken major steps to align its legislation with the *acquis*. But it still has to establish the operators and operation of standardization, testing, certification, inspection, accreditation, and metrology according to the same principles and obeying the same rules as in the EU. Once these problems are solved, competition will increase in the economy, leading to decreases in markups and concentration ratios, provided it is complemented with privatization and adoption of appropriate competition policies. Thus, to benefit from free trade between the parties, Turkey has to adopt and implement the whole body of EU legislation—that is, the *acquis communautaire,* and in particular the rules on competition, intellectual, industrial, and commercial property rights, and the whole body of technical legislation on a sectoral as well as a horizontal level.

Notes

1. The authors wish to thank their discussant, Bernard Hoekman, and anonymous referees for helpful comments. İbrahim Yılmaz and Harun Çelik provided excellent research support.

2. For a discussion of the trade regime during the 1980s, see Togan (1994).

3. All dollar amounts are U.S. dollars unless otherwise indicated.

4. EU15 refers to the 15 members of the EU prior to the 2004 enlargement in which 10 more countries joined the EU. The 15 countries are Austria, Belgium, Denmark, Finland, France, Germany, Greece, Ireland, Italy, Luxembourg, Netherlands, Portugal, Spain, Sweden, and the United Kingdom.

5. The mass housing fund tax is a specific tariff imposed mainly on agricultural commodities.

6. The average rates of nominal protection were derived by weighting nominal rates estimated as applied rates for the sectors by sectoral outputs valued at world prices. The average rates of effective protection were obtained by weighting effective rates estimated for the sectors by sectoral value addeds evaluated at world market prices.

7. These are the sectors with negative EPRs and with values greater than -100.

8. The classification of the sectors into four trade groups follows the same rule adopted by Balassa and others (1982). The export category includes sectors whose exports amount to more than 10 percent of domestic production and whose imports account for less than 10 percent of domestic consumption. For sectors classified as export and import competing, both of these shares exceed 10 percent. The import-competing and non-import-competing categories include sectors whose exports amount to less than 10 percent of domestic production. In sectors in the import-competing category, imports exceed 10 percent of domestic consumption. In sectors in the non-import-competing category, imports are less than 10 percent of domestic consumption.

9. The authors are grateful to Ela Yazıcı İnan for her contributions to this section. On technical barriers to trade, see Sykes (1995).

10. Directive 83/189/EEC, amended by Directive 98/34/EC, established the requirements that member states notify draft regulations and that national standards bodies notify work on new standards.

11. Consider the machinery directive that applies to all machinery and to safety components. The directive defines a machine as "an assembly of linked parts or components, at least one of which moves." Annex I of the directive gives a comprehensive list of the hazards that may arise from the design and operation of machinery, and gives general instructions on what hazards must be avoided. The directive requires the machine manufacturer to produce a "technical file" of documentary evidence that the machinery complies with the directive, the form and content of which is dictated in the directive. Machinery

meeting the requirements of the directive is required to have the CE symbol clearly affixed to indicate compliance. An item of equipment may only display the CE mark when the equipment satisfies all relevant directives—for example, machines with electrical controls must also comply with the requirements of the low voltage and electromagnetic compatibility (EMC) directives. For most items of machinery, the manufacturer (or its authorized representative) can self-certify—that is, it designs its products to meet the requirements of the directive and signs a Declaration of Conformity. This declaration of conformity must be backed up with the technical file. The file must be retained for a period of 10 years after the manufacture of the machine (or the last machine of a production run). For certain especially dangerous items of machinery (known as Annex IV machines), justification of use of the CE mark must be independently verified by a recognized authority (called an "approved body" or "notified body"). Manufacturers of Annex IV machines are required to compile a technical file that shows how the machinery has been constructed to meet the requirements of the directive. The file is then audited by the notified body to confirm that the directive's requirements have indeed been met, and a sample of the machinery is examined to confirm that it is constructed as described in the file. If a harmonized standard for a particular type of Annex IV machine exists, the manufacturer can avoid the expense of type examination by manufacturing the machine fully in accordance with the standard. All that is then required is that the file be lodged with a notified body, but the notified body does not have to give an opinion on the machine—it simply acts as an independent repository for the file. This procedure can only be applied to machines that are manufactured fully in accordance with the harmonized standard. If there are any deviations from the standard (e.g., a light guard is fitted where the standard says a physical guard is required), the full type approval route must be followed.

12. This section reports the state of affairs on technical barriers to trade in Turkey as of 2003.

13. Law 4703 is based on Council Directive 92/59/EEC on general product safety, Council Regulation 85/C 136/01 on the new approach to technical harmonization and standards, and the Council resolution of December 1989 on the global approach to conformity assessment.

14. The legislation on market surveillance was prepared using Council Directive 92/59/EEC on general products safety, the Council resolution of December 1989 on the global approach to conformity assessment, Council Directive 88/378/EEC on the approximation of the laws of the member states on the safety of toys, and on a European Commission implementation guide (2000). The legislation on working principles and procedures for the conformity assessment bodies and notified bodies was prepared using the material in chapter 6 of the European Commission guide (2000). The legislation on the use and affixing of the CE conformity mark is based on Council Decision 93/465/EEC on the modules for the various phases of the conformity assessment procedures and the rules for affixing and the use of the CE conformity marking. Finally, the legislation on notification procedures between Turkey and the EU for technical legislation and standards is based on Council Directive 98/34/EC, laying down a procedure for the provision of information in the field of technical standards and regulations and the relevant section of Decision 2/97 of the EC-Turkey Association Council.

15. Under a law published on October 27, 1999, TURKAK is the national accreditation body in all fields. But the regulations that gave the Turkish Standards Institute (TSE) and Turkish Scientific and Technical Research Council (TUBITAK) the power to accredit are still in force.

16. The TSE was established in 1954 to draw up standards for all kinds of products and services.

17. For automotive products, the "e" sign confirms conformity.

18. UME is organized as part of TUBITAK. UME has calibration laboratories in mechanics, physics, electricity, ionizing radiation, and chemicals. The laboratories under construction include EMC, acoustics, and liquid flow.

19. We use four-digit SITC trade data and correspondences between the NACE, International Standard Industrial Classification, and Standard Identification Trade Classification classifications provided by the Eurostat's Classification Server (http://europa.eu.int/comm/eurostat/ramon/).

20. *Manufactures* are defined as consisting of sectors under SITC sections 5, 6, 7, and 8 minus division 68 and group 891.

21. Although Turkey realizes that the major pillars of a competition policy must comprise privatization, liberalization of entry and exit, imposition of hard budget constraints on all public and private enterprises, and a very liberal trade regime, it faces difficulties in implementing these principles.

22. For concentration ratios in Slovakia and Belgium, see Djankov and Hoekman (1998).

References

Balassa, B. 1982. *Development Strategies in Semi-Industrial Economies.* Baltimore: Johns Hopkins University Press.

Baldwin, R. E. 2001. "Regulatory Protectionism, Developing Nations and a Two-Tier World Trade System." *Brookings Trade Forum* 3: 237–80.

Breton, P., J. Sheehy, and M. Vancauteren. 2001. "Technical Barriers to Trade in the European Union: Importance for Accession Countries." *Journal of Common Market Studies* 39: 265–84.

Djankov, S., and B. Hoekman. 1998. "Conditions of Competition and Multilateral Surveillance." *World Economy* 21: 1109–28.

European Commission. 1998. *Technical Barriers to Trade.* Vol. 1, Subseries III, *Dismantling of Barriers, The Single Market Review.* Luxembourg: Office for Official Publications of the European Communities (OOPEC).

————. 2000. *Guide to the Implementation of Directives based on the New Approach and the Global Approach.* Brussels.

————. 2002. *2002 Regular Report on Turkey's Progress towards Accession.* Brussels.

European Committee for Standardization. 2003. *Support to the Quality Infrastructure in Turkey: Country Report 2003.* Brussels: CEN.

Messerlin, P. A. 2001. *Measuring the Costs of Protection in Europe: European Commercial Policy in the 2000s.* Washington, DC: Institute for International Economics.

OECD (Organisation for Economic Co-operation and Development). 2002. *Turkey: Crucial Support for Economic Recovery.* OECD Reviews of Regulatory Reform. Paris: OECD.

Sykes, A. O. 1995. *Product Standards for Internationally Integrated Goods Markets.* Washington, DC: Brookings Institution.

Togan, S. 1994. *Foreign Trade Regime and Trade Liberalization in Turkey during the 1980's.* Avebury, UK: Ashgate Publishing.

Undersecretariat of Foreign Trade. 2002. "Türkiye'nin AB Teknik Mevzuatına Uyumu—Çerçeve Kanun, Uygulama Yönetmelikleri" [Harmonization of Turkish Regulations on Technical Barriers to Trade to EU Approaches]. Ankara: UFT.

4

ACCESSION OF TURKEY TO THE EUROPEAN UNION: MARKET ACCESS AND REGULATORY ISSUES

Joseph Francois

The European Union (EU) has been at the center of a recent explosion in regional trading schemes. A combination of economic and political factors—including greater peace and stability in the EU hinterland, support for democratic reforms in developing countries, greater trade and investment liberalization in developing countries, and access to new markets for EU exports—have been advanced as motives for the EU to conclude such agreements. For developing countries, the attraction has been preferential access to the large EU market and the prospect of increased EU aid. The reality is that everybody, except the North American and high-income Asian economies, now seems to have preferential access to the EU.[1]

For those countries that are immediate neighbors of the EU, the big prize has been the promise of accession to the EU (see Baldwin and Francois 1997). Turkey is no exception. Although Turkey was not included in the list of new members for the next round of accession, an ongoing process (with a very long history) is supposed to lead eventually to EU membership.

This chapter explores the implications of eventual Turkish accession to the EU. The potential impacts of regulatory reform under such a process are examined by focusing on the transport sector, broadly defined to include air, land, rail, and other. Two issues studied are the linkage between trade effects and the transport sector, and the implica-

tions of EU regulation for the sector. The first section discusses the context of membership, especially the Customs Union between the EU and Turkey, but also the other protocols agreed to and under negotiation between the EU and Turkey. That section is followed by a brief quantitative discussion of the likely impact of full membership on trade and on the transport sector itself. Because the customs union covers many of the steps needed for membership, the incremental impact of the last necessary steps for the transport sector is relatively minimal. Other possible effects are then identified through a detailed assessment of the regulatory regime in Turkey for transport as compared with the one in effect for the rest of the EU. Here, too, the major steps have already been taken, implying that EU membership will have little direct impact, institutionally or economically, on the domestic transport sector. Effects may be related to EU structural funds (which was the case in Spain and Portugal), but in view of the size of the looming enlargement, such funds are likely to be limited.

The Customs Union

The primary difference between the current list of new EU members and membership for Turkey is the depth and long history of trade integration in place between the EU and Turkey. The EU-Turkey customs union has been a long time in the making. In

1963 the Treaty of Ankara envisaged Turkey becoming a full member of the EU, with preparation occurring over a series of stages. In 1970 a protocol to this Ankara agreement outlined a framework of the customs union between the EU and Turkey. Even though Turkey's 1987 application for full membership in the EU was rejected, it continued to pursue unilateral trade liberalization with the EU. As a result, when the customs union was finally established for *industrial products* on January 1, 1996, after a transition period of 22 years, much of the required tariff changes for industrial products had already been implemented.

The existence of the customs union, along with the protocols that go with it, has important implications for the discussion that follows of the likely effects of full EU membership. The average reduction in tariffs required by the CU for Turkey has been estimated to be only 7 percent (Harrison, Rutherford, and Tarr 1997). The combination of adopting the Common Customs Tariff (CCT) structure and Uruguay Round commitments should have produced a trade-weighted average tariff on industrial goods of 3.5 percent by 2001 (WTO 1998). In theory, the objective of the customs union agreement is to prepare Turkey for full membership in the EU, and the agreement is, therefore, not only deeper than the EU's free trade agreements, but also goes well beyond the basic requirements of a customs union agreement. In particular, it requires Turkey to introduce a wide range of legislation covering all aspects of trade; competition law; industrial, commercial, and intellectual property rights; and to adopt EU technical standards.[2] In this sense, the customs union agreement carries with it many of the consequences that would follow from full EU membership.

Table 4.1 compares the current EU arrangement with Turkey with recent and ongoing agreements (in the form of free trade agreements, FTAs) with selected developing countries and regions. Behind all of these agreements is a mix of politics and economics. A basic dilemma facing EU negotiators of these free trade agreements is that, according to their negotiating mandate, they must not undermine the finely tuned border protection of the EU's Common Agricultural Policy (CAP) and the Common Fisheries Policy. At the same time, they must ensure that agreements are compatible with

Article XXIV of the General Agreement on Tariffs and Trade (GATT) of 1994, particularly Section 8 requiring coverage of "substantially all trade" and the Understanding on Article XXIV (especially the preamble, which states that "no major sector is excluded"). The EU seeks to resolve this dilemma by interpreting World Trade Organization (WTO) rules as requiring free trade to be established on 90 percent of total bilateral trade flows.

Because EU tariffs on most industrial products are zero or very low (exceptions are, for example, clothing and motor vehicles), the EU has little difficulty in liberalizing imports of all, or practically all, industrial products. Moreover, because imports of agricultural and fisheries products are limited by (sometimes prohibitive) border protection, they account for only a small proportion of existing total imports from the partner country. As a result, the EU is able to make a sufficient contribution to the fulfillment of the 90 percent criterion by liberalizing only around 60 percent of its imports of agricultural products. Similar calculations, it is argued by the EU, also enable the partner country to protect sensitive industrial and agricultural sectors of its economy while remaining within the EU's interpretation of the requirements of Article XXIV.

Given these constraints, the pattern of tariff reductions in the developing country usually takes the form of abolishment of the duties on capital and intermediate goods before duties on final consumer goods, which are also subject to significantly higher initial duties and which are liberalized only toward the end of the transitional period. It is in the area of trade in agricultural and fisheries products that the agreements fall significantly short of free trade. The EU routinely excludes products such as beef, sugar, a range of dairy products, some cereals and cereal products, rice, some fresh fruits and vegetables, some cut flowers, and fisheries products. The partner developing country also excludes a range of agricultural products, not least to protect its agriculture from imports of subsidized agricultural goods from the EU, such as beef, sugar, dairy products, and cereals. As a result, in the agreement with Mexico only 62 percent of bilateral trade in agricultural products is fully liberalized. In the agreement with South Africa, 62 percent of EU imports are liberalized, while South Africa fully liberalizes 82 percent of its imports from the EU. No

TABLE 4.1   Structure of EU Free Trade Agreements with Selected Developing Countries

	Egypt	South Africa	Mexico	Turkey
Rationale:				
EU	Security	Reinforce democracy; regional hub	Access to NAFTA; regional hub	Customs union agreement in industrial products; objective of membership in EU
Partner	Maintain preferences; lock in reforms; attract FDI	Improve access to EU market; attract FDI; lock in reforms	Reduce dominance of United States; improve access to EU market; attract FDI	
Transitional period:				
EU	Immediate	10 years	10 years	Turkey's customs legislation now almost same as that of EU
Partner	12–15 years	12 years	10 years	
Industry coverage:				
EU	All	Almost all, most by 2006	All by 2003	All
Partner	All, less than half by year four, end-weighted on most protected	87% and end-weighted	All by 2007, most by 2003	All
Agricultural coverage:				
EU	Approx. 60%+ of imports, entry prices, plus preferences with tariff quotas			Separate preferential agreement covering range of products, some with tariff quotas
Partner	Very limited; some duty reductions within tariff quotas	Substantial; some wines subject to tariff quotas	Some, such as dairy, tobacco, processed foods	
Rules of origin:				
EU	EU rules; bilateral cumulation with EU; derogations can be requested.			EU rules
Partner	Part MEDA cumulation an objective	Full SACU cumulation; partial SADC cumulation with one country	Relaxation in some sectors due to lack of raw materials and components	
Safeguards	Standard EU clause for both parties plus transitional arrangements for partner			EU rules
Antidumping	Standard WTO rules			
Intellectual property rights	Protected under TRIPS plus list of international agreements		Special committee to solve difficulties	TRIPS plus list of international agreements

TABLE 4.1   (Continued)

	Egypt	South Africa	Mexico	Turkey
Competition rules	Outlaws collusion/ abuse of dominant position of enterprises, which distorts competition in trade (except for ECSC products)	Each retain own rules; outlaws collusion/abuse of market power, etc.; cooperation plus EU assistance	Own laws; detailed statement on cooperation; technical assistance	EU policy
State aids	Must not distort competition in trade between EU and partner, but are permissible for public or policy objectives (EU Article 92)			
Public procurement	Consultation with aim of liberalization	"Fair, equitable and transparent"	National treatment and nondiscrimination phased in over 10 years, except some public utilities and transport	Agreement to be reached in future
Rights of establishment and services	GATS plus possibility of further liberalization		Trade in most services liberalized plus most modes of supply by 2004; transitional period of 10 years; national treatment	National treatment; services agreement under negotiation as part of customs union
Capital movements	Free movement of capital relating to direct investment plus interest profits and dividends		Program of liberalization relating to investment plus protection of investment	Export of large sums from Turkey unclear
Standards	Aim of reducing differences (especially SPS) and mutual recognition		Cooperation; Special Committee on SPS Measures	Working toward implementation of EU rules
Custom cooperation	For example, exchange of information, introduction of single administration document, simplification of controls and procedures for clearance, cooperation on rules of origin			EU commercial policy and rules
Aid, economic development cooperation	MEDA programs (grants) to support all Euro-Med agreements; three-year rolling national indicative programs	Multiannual indicative programs of grants and loans	n.a.	MEDA plus EIB preaccession loan facility
Institutions	Joint EU/Partner Association/Cooperation Council at ministerial level supported by committees (high official) and technical working groups			Association Council; CU Joint Committee; Joint Consultative Committee

	Egypt	South Africa	Mexico	Turkey
Dispute settlement	Association Council by "decision" or by arbitration binding on both parties; no time limit or enforcement procedures	Cooperation Council or arbitration; stages time limited; no enforcement procedures	Joint Committee or arbitration; rules for procedures, time-limited, stages, compensation	Association Council or arbitration
General	Political dialogue; social and cultural cooperation; democratic principles and respect for human rights; scientific, technical, and technological cooperation			
Other	Money laundering; drug trafficking; migrant workers and illegal immigration; regional integration	Wine and spirits agreement; fisheries (not concluded); regional cooperation		Turkey to adopt all of EU's preferential trade agreements

n.a. Not applicable.

Note: NAFTA = North American Free Trade Agreement; FDI = foreign direct investment; MEDA is the financial instrument of the Euro-Mediterranean Partnership; SACU = South African Development Community; SADC = South African Development Community; WTO = World Trade Organization; TRIPS = Agreement on Trade-Related Aspects of Intellectual Property Rights; ECSC = European Coal and Steel Community; GATS = General Agreement on Trade in Services; SPS = sanitary and phytosanitary; EIB = European Investment Bank; CU = Customs Union.

Source: Francois, McQueen, and Wignaraja 2003.

comparable figures are published for trade in agricultural products with Egypt or Turkey.

Agricultural products are not included in the customs union agreement with Turkey, but because the objective is full membership in the EU, both parties have agreed to progressively improve their preferential regime in the agricultural sector with the aim of allowing Turkey to adapt its agricultural policy to the EU's Common Agricultural Policy. However, no time frame has been applied to this process, and the system of preferences does not "restrict in any way the pursuance of the respective agricultural policies of the Community or Turkey."[3] In addition, both countries have a safeguard clause that can be activated if "either quantities or the prices of imported products from the other Party in respect of which a preferential regime has been created, causes or threatens to cause a disturbance of the Community or Turkish market." The European Commission estimates that 93 percent of Turkey's agricultural exports to the EU and 33 percent of EU agricultural exports to Turkey are covered by the 1998 scheme of preferences.

The customs union agreement is part of the more general program of preparation for EU membership, signaled in particular by the Helsinki agreement to include Turkey as a candidate country for accession to the EU and by Turkey's adoption on March 19, 2001, of the "National Programme for the Adoption of the Acquis" (the *acquis communautaire* is the entire body of legislation of the European Communities and Union). This program includes the economic aspects of the *acquis*, in particular the "four freedoms" (related to goods, persons, services, and capital) that form the basis for the operation of the internal market. As discussed in other chapters in this volume, these economic aspects have immediate implications for services trade.

A Quantitative Assessment

As noted earlier, the customs union between the EU and Turkey already covers most, if not substantially all, trade. To analyze the impact of Turkey's accession to the EU, this section describes the application of a global general equilibrium model (the model, which is described in annex 2, is based on Francois, McQueen, and Wignaraja 2003). The policy experiments involve a summary of the estimated economic effects of the customs union and of its extension, under membership, to cover all trade.

The EU-Turkey customs union agreement is really designed for industrial products; the final stage was completed in 2000. As such, there is unrestricted trade in all industrial products between the two countries, and Turkey applies the CCT to imports of industrial products from third countries. Agriculture is largely excluded from the agreement, although there is a preferential trade regime for a limited range of agricultural products (see table 4.2 for a summary).

EU imports of products not listed in table 4.2 are exempt from ad valorem duties, but they are still subject to specific duties and quotas. Even where preferences are given for some food products (fruits and vegetables), they are only available between certain dates. Turkey has liberalized even less in the area of food and agriculture. Most-favored-nation (MFN) duties have been abolished for live bovine (pure breeding animals) and meat or fish unfit for human consumption. For a fairly short list of other products, duties are abolished within small tariff quotas, including products listed in table 4.2.

Turkey has undertaken "far-reaching structural and legislative reforms within the framework of the customs union agreement" (WTO 1998). The adoption of the CCT has meant that Turkey's level of border protection on industrial products and the industrial component of processed foods has declined significantly. As a result, even though there may be some concerns about the possibility of relative trade diversion, the absolute level of imports from third countries should have increased, not only because border measures of protection have declined significantly, but also because the adoption of EU customs regulations has provided exporters with greater certainty of treatment. Turkey illustrates as well some of the substantial difficulties that developing countries experience in implementing far-reaching structural reforms even when, like Turkey, they have both the

TABLE 4.2   Processed Food Concessions under the EU-Turkey Customs Union

EU Concessions	Turkey Concessions
Tomato paste	Live bovine animals
Poultry meat	Frozen meats
Sheep and goat meat	Butter
Olive oil	Cheese
Cheese	Vegetable and flower seeds
Some fresh fruit and vegetables	Flower bulbs
Hazelnuts	Apples and pears
Fruit juices	Potatoes
Marmalade and jams	Cereals
	Refined/raw vegetable oil
	Sugar
	Tomato paste
	Some alcoholic beverages
	Some animal foods

Note: Products not listed by the EU are exempted from ad valorem duties, but they are still subject to quotas and specific duties. Examples are beef and sugar. Turkey has liberalized some agricultural tariffs within very narrow tariff-rate quotas.

Source: Francois, McQueen, and Wignaraja 2003.

incentive of full membership in the EU and the backing of substantial financial and technical resources.

Because the customs union reflects political sensitivities in the EU and Turkey, areas of significant potential (agricultural) trade have been excluded by both parties to the agreement. Reflecting the customs union as just described, the scenario for application of the computable general equilibrium (CGE) model is summarized in table 4.3.[4]

Of immediate interest here is the sectoral impact of the actual customs union and of a full free trade scenario. The omission of the agricultural sector from the customs union agreement almost certainly means that the agreement does not conform with Article XXIV of the GATT. Interestingly, this issue was raised in the WTO review of the report of the Trade Policy Review Board (TPRB) on Turkey (no response by Turkey was recorded), but no WTO member state has so far challenged the agreement, presumably because those states feel that adoption of the CAP by Turkey would increase the current level of discrimination against their exports.

Agriculture is, however, an important sector of the Turkish economy, accounting for about 11.4 percent of its gross domestic product and 34 percent of employment. The omission of this sector from the customs union agreement must produce significant distortions in the allocation of resources in the economy and in the economic effects of the agreement.

The macroeconomic effects of the customs union are summarized in table 4.4. Consider first national welfare (measured as current welfare derived from economy-wide consumption patterns). The customs union, as currently constructed, yields a boost in Turkish welfare (measured as a percentage of base national income) of over 1.3 percent relative to the baseline with MFN industrial tariffs. Based on 1997 values, this gain is comparable to a boost in real GDP of US$2.2 billion.[5] The static effect is slight, adding less than 0.1 percent to welfare through induced capital accumulation.

TABLE 4.3 Customs Union Scenario

	Full Liberalization	Partial Liberalization	No Liberalization
Grains		Turkey	EU
Other agriculture		EU, Turkey	
Mining	EU, Turkey		
Other primary production	EU, Turkey		
Sugar		Turkey	EU
Dairy		Turkey	EU
Meats			EU, Turkey
Processed foods		EU, Turkey	
Textiles	EU, Turkey		
Clothing	EU, Turkey		
Leather	EU, Turkey		
Wood and paper	EU, Turkey		
Chemicals	EU, Turkey		
Refineries	EU, Turkey		
Steel	EU, Turkey		
Nonferrous metals	EU, Turkey		
Motor vehicles	EU, Turkey		
Electronics	EU, Turkey		
Other machinery	EU, Turkey		
Manufactures, NEC	EU, Turkey		

Note: Partial liberalization is modeled as 50 percent. NEC = not elsewhere classified.
Source: Author's definition of model aggregation.

TABLE 4.4   Summary of Macroeconomic Effects of Customs Union for Turkey

	A	B	C = A + B	D
	Static Effects	Dynamic Effects	Long-Run Effects of Actual Customs Union	Long-Run Effects of Full EU Membership
Welfare (% of national income)	0.91	0.4	1.31	1.36
Welfare (millions of US$)	1,558.92	678.31	2,237.23	2,335.73
Terms of trade (%)	2.64	0.91	1.73	1.95
Value of exports (%)	10.6	3.46	14.06	15.21
Unskilled worker wages (%)	2.02	0.22	2.24	2.62
Skilled worker wages (%)	1.28	0.43	1.71	1.72
Capital stock (%)	0.00	1.24	1.24	1.24
Value of GDP in dollars (%)	3.17	0.36	2.81	3.01
Real exchange rate (%)[a]	3.05	1.1	1.95	2.16
GDP quantity index (%)	0.11	0.74	0.85	0.84

a. Real exchange rate is the dollar price of the base period GDP basket.
Source: Author's calculations.

A comparable improvement appears in Turkey's terms of trade through static effects—the gap between export and import prices widens by over 2.5 percent. However, there is an interaction between long-run capital accumulation and the terms of trade that erodes terms-of-trade gains over the medium run. The agreement, as modeled, yields a considerable boost in the capital stock (1.24 percent). Normally, a large boost in real income would follow. In fact, the quantity index for GDP does expand. But because of the erosion in the terms of trade in the medium to long run, the value of GDP (in dollar terms) falls somewhat. Even so, the initial terms-of-trade gains are strong enough to outweigh these effects.

Consider next the impact on wages. Both skilled and unskilled workers gain from the agreement, with a 2.2 percent and 1.7 percent boost, respectively, to real incomes (net of changes in the consumer price index, CPI) over the long run. Such wage changes are considerable, given that they are realized in the context of a trade agreement. The positive wage effects imply that, overall, the customs union will not make labor market conditions worse.

The next set of indicators reported in table 4.4 relate to real exchange rates and GDP. GDP is not an appropriate measure of economic welfare—it

misses substitution effects in production and consumption—but it is a common metric for government monitoring of economic climate. The changes in both the value and quantity of GDP (based on a fixed 1997 basket of goods and services) fail to track welfare gains in any meaningful way.

How does the actual customs union compare with a full customs union? A comparison of the last two columns of table 4.4 reveals the differences. The EU-Turkey customs union does not cover all potential EU-Turkey trade, but Turkey is at a stage of development where critical market access revolves around manufactured goods rather than agriculture. As a result, the actual customs union does cover enough trade to generate gains that are broadly similar to those of a full customs union. The differences between the two columns are within the margin of error for this kind of modeling exercise. Broadly speaking, the table does not reveal a significant difference, in terms of welfare, between a full customs union and the EU-Turkey customs union. But there is some expansion of trade (primarily in food) under full membership.

Although the overall macro effects of the actual customs union are comparable with those of a full customs union, some slight differences emerge at

TABLE 4.5 Change in Output by Sector in Turkey
(percent)

Sector	A Static Effects	B Dynamic Effects	C = A + B Long-Run Effect of Actual FTA	D Long-Run Effect of Full EU Membership
Grains	0.76	0.67	0.09	1.18
Other agriculture	0.89	0.78	0.11	2.3
Mining	4.14	0.65	3.49	4.67
Other primary production	0.28	0.34	0.62	0.4
Sugar	0.4	0.61	0.21	4.6
Dairy	0.09	0.39	0.48	0.09
Meats	0.77	1.03	0.26	2.96
Processed foods	0.84	1.06	1.9	1.61
Textiles	21.81	4.43	26.24	25.46
Clothing	49.16	6.46	55.62	54.86
Leather	0.81	3.92	4.73	4.88
Wood and paper	0.76	0.05	0.71	0.87
Chemicals	2.31	1.21	1.1	1.14
Refineries	0.85	0.97	0.12	0.1
Steel	3.93	0.74	3.19	3.67
Nonferrous metals	7.09	2.23	4.86	5.5
Motor vehicles	17.12	2.05	−15.07	15.73
Electronics	11.6	1.46	13.06	12.7
Other machinery	6.35	1.81	4.54	5.08
Manufactures, NEC	1.0	0.39	0.61	0.81
Transport	0.43	0.87	0.44	0.35
Construction	3.47	2.77	0.7	0.64
Business services	3.71	1.83	1.88	2.13
Other services	1.07	0.78	0.29	0.41

Note: NEC = not elsewhere classified.
Source: Author's calculations.

the sectoral level (see table 4.5). Under a full customs union, EU grain production squeezes Turkey's production, with a projected drop in output of 1.18 percent. However, under the actual agreement this sector is largely sheltered, with production projected to drop only 0.09 percent from baseline levels. A similar story holds for meat production, which is largely insulated under the current agreement.

Outside of food production, the largest effects are in textiles, clothing, and motor vehicle production. Textiles and clothing have benefited tremendously from improved EU access. Production is 25 percent and 50 percent higher, respectively, than without preferred access. At the same time, the motor vehicle sector in the EU applied strong pressure on the motor vehicle and parts sector in Turkey, which shrank by 15 percent. Another sector that benefits is (consumer) electronics, which enjoyed a 12 percent increase in production.

The sector-level results also point to no real great adjustment pressures within Turkey, except in heavy manufacturing. The motor vehicle, machinery, and equipment sectors are squeezed. This situation is consistent with expectations about Turkey's comparative advantage, with an advantage in lighter manufactures and a relative disadvantage in some heavy manufacturing sectors.

The trade results largely mirror the results for production. One outlier is motor vehicles. Although production is squeezed and imports go up substantially, exports also go up substantially. Mexico's experience with the North American Free Trade Agreement (NAFTA) was similar. The motor vehicle sector is forced to restructure, and in the process it becomes more deeply integrated with the European industry. As a result, significant growth is projected in both imports and exports in the sector relative to a baseline with continued MFN protection for the sector. The result for sugar under the full customs union reflects the subsidies to EU production and a large increase in a small export base for Turkey (small changes in small flows can lead to large percentage changes). In the actual customs union agreement, these effects are sterilized.

What happens to the transport sector under the customs union? The static effect is contraction, as resources are pulled out of the sector and into manufacturing. However, because the customs union is estimated to have positive investment effects (i.e., the capital stock expands), there is a projected expansion of the sector in the medium term of roughly 0.44 percent. Because the agreement is already in place, the interpretation is that the transport sector is almost a half percent larger than it would be otherwise.

What happens to the transport sector under actual EU membership (the focus here is on the trade-related effects)? Again, the impact is positive relative to no preferential trade at all. However, because full membership would extend access to the EU food markets (food production is a large share of Turkey's economy), resources would be pulled out of the service sectors and into agriculture.

Finally, what happens to direct trade in transport services? The Global Trade Analysis Project (GTAP) database reveals that Turkey's trade in transport services is relatively small, with imports of roughly $1.207 billion in 1997. Based on gravity estimates of services trade barriers, the import tariff equivalent for cross-border transport service imports into Turkey is roughly 8.9 percent (see annex 1). Assuming an import demand elasticity of −3.9 (equal to the import substitution elasticity in demand in the GTAP model for this sector) and deadweight trade costs, a back-of-the-envelope calculation yields gains of roughly $126 million per year from full trade liberalization in the sector. The EU accounts for roughly 25 percent of this total, or only about $30 million per year in welfare gains in the sector from direct trade related to liberalization vis-à-vis

the EU. This would follow from roughly $100 million in additional services imports from the EU.

A Factor Analysis of Regulatory Structures

Membership in the EU involves not only market access, but also community rules and regulations. In this section, the regulation database of the Organisation for Economic Co-operation and Development (OECD) is used to examine the structure of competition and regulation in the transport sector across OECD countries. The goal is to compare the regulatory status of Turkey's transport sector with those of EU members. In the end, it turns out that the Turkish regulatory regime is not at all inconsistent, by these measures, with the broad pattern observed within the EU. This finding may reflect the long, ongoing process of Turkish integration. In any event, it suggests that the sector may require little overall realignment of regulation in view of what is currently allowed within the EU.

The 2000 OECD International Regulation Database includes more than 1,100 variables for each OECD member on both economy-wide product market regulation and regulation at the sector level. For the purposes of this study, it includes data on regulation in road transport, national and international air transport, and rail transport (see Nicoletti, Scarpetta, and Boylaud, 1999, for a detailed description of the data). In general, the data of interest here are centered around 1998.

The OECD database may contain over 1,100 variables, but only a limited number apply to transport. In addition, many remain unanswered by a large number of members, and many others simply defy quantification. For this reason, the full set of transport questions has been reduced to the set covered in table 4.6. The 18 variables listed for air transport are classified into domestic competition, international competition, and government ownership and regulation. The 15 variables for road transport and the six for rail are roughly classified into domestic competition and government ownership and regulation.

Within each set of variables, the assigned values range from 0 to 6 (so that for dummies, yes is generally 6 and no is 0), and the assigned weights are based on the number of variables in a sector:category set. In this factor analysis of the variables, the result of this scaling is a set of regulatory indexes ranging

TABLE 4.6   Variables Used from OECD International Regulation Database

OECD Survey Question No.	Question	Data Set Variable Name
17	Does national, state, or provincial government hold equity stakes in business company? 7,131 air transport carriers	ATOR1
52	Do national, state, or provincial laws or other regulations restrict in at least some markets the number of competitors allowed to operate a business? 7,131 air transport carriers	ATOR2
547	Air travel/national market structures: domestic market share of the largest airline (incl. subsidiaries) (more than 500,000 passengers a year)	ATDC1
548	Air travel: market structure: domestic routes (all routes): share of traffic (passengers/km) of the incumbent carrier	ATDC2
558	Air travel: market structure: international routes (all routes): share of traffic (passengers/km) of the largest carrier in the international traffic of national carriers	ATIC1
566	Air travel: Is the largest operator in international routes also the largest operator in domestic routes? (all routes)	ATIC2
567	Air travel/national market structures: share of 100 international routes with more than three carriers	ATIC3
572	Air travel/national regulations and government ownership: government ownership in largest airline (%)	ATOR3
573	Air travel/national regulations and government ownership: government golden share in a major airline	ATOR4
579	Air travel/national regulations and government ownership: government loss makeups in major airlines in the past five years	ATOR5
580	Air travel/national regulations and government ownership: the largest airline has public service obligations	ATOR6
611	Air travel/national regulations and government ownership: domestic market deregulated	ATOR7
612	Air travel/national regulations and government ownership: Open Sky agreement with United States	ATIC4
613	Air travel/national regulations and government ownership: Open Sky agreement older than six years	ATIC5
618	Air travel/national market structures: international market share of the largest airline (incl. subsidiaries) (more than 500,000 passengers a year)	ATIC6
619	Air travel/national market structures: Herfindahl concentration index in domestic market	ATDC3
620	Air travel/national market structures: Herfindahl concentration index in international market (%)	ATIC7
1120	Air travel: ceiling on foreign ownership allowed in national air transport carriers	ATOR8
13	Does national, state, or provincial government hold equity stakes in business company? 7,114 road freight	RTOR1
48	Do national, state, or provincial laws or other regulations restrict in at least some markets the number of competitors allowed to operate a business? 7,114 road freight	RTDC1
492	Road freight: Is there a firm in the road freight sector that is publicly controlled (i.e., national, state, or provincial governments hold the largest single share)?	RTOR2
493	Road freight: Is registration in any transport register required in order to establish a new business in the road freight sector?	RTOR3
494	Road freight: In order to operate a national road freight business (other than for transporting dangerous goods or goods for which sanitary assurances are required) do you need to be granted a state concession or franchise by any level of government?	RTOR4

TABLE 4.6 **(Continued)**

OECD Survey Question No.	Question	Data Set Variable Name
495	Road freight: In order to operate a national road freight business do you need to obtain a license (other than a driving license) or permit from the government or a regulatory agency?	RTOR5
496	Road freight: In order to operate a national road freight business do you need to notify any level of government or a regulatory agency and wait for approval before you can start operation?	RTOR6
505	Road freight: Does the regulator, through licenses or otherwise, have any power to limit industry capacity?	RTDC2
513	Road freight: Are there any regulations setting conditions for driving periods and rests?	RTOR7
515	Road freight: Do regulations prevent or constrain: backhauling?	RTDC3
516	Road freight: Do regulations prevent or constrain: private carriage?	RTDC4
517	Road freight: Do regulations prevent or constrain: contract carriage?	RTDC5
520	Road freight: Within the last five years, have laws or regulations removed restrictions on: commercial, for-hire shipments?	RTOR8
521	Road freight: Are retail prices of road freight services in any way regulated by the government?	RTOR9
522	Road freight: Does the government provide pricing guidelines to road freight companies?	RTDC6
10	Does national, state, or provincial government hold equity stakes in business company? 7,111 railways	RROR1
45	Do national, state or provincial laws or other regulations restrict in at least some markets the number of competitors allowed to operate a business? 7,111 railways	RRDC1
528	Railways: freight transport: total number of operators	RRDC2
538	Railways: Please indicate if the government has any liability for losses made by a railway company (excluding subsidies related to service obligations).	RROR2
539	Railways: Did the government in the past five years make up for any losses made by railway companies?	RROR3
540	Railways: Are companies operating the infrastructure or providing railway services subject to universal service requirements (e.g., obligation to serve specified customers or areas)?	RROR4

Note: Questions have generally been rescaled from 0 to 6, with 0 being a positive indicator (more competition, less regulation, less participation by government through ownership, golden shares, price setting, and so forth). Questions have also been assigned inverse weights (i.e., if there are four domestic competition questions for air, each gets a 1/4 weighting for the domestic competition for air transport factoring and scoring exercise).
Source: OECD International Regulation Database, 2001.

from 0 (generally open, competitive regimes with minimal regulation) to 6 (generally more regulated, with less or no competition).

Multivariate factor analysis is a standard technique for summarizing patterns in regulatory data (see Nicoletti, Scarpetta, and Boylaud 1999 and Boylaud 2000). Factor analysis yields factors that are linear combinations of the variables observed and that, in theory, identify latent variables or indicators that lurk behind the observed data. In the present context, this approach allows the construction of indexes of regulatory frameworks in the sample.

Factor analysis is applied first to the regulatory variables grouped by sector and type of regulation, thereby yielding a set of indicators for road transport, air, and rail, which are listed in tables 4.7, 4.8, and 4.9. The critical point to pick up from these indexes is that in all three transport sectors Turkey's regulatory regime is fully consistent with the regimes of current EU members. For example, the road transport regime in Turkey has fewer limits on competition (including pricing guidelines) than Germany, Greece, Finland, and the Netherlands. Overall, the road transport sector compares favorably

TABLE 4.7 Regulation Indexes, Air Transport

	Overall	Government Ownership or Management	Government Bailouts	Regulation and Limits on Restructuring	Public Service Obligations and Custom Guarantees	Domestic Competition	International Competition	International Reservation for Dominant Domestic Carrier(s)	Air	Road	Rail	Competition and Price Regulation	Regulation of Industry Structure	Public Service Obligation, Regulated Customer Access	Government Ownership and Bailouts
United States	2.1	2.5	2.7	1.7	0.8	1.1	2.4	3.7	2.1	1.4	2.6	0.827486135	0.639225018	0.373642805	0.451764654
Japan	3.6	2.5	2.6	1.3	0.9	2.2	4.7	3.8	3.6	1.2	1.7	1.608383946	0.398000994	0.440217734	0.397295435
Germany	4.6	2.7	2.5	2.7	1.5	3.4	5.9	4.0	4.6	1.6	1.2	2.001897264	0.760787878	0.464155476	0.478902558
France	3.8	4.7	3.5	2.1	1.3	2.5	5.7	3.4	3.8	1.0	1.9	1.648319644	0.690636245	0.58446881	0.551299765
Italy	4.1	4.6	3.5	2.1	2.2	3.1	5.8	3.5	4.1	2.1	2.0	1.802392871	0.653592598	0.710903353	0.539211452
United Kingdom	3.7	2.7	1.7	2.3	2.8	1.9	4.7	4.4	3.7	1.9	0.9	1.41077272	0.838287495	0.998012427	0.190062094
Canada	3.4	2.5	1.9	0.7	1.2	2.3	4.7	3.2	3.4	1.4	1.8	1.634645345	0.316644254	0.4247025	0.304681501
Finland	4.0	4.4	1.4	2.4	1.2	3.4	6.0	2.8	4.0	2.1	1.9	1.854702305	0.722343477	0.560720801	0.32557426
Greece	4.2	4.7	3.4	1.5	2.2	3.8	5.9	3.0	4.2	2.4	2.1	1.95420938	0.461873888	0.714813349	0.543616231
Mexico	2.1	4.2	3.5	1.7	1.1	2.0	3.4	1.8	2.1	1.0	1.3	1.353502801	0.694882568	0.570964691	0.522586274
Netherlands	4.0	4.0	2.2	3.7	0.2	3.6	5.4	3.2	4.0	1.8	1.6	1.768005014	1.039911684	0.309726703	0.337963967
New Zealand	4.5	2.7	2.7	3.5	1.2	3.7	6.0	3.0	4.5	2.8	0.7	2.010288982	0.905292063	0.478973959	0.385442689
Norway	3.3	4.3	1.4	2.4	1.1	2.2	5.6	1.9	3.3	2.8	1.9	1.550070023	0.703961664	0.571637512	0.309285763
Portugal	4.2	4.7	3.4	1.5	2.2	3.9	5.9	3.1	4.2	1.4	1.9	1.927716035	0.537816601	0.712804139	0.52197316
Spain	3.7	4.7	3.6	2.9	1.0	2.5	5.6	3.1	3.7	1.2	1.9	1.682086662	0.927405698	0.473408351	0.55497655
Sweden	4.0	4.2	2.1	2.8	0.7	3.1	6.0	2.9	4.0	1.7	1.9	1.836297304	0.773933652	0.427582084	0.399262966
Switzerland	4.2	3.7	1.4	1.6	0.5	3.5	6.0	3.0	4.2	2.2	1.9	1.90027128	0.545283018	0.315114694	0.280302128
Turkey	4.1	4.8	1.3	1.6	2.2	3.7	5.8	3.3	4.1	2.3	1.9	1.740053875	0.631766305	0.758792739	0.343861905
Czech Rep.	3.8	4.7	1.3	1.7	1.3	3.8	5.9	1.9	3.8	1.5	1.4	1.976677595	0.599534062	0.47354244	0.250246189
Hungary	2.8	4.4	1.3	1.8	1.1	2.6	4.9	1.0	2.8	2.1	1.9	1.512782968	0.653479446	0.495375794	0.162857349
Korea, Rep. of	3.9	2.6	2.5	2.1	1.5	3.2	4.8	3.6	3.9	0.6	0.3	1.830529419	0.767582267	0.66823034	0.245312432
Poland	3.7	4.9	1.3	1.6	1.3	3.7	5.7	2.1	3.7	1.4	1.7	1.875180579	0.60420922	0.557323214	0.26365386

Note: Indexes, which range from 0 to 6, are based on rotated factor loadings. The overall index is based on the first factor for the summary indexes, with 90 percent of the variance explained.

Source: Author's calculations.

TABLE 4.8   Regulation Indexes, Road Transport

	Overall	Government Licensing	State Ownership/ Concessions	State Concession Requirements and Price Regulation	Regulatory Approval Required for Establishment	Other Regulations	Limits on Backhauling, Private Carriage, and Contract Carriage	Limits on Competition (Including Price Guidelines)
United States	1.4	4.7	1.9	1.3	1.8	1.2	0.8	1.7
Japan	1.2	4.7	1.4	2.3	0.6	1.4	0.5	1.7
Germany	1.6	4.6	2.3	1.2	2.1	1.3	1.2	2.4
France	1.0	4.9	3.5	1.1	0.3	1.3	0.5	1.7
Italy	2.1	4.4	1.6	3.9	1.8	2.0	0.7	1.5
United Kingdom	1.9	4.6	1.8	1.4	1.7	2.1	0.9	1.7
Canada	1.4	4.7	1.9	1.3	1.8	1.2	0.8	1.7
Finland	2.1	4.4	2.2	1.3	1.2	2.2	1.2	3.9
Greece	2.4	4.4	1.6	3.9	1.8	2.0	0.7	4.1
Mexico	1.0	4.8	1.7	1.2	1.8	0.2	0.7	3.4
Netherlands	1.8	4.5	1.8	1.4	1.0	2.1	0.8	2.9
New Zealand	2.8	3.0	1.8	1.4	2.7	2.1	0.0	1.7
Norway	2.8	3.2	3.9	1.1	2.2	2.3	0.2	2.1
Portugal	1.4	4.7	1.9	1.3	1.8	1.2	0.8	1.7
Spain	1.2	4.6	1.9	1.3	1.1	1.2	0.8	1.8
Sweden	1.7	4.5	1.8	1.4	1.0	2.1	0.8	1.7
Switzerland	2.2	1.8	1.8	1.6	0.6	1.4	0.9	3.4
Turkey	2.3	1.8	2.3	1.5	1.6	1.5	1.4	1.7
Czech Rep.	1.5	4.6	4.2	2.6	1.9	1.1	1.1	1.7
Hungary	2.1	4.6	1.8	1.4	1.7	2.1	0.9	3.2
Korea, Rep. of	0.6	4.7	1.7	1.2	1.1	0.2	0.6	1.7
Poland	1.4	4.5	4.2	2.6	1.2	1.1	1.0	1.7

Note: Indexes, which range from 0 to 6, are based on rotated factor loadings. The overall index is based on the first factor for the summary indexes, with 90 percent of the variance explained.

Source: Author's calculations.

TABLE 4.9 Regulation Indexes, Rail Transport

	Overall	Government Financial/ Operational Interventions	Government Ownership	Domestic Competition
United States	2.6	1.9	1.7	0.2
Japan	1.7	1.7	1.8	1.3
Germany	1.2	1.7	1.8	1.9
France	1.9	3.4	1.8	1.3
Italy	2.0	3.4	1.8	1.2
United Kingdom	0.9	2.2	0.3	1.3
Canada	1.8	1.9	1.7	1.2
Finland	1.9	1.3	2.2	1.3
Greece	2.1	3.0	2.2	1.3
Mexico	1.3	1.7	1.8	1.8
Netherlands	1.6	2.3	1.4	1.3
New Zealand	0.7	1.3	1.1	1.9
Norway	1.9	1.3	2.2	1.3
Portugal	1.9	3.4	1.8	1.3
Spain	1.9	3.4	1.8	1.3
Sweden	1.9	1.3	2.2	1.3
Switzerland	1.9	3.4	1.8	1.3
Turkey	1.9	3.4	1.8	1.3
Czech Rep.	1.4	3.4	1.8	1.9
Hungary	1.9	3.4	1.8	1.3
Korea, Rep. of	0.3	2.2	0.3	1.9
Poland	1.7	1.9	1.7	1.3

Note: Indexes, which range from 0 to 6, are based on rotated factor loadings. The overall index is based on the first factor for the summary indexes, with 90 percent of the variance explained.
Source: Author's calculations.

with that of the EU, as does air and rail (see figure 4.1, which compares Turkey with 21 other OECD members on the overall sector indexes).

Another set of indicators, for the transport sector broadly defined, is presented in table 4.10. Like those in tables 4.7, 4.8, and 4.9, these indicators are based on a factor analysis of the regulatory variables. In table 4.10, however, the full set of sector indicators in the previous three tables are combined to yield a set of four factors used to construct the composite index—that is, a set of overall regulatory indicators for competition, regulation of industry structure, public service obligations, and financial involvement of government—as well as an overall index, based on these four factors and aggregated using rotated factor loadings. These four factors explain roughly 90 percent of the regulatory variable variance, because they are constructed from sector indicators. For the overall index, the most

important summary indictor is competition and price regulation (37.4 percent), followed by regulation of industry structure (23.2 percent), public service obligations and regulation of customer access (22.5 percent), and indicators of government ownership and bailouts (16.9 percent).

The indexes in table 4.10 are summarized in figure 4.2. The figure presents a breakdown (based on the weights in table 4.10) of the contribution of each factor to the total index. Note the level of Turkey in relation to the average level for the EU. It reveals for all of transport, as it was for the individual subsector indicators, a rough congruence between the Turkish regulatory regime and the range of regimes tolerated by the European Union.

What do these indicators say? Overall, the regime in Turkey appears to be consistent with regimes existing within the EU, including, for example, Greece, Spain, Italy, Germany, and Portugal. Thus,

FIGURE 4.1   Comparison of Regulatory Regimes

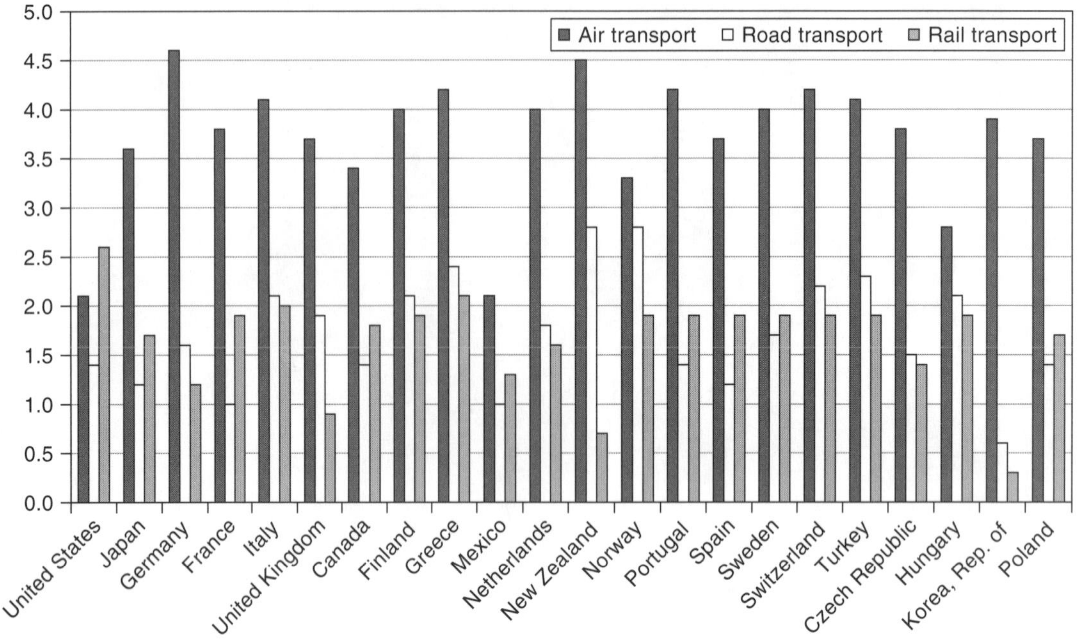

Source: The author.

TABLE 4.10   Regulation Indexes, All Transport

	Overall	Competition and Price Regulation	Regulation of Industry Structure	Public Service Obligation, Regulated Customer Access	Government Ownership and Bailouts
United States	2.3	2.2	2.8	1.7	2.7
Japan	2.8	4.3	1.7	2.0	2.4
Germany	3.7	5.3	3.3	2.1	2.8
France	3.5	4.4	3.0	2.6	3.3
Italy	3.7	4.8	2.8	3.2	3.2
United Kingdom	3.4	3.8	3.6	4.4	1.1
Canada	2.7	4.4	1.4	1.9	1.8
Finland	3.5	5.0	3.1	2.5	1.9
Greece	3.7	5.2	2.0	3.2	3.2
Mexico	3.1	3.6	3.0	2.5	3.1
Netherlands	3.5	4.7	4.5	1.4	2.0
New Zealand	3.8	5.4	3.9	2.1	2.3
Norway	3.1	4.1	3.0	2.5	1.8
Portugal	3.7	5.2	2.3	3.2	3.1
Spain	3.6	4.5	4.0	2.1	3.3
Sweden	3.4	4.9	3.3	1.9	2.4
Switzerland	3.0	5.1	2.3	1.4	1.7
Turkey	3.5	4.6	2.7	3.4	2.0
Czech Rep.	3.3	5.3	2.6	2.1	1.5
Hungary	2.8	4.0	2.8	2.2	1.0
Korea, Rep. of	3.5	4.9	3.3	3.0	1.5
Poland	3.3	5.0	2.6	2.5	1.6
Weight		0.374	0.232	0.225	0.169

Note: Indexes, which range from 0 to 6, are based on rotated factor loadings. The overall index is based on the first factor for the summary indexes, with 90 percent of the variance explained.

Source: Author's calculations.

FIGURE 4.2   Decomposition of Overall Transport Regulation Index

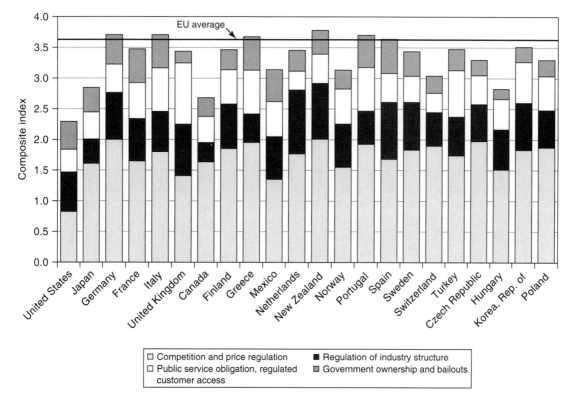

Source: The author.

given what is tolerated within the EU, there is no clear indication that Turkey will need to realign its regulatory stance upon accession to the EU. This situation probably reflects, in part, the country's already long history of regulatory alignment.

Summary and Conclusions

This chapter has explored the possible implications of Turkish accession to the EU, particularly regulatory issues in the transport sector in Turkey. The transport sector is important to the general conditions for economic performance and growth. Because it serves as an important intermediate input, both nationally and internationally, changes in the trade and regulatory regime of the sector can have important economic effects. The chapter has addressed two sets of issues. The first is the quantitative impact, through direct trade and economy-wide effects, of full membership. These effects have been examined through reference to computable general equilibrium analysis and partial equilibrium analysis. Because of the existence of the EU-Turkey customs union, deeper integration along this front does not appear to carry significant

threats of pressure for restructuring, surges in imports, or, as a consequence, significant income gains from the sector. The second set of issues involves regulatory convergence. Here, factor analysis of a database of regulatory variables indicates that, overall, the two regimes (Turkey and the EU) are broadly consistent in their regulatory stance (e.g., degree of competition, price regulation, government financial intervention). This consistency most likely reflects the long process of negotiation and regulation that has accompanied evolution of the customs union. It means as well that pressure to restructure for broad regulatory reasons may be minimal.

Annex 1: Tariff Equivalents for Transport Services

This annex describes a basic methodology for the estimation of sector-specific gravity equations in relation to global trade levels. The results are reported in table 4.11. Basically, services trade data are fitted to a simple gravity model of total imports by country. These equations have been estimated at the level of transport services.

TABLE 4.11 Regression Results for Gravity Equation on Cross-Border Trade

Regression Statistics		
Multiple R	0.967335	
R-square	0.935736	
Adjusted R-square	0.926556	
Standard error	0.179688	
Observations	25	

ANOVA					
	df	SS	MS	F	Significance F
Regression	3	9.872914	3.290971	101.9261	1.12E-12
Residual	21	0.678044	0.032288		
Total	24	10.55096			

	Coefficients	Standard Error	t Statistic
Intercept	2.48491	1.213893	2.04706
log(POP)	0.901064	0.064715	13.92348
LOG (PCGDP)	1.43188	0.693996	2.063239
log(PCGDP)sq	0.0585	0.098696	0.59275

Source: Author's calculations.

The gravity equations are estimated using ordinary least squares with the variables

(4.1) $$X_i = a_1 \cdot \ln(POP_i) + a_2 \cdot \ln(PCGDP)_i + a_3 \cdot \ln(PCGDP)_i^2 + \varepsilon_i$$

where X_i represents imports from the world, *POP* represents population, and *PCGDP* per capita income in the importing country.

In the regressions, Hong Kong (China) is broken out as a free trade "benchmark." Deviations from predicted imports, relative to this free trade benchmark, are taken as an indication of barriers to trade. These tariff equivalent rates are then backed out from a constant elasticity import demand function as follows:

(4.2) $$\frac{T_1}{T_0} = \left[\frac{M_1}{M_0} \right]^{1/e}$$

Here, T_1 is the power of the tariff equivalent $(1 + t_1)$ such that in free trade $T_0 = 1$, and $[M_1/M_0]$ is the ratio of actual to predicted imports (normalized relative to the free trade benchmark ratio for Hong Kong). In this reduced form, actual prices and constant terms drop out because ratios are formed. The term *e* is the demand elasticity (taken to be -3.9).

This approach yields an estimated tariff equivalent for Turkey's imports of transport services of 8.9 percent, and the EU data reveal no barriers to

cross-border trade in the sector at the EU15 level— that is, including all 15 member states. Barriers may emerge, however, at the level of individual member states (see Francois, van Meij, and van Tongeren forthcoming).

Annex 2: The Model

This annex describes the basic structure of the standard multiregion computable general equilibrium model used in this study. The model is implemented in GEMPACK, a software package designed for solving large applied general equilibrium models.[6] It is solved as an explicit nonlinear system of equations, using techniques described by Harrison, Horridge, and Pearson (2000).[7] The national accounts data were organized into 24 sectors and 29 regions. The sectors and regions for this 24 × 29 aggregation of the data are detailed in table 4.12.

The data were taken from various sources. Data on production and trade are based on national accounting data linked through trade flows and drawn directly from the GTAP Version 5 dataset (GTAP 2001; also see Reinert and Roland-Holst, 1997, for a discussion of the organization of such data for CGE models). The GTAP Version 5 dataset is benchmarked to 1997 and includes detailed national

TABLE 4.12 Sectoring Scheme of Model

Model Regions	Model Sectors
Australia and New Zealand	Grains
China	Other agriculture
Hong Kong (China)	Mining
Japan	Other primary production
Korea	Sugar
Taiwan	Dairy
Other ASEAN	Meats
Vietnam	Processed foods
Bangladesh	Textiles
India	Clothing
South Asia	Leather
Canada	Wood and paper
Mexico	Chemicals
United States	Refineries
Caribbean Basin Initiative countries	Steel
Andean Trade Pact	Nonferrous metals
MERCOSUR	Motor vehicles
Chile	Electronics
Other Latin America	Other machinery
European Union (EU15)	Manufactures, NEC
Central European Associates	Trade, transport, communications
Turkey	Construction
SACU	Business services
Botswana	Other services
Malawi	
Mozambique	
Rest of Southern Africa	
North Africa and Middle East	
Rest of world	

Note: ASEAN = Association of South East Asian Nations; MERCOSUR = Southern Cone Common Market (Mercado Común del Sur); SACU = Southern African Customs Union; NEC = not elsewhere classified.
Source: Author's definition of model aggregation.

input-output, trade, and final demand structures. Significant modifications were made to the basic GTAP database. The basic social accounting and trade data were supplemented with trade policy data, including additional data on tariffs and nontariff barriers. The dataset was also updated to better reflect actual import protection for goods and services (for example, the basic GTAP database includes no information at all on trade barriers for services).

General Structure

The general conceptual structure of a regional economy in the model is represented in figure 4.3. Within each region, firms produce output, employing

land, labor, and capital and combining these with intermediate inputs. Firm output is purchased by consumers, government, the investment sector, and other firms. Firm output also can be sold for export. Land is employed only in the agricultural sectors, while capital and labor (both skilled and unskilled) are mobile between all production sectors. Moreover, capital is fully mobile within regions. However, capital movements between regions are not modeled, but rather are held fixed in all simulations. Labor mobility is discussed below.

All demand sources combine imports with domestic goods to produce a composite good, as indicated in figure 4.3. These are Armington composites.

FIGURE 4.3   Armington Aggregation Nest

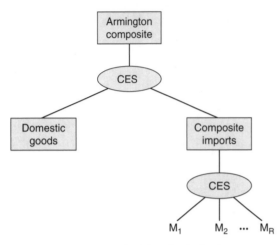

Note: CES = constant elasticity of substitution.
Source: The author.

Dynamics

An important feature of the model is a dynamic link, whereby the static or direct income effects of trade liberalization induce shifts in the regional pattern of savings and investment. These effects have been explored extensively in the trade literature, including Baldwin and Francois (1999), Smith (1976, 1977), and Srinivasan and Bhagwati (1980). Several studies of the Uruguay Round have also incorporated variations on this mechanism. Such effects compound initial output welfare effects over the medium run and can magnify income gains or losses. How much these "accumulation effects" will supplement static effects depends on various factors, including the marginal product of capital and underlying savings behavior. This application employs a classical savings-investment mechanism (Francois, McDonald, and Nordstrom 1997), which means modeling medium- to long-run linkages between changes in income, savings, and investment. The results reported here therefore include changes in the capital stock and the medium- to long-run implications of such changes.

Taxes and Policy Variables

Taxes are included in the theory of the model at several levels. Production taxes are placed on intermediate or primary inputs, or on output. Some trade taxes are modeled at the border. Additional internal taxes can be placed on domestic or imported intermediate inputs and may be applied at differential rates that discriminate against imports. Where relevant, taxes are also placed on exports and on primary factor income. Finally, where relevant (as indicated by social accounting data), taxes are placed on final consumption and can be applied differentially to consumption of domestic and imported goods.

Trade policy instruments are represented as import or export taxes/subsidies. This includes applied most-favored-nation tariffs, antidumping duties, countervailing duties, price undertakings, export quotas, and other trade restrictions. The one exception is services sector trading costs, which are discussed in the next section.

The basic data on current tariff rates are taken from the UN Conference on Trade and Development (UNCTAD) and WTO data on applied and bound tariff rates, and they are integrated into the core GTAP database. These data are supplemented with those from the U.S. Trade Representative (USTR) and U.S. International Trade Commission (USITC) on regional preference schemes in the Western Hemisphere. For agriculture, protection is based on OECD and U.S. Department of Agriculture (USDA) estimates of agricultural protection, as integrated into the GTAP core database. Tariff and nontariff barrier estimates are further adjusted to reflect the remaining Uruguay Round commitments, including the phasing out of the remaining textile and clothing quotas under the Agreement on Textiles and Clothing (ATC). Data on post–Uruguay Round tariffs are taken from recent estimates reported by Francois and Strutt (1999), which are taken, in turn, primarily from the WTO's integrated database, with supplemental information from the World Bank's recent assessment of detailed pre– and post–Uruguay Round tariff schedules. All of this tariff information was concorded to the model sectors. The services trade barriers are based on the estimates described in Annex 1.

Trade and Transport Costs

International trade is modeled as a process that explicitly involves trading costs, which include both trade and transportation services. These trading costs reflect the transaction costs of international trade, as well as the physical activity of transportation itself. Those trading costs related to the international movement of goods and related logistic services are met by composite services purchased from a global trade services sector in which the composite "international trade services" activity is produced as a Cobb-Douglas composite of regional exports of trade and transport services. Trade cost margins are based on reconciled free on board (FOB) and cost, insurance, and freight (CIF) trade data, as reported in Version 5 of the GTAP dataset.

A second form of trade costs, known in the literature as frictional trading costs, is implemented in the services sector. These costs represent the real resource costs associated with producing a service for sale in an export market instead of the domestic market. Conceptually, a linear transformation technology was implemented between domestic and export services. This technology is represented in figure 4.4. The straight line AB indicates, given the resources needed to produce a unit of services for the domestic market, the feasible amount that can instead be produced for export using those same resources. If there are no frictional barriers to trade in services, this line has a slope of 1. This free trade case is represented by the line AC. As trading costs fall, the linear transformation line converges on the free trade line, as indicated in the figure.

FIGURE 4.4 Trading Costs in the Services Sector

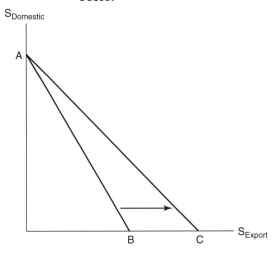

Source: The author.

Production Structure

The basic structure of production is depicted in figure 4.5. Intermediate inputs are combined, and this composite intermediate is in turn combined in fixed proportions with value added. This yields sector output Z.

Composite Household and Final Demand

Final demand is determined by an upper-tier Cobb-Douglas preference function that allocates income in fixed shares to current consumption, investment, and government services. This process

FIGURE 4.5 Basic Features of the Simulation Model

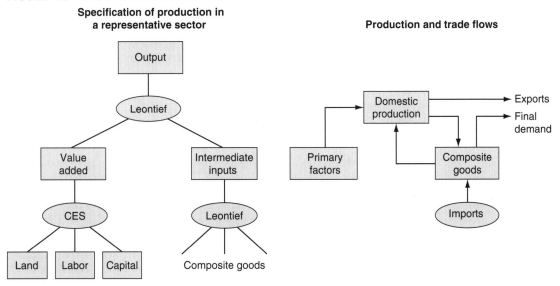

Note: CES = constant elasticity of substitution.
Source: The author.

yields a fixed savings rate. Government services are produced by a Leontief technology, with house-hold/government transfers being endogenous. The lower-tier nest for current consumption is also specified as a CDE (constant difference of elasticities) demand function. The regional capital markets adjust so that changes in savings match changes in regional investment expenditures. (Note that the Cobb-Douglas demand function is a special case of the CDE demand function, as is the CES or constant elasticity of demand specification. The Cobb-Douglas version of the CDE is implemented through GEMPACK parameter files.)

Labor Markets

The default closure involves modeling labor markets as clearing with flexible wages. This fits with the "long-run" approach in which labor markets tend to be more flexible. A situation is specified in which the basic structural rigidities of labor markets (and the aggregate employment levels implied) are unaffected by the simulations in the long run. However, in implementation the mobility of labor between sectors is slightly "sluggish" in the sense that there is not a perfectly linear transform technology for the movement of labor between sectors. The implementation of sluggish factor mobility represents the assumption that, for institutional reasons (and because some skills are sector-specific), labor is not fully flexible in its application across sectors. This representation of labor markets seems reasonable. To the extent that wage rigidities are important, the direction of aggregate employment effects may be inferred from wage effects. (Hertel, 1996, refers to this as "sluggish" factor movements). A theoretical discussion of factor mobility, along the lines developed in Hertel and employed here, can be found in Casas (1984). In practice, the transformation elasticities are set very high (25.0), but not infinitely so. This effectively allows for almost full mobility.

Notes

1. One might say that, in the eyes of the EU, when it comes to trading partners, "Everybody is special and unique, just like everybody else."

2. The procedures for implementing the final phase of the customs union in industrial products are set out in the *Official Journal of the European Communities* 13.02.95 L 035, and in a bilateral steel agreement.

3. Decision No. 1/98 of the EC–Turkey Association Council, February 25, 1998, on the trade regime for agricultural productions (98/223/EC).

4. See Francois, McQueen, and Wignaraja (2003; technical annex) for a detailed discussion of the model. Also see the related background report cited therein.

5. All dollar amounts are U.S. dollars unless otherwise indicated.

6. See Hertel (1996: chap. 2) for a detailed discussion of the basic algebraic model structure represented by the GEMPACK code. The capital accumulation mechanisms are described in Francois, McDonald, and Nordstrom (1996).

7. More information can be obtained at http://www.monash.edu.au/policy/gempack.htm. Social accounting data are based on Version 5 of the GTAP dataset (GTAP 2001), with an update to reflect post–Uruguay Round protection.

References

Baldwin, R. E., and J. F. Francois. 1997. "The Costs and Benefits of Eastern Enlargement: The Impact on the EU and Central Europe." *Economic Policy* 12 (24): 125–76.

———. 1999. *Applied Issues in Dynamic Commercial Policy Analysis.* Cambridge: Cambridge University Press.

Boylaud, O. 2000. "Regulatory Reform in Road Freight and Retail Distribution." Economics Department Working Paper No. 225, Organisation for Economic Co-operation and Development, Paris, August.

Casas, F. R. 1984. "Imperfect Factor Mobility: A Generalization and Synthesis of Two-Sector Models of International Trade." *Canadian Journal of Economics* 17(4).

Francois, J. F., and A. Strutt. 1999. "Post Uruguay Round Tariff Vectors for GTAP Version 4." Manuscript, Erasmus University.

Francois, J. F., B. McDonald, and H. Nordstrom. 1996. "Trade Liberalization and the Capital Stock in the GTAP Model." GTAP consortium technical paper, http://www.agecon.purdue.edu/gtap/techpapr/tp-7.htm.

———. 1997. "Capital Accumulation in Applied Trade Models." In *Applied Methods for Trade Policy Analysis: A Handbook,* ed. J. F. Francois and K. A. Reinert. Cambridge: Cambridge University Press.

Francois, J. F., M. McQueen, and G. Wignaraja. 2003. "An Overview of EU FTAs." Paper presented at the Vienna World Economics Institute Workshop on WTO Issues, April.

Francois, J. F., H. van Meij, and F. van Tongeren. 2005. "Trade Liberalization under the Doha Round." *Economic Policy* 20(42): 349–390.

GTAP (Global Trade Analysis Project). 2001. "The GTAP Version 5 Dataset." Centre for Global Trade Analysis, Purdue University.

Harrison, G., D. Rutherford, and D. Tarr. 1997. "Economic Implications for Turkey of a Customs Union with the European Union." *European Economic Review* 41 (3–5): 861–70.

Harrison, W. J., J. M. Horridge, and K. Pearson. 2000. "Decomposing Simulation Results with Respect to Exogenous Shocks." *Computational Economics* 15: 227–49.

Hertel, T., ed. 1996. *Global Trade Analysis.* Cambridge: Cambridge University Press.

Nicoletti, G., S. Scarpetta, and O. Boylaud. 1999. "Summary Indicators of Product Market Regulation with an Extension to Employment Protection Legislation." Economics Department

Working Paper No. 226, Organisation for Economic Co-operation and Development, Paris.

Reinert, K. A., and D. W. Roland-Holst. 1997. "Social Accounting Matrices." In *Applied Methods for Trade Policy Analysis: A Handbook,* ed. J. F. Francois and K. A. Reinert. New York: Cambridge University Press.

Smith, M. A. M. 1976. "Trade, Growth, and Consumption in Alternative Models of Capital Accumulation." *Journal of International Economics* 6 (November): 385–88.

————. 1977. "Capital Accumulation in the Open Two-Sector Economy." *Economic Journal* 87 (June): 273–82.

Srinivasan, T. N., and J. N. Bhagwati. 1980. "Trade and Welfare in a Steady-State." In *Flexible Exchange Rates and the Balance of Payments*, ed. J. S. Chipman and C. P Kindelberger, chap. 12. Amsterdam: North-Holland Publishing.

WTO (World Trade Organization). 1998. *Trade Policy Review: European Union 1997.* Geneva: WTO.

5

THE TURKISH TELECOMMUNICATIONS SECTOR: A COMPARATIVE ANALYSIS

Erkan Akdemir, Erdem Başçi, and Gareth Locksley

The telecommunications industry has many interesting aspects.[1] First, it is a network industry, with high fixed costs and low marginal costs. Second, it is subject to rapid technological progress. Third, it serves as the infrastructure for the information society and knowledge economy. Finally, it provides direct utility to the end users of telecommunications services.

The first aspect—the telecommunications industry as a network industry—has been a challenge to both economic theorists and policymakers in general. How to maintain an efficient outcome by an appropriate mix of competition and regulation policies is still an active research area (e.g., Baumol and Sidak 1994; Laffont and Tirole 1996, 2000; Armstrong 1997, 1998; Shy 2001). The legal and regulatory arrangements have been evolving quite fast in the last decade as well (e.g., World Bank 2000; OECD 2003; 1997 and 2002 *acquis communautaire* of the European Union on telecommunications services). Turkey has already adopted the 1998 *acquis* of the European Union (EU) in telecommunications, and it has shown some progress in regulatory capacity building and liberalization of mobile phone (GSM) services. A crucial milestone was reached in May 2004, when the first licenses for the provision of voice telephony services by alternative operators were issued.

The second and third aspects of the telecommunications industry—its rapid technological progress and its role in providing the infrastructure for the information society and knowledge economy—are central to investments and economic development. Private investments are becoming the main source of technology development and capacity building in the telecommunications industry. Licensing and privatization are the two main channels to attracting initial private capital and paving the way for further investments. Human capital formation and innovation are facilitated by means of sharing knowledge at almost no cost. The easy interaction between universities and research institutions also encourages research and innovation. Moreover, easy access to networks promotes social cohesion and inclusiveness. Finally, government-citizen and government-business relations are simplified through e-government projects. In this area, Turkey has signed the eEurope+ 2003 Action Plan along with other EU candidate countries. Some progress has been made in areas of liberalization and licensing, but very little progress has been made in privatization.

The fourth aspect of the telecommunications industry—its direct utility to the end users of telecommunications services—can be measured roughly by the share of telecommunications spending of households as a fraction of gross domestic product (GDP). Other indicators are per capita number of fixed plus mobile lines (teledensity) and Internet use and the urban-rural teledensity ratio. In some of these measures, Turkey has shown substantial progress; in others, it is still lagging behind.

The focus in recent years, however, has shifted from building infrastructure to regulatory and market structure issues. For example, using data from 23 Organisation for Economic Co-operation and Development (OECD) countries over the 1991–97 period, Boylaud and Nicoletti (2000) find significant price, quality, and productivity effects for both *prospective* and *effective* competition. They measure prospective competition by the number of years remaining until liberalization and measure effective competition by the share of new entrants or by the number of competitors. Legal competition in fixed lines became effective in Turkey as of January 2004.

Likewise, a recent paper by Fink, Mattoo, and Rathindran (2002) based on data from 86 developing countries finds that both the privatization and liberalization of fixed lines significantly increase mainline penetration and productivity. They also show that competition without privatization is not significant on these two performance measures. The sequencing also matters. According to Fink and his colleagues, simultaneous privatization and competition have a greater impact on mainline penetration than the privatization-before-competition scenario. The estimated quantitative impact of complete reform is 8 percent higher mainline penetration and 21 percent higher productivity compared with the case of no reform.

This chapter is organized as follows. The first section gives a quantitative comparison of recent indicators for price, quantity, and quality of various services for Turkey, EU member countries, and EU accession countries. The second section summarizes developments in the liberalization and regulation of the sector, and the third discusses the brief history of the privatization process for Türk Telekom. A comparison of the legal infrastructure and institutional aspects of Turkey's telecom sector with those of the EU follows in the fourth section. The concluding section provides an overview of needs assessment in market structure, legislative, regulatory, and taxation issues in light of EU accession and the eEurope+ Action Plan.

A Quantitative Comparison

Broadly speaking, the Turkish telecommunications sector is comparable with those of the accession countries[2] that have with a similar level of GDP. Turkey scores better in terms of total teledensity and the urban-rural teledensity ratio, but lags behind in Internet usage.

The total expenditure on telecommunications services constitutes a significant portion of GDP in both EU members and candidate countries. Figure 5.1 shows this statistic to be about 3 percent for both Turkey and candidate countries and slightly lower for EU members.

Figure 5.2 shows that in terms of fixed-line telephones per household, Turkey scores better than both the candidate countries and the EU. However, in terms of the fixed-line penetration rate (i.e., the number of fixed lines per 100 inhabitants) Turkey seems to lag behind (figure 5.3). The striking difference between figures 5.2 and 5.3 can be attributed to the large families in Turkey. Therefore, the relatively low penetration rate in fixed lines need not be seen as a deficiency.

The urban-rural teledensity ratio (Istanbul versus the rest of the country) is shown in figure 5.4. This figure reflects the fact that most of the investments of Türk Telekom were carried out with the implicit understanding that it would provide universal service throughout the country. The figure also is indicative of the significant investments

FIGURE 5.1   Telecommunications Revenue in GDP

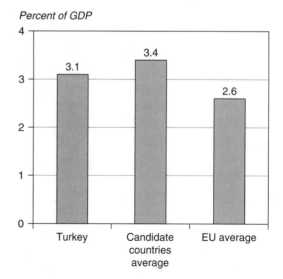

Percent of GDP

Source: ITU 2001.

FIGURE 5.2   Households with Fixed-Line Telephone Service

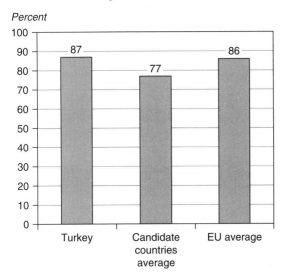

Source: eEurope+ 2003.

FIGURE 5.3   Fixed-Line Penetration Rates
(fixed lines per 100 inhabitants)

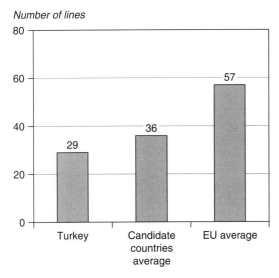

Source: eEurope+ 2003.

FIGURE 5.4   Largest City/Overall Country Teledensity Ratio

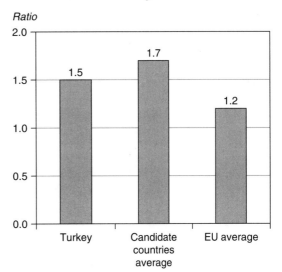

Source: ITU 2001.

FIGURE 5.5   Investment in Telecommunications

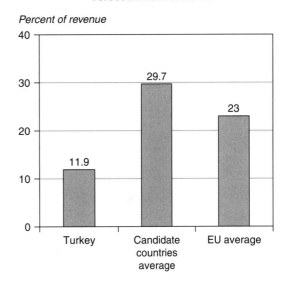

Source: ITU 2001.

made by Türk Telekom during the 1980s. In 1980 the ratio of Türk Telekom investments to the gross national product (GNP) was about 0.3 percent. This ratio steadily increased to 1 percent of GNP in 1987. Afterward, it sharply declined and fell back on average to about 0.3 percent during the second half of the 1990s (Yılmaz 2000). The significant slowdown in investments by TT brought stagnation in improvements in the fixed-line teledensity.

Figure 5.5 also supports the investment slowdown reported by Yılmaz (2000). The slowdown can be attributed largely to the financial squeeze in the government's budget and the use of TT profits to contribute to the primary budget surplus of the general government under the International Monetary Fund (IMF) program.

The mobile penetration rate is also significant. According to figure 5.6, Turkey has a mobile

FIGURE 5.6   Mobile Penetration Rates
(per 100 inhabitants)

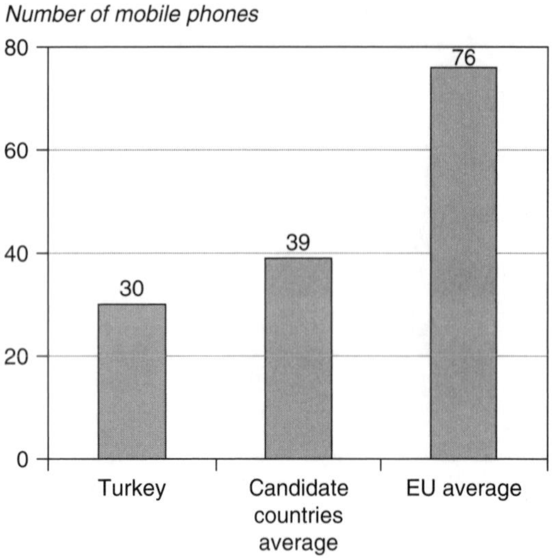

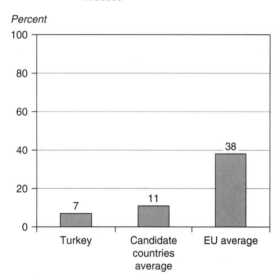

Number of mobile phones

Source: eEurope+ 2003.

FIGURE 5.8   Regular Users of Internet in Population

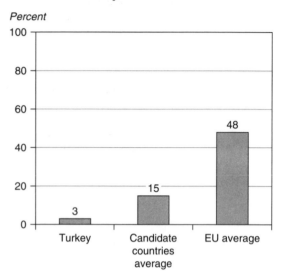

Percent

Source: eEurope+ 2003.

FIGURE 5.7   Households with Internet Access

Percent

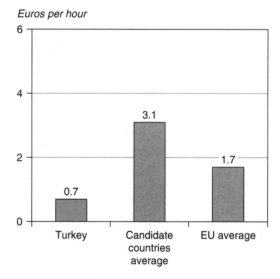

Source: eEurope+ 2003.

FIGURE 5.9   Internet Access Costs
(purchasing power standard [PPS]–adjusted)

Euros per hour

Source: eEurope+ 2003.

penetration rate comparable with that of the candidate countries. Given Turkey's population, this rate translates into a large mobile market in Europe.

In line with the 2002 *acquis* and the eEurope+ 2003 Action Plan, Internet use and related data services are also important. Figures 5.7 and 5.8 indicate that both the Internet availability per household and Internet use per individual are low in Turkey compared with the rates even in the candidate countries. There are two possible explanations for this observation. One is related to the

price of Internet services, and the second is related to the availability of Internet facilities—that is, data lines and personal computers (PCs).

Figure 5.9 shows that the cost of connecting to the Internet is significantly lower in Turkey than in the other countries. Connection prices are less than half of the EU average and less than a quarter of the candidate countries' average. Thus the only possible obstacle to use of the Internet in Turkey would be the availability of PCs. Although significant progress has been achieved in recent years, mobile Internet technologies serve a niche market and do not seem to contribute to Internet penetration.

Likewise, figures 5.10 and 5.11 show Turkey as an outlier to the negatively sloped demand curve on cost versus use of the Internet.

In Turkey, the PC penetration is low—only about 4 PCs per 100 persons, compared with about

FIGURE 5.10   Regular Use versus Dial-up Access Costs of Internet
(cost per hour, PPS–adjusted)

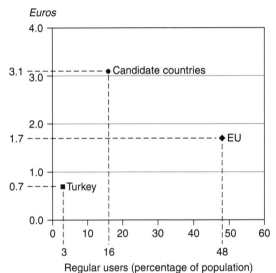

Source: eEurope+ 2003.

FIGURE 5.11   Penetration versus Dial-up Access Costs of Internet
(cost per hour in euros, PPS–adjusted)

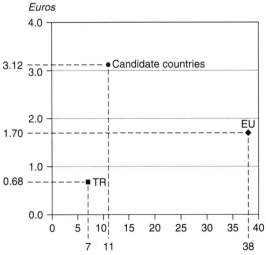

Source: eEurope+ 2003.

FIGURE 5.12   Personal Computer Use
(estimated number of PCs per 100 inhabitants)

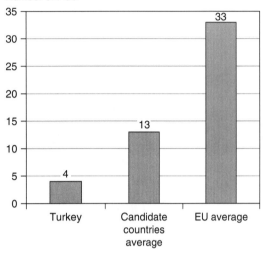

Source: eEurope+ 2003.

13 PCs for candidate countries and 33 PCs for the EU member states (figure 5.12). Therefore, low Internet use can be linked to low PC penetration rates in Turkey. The 2002 "Progress Report" of eEurope+ 2003 (2003) elaborates on the low PC use in primary, secondary, and higher education in Turkey. The same document also points out that Turkey does not have any public Internet access points (PIAPs or telecenters).[3]

As for the prices of fixed-line telephone services, both Turkey and other candidate countries have relatively high call rates and relatively low fixed monthly fees (see figure 5.13 for a comparison of the fixed monthly access fees). Turkey, with an average monthly fee of about €4, is below the averages of both the EU and candidate countries. The country-specific fixed access fees are reported in tables 5.1 and 5.2 in the chapter annex.

Figure 5.14 compares local call rates. Turkey's price is slightly above the average for the candidate countries and significantly above the EU average. Turkey's position can be attributed to Türk Telekom's monopoly in fixed-line services. The country-specific local charges are given in tables 5.1 and 5.2 in the chapter annex as well.

One measure of quality of service is faults per 100 main lines per year. In this area, Turkey scores worse than both the candidate and EU countries (see figure 5.15).

FIGURE 5.13   Residential Monthly Access Fee (Including Value Added Tax) for Fixed-Line Telephone Service

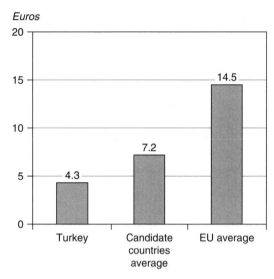

Source: World Bank 2002.

FIGURE 5.14   Cost (Including Value Added Tax) of a Three-Minute Economy Local Call

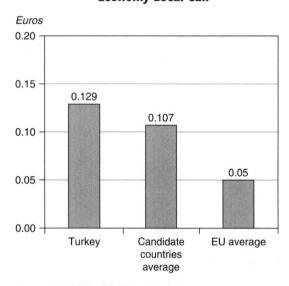

Source: World Bank 2002.

FIGURE 5.15   Quality of Service
(faults per 100 main lines per year)

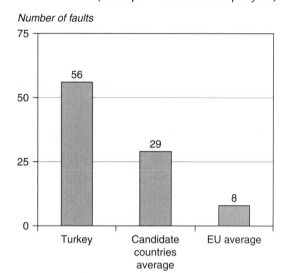

Source: ITU 2001.

FIGURE 5.16   International Telephone Traffic
(minutes per subscriber)

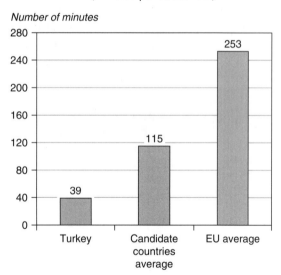

Source: ITU 2001.

In the final measure—international calling—Turkey, possibly because of its high international tariffs, ranks far behind both the candidate and EU countries.

Competition Policy and Regulation

As of January 2004, Turkey's telecommunications sector was fully open to competition, making Turkey the last of the OECD countries to fully liberalize its sector. To this end, in 1998 the Turkish government had committed itself, in accordance with World Trade Organization (WTO) guidelines, to liberalize its fixed-line telephone network and services no later than the end of 2004. However, the telecommunications law (No. 4502) enacted in January 2000 shifted the liberalization timetable to the end of 2003.

After taking the important step of opening up fixed lines for competition, the government addressed the institutional capacity of the independent Telecommunications Authority (TA), Telekomünikasyon Kurumu. The TA was established by the 2000 telecommunications law. Some criticism was directed at the authority's initial composition and the excessive amount of power that it was given to apply sanctions if national security or public order were imperiled (OECD 2002; Goldstein 2003). Nevertheless, the secondary legislation was broadly completed by the TA before January 2004.

In fact, limited competition had been under way in mobile phone services since 1994, when two private firms, Turkcell and Telsim, were given the rights to offer GSM services through revenue-sharing agreements with Türk Telekom. In 1998 the government sold the two operators licenses, by means of a concession agreement, to operate their GSM 900 networks for 25 years in return for US$500 million apiece.[4]

In April 2000, the Ministry of Transportation tendered two new GSM 1800 licenses by means of concession agreements. A third license was reserved for Türk Telekom at the price of the first auction. Because of the auction design, only one of the licenses was sold, but the revenue generated was higher than expected. İşbank-Telecom Italia Mobile (TIM) consortium (Aria) won the first auction with a bid of $2.5 billion. This number was then the minimum price for the second auction, and thus the auction attracted no bidders.[5] Türk Telekom decided to launch its own GSM 1800 operator, Aycell. As of the end of 2003, the four GSM operators—Turkcell, Telsim, Aria, and Aycell—had market shares of 68 percent, 18 percent, 7 percent, and 7 percent, respectively. The two small operators, Aria and Aycell, merged in 2004 under TT-İşbank-TIM with the brand name Avea.

Privatization of Türk Telekom

The already delayed privatization of Türk Telekom bears urgency, because competition between the company and potential private entrants will not be easy. Some of the difficulties facing Türk Telekom in its competition with others are as follows:

- Turkey's Treasury does not permit the state-owned corporation to borrow funds for investments.
- Only a small fraction of net profits can be used for investments.[6]

- As a state-owned corporation, Türk Telekom would find it difficult to undertake risky and ambitious projects and restructuring plans.

Since 1994, when the postal and telecommunications services of the General Directorate of Post, Telegraph, and Telephone (PTT) were separated, various attempts have been made to privatize Türk Telekom. Earlier attempts were turned down by the Supreme Court. After addressing the legal issues more carefully, the government offered a tender in 2000 that left 51 percent of the shares with the Treasury, but it was not successful in part because of poor market conditions in the telecommunications sector worldwide. Law No. 4673 of May 2001 left a golden share of Türk Telekom to the Treasury, which means, in fact, to one strong member of the board of directors. Türk Telekom employees are entitled to 5 percent of the shares, and the remaining are available for block sale or for initial public offerings (IPOs). The restriction on foreign ownership was removed by the foreign direct investment law of 2004.

In December 2003, the Council of Ministers adopted a new privatization plan for Türk Telekom. The plan called for a block sale of 51 percent of shares in 2004. Since then, the valuation committee and the tender committee have been preparing for that sale. Law No. 5189 of July 2004 provided further amendments to foster the privatization process.

Legal and Institutional Comparisons with the EU

The most recent legal development in the EU is the acceptance of the 2002 *acquis* in telecommunications. The European Parliament and the European Council approved and published a set of new directives in 2002. The directives considered here are the framework directive, authorization directive, access directive, and universal service directive. This section, in light of the EU directives, describes the recent progress of Turkey in each area. It also compares price regulation practices in EU and Turkey.

Framework

The purpose of the 2002 EU legislation is to provide a common regulatory framework and competition principles and practices for the electronic communications sector, comprising telecommunications, media, and information technology services (the framework does not regulate content). The purpose of introducing the new directives is to address the technological convergence observed in these three sectors. Under the framework directive,

- Member states are to guarantee the independence of the national regulatory authority (NRA).
- Telecommunication service providers have the right of appeal against NRA decisions.
- NRAs are responsible for the gathering and dissemination of sector-related information.
- All potential service providers have the right to install facilities in a timely, nondiscriminatory, and transparent manner.
- Facility sharing among service providers is normally voluntary, but the NRAs can also make it compulsory under exceptional circumstances.
- NRAs are responsible for identifying service providers that have a "significant market power" in the relevant market.
- In cases in which significant market power is identified, the NRAs are supposed to impose regulations ex ante on the company with significant market power.
- If access and interconnection negotiations between companies fail, the NRA resolves the dispute within four months.

In Turkey, an important reform process began in 2000 in the telecommunications sector. The previous legislation, which dates back to 1924, was amended. The new legislation is broadly compatible with the EU perspective. In June 2001, Turkey, along with the other EU candidate countries, was a signatory to the eEurope+ Action Plan by which it committed itself to achieving certain measurable goals in the electronic communications sector.

Authorization

The most recent EU document on licensing and related issues is the authorization directive (2002/20/EC). The objective of the directive is

> to create a legal framework to ensure the *freedom to provide electronic communication networks and services,* subject only to the conditions laid down in this Directive and to any restrictions in

conformity with Article 46(1) of the Treaty, in particular, measures regarding public policy, public security and public health. (Emphasis added.)

A general authorization is available for every service provider. Yet the member states may at most require a notification from the service provider. Other than the notification, no permissions or other administrative barriers to entry will be imposed (Article 3.2). In cases in which there is a technical need to limit the number of rights of use granted, such as the allocation of radio frequencies, the selection criteria must be objective, transparent, nondiscriminatory, and proportionate. Time limits are imposed on the administration to finalize the applications (Articles 5.2, 7.4).

Although obtaining a general authorization is as simple as it can be, an undertaking that does not comply with the general conditions laid down by the NRAs may be subject to financial penalties and even be prevented from providing service (Article 10).

In Turkey, the government monopoly on fixed-line services dates back to 1924 and the telegram and telephone law (No. 406). This monopoly ended, however, at the beginning of 2004 under the telecommunications law (No. 4502). Licensing was mentioned in legal arrangements for the first time in 1995, when a value added telecommunications services regulation was enacted. In 2000 the telecommunications law brought with it a new approach to licensing. Based on this approach, the Ministry of Transportation issued a new telecommunications services regulation.

In May 2001, by means of Law No. 4673, the right to issue licenses was transferred to the Telecommunications Authority. Accordingly, the TA published a Licensing Communiqué in 2002. The communiqué states the conditions to be met by applicants, the time limits, and the other procedural details for issuing licenses. The minimum license fees are determined by the Council of Ministers. These fees are broadly consistent with the average administrative fees set in the EU.

In 2002, new licenses were issued by the TA. These were general authorizations and telecommunications licenses for some existing Internet service provider, very small aperture terminal, and satellite platform operators. The licenses for long-distance telephony operators have been issued since

May 2004. Although some applications for telecommunications services, such as fixed wireless access, are outstanding, the TA is expected to issue licenses in the fourth quarter of 2004.

The 2000 telecommunications law contains clauses on licensing with four types of authorization: (1) authorization agreement, (2) concession agreement, (3) telecommunications license, and (4) general authorization. The approach in the EU is general authorization and allocation rules for individual licenses for radio frequencies based on competitive principles. In Turkey, the four different arrangements for licensing are confusing and difficult to implement.

The latest telecommunications services regulation should be updated to reflect changes in legislation (mainly Law No. 4502 and No. 4673). Authorization agreements and concession agreements could be converted to individual licenses, and telecommunications licenses could be converted to general authorizations or permits. Revenue share agreements also could be converted to licenses. There is no genuine license concept in current arrangements because the TA can change license conditions unilaterally.

Access

The most recent EU documents regulating access to the network of other firms are the access directive (2002/19/EC) and the regulation on unbundled access to the local loop (No. 2887/2000). The access directive defines *access* as "the making available of facilities and/or services, to another undertaking, under defined conditions, on either an exclusive or non-exclusive basis, for the purpose of providing electronic communication services" and *interconnection* as

> the physical and logical linking of public communications networks used by the same or a different undertaking in order to allow the users of one undertaking to communicate with users of the same or another undertaking, or to access services provided by another undertaking. . . . Interconnection is a specific type of access implemented between public network operators.

Local loop unbundling is based on the definition in the local loop regulation in which the "'local loop' is the physical twisted metallic pair circuit in the fixed public telephone network connecting the network termination point at the subscriber's premises to the main distribution frame or equivalent facility."

The access directive establishes the rights and obligations of operators regarding interconnections and access. It also defines the NRA objectives and procedures regarding access. The main points are as follows:

- Private negotiations between undertakings for interconnections cannot be restricted by member states.
- Operators cannot be obliged to discriminate between different undertakings for equivalent service.
- Operators are obliged to negotiate interconnection when others ask for it.
- The NRAs can impose, when necessary, obligations on an operator to facilitate interconnections.
- The obligations may be imposed only on an objective, transparent, proportionate, and nondiscriminatory basis.
- With the permission of the European Commission, the NRAs can impose additional measures related to access on operators with significant market power.

Likewise, the local loop unbundling regulation aims to facilitate access to the "least competitive segments of the liberalized telecommunications market." It is recognized that the new entries will be difficult, given the high costs of fixed-line infrastructure, and that the existing infrastructure has been financed by monopoly rents. Yet the eEurope+ Action Plan, in order to substantially reduce the costs of using the Internet, identifies unbundled access to the local loop as a short-term priority.

According to the local loop unbundling regulation, the NRA has the following responsibilities:

- To identify *notified operators* (NOs) as those that have significant market power in fixed public telephone networks
- To ask NOs to publish a reference offer for unbundled access to their local loops and related facilities
- To supervise NOs in their cost-based pricing and in providing other operators with transparent, fair, and nondiscriminatory unbundled access to the local loop.

The clauses in Turkey's Law No. 4502 on interconnection and roaming are in harmony with the EU *acquis*. The law also includes a dispute resolution mechanism for interconnection via the TA. However, no direct legal basis exists for local loop unbundling. The secondary legislation for national roaming, interconnection, and local loop unbundling were put in place in 2002, 2003, and 2004, respectively.

Universal Service

Universal service is defined in the 2002 *acquis* as "the provision of a defined minimum set of services to all end-users at an affordable price." The EU views universal service as an obligation of its member states (see Article 3.1 of the universal service directive). However, care is taken not to distort the market mechanism while safeguarding the public interest (Article 3.2).

The minimum service requirements in the universal service directive can be summarized as the provision of

- Access to a fixed telephone at every reasonable fixed location
- Directory inquiry services and directories
- Public pay phones
- Special measures for disabled users
- Affordable tariffs
- Adequate quality of service
- Number portability.

How much of the obligation of universal service that should be allocated on the service providers has been greatly debated (see, e.g., Choné, Flochel, and Perrot 2002 for a theoretical investigation). The universal service directive of the 2002 *acquis* imposes certain obligations on all undertakings, including the competitive ones, but it imposes extra obligations on firms with significant market power (Articles 16–19). Nevertheless, the financing of an important part of the universal service obligations is left to the member states (Articles 12–14).

In Turkey, universal service is covered by various laws, but no explicit mechanism is in place. The Ministry of Transportation is responsible for universal service policy, and the burden is carried mostly by Türk Telekom. As for the rights of users, the legislation contains no solid regulation, except for the general consumer rights protection law.

Thus the main and secondary legislation for universal service needs to be put in place, and new programs should be developed for a low-user scheme and special needs. As for financing the burden of the universal service organization, a fund or a budgetary mechanism must be established.

Price Regulation

According to the EU *acquis*, only firms with significant market power can be regulated. The same principle carries over to the telecommunications services. National regulatory authorities are supposed to define the relevant markets and then, in each relevant market, determine the presence of firms with SMP. Where SMP exists, the NRA would implement price regulation.

The economics literature discusses two possible ways of price regulation: price cap regulation and rate of return (or cost plus) regulation. For price cap regulation, the regulator determines a "reasonable price" for the base year and then for the following years applies a consumer price index (CPI) inflation − X percent adjustment on the base year's price. Price cap regulation is desirable because it provides an incentive for a firm to find ways to cut its production cost. The disadvantages are a greater need to regulate the quality of services and the difficulty encountered in setting the base price and the X factor—that is, the expected growth in productivity (see Weisman 2002 for an interesting discussion). Rate of return regulation also has negative aspects. First, the NRA must be cautious about the costs reported by the firm. Second, the incentives to improve productivity and thus cut costs are not there.

The trend in Europe, as well as in Australia, the United States, and South America, over the past 15 years has been toward implementing price cap regulation (Weisman 2002: 350). In Turkey, the price cap method is also used. Turkish telecom law has several clauses on price regulation. The 2001 Pricing (Tariff) Regulation and 2001 Price Cap Communiqué for SMP operators are in force. GSM tariffs are subject to price regulation based on the operators' concession agreements. But their X factor is fixed at 3 percent (CPI − 3 percent [CPI]), which is much lower than that of Türk Telekom.

Türk Telekom is subject to price regulation as well. For the years 2002–03, the voice telephony services of TT were subject to an X factor of 7.5 percent, which was changed to 4 percent in 2004. By contrast, the leased-line tariffs price cap method was used for 2002. The TA approved cost-based tariffs for leased lines in 2004, which were in force by June 2004.

Another important issue lagging behind schedule for the TA and Türk Telekom is the rebalancing of the local, long-distance, and international prices of TT. Rebalancing is central to price regulation. The new structure, which is based on a monthly rental fee and a reduction in the tariffs of national and international calls in order to eliminate cross subsidy, came into effect in August 2004. A wholesale tariff is needed for resale and new entrants.

For GSM operators, the inconsistency between their concession agreements and tariff regulation should be removed. For operators with significant market power, a flexible price regulation similar to the one in the EU should be followed.

Conclusion and Recommendations

The liberalization of telecommunications services in the EU has had a substantial impact. During 1998–2002, the prices of telecommunications services fell substantially, ranging from 14 percent in residential national calls to 70 percent in international business calls (see figures 5.17 and 5.18 in the chapter annex). Turkey is also expected to benefit from a reduction in prices and increase in quality by adopting the EU regulatory framework and by liberalizing the market for fixed lines.

This chapter has shown that Turkey scores reasonably well when compared with the EU candidate countries in terms of the significance of telecommunications services in GDP, the mainline and mobile penetration rates, the urban to rural penetration rates (i.e., universal service), and Internet service prices. However, performance needs to be improved in some areas. Examples are investments in fixed lines such as fiber cables, Internet usage, tariff rebalancing by means of higher fixed access fees and lower marginal fees, and the quality of services offered by Türk Telekom.

Therefore, a clear need exists for a new, single telecommunications act that would update the century-old telegraph and telephone law (Law No. 406), eliminate conflicting clauses in the amending laws, and harmonize with EU regulations. The main problems facing Turkey are related to the implementation of the new legislation and, by implication, the quantitative targets. It is also important

that the TA be strengthened in its technical, legal, and economics capabilities. Finally, after full liberalization of the sector, the successful privatization of Türk Telekom would benefit not only the sector but also significantly benefit the Turkish economy.

Annex: Price Comparisons

FIGURE 5.17 Basket of National Calls

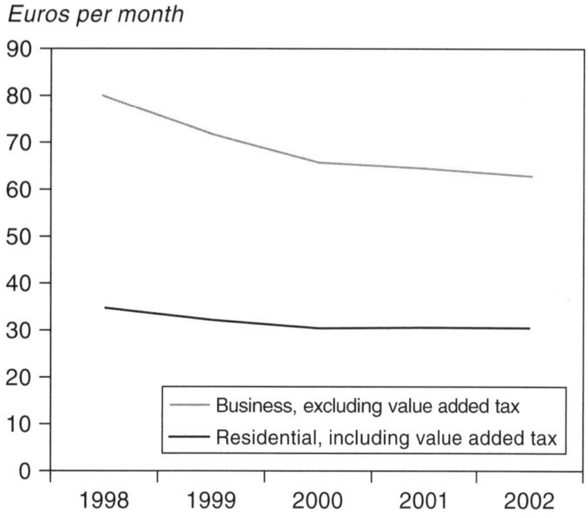

Euros per month

Note: Figure shows estimates of the average monthly spending by a typical "European business/residential user" for fixed national calls.

Source: European Commission 2002.

FIGURE 5.18 Basket of International Calls

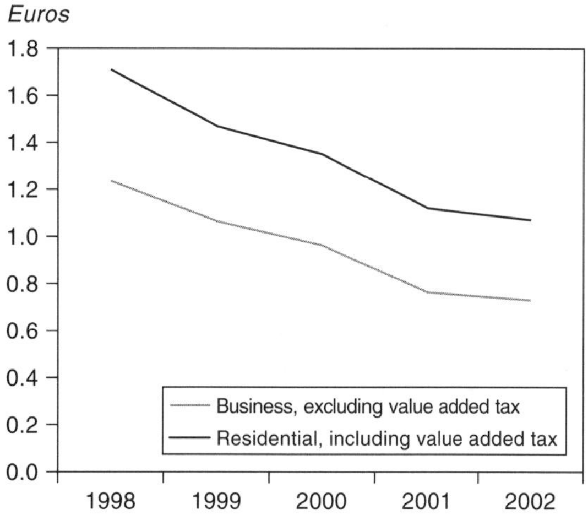

Euros

Note: Figure shows the average price of a single call from the originating country to all other OECD destinations. A full description of the methodology can be found in OECD 1990.

Source: European Commission 2002.

Annex:

TABLE 5.1 Monthly Residential Access Fee and Local Call Tariffs: 15 EU Member States and Washington, DC, July 1, 2002

Country	Monthly Residential Access Fee, Including Value Added Tax (euros)	Cost of Three-Minute Local Economy Call, Including Value Added Tax (euros)
Austria	17.44	0.09
Belgium	16.20	0.12
Denmark	15.74	0.08
Finland	13.79	0.16
France	12.55	0.13
Germany	12.69	0.05
Greece	11.77	0.09
Ireland	19.60	0.04
Italy	14.88	0.07
Luxembourg	18.40	0.05
Netherlands	16.42	0.07
Portugal	14.10	0.17
Spain	13.54	0.08
Sweden	13.25	0.08
United Kingdom	15.51	0.05
EU average	14.46	0.05
Washington, DC (Verizon), low-user, flat fee per call (excluding tax of $2.69 and other charges and levies of $6.00)	10.67	0.05

Source: World Bank 2002.

TABLE 5.2 Monthly Residential Access Fee and Local Call Charges: 13 EU Preaccession Countries (PAC), March 31, 2002

Country	Monthly Residential Access Fee, Including Value Added Tax (euros)	Cost of Three-Minute Local Economy Call, Including Value Added Tax (euros)
Bulgaria	3.00	0.022
Cyprus	9.50	0.076
Czech Republic	9.70	0.136
Estonia	5.90	0.096
Hungary	12.30	0.111
Latvia	6.30	0.143
Lithuania	5.50	0.130
Malta	5.30	0.132
Poland	11.80	0.970
Romania	3.50	0.940
Slovakia	5.90	0.141
Slovenia	9.90	0.084
Turkey	4.30	0.129
PAC average	*7.15*	*0.107*

Source: PWC Consulting 2002.

Notes

1. The authors would like to thank İzak Atiyas, Andrea Goldstein, Sübidey Togan, Kamil Yılmaz, Tolga Kılıç, and Şahin Ardıyok for their comments and encouragement. The usual disclaimer applies.

2. In this chapter, the term *accession* or *candidate countries* refers to the 10 countries that joined the EU in May 2004, together with Bulgaria and Romania.

3. PIAPs are government-initiated centers within the context of universal service policies.

4. All dollar amounts are U.S. dollars unless otherwise indicated.

5. The auction design for mobile phone service licenses is heavily discussed in the literature, especially after the so-called UMTS auction tragedy in Europe (UMTS is a third-generation mobile system). See Klemperer (2002) and van Damme (2002) for possible reasons why the UMTS auctions in Europe during 2000 and 2001 produced incredibly different outcomes.

6. See the paper by Li, Qiang, and Xu (2001) for cross-country evidence that supports the "cash cow" hypothesis, among other reasons, for delayed privatization of the telecommunications sector.

References

Armstrong, M., 1997. "Competition in Telecommunications." *Oxford Review of Economic Policy* 13: 64–82.

————. 1998. "Network Interconnections." *Economic Journal* 108: 545–64.

Baumol, W. J., and G. Sidak. 1994. *Toward Competition in Local Telephony.* Cambridge, MA: MIT Press.

Boylaud, O., and G. Nicoletti. 2000. "Regulation, Market Structure and Performance in Telecommunications." Economics Department Working Paper No. 237, Organisation for Economic Co-operation and Development, Paris.

Choné, P., L. Flochel, and A. Perrot. 2002. "Allocating and Funding Universal Service Obligations in a Competitive Market." *International Journal of Industrial Organization* 1247–76.

eEurope+ 2003. 2003. "eEurope+ Progress Report." Prepared by the EU membership candidate countries with the assistance of the European Commission, Ljubljana, June 3–4, 2002.

European Commission. 2002. "Eighth Report from the Commission on the Implementation of the Telecommunications Regulatory Package. COM(2002) 695. Brussels.

Fink, C., A. Mattoo, and R. Rathindran. 2002. "Liberalizing Basic Telecommunications: Evidence from Developing Countries." Paper presented at the OECD-World Bank Services Experts Meeting, Organisation for Economic Co-operation and Development, Paris.

Goldstein, A. 2003. "The Political Economy of Regulatory Reform: Telecoms in the Southern Mediterranean." Paper presented at the Fourth Mediterranean Social and Political Research Meeting, Florence-Montecatini Terme.

ITU (International Telecommunications Union). 2001. "World Telecommunications Indicator." March.

Klemperer, P. 2002. "How (Not) to Run Auctions: The European 3G Telecom Auctions." *European Economic Review* 46: 829–45.

Laffont, J. J., and J. Tirole. 1996. "Creating Competition through Interconnection: Theory and Practice." *Journal of Regulatory Economics* 10: 227–56.

————. 2000. *Competition in Telecommunications.* Cambridge, MA: MIT Press.

Li, W., C. Z. Qiang, and L. C. Xu. 2001. "The Political Economy of Privatization and Competition: Cross Country Evidence from Telecommunications Sector." World Bank, Washington, DC.

OECD (Organisation for Economic Development and Co-operation). 2002. "Regulatory Reform in the Turkish Telecommunications Industry." In *Review of Regulatory Reform in Turkey.* Paris: OECD.

————. 2003. *Communications Outlook.* Paris: OECD.

PWC Consulting. 2002. "1st Report on Monitoring of EU Candidate Countries (Telecommunication Services Sector)." July 25, Brussels.

Shy, O. 2001. *The Economics of Network Industries.* Cambridge: Cambridge University Press.

van Damme, E. 2002. "The European UMTS-Auctions." *European Economic Review* 46: 846–58.

Weisman, D. L. 2002. "Is There 'Hope' for Price Cap Regulation?" *Information Economics and Policy* 14: 349–70.

World Bank. 2000. *Telecommunications Regulation Handbook.* http://www.infodev.org/projects/314regulationhandbook.

————. 2002. *European Universal Service Atlas.* Washington, DC: World Bank.

Yılmaz, K. 2000. "Türk telekomünikasyon sektöründe reform: özelleştirme, düzenleme ve serbestleşme" [Reform in the Turkish Telecommunications Sector: Privatization, Regulation and Liberalization]. In *Devletin Düzenleyici Rolü* [The Regulatory Role of the State], ed. İzak Ati yas. Istanbul: TESEV Yayınları.

6

ACCESSION TO THE EUROPEAN UNION: POTENTIAL IMPACTS ON THE TURKISH BANKING SECTOR

Ceyla Pazarbaşıoğlu

Turkey's prospects of accession to the European Union (EU) are highly dependent on the progress made with political and economic reforms.[1] Of these reforms, financial sector–related issues are an important component of the criteria associated with full membership. Most of the issues are concentrated in the banking sector, because banks account for more than 90 percent of the total assets of the Turkish financial system.

Turkey adopted a comprehensive disinflation program, supported by the International Monetary Fund (IMF), at the beginning of 2000. Before adoption of this program, macroeconomic instability, crowding out by the public sector, systemic distortions created by state banks, inadequate risk assessment and management systems, and a lack of independent and effective supervision were all factors contributing to the major structural weaknesses of the Turkish banking system. In September 2000, the Banking Regulation and Supervision Agency (BRSA), an independent institution with responsibility for regulating and supervising the banking sector, began operations. Soon after its formation, the BRSA had to manage a major banking crisis brought on by the escalating political uncertainties, the loss of credibility by the exchange rate regime, and, finally, the abolition of the pegged exchange rate system in February 2001.

As in many other countries, the restructuring of Turkey's banking sector has been very costly. The initial fiscal costs of the resolution of the Turkish banking crisis were about €50 billion (about 34 percent of the gross domestic product, GDP), which, with servicing costs, implies an annual cost of €5 billion. These restructuring costs must be taken into account in an assessment of the potential costs to the Turkish banking sector of EU accession. In effect, much of the adjustment costs have already been borne because of the major bank restructuring that took place during 2001–03.

In implementing structural reforms, Turkey has met nearly all of the conditions set for the banking sector so that it complies with EU norms. Indeed, the sector has made the necessary amendments as dictated by the Turkish "National Program," which puts forth the criteria for accession to the EU. Setting capital adequacy standards, redefining "own funds" and subsidiaries, setting related lending limits, regulating accounting practices, and ensuring transparency of financial reporting are among the issues addressed in the recent regulations that have been adopted and that are in full compliance with EU principles.

Despite the relatively small asset size and low degree of intermediation of the Turkish financial system, Turkey's potential and its regional situation make it an attractive market. The entry of foreign banks into Turkey's financial markets is expected to enhance competition in the financial sector and improve the quality of banking services and financial products. Furthermore, the Turkish banking

161

system, with its high-technology systems and regulatory compliance, is a strong candidate for becoming a member of the EU financial system.

The remainder of this chapter is organized as follows. The next section provides an overview of the major reforms undertaken in restructuring the Turkish banking sector during 2001–03 and the associated costs.[2] That overview is followed by a comparison of the Turkish banking sector with those of the EU member states and other EU accession countries in order to evaluate the impact of the greater competition that may result from joining the EU. The chapter then summarizes the current situation in relation to compliance with EU banking legislation. The final section is devoted to an assessment of the general findings.

The Restructuring of the Turkish Banking Sector and Related Fiscal Costs

In the early 1980s, the Turkish economy underwent a significant policy shift from financial repression toward liberalization. Compared with its stance before the 1980s, Turkey became an outward-oriented economy and experienced significant changes in foreign trade and external capital movements. During the same period, Turkey also experienced high inflation, coupled with high public sector deficit financing. High real interest rates and greater macroeconomic instability became the defining features of the Turkish economy after the 1980s.

Turkey's banks therefore found themselves operating in an environment of macroeconomic instability, characterized by high and volatile inflation rates and fragile external capital flows. Because of the high interest rates resulting from the high public sector deficits, banks invested in risk-free government securities. The systemic distortions created by the state banks and the inadequate risk management and internal control procedures of the sector exacerbated the vulnerability of the banks to financial crises. In the aftermath of the 1994 financial crisis, the strength of the Turkish banking sector was severely tested. The recovery that began in 1995 was negatively affected by the East Asian and Russian crises of 1997–98. The devastating earthquakes of 1999 also had negative effects on the Turkish economy in general and the banking sector in particular.

The exchange rate–based disinflation program introduced in January 2000 had a major impact on banks' balance sheets. Deposit and lending rates fell sharply during the initial stages of the program's implementation phase. Funding in foreign currency became cheaper because of the preannounced exchange rate and the real appreciation of the Turkish lira. As a result, banks borrowed short term, leading in turn to a maturity mismatch because outstanding loans had longer durations. Moreover, open foreign currency positions increased sharply. The financial crises of November 2000 and February 2001 led to the abolition of the pegged exchange rate system and triggered another severe hit on the Turkish banking sector.

The Bank Restructuring Strategy

The Banking Regulation and Supervision Agency, established in 2000, is a financially and administratively independent institution funded by the premiums collected from Turkish banks. Before the formation of the BRSA, the Undersecretariat of Treasury was responsible for preparing and issuing prudential banking regulations and conducting bank examinations under the Banks Act, and the Central Bank of the Republic of Turkey conducted off-site monitoring of banks under the Central Bank Act.

In May 2001, in the aftermath of the crises, the BRSA announced the Banking Sector Restructuring Program (see BRSA 2001). The main objective of the program was to eliminate distortions in the financial sector and adopt regulations to promote an efficient, globally competitive, sound Turkish banking sector (see figure 6.1). The restructuring program was based on four main pillars: (1) restructuring the state banks, (2) seeking prompt resolution of the intervened banks, (3) strengthening the private banks, and (4) strengthening the regulatory and supervisory framework. Despite various challenges, much progress has been achieved in all of these areas.

As in many other countries, the costs of restructuring the banking sector have been high (see table 6.1). During the restructuring of the state banks (the *first pillar*), the Treasury issued government bonds worth about €18 billion in 2001 to securitize the state banks' losses arising from subsidized lending (so-called duty losses). At the same

FIGURE 6.1 Turkish Bank Restructuring Strategy

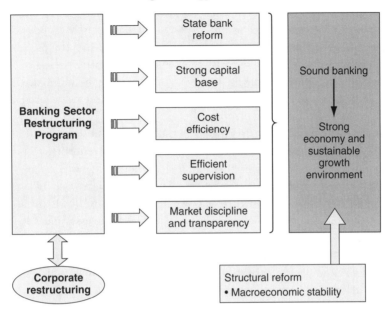

Source: The author.

TABLE 6.1 Initial Fiscal Costs of Turkish Banking Crisis, 2000–01

	Cost in 2001 (billion euros)	Ratio of Cost to 2001 GDP (%)
State banks' duty losses	18.5	12.8
Capital support to state banks	2.9	2.0
Resolution of SDIF banks	27.1	18.7
Public resources	24.6	17.0
Private resources	2.5	1.7
Total costs	48.5	33.5

Source: Banking Regulation and Supervision Agency of Turkey.

time, legislation was introduced to prevent the future accumulation of duty losses. Meanwhile, the banking license of the third largest state bank (Emlak) was revoked, and the management of the remaining two state banks, Ziraat and Halk, was strengthened through the establishment of a joint board of management. The total resources transferred to the state banks to eliminate duty losses and to provide capital support amounted to about €22.5 billion as of the end of 2001.

Operational restructuring was a very important component of the overall restructuring of the state banks. The number of branches was reduced from 2,494 as of December 2000 to 1,685 as of December 2002, and the number of personnel was reduced to 30,399 from 61,601. State banks became more efficient in organization, technology, human resources, financial control, planning, and risk management, so that they can operate in line with the requirements of modern banking and international competition.

The *second pillar* of the restructuring strategy was the resolution of the banks taken over by the Savings Deposit Insurance Fund (SDIF). The SDIF, run by the Central Bank of Turkey since 1983 with the mandate to insure saving deposits, was also charged with resolving insolvent banks in 1994. It was transferred to the BRSA on August 31, 2000. Twenty banks were transferred to the SDIF during 1997–2002. An Asset Management Unit was created and charged with recovering the value of the assets of the banks taken over by the SDIF. As of the date of transfer, the total liabilities of the banks taken over were €33 billion, and the total losses of these banks amounted to about €18 billion.

The funds needed for the resolution of the banks in which the SDIF intervened were met by government bonds issued by the Treasury (€18.5 billion) and the SDIF's own resources (€5 billion). The main source of the SDIF revenues were premiums collected from the banking sector, as well as proceeds from the sale and collection of the assets of the intervened banks. Thus the private sector also shared the burden of the costs of restructuring.

To avoid even greater losses and to accelerate the resolution process, the SDIF has subjected the troubled banks to an intensive financial and operational restructuring. The speed of the resolution has been very rapid compared with the international experience. As of May 2003, only two banks remained under management of the SDIF. One was a bridge bank used for asset management purposes; the other bank was put up for sale.

The *third pillar* of the restructuring strategy was the establishment of a sound private banking sector. The financial structure and profitability of the private banks deteriorated sharply in the aftermath of the crises. During the first stage of the restructuring program, measures were put in place to recapitalize the private banks, limit foreign currency open positions, and encourage mergers and acquisitions. In line with the program, important steps were taken toward strengthening the capital base of the private banks with their own resources.

The deeper-than-expected recession in 2001 and the general global economic conditions highlighted the need to further bolster the private banks by strengthening their capital through public support if necessary, by resolving the nonperforming loans of the banking sector through the Istanbul Approach,[3] and by establishing asset management companies.

The recapitalization program consisted of three phases.[4] During the a*ssessment phase,* the financial status of all private commercial banks using international accounting standards was obtained by means of a three-phase audit procedure carried out on a fair and impartial basis. An independent audit company appointed by the bank undertook the first audit. A second audit was conducted by another independent audit company to ensure that the first audit was carried out according to the agreed-on principles. The BRSA conducted the final audit. This multiphase auditing procedure was utilized to increase transparency and credibility. The audits were based on the financial statements of the banks, as well as on the supplementary reporting schedules completed, based on the detailed instructions of the BRSA. The supplementary reporting

schedules and statements focused on four areas: (1) capital adequacy, (2) credit portfolio and counterpart risk, (3) risk groups to which the bank belongs, and (4) structured transactions and other income recognition issues.

In preparation of the financial statements the following central issues were taken into consideration:

- Inflation accounting
- Consolidated reporting
- Inclusion of material changes to financial statements after December 2001
- Special issues related to the assessment
- Loan portfolio assessment and provisioning
- Evaluation of derivative instruments
- Evaluation of swap bonds
- Valuation of foreign currency accounts.

The *bank recapitalization phase* began with the BRSA's notification to the banks. During this phase, ordinary general assemblies were convened, and the financial situation of the banks, as determined during the assessment phase, was presented to the shareholders. The shareholders made the required resolutions for the recapitalization of the banks whose capital adequacy ratio fell below the 8 percent minimum required.

The *public recapitalization phase* was designed to provide public capital support for solvent banks that did not satisfy the minimum capital adequacy ratio (8 percent) on a *pari passu* basis with the majority shareholders. The public support took the form of a capital injection or subordinated debt with the appropriate contingencies and safeguards.

Banking Sectors in the EU and Turkey: A Comparison of Structural Indicators

This section presents an overview of the structural characteristics of the Turkish banking sector and compares these characteristics with those of the banking sectors of the EU member countries as well as the countries included in the EU enlargement process.[5]

Concentration Ratio, Entry to the Sector, Public Share, and Capital Adequacy

The five largest Turkish banks have a market share of 60 percent of total assets, which is similar to the average for the EU's five largest banks (see figure 6.2

FIGURE 6.2 Concentration Ratios of Five Largest Banks, 2003
(percent)

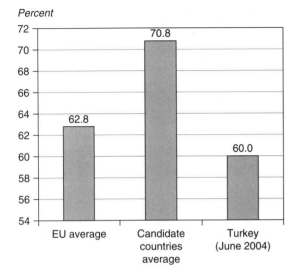

Sources: World Bank, and the Banking Regulation and Supervision Agency of Turkey.

FIGURE 6.3 Share of Assets of State-Owned Banks, 2003
(percentage of total assets)

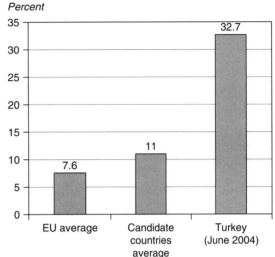

Sources: World Bank, and the Banking Regulation and Supervision Agency of Turkey.

and annex 1).[6] This ratio is a little higher for the EU candidate countries, reflecting the entry of large foreign banks in the financial markets of these countries. The concentration of the large Turkish banks is significantly higher than in the late 1990s because of the significant merger and acquisition activities, as well as the state's intervention into the failed banks. The launching of negotiations with the EU and thus the expected "convergence play" are likely to generate more consolidation in the banking industry and increased interest by both domestic and foreign participants.

The €11 million in capital required to license a bank in Turkey is in line with the EU average of €12 million (see annex 1, table 6.3). Licensing requirements have become much more onerous in Turkey since the bank failures of 2000–01.

Although the withdrawal of the state from the banking sector in many EU member countries is significant, state banks still play a dominant role in Turkey, accounting for one-third of total assets as of June 2004 (see figure 6.3). However, a key pillar of the bank restructuring strategy (as discussed in the earlier section) is the restructuring and privatization of state banks.

The average capital adequacy ratio of the Turkish banking system is high compared with the EU average and that of the candidate countries (see figure 6.4). A minimum capital adequacy ratio—the

FIGURE 6.4 Capital Adequacy Ratios, 2003
(percent)

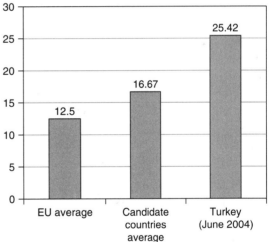

Sources: World Bank, and the Banking Regulation and Supervision Agency of Turkey.

ratio that measures a bank's capital as a percentage of its risk-weighted assets—is a regulatory requirement intended to ensure that banks maintain adequate capital to support their risk exposures. The capital adequacy ratio of a bank is a good indication of its vulnerability to potential shocks and thus the health of that bank. The capital adequacy regulations in Turkey are in line with those of the EU.

Deposit Insurance

An explicit full deposit guarantee for the banks in which the state intervened was extended to avoid the deposit runs that occurred during the 2001 financial crisis in Turkey. However, because of the distortions and the moral hazard such a blanket guarantee creates, the BRSA subsequently implemented a partial deposit guarantee system in line with EU regulations. This system was put into place in 2004 with a one-year notice period.

Compared with the GDP and per capita national income of the EU countries, it can be argued that the level of protection of deposits in Turkey—€27,000 per account holder—is very high.[7] Although the level of deposit protection (guarantee or insurance) varies between €20,000 and €60,000 in the EU countries, the average amount of insured deposits is about €29,000 (figure 6.5). The average deposit guarantee amounts to nearly €13,000 in the candidate countries.[8]

Number of Banks, Average Size, and the Staff Employed

Compared with EU averages, the Turkish banking system has fewer banks that have a high-density networks and a high level of employment. Although there is wide variance among EU member countries,

as of the end of 2003 an EU member country had on average 500 banks with 11,500 branches and 140,000 employees (see annex 1, table 6.3). As of end of June 2004, Turkey had 49 banks with 6,000 branches and 126,000 employees.

An average EU bank is almost twice as large as an average Turkish bank. The average asset size per bank (calculated as total assets divided by number of banks) in EU countries is about €5.3 billion, compared with about €3.1 billion in Turkey. The average asset size of banks in the candidate countries is about €1 billion (see figure 6.6).

An average bank in Turkey has 125 branches, much higher than the comparable number for EU member and EU candidate countries. In the EU member countries, the average number of branches per bank is 36, and the average number of employees per branch is 27 (see figures 6.7 and 6.8). Similar figures apply to the EU candidate countries. The average number of personnel per branch in Turkey is 21, which is comparable to that of EU member and candidate countries.

Asset, Deposit, and Loan Indicators

The total asset size of the banking system of Turkey is about €152 billion, compared with the EU average of €1.7 trillion. One of the large banks in

FIGURE 6.5 Size of Deposits Subject to Insurance, 2003
(euros)

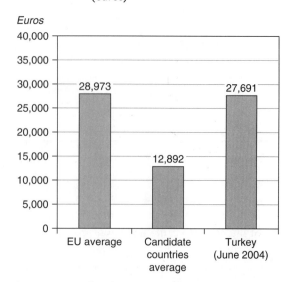

FIGURE 6.6 Average Bank Size, 2003
(total assets per number of banks, in millions of euros)

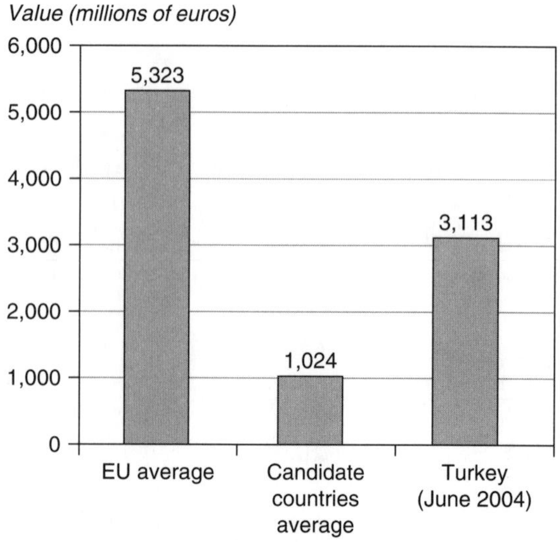

Sources: World Bank, and the Banking Regulation and Supervision Agency of Turkey.

Sources: European Banking Federation and Banking Regulation and Supervision Agency of Turkey.

**FIGURE 6.7   Number of Branches
per Bank, 2003**

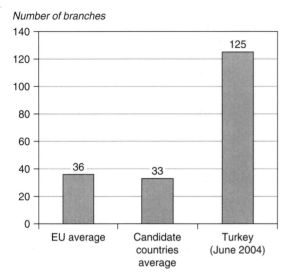

Sources: European Banking Federation and Banking Regulation and Supervision Agency of Turkey.

**FIGURE 6.8   Number of Personnel
per Branch, 2003**

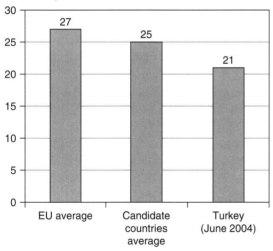

Sources: European Banking Federation and Banking Regulation and Supervision Agency of Turkey.

Europe, Deutsche Bank, had total assets of about €803 billion as of December 2003, which is five and a half times larger than that of the whole Turkish banking sector.

In terms of the ratio of loans to GDP, Turkey fares poorly, reflecting the crowding out of the real sector by the government. The loans-to-assets ratio was 20 percent in Turkey in June 2004, compared with

FIGURE 6.9   Selected Indicators, 2003
(percent)

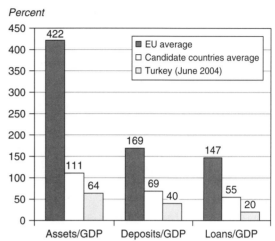

Sources: World Bank, Banking Regulation and Supervision Agency of Turkey, European Banking Federation, and Eurostat.

147 percent in the EU member countries and 55 percent in candidate countries. Similar observations can be made about deposit mobilization (figure 6.9).

Profitability

The return on equity of Turkish banks has been very volatile, reflecting the macroeconomic developments. For example, the ratio of the term profit[9] of the Turkish banking sector to total equity (return on equity) was −80 percent as of December 2001,[10] reflecting the financial crises of 2000–01 and the adoption of inflation accounting (figure 6.10). During 1995–2000, this ratio averaged about 22 percent. However, these figures are estimated to be close to the 8–10 percent levels under inflation accounting. The average return on equity of the EU member countries' banks was about 10 percent (after deduction of tax and extraordinary items) in 2003 (see figure 6.11 and annex 1).[11] However, the return on equity of the large-scale banks is much higher than that of the other bank segments.

Income, Expenditure, and Cost Structure

In banks in the EU countries, net interest income accounts for almost 60 percent of total income, but it accounts for only 14 percent of the total income of Turkish banks. The share of other operating

FIGURE 6.10 **Return on Equity: Turkey and EU Banking Sectors, 2003**
(percent)

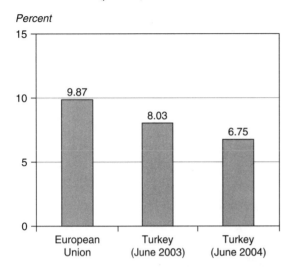

Sources: EU Banking Sector Stability (European Central Bank 2004) and Banking Regulation and Supervision Agency of Turkey.

FIGURE 6.11 **Return on Equity of EU Banks by Asset Size, 2003**
(percent)

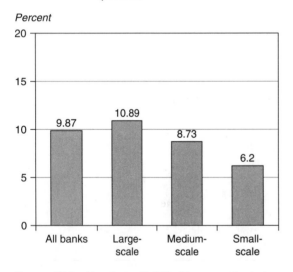

Source: EU Banking Sector Stability (European Central Bank 2004).

FIGURE 6.12 **Personnel Expenses to Total Assets, 2003**
(percent)

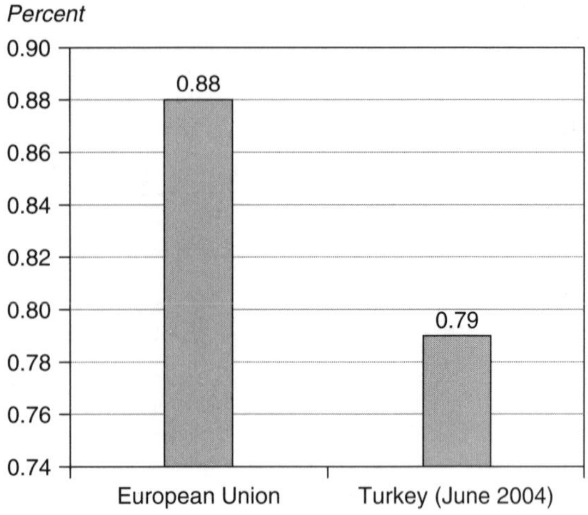

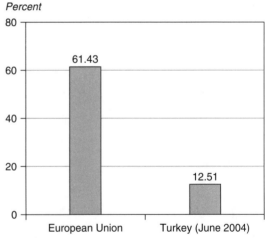

Sources: EU Banking Sector Stability (European Central Bank 2004) and Banking Regulation and Supervision Agency of Turkey.

Figure 6.13 **Personnel Expenses to Total Expenditures, 2003**
(percent)

Sources: EU Banking Sector Stability (European Central Bank 2004) and Banking Regulation and Supervision Agency of Turkey.

Asset Quality

The ratio of nonperforming loans to total loans in Turkish banks (6.3 percent) is more than double that for the average EU bank (figures 6.14 and 6.15). With the onset of the severe financial crises in Turkey in 2000–01, the quality of the assets of Turkish banks deteriorated sharply, with the ratio of nonperforming loans reaching about 22 percent in 2001. The

income (net) is the largest item in the total income of Turkish banks.

The staff expenses of EU banks constitute about 61 percent of total expenditures (figures 6.12 and 6.13), whereas such expenses account for only 13 percent of the total expenditures of Turkish banks.

FIGURE 6.14   Total Loans to Total Assets, 2003
(percent)

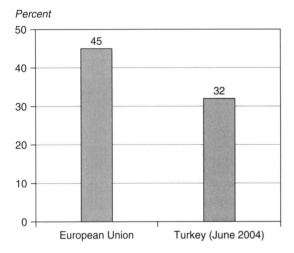

Sources: European Banking Federation and Banking Regulation and Supervision Agency of Turkey.

FIGURE 6.15   Nonperforming Loans (Gross) to Total Loans, 2003
(percent)

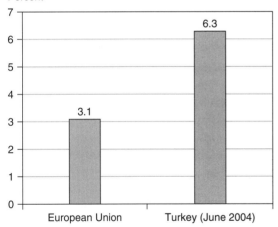

Sources: European Banking Federation and Banking Regulation and Supervision Agency of Turkey.

situation improved during 2002–03 because of the acceleration of out-of-court settlements and voluntary debt restructuring arrangements.

Share of Government Debt Securities

Government debt securities held by Turkish banks amounted to 40 percent of total assets as of June 2004, compared with less than 2 percent for EU banks at the end of 2003. This ratio increases to 22.6

FIGURE 6.16   Debt Securities to Total Assets, 2003
(percent)

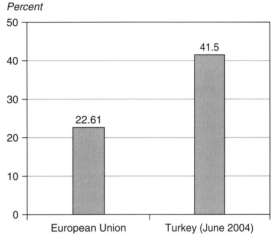

Sources: EU Banking Sector Stability (European Central Bank 2004) and Banking Regulation and Supervision Agency of Turkey.

percent for the EU banks when nongovernment securities are included, indicating the dominance of the real sector in the securities portfolio (figure 6.16). The nongovernment securities holdings of Turkish banks are about 1.5 percent of total assets.

Financial Strength Ratings

Turkish banks have much lower financial strength ratings than banks in the EU member countries. In a study conducted by Moody's Investors Service in March 2003, all countries were rated by their financial strength by assigning weights to their assets (figure 6.17). E was the lowest rating and A was the highest. The average rating mark of the EU member states was B–; the average rating mark of the candidate countries was D; and Turkey's rating mark was D– (figure 6.17).

Foreign Bank Entry

The low share of foreign banks in Turkey (less than 10 percent) offers a striking contrast with the shares of foreign banks in newly liberalized or liberalizing Central and Eastern European countries (close to 70 percent). Persistent macroeconomic instability appears to be the main reason for the very small share of foreign banks in Turkey. A positive correlation exists between the volume of foreign direct

FIGURE 6.17   Financial Strength Rating of the Sector (Moody's), 2003

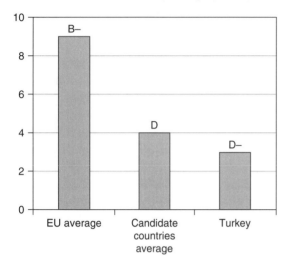

Source: Moody's Investors Service (http://www.moodys.com).

investment and foreign bank expansion in the host country originating from the same parent country. In 2003 the net foreign direct investment in Turkey was about $1 billion. In addition to macroeconomic instability, the delays in implementing financial sector reforms in Turkey have prevented foreign investors from entering the Turkish market. Host country regulations also determine foreign bank entry. Foreign banks prefer countries with fewer regulatory restrictions for investment.

Since completion of the Turkish bank restructuring program, the banking sector has become more resilient to economic shocks, regulations have been streamlined with international standards, and overall bank soundness has improved. As a result, the interest of foreign investors in Turkish banks has begun to increase. Ongoing efforts to decrease high intermediation costs and implement limited deposit insurance are expected to accelerate foreign entry.

Compliance with EU Banking Legislation

Because of the European Commission's work in parallel with the Basel Committee on Banking Supervision, Turkey's efforts to prepare changes in the banking system regulations serve both bodies' proposals (and thus directives). Specifically, Turkey's compliance with EU banking legislation is mainly in the area of EU directives. Several initiatives have been taken in the context of the ongoing regulatory efforts of the EU.

After establishing the BRSA,[12] Turkey increased its effort to harmonize Turkish legislation with the related EU directives. The new Banks Act and the regulations issued by the BRSA are in line with international standards, and the Turkish banking legislation in force is almost fully in compliance with the EU in many areas.

The remaining pieces of legislation that need to be introduced or amended in order for Turkey to achieve full alignment with the EU legislation are on the agenda, and they are expected to be realized within the framework of the National Program that is currently being revised by the Secretariat General for the EU in cooperation with the related Turkish authorities, including the BRSA. The comprehensive table in annex 2 of this chapter describes both the legislation in force in banking in the EU and the corresponding Turkish legislation to give a picture of the current state of play in legislative compliance.

Adoption of the Capital Adequacy Directive

Parallel with the consultative process of the Basel Committee on Banking Supervision for the finalization of the New Basel Accord (Basel II), the European Union released an advance draft of a new directive on the EU capital framework known as Capital Adequacy Directive 3 (CAD 3), which translates Basel II into EU legislation and applies Basel-type provisions to investment firms and domestic credit institutions as well as to international banks. Unlike Basel II, which addresses internationally active banks, CAD 3 will be applied to all credit institutions in the EU (including building societies). It also will be applied to nonbank investment firms authorized under the Investment Services Directive (ISD). The directive will take effect in 2007.

In parallel with CAD 2 principles, the communiqué on capital adequacy was amended in February 2001 to cover market risks, and further amendments were made in January 2002 to include options and to address some other specific issues, such as the inclusion of Tier 3 capital and structural positions. The regulation requires banks to incorporate their market risks into their regulatory capital calculation, and it stipulates that banks must separate their books into a banking book and a trading book. The calculation of market risk covers the interest rate risk and equity risk of the trading book, and the foreign exchange risk covers both the trading book and the banking book. Banks are permitted to use either the standard approach or the model approach to calculate their market risks. Banks implementing the internal model approach will calculate their market risk–based capital requirements on the basis of their their value-at-risk (VaR) figure. Banks are also required to conduct a regular stress testing program. Whether a bank can use the model approach is determined by compliance with the qualitative and quantitative criteria defined in the regulation. Currently, all banks are using the standard approach to report their market risk capital charges on both a solo basis (since January 2002) and on a consolidated basis (since July 2002).

The BRSA has prepared a draft "Circular Regarding the Evaluation of Risk Measurement Models of Banks by the Agency," which sets out the principles and procedures for assessment of the risk measurement models to be used for regulatory reporting purposes by banks. Whether a bank can use the model is determined on the basis of a careful and comprehensive set of checks to grant permission for its use.

To gauge the impact of Basel II (and CAD 3), six of the top 10 Turkish banks (ranked by asset size) participated in the third Quantitative Impact Study (QIS 3) under the guidance of the BRSA (Basel Committee 2003). The study focused on the proposed minimum capital requirements under pillar

one of Basel II. The results of the study, in which participant Turkish banks have applied simpler approaches for credit and operational risks,[13] have been shared with the QIS Working Group of the Basel Committee on Banking Supervision.

The results of the QIS 3, in which 365 banks from 43 countries participated, convey significant information about the potential impact of Basel II on Turkey as well as other on participant countries. The results are generally in line with the Basel Committee's objectives: the minimum capital requirements would be broadly unchanged for large, internationally active banks under the internal ratings–based (IRB) approach, and the proposals would offer an incentive for internationally active banks to adopt more sophisticated approaches. The summary of worldwide results, which reflects the impact of the last consultative paper of Basel II (Consultative Paper 3), is presented in table 6.2.

The results show that under three different approaches for credit risk (standardized approach, foundation IRB approach, and advanced IRB approach), both the G-10 countries and the EU countries have lower capital requirements.[14] However, other countries incur a small increase in credit risk capital requirements under the standardized approach. For operational risk capital charges, all banks incur on average nearly an 8–10 percent increase in risk-weighted assets.

The table also reveals that there is considerable variation in the extent to which capital requirements will rise or fall under Basel II for different banks.

TABLE 6.2   Results, Quantitative Impact Study, 2003
(percent)

		Standardized Approach			Foundation IRB Approach			Advanced IRB Approach		
		Average	Max	Min	Average	Max	Min	Average	Max	Min
G-10	Group 1	11	84	−15	3	55	−32	−2	46	−36
	Group 2	3	81	−23	−19	41	−58			
EU	Group 1	6	31	−7	−4	55	−32	−6	26	−31
	Group 2	1	81	−67	−20	41	−58			
Other	Groups 1 and 2	12	103	−17	4	75	−33			

Note: IRB = internal ratings–based approach; for definition of G-10 countries, see note 14.
Sources: Quantitative Impact Study Results, Basel Committee on Banking Supervision, 2003.

This variation reflects the differences between bank portfolios. The variation in results for the standardized approach also largely stems from the relative importance of retail portfolios for different banks. Moreover, the level of specialization in different lines of activities will imply different capital charges for operational risk between banks.

The results of the third quantitative impact study (QIS 3) imply that the implementation of new capital adequacy regulations will mean that Turkish banks must incur significant costs to meet their credit and operational risk capital requirements and the cost of funding. Even though the said effects have been verified by the QIS 3, the potential effects of CAD 3 are not expected to be significantly different from the effects of Basel II. This expectation is based on the assumption that there is a negligible difference between CAD 3 and Basel II, in view of the fact that CAD 3 has so far suggested Basel-type provisions. Because the new directive requires additional inputs and new methodologies for capital adequacy, the inherent costs appear in three main areas: input gathering, system design, and additional charges for capital requirements and cost of funding.

Contrary to the relatively low data intensiveness of CAD 2, which basically requires the location of the counterparty (whether it is an Organisation for Economic Co-operation and Development country or not) and the type of collateral, CAD 3 requires a comprehensive amount of technical data, such as external ratings, probability of default or of a loss-given event for credit risk, and a new type of data for operational risk (such as event data or gross income by business lines). Providing this data will obviously be a difficult task for Turkish banks and banks elsewhere and will require modifications in the accounting and reporting framework and information technology restructuring. New data requirements can be met only by means of an efficient infrastructure such as the existence of a well-functioning rating system and liquid markets for collaterals.

The BRSA aims to implement CAD 3 by 2007. This target also includes working on the potential effects of Basel II and CAD 3, as well as clarification of the provisions of CAD 3 by taking the country-specific issues into consideration. To serve this purpose, a steering committee, pioneered by the BRSA and consisting of representatives of the member banks of the Banks Association of Turkey, was formed in February 2003 to prepare a road map for the adoption and implementation of Basel II and CAD 3 principles by the Turkish banking sector.

Conclusion

Turkey has fulfilled most of the conditions required for the banking sector to comply with the integration process for the EU. Within the National Program, the necessary legislation on various issues has been amended or enacted in line with EU directives. Examples are indirect loans; definitions of capital and subsidiary; related lending limits; principles on the establishment and operations of banks and special finance houses; regulation on accounting practices; steps to ensure transparency on financial reporting; principles on bank mergers and acquisitions; the issues surrounding decreasing the public share within the financial sector; steps to ensure the efficiency of supervision and surveillance in cross-border banking; capital adequacy, including market risk; and risk management and internal control systems.[15]

The BRSA has revised the regulations on deposit insurance in line with international standards; the introduction of the new scheme was announced in 2004 (with a one-year transition period). Areas that need further improvements in regulations are the business of electronic money institutions and supplementary supervision of financial conglomerates. Various directives such as the one for cross-border payments in euros will become effective with full EU membership. Thus the preparation at this stage is restricted to the technical evaluations.

Despite the adverse macroeconomic conditions, the core Turkish banking sector proved to be resilient. Many of these banks are comparable to their European counterparts in terms of selected indicators, such as high quality of human resources, technological infrastructure, a nationwide branch network, and high-quality service provided in a variety of financial products. However, it will be difficult for Turkish banks to compete with the larger European banks with their large assets and capital strength. Thus the initiation of negotiations with the EU and the expected "convergence play" are likely to generate more consolidation in the banking industry and increased interest of both domestic and foreign participants.

Because of the crowding out by the government, the share of consumer and corporate loans of total assets or deposits is very low. However, under a convergence scenario it is clear that the Turkish financial sector has important future growth potential. The convergence to the EU implies not only convergence of the capital structure, profitability, and management techniques, but also of accounting standards, transparency guidelines, and corporate structure.[16]

There is no doubt but that the Turkish banking sector will be exposed to certain costs during integration with the EU. EU banks tend to keep their profitability high through restructuring their activities and improving their risk management techniques. Competitive pressure on the Turkish banking sector may arise from EU banks that are well known for their strong capital base and their capability for managing risks. It appears that, to be competitive in the EU banking sector, or at least to form partnerships based on solid ground with EU banks, Turkish banks must further strengthen their equity structures during the transition period.

The Turkish banking system has become more resilient and sound since the extensive restructuring program and implementation of international standards. This development inevitably implied a large fiscal cost in which the initial fiscal burden of the bank restructuring reached levels close to one-third of GDP. Thus a large portion of the cost that will emerge from full membership and full convergence to the EU banking sector has already been borne. Furthermore, the confidence that will result from the convergence to the EU is expected to have significant positive externalities on the banking sector that should at least partially offset the impact of competition from strong EU banks.[17]

Annex 1: Banking Sector Statistics—The EU, New Member States, and Turkey

TABLE 6.3 Statistics on Banking Sectors of EU15 and Turkey, 2003

	Concentration Ratio of Five Largest Banks (%)	Minimum Capital Entry Requirement (€ millions)	Number of Banks	Number of Branches	Number of Staff	CAR (%)	Risk-Adjusted Capital Ratio (%)	Percentage of Banking System's Assets in Banks 50% or More Government-Owned	Percentage of Banking System's Assets in Banks 50% or More Foreign-Owned	Deposit Insurance per Account (€)	Total Assets (€ billions)	Total Deposits (€ billions)	Total Credit (€ billions)	GDP (€ millions)	Moody's Rating (March 2003)	Scale Corresponding to Moody's Rating
Austria	—	5	896	4,401	62,674	8	—	0.0	—	20,000	605	370	288	199,603	C+	8
Belgium	88.0	62.5	109	4,935	72,210	8	12.7	0.0	—	20,000	891	420	397	269,546	B	10
Denmark	90.0	5	198	2,014	38,740	8	9.7	0.0	0.0	47,728	312	125	126	187,951	B	10
Finland	99.5	5	343	1,527	23,372	8	10.5	0.0	6.2	25,000	177	64	81	142,518	B–	9
France	60.0	7	925	25,789	—	8	—	0.0	—	70,000	3,779	978	1,196	1,557,245	B–	9
Germany	20.0	5	2,465	36,599	712,000	8–12.5	10.6	42.2	4.3	20,000	6,471	2,448	3,025	2,128,200	C	6
Greece	73.9	18	59	3,095	61,074	8	13.6	22.8	10.8	20,000	200	116	101	153,045	D+	5
Ireland	—	6.3	91	856	42,126	8	—	—	—	20,000	575	160	249	134,786	B–	9
Italy	51.2	6.3	788	30,502	337	8	13.4	10.0	5.7	—	2,170	596	1,039	1,300,926	C+	8
Luxembourg	27.9	8.7	169	200	22,529	8	12.7	5.1	94.6	20,000	656	218	118	23,956	B–	9
Netherlands	88.1	5	147	4,000	144,000	8	11.5	3.9	2.2	—	1,911	1,263	1,096	454,276	B+	11
Portugal	79.8	17.5	52	5,431	54,089	8	9.5	22.8	17.7	—	318	139	181	129,908	C+	8
Spain	53.2	18	265	39,506	240,210	8	13.0	0.0	8.5	—	1,430	807	813	744,754	B	10
Sweden	62.0	5	126	1,900	38,200	8	19.9	0.0	—	27,000	287	123	123	267,251	B	10
U.K.	23.0	5	356	11,624	455,500	8	—	0.0	46.0	—	6,786	3,493	3,283	1,591,412	B+	11
EU average	62.8	12	466	11,492	140,504	8	12.5	7.6	20	28,973	1,771	755	808	619,025	B–	9
Turkey	60.0	11.1	49	6,126	126,274	8	25.4	32.7	3.2	27,691	152.5	95	48	237,723	D–	3

— Not available, not applicable, or negligible.

Note: In June 2004, 1 euro = TL 1,805.605; in December 2003, 1 euro = TL 1,757.480.

Sources: Data on concentration, minimum capital, capital adequacy ratio (CAR), public share, foreign share, deposit insurance: "2003 World Bank Banking Survey," http://www.worldbank.org; other banking indicators: European Banks Federation (FBE), http://www.fbe.org; GDP figures: Eurostat, http://www.europa.eu.int.

Unless otherwise stated, data on Turkey are from national sources. Concentration, number of banks, number of branches, realized capital ratio data are as of June 2004, http://www.bddk.org.tr. Turkish data can be found in BRSA 2004.

TABLE 6.4 Statistics on Banking Sectors of EU15 and Turkey, 2001

	Personnel per Branch	Number of Branches per Bank	Total Assets/ GDP (%)	Total Deposits/ GDP (%)	Total Credit/ GDP (%)	Deposits/Credit (%)	Credit/Assets (%)	Assets/Number of Banks (€ millions)
Austria	14	5	303	185	144	128	48	675
Belgium	15	45	331	156	147	106	45	8,173
Denmark	19	10	166	67	67	100	40	1,577
Finland	15	4	124	45	57	80	46	517
France	—	28	243	63	77	82	32	4,085
Germany	19	15	304	115	142	81	47	2,625
Greece	20	52	130	76	66	114	51	3,384
Ireland	49	9	427	119	185	64	43	6,321
Italy	0	39	167	46	80	57	48	2,754
Luxembourg	113	1	2,737	912	491	185	18	3,880
Netherlands	36	27	421	278	241	115	57	13,002
Portugal	10	104	245	107	139	77	57	6,110
Spain	6	149	192	108	109	99	57	5,395
Sweden	20	15	107	46	46	100	43	2,278
U.K.	39	33	426	220	206	106	48	19,061
EU average	27	36	422	169	147	100	45	5,323
Turkey	21	125	64	40	20	196	32	3,113

— Not available, not applicable, or negligible.

Note: In June 2004, 1 euro = TL 1,805.605; in December 2003, 1 euro = TL 1,757.480.

Sources: Banking indicators: European Banks Federation (FBE), http://www.fbe.org; GDP figures: Eurostat, http://www.europa.eu.int.

Unless otherwise stated, data on Turkey are from national sources. Concentration, number of banks, number of branches, realized capital ratio data are as of June 2004, http://www.bddk.org.tr. Turkish data can be found in BRSA 2004.

TABLE 6.5 Statistics on Banking Sectors of Enlargement (Candidate) Countries and Turkey, 2003

	Concentration Ratio of Five Largest Banks (%)	Minimum Capital Entry Requirement (millions)	Number of Banks	Number of Branches	Number of Staff	CAR (%)	Risk-Adjusted Capital Ratio (%)	Percentage of Banking System's Assets in Banks 50% or More Government-Owned	Percentage of Banking System's Assets in Banks 50% or More Foreign-Owned	Deposit Insurance per Account (euros)	Total Assets (€ billions)	Total Deposits (€ billions)	Total Credit (€ billions)	GDP (€ millions)	Moody's Rating (March 2003)	Scale Corresponding to Moody's Rating
Bulgaria	56.52	Lev 10 (approx. US$5.40)	35	727	21,434	12	31.1	17.6	74.6	6,843	9	6	5	15,793	D–	3
Cyprus	89.2	£C 3	13	940	10,300	10	14.0	4.2	12.7	—	36	28	20	11,645	D+	5
Czech Rep.	69	CZK 500	35	1,647	39,004	8	15.4	3.8	90.0	No limit	78	52	31	80,097	D	4
Estonia	98.9	EEK 75	7	206	4,018	8	15	0.0	98.9	20,000	7	3	5	125,832	C–	6
Hungary	62.5	Ft 2,000	38	1,126	27,200	8	15.6	9.0	88.8	No limit	51	31	32	73,213	C–	6
Latvia	66.2	€5	23	206	8,895	12	14.2	3.2	65.2	—	9	6	4	9,868	D	4
Lithuania	87.9	€5	13	485	7,027	10	15.7	12.2	78.2	10,000	6	4	4	16,271	—	
Malta	84.13	Lm 2	15	106	3,407	8	18.4	0.0	60.0	16,488	18	8	8	4,333	D+	5
Poland	57.4	€5	660	4,394	151,257	8	15.1	23.5	68.7	—	104	61	44	185,227	D	4
Romania	42.8	Rol 370 000	38	2,921	46,535	11	20.3	41.8	47.3	No limit	14.7	10.23	7.27	47,936	D–	3
Slovak Rep.	66.5	Sk 500	21	553	19,797	8	13.4	4.4	85.5	11,129	24	17	9	28,822	E+	2
Slovenia	69	SIT 1,100 (approx. US$5.10)	20	636	11,397	8	11.9	12.2	20.6	No limit	21	14	11	24,576	D+	5
Candidate countries average	70.8	—	77	1,162	29,189	9	16.67	11	66	12,892	31	20	15	51,968	D	4
Turkey	60	11.1	49	6,126	126,274	8	25.42	32.7	3	27,691	152.5	95	48	237,723	D–	3

— Not available, not applicable, or negligible.

Note: In June 2004, 1 euro = TL 1,805.605; in December 2003, 1 euro = TL 1,757.480.

Sources: Concentration, minimum capital, capital adequacy ratio (CAR), public share, foreign share, deposit insurance: "2003 World Bank Banking Survey," http://www.worldbank.org; other banking indicators: European Banks Federation (FBE), http://www.fbe.org; GDP figures: Eurostat, http://www.europa.eu.int.
Unless otherwise stated, data on Turkey are from national sources. Concentration, number of banks, number of branches, realized capital ratio data are as of June 2004, http://www.bddk.org.tr. Turkish data can be found in BRSA 2004.

TABLE 6.6   Statistics on Banking Sectors of Enlargement (Candidate) Countries and Turkey, 2001

	Personnel per Branch	Number of Branches per Bank	Total Assets/ GDP (%)	Total Deposits/ GDP (%)	Total Credit/ GDP (%)	Deposits/ Credit (%)	Credit/ Assets (%)	Assets/Number of Banks (€ millions)
Bulgaria	29	21	56	39	29	134	52	253
Cyprus	11	72	307	238	171	139	56	2,750
Czech Rep.	24	47	97	64	38	167	40	2,229
Estonia	20	29	5	3	4	76	69	931
Hungary	24	30	70	43	43	99	62	1,350
Latvia	43	9	87	57	46	124	53	372
Lithuania	14	37	37	24	22	112	58	462
Malta	32	7	412	189	195	97	47	1,191
Poland	34	7	56	33	24	140	42	157
Romania	16	77	31	21	15	141	49	387
Slovak Rep.	36	26	83	59	31	193	37	1,140
Slovenia	18	32	87	57	44	130	50	1,069
Candidate countries average	25	33	111	69	55	129	51	1,024
Turkey	21	125	64	40	20	196	32	3,113

Note: In June 2004, 1 euro = TL 1,805.605; in December 2003, 1 euro = TL 1,757.480.

Sources: Banking indicators: European Banks Federation (FBE), http://www.fbe.org; GDP figures: Eurostat, http://www.europa.eu.int.

Unless otherwise stated, data on Turkey are from national sources. Concentration, number of banks, number of branches, realized capital ratio data are as of June 2004, http://www.bddk.org.tr. Turkish data can be found in BRSA 2004.

TABLE 6.7 Income, Costs, and Profits of EU Banks in Different Size Groups, 2003

	All		Large	Medium	Small
	Change 2002–03	2003			
	(% of total assets)				
Income					
Net interest income	−0.02	1.38	1.22	1.64	2.54
Fees and commissions (net)	−0.02	0.64	0.65	0.57	0.84
Trading and foreign exchange results	0.04	0.20	0.25	0.06	0.09
Other operating income (net)	0.00	0.17	0.16	0.17	0.31
Total income	0.00	2.38	2.28	2.44	3.78
Expenses					
Staff costs	−0.03	0.88	0.86	0.84	1.47
Other	−0.01	0.11	0.09	0.13	0.28
Total expenses	−0.07	1.44	1.37	1.43	2.62
Profitability					
Profits I (operating profits)	0.08	0.94	0.91	1.00	1.16
Specific provisions	−0.02	0.36	0.32	0.44	0.47
Funds for general banking risks (net)	0.00	0.01	0.00	0.01	0.02
Profits II (before tax and extraordinary items)	0.10	0.59	0.59	0.56	0.67
Extraordinary items (net)	−0.02	0.01	−0.01	0.05	0.08
Tax charges	0.03	0.18	0.18	0.20	0.27
Profits III (after tax and extraordinary items)	0.05	0.41	0.40	0.42	0.48
	(% of Tier 1 capital)				
Return on equity					
Profits III (after tax and extraordinary items)	1.08	9.87	10.89	8.73	6.20
	(% of total income)				
Income structure					
Net interest income	−0.71	58.05	53.48	67.29	67.15
Fees and commissions (net)	−1.02	26.80	28.55	23.42	22.22
Trading and foreign exchange results	1.42	7.33	9.64	2.34	2.28
Other operating income (net)	0.11	6.94	6.88	6.79	8.22
	(% of total expenses)				
Expenditure structure					
Staff costs	0.94	61.43	63.02	58.84	56.28
Administrative costs	−0.68	31.10	30.42	32.19	33.33
Other	−0.26	7.47	6.56	8.97	10.51
Cost-to-income ratio	−3.18	60.39	60.15	58.89	69.31

Source: European Central Bank 2004.

TABLE 6.8   Indicators of 50 Major EU Banks, 2002 and 2003
(percent)

	2002	2003
Profitability		
Cost-to-income ratio	67.9	64.5
Return on assets (after tax and extraordinary items)	0.4	0.4
Return on equity A9 (after tax and extraordinary items)	8.0	8.7
Net interest income/total assets	1.4	1.3
Net noninterest income/total assets	1.2	1.2
Noninterest income/total operating income	48.9	47.5
Solvency		
Tier 1 ratio	6.7	6.7
Total capital ratio	9.6	9.9

Note: The sample of large banks in table 6.8 differs from that in table 6.7. Table 6.8 covers the weighted average figures for 50 major banks of EU15 countries.
Source: European Central Bank 2004.

TABLE 6.9   Nonperforming Assets and Provisioning of EU Banks, 2003
(percent)

	All		Large	Medium	Small
	Change from 2002	2003			
Nonperforming and doubtful loans (gross; % of loans and advances)	−0.1	3.1	2.7	3.6	6.5
Nonperforming and doubtful loans (gross; % of own funds)	−1.9	51.1	46.6	55.7	61.6
Nonperforming and doubtful loans (net; % of own funds)	−1.9	16.7	12.1	22.7	28.3
Provisioning (stock; % of nonperforming and doubtful assets)	2.3	67.4	74.1	59.1	54.0

Source: European Central Bank 2004.

TABLE 6.10 Regulatory Capital Ratios and Risk-Adjusted Items of EU15 Banks, 2003

	All Banks	Change from 2002
Tier 1 ratio	8.8	0.3
Overall solvency ratio	12.4	0.4
Overall solvency ratio below 9%		
Number of banks	98	−74
Asset share (% of total banking sector assets)	0.7	−1.26
Risk-adjusted items (% of total risk adjusted assets)		
Risk-weighted assets	82.3	−0.16
Risk-weighted off-balance-sheet items	11.1	0.0
Risk-adjusted trading book	6.6	0.1

Source: European Central Bank 2004.

TABLE 6.11 EU Balance Sheet Structure of EU Banks, 2003

	All Banks (% of total assets)	Change from 2002 (%)
Assets		
Cash and balances with central bank	1.24	0.1
Treasury bills	1.0	0.0
Loans to credit institutions	15.8	−0.2
Debt securities (public bodies)	7.8	0.8
Debt securities (other borrowers)	10.5	0.1
Loans to customers	50.6	−0.4
Shares and participating interests	3.3	0.0
Tangible assets and intangibles	1.6	0.0
Other assets	8.0	−0.2
Liabilities		
Amounts owed to credit institutions	30.4	0.1
Amounts owed to customers	41.9	−0.2
Debt certificates	20.7	0.1
Accruals and other liabilities	8.8	0.0
Fund for general banking risks	0.14	0.0
Provisions for liabilities and charges	1.2	0.0
Subordinated liabilities	1.8	0.0
Equity capital	4.2	0.0
Other liabilities	0.5	0.0
Profit/loss for financial year	0.4	0.1
Selected off-balance-sheet items		
Credit lines	14.2	0.7
Guarantees and other commitments	6.5	0.7

Source: European Central Bank 2004.

Annex 2: EU Banking Directives in Force, Main Issues

EU Banking Directives in Force	The Directive . . .	Turkish Equivalent
Directive No. 2002/87/ EC of European Parliament and European Council, December 16, 2002, on the supplementary supervision of credit institutions, insurance undertakings, and investment firms in a financial conglomerate	• Lays down rules for supplementary supervision of "regulated entities" that are part of a financial conglomerate. • Defines the term *regulated entity* as a credit institution, an insurance undertaking, or an investment firm. • Defines the term *financial holding company* as a financial institution, the subsidiary undertakings of which are either exclusively or mainly credit institutions or financial institutions. • Makes it compulsory for all financial conglomerates that are subject to supplementary supervision to have a *coordinator* appointed from among the competent authorities involved. The coordinator does not affect the tasks and responsibilities of the competent authorities as provided for by the sectoral rules, but works in cooperation and exchanges information with these authorities. • Specifies that the activities of a group occur mainly in the financial sector if the ratio of the balance sheet total of the regulated and non-regulated financial sector entities in the group to the balance sheet total of the group exceeds 40 percent. Sets out the thresholds for identifying a financial conglomerate, taking into account the regulated entities and the other undertakings and their significance among the whole. • Sets out that regulated entities shall be subject to supplementary supervision. • Requires regulated entities to have in place adequate capital adequacy policies and lays down the rules for the supplementary supervision of the capital adequacy of the regulated entities. • Requires regulated entities to report on a regular basis and at least annually to the competent authority any significant risk concentration at the level of financial conglomerate. • Requires regulated entities to report on a regular basis and at least annually to the coordinator all significant intragroup transactions and requires the supervisory overview of these transactions to be carried out by the coordinator. • Requires regulated entities to have adequate risk management process and internal control mechanisms. • Requires the member states to decide or give their competent authorities the power to decide according to which sectoral rules asset management companies shall be included in the consolidated or supplementary supervision.	No corresponding regulation. The introduction of compliant legislation may bring about some costs because of reorganization and related changes at the institutional level, but it is expected that the ultimate overall outcome is likely to produce efficiency gains for the banking sector and the whole economy.

Annex 2: (Continued)

EU Banking Directives in Force	The Directive . . .	Turkish Equivalent
	• Amends Directives No. 93/6/EC and No. 2000/12/EC.	
Regulation (EC) No. 2560/2001 of European Parliament and European Council, December 2001, on cross-border payments in euros	• Lays down rules on cross-border payments in euros to ensure that charges for these payments are the same as those for payments in euros within a member state. • Applies to cross-border payments in euros up to €50,000 within the European Community. • Specifies that cross-border payments made between institutions for their own account are not covered. • Specifies that the charges levied for cross-border payments and for payments effected within the member state shall be transparent. • Requires that prior to exchanging currencies into and from euros, customers be informed about the exchange charges the institutions propose to apply and about the various charges that have been applied.	No need for any national implementing legislation, because the EU regulation becomes binding and directly applicable upon full membership. Its implementation is not expected to incur a major cost for the banking sector.
Directive No. 2001/24/ EC of European Parliament and European Council, April 4, 2001, on the reorganization and winding up of credit institutions	• Applies to credit institutions and their branches set up in member states other than those in which they have their head offices. • Stipulates that the administrative or judicial authorities of the home member state shall be the sole authority to decide on the implementation of reorganization measures. • States that the home member state shall without delay inform the competent authorities of the host member state of decisions on reorganization. • Calls for the home member state to publish an extract from the decision to adapt a reorganization measure in the *Official Journal of the European Communities* to facilitate the exercise of right of appeal. • Mandates that the administrative or judicial authorities of the host member state of a branch of a credit institution having its head office outside the community shall without delay inform the other authorities of their decision to adopt any reorganization measure. • Specifies that the home member state shall be the sole authority to decide on the opening of winding-up proceedings. • Calls for the home member state to, without delay, inform the competent authorities of the host member state of its decision to open winding-up proceedings. • Sets out that where the opening of winding-up proceedings is decided after the failure of reorganization measures, the authorization of the institution shall be withdrawn.	Banks Act as amended by Act No. 4743.

EU Banking Directives in Force	The Directive . . .	Turkish Equivalent
Directive No. 2000/46/EC of European Parliament and European Council, September 18, 2000, on the taking up, pursuit, and prudential supervision of the business of electronic money institutions	• Defines an electronic money institution as an undertaking or any other legal person, other than a credit institution, that issues means of payment in the form of electronic money. • Restricts the business activities of electronic money institutions, other than the issuing of electronic money, to the provision of closely related financial and nonfinancial services and to the storing of data in electronic devices on behalf of other undertakings or public institutions. • Sets out the redeemability of the bearer of electronic money during the period of validity and depending on the contract between issuer and bearer. • Sets out that electronic money institutions should have initial capital of not less than €1 million. • Specifies that the maximum storage amount of the electronic storage device shall not exceed €150.	No corresponding Turkish legislation. The introduction of such legislation would enrich the scope of financial services.
Directive No. 2000/12/EC of European Parliament and European Council, March 20, 2000, on the taking up and pursuit of the business of credit institutions	• Defines the term *credit institution* as an undertaking whose business is to receive deposits or other repayable funds from the public and to grant credits for its own account. • Prohibits undertakings other than credit institutions from carrying on the business of taking deposits or other repayable funds from the public and makes it compulsory for credit institutions to obtain authorization from member states before commencing their activities. • Stipulates that credit institutions should possess their separate own funds and that the initial capital for access to the taking up of credit institutions should be equal to or greater than €5 million. • States that the competent authorities shall not grant authorization (1) unless at least two persons are effectively directing the business of the credit institution and (2) before they have been informed of the identities of the shareholders or members. • Calls for any natural or legal person who proposes to hold, directly or indirectly, a qualifying holding in a credit institution to first inform the competent authorities. • Permits the competent authorities of the host member state to, in emergencies, take any precautionary measures necessary to protect the interests of depositors, investors, and others to whom services are provided. • Specifies that the state is responsible for the prudential supervision of a credit institution. • States that the competent authorities of the member states concerned shall collaborate closely in order to supervise the activities of the credit institutions operating.	• Banks Act as amended by Act No. 4743. • Regulation on the Establishment and Operations of Banks. • Regulation on Measurement and Assessment of Capital Adequacy of Banks.

Annex 2: (Continued)

EU Banking Directives in Force	The Directive . . .	Turkish Equivalent
	• Specifies that the solvency ratio expresses own funds as a proportion of risk-adjusted total assets and off-balance sheet items, and requires the competent authorities to ensure that the ratios are calculated not less than twice each year, either individually or consolidated, where required.	
	• Requires credit institutions to permanently maintain the solvency ratio at a level of at least 8 percent, but the competent authorities may prescribe any higher minimum ratios they consider appropriate.	
	• Limits a credit institution's large exposure to a client or group of connected clients to 25 percent of its own funds and limits the large exposures in total to 800 percent of the credit institution's own funds.	
	• States that no credit institution shall have a qualifying holding, the amount of which exceeds 15 percent of its own funds, in an undertaking that is neither a credit institution nor a financial institution.	
	• Limits the total amount of a credit institution's qualifying holdings in undertakings other than credit institutions and financial institutions to no more than 60 percent of its own funds.	
	• Subjects every credit institution that has a credit institution or a financial institution as a subsidiary or that holds a participation in such institutions to supervision on the basis of its consolidated financial situation.	
	• Sets up a Banking Advisory Committee alongside the European Commission in order to ensure the proper implementation of this regulation and to assist the Commission in the preparation of new proposals to the European Council.	
Directive No. 94/19/EC of European Parliament and European Council, May 30, 1994, on deposit guarantee schemes	• Defines *deposit* as any credit balance that results from funds left in an account or from temporary situations deriving from normal banking transactions, which a credit institution must repay under the legal and contractual conditions applicable, and any debt evidenced by a certificate issued by a credit institution.	Decree No. 2000/682 on Savings Deposit Insurance and Premiums Collected by the Saving Deposit Insurance Fund.
	• Specifies that the scheme does not cover deposits made by other credit institutions on their own behalf, all instruments that fall within the definition of own funds, and deposits arising out of transactions in connection with which there has been a criminal conviction for money laundering.	
	• Permits credit institutions authorized in a member state to take deposits only if they are members of such a scheme.	

EU Banking Directives in Force	The Directive . . .	Turkish Equivalent
	• States that the aggregate deposits of each depositor shall be covered up to 20,000 European currency units (ECUs). • States that this regulation shall not preclude the retention or adoption of provisions that offer a higher or more comprehensive cover for deposits. • Allows deposit guarantee schemes to, on social considerations, cover certain kinds of deposits in full. • Calls for depositors to be informed of the provisions of the deposit guarantee.	

Notes

1. This chapter was written while the author was vice president of the Banking Regulation and Supervision Agency of Turkey. She is grateful to Münür Yayla and Serdar Özdemir for their contributions to this chapter. The views expressed in it are hers and do not necessarily represent those of the Banking Regulation and Supervision Agency of Turkey.

2. Details of the restructuring program can be found in "Banking Sector Restructuring Program—Progress Reports of BRSA" at http://www.bddk.org.tr.

3. The Istanbul Approach is a voluntary corporate debt restructuring scheme based on the London Approach. It was introduced by amendments to the Banks Act. A Financial Restructuring Framework Agreement was prepared and submitted to the banks by the Banks Association of Turkey on May 24, 2002. The agreement was signed by 25 banks and 17 financial institutions and approved by the BRSA on July 4, 2002.

4. Detailed explanations about and the results of the audit and assessment phases of the program have been released to the public through the "Introductory Report" and "Progress Report." These reports are available on the BRSA Web site, http://www.bddk.org.tr.

5. The description of the EU banking sector in this study is based on the report *EU Banking Sector Stability* (European Central Bank 2003a).

6. Data for the figures that follow are reported in annex 1 and were drawn from World Bank (http://www.worldbank.org), European Central Bank (2003a, 2003b; see http://www.ecb.int), and European Banking Federation (http://www.fbe.be) sources. These data are based on Banking Supervision Committee (BSC) sources. The banks of current member countries are classified by asset size as large, medium, and small. The data on banks cover 99 percent of the credit institutions in EU countries. Large, medium, and small banks account for 66 percent, 30 percent, and 4 percent of total assets, respectively. The data for 2003 cover 57 large banks, 968 medium banks, and 3,600 small banks.

7. The euro–Turkish lira exchange rate for June 2004 was used in these calculations.

8. These figures should be considered with caution, because data were not available for five of the candidate countries.

9. Based on the historical cost and for the whole banking sector, including the intervened banks.

10. For the same period, this ratio is −33 percent for state banks, −132 percent for privately owned banks, −12 percent for development and investment banks, −242 percent for SDIF banks, and 1.6 percent for foreign banks.

11. Because consistent data for candidate countries are not available, comparisons are made only between the EU countries and Turkey in the rest of this chapter.

12. The BRSA was established by the Banks Act (Law No. 4389), issued on June 23, 1999.

13. They applied the standardized approach for credit risk and the basic indicator and standardized approaches for operational risk.

14. The Group of Ten is made up of 11 industrial countries—Belgium, Canada, France, Germany, Italy, Japan, the Netherlands, Sweden, Switzerland, the United Kingdom, and the United States—that consult and cooperate on economic, monetary, and financial matters. The ministers of finance and the central bank governors of the Group of Ten usually meet once a year in connection with the fall meetings of the Interim Committee of the International Monetary Fund. The governors of the Group of Ten normally meet bimonthly at the Bank for International Settlements.

15. For recent information on actions taken to satisy accession requirements, see "Monitoring the Implementation of the National Program," http://www.abgs.gov.tr.

16. It is believed that an assessment of new organizational models, such as a financial holding company, within the same scope will be useful.

17. In fact, the economic criteria that are a precondition for EU membership will independently be an important development for ensuring confidence and stability in the markets. Membership might further strengthen this confidence.

References

Basel Committee on Banking Supervision. 2003. "Quantitative Impact Study 3: Overview of Global Results." Bank for International Settlements, Basel.

BRSA (Banking Regulation and Supervision Agency of Turkey). 2001. *Towards a Competitive Turkish Banking Sector*. June.

———. 2003. *Banking Sector Assessment Report*. Various issues.

———. 2004. "Banking Sector Evaluation Report." Ankara: BRSA.

European Central Bank. 2003a. *EU Banking Sector Stability*. Frankfurt: ECB, February.

———. 2003b. *Report on EU Banking Structure*. Frankfurt: ECB.

———. 2004. *EU Banking Sector Stability*. Frankfurt: ECB, November.

7

COMPETITION AND REGULATORY REFORM IN TURKEY'S ELECTRICITY INDUSTRY

İzak Atiyas and Mark Dutz

Turkey has begun a major overhaul of the legal and regulatory framework surrounding its electricity industry.[1] The reform program entails liberalization as well as a radical restructuring of the industry—that is, its generation, transmission, and distribution segments, including its wholesale and retail activities. The purpose of this chapter is to review and assess the new regulatory regime, identify the main competition-related challenges the industry is likely to face, and discuss future prospects. The chapter will attempt to evaluate the reform process in light of the regulatory framework established at the level of the European Union (EU) and the current debate on the proposals about its amendment.

The chapter is organized as follows. The first section reviews the physical peculiarities of the electricity industry and discusses how they have shaped the evolution of its industrial organization. The second section presents an overview of regulatory reform in the EU, the electricity directive issued by the European Parliament in 1996, and the recent proposals for amendment advanced by the European Commission. The pre-and postreform structure of the electricity industry in Turkey and the main features of the new regulatory regime are featured in the third section. The fourth section identifies the main challenges that the industry is likely to face in the process of developing effective competition. A final section discusses possible competition-enhancing solutions.

Characteristics and Evolution of the Industry

The electricity industry is made up of three main interrelated segments. Electricity is *generated* in plants by harnessing the flow of water or the power of the wind, sun, or earth (geothermal); burning fossil fuels (thermal); or capturing nuclear fission. *Distribution* refers to supplying residences or businesses with electricity through lower-voltage wires and transformers. The *transmission* of electricity refers to the actual transportation of higher-voltage electricity between generation plants and distribution facilities, the interconnection of geographically dispersed generation plants, their scheduling, and orderly dispatch. The operation and commercial principles of related wholesale and retail supply activities are quite similar; both involve metering, computing, and billing. An important distinction is that the wholesale trade business is carried out mostly at the transmission level on a larger scale, and the retail trade business is carried out through the distribution system at the end user level with both smaller business and household customers.

Several characteristics of the electricity industry distinguish it from other industries. For one thing, there is no economical way to store electricity. This situation implies that the demand for and supply of electricity must be balanced almost continuously in real time. In addition, the demand for electricity varies hourly and daily, as well as across months and seasons. Consumers can obtain electricity as long as they are connected to the network, because there is no cost-effective way to establish physical contact between specific consumers and generators. Rather, electricity from generating plants flows to a common pool and is retrieved by consumers from that pool. In the short run, the price elasticity of demand is very low. Because generating plants have rigid, nonflexible capacity constraints, supply is relatively inelastic, especially at peak demand times. In addition, several physical constraints, such as voltage, have to be met. The most binding constraint affecting system operations is the limitation on the power-carrying capacities of lines and transformers. Congestion resulting from this constraint can, in principle, so severely limit system operation that it could impede the transfer of production from a least-cost plant to a load, even though both parties would like to make the requisite sales agreement. Thus, balancing supply and demand requires coordinating and scheduling the production of different plants, taking the existing capacity of lines and transformers into account. The use of generators will allow the system to respond to changes in demand or supply. The generators must hold a minimum level of reserve capacity to keep the probability of system failure below an acceptable threshold. Failure at one point in the network (e.g., failure of a generation plant) can have serious repercussions for the whole network if not managed properly. Thus there are strong externalities in terms of network security.

The need to coordinate generation and supply on an almost minute-by-minute basis is an incentive to integrate these two activities vertically. Indeed, in most countries electricity services historically have been supplied through vertically integrated enterprises encompassing generation, transmission, and distribution activities. In Europe, such enterprises have been organized as monopolies under public ownership. In the United States, the predominant form of industrial organization has been privately owned but regulated franchises with monopoly rights to serve specific geographic regions.

Because the transmission and distribution of electricity involve large sunk capital costs with strong economies of scale (in the sense that duplication of lines would be economically wasteful), there is little scope for competition in these segments of the industry. By contrast, the generation of electricity is now regarded as potentially competitive, especially with the advent of the smaller-scale combined-cycle gas turbine (CCGT) technology. Generation is generally believed to exhibit increasing returns of scale at low levels of production and constant returns to scale otherwise (Armstrong, Cowan, and Vickers 1994: 282). Armstrong and others report Joskow and Schmalensee's estimate of minimum efficient scale for fossil-based plants at 400-megawatt capacity.

In the last 10–15 years, the predominant view has evolved to favor the introduction of competition into generation and retail supply activities. Some countries, such as Chile and the United Kingdom, were pioneers, but the wave of liberalization has been widespread, covering developing and developed economies alike.

Regulatory Reform in the EU

The European Commission's effort to liberalize electricity markets in the EU was driven primarily by the quest for a single market, but it was met with resistance by many national governments.[2] In 1991 the Commission proposed allowing third-party access within the electricity markets of all member states, but the Council of Ministers rejected the proposal. By 1993 the concept of negotiated (as opposed to full or regulated) third party access was being presented as one of the options under discussion. In 1994 France introduced the single buyer model as an alternative to negotiated third party access. Eventually, in 1996, an agreement was reached on a timetable for liberalization, and each member state was given a choice between the three alternatives for access. The agreement culminated in the European Parliament's electricity directive.[3]

Liberalization of the electricity sector was strongly supported by the Competition Directorate General of the European Commission (the former DG IV) through its threats that no liberalization would call for tougher action on the basis of Articles 81 and 82 of the Treaty Creating the European Community (Pollitt 1999: 50).

The Electricity Directive of 1996

The basic idea behind the electricity directive is to introduce competition to the potentially competitive segments of the electricity industry—generation and retail supply—and to regulate transmission and distribution, which retain natural monopoly characteristics. This section examines four aspects of the directive: market opening, unbundling, third party access, and public service obligations and regulation

Market Opening   On the demand side, the directive envisaged market opening targets on the basis of consumers being designated to have freedom to contract their consumption of electricity (so-called eligible customers). Thus, according to the directive, each member state would "open" a given and increasing percentage of its market over the next six years. That percentage was to be calculated as the share, in overall European Community consumption, of final customers consuming more than 40 gigawatt-hours per year. The threshold was to be reduced to 20 gigawatt-hours in the second stage (within three years) and 9 gigawatt-hours in the third step (within six years). Those thresholds have been estimated to correspond to market share openings equal to 27 percent, 28 percent, and 33 percent, respectively, in 1999, 2000, and 2003.[4] Each member state was to designate its own set of eligible customers, but consumers with more than 100 gigawatt-hours of consumption were to be definitely included in that designation. To address problems that might arise if the degree of market opening differed across states, the directive included provisions for reciprocity: a member state has the right to refuse access for companies from states that have not *liberalized to an equal extent.*

On the supply side, the directive provided for two mechanisms for the development of new capacity in generation, both aimed at introducing competition:

- *Authorization.* Companies offer to build new power plants under an open and impartial procedure that decides whether they should go ahead.
- *Tendering.* An authority decides what new capacity is required. It solicits tenders, which are then assessed through an impartial procedure.

Unbundling   To prevent discrimination, cross subsidization, and distortion of competition, the directive obliged integrated operators to separate the management of the generation, transmission, distribution, and nonelectricity activities and to keep separate accounts for each. To ensure nondiscrimination, it envisaged creation of an independent authority for dispute settlement.

Each member state was required to specify a transmission system operator (TSO), whose task was to ensure dispatch of a generation plant under fair and transparent rules that did not favor plants owned by the same company as the TSO. The unbundling of the TSO was deemed crucial (management, legal, or ownership unbundling).

As for distribution, the system was to operate on the same nondiscriminatory basis as transmission.

Third Party Access   One of the main objectives of the directive was to enable independent generators to have access to the transmission and distribution networks in order to supply final customers. The directive prescribed three types of access arrangements (but member countries could also choose hybrid arrangements):

- *Negotiated third party access (nTPA).* Consumers and producers contract directly with each other and then negotiate with the transmission and distribution companies for access to the network.
- *Regulated third party access (rTPA).* Access prices are not negotiated, but rather are published by the regulator.
- *Single buyer model (SBM).* There is a single wholesale buyer of electricity. Competition in generation is allowed, but retail competition is limited. Eligible consumers not tied to a specific distributor or retailer can still contract with producers. The single buyer pays the producer its regulated sales price minus network charges. The producer can then compensate the consumer so that the consumption prices become equal to the contract price.

Public Service Obligations (PSOs)   The directive also recognized that some objectives deemed desirable from a social point of view may not be achieved through unfettered competition. To achieve these objectives, the directive provided that member states may impose such obligations on electricity undertakings. The objectives mentioned in the directive were security (including security of supply), regularity, quality, price, and environmental protection. The obligations would be defined by the member states.

Progress with Implementation and Proposed Amendments

In March 2001, the European Commission issued a communication that assessed the progress in development of the internal market for electricity and the effects of implementation of the 1996 directive (European Commission 2001a) and proposed a series of amendments (European Commission 2001b). The communication underlined the importance of fully opening energy markets to improving Europe's competitiveness. According to the Commission, the effects of market opening were positive. However, it also stated that to complete the internal market, further measures were necessary. The key points of the communication are described in this section.

By 2000 the average market openness in the European Community had reached 66 percent—a figure higher than the thresholds established in the directive. However, progress was very uneven across countries. Some countries had full market opening; in others, market opening was limited to 30 percent. It also was observed that the reciprocity provisions of the directive had proved unable to address problems of unevenness in the competitive environments between member states. There was concern that if this unevenness persisted over a longer period, a level playing field would not develop within the internal market.

For access, 14 member states had chosen rTPA; only Germany had selected the nTPA regime. Italy and Portugal had chosen SBM for captive (i.e., noneligible) customers and rTPA for eligible customers. Most member states had chosen authorization as the procedure to elicit additions to generation capacity. However, the ultimate goal of nondiscriminatory access to the network was not fully achieved. The absence of standard and published third party access tariffs was thought to be a significant barrier to entry. Another barrier was the absence of effective unbundling in member states. Germany and France chose management unbundling, seven countries chose legal unbundling,

and five countries chose ownership unbundling. Thus effective access required further strengthening of unbundling.

The communication underlined the benefits of progress in competition. Prices for industrial users had come down in all member states, but larger price decreases occurred in countries where liberalization was 100 percent. Household prices fell, though to a lesser extent overall than prices for industrial users. Overall, larger reductions occurred in countries in which customers were free to change suppliers and in which changing suppliers was actually easy to do.

The communication also raised concerns about the pace of cross-border trade: "The objective of the Electricity and Gas Directives is the creation of one truly integrated single market, not fifteen more or less liberalized but largely national markets." It pointed out that even though the number of customers who switched suppliers rose overall, most customers tended to opt for national suppliers. In general, cross-border trade was limited. Its expansion would require developing appropriate rules on the pricing of this trade, developing rules for the allocation and management of scarce interconnection capacity, and, where necessary, increasing such capacity.

In short, the Commission indicated that there were "several weaknesses in the current legal framework which needed to be remedied if a fully operational internal market for gas and electricity is to be achieved" (European Commission 2001a: 6). On the basis of these findings, the Commission developed proposals to amend the directive (European Commission 2001b). The most important proposed amendments were as follows:

- *Market opening.* Allow all electricity customers freedom to choose suppliers (end domestic customer franchise monopoly) by January 1, 2005. This was called the quantitative proposal.
- *Unbundling.* Strengthen unbundling to legal and functional separation of transmission from generation (thus management separation alone was no longer sufficient, and ownership separation is now appropriately promoted as a form of unbundling stronger than legal separation).
- *Access.* Strengthen access by requiring rTPA with published tariffs. Do not permit the single buyer model.

- *Public service obligations.* Make explicit mention of the obligation that member states should ensure universal service, defined as "supply of high quality of electricity to all customers in their territory," as well as protection of vulnerable customers and final consumers' rights.
- *Regulation.* Establish an independent regulatory authority to approve tariffs and conditions for access to transmission and distribution networks ex ante and to monitor and report to the Commission on the state of the electricity markets (especially supply-demand balances).

The proposals did not prescribe a specific model for organization of wholesale activities. Some of the proposals initially met with opposition. In particular, Germany opposed the requirement for an independent regulator and ex ante regulation of access prices and conditions (Newbery 2002a). The principles of nondiscriminatory access to the network, based on transparent and published tariffs, and the establishment of independent regulators were adopted by the Barcelona European Council in March 2002 (European Commission 2002b). The Barcelona council also pointed out the need to take measures on PSO, in particular for remote areas and vulnerable groups. During their November 2002 meeting, EU energy ministers agreed that full market opening would be achieved in 2004 for nonhousehold customers and in 2007 for household customers (European Commission 2002a). Unbundling was to be achieved by July 2004 for transmission and 2007 for distribution. The proposed amendments were finally adopted in June 2003.[5]

The Current Structure of Turkey's Electricity Industry

As in many European countries until recently, the Turkish electricity industry was dominated by a state-owned vertically integrated company, TEK.[6] In 1993, in an attempt to prepare TEK for privatization, the government separated TEK into the Turkish Electricity and Transmission Company (TEAS) and the Turkish Electricity Distribution Company (TEDAS).

Background

Beginning in the 1980s, the government sought to attract private participation in the industry. Its motivation was both the general disposition toward the private sector that emerged in the 1980s and fiscal constraints, purportedly to ease the investment load on the general budget. This effort was constrained, however, by the constitutional regime that interpreted the provision of electricity as a public service—that is, something that had to be supplied by the government. Instead of responding directly by seeking to remove this constitutional challenge, the governments of the 1980s and 1990s chose to create shortcuts[7] through various private sector participation models short of privatization. The first law setting up a framework for private participation in electricity was enacted in 1984 (Law No. 3096).[8] This law forms the legal basis for private participation through build-operate-transfer (BOT) contracts for new generation facilities, transfer of operating rights (TOOR) contracts for existing generation and distribution assets, and the autoproducer system for companies wishing to produce their own electricity. Under a BOT concession, a private company would build and operate a plant for up to 99 years (later reduced to 49 years) and then transfer it to the state at no cost.[9] Under a TOOR contract, the private enterprise would operate (and rehabilitate, where necessary) an existing government-owned facility through a lease-type arrangement.

In 1994 Law No. 3996 and Implementing Decree 5907 were enacted to enhance the attractiveness of BOT projects. The laws authorized the Undersecretariat of the Treasury to grant guarantees and provided tax exemptions (as well as extended the purview of the model to other public services such as water and wastewater, transport, and communications).[10] An additional law was enacted in 1997 for private sector participation in the construction and operation of new thermal power plants through a licensing system rather than concession award. The build-operate-own (BOO) law (Law No. 4283) again provided guarantees by the Treasury. Under the BOO model, investors retain ownership of the facility at the end of the contract period.

A typical BOT, BOO, or TOOR generation contract, signed between the private party and TEAS or TEDAS, includes exclusive "take-or-pay" obligations with fixed quantities and prices (or price formulas) over 15–30 years. Thus it does not provide a framework for competition *in the market*, but only potentially for competition *for the market* if the contracts are granted through a competitive process in which the lowest-cost proposals are accepted. The main benefits, in principle, of such private sector participation contracts arise from (1) transferring those risks to the private sector that is best able to manage them (including most commercial risk during the operating phase), (2) accessing strong and effective private sector commercial and managerial skills for reduced operational costs and improved service quality, and (3) spurring adoption of innovation at both the design and implementation phases of projects. Such efficiency-related benefits are only likely to arise, however, from competitively tendered projects. Unfortunately, no rigorous framework was in place to ensure implementation of competitive tendering. On the contrary, under the Turkish BOT model there was no requirement for prequalification, nor for a competitive open tender, nor even for a closed tender (the "method of sealed bid from selected companies" merely requires that at least three interested companies submit their offers). Unsolicited bids could be brought forward and negotiated solely on the basis of an investor-completed feasibility study (through "the method of negotiation").

Compounding these problems, under the Turkish BOT, BOO, and TOOR generation models the government has retained most of the commercial risks while providing the private sector with substantial rewards. Under these contracts, the Treasury has provided guarantees to cover critical commercial take-or-pay payment obligations, such as minimum electricity generation levels and minimum quantities of gas in power station gas purchase contracts, at associated predetermined prices in U.S. dollars over the life of the contracts.[11] Although the fixed-price nature of the contracts creates incentives for cost efficiencies, the contracts preclude any possibility of making consumers share in any efficiency gains: all cost savings are appropriated by the generator. In addition to the relatively high electricity cost of many of these projects, the BOT and TOOR contracts are heavily front-end loaded with higher capacity charges in the first years of operation to allow for early recovery of investment costs (OECD 2002). As discussed below, the current structure of these contracts acts as a major barrier to the development of competition in the generation sector.[12]

A large number of BOT proposals or projects have not been completed.[13] Initially, the main constraint was the prevailing interpretation of Turkey's constitution—that is, that even though Law No. 3996 stated that BOT contracts would be subject to private law, the Constitutional Court decided that electricity was a public service and that therefore the BOTs were to be considered as concessions under public administrative law. This ruling meant that the development and eventual completion of a BOT contract required intervention and approval from a multitude of government agencies, including the Ministry of Energy and Natural Resources (MENR), the High Planning Council (referred to by its Turkish initials, YPK), the State Planning Organization (SPO), and the Treasury. In addition, the public law character of the contract meant that investors did not have recourse to international arbitration and that contracts had to be reviewed by Danıştay, the Council of State, which was a lengthy process.

In August 1999, a constitutional amendment opened the way for privatization in the electricity sector, for the application of private law to contracts, and for limits to the scope and duration of the Danıştay review.[14] Although the constitutional amendment (and the subsequent Law No. 4501 of January 2000, which implemented these changes) simplified the legal framework for private participation, the new obstacle to the development of BOT contracts was the unwillingness of the Treasury to provide new guarantees in light of the implied contingent liabilities.

By the end of the 1990s, it had become clear that quasi-privatization with Treasury guarantees was not going to be feasible because of the rapidly deteriorating fiscal stance. In addition, there was wider appreciation that these types of contracts, which locked generation companies into long-term exclusive sale agreements with predetermined, fixed prices, did not serve the overall objective of developing competition in electricity markets. Several government agencies (e.g., MENR, SPO, the Treasury) were already working on the design of a competitive electricity sector regulated through an independent agency. In 2001 Law No. 4628 (the electricity market law, or EML) provided a new and radically different legal framework for the design of electricity markets and established a new, independent Energy Market Regulatory Authority (EMRA).

The Current Model

The main drivers for liberalization in Turkey were very different from those that preoccupied the EU or the leaders of electricity liberalization such as the United Kingdom. The EU was primarily concerned with creating an internal market. Countries such as the United Kingdom were motivated by the ineffi- ciency of public enterprises (the ownership dimen- sion) and the opportunities generated by techno- logical changes that made competition possible in generation (the market structure dimension).[15] In Turkey, the main driver of and the public justifica- tion for private participation under the pre-2001 regime, and liberalization under the new regulatory regime, were rapid growth in demand, combined with the inability of the government to meet that demand through public investments or Treasury- guaranteed private investments because of the deteriorating fiscal situation.

Still, the degree of competition envisaged in the new framework is more advanced than the EU directive of 1996. In most respects, it is compatible with (if not more competitive than) the proposed amendments to the directive currently under dis- cussion. As described in the next section, the main challenge for Turkey is that, the competitive frame- work notwithstanding, the actual development of competition is likely to take some time because of the legacy of Turkey's recent past: the current struc- ture of ownership (dominance of state-owned assets in generation) and even more problemati- cally the uncompetitive, tied nature of the contracts governing the privately operated assets.

The new regime contained in primary legislation and implementing regulations emphasizes competi- tion in ordering the market. The main principles of the EML, and their status in relation to the 1996 directive, are as follows.

Market Opening On the demand side, customers that consume more than 9 gigawatt-hours per year are designated as eligible consumers who are free to choose their suppliers—a measure that meets the targets of the directive. The main operational diffi- culty in market opening is estimating the number of expected eligible customers, because higher numbers mean more measuring, telemetering, and computing hardware and software, which means larger investments by wholesale and retail companies. These costs must be reflected in con- sumer tariffs. As of May 2003, the estimated eligible customers above 9 gigawatt-hours per year were 103 at the transmission level and 507 at the distri- bution level, accounting for 13.5 percent of overall consumption (Sevaioğlu n.d.).[16] This number is likely to increase, however, because additional industrial users are expected to enroll as eligible customers through demand aggregation, with users having similar demand characteristics.

On the supply side, the authorization-type licensing framework established in the new regime also appears to be fully compatible with the direc- tive. It provides entry opportunities into the gener- ation (independent power producers, or IPPs, and autoproducers who can sell up to a maximum of 20 percent of their annual production to consumers other than their shareholders), wholesale trade, distribution, retail trade, import, and export of electricity. Distribution companies may also oper- ate as retail sales companies in their regions by obtaining a retail sales license and may import elec- tricity if allowed in their license. Distribution com- panies may establish joint ventures with generation companies or set up generation units (not exceed- ing a market share of 20 percent). Transmission remains a state monopoly, but private generators can establish private direct transmission lines. The only limitation is that the EMRA's granting of gen- eration licenses is conditional on no congestion in the transmission-distribution link connecting the new plant to the grid or directly to customers. According to EMRA, congestion in the transmis- sion network is most likely to be resolved through some type of auctions among the companies that would benefit from the transmission investments (Sevaioğlu n.d.).

Unbundling TEAS has been further unbundled into the Turkish Electricity Generation Company (EUAS), Turkish Electricity Wholesale Company (TETAS), and Turkish Electricity Transmission Company (TEIAS), each organized as a separate legal entity. Thus, the degree of unbundling between generation, transmission, and distribution envis- aged and carried out under the EML goes beyond the minimum directive requirements of manage- ment separation and unbundling of accounts. The secondary legislation regulating these activities is being prepared by EMRA.

FIGURE 7.1 Structure of the Electricity Market, Turkey

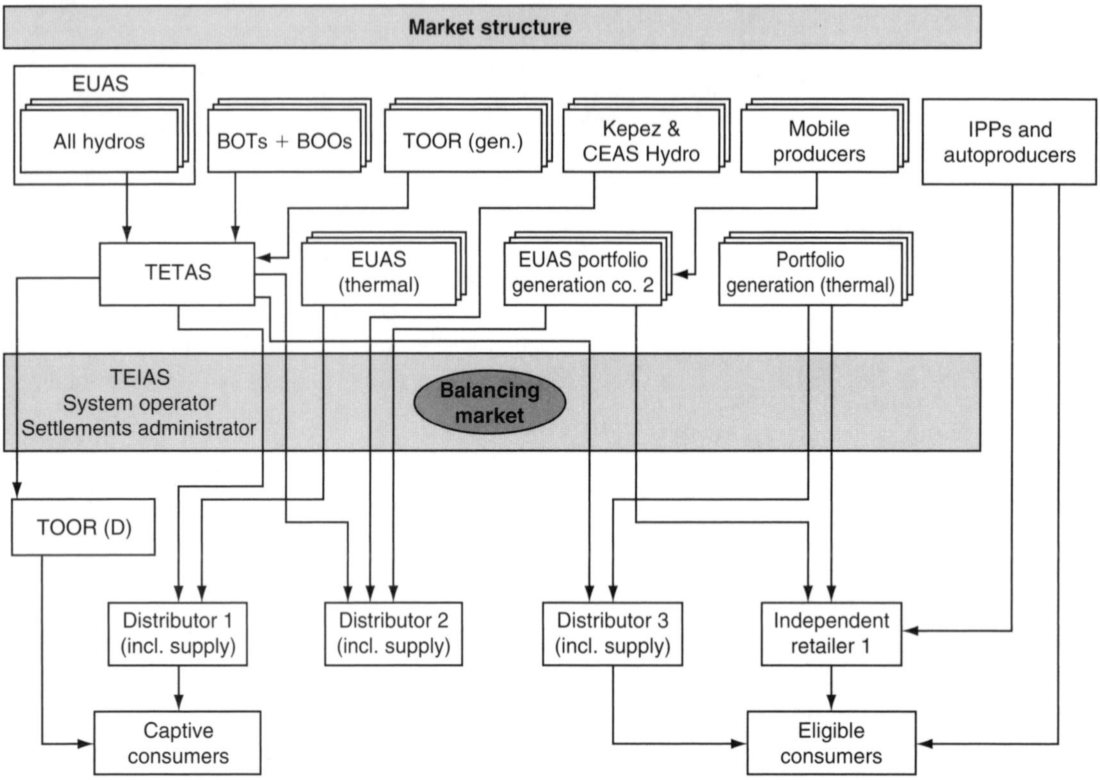

Source: Modified from *Draft Electricity Market Implementation Manual* (see EMRA 2003).

Under the new structure, EUAS will take over, operate, or close down the state's existing power plants that are not transferred to the private sector. TETAS is created to carry out wholesale operations. It will take over all existing energy sale and purchase agreements from TEAS and TEDAS (distribution). TEIAS is responsible for transmission assets, for system operation and maintenance, for planning of new transmission investments and building of new transmission facilities, and, critically, for the balancing and settlement procedure that will balance the power transactions among parties, both physically and financially. Thus, in the words of the directive, TEIAS is the transmission system operator. It is envisaged that all transmission facilities owned and operated by other companies will be transferred to TEIAS under the EML. In line with this requirement, the transmission facilities that had been awarded to private investors through concessions to the two companies Kepez Elektrik (Antalya region) and Cukorova Elektrik, or CEAS (Adana, Mersin, Hatay, and Osmaniye regions), were seized by the Ministry of Energy[17] and handed over to TEIAS in June 2003, because the companies had failed to hand them over by February 2003 as required.[18]

Third Party Access EML requires the rTPA regime for access to transmission and distribution. An independent regulatory authority was created that, among other things (see later discussion), will settle disputes between parties.

Market Design As highlighted in figure 7.1, at the heart of the new regime is a bilateral contracts market in which generation companies contract with wholesale trade companies (TETAS and any eventual new entrants), distribution companies, any new independent retail companies, and eligible customers (EMRA 2003). On the generation side, EUAS is likely to be split into a hydro generator (holding all state-owned hydro plants transferred from DSI, the Directorate General of State Water Works) and a small number of affiliate portfolio generation companies (holding the state-owned thermal plants and mobile plant contracts). EUAS also will hold the physical assets associated with any TOOR (generation) contracts. For any excess capacity, existing and new autoproducers (generation by industrial facilities for own use) will compete with other generators for contracts with distribution companies and independent retailers, and directly with eligible consumers. As illustrated in figure 7.1, the dominant state-owned wholesaler TETAS also holds all previous BOO, BOT, and TOOR (generation) contracts and will assume other stranded costs such as the debts and employment liabilities of EUAS and TEIAS.[19] In fact, dealing with stranded costs is one of the main reasons for the creation of TETAS.

As for end users, eligible customers may buy electricity from their regional distributor/retailer or TOOR distributor, but they also may buy directly from a wholesaler, from a new independent retailer, or from an independent generator. Captive customers, by contrast, must buy their electricity from a distributor/retailer in their region, but they have the right to buy from any retailer carrying out the same commercial activity in the region—that is, either their existing regional distributor or retailer or TOOR distributor or any other new retailer in the region.

The current market design does not envisage a centralized pool or power exchange. Therefore, dispatch is separated from the operation of the wholesale market. The actual real-time equality of demand and supply, given the bilateral contracts, will be carried out by the system operator through purchases and sales in a balancing market. For this purpose, a market System Balancing and Settlement Center[20] is to be established within TEIAS. In principle, it is expected that the balancing market will make up a small percentage of total demand and will be used for adjustments at the margin.

Privatization   The new regime envisages eventual direct privatization in generation and distribution. Transmission assets are to remain under government ownership. Foreign investors cannot assume a controlling interest in the generation, transmission, and distribution sectors.

The details of licensing procedures, market operation, tariffs, vesting contracts, privatization, and stranded cost mechanisms have been left to secondary legislation and decisions.

Vesting Contracts   Vesting contracts are an initial set of bilateral contracts put in place by the government between companies it owns (or between state-owned companies and private companies such as independent retailers when the government decides the contract structure and when the retailer decides whether to buy it) to provide a smooth transition to competitive markets and to improve the predictability of revenues during this transition. The contracts remain with the companies when they are privatized—the private buyer pays for the company and its package of contracts. Vesting contracts are intended to cover a large portion of sales (90–100 percent) of each supplier initially. This share is reduced gradually in later years and replaced by freely negotiated bilateral contracts as the vesting contracts expire.

Vesting contracts are expected to include purchases by TETAS from all EUAS hydro plants, sales from TETAS to all distribution companies and distribution TOORs to cover franchise captive consumer demand (with part of hydro capacity available for the balancing market), and sales from affiliate portfolio generation companies to all distribution companies.

The main objectives of vesting contracts are as follows (OECD 2002, EMRA 2003):

- Avoid large physical imbalances or large financial risks to participants.
- Avoid chaotic prices.
- Ensure that distribution companies are not overexposed in the balancing market.
- Allow a period of time for learning how the bilateral market works before distribution companies undertake their own contracting.
- Allow companies to be privatized with a set of matching purchase and sale contracts so that potential buyers can value them.
- Allow government to influence the portfolio mix of generation purchased by each distributor to ensure reasonable regional balance.
- Allow determination of a reasonable flow of funds between companies (e.g., minimum sales levels for generation companies).

Public Service Obligations   The EML under the consumer support section of Article 13 and the tariff regulation under Article 20 allow for an explicit cash subsidy: direct cash refunds to consumers without affecting the price structure and the prices "in cases where consumers in certain regions and/or in line with certain objectives need to be supported." The mechanism for allocation of these direct cash refunds ("amount, procedure and principles") has not been defined in the primary legislation; it will be established by the Council of Ministers upon proposal by the MENR.

The Independent Regulatory Authority The new regime establishes the independent Energy Market Regulatory Authority, which is governed by its own board.[21] The main functions of the authority include:

- Applying and overseeing the new licensing framework
- Preparing and publishing secondary legislation on electricity and natural gas markets[22]
- Enforcing regulated third party access
- Applying a new transmission and distribution code
- Determining eligible customers over time
- Regulating tariffs for transmission and distribution activities (connection and use of system), as well as provision of retail services to noneligible customers, and the wholesale tariff of TETAS
- Performing tenders for city gas distribution networks
- Following the performance of all actors in the market
- Following and protecting customer rights
- Applying sanctions to parties violating the established rules.

Main Challenges

The actual development of competition in the Turkish electricity market is likely to take time because of various challenges and difficulties, especially those related to the exit from the old system. Primary among these challenges is the fact that most generation capacity is currently either under government ownership or tied up in take-or-pay contracts that leave no room for competition. Additional challenges lie in the financial difficulties that may persist in distribution. Finally, liberalization will entail significant tariff rebalancing, which may pose serious political challenges.

Stranded Costs and Competition in the Generation Market

As of 2002, private generators in Turkey accounted for a total of about 37 percent of capacity, including 12 percent for autoproducers (table 7.1). Under currently committed BOO, BOT, and TOOR contracts (see table)—assuming no privatization in generation, a significant increase in autoproduction capacity, but little additional new entry for the foreseeable

TABLE 7.1   Turkey's Electricity Generating Capacity: 2002, 2005, 2010

	2002 Megawatts	Percent	2005 Megawatts	Percent	2010 Megawatts	Percent
Non-EUAS plant						
Build-own-operate (BOO)	3,830	11.3	5,810	14.4	5,810	13.5
Build-own-transfer (BOT) thermal	1,450	4.3	1,450	3.6	1,450	3.4
BOT hydro and wind	899	2.7	899	2.2	899	2.1
Transfer of operating rights (TOOR) transferred	650	1.9	650	1.6	650	1.5
Mobile	623	1.8	823	2.0	823	1.9
Kepez and CEAS	1,120	3.3	1,120	2.8	1,120	2.6
Autoproduction	3,944	11.7	5,344	13.2	6,844	15.9
Subtotal	12,516	37.0	16,096	39.8	17,956	41.7
EUAS plant						
Natural gas	3,983	11.8	3,983	9.8	3,983	9.3
Hydro	10,326	30.6	11,685	28.9	12,762	29.7
Coal/lignite and fuel oil	6,972	20.6	8,692	21.5	8,692	20.2
Subtotal	21,281	63.0	24,360	60.2	25,437	59.1
Total capacity	33,796	100.0	40,455	100.0	43,032	100.0

Note: The forecasts in the table exclude additional hydro plants with signed intergovernmental protocols scheduled for 2007 and after.

Source: ECA 2002.

future—the public sector's share of capacity will remain at about 60 percent in 2010. Publicly owned hydro assets alone account for about a third of total generation capacity.

Because a significant share of privately operated assets are tied to contracts entailing fixed amounts and prices, those assets will not be deployed under competitive forces. As highlighted in table 7.1, as of 2002 the three BOO plants in operation accounted for the largest share. Total energy sold by the BOO plants in 2002 was 36.4 gigawatt-hours, or 34.3 percent of the total energy purchased by TETAS in 2002. Four natural gas plants, 17 hydroelectric plants, and two wind BOT plants are already in operation. These BOT projects sold 12.7 gigawatt-hours of energy in 2002, which accounted for an additional 11.9 percent of total TETAS consumption. Therefore, 46.2 percent of all purchases made by TETAS is based on existing tied BOO and BOT contracts.

Procedures are not complete for an additional 30 BOT projects with a capacity of 2,771 megawatts, and their legal status is still not clear. The anticompetitive nature of these contracts and their apparent high cost have roused public reaction against them. As for TOORs, two generators (one lignite and one hydro) are operating. TOOR contracts accounting for an additional 3,926 megawatts have not been transferred; their legal status is not clear (and their transfer would have little effect on available capacity, because they represent existing production).

Stranded costs—that is, the costs incurred within the previous market structure that cannot be economically recovered within a competitive market structure—include the high operating costs of old and inefficient generators, long-term power purchase agreements with high prices, removal of production subsidies, and high staffing costs (payments of redundancies resulting from the transfer of operations to the private sector, including pension liabilities for workers able to retire). Stranded costs create uncertainty for new investors and risk stifling competition.

Stranded costs have two main sources. The first is the substantial surplus generating capacity. Reserve margins were over 60 percent in 2002 and may remain substantially above the minimum 25 percent or so required for system security for the next few years, depending on the evolution of demand. This substantial level of excess capacity creates a situation in which facilities have low capacity

factors and thus lower revenues than required to recover full costs. Surplus generating capacity may have been driven at least in part by overly optimistic demand forecasts, a natural occurrence in a system in which the costs of substantial publicly promoted overbuilding are not apparent, and the costs of underbuilding are immediately obvious and extremely high. The two earthquakes and the economic crises that Turkey suffered in recent years also play a significant role in explaining the deviation between initial demand forecasts and actual demand. The second main source of stranded costs is the long-term power purchase contracts between the state and private producers with especially high front-end costs. The high cost of electricity from many of these contracts makes it difficult to generate the required revenues to service these contracts without increasing average wholesale and retail prices.

The long-term, Treasury-guaranteed generation contracts and associated stranded costs have two important implications. The first relates to competition. The prospects for competition among generators are poor for the immediate future unless there is new entry by IPPs or autoproducers. However, new entry may exacerbate the problem of stranded costs, because generation capacity is already expected to be in substantial surplus. Furthermore, the existing finalized BOT, BOO, and TOOR (generation) contracts adversely affect the possibilities of market liberalization by preserving an uneven playing field (in which favored generators benefit from state guarantees, privileged trading relationships, and noncompetitive pricing, and thereby face substantially fewer market risks), by preventing pressures on prices from new entry, and by preventing flexible price and quantity adjustments to unanticipated market shocks (such as the recent macro crisis).

The second implication has to do with the contingent liabilities created for the government. If revenues to the electricity sector do not cover payments to the Treasury-guaranteed generators, then the guarantees would be activated and payments from the government's constrained budgetary resources would be needed to subsidize electricity (whether it is actually used or not). The substantial state-owned hydro resources that have been developed to date go some way toward minimizing these potential liabilities, because the low cost of hydro can be considered a "stranded benefit" that can be used to help offset the sizeable transition-related stranded costs.

Indeed, the idea behind initially contracting all state-owned hydro assets to TETAS is to enable it to cover a substantial part of the stranded costs through the profits on sales at market levels of this low-cost power. However, under some low demand scenarios, even with hydro fetching the very low price of US$0.002 per kilowatt-hour,[23] TETAS may be faced with a substantial revenue deficit. Under the worst-case but not necessarily zero-probability scenarios, Economic Consulting Associates calculates these deficits to be between $100 million and $800 million annually (adding to a total of $4.1 billion) between 2003 and 2010 (ECA 2002: table 29).[24]

Revenue Deficits, Technical Losses, and Private Participation in Distribution

The main challenge in distribution when trying to create competition is to ensure the creation of creditworthy entities that can act as counterparts to incumbents and potential entrants on the generation side.

Turkey presently has 33 distribution areas. In a few regions (including those served by Kepez and CEAS, concessions that had permitted operation of the networks by private investors have been cancelled. Additional tenders for TOORs were held for other regions in 1996. Bidding occurred through offers of distribution tariffs over the concession period, with the lowest bidder winning. Thus, as for the fixed-price BOT, BOO, and TOOR generation contracts, any efficiency gains over the franchise period will not be passed on to consumers. In addition, winners had to commit to reducing technical electricity losses; gains or losses generated by changes in electricity losses would be appropriated fully by the company. An additional problem with distribution TOOR contracts is that they may prevent the subsequent imposition of a harsh efficiency-enhancing, incentive-based tariff formula, because these companies would then lose profits relative to the initially promised fixed-cost-plus tariffs, and they would therefore seek (and have grounds for) compensation. Finally, to the extent that the desirable distribution regions were cherry-picked through the TOOR process, sufficiently marketable and competitive groupings could not be formed from the remaining regions, and the most desirable subregions could not be matched with least desirable subregions, thereby

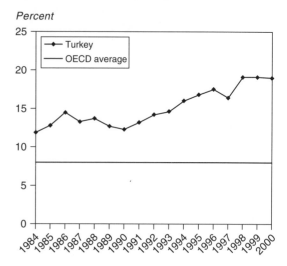

FIGURE 7.2   Electricity Losses of Turkey versus OECD, 1984–2000

Source: OECD 2002.

jeopardizing distribution privatization and possibly resulting in nonsalable assets. In 2003 most of those contracts were canceled by the Council of State.

The distribution sector suffers from growing operating revenue deficits, which are driven by electricity theft and nonpayment (about 14 percent of total energy purchased by TEDAS with large regional variation), technical losses (about 7 percent), and a free or unbilled electricity supply (4 percent, especially street lighting). In member countries of the Organisation for Economic Co-operation and Development (OECD), the average of electricity losses (which are driven mainly by technical losses) is about 8 percent (figure 7.2). Theft and nonpayment are fundamentally a political economy and distribution problem that has implications for rebalancing tariffs.

Tariff Rebalancing, Social Protection, and Industrial Competitiveness

Industrial prices are almost as high as household prices, unlike in more liberalized markets where industrial prices are often less than half those of households (lower industrial prices reflect the lower unit cost of delivery of large amounts of electricity to industrial customers). According to data on end-user prices, Turkish industry faces one of the highest costs in Europe. However, equally noteworthy is that Turkish household prices are not particularly high, in the lower end of

TABLE 7.2 Retail Prices for Electricity
(US¢ per kilowatt-hour)

	Electricity for Industry	Electricity for Households
EU12		
Austria	9.21	12.14
Belgium	4.77	13.23
Denmark	5.97	19.53
Finland	3.94	7.89
France	3.58	10.17
Germany	7.90	16.66
Greece	4.31	7.75
Ireland	4.62	9.57
Italy	9.30	13.42
Portugal	6.59	11.77
Spain	5.58	14.33
United Kingdom	4.96	10.10
Central and Eastern Europe		
Czech Republic	4.68	6.11
Hungary	5.21	6.98
Poland	4.76	8.34
Slovak Republic	4.35	6.28
North America		
Canada	3.86	6.01
United States	4.27	8.50
Turkey	8.05	8.49

Source: IEA 2002.

the range for Europe. Out of 32 countries listed in the International Energy Agency (IEA) report *Key World Energy Statistics 2002,* Turkey is the only country (apart from India) in which consumer prices are so close to industrial prices (IEA 2002). Consumer prices are more than double industrial prices in 8 of the 12 EU countries in table 7.2 and in Denmark they are three times higher. The numbers in table 7.2 suggest that, although large industrial users are likely to see substantial price decreases from increased competition, households and smaller industrial users are likely to see substantial price increases.

This large cross subsidy to households will not survive with liberalization, because eligible consumers are entitled to switch to lower-cost sources under bilateral agreements, and because less efficient or higher-cost regional distribution systems

reflect these costs in user tariffs. This issue of tariff rebalancing toward cost-reflective tariffs, if not properly handled, could jeopardize the entire reform effort by creating political pressures for backtracking. Rebalancing will have effects on poverty and relocation incentives—poorer households in the east are likely to see their prices rise most in the short term, while already overpopulated cities in the west with more efficient distribution systems will face somewhat less steep tariff increases. And it will have effects on employment and industrial competitiveness—business users with annual consumption below the threshold, including all small and medium-size enterprises (SMEs), will also likely see substantial price rises.

The recent difficulties over the creation of distribution regions reflected the income distribution dilemma faced by the authorities. The agreement reached ultimately among EMRA, MENR, TEDAS, and the Treasury after months of work was rejected by the government because of intense pressures from localities that did not want to be included in regions designated as high-cost areas. EMRA responded by proposing instead province-based, cost-reflective retail tariffs. The highest proposed tariff was for Hakkari, which is both one of the poorest provinces and the one with the highest incidence of theft (*Radikal,* March 3, 2003).

Wholesale Market Concentration and the Dominant Role of TETAS

In the design of the new market model, the role of TETAS is critical as an instrument to help resolve transitional stranded costs through market mechanisms, and thereby help protect captive consumers from sudden and large increases in wholesale prices. It is with this purpose in mind that TETAS was designated to hold all legacy state-owned contracts and liabilities—including BOT, BOO, and TOOR contracts as well existing import and export contracts—and play a key role as a wholesaler trader of electricity. The EML requires TETAS to be financially viable and authorizes TETAS to charge a wholesale price sufficient to cover its stranded cost obligations (based on the weighted average costs of the generation plants selling to it, including BOT, BOO, and TOOR plants). However, there is no requirement for profitability on a year-by-year basis. Rather, surpluses and deficits must balance over a reasonable period. The initial contracting to TETAS of all state-owned hydro plants is intended to help it meet this financial viability criterion.

As the holder of the majority of generation contracts, TETAS will be the dominant seller in the market for the foreseeable future. Through its rights to hydro capacity, TETAS also will be the dominant participant in the balancing market. Given its dominant position, it will be critical that TETAS be effectively regulated. In the absence of effective regulation, TETAS has no incentive to keep its costs as low as possible, because it passes its costs fully to captive customers.

In practice, the ability of TETAS to raise the wholesale price to cover its stranded cost obligations is constrained by the prices that could be offered by new entrants (such as the cost of electricity from a new gas-fired CCGT power plant), to the extent that new developers are willing to take the risk of building new power plants over the next few years. If the TETAS wholesale price is above the price offered by IPPs, then distribution companies and eligible consumers will choose to buy from IPPs, causing TETAS's sales to fall. However, because TETAS's costs have a large take-or-pay component from BOT, BOO, and TOOR plants, those costs will remain high as TETAS's market share falls, forcing the company to recover its fixed costs over a lower level of sales. To avoid such a vicious cycle of falling sales and required higher wholesale prices, TETAS cannot afford to charge a wholesale price significantly above that offered by a new gas-fired plant.

Interinstitutional Coordination and a National Electricity Policy

Turkey's electricity policy lacks the strong, centralized leadership needed to take an overall perspective of the electricity reform program—including tariffs, market structure, promotion of competition, and privatization issues—and to ensure coordination of the eight or more entities with separate management teams: MENR, EMRA, PA (Privatization Authority), EUAS, TETAS, TEIAS, TEDAS, and the Treasury. It would be highly desirable to achieve consensus among all main national stakeholders around a national electricity policy that presents a coherent strategy for market structure, that outlines what is meant by competition in Turkey's

electricity market for the foreseeable future and how more room could be made for additional competition, and that articulates a well-defined end state for the industry and a strategy for achieving it.

Possible Competition-Enhancing Solutions

Evidence of the benefits of electricity reform is rather recent, and most of the detailed studies concentrate on well-known cases such as the United States, United Kingdom, and Scandinavian countries. Some studies do not provide strong conclusions. For example, a recent study by the OECD (Steiner 2002) fails to find that regulatory variables such as third party access and unbundling have a significant effect on industrial prices. Such variables are found to have an impact on the *ratio* of industrial to residential prices, but this finding may be capturing the impact of rebalancing rather than the impact of the other components of reform. Privatization is found to *increase* industrial prices. Yet the same regulatory variables are found to have a positive impact on a proxy for efficiency.

Nevertheless, there is a general consensus among analysts that the key to welfare-enhancing electricity reform is adequate competition in generation. Efficiency gains, especially those stemming from cost reduction, are easiest to obtain in this segment of the industry. However, enhanced competition is necessary for those efficiency gains to be passed on to consumers. The rest of this section discusses some options that can accelerate the development of competition in the Turkish context.

Transitional Regimes for Tackling Stranded Costs

In minimizing and addressing stranded costs, the government will have to consider several options. Lowering and more rapidly resolving stranded costs will have benefits—in particular, allowing the more rapid introduction of competition. Such a step also would allow a more rapid release of hydro plants for privatization, which would have the added benefits of enabling generators and retailers to offer more valuable contract shapes and of providing flexible energy to the balancing market. Possible options include

- *A final resolution of all outstanding nonfinalized BOT and TOOR generation contracts that does not increase stranded costs.* In view of the potential costs to the economy and the electricity sector in both additional fiscal costs and foregone competition benefits, it appears to be in the public interest not to provide Treasury guarantees for most of the nonfinalized BOT and TOOR projects, while remaining open to negotiated win-win solutions subject to this constraint. The basic strategy of EMRA has been to encourage project sponsors to apply for generating licenses and to act according to the dictates of the new market model. Because of the potential reputational costs to Turkey as a destination for foreign direct investment (FDI) inflows from such a unilateral government decision, the government should remain open to negotiating with project sponsors on a case-by-case basis to seek acceptable solutions that do not burden Turkey with additional expensive and unneeded power. The broader international impact should not be too negative, as long as the underlying public policy reasons are clearly explained and the initially agreed-upon contractual terms are met, including the appropriate compensation being offered after arbitration if a negotiated solution is not possible.

- *Voluntary win-win renegotiation of tariffs.* The existing BOT contracts are heavily front-loaded with higher capacity charges in the first 5–10 years of operation. By exploring the scope for nonunilateral improvements to the contracts in the spirit of the basic principles of the EU's 1996 directive, the government could lower the level of stranded costs. Possible win-win modifications include lowering the average tariff level over time and flattening the tariff slope in exchange for removing the "T" (transfer requirement) in BOT or using alternate approaches to providing an equity return over a longer period. To facilitate negotiations, the following potential win-win modifications that would transform the existing BOT contracts into IPPs should be unbundled and discussed separately (Sevaioğlu n.d.): (1) tariff smoothing, flattening the payment curve by retarding the higher payments of the first years; (2) ownership transfer, transforming the BOT to a BOO model by subtracting the value of the assets from the tariff profile; (3) price risk transfer, removing the take-or-pay condition by compensating the difference between the agreed-on and estimated stabilized

market price; and (4) volume risk transfer, compensating the estimated revenue loss when the company fails to find customers paying the same price as agreed to in the initial take-or-pay clause. The potential for outsiders to challenge any such negotiated solution should be minimal, so long as project sponsors are no better off than they were prior to the renegotiation. Stranded costs also could be reduced by agreeing to lower the gas prices charged in individual contracts by BOTAŞ, the state-owned national gas company.

- *Postponing or canceling of nonfinalized intergovernmental protocols on hydro.* Intergovernmental protocols refer to commitments between two or more sovereign governments for specific investments. To help lower the extent of excess generation capacity on the system, authorities should consider altering the existing pipeline of country-to-country protocols. Because such protocols are political undertakings rather than established private contractual rights, modifications in line with unexpected public policy imperatives may be easier to achieve.

- *Low pricing of TETAS-contracted, state-owned hydro generation assets.* By pricing hydro at its operations and maintenance cost, TETAS could reduce the revenues required to pay the stranded costs. However, depending on the demand scenario, low pricing of hydro may not be adequate on its own.

- *Stranded cost levy.* A levy or additional surcharge could be applied in various ways to obtain revenue to cover any deficit, but the simplest way would be to apply it to final electricity consumption. Imposing the levy on final consumption ensures that eligible consumers and distribution companies cannot avoid the levy when they buy power from sources other than TETAS. A stranded cost levy may be the easiest and best solution from an economic point of view. However, the levy would result in an increase in prices to end consumers: the approach suffers from the obvious drawback that the tariff would raise.

- *Sale of hydropower plants.* Selling (or leasing) hydropower plants to the private sector and using these sales revenues to cover the stranded cost deficits is an option that also should be considered. This would have an impact similar to that produced by diluting the high BOT, BOO, and TOOR generation costs with low-cost hydro, but the advantages would be twofold. First, revenues would be realized immediately, at a time when Treasury resources are particularly constrained. Second, such an approach would allow market liberalization to go ahead more rapidly. However, an important consideration for the government is whether adequate revenues would be realized from the sale of what are potentially extremely valuable assets in the balancing market in the immediate term, or whether higher revenues could be realized once the market begins functioning, once experience accumulates on how the new market would value hydro plants and hydro electricity, and once investor confidence increases with additional regulatory oversight experience. Yet the benefit of more rapid liberalization or at least a staged privatization approach with annual auctions for some hydro (either for capacity in, say, 1-megawatt tranches of all hydro or for all of a specific plant for one-year leases) may well outweigh the foregone higher revenue proceeds of a later sale, in particular if the earlier prospect of privatization helps to spur better regulatory oversight and other market-friendly policy decisions during the shorter preprivatization period (driven by the pressures of an incipient privatization).

Tariffs and Universal Service

Under the electricity reforms, industrial tariffs are expected to fall, and household tariffs are expected to increase from tariff rebalancing. However, in any assessment of the impact of overall tariff changes on consumer welfare, it is important to take into account the decrease in the prices of all goods in the household consumer basket that will result from the lower cost of this key intermediate input. More generally, efficiency gains from cost-reflective prices are expected throughout the economy.

To mitigate the effect of rising household tariffs, the first priority should be to reduce costs by eliminating theft and nonpayment rather than by adjusting household tariffs upward by the full margin required to cover costs (inclusive of theft and nonpayment). In addition, a means-tested system is needed to provide support to those who cannot afford the higher retail prices and are eligible for such social protection (in part replacing the current reliance on theft and nonpayment of bills

as a social safety net). Such support has fiscal implications for forthcoming budgets. It also requires the implementation of workable eligibility and delivery mechanisms.

As part of a possible policy solution, the EML and the tariff regulation allow an explicit cash subsidy under a mechanism to be established by the Council of Ministers. Provisional Article 12 of the licensing regulation allows vesting contracts, which could be bundled in order to offer lower-cost contracts to higher-cost distribution regions and thereby ease cross-regional adjustment. One additional mechanism that might help to ease the cost burden on residents in the eastern part of Turkey is the use of meters with a three-term tariff structure. By using such meters, the electricity sector could offer extremely low prices during off-peak periods and thereby help to reduce illicit utilization.

Cross-Border Trade and the Benefits of EU Accession

EU countries have reported benefits from adopting the electricity directive, but problem areas remain (European Commission 2002c):

- *Differential rates of market liberalization.* By 2002, five countries had implemented 100 percent market liberalization, but the rest had opened up less than 60 percent of their markets. Indeed, Denmark, France, and Greece had opened up only 35 percent of their markets.
- *Disparities in access tariffs between network operators.* Because of a lack of transparency caused by insufficient unbundling (e.g., management or accounting but not legal or ownership separation) and inefficient regulation, these disparities may form a barrier to competition.
- *The high level of market power among existing generating companies associated with a lack of liquidity in wholesale and balancing markets.* Such high market power impedes new entrants. For example, only in three member states do the top three companies have less than 50 percent market share; in nine member states the top three companies have more than 75 percent market share. Large divergences in prices continue to exist across member states.

A central implication of the full internal market is that an important source of competition in countries where the generation market is concentrated would be cross-border transactions. However, the ratio of import capacity to installed capacity is more than 25 percent in only four out of the 15 EU countries to date. A heavier reliance on cross-border transactions requires better cross-border arrangements. The problem is insufficient interconnection infrastructure between member states and, where congestion exists, unsatisfactory methods for allocating scarce capacity. But it is encouraging that participants in the sixth Florence forum in September 2001 agreed on common guidelines on congestion management. There has been more progress on cross-border tariffication. Since the adoption of a temporary mechanism for cross-border electricity exchanges in March 2002, EU market players involved in cross-border exchanges no longer have to pay a series of uncoordinated charges to transmission networks ("pancaking") because all transit and import charges have been removed. Under the new regime, only a single export charge is allowed (€1 per megawatt-hour). Nevertheless, the European Commission remains worried about the pace of development of cross-border trade. By the end of 2000, four years after adoption of the electricity directive, the physical cross-border trade in electricity did not exceed 8 percent of total consumption, which left "the EU far from a real, competitive internal market" (European Commission 2002c: 22)

As for Turkey, obstacles to increased cross-border trade include:

- *Operating standards and interconnector capacity.* Currently, Turkey does not comply with the main continental European UCPTE (Union for the Coordination of Production and Transmission of Electricity) operating standards, and therefore it cannot connect its network synchronously. In 2006 Turkey is expected to be part of the UCPTE network. A 400-kilowatt overhead line to Greece is expected to be commissioned by 2006 (with a subsea cable connecting Greece with Italy and the Western Europe network). A connection exists with Bulgaria when a portion of the Turkish network in Thrace is disconnected (according to the OECD, imports from Bulgaria account for 3 percent of domestic consumption).
- *Cross-border transmission pricing and settlement coordination.* The tariff framework for cross-border transactions is not yet very well developed, so it is still organizationally and economically difficult for individual electricity customers to choose suppliers situated in another EU member state, although proposals for more refined systems of cross-border pricing are being developed.
- *Technological transmission losses over distance.* Absent a DC (direct current) direct transmission link (like the one between Greece and Italy), the cost of running electricity through intermediary transmission networks makes shipping electricity from Turkey to France or the United Kingdom prohibitive. Therefore, trade in the medium term will remain fairly localized, possibly including Greece, Italy, and Bulgaria-Romania. Because Turkey has lower-cost endowments than neighboring countries, it is likely that the eventual flow will be from Turkey to neighboring countries, implying a gradual increase in Turkish prices as low-cost assets are fully utilized.

Without a doubt, one of the most significant benefits of EU accession for Turkey in the electricity sector would be the stability provided by anchoring Turkish regulations and practices to EU norms and practices. Because of the degree of political instability in Turkey (especially, until recently, the predominance of coalition governments and the short tenure of governments), and because in the past the discretionary authority of the state has not always been used in the clear interest of the public (the existing stranded contracts in electricity are an example), the European anchor will provide a strong signal of discrete and irreversible regime change from past practices that may have caused concern among both foreign and domestic players in the electricity industry. The confidence-boosting effect on potential investors, who otherwise may continue to be reluctant to enter the Turkish electricity market, is likely to be significant.

Privatization and Entry Promotion Strategies for Generation and Distribution Assets

It has been asserted that one of the worst features of EU electricity reforms until the recent proposals was the continued presence of vertical integration—in Europe, common ownership of generation and distribution is increasing. Vertical ownership separation or unbundling of distribution from generation at the time of privatization seems to have become the consensus approach in the rest of the world; it has been adopted successfully in England/Wales, Latin America (Argentina, Bolivia, Chile, Colombia, El Salvador, Guatemala, and Peru as the most-cited examples), several transition economies, and Australia and New Zealand. Malaysia and many EU countries are exceptions to this pattern.

The recent crisis in California, however, raised doubts, including in Europe, about the stability and viability of unbundled electricity markets (Newbery 2001, 2002a). It has been argued that generating companies in California had the incentives and ability to behave strategically, withhold capacity, and thereby manipulate and increase wholesale prices (although other factors were at work as well, including flawed market design—see box 7.1). By contrast, it is argued that integration of generation with distribution eliminates these incentives and creates a more stable market structure.

An assessment of which way to go must include weighing the benefits of mitigating the wholesale price risk that vertical integration can provide against the costs of foregone competition and foregone effective regulation. The arguments point to vertical separation as the preferred initial configuration, allowing markets to reconfigure assets at a later stage if desirable (subject to oversight by the competition authorities). Whether Turkey's state-owned thermal generation plants should be privatized as a small number of bundled portfolio companies or sold as separate units depends at least in part on how geographically apart from each other they are.

Mitigating Wholesale Price Risk The recent rush toward vertical mergers in England/Wales has been driven at least in part by their move from a compulsory, single-price power pool to a bilateral contracts framework in which there would no longer be a single price for the delivery of electricity at any particular time but rather directly negotiated prices between buyers and sellers (and substantial penalties for generators and customers who deviate from their contracted levels). The wholesale price risk that arises in a bilateral contracting environment translates directly into profit risk in an

unbundled structure: a high price shifts profits to generators and away from the retailing business, and a low price benefits retailing at the expense of generators. This risk can be reduced by vertical integration in which generators are assured of a captive market. Vertical integration also reduces the transaction costs of contracting, as well as the risk of failing to find a buyer and thus being forced into a distress sale in the short-term balancing market. Yet the larger the share of the market covered by vertically integrated companies, the harder new entry will be and the more disadvantaged will be those companies that remain nonintegrated.

Developing Competition Where Possible If a key objective of reform is to stimulate the stable provision of low-cost, low-priced electrical energy, international evidence suggests that sufficient competition is the best means to achieve it. A negative aspect of vertical integration is that the monopolist distributor will, in many circumstances, be able to increase its profits (together with delayed innovation) at the expense of society by favoring its own integrated generating companies over more efficient (existing and potential that may not enter) generators. Ownership separation removes the incentive for market foreclosure. Although there remain economies of scope between generation and transmission/distribution that may suggest benefits from full vertical integration, there is also substantial evidence that the benefits of unbundled competition may be substantial. A telling example is the early experience of Scotland, where the two producers were privatized as vertically integrated companies, and England/Wales, where there was strict vertical separation at the time of privatization. Prior to the reforms in 1990, prices in Scotland were about 8 percent lower than those in England/Wales. In 2000, Scottish prices were 5 percent higher, a swing of 13 percent (OECD 2001).

Facilitating Effective Regulation If the regulators of the distribution monopolies are unable to detect or prevent discriminatory treatment toward favored generators, many of the benefits of competition would be lost, casting doubt on the benefits of the overall liberalization project. Vertical ownership separation facilitates the job of the regulator by removing incentives for nontransparent transfer pricing, differential quality of access to the wires, or

BOX 7.1   California's Electricity Crisis

In 1996 the California electricity industry underwent a fundamental restructuring. Before reforms, three vertically integrated utilities owned and operated generation, transmission, and distribution assets. Retail prices were regulated by the state, and wholesale prices were regulated at the federal level by the Federal Energy Regulatory Commission (FERC). Prices were higher than U.S. averages, a situation that was blamed on the vertically integrated structure and long-term contracts with independent power producers (IPPs). Thus, the public demanded reform.

The most important features of the Restructuring Law of 1996 were as follows:

- Customers could choose a competitive electricity service provider (ESP) or buy default service from the local utility distribution company (UDC).
- Incumbents were required to provide competing generators, wholesale marketers, and ESPs with open access to their transmission and distribution networks at regulated prices.
- The UDC default service price was set equal to the wholesale spot market prices determined in the day-ahead real-time markets.
- A retail rate freeze of a maximum of four years was set to recover the stranded costs of generating assets (the assumption was that wholesale prices would be lower than frozen retail levels).
- The California Independent System Operator (ISO) and California Power Exchange were created.
- The two largest investor-owned utilities (IOUs) were ordered to divest at least half of their fossil fuel generating capacity.
- The IOUs were required to meet default service obligations by purchasing from the spot market (i.e., they had to sell power from their remaining assets and then buy it back to meet their default service demand). They were "short" for the difference between what they could sell and what they had to meet in terms of default demand; and they were not allowed to hedge by forward contracts with generators, because it was feared that such contracts could be anticompetitive.

Market design represented a series of incoherent and fragmented compromises between interest groups (bits and pieces from different designs) rather than a well-thought-out strategy. It also was very complicated. The design relied more on individual generator owners to make commitment and dispatch decisions and to manage congestion based on their self-interests (in that sense, it was closer to the "New Trading Arrangements" in the United Kingdom than the previous pool system). Meanwhile, serious episodes of horizontal market power problems began to emerge: because of the rigid capacity constraints, small amounts of withheld capacity resulted in large price increases. But the buildup of new capacity turned out to be very slow, and California found itself also experiencing a rapid increase in demand. In response, the IOUs became increasingly reliant on the spot market. Customer switching to ESPs was slower than expected, which meant large default service obligations for the IOUs. The ban on hedging contracts made their situation even more difficult. As a result, a large portion of demand was served through the volatile wholesale market.

The meltdown of the system was triggered by dramatic increases in the wholesale prices that utilities had to pay. The main reasons for the increase were rising natural gas (input) prices, a large increase in demand (due to abnormally hot weather, high economic growth), reduced imports, and rising prices for nitrogen oxide emissions credits. In addition, there were serious market power problems. It has been estimated that about a third of price increases were attributable to market power and strategic behavior by players. High prices also further distorted incentives. For example, ESPs lost incentives to sell in the retail market because they could increase profit by selling in the wholesale market.

Because retail prices were frozen, the utilities began to experience financial problems and creditworthiness declined. Their requests to increase retail prices were turned down by the state regulator. Finally, they went bankrupt. The state government practically took over supply.

Bad luck played an important role in the Californian crisis in the sense that a large number of adverse events jointly triggered wholesale prices. However, flawed design and existence of market power made the system vulnerable to adverse shocks.

Sources: Joskow 2001; Cabral 2002.

other discriminatory treatment between distributors and generators, and thereby making it easier for regulators to get information about the true underlying costs and to secure fair access to the networks. The much more difficult task of effectively regulating vertically integrated companies, if that is to be an outcome preferred by the markets at a subsequent stage, should only be attempted by more seasoned regulators after a significant period of learning-by-doing in an unbundled environment.

As for sequencing, it is appropriate first to privatize distribution companies and ensure commercial management of those assets. This approach will allow the creation of financially viable companies that, in turn, allow private generators to structure bankable projects without government guarantees.

According to Newbery (2002a, 2002b), four conditions must be met for unbundled electricity markets to create socially beneficial outcomes. The first is that potential suppliers must have access to the transmission system. Access is best achieved by unbundling transmission from generation and securing third party access, both of which are satisfied in the Turkish design.

The second condition is the existence of adequate and secure supplies of electricity, which implies the existence of adequate transmission and generation capacity. This condition also seems to be satisfied in the Turkish case, at least in the short to medium term, because of the substantial amounts of excess capacity available at present.

The third condition is the presence of a sufficient number of untied generation companies, so that generation is truly competitive. This situation is perhaps the most problematic in the current Turkish context because of the sizable amount of generation capacity that is either state-owned or has tied quantities and prices through long-term contracts. Thermal generation assets under public ownership can, in principle, be regrouped prior to privatization to create a number of viable companies. These affiliate portfolio generation companies can be granted managerial and financial independence so that they can perform their activities in accordance with more competitive conditions even prior to privatization. This situation would be desirable in any case in order to put at least a minimum amount of structurally based competitive pressure on existing state-owned thermal plants for increased productive efficiency and lower costs.

However, the weight of tied generation assets that have been contracted to private parties through BOT, BOO, and TOOR contracts may continue to prevent sufficient competition from emerging for some time, particularly to the extent that hydro assets also remain contracted to TETAS over the medium term to ensure its financial viability. In this area, bold policy measures that reduce stranded costs and allow earlier hydro release to the market could yield substantial benefits.

An alternate but complementary way in which to increase competition and reduce market power in generation markets is through policies that work on the demand rather than the supply side by increasing the elasticity of demand—that is, by promoting stronger customer response to price changes. Traditionally, all customers pay fixed prices (for industrial customers, these are based on annually negotiated fixed-price contracts) that may vary in a mutually agreed-upon manner on a daily or weekly basis, but independent of fluctuations in wholesale prices. As a result, the drop in demand in response to a rise in market price is negligible, greatly facilitating the exercise of market power. The key here is to induce customers to reduce consumption when prices rise. Two options are possible. For the first, interruptible contracts, which give the electricity supplier the right to curtail supply or to ripple off specific appliances for short periods of time when price exceeds some level, could be promoted—if necessary through subsidies because of their positive externality—for customers who can switch to other fuels or self-generation. But the preferred option, again promoted through subsidies if necessary because of their positive spillover, is to subject customers, especially the largest, to real-time (time-of-use) metering and billing. Once end users receive the technology not only to observe but also to respond to real-time prices, they are empowered to modify their purchasing habits accordingly.

A powerful additional mechanism for enhancing customer response to price changes is the promotion of competition in retail activities. As discussed earlier, the EML allows for several retail companies to undertake activities in a distribution region along with the retailer that belongs to the distribution company.

Newbery's fourth and final condition is that the liberalized markets should be adequately regulated.

This condition means, among other things, that regulation should not be limited to naturally monopolistic segments, but also should include wholesale markets. The argument here is that relying solely on ex post competition policy remedies to discipline strategic behavior in wholesale markets may be insufficient for preventing large welfare losses. Instead, regulators may need competition powers to ensure that pricing in wholesale markets does not deviate too much for too long from costs.[25] This area seems to have been overlooked in the proposed amendments to the electricity directive in Europe.

In the Turkish market design, the wholesale tariff applicable to electricity sales by TETAS will be regulated to reflect TETAS's average purchase prices as well as its financial obligations (see Provisional Article 1 of the electricity market tariff regulation). In addition, the vested contracts discussed earlier should prevent high volatility as the non-TETAS segment of the market develops. Because of the initial monopolistic structure of the wholesale market in Turkey, it is appropriate that the behavior of TETAS be closely regulated. However, as noted earlier, it may be desirable that the regulator be granted additional oversight powers over the wholesale market even as the dominant power of TETAS dissipates over time.

Conclusion

It will take some time before electricity reform in Turkey starts showing benefits that are appreciated by consumers. In fact, in the short run some consumers may be adversely affected as measures are undertaken to correct for past mistakes. Yet the slow pace of market development may be turned into a blessing. Electricity reform of the Turkish type is radical and entails huge uncertainties. The slow pace of liberalization stemming from inherited stranded costs should allow market players and regulators alike to experiment and adjust the rules wherever necessary.

Notes

1. The authors are grateful for extremely helpful written comments on an earlier draft provided by Osman Sevaioğlu, board member of Turkey's Energy Market Regulatory Authority, and for additional feedback from conference participants.

2. This section builds on Pollitt (1999) and Newberry (2002b, 2002c).

3. Directive 96/92/EC of the European Parliament and of the Council of 19 December 1996 Concerning Common Rules for the Internal Market in Electricity. The text of the directive, as well as the accompanying explanatory memorandum and proposed amendments (discussed later in this chapter), can be found at http://europa.eu.int/comm/energy/en/elec_single_market/index_en.html.

4. See the guide to the electricity directive at http://europa.eu.int/comm/energy/en/elec_single_market/memor.htm.

5. See "Directive 2003/54/EC of the European Parliament and of the Council of 26 June 2003 Concerning Common Rules for the Internal Market in Electricity and Repealing Directive 96/92/EC." The new directive is available at http://europa.eu.int/comm/energy/electricity/legislation/index_en.htm.

6. For background on the Turkish electricity sector, see Kulalı (1997), Zenginobuz and Oğur (2000), and OECD (2002).

7. OECD (2002) calls this "policy work-arounds."

8. The law is titled Law Concerning the Authorization of Enterprises Other than Turkish Electricity Authority for the Production, Transmission, Distribution and Trade of Electricity.

9. In practice, most BOT contracts have been for 20 years.

10. Law No. 3996 is titled Law for Certain Investments and Services to be Carried Out under the Build-Operate-Transfer Model. The scope of the BOT model under this new law (Article 2) appears to limit its application to greenfield projects and to require TOOR projects for existing assets to be governed by the privatization law (Law No. 4046, also dated 1994). The electricity sector was removed from the domain of Law No. 3996 in 1994 (through Law No. 4047), but was reinstated in 1999 (through Law No. 4493).

11. The take-or-pay element of the contracted gas varies from contract to contract, but on average it is 80 percent, implying, for example, that in 2005 some 33 billion cubic meters of gas must be purchased whether needed or not (ECA 2002).

12. Although there now is general agreement that these contracts are not in the best public interest, it is still not clear why they were awarded in the first place. One explanation, mentioned earlier in this chapter, is that the government saw an urgent need to attract private investors (both to deal with fiscal constraints and to reduce state dominance), and that it had to pay high risk premiums because of macroeconomic uncertainty and, in general, weak protection of property rights. Others argue that that view is naïve, and they point to lobbying and capture by investor groups and weaknesses in checks and balances.

13. The evolution of BOT and TOOR projects in generation and distribution is further discussed later in this chapter.

14. Law No. 4446 Regarding Amendments on Certain Articles of the Constitution of the Republic of Turkey, published in the *Official Gazette* on August 14, 1999.

15. Many authors also point to the Conservative Party's overall—ideological—dislike of government intervention in the economy (see, e.g., Newbery 2001).

16. Data provided by Osman Sevaioğlu, board member, EMRA, May 11, 2003.

17. EML Article 2.b states that TEIAS is to take over all "publicly owned" transmission facilities. A communiqué issued by EMRA in November 2002 envisaged the transfer of all transmission assets to TEIAS by December 31, 2002. This deadline was moved a month by the decision of the board of EMRA (Communiqué on the Amendments of Contracts of Undertakings Active in More than One Market and on Transfer of Transmission Activities and Activities Which Are to Be Withdrawn From). Apparently, CEAS and the government disagree about the ownership of transmission facilities that were operated by CEAS.

18. All production, distribution and commercial facilities of these two companies were also seized in June 2003, on grounds that the companies persistently violated provisions of the TOOR concession agreements that they had signed with the government to run the power stations and distribute electricity.

19. Stranded costs are those incurred within the previous market structure that cannot be economically recovered within a competitive market structure.

20. In the English translation available on EMRA's Web site, it is called the Market Financial Reconciliation Center.

21. The EML provided for an authority responsible for regulating the electricity sector. This provision was changed, however, through Law No. 4646 (the natural gas market law), which designated a single authority for both the electricity and gas sectors.

22. For the electricity market, EMRA has issued, among other things, regulations on licensing, tariffs, exports and imports, and eligible consumers, as well as a grid code and a distribution code. These are available at http://www.epdk.gov.tr/english/regulations/electricity.htm.

23. All dollar amounts are U.S. dollars unless otherwise indicated.

24. The worst-case scenario entails demand growth at levels projected by the Organisation for Economic Co-operation and Development (OECD), which are lower than those projected by MENR and with all pending BOT and TOOR projects going ahead. In addition to assumptions on demand, results also are sensitive to the assumed level of wholesale prices that might emerge with new entry (lower wholesale prices will create larger operating deficits for the relevant generation plants selling to TETAS) and to the assumed minimum unavoidable costs of the state-owned plants that must be covered (sustainable operating cost levels, rather than those required just to cover operations and maintenance, fuel, and debt service costs, could lead to revenue deficits even with the higher MENR demand levels).

25. For example, in the United States FERC has a statutory responsibility to ensure that prices are "just and reasonable," which gives it the authority it needs to replace market-determined prices with regulated prices. See the discussion in Newbery (2002b).

References

Armstrong, Mark, Simon Cowan, and John Vickers. 1994. *Regulatory Reform: Economic Analysis and British Experience.* Cambridge, MA: MIT Press.

Cabral, Luis. 2002. "The California Energy Crisis." *Japan and the World Economy* 14: 335–39.

ECA (Economic Consulting Associates). 2002. "Turkey Power Sector Review Study." Draft, October.

EMRA (Energy Market Regulatory Authority). 2003. *Electricity Market Implementation Manual.* Ankara.

European Commission. 2001a. *Communication from the Commission to the Council and the European Parliament: Completing the Internal Energy Market.* COM(2001)125 final, March 13, 2001. http://europa.eu.int/comm/energy/en/elec_single_market/index_en.html.

————. 2001b. *Proposal for a Directive of the European Parliament and the Council Amending Directives 96/92/EC and 98/30/EC Concerning Rules for the Internal Markets in Electricity and Natural Gas.* COM(2001)125 final, March 13, 2001. http://europa.eu.int/comm/energy/en/elec_single_market/index_en.html.

————. 2002a. "Energy Council: Loyola de palacio. European Energy Market Revolutionized." EC Press Release, IP/02/1733, November 26.

————. 2002b. "Presidency Conclusions Barcelona European Council 15 and 16 March 2002." EC Press Release, C/02/930, March 20.

————. 2002c. "Second Benchmarking Report on the Implementation of the Internal Electricity and Gas Market." SEC (2002)1038, Brussels, January 10.

IEA (International Energy Agency). 2002. *Key World Energy Statistics 2002.* Paris.

Joskow, Paul. 2001. "California's Electricity Crisis." *Oxford Review of Economic Policy* 17(3): 365–88.

Kulalı, İhsan. 1997. *Elektrik Sektöründe Özelleştirme ve Türkiye Uygulaması* [Privatization in the Electricity Sector and Application to Turkey]. Ankara: DPT Uzmanlık Tezi.

Newbery, David M. 2001. "Regulating Unbundled Network Utilities." http://www.econ.cam.ac.uk/dae/people/newbery/files/dublin.pdf.

————. 2002a. "Mitigating Market Power in Electricity Markets." http://www.econ.cam.ac.uk/dae/people/newbery/files/rome.pdf.

————. 2002b. "Problems of Liberalising the Electricity Industry." *European Economic Review* 46: 919–27.

————. 2002c. "Regulatory Challenges to European Electricity Liberalization." Department of Applied Economics Working Paper No. 0230, University of Cambridge.

OECD (Organisation for Economic Co-operation and Development). 2001. *OECD Review of Regulatory Reform, UK.* Paris.

————. 2002. "Regulatory Reform in Electricity, Gas and Road Freight Transport." Background paper for *OECD Review of Regulatory Reform: Regulatory Reform in Turkey.* http://www.oecd.org/regreform/backgroundreports.

Pollitt, Michael. 1999. "Issues in Electricity Market Integration and Liberalization." In *A European Market for Electricity,* ed. Lars Bergman, Gert Brunekreeft, Chris Doyle, Nils-Henrik M. von der Fehr, David M. Newbery, Michael Pollitt, and Pierre Regibeau. London: Centre for Economic Policy Research.

Sevaioğlu, Osman. n.d. "Discussion Notes on the Paper: 'Competition and Regulatory Reform in the Turkish Electricity Sector.'" Middle East Technical University.

Steiner, Faye. 2002. "Regulation, Industry Structure and Performance in the Electricity Supply Industry." Economics Department Working Paper ECO/WKP(200)11, Organisation for Economic Co-operation and Development, Paris.

Zenginobuz, Ünal, and Serhan Oğur. 2000. "Türkiye Elektrik Sektöründe Yeniden Yapılanma, Özelleştirme ve Regülasyon" [Restructuring, Privatization and Regulation in the Turkish Electricity Sector]. In *Devletin Düzenleyici Rolü* [The Regulatory Function of the State], ed. Izak Atiyas. Istanbul: TESEV Publications.

8

INSTITUTIONAL ENDOWMENT AND REGULATORY REFORM IN TURKEY'S NATURAL GAS SECTOR

Maria Rita Mazzanti and Alberto Biancardi

This chapter focuses on Turkey's natural gas market and the regulatory reforms recently adopted to liberalize the sector and comply with European Union (EU) requirements for accession.[1] To this end, the first section of the chapter analyzes the present situation of the gas market from the point of view of its structural parameters—that is, the structure of its demand and supply and the present status of its import and export interconnections and national networks, as well as its future development. The section then goes on to analyze the issues related to the long-term take-or-pay contracts by the national transportation company and their impact on liberalization. The second section of this chapter addresses questions related to the present ownership and industry structure, and it compares the Turkish case with that of some EU countries. In doing so, the section discusses similarities with other emerging gas markets as well as differences with more mature markets. The third section is devoted to regulatory reforms. It analyzes the new Turkish gas law and compares it with the solutions adopted in selected EU countries, with particular reference to the gas release program and measures that might be taken to limit the market power of the incumbent. A concluding section follows.

The Present Situation in the Turkish Gas Market

The Turkish natural gas market is still an emerging one. Turkey has limited gas resources, and it began production and distribution only in 1976. A considerable part of the country is still not served by natural gas.

The use of natural gas by industry is also relatively new. It began in 1989—after the initiation of gas imports from the Russian Federation and is rapidly growing. Demand in the power generation sector is expected to grow even more rapidly, doubling between 2001 and 2010. In 2001 total gas demand was 15.5 billion cubic meters. Of this, the power industry accounted for about 10.6 billion cubic meters, followed by residential demand at about 2.7 billion cubic meters and industry demand at 2.0 billion cubic meters.[2]

Between 1990 and 1998, the average annual primary gas demand increased by 15.3 percent, with peak growth of 18.4 percent in 1999. Past government forecasts had predicted that demand would grow by almost 26 percent per year between 1999 and 2005; for the next 15 years it was expected to grow at a rate of between 3.5 percent and 4 percent. Figures published recently by Turkey's state-owned gas company, BOTAŞ, indicate that the company expects the Turkish gas market to double in size over the next years, with 55 cities receiving natural gas for the first time. Many independent observers have expressed doubts about these figures, however. They believe BOTAŞ's demand forecasts were overly optimistic and point to the fact that subsidies and below-cost pricing would have to be phased out during the process of liberalization of the energy sector.

Import and Export Infrastructure and Future Developments

The state-owned company, BOTAŞ, has enjoyed monopoly rights for oil and gas pipeline transportation, as well as for import, export, and wholesale trading, since 1987. BOTAŞ owns seven natural gas pipelines and related facilities: Russian Federation–Turkey Natural Gas Main Transmission Line, Marmara Ereğlisi Liquefied Natural Gas (LNG) Import Terminal, İzmit-Karadeniz Ereğli Natural Gas Transmission Line, Bursa-Çan Natural Gas Transmission Line, Çan-Çanakkale Natural Gas Transmission Line, Eastern Anatolia Natural Gas Main Transmission Line, and Karacabey-İzmir Natural Gas Transmission Line.

In view of the expected rapid increase in natural gas consumption, in 1984 the government of Turkey signed an intergovernmental agreement with the former Soviet Union. Consequently, in 1986 BOTAŞ and SOYUZGAZEXPORT signed a natural gas sale and purchase agreement for a 25-year period. Natural gas began flowing to Turkey in 1987, and the volume transported gradually increased, reaching 6 billion cubic meters per year in the plateau period in 1993.

The 842-kilometer Russian Federation–Turkey Natural Gas Main Transmission Line enters Turkey at Malkoçlar at the Bulgarian border and then follows the Hamitabat, Ambarlı, İstanbul, İzmit, Bursa, Eskişehir route to reach Ankara. The main dispatching center is located in Yapracık-Ankara. Construction of the pipeline began on October 26, 1986, and the line reached Hamitabat on June 23, 1987. Since then, imported natural gas has been used together with domestic gas for power generation at the Trakya Combined Cycle Power Plant in Hamitabat. The pipeline reached Ankara in August 1988. The İstanbul Fertilizer Industry Company (IGSAŞ) began to receive natural gas in July 1988,

the Ambarlı Power Plant in August 1988, and Ankara for residential and commercial purposes in October 1988. In 1996, the transmission pipeline was extended to the western Black Sea region via the İzmit-Karadeniz Ereğli line (209 kilometers); the main customers are the Ereğli Iron and Steel Works plants. In the same year, the main transmission line also was extended to Çan.

The Bursa-Çan Natural Gas Transmission Line was completed in 1996 for the purpose of supplying natural gas to the Çanakkale Ceramic Factory, together with other industrial establishments along the route. In 2000, the Çan-Çanakkale Natural Gas Transmission Line was completed.

In 1998, BOTAŞ signed an agreement with Russia to import 8 billion cubic meters per year of natural gas from the West through TURUSGAZ—a BOTAŞ, GAZPROM (Russia), and GAMA (Turkey, civil contractor) joint venture. Another agreement was signed with the Russian Federation on December 15, 1997, to import 16 billion cubic meters of gas per year through a pipeline beneath the Black Sea. A joint venture was also established by GAZPROM and ENI (Italy) to lay the "Blue Stream" pipeline, and on December 29, 2002, the first Blue Stream pipeline gas from Russia entered Turkey, crossing the Black Sea at a depth of down to 2,150 meters. Deliveries were expected to amount to 16 billion cubic meters by 2007 in accordance with the natural gas sale and purchase agreement.

In August 1996, Turkey and the Islamic Republic of Iran signed a 25-year natural gas sale and purchase agreement that called for the delivery of natural gas to start at a volume of 3 billion cubic meters per year, to reach 10 billion cubic meters per year in the plateau period in 2007. The agreement was then amended in August 2000. A dedicated pipeline, the Eastern Anatolia Natural Gas Main Transmission Line, running between Dogubayazit on the Turkish-Iranian border and Ankara/Seydisehir (Konya) was completed at the end of 2001 after some delay. On December 2001, the delivery of natural gas began through the Eastern Anatolia line. In April 2002 the construction works of the Karacabey-İzmir Natural Gas Transmission Line were completed, and the line became operational.

In 1999, BOTAŞ signed an agreement with Turkmenistan for the purchase of 16 billion cubic meters of natural gas per year. The Turkmen gas would be transported to Turkey for a period of

30 years. On February 19, 1999, the Turkmen government commissioned project studies to a consortium comprising PSG–General Electric Capital and Bechtel. Shell joined this consortium on August 6, 1999. This project involves construction of a pipeline from Turkmenistan to Turkey, running parallel to the Baku-Tbilisi-Ceyhan crude oil pipeline until it joins the Eastern Anatolia Natural Gas Main Transmission Line near Erzurum. Gas imports were expected to begin between 2002 and 2004; however, no progress has been made on this gas pipeline. Meanwhile, the Turkish Petroleum Corporation (TPAO) has conducted the relevant studies needed to join the international consortium that will develop and produce gas from six dedicated gas fields (including the Körpece, Zeagli, Darvaza, Garacaovlak, and Malay fields) to feed the Trans-Caspian gas pipeline.

In April 2002, after two years of planning, Turkey and Greece signed a memorandum of understanding for a gas pipeline linking the two countries. The Ankara–Dedeagac link, which forms part of the EU's INOGATE (Interstate Oil Gas Transport to Europe) program, will feed Iranian gas through western Turkey to the Greek frontier. INOGATE is a technical assistance program of the EU (covering central and eastern Europe, including the newly independent states) that seeks to integrate the hydrocarbon transport networks between the Caucasus, central Asia, and central and eastern Europe. Start-up is planned for 2005, with an initial capacity of 0.5 billion cubic meters per year, rising to a plateau of 3.6 billion cubic meters per year. The link is capable of carrying 13 billion cubic meters of gas per year, with Turkey's share set to plateau at 10 billion cubic meters per year in 2007. The pipeline will connect Karacabey in western Turkey to Komotini city in northeast Greece, enabling Turkey to sell Greece some of the gas surplus. The cost of this project is estimated at €250 million, and it should be completed in 2005. An economic feasibility study for the project, conducted by Société Générale, was funded equally by DEPA (the Greek national gas company) and the European Commission. Countries that could be interested in selling gas to the European market via this pipeline include Azerbaijan, the Islamic Republic of Iran, Kazakhstan, Turkmenistan, and Uzbekistan. In particular, Iran hopes to export the extra 3 billion cubic meters per year to the European market.

The natural gas could reach Italy by means of an offshore connection, where it could eventually compete with Algerian and Libyan natural gas. Another possibility is to export gas to Bosnia and Herzegovina. A further possibility could be the construction of a pipeline to Austria through Bulgaria, Romania, and Hungary.

In fact, in November 2002 five companies signed an agreement to carry out a joint feasibility study on the construction of a natural gas pipeline from Turkey to Austria via Bulgaria, Romania, and Hungary. Participants in the project are BOTAŞ, (Turkey), Bulgargaz (Bulgaria), Transgaz (Romania), MOL (Hungary), and OMV Erdgas (Austria). The study received approval from the EU in July 2003. At the beginning of 2004, the Nabucco Company began its financial and market studies, and the final report of the feasibility study is due by the beginning of 2005. The construction phase is scheduled to start in mid-2006, and operations are expected to begin at the end of 2009. Once contracted, the pipeline will stretch about 3,400 kilometers, with total capacity from Turkey of 25 billion to 30 billion cubic meters per year. The expected offtake in transit countries would be 8 billion to 10 billion cubic meters per year, and the total capacity to Austria's Baumgarten region would be 17 billion to 20 billion cubic meters per year. Total costs are projected to be about €4.4 billion. The idea behind the project is that Turkey would act as an "energy corridor" for the export of Caspian oil and gas. Turkey finds the idea attractive, because it would allow the country to reduce the gas surplus it seems to be facing in the near future. In view of its geographic position, Turkey could, in fact, play a pivotal role in enhancing the security of supply and competition in the EU, connecting the Caspian gas reserves with the Mediterranean region and Europe.

Long-Term Purchase Contracts

BOTAŞ has signed eight long-term sales and purchase contracts with six different supply sources. Six contracts are presently in effect. Of these, three are with Russia for plateau volumes of 6 billion cubic meters per year, 16 billion cubic meters per year, and 8 billion cubic meters per year, respectively, through the Blue Stream pipeline across the Black Sea; one is with Iran for 10 billion cubic meters per year; and two are liquefied natural gas

TABLE 8.1   Existing Gas Agreements, Turkey

	Amount (billion cubic meters per year)	Signature Date	Duration (years)
Russian Federation (West)	6	February 1986	25
Algeria (LNG)	4	April 1988	20
Nigeria (LNG)	1.2	November 1995	22
Islamic Republic of Iran	10	August 1996	25
Russian Federation (Black Sea)	16	December 1997	25
Russian Federation (West)	8	February 1998	23
Turkmenistan	16	May 1999	30
Azerbaijan	6.6	March 2001	15

Source: BOTAŞ, http://www.botas.gov.tr/.

(LNG) contracts—one with Algeria for 4 billion cubic meters per year and the other with Nigeria for 1.2 billion cubic meters per year. These agreements are summarized in table 8.1.

Of the two contracts that are not yet in effect, one was signed with Turkmenistan for 16 billion cubic meters per year, and the Shah Deniz contract with Azerbaijan is for 6.6 billion cubic meters per year, starting in 2005 (see table 8.1). It is likely, however, that these two contracts will prove mutually incompatible. Although progress has been reported on imports from Azerbaijan, the pipeline project from Turkmenistan appears to be stalled.

On December 26, 1996, a framework agreement was signed between Iraq and Turkey to pipe 10 billion cubic meters of Iraqi gas per year to Turkey after development of the gas fields in Iraq. On the Turkish side, BOTAŞ, TPAO, and TEKFEN have been involved in this project. ENI was designated as coordinator of the upstream activities.

Finally, a natural gas sale and purchase agreement was initialed on March 31, 2001, by BOTAŞ and EMG (Eastern Mediterranean Gas Company) of Egypt to supply Turkey with 4 billion cubic meters per year of natural gas.

To diversify natural gas supply sources, BOTAŞ entered into a 20-year LNG sale and purchase agreement with SONATRACH (Algeria) in 1988. In order to receive the imported LNG, BOTAŞ began construction of the Marmara Ereğlisi LNG Import Terminal in September 1989. The terminal, which began operations in 1994, is used both as a LNG regasification plant and as a storage facility for imported LNG.

In addition to long-term contracts, BOTAŞ has also purchased natural gas on the spot market. The first spot LNG was from Australia within the scope of an agreement signed with North West Shelf LNG in 1995. Spot LNG was also purchased from Qatar and Algeria under two different agreements signed with Qatar Gas and SONATRACH in 1998.

In 2001 BOTAŞ purchased a total of 16,368 million cubic meters of natural gas. The Russian Federation was the main natural gas supplier with 10,931 million cubic meters, followed by Algeria (3,985 million cubic meters) and Nigeria (1,337 million cubic meters). Iran provided 115 million cubic meters (BOTAŞ 2001).

BOTAŞ justified signing these long-term purchase contracts by pointing to the expected rapid growth in the Turkish gas market; it predicted that gas demand would reach 55 billion cubic meters in 2010 and 83 billion cubic meters in 2020. As noted earlier, however, most observers believed the ambitious BOTAŞ demand forecasts were overly optimistic, and they cautioned as well about the country's economic crisis. Some analysts foresee that in 2010 Turkey will have surplus gas of 10 billion to 25 billion cubic meters, increasing to 50 billion cubic meters in 2020 (Hafner 2002).

Oversupply also seems to be the basis of the dispute that arose between Turkey and Iran in 2001 in connection with a natural gas purchase agreement for 10 billion cubic meters per year signed in 1996. Under the contract, Iran was to export to Turkey a total of 192 billion cubic meters of Iranian gas over 22 years, with deliveries starting in January 2000. However, when deliveries were scheduled to start,

BOTAŞ had not completed the necessary import infrastructure, and an amendment to the original deal was negotiated under which first gas was delayed to July 2001, and the duration of the contract was extended to 25 years. The total contractual volume was also increased to 228 billion cubic meters, with annual volumes scheduled to reach their plateau level of 10 billion cubic meters per year in 2007. But again, when the July 2001 date arrived, BOTAŞ claimed that Iran had not constructed the necessary border metering facilities, and gas did not actually start flowing until December 2001.

In June 2002, BOTAŞ announced that gas imports from Iran had been halted because of an alleged quality problem. Iran accused Turkey of using the quality issue as a pretext, and said that the real reason for the halt was that Turkey was not in a position to consume the gas. The dispute was resolved after a reduction in the contract price (in line with the reduction that BOTAŞ agreed to with the Blue Stream consortium—about 9 percent) and in the take-or-pay level (down from the original 87 percent of annual contract quantity to 70 percent, which means that BOTAŞ will need to take only 7 billion cubic meters per year at the plateau).

National Networks and Future Development

Residential users in Ankara began receiving natural gas in 1988. In 1992 Istanbul and Bursa also began to receive supplies of natural gas; İzmit and Eskişehir received supplies in 1996. The distribution of natural gas is undertaken by local distribution companies; EGO in Ankara, İGDAŞ in İstanbul, İZGAZ in İzmit, and BOTAŞ in Bursa and Eskişehir. The distributors are owned or co-owned by the municipalities they serve, except in Bursa and Eskişehir. The gas supply continues to be restricted to limited areas of western Turkey, but there are plans to extend the system.

The city distribution networks have been enlarged over the years, parallel with demand. In 2001 the number of consumers increased to 197,303 in Bursa and 76,484 in Eskişehir because of the work under way to enlarge the city distribution networks in these cities. In view of the growth scenario described earlier, BOTAŞ has planned to connect local distribution networks in 55 new cities. The connection dates for all of these projects are in 2002–04.

In order to become "a Bridge to Europe" and boost its internal demand, Turkey will have to improve its national transmission and distribution network. Five projects are already under study and slated to become operational in 2005: the Southern Natural gas transmission line project; the Konya-İzmir natural gas transmission line project; the eastern Black Sea gas transmission line project; the western Black Sea natural gas transmission line project; and the Georgian border–Erzurum (Horasan) natural gas transmission line project.

The Southern Natural gas transmission line project is aimed at meeting natural gas demand in the southern and southeastern regions of Turkey by transmitting natural gas through a branch line to be extended from the Eastern Anatolia Natural Gas Main Transmission Line near Sivas. The total length of this 40-inch pipeline from Sivas to Mersin via Malatya, Kahramanmaraş, Gaziantep, Osmaniye, and Adana will be 565 kilometers.

By means of the Konya-İzmir natural gas transmission line project, the Eastern Anatolia Natural Gas Main Transmission Line will be extended from Konya to İzmir, and will supply natural gas to cities such as Burdur, Isparta, Denizli, and Nazilli. The 618-kilometer 40-inch line will have branches to the cities in the vicinity of Afyon and Antalya.

The eastern Black Sea gas transmission line project will supply Hopa, Artvin, Rize, Trabzon, Giresun, Ordu, and Samsun via Bayburt and Gümüşhane by extending a branch from the Eastern Anatolia Natural Gas Main Transmission Line at Erzincan. The plan is to supply natural gas to Gümüşhane, Bayburt, Trabzon, and Rize as the first stage of the project. Through the western Black Sea gas transmission line project, natural gas will be supplied to Bartın, together with the industrial and residential sectors along the route via Zonguldak, Devrek, and Çaycuma, by extending a branch from Karadeniz Ereğli. It is foreseen that the 141-kilometer line will consist of a 78-kilometer line of 16-inch pipe and a 63-kilometer line of 12-inch pipe. In addition, a 65-kilometer loop line of 16-inch pipe will be constructed on the İzmit-Karadeniz Ereğli Natural Gas Transmission Line.

To transport Turkmenistan and Azerbaijan natural gas within Turkish territories, an approximately 225-kilometer pipeline will be constructed from the Georgian border of Turkey to Erzurum (Horasan). This line will be connected to the Eastern Anatolia

Natural Gas Main Transmission Line at Horasan. The project includes a commercial metering station and a compressor station.

Ownership and Industry Structure

This section addresses questions related to the present ownership and industry structure of Turkey's natural gas sector, with the goal of comparing the Turkish case with that of some EU countries. In doing so, the section discusses similarities with other emerging gas markets as well as differences with more mature markets.

Turkey

Turkey's natural gas sector is dominated by BOTAŞ. BOTAŞ Petroleum Pipeline Corporation was established as an affiliated company of the Turkish Petroleum Corporation on August 15, 1974, to transport Iraqi crude oil to the Gulf of Iskenderun. In 1995 the company was restructured as a state economic enterprise (SEE) by Decree of the Council of Ministers No. 95/6526, thereby obtaining the status of an independent company. Since 1987, BOTAŞ has expanded its original mission of transporting crude oil through pipelines to cover the natural gas transportation and trading activities. In 1995 all kinds of petroleum-related activities such as exploration, drilling, production, transportation, storage, and refining for the purpose of providing crude oil and natural gas from sources abroad was added to BOTAŞ's activities.

BOTAŞ is made up of a series of sectoral and provincial organizations: Petroleum Operations Management, Natural Gas Operations Management, LNG Operation Management, Dörtyol Operation Management, Kayseri Operation Management, İstanbul Operation Management, Bursa Operation Management, and Eskişehir Operation Management.

By Decision of the High Planning Council No. 2002/T-15 of June 6, 2002, the Bursa and Eskişehir Operation Managements were restructured and transformed into affiliate companies of BOTAŞ that took the form of joint stock companies. The new companies were the Bursa City Natural Gas Distribution, Trade and Contracting Corporation (BURSAGAZ) and the Eskişehir City Natural Gas Distribution, Trade and Contracting Corporation (ESGAZ).

BOTAŞ's monopoly rights to natural gas import, distribution, sales, and pricing, granted by Decree No. 397 of February 9, 1990, were abolished by the natural gas market law (No. 4646) enacted on May 2, 2001, to establish a stable and transparent natural gas market based on competitive rules. The new law covers the import, transmission, distribution, storage, wholesale trading, and export of natural gas, and the transmission and distribution of compressed natural gas (CNG), as well as the rights and obligations of all real and legal persons related to these activities. Under the law, BOTAŞ will competitively tender and release the import contracts to new private entrants until its import share falls below 20 percent by the year 2009. The company must auction at least 10 percent of its gas purchase rights a year, starting from the enactment date of the law. BOTAŞ will also undergo further restructuring, and separate companies will be established for trade, transmission, and storage after the year 2009.

The 2001 natural gas market law also set the minimum annual consumption limit for qualification as an eligible consumer to 1 million cubic meters, which corresponds to a market opening of approximately 80 percent (European Commission 2003).

EU Emerging Gas Markets

Within the European Union, Greece and Portugal are considered to be emerging gas markets. As a result, both countries obtained derogation to the liberalization schedule foreseen in Directive 98/30/EC of the European Parliament and of the Council of June 22, 1998, on common rules for the internal market in natural gas.

Greece   Greece is not directly linked to the interconnected system of any other member state, and it has only one main external supplier of imported gas, Russia, which has a market share of more than 75 percent. So far, Greece has only a vertically integrated gas company, DEPA (Public Gas Corporation). Plans are under way to separate DEPA's activities into transmission and supply. At present, there is no unbundling of gas supply and high-pressure transmission.

Low-pressure gas distribution is performed (for individuals and small industrial consumers) by three independent private companies, each covering a specific geographic area. An energy regulatory authority was established by Law No. 2773/99. Greece has an LNG terminal, which may serve as storage. No underground gas storage is yet in operation. The opening of the Greek gas market is scheduled for 2006.

Portugal The Portuguese gas market is very small. Transgas, the main operator for the high-pressure network, was set up in 1993, and its major shareholder is Gas de Portugal, which previously was in charge of supply and transmission. Industrial and commercial consumers with a gas consumption profile of over 10,000 thousand cubic meters are served directly by Transgas, along with the four distribution companies in Portugal (Gas de Lisboa for the capital city, Portgas for the northern region, Lusitania Gas for the central region, and Set Gas for the southern region). These four companies sell, in turn, to smaller distribution companies (less than 2,000 cubic meters purchased annually). To promote investment in the enlargement of the three provincial distribution networks, the Portuguese government conducted in the 1990s an international tender to select strategic investors for each network. Italgas, a subsidiary of ENI, was selected as the strategic investor for two out of three (Lusitania Gas and Set Gas).

In 2000 the government merged the state-owned oil and gas operators with the intention of privatizing them. A holding was then set up (Galp-SGPS) in which Eletricidade de Portugal is the major shareholder. ENI took 33 percent of the capital. As an emerging market, Portugal has applied for derogation; therefore, the EU natural gas directive will not be implemented before 2007.

EU Mature Gas Markets: The Italian Case

Italy produces only about one-fifth of its internal gas consumption, and production is falling, in absolute and relative terms, in relation to needs. In the production sector, ENI is the dominant operator (in 2001 it accounted for 88 percent of total production), followed by Edison T&S SpA (12 percent of total production). Proven overall reserves amount to about 215 billion cubic meters, the

equivalent of 13 years of production at current levels. Imports fulfill most of the country's requirement (just under 80 percent), and their share is expected to cover 88 percent of the total requirement by 2005 and 90 percent by 2010. As for imports, the ENI Group is again the dominant operator, accounting for about 85 percent of the total in 2001. The second importer after ENI is Enel SpA (the former electricity monopoly), with about 11 percent of imports in 2001.

In 2004, Italy started importing gas from Libya, and in 2007 the operator Edison will begin importing liquefied natural gas from Qatar upon the construction of a regasification terminal in the upper Adriatic. The import contracts that are signed will satisfy expected requirements until 2010.

The contracts for the vast majority of imports are long term; in 2001 they accounted for about 98 percent of the imported volume. Nearly 93 percent of imported gas is transported by pipeline to entry points in Italy. The transportation rights paid by importers on foreign pipelines serving the national gas system go mainly to companies of the ENI Group, which was responsible for constructing and funding the infrastructure. Snam Rete Gas SpA[3] owns 96 percent of the transportation capacity in Italy in terms of invested capital. The network of the second operator, Edison, is geographically complementary to that of Snam Rete Gas, especially in the central part of the country. The section of pipeline passing under the territorial waters of the Channel of Sicily is also part of the national system. It is owned by Transmediterranean Pipeline Company Limited (TMPC, an Italian-Algerian company in which SONATRACH and ENI hold equal stakes).

Access to Italy's transportation networks is regulated in accordance with Legislative Decree 164/2000 implementing the EU directive on the internal market for natural gas. Tariffs, access criteria, and the obligations to be met by the transportation companies are set by the Electricity and Gas Regulatory Authority.

Legislative Decree 164/2000 also defined the national network of gas pipelines, which is made up of import pipelines, connections to storage facilities and the principal interregional pipelines. For this network, as defined and updated by ministerial decree, access has been regulated since October 2001 along entry-exit lines.

The Italian storage system consists of depleted fields. The storage sites currently in operation are managed by Stoccaggi Gas Italia SpA (Stogit), a company set up in 2001 by the ENI Group, after hiving off its storage branch, and Edison. Stogit manages eight storage facilities, and Edison has two storage facilities. The energy authority sets the tariffs, criteria, access priorities, and obligations that storage companies are required to respect. The only regasification terminal in Italy at present is the one at Panigaglia, which is run by Snam Rete Gas. Its capacity is presently entirely taken up. Six new terminals are planned.

The Italian market has been fully open since January 1, 2003. Article 1 of Legislative Decree 164/00 implementing European Commission Directive 98/30/EC on common rules for the internal natural gas market provides that the importation, exportation, transportation, dispatch, distribution, and sale of natural gas are free.

Imports from non-EU countries are subject to authorization by the Ministry of Industry on the basis of objective, nondiscriminatory published criteria on technical and financial capabilities; assurances about the origin of the gas; the availability of strategic storage capacity in Italy in proportion to the quantity of gas imported annually; and the ability to contribute to the development and safety of the system or to the diversification of supply. LNG imports are facilitated through the reduction of strategic storage obligations. Two transitional annual constraints have been introduced to facilitate the entry of new operators: a ceiling on the national consumption level that can be served by a single company from 2003 to 2010 (50 percent) and a ceiling on the deliveries to the national network by any single company from 2002 to 2010 (initially 75 percent of national consumption, with a reduction of 2 percentage points per year, to 61 percent).

Transportation and dispatch are public service activities, with connection and network access obligations according to the criteria and tariffs laid down by the energy authority. Storage is conducted on a licensing basis lasting no more than 20 years, and is subject to access obligations under the criteria, priorities, and tariffs laid down by the authority. Storage and exploitation activities must be separated.

Distribution is a public service activity. The service is entrusted to a concessionaire through an open tendering process for a period not exceeding 12 years. The local authorities that grant the concession are entrusted with the orientation, supervision, and control powers, and their relation with the distributors are regulated on the basis of a standard contract prepared by the regulatory authority and approved by the Ministry of Productive Activities.

The legislative decree implementing the EU directive completely transformed the structure of the gas sector in Italy and provided a new impetus to the reorganization of the sector. The major energy companies acquired many distribution companies so that they could increase their market share and create new consortia. Companies that use gas have also set up consortia with a similar goal of purchasing gas on competitive terms.

The Italian case represents a median case of liberalization in the EU context. The U.K. market is considerably more competitive than the Italian one, because the country has, until recently, been self-sufficient in natural gas. In almost all other EU countries, the market is less competitive: in Germany, a regulatory authority has not yet been introduced, although it was recently decided to introduce one; in France, the incumbent controls the market almost completely; in Spain, competition is facilitated by the presence of multiple regasification terminals, and a model gas release program was implemented to reduce the share of the incumbent, Gas Natural.

Regulatory Reform in Turkey

On May 15, 2001, the executive board of the International Monetary Fund (IMF) approved a new three-year standby arrangement for Turkey amounting to US$19 billion. As part of the package of economic measures, which were a condition of IMF support, Turkey passed new electricity and gas laws.

The new natural gas market law (Law No. 4646) was adopted on May 2, 2001. The law came into force immediately, but its implementation was subject to a 12-month transition period, extendable to a maximum of 18 months. The transitional period was in fact extended until November 2002. Implementing legislation on gas market licensing was issued in September 2002.

The law is intended to establish a competitive gas market and to ensure independent regulation of the sector. The law also seeks to harmonize Turkish legislation with EU law in view of Turkey's future accession. The main features of the law are the following:

- All legal entities can carry out import, export, wholesale trade, transportation, distribution, storage, and CNG transmission and distribution activities under license from the energy market regulator.
- The natural gas activities of BOTAŞ are to be unbundled. BOTAŞ is to be split into three state economic enterprises after the year 2009, responsible for trading, storage, and transmission, respectively. The two local distributors owned by BOTAŞ in Bursa and Eskişehir will later be corporatized and privatized.
- No importer will be allowed to import more than 20 percent of Turkey's gas consumption during any one year. BOTAŞ will be required to sell part of its gas import contracts to comply with this provision. This sale will be accomplished through a series of annual competitive tenders to sell existing import contracts to new importers for no less than 10 percent of total imports each year. No new natural gas purchase agreement can be executed by any import company with countries that have existing contracts with BOTAŞ. This limitation shall apply for the entire duration of the agreement.
- No legal entity is allowed to sell more than 20 percent of annual gas consumption. Only national gas producers may sell more than 20 percent of annual gas consumption in the domestic market, provided that the amount sold directly to eligible consumers does not exceed 20 percent. The remaining gas could be sold through importers, distributors, or wholesalers.
- Gas companies will not be allowed to establish another company in the same field of activity, but will be allowed to own participations in a company operating in another field. They may not, however, directly or indirectly hold the majority of the capital or commercial assets of the company, nor do they have the right to use the majority of voting rights of the company.

The rights of BOTAŞ on existing participations are preserved.

- To ensure security of supply, gas importers and wholesalers must inform the Energy Market Regulatory Authority (EMRA) about the source and security of their gas imports, and they must store 10 percent of the gas they import in five years. Importers also must prove that they can contribute to the improvement and security of the national transmission system.
- Transportation companies that own transportation networks and the owners and operators of LNG and storage facilities are to offer services at nondiscriminatory conditions.
- Third parties also will be allowed to build pipelines. BOTAŞ and other potential grid operators are to undertake investment, which is subject to EMRA's approval. The regulatory agency is to control this investment, along with service quality. Existing and planned national transmission networks as well as transmission networks under construction remain under the ownership of BOTAŞ.
- Eligible consumers will be free to select the supplier of their choice. Eligibility will be determined by the regulator. Consumers purchasing more than 1 million cubic meters of natural gas a year and users unions (consortia), power generators, and cogenerators are considered eligible.
- Distribution rights for cities and municipalities must be awarded under a tender. Once a distributor has won a tender, it applies the unit service and the amortization price as specified in the tender announcement. After this period, its prices and conditions will be reviewed every year by the regulator. Distributors must construct, operate, and extend distribution equipment as specified in the license. Once the license for a distribution area has been awarded, the selected operator has to allow the local government to participate up to 20 percent in the company capital. The size of public participation, to be remunerated at the nominal share price, is to be determined by the regulator. Distribution companies may hold a license for no more than two cities within the country.
- EMRA has to develop five different categories of gas prices: for connection, transmission, storage, wholesale sales, and retail sales. Prices for

connection will be determined between the regulator and distribution companies. Network tariffs will be based mainly on distance and volume. Storage tariffs will be freely determined between storage companies and users. Transmission and storage companies will have an obligation to prove to the regulator that their services are economical and safe. Wholesale prices will be negotiated by the trading parties, but the regulator will maintain some oversight of wholesale prices. The distribution companies must prove that they provide gas from the cheapest source, and they must operate efficiently and safely during their license period. Distributors' retail sales prices for captive consumers are subject to rate-of-return regulation.

The Energy Market Regulatory Authority, which opened its doors in November 2001, was established to meet a condition of the IMF's support for Turkey. EMRA is an independent, administratively and financially autonomous public administration related to the Ministry of Energy and Natural Resources. According to Article 4, paragraph 3, of the electricity market law (No. 4628), "The headquarters of the Authority shall be located in Ankara and the ministry to which it is related shall be the Ministry of Energy and Natural Resources. The Authority may establish representative offices in distribution regions in order to carry out customer relations." Most of the technical specialists have so far been recruited through temporary assignments from various public administrations, including the Ministry of Energy and Natural Resources, BOTAŞ, the former Turkish Electricity and Transmission Company (TEAS), the Treasury, and public banks. By March 2003, its overall personnel, including support staff, totaled 270. Its budget is €4.3 million.

EMRA has begun to develop some of the secondary regulation for the liberalization of the energy sector. In September 2002, EMRA issued a regulation on principles and procedures pertaining to connection, transmission and dispatch, storage, and wholesale and retail sale tariffs. In January 2003, the new transmission tariff was announced. The tariff—the maximum that system operator BOTAŞ can charge to shippers—is a flat rate postal tariff equivalent to $0.4 per million Btus. This tariff is lower than many expected, indicating that EMRA seriously intends to create a competitive market and that the prices for industrial consumers will probably go down as a result of liberalization. Secondary legislation on licensing procedures and on network operation rules to be determined by transmission companies was also adopted.

Comparative Analysis of Turkey's Gas Legislation

Even though Turkey is an emerging market, its industry structure does not differ considerably from that of other countries of the EU, including more mature markets. Furthermore, its new legislation goes even further than the laws in force in many EU countries. Although liberalization was postponed in Greece and Portugal until 2006 and 2007, respectively, in Turkey the threshold of 1 million cubic meters per year for eligibility represents a market opening of approximately 80 percent. This figure may, however, be a result of the structure of the demand, mainly consisting of large consumers. The average market opening within the EU is about 78 percent.

As for unbundling, the obligation imposed on BOTAŞ to divest all distribution activities, in addition to separating trading and transmission activities, is more stringent that that found in other EU countries. In Italy, for example, ENI has substantial interest in distribution (100 percent of Italgas through Snam Rete Gas) and was not requested to divest its distribution arm, which owns 35 percent of the distributors. In Spain, Gas Natural is strongly linked to Enagas and Repsol. In Germany, Ruhrgas has a minority interest in regional companies and distributors at least sufficient to influence them. RWE Gas and E. ON cover the whole chain, including small production interests. In France, over 90 percent of distribution is undertaken by EdF-GdF. In Austria, the regional gas companies may be connected with their distributors.

The limit on BOTAŞ's share of imports is much more stringent than what is imposed in Italy and in Spain. No limit was imposed in France or Germany. Likewise, the limit on BOTAŞ's domestic market share is more stringent than what was imposed on Snam Rete Gas in Italy. The 10 percent storage obligation is similar to that existing in Italy. However, Turkey's situation is different because it is a transit country that eventually will have access to much more gas than it consumes domestically, but it has little opportunity to create underground storage sites (which instead are available "downstream," in the Balkans).

The most interesting feature of the new gas law, however, is the gas release program. If managed wisely, the program has the potential to create real competition within the country. The natural gas law states (temporary article 2) that every year until the aggregate of the annual import amount falls to 20 percent of the annual consumption amount, BOTAŞ shall release part of its contracts to competitors by means of a tender. However, it is not yet clear how such a system will work in practice. BOTAŞ has a final say on the winner of the tender procedure. If BOTAŞ is left free to choose the operator to whom it will cede its purchase agreements, the program may turn out to be not too effective. Also, in view of the Italian experience, it would be preferable that the gas be released by means of a tendering procedure based on objective criteria.

Italian legislation implementing the EU directive introduced two constraints on the incumbent, ENI, to facilitate the entry of new operators. The first is a ceiling on the national consumption level that can be served by a single company from 2003 to 2010 (50 percent). This measure, however, excludes gas for self-consumption.[4] The second is a ceiling on the deliveries to the national network by any single company from 2002 to 2010 (initially 75 percent of national consumption, with a reduction of 2 percentage points a year, to 61 percent).

ENI was left free to decide how to resell part of the gas for which it had already contracted through long-term take-or-pay contracts. The result was that only Italian companies (Plurigas SpA, Dalmine Energia, and Energia SpA) benefited from the measure; major international gas companies, especially producers, were not offered an opportunity to enter the market.

The solution adopted in Italy thus, in the end, reinforces the position of some weak competitors that represent no real threat to the incumbent, but it does not seem very effective as a means of reducing prices and building competition. The three companies that benefited from the measure are too small to effectively compete with ENI. On the contrary, it is more likely in practice that smaller firms will adjust their prices to be in line with that of the incumbent.

In the United Kingdom, competition effectively started only in the early 1990s, when a gas release program was introduced. Each year, the release gas was allocated on a pro rata basis to successful applicants (32 in the first year and an additional 70 in the second year—albeit including some multiple bids), who paid BG (British Gas) a price equal to BG's weighted average cost of gas. Previous attempts by the British government to introduce supply side competition through voluntary commitments by BG (including the 90/10 rule under which BG would contract no more than 90 percent from new fields, leaving 10 percent to other companies) were less effective than hoped, because most of the 10 percent gas contracts were bought for new power generation rather than competing in the industrial market.

One example of a competition-enhancing release program was undertaken in Spain. By Royal Decree Law 6/2000 of June 23, 2000, and by an order of June 29, 2001, the Spanish government conducted a gas release program for 25 percent of the gas supplies that Spain received from Algeria through the Maghreb pipeline from October 2001 to January 1, 2004—that is, for about 26 months. This program, like the gas release program in the United Kingdom, was based on the principle of keeping the incumbent neutral.

The release was designed to give competitors to Gas Natural access to gas, so that customers in the large industrial market would receive offers from alternative suppliers. Trading companies with a market share of more than 50 percent of the market were excluded from the bidding. Fourteen bids were made by different company groups (the total bid was for two and a half times the amount of gas being offered). Bids could be made for only up to 25 percent of the total volume offered. The average price paid by bidders was equivalent to Gas Natural's purchasing cost (oil-related gas price) plus a fixed management fee.

The final awards were made on October 22, 2001. Among the winning applicants were three Spanish companies—Iberdrola Gas (25 percent), Unión Fenosa Gas Comercializadora (20 percent), and Endesa Energía (18 percent)—and two international companies—BP Gas (25 percent) and Shell (2 percent)—through their Spanish subsidiaries.

Spanish imports from Algeria by pipeline totaled 6.54 billion cubic meters in 2001; total imports were almost 17.5 billion cubic meters. Spain's gas release program was therefore equal to about 16 percent of Spanish consumption, whereas the planned gas release for Turkey will be for 80 percent of total imports.

Conclusion

Turkey plays a central role as a transit country for oil and gas from the Caspian Sea, Black Sea, and Central Asia regions to the EU. Because of its strategic position, Turkey can help to improve natural gas supply diversification and security in Europe as well as to enhance competition. It is expected that the EU will have a gas supply deficit of about 13 percent in 2010 and about 28 percent in 2020 (European Commission 2002).

To perform this role effectively, Turkey will have to develop its national infrastructure and stimulate internal gas demand. The development of distribution networks is important to maintain market growth, which itself will be vital if the gas that BOTAŞ has contracted is to be absorbed and if the country is to attract international investors. In that respect, clear regulations on access rules, tariffs, and new investments are vital. Experience in other countries reveals that uncertainty over the applicable regime may seriously prevent investments.

To develop the internal market, regulators should also enact the appropriate secondary legislation that will allow prices to domestic consumers to go down while maintaining good quality standards. Time limits must be imposed on the licensing system for distribution.

Finally, the release program must be implemented soon to increase the number of market participants.

Notes

1. The authors wish to thank the participants in the conference "Turkey: Towards EU Accession" for their comments, and especially Ahmet Aydin, who sent them detailed comments and additional information that allowed them to substantially improve the first draft of this chapter.

2. These numbers were provided by the state-owned gas company, BOTAŞ.

3. In 2001 both Snam Rete Gas and Edison were separated from their respective vertically integrated groups (ENI and Edison) in compliance with the provisions of Legislative Decree 164/2000 on the unbundling of activities in the gas sector. At the end of 2001, 40.24 percent of the shares of Snam Rete Gas were floated, with ENI continuing to own the remaining stake.

4. The fact that gas for self-consumption has been excluded from the ceiling means that Snam can minimize the amount of gas it releases by entering the electricity market through the construction of gas-fired power generators, thus reducing the effect of the program.

References

BOTAŞ. 2001. *2001 Annual Report.* http://www.botas.gov.tr/raporlar/Botas/index.htm.

European Commission. 2002. "Discussion Document on Long-Term contracts, Gas Release Programmes and the Availability of Multiple Gas Suppliers." Draft paper for discussion of the Fifth Meeting of the European Gas Regulatory Forum, January 22.

———. 2003. "Second Benchmarking Report on the Implementation of the Internal Electricity and Gas Market." Commission Staff Working Paper SEC (2003) 448, July 4. http://www.europa.eu.int/comm/energy/gas/benchmarking/doc/2/sec_2003_448_en.pdf.

Hafner, Manfred. 2002. "Future Natural Gas Supply Options and Supply Costs for Europe." Observatoire Méditerranéen de l'Energie, Workshop on the Internal Market for Gas, Brussels, November 7–8.

PART III

ECONOMIC CHALLENGES

9

LABOR MARKET POLICIES AND EU ACCESSION: PROBLEMS AND PROSPECTS FOR TURKEY

Erol Taymaz and Şule Özler

The process of European Union (EU) accession has provided a strong stimulus for various institutional changes in Turkey. The recognition of Turkey as a candidate state for accession by the European Council at Helsinki on December 10–11, 1999, was an important turning point in this process.[1] The Accession Partnership (AP), which followed the Helsinki summit, identified the short-term and medium-term priorities, intermediate objectives, and conditions on which accession preparations must concentrate in light of the political and economic criteria. One of the most important issues for Turkey in adopting and implementing the EU *acquis communautaire* (the entire body of legislation of the European Communities and Union) is labor market regulations and employment policies. Adoption of the EU *acquis* will certainly bring radical changes to the functioning of the labor market in Turkey, with vital consequences for firms, workers, and the long-term performance of the economy.

As noted, the Accession Partnership identified short-term and medium-term priorities and objectives in employment and social affairs. In the short term, Turkey was expected to strengthen efforts to tackle the problem of child labor, to ensure that the conditions are in place for an active and autonomous social dialogue, and to support the social partners' capacity-building efforts to develop and implement the *acquis*. The AP envisaged, in the medium term, removal of all forms of discrimination, adoption of EU legislation in the field of labor law, effective implementation and enforcement of the social policy and employment *acquis*, and preparation of a national employment strategy with a view toward later participation in the European Employment Strategy (EES). These institutional changes are expected to enhance Turkey's capacity to develop and implement, together with the European Community, strategies for "employment and particularly for promoting a skilled, trained and adaptable workforce and labour markets responsive to economic change" (Treaty Establishing the European Community, Article 125; also see the EU's *Official Journal*, C 325, December 24, 2002).

Adoption of the EU *acquis* on employment and social affairs is likely to put a burden on the firms and workers that need to adapt themselves to the new competitive environment. The adverse effects of this process of transformation would be minimized if the government, the private sector, and labor understand what needs to be changed and then adopt effective policies and strategies. The main aim of this study is to provide, for use by these agents, information on the employment and labor market issues that are important during the EU accession process. A study of labor markets in the process of EU membership is crucial for Turkey, because, as in all other European countries, the

223

labor market is the single largest market whose efficient operation has significant repercussions for the performance of the whole economy. Moreover, being a social institution, the labor market, and the rules and regulations defining how it should operate, have a direct impact on the lives of almost all citizens.

Because the topic is rather broad, this study concentrates on the possible effects of the adoption of the employment *acquis* regulating work and employment conditions, and it ignores some issues such as child labor, discrimination, and social protection. The chapter thus focuses on employment protection and labor market flexibility issues. It begins by briefly summarizing the literature on labor market policies, institutions, and economic performance. It then presents basic employment indicators for Turkey, the EU, and some accession countries to set the background for the study. The next section compares EU and Turkish labor law and discusses the main characteristics of the rationale and implementation of the European Employment Strategy. The sections that follow analyze the measurement of labor market flexibility and the flexibility of the Turkish labor market and describe the impact of the accession process and the adoption of the *acquis*. The final section summarizes the basic findings and policy proposals.

Labor Market Policies, Institutions, and Economic Performance

Although the link between labor market institutions and economic performance has received considerable attention in the literature beginning with the classical economists, since the mid-1970s it has become a major contentious issue among economists and policymakers. The member countries of the Organisation for Economic Co-operation and Development (OECD) experienced a rapid increase in inflation and unemployment rates in the second half of the 1970s. Almost all the OECD countries (with a major exception, Turkey) were successful in curbing the inflation, but high unemployment rates have persisted in European countries.

The difference in the labor market performances of the United States and European countries has instigated an intensified debate on the link between labor market institutions and economic performance. Many economists and international

organizations such as the OECD have pointed to inefficient and inflexible labor markets as a reason for the high and, in many cases increasing, unemployment in European countries. The concept of "labor market flexibility" has played a key role in these discussions.[2]

The concept of labor market flexibility refers to the functioning of labor markets ("external flexibility"), and it focuses mainly on wage and numerical flexibility. Wage flexibility refers to the speed of adjustment in wages in the labor market. What is usually meant by wage flexibility is the downward flexibility of real or nominal wages. Specific wage-setting institutions (centralized collective bargaining, wage indexation, and minimum wage legislation) and tax and social spending policies (such as high unemployment benefits, high nonwage labor costs, and high marginal tax rates) are blamed for reducing wage flexibility. Numerical flexibility refers to how fast and at what cost a firm can adjust the composition and the number of workers it employs by hirings, layoffs, and firings. Employment protection legislation (EPL) is one of the main institutions that determines numerical flexibility. Because numerical and wage flexibility are closely related (as will be discussed later—rigidities in EPL may lead to higher wages), in this chapter we use only the term *labor market flexibility* to cover both aspects of external flexibility.

In the 1990s, some researchers emphasized the importance of functional (or "internal") flexibility—that is, flexibility in job description and job design for multiskilled workers. Although external and internal flexibility could be substitutes, or options, for alternative corporate strategies, we do not study the issue of internal flexibility.

As noted earlier, Article 125 of the Treaty Establishing the European Community calls for a coordinated strategy for promoting a "skilled, trained and adaptable workforce and labour markets responsive to economic change." The concept of adaptability is certainly broader than the concept of flexibility. For example, it is suggested in a report financed by the European Commission that *adaptability* refers to "the broad process by which labour markets adjust to exogenous developments over a period of time." whereas *flexibility* is now used to refer to the "short-term response of wages and labour costs, in particular, to variations in the demand for labour relative to supply, or to the ability of employers to adjust their work force to changes in economic activity." Therefore, "[w]hile flexibility defined in these terms may be an important part of the wider concept of adaptability, it is far from being the only aspect of labour market behavior which is of significance. Indeed, a high degree of flexibility so defined may not only conflict with the achievement of wider objectives than simply the maintenance of a high level of employment but might also make it more difficult to secure longer-term growth objectives" (Algoé Consultans 2002: 2). Keeping in mind these differences, this study focuses on labor market flexibility, especially on changes needed in the EPL during the accession process in Turkey.

Researchers disagree about the effects of labor market flexibility on economic performance. One group claims that labor market flexibility is required for the good functioning of competitive markets and thus for the efficient allocation of resources. Because employment protection and rigidities in wage setting are costs incurred by firms, they have profound effects on firms' decisions (OECD 1994a, 1994b, 1999; Salvanes 1997; Blanchard 2000; Scarpetta and Tressel 2002; Heckman and Pagés 2004). These researchers suggest, first, that stricter labor market regulations may lead to higher unemployment (and lower output) and change the composition of unemployment, because they affect the flows to and from employment—that is, hiring and layoffs. EPL costs affect layoffs directly, because these costs are added to the cost of layoffs, and the cost of hiring indirectly, because firms will take into consideration the (potential) costs of layoffs (including EPL costs) in their hiring decisions. If the second effect dominates the first one, then the unemployment rate will be higher. EPL will also increase unemployment duration because of the decrease in the exit rate from unemployment.

Second, strict EPL is likely to strengthen the bargaining power of workers and, depending on the structure of product and labor markets, may lead to wages higher than the market-clearing wages and higher unemployment. Moreover, EPL provides protection for insiders, those workers who have regular jobs in the formal sector. Thus, strict EPL may cause a widening gap between insiders and outsiders and may encourage firms to operate in the informal sector.

Although there is almost a consensus on the effects of EPL on the composition and rate of unemployment among neoclassical economists, another group of researchers suggests that excessive labor market flexibility may hinder investment in training and innovative activities, diminish the accumulation of human and knowledge capital, and thus have a negative impact on growth and employment in the long run. According to Michie and Sheehan (2003), "The sort of 'low road' labor flexibility practices encouraged by labor market deregulation—short term and temporary contracts, a lack of employer commitment to job security, low levels of training, and so on—are negatively correlated with innovation." Firms that rely on labor market flexibility to be more competitive will have weak incentives for conducting innovative activities. Moreover, reduced innovative activities will, in turn, have a negative impact on employment and company profits because "(1) lower wage increases will lead to a slower replacement of the capital stock, (2) lower wages prevent the Schumpeterian process of creative destruction, and (3) lower wages will lead to a lack of effective demand" (Kleinknecht 1998).[3] Patterns of sectoral specialization also may be influenced by labor market flexibility. For example, Bassanini and Ernst (2002) show in an empirical study that "countries with coordinated industrial relations systems and strict employment protection tend to specialize in industries with a cumulative knowledge base because coordinated industrial relations and employment protection encourage firm-sponsored training as well as the accumulation of firm-specific competencies."

Rigidities and frictions in the labor market may reduce labor flows and lead to wage compression (lower wage differentials). These factors, however, may induce firms to provide more training for their employees and contribute to the accumulation of human capital, both at the firm level and at the economy level (see, e.g., Acemoglu and Pischke 1998, 1999; Agell 1999; Ballot and Taymaz 2001). The stability of the employment relationship, complementarities between training and innovation activities, and wage compression all make training activities more profitable. Thus, firms will achieve higher productivity and a higher rate of growth in productivity as a result of employing more skilled and well-educated employees.

Although the issue of the effects of labor market institutions on economic performance has yet to be resolved, some remarkable contributions in recent years have improved understanding of how labor market institutions function. For example, Belot, Boonez, and van Ours (2002) have developed a model that proves that there is an optimal degree of employment protection. In other words, both excessive and limited labor market flexibility could be detrimental to economic growth. More important, it has been shown that the impact of labor market regulations and institutions depends on other market and technology conditions (Scarpetta and Tressel 2002). Blanchard has developed models in which he studies the interactions between labor and product markets (e.g., Blanchard 2000). He shows that institutions play a more important role in the process of wage setting if product markets are monopolistic or oligopolistic, because only in those markets would workers be able to bargain over rents. Therefore, (de)regulation of labor and product markets must be implemented together. Finally, Belot (2002) develops the idea that labor market flexibility itself could be an endogenously determined variable, and he shows in a model that countries with low migration costs and high economic heterogeneity (such as the United States) may prefer no employment protection.

Numerous empirical studies have attempted to test the effects of labor market flexibility on economic performance. Most of these studies show that the effect on the composition of unemployment is unambiguous: employment protection increases the duration of unemployment by slowing down the flows through the labor markets (more long-term unemployment and less short-term unemployment), but the effect on the rate of unemployment and output is ambiguous. Labor market flexibility has an adverse impact on specific groups of workers such as youth and marginal groups (for extensive surveys, see Nickell and Layard 1999; Addison and Teixeira 2001; Baker and others 2002; Heckman and Pagés 2004). As for growth and productivity, Nickell and Layard (1999) suggest that "there seems to be no evidence that either stricter labor standards or employment protection lowers productivity growth rates. If anything, employment protection can lead to higher productivity growth if it is associated with other measures taken by firms to enhance the substantive participation of the workforce."

Labor Market Indicators for Turkey

Turkey, with its population of 64 million, is the largest of the 13 accession and candidate countries.[4] Its eventual membership in the EU will have a profound impact on both Turkey and the EU countries, and the impact of membership will be determined, to a large extent, by the peculiarities of the structure of the population and labor markets in Turkey.

One of the most important characteristics of the population of Turkey is its age composition. The share of young people is relatively high because of the country's high birthrate. The birthrate is declining, but it is predicted to remain higher than the European average in the coming decades (the population growth rate was about 1.8 percent in the 1990s). The high proportion of young people could be an advantage for Turkey because it includes a high share of active population, but it imposes a heavy burden on the educational system and makes employment generation one of the main social issues.

The employment rate as a percentage of working-age population (aged 15–64) is lower in Turkey than in the EU and other candidate countries. In 2000 the employment rate was only 48.2 percent in Turkey, whereas it was 63.2 percent in the EU and well above 50 percent in all candidate countries (see table 9.1 for data on Turkey, the EU, and candidate countries with more than 5 million population). One of the main reasons for the low employment rate in Turkey is the fact that the participation rate is also low, especially for urban women. Turkey is expected to experience an increase in its participation rate in the future, which may intensify pressures for employment generation.

Self-employment rates and part-time and fixed-term employment rates[5] seem to be quite high in Turkey (24.5 percent, 20.7 percent, and 10.0 percent, respectively). However, the majority of the self-employed and part-time employed are working in agriculture, and the fixed-term employment is dominant in the construction sector. Therefore, these rates basically reflect sectoral specificities and the importance of these sectors (agriculture and construction) in total employment.

In Turkey, the share of agriculture in total employment is extremely high (34.5 percent); among all candidate countries, it is second to that

TABLE 9.1   Employment Indicators: EU and Selected Group of Candidate Countries, 2000[a]

	Turkey	EU	Bulgaria	Hungary	Poland	Romania
Total population (thousands)	64,059	370,914	6,832	9,927	30,535	22,338
Population aged 15–64 (thousands)	41,147	247,708	5,502	6,760	25,652	15,213
Total employment (thousands)	20,579	165,537	2,872	3,807	14,518	10,898
Employment rate (% population aged 15–64)	48.2	63.2	51.5	55.9	55.1	64.2
FTE employment rate (% population aged 15–64)[c]	49.3	57.9	50.3[b]	56.0	53.0[b]	63.8
Self-employed (% total employment)	24.5	15.0	14.7	14.5	22.5	25.4
Part-time employment (% total employment)[c]	20.7	17.8	3.4[b]	3.6	10.6	16.4
Fixed-term contracts (% total employment)[c]	10.0	13.6	5.7[b]	5.8	4.2	1.6
Employment in services (% total employment)	47.3	69.0	54.0	59.8	50.3	29.0
Employment in industry (% total employment)	18.2	26.7	32.8	33.8	31.1	25.8
Employment in agriculture (% total employment)	34.5	4.3	13.2	6.5	18.7	45.2
Unemployment rate (% labor force)	6.6	7.9	16.2	6.6	16.3	7.0
Youth unemployment rate (% labor force aged 15–24)	13.2	15.5	33.3	12.3	35.7	17.8
Long-term unemployment rate (% labor force)	1.3	3.7	9.5	3.1	7.3	3.4

Note: FTE = full-time equivalent.

a. Candidate countries with more than 5 million population in 2000.

b. Data for 2001.

c. Calculated from Turkish State Institute of Statistics; *Household Labour Force Statistics* (SIS 2000b).

Sources: Turkey: SIS 2000b; all other countries: European Commission DG for Employment and Social Affairs 2002.

of Romania (45.2 percent). Because the share of agriculture is expected to decline in the future, this transformation may tend to lower the participation rate (the participation rate for urban women is much lower than that for rural women) and add another source of demand for urban male jobs, mainly in the services sector. The share of services in total employment in Turkey is much lower than that in the EU and candidate countries, but again with the exception of Romania where the agricultural sector is predominant.

The unemployment data reveal that there could be substantial differences between the labor markets in Turkey and the EU. The unemployment rate in Turkey is relatively lower. Moreover, the youth unemployment rate is significantly lower, especially compared to major candidate countries, in spite of a huge influx of the young people into the labor force. Most interesting, the long-term unemployment rate[6] (as a percentage of labor force) is very low, only 1.3 percent, although it is 3.7 percent in the EU, 9.5 percent in Bulgaria, 3.1 percent in Hungary, 7.3 per-

cent in Poland, and 3.4 percent in Romania. The proportion of long-term unemployed in total unemployed in Turkey is also very low, only 20 percent in 2000. Among all large candidate countries, the lowest rate after Turkey is observed in Poland (45 percent), and the EU average is about 47 percent. These data seem to suggest that Turkey has maintained a high rate of labor market flows so that, in spite of a huge youth population and the growing demand for new jobs, the rate of long-term unemployment remains relatively low. In other words, Turkey has quite a dynamic labor market.

The labor market indicators summarized in table 9.1 also reveal that employment generation is a major issue in Turkey. The demand for labor must increase at a high rate to keep the rate of unemployment at the existing level. One of the main determinants of labor demand is, of course, the cost of labor. Table 9.2a presents the data on labor costs, income tax, and employees' and employers' social security contributions (SSCs) for a single individual without children in OECD countries in 2002.

TABLE 9.2a Income Tax Plus Employees' and Employers' Social Security Contributions, 2002[a]
(percent of labor costs)

	Income Tax	Social Security Contributions		Total	Labor Costs (US$)[b]
		Employee	Employer		
Australia	24	0	0	24	33,964
Austria	8	14	23	45	34,030
Belgium	21	11	24	55	43,906
Canada	18	6	7	31	34,793
Czech Rep.	8	9	26	43	18,631
Denmark	32	11	1	43	36,690
Finland	20	5	20	45	35,513
France	9	9	29	48	32,856
Germany	17	17	17	51	42,197
Greece	0	12	22	35	20,570
Hungary	13	9	24	46	11,934
Iceland	21	0	5	26	25,379
Ireland	10	4	10	24	27,775
Italy	14	7	25	46	35,709
Japan	6	9	10	24	32,287
Korea, Rep. of	2	6	8	16	32,116
Luxembourg	7	12	12	32	37,573
Mexico	2	1	13	16	10,295
Netherlands	6	19	10	36	36,019
New Zealand	20	0	0	20	26,629
Norway	19	7	11	37	36,262
Poland	5	21	17	43	16,268
Portugal	4	9	19	32	15,376
Slovak Rep.	5	9	28	42	13,249
Spain	10	5	23	38	27,156
Sweden	18	5	25	48	33,345
Switzerland	9	10	10	30	37,710
Turkey	12	12	18	42	17,367
United Kingdom	14	7	8	30	32,557
United States	15	7	7	30	34,650

a. Single individual without children at the income level of the average production worker. Note that such workers do not receive family benefits.
b. Annual labor cost per worker, U.S. dollars with equal purchasing power.
Source: OECD 2002.

Table 9.2b presents the same data for various family types and wage levels.

Three striking observations about Turkey emerge from the data presented in tables 9.2a and 9.2b. First, the average labor cost for employers is substantially lower in Turkey than in the developed OECD countries, but it is relatively higher than in some major candidate countries (Hungary, Poland, and the Slovak Republic). The tax wedge (the proportion of income tax and employers' and employees' SSCs in labor cost) for a single individual without children is close to the EU average and lower than the one observed in most of the candidate countries.

Second, the tax wedge does not differ much in Turkey across family types and wage levels. For example, the lowest tax wedge exists for an individual without any children earning 67 percent of the average wage rate (41.3 percent) and the highest for an individual without any children earning 167 percent of the average wage rate (44.3 percent); the difference is only 3 percentage points. In all EU countries (with the exception of Greece), the tax

TABLE 9.2b   Income Tax Plus Employees' and Employers' Contributions Less Cash Benefits, by Family Type and Wage Level, 2002
(percent of labor costs)

Family Type	Single, No Child	Single, No Child	Single, No Child	Single, 2 Children	Married, 2 Children	Married, 2 Children	Married, 2 Children	Married, No Child
Wage Level[a]	67	100	167	67	100–0	100–33[b]	100–67[b]	100–33[b]
Australia	19.7	23.6	32.0	−10.5	14.7	16.8	19.2	20.3
Austria	39.9	44.8	50.0	16.3	29.6	31.9	34.4	42.5
Belgium	48.9	55.3	61.1	32.9	40.1	42.5	48.5	49.8
Canada	26.8	30.8	31.8	4.6	20.9	24.5	27.4	27.9
Czech Rep.	41.8	43.5	45.8	18.0	28.7	35.4	39.3	42.3
Denmark	40.4	43.4	51.2	15.8	30.9	35.7	38.4	40.5
Finland	40.4	45.4	51.2	26.7	38.5	37.4	39.3	42.5
France	37.8	47.9	50.5	30.1	39.2	37.8	39.9	43.0
Germany	45.9	51.3	55.8	29.1	32.5	38.7	43.0	45.9
Greece	34.3	34.7	40.2	34.3	35.1	34.9	34.8	35.3
Hungary	42.0	46.3	54.8	17.7	30.2	32.1	34.9	44.2
Iceland	19.4	25.8	31.0	−6.4	1.9	12.3	19.0	19.4
Ireland	16.6	24.5	34.4	−13.3	9.0	13.5	16.9	19.1
Italy	42.7	46.0	49.9	25.4	34.0	39.3	41.8	42.9
Japan	23.2	24.2	27.1	20.4	20.3	21.8	22.6	23.3
Korea, Rep. of	14.8	16.0	20.3	14.4	15.4	15.0	15.3	15.3
Luxembourg	27.3	31.5	39.0	1.3	9.0	12.8	15.4	25.9
Mexico	11.4	16.1	22.4	11.4	16.1	13.4	14.2	13.4
Netherlands	37.2	35.6	40.4	18.2	25.2	29.1	32.6	33.6
New Zealand	18.8	20.0	25.7	1.6	18.2	19.2	19.5	19.2
Norway	33.8	36.9	43.5	14.0	27.2	29.2	31.4	34.5
Poland	41.4	42.7	43.8	36.5	37.7	41.4	42.2	41.4
Portugal	29.5	32.5	38.0	18.9	23.4	24.6	27.1	30.2
Slovak Rep.	40.3	41.4	44.7	23.8	29.6	34.1	35.9	40.5
Spain	33.9	38.2	41.9	28.3	31.4	34.5	34.7	35.7
Sweden	45.9	47.6	52.0	35.3	40.5	41.3	42.7	46.6
Switzerland	27.0	29.6	33.8	12.6	18.1	20.5	23.6	27.3
Turkey	41.3	42.4	44.3	41.3	42.4	41.7	41.9	41.7
United Kingdom	24.7	29.7	32.9	−10.8	18.2	18.0	22.4	24.7
United States	27.3	29.6	35.2	5.0	17.6	22.7	25.0	27.8

a. Percentage of the wage rate for an average production worker.
b. Two-earner family.
Source: OECD 2002.

wedge differences between various categories of workers are much wider. These figures show that income tax and social security structures in Turkey do not have a social policy component that favors disadvantaged groups.

Third, significant differences appear across countries in terms of the shares of income taxes and SSCs. For example, the tax wedge is almost the same for Denmark and Austria, but the share of income tax is 32 percent in Denmark and only

8 percent in Austria. In other words, there are substantial intercountry differences in the composition of cuts on labor costs.

These observations indicate that anyone making intercountry comparisons should be extremely careful. There are significant differences in the institutional setups: different institutions may have similar functions, and there may be complementarities or substitutions between various institutions and functions. Therefore, issues such as labor market flexibility must be studied within a larger framework that encompasses all institutions interacting with each other.

Turkey and EU Labor Market Policies

Turkey must fulfill the accession criteria and adopt the regulatory framework required for EU membership. This process will lead to a rather dramatic transformation in the Turkish labor market through two channels. First, the membership process implies economic integration with the EU, and competition in all markets will be intensified. Indeed, Turkey should ensure "the existence of a functioning market economy as well as the capacity to cope with competitive pressure and market forces within the Union" to satisfy the economic criteria for membership—that is, the so-called Copenhagen criteria. Second, Turkey is required to apply fully the *acquis* of the EU in force,[7] including all rules and regulations in the field of employment and social policy that form Chapter 13 in accession negotiations.

Turkey has had a customs union with the EU since 1996. Therefore, the impact of the process of membership on the labor market through changes in product markets could be expected to be limited. The adoption of the *acquis* would have a direct impact on the labor market, because it requires a new institutional setup and a new way of forming policy. In this section, we compare the labor law in Turkey with the EU directives and assess the effects of adopting the *acquis*. We focus on the labor law and issues related to labor market flexibility.[8] We also briefly analyze how employment policies are formed in the EU (the European Employment Strategy) and how the candidate countries are expected to adjust employment policies and coordinate them with the EU during the membership process.[9]

The EU Law

The EU law is composed of three different types of legislation: primary legislation, secondary legislation, and case law. These types of legislation compose the *acquis communautaire*.[10]

Primary Legislation   Primary legislation includes the treaties establishing the European Union and other agreements having similar status. The treaties have been revised several times (for all treaties, see the EU Web site, http://europa.eu.int/eur-lex/ lex/en/treaties/index.htm). The Treaty of Amsterdam, which was signed by the heads of state or government of the member states on October 2, 1997, and entered into force on May 1, 1999, promoted a series of social policy priorities at European Community level, especially in the area of employment. The change in emphasis on employment is reflected in the fact that the employment articles are included in the treaty as a title (like the monetary and economic articles), not as a mere chapter. The employment title (Title VIII of the treaty) lays down the principles and procedures for developing a coordinated strategy for employment. Article 125 sets the basic objectives as follows:

> Article 125: Member States and the Community shall, in accordance with this title, work towards developing a coordinated strategy for employment and particularly for promoting a skilled, trained and adaptable workforce and labour markets responsive to economic change with a view to achieving the objectives defined in Article 2 of the Treaty on European Union and in Article 2 of this Treaty.

The treaty maintains the commitment to achieving a high level of employment as one of the key objectives of the EU, and it calls attention to promoting "a skilled, trained and adaptable workforce and labour markets responsive to economic change." This objective is an issue of "common concern" for all member states.

The Treaty of Amsterdam, like earlier treaties, leaves the implementation of employment policy to the member states, but it obliges member states and the Community to work toward developing a "coordinated strategy for employment," because the labor market policies of a member state will have a direct impact on other member states as well. Article 128 sets out the specific steps leading to the formulation of such a strategy, including, on an annual basis, guidelines for employment, possible recommendations to the member states, and a joint report by the Council of the European Union and the Commission to the European Council that describes the employment situation in the European Community and the implementation of the guidelines. Each member state is to provide the Council of the European Union and the Commission with an annual report on the principal measures taken to implement its employment policy in light of the guidelines for employment.

Finally, the treaty provides a legal base for the analysis, research, exchange of best practices, and promotion of incentive measures for employment (Article 129), and it establishes permanent, constitutionally based institutional structures (Article 130, Employment Committee) that will help to develop employment policies.

Secondary Legislation   The EU secondary legislation is based on the treaties and takes the following forms:

- *Regulations,* which are directly applicable and binding in all member states without the need for any national implementing legislation.
- *Directives,* which bind member states as to the objectives to be achieved within a certain time limit while leaving to the national authorities the choice of form and means to be used. Directives have to be implemented in national legislation in accordance with the procedures of the individual member states.
- *Decisions,* which are binding in all their aspects for those to whom they are addressed. Thus, decisions do not require national implementing legislation. A decision may be addressed to any or all member states, to enterprises, or to individuals.
- *Recommendations and opinions,* which have no binding force. The Commission can make a recommendation for a party to behave in a particular way without any legal obligation, or it can deliver an opinion to assess a given situation or development in the Community or individual member states.

The EU secondary legislation on employment is mainly regulated through European Council directives, which bind member states to the objectives to be achieved within a certain time limit but leave them the choice of form and means to be used. In other words, the directives are implemented in national legislation in accordance with the procedures of the individual member states. Most of the employment directives can be implemented through collective agreements, provided such agreements apply to all workers that the directive intends to cover or to protect.

The secondary legislation, like the treaty itself, directly confers certain individual rights on the citizens of member states under the protection of the judicial system. Moreover,

[u]nder article 226 EC (ex article 169 EC) the European Commission or a Member State may bring a complaint, alleging the failure by a Member State to fulfil an obligation under the Treaty, before the European Court of Justice (ECJ or the Court). Grounds for a complaint may be, for example, the lack of transposition of a binding Directive, or the non repeal of a national rule that is not consistent with the Treaty or a Directive. If the Court finds that the obligation has not been fulfilled, the Member State concerned must comply without delay. If, after new proceedings are initiated by the Commission, the Court finds that the Member State concerned has not complied with its judgment, it may impose a fixed or a periodic penalty. (Bronstein 2003)[11]

Case Law   Case law includes judgments of the European Court of Justice and of the European Court of First Instance, for example, in response to referrals from the Commission, national courts of the member states, or individuals. In this study, we do not cover the case law on employment regulations.

Council Directives on Employment and the Turkish Labor Law

Turkey has begun to change its laws and regulations in accordance with the *acquis.* In this section, we compare the European Council directives on employment with the Turkish labor laws, both the new Labor Law No. 4857 enacted by the Turkish Parliament on May 22, 2003, and the former Labor Law No. 1475 that regulated the labor market for decades. We compare both the former and new labor laws because the new law has been in force for a few months and the agents in the labor market are in the process of adapting to the new circumstances. This comparison will also make it possible to show how far the new law goes in adopting the *acquis.* As mentioned earlier, we focus only on employment directives and not on directives on other labor-related issues such as discrimination, free mobility of workers, and health and safety regulations (for a comprehensive study of all directives as of 2001, see Hermans 2001). Table 9.3 compares the EU directives,[12] the existing labor law, and the former labor law.[13] It summarizes the main issues and regulations addressed in each directive.

TABLE 9.3 EU Directives and Turkish Labor Law

Directive Date of Issue (Entry into Force)	Issues/Regulations	Former Labor Law No. 1475 (Relevant Articles)	New Labor Law No. 4857 (Relevant Articles)
93/104 *Organization of working time* November 23, 1993 (November 23, 1996)	• Normal weekly work • Maximum week time • Minimum period of daily rest • Minimum period of weekly rest • Minimum period of annual leave • Shift work • Night work (information/health) • Patterns of work	• + • − • + • + • − • + • − (excl. men) • − (Articles 41, 43, 49, 61–65, 73)	• + (45 hours) • − • + • + • − • + • + • − (Articles 41, 46, 53–70)
99/70 *Framework agreement on fixed-term work* (UNICE/CEEP/ETUC) June 28, 1999 (July 10, 1999)	• Definition of fixed-term work • Definition of "comparable permanent worker" • Abuse arising from the use of successive fixed-term contracts • Rights of fixed-term workers • Information/training	No specific clause on fixed-term work (Article 8 defines only temporary and permanent work)	• + • ? • ? (no limit) • + • ? / − (Articles 11–12)
97/81 *Framework agreement on part-time work* (UNICE/CEEP/ETUC) December 15, 1997 (January 20, 2000)	• Definition of fixed-time work • Definition of "comparable full-time worker" • No shift from full-time to part-time work without consent • Rights of part-time workers • Information/training	No specific clause on part-time work (Article 8 defines only temporary and permanent work)	• + • ? • + • + • ? / − (Article 13)
98/59 *Collective redundancies* July 20, 1998 (September 1, 1998)	• Definition of collective redundancy • Information and consultation • Procedure	• −/+ (changed by Law No. 4773) • −/+ (changed by Law No. 4773) • −/+ (changed by Law No. 4773) (Article 24)	• + • + (excl. A 2.3.b.v and vi) • + (Article 29)

EU Directive	Issue		
2001/23 Employees' rights in the event of transfers March 12, 2001 (April 12, 2001)	• Employees' rights	+	+
	• Employers' liabilities	+	+
	• Information and consultation	(Articles 14, 53; Law No. 2822, Article 8)	− (Article 6)
80/987 Protection of employees in the event of insolvency (Amended by 2002/74) Oct. 20, 1980/Sept. 23, 2002 (Oct. 28, 1983/Oct. 8, 2002)	• Claims	No specific clause (Law No. 2004 on bankruptcy, Article 206; workers' claims have priority in the event of insolvency)	+
	• Guarantees (guarantee institution)		+
	• Coverage		+ (Article 33)
94/33 Protection of young people at work June 22, 1994 (June 22, 1996)	• Definition of "young"	−	+
	• Employers' obligations	−	+
	• Restrictions	− (Article 67; also regulated by the law on apprenticeship and vocational training, No. 3308)	(to be regulated by MESS) (Articles 71–73, 85, 87)
91/533 Information for employees October 14, 1991 (June 30, 1993)	• Information content	+?	+?
	• Time limits	−	+
	• Enforcement	+ (Articles 9 and 11)	+ (Article 8)
2002/14 Consultation and employee representation March 11, 2002 (March 23, 2005/2007)	• Information content	−	−
	• Coverage	−	−
	• Procedures/enforcement	−	−

Note: A positive mark (+) for a labor law indicates that it is in conformity with the directive. A negative sign (−) indicates either that the law does not satisfy the requirements set by the directive or that there is some difference between the law and the directive. A question mark (?) indicates that the issue is not addressed in a well-defined way or that there are some differences between the law and the directive. The third and fourth columns refer to relevant articles of the new labor law. UNICE = Union of Industrial and Employers' Confederations of Europe; CEEP = European Centre of Enterprises with Public Participation; ETUC = European Trade Union Confederation; MESS = Ministry of Employment and Social Security.

Source: The authors.

Turkey, like the member states, can comply with the directives either by adopting the laws, regulations, and administrative provisions, or by introducing the required provisions through an agreement between the employers' and workers' representatives. For example, some directives have been introduced in some member states through collective agreements. However, Turkish lawmakers seem to prefer to cover almost all provisions of the directives in the new labor law. Therefore, the lack of regulations in the labor law may require further legislative work.[14]

Council Directive 93/104 on certain aspects of the organization of working time is one of the main directives regulating working conditions. The directive lays down minimum safety and health requirements for the organization of working time; it applies to minimum periods of daily rest, weekly rest, and annual leave; to breaks and maximum weekly working time; and to certain aspects of night work, shift work, and patterns of work. The directive brings flexibility to working time by setting the minimum requirements for the "average working time" for a reference period not exceeding four months. Labor Law No. 1475 does not comply with the directive for the maximum average work week (48 hours). Although the proposal for the new law prepared by the Scientific Committee introduced the maximum limit to the average work week, Parliament failed to adopt the provisions and did not set any explicit limit for the weekly working time. This is surprising because the new law was promoted by its proponents as introducing flexible working arrangements, including *part-time* work. The new law also failed to meet the requirement of the directive on annual leave. Although the directive states that "every worker is entitled to paid annual leave of at least four weeks," the new law sets shorter periods on the basis of a worker's tenure (if a worker is employed 1–5 years, annual leave is only 14 days; 6–14 years, 20 days; and more than 14 years, 26 days). The former labor law had a similar scheme, but two days shorter leave for all categories. Both the new and former labor laws also fail to take the measures necessary "to ensure that an employer who intends to organize work according to a certain pattern takes account of the general principle of adapting work to worker, with a view, in particular, to alleviating monotonous work and work at a predetermined work-rate, depending on the type of activity, and of safety and health requirements, especially as regards breaks during working time" (Article 13 of Directive 93/104).

Directive 97/81 on part-time work and *Directive 99/70* on fixed-term work have adopted the framework agreements on part-time and fixed-term work, respectively, between the general cross-country organizations UNICE (Union of Industrial and Employers' Confederations of Europe), CEEP (European Centre of Enterprises with Public Participation), and ETUC (European Trade Union Confederation). The social partners (UNICE, CEEP, and ETUC) recognize that "contracts of an indefinite duration are, and will continue to be, the general form of employment relationship between employers and workers," but follow the conclusions of the Essen European Council on the need to take measures with a view toward "increasing the employment-intensiveness of growth, in particular by a more flexible organization of work in a way which fulfills both the wishes of employees and the requirements of competition." Thus, the main aim of these directives is to facilitate the development of part-time and fixed-term work on a voluntary basis and to contribute to the flexible organization of working time *by providing measures for the removal of discrimination against part-time and fixed-term workers* and by improving the quality of part-time and fixed-term work. These directives require that, in relation to employment conditions, part-time and fixed-term workers not be treated in a less favorable manner than comparable full-time and permanent workers. The former labor law did not specifically define part-time and fixed-term contracts. Although the new law complies with the directives to a large extent, it does not include the reference to the "applicable collective agreement" in the definition of "comparable worker."[15] The directive on fixed-term work explicitly calls for the prevention of abuse arising from the "use of successive fixed-term employment contracts or relationships." The new law, however, does not impose any restriction on the cumulative duration or the number of successive contracts, but allows successive fixed-term contracts if there is a "sound reason" (*esaslı neden*) to do so.

Directive 98/59, which deals with the approximation of the laws of the member states related to collective redundancies, introduced the procedures an employer should follow in contemplating collective redundancies. The former labor law had not envisaged any formal procedure for collective redundancies. However, the law on employment protection (No. 4773), adopted by Parliament on August 15, 2002, and effective as of March 15, 2003, after a lengthy political struggle, replaced Article 24 in compliance with the directive. Law No. 4773 has been repealed by the new labor law, which endorses the same procedure for collective redundancies (Article 29).

Directive 2001/23 (which repealed Directive 77/187) and its amending directive (98/50) are related to the protection of workers' rights in the event of transfers of undertakings, businesses, or parts of undertakings or businesses. *Directive 80/987* (which was amended by Directive 2002/74) regulates the protection of employees in the event of the insolvency of their employers. The directive on transfers stipulates that the "transferor's rights and obligations arising from a contract of employment or from an employment relationship existing on the date of transfer shall, by reason of such transfer, be transferred to the transferee," and the transferor and the transferee shall be jointly and individually liable with respect to obligations, including collective agreements, that arose before the date of transfer from a contract of employment or from an employment relationship existing on the date of transfer (Article 3). Moreover, both the transferor and the transferee shall be required to inform representatives of their respective employees affected by the transfer. The labor law and the law on collective bargaining agreements (Law No. 2822) have provided similar safeguards to protect employees' rights. The new labor law complies with most of the provisions of the directive, with the exception of those on "information and consultation" with employees (the third chapter).

Directives 80/987 and *2002/74* set rules to protect employees' claims arising from contracts of employment or employment relationships in the event of their employer's insolvency. The directive states explicitly that the member states may not exclude from its scope part-time employees, workers with fixed-term contracts, and workers with a temporary employment relationship. Member states "shall take the necessary measures to ensure that guarantee institutions guarantee . . . payment of employees' outstanding claims, resulting from contracts of employment or employment

relationships, including, provided for by the national law, severance pay on termination of employment relationships" (Article 3). The former labor law did not specifically address the issue of employees' rights in the case of insolvency. However, the law on bankruptcy (No. 2004) assigns priority to workers' outstanding claims. The new law calls for the creation of a Wage Guarantee Fund as a part of the Unemployment Insurance Fund to protect employees' claims, excluding severance pay.[16]

Directive 94/33 provides the measures necessary to prohibit work by children (any person under 15 years of age or who is still subject to compulsory full-time schooling under national law) and the minimum working conditions for young people (any person under 18 years of age). The labor law prohibits employment of any person under 13 years of age and restricts employment of people under 15. The law on apprenticeship and vocational training (No. 3308) also regulates the employment of children and young people. The new law satisfies most of the provisions set by the directive, and refers to the Ministry of Employment and Social Security (MESS) for regulation of the employment conditions for young people.

Directive 91/533 states that employers have an obligation to provide an employee with information in the form of a written document on the essential aspects of the contract or employment relationship not later than two months after the commencement of employment. The former labor law had a similar clause but did not specify the time limit in which the information has to be provided to the employee. The new law, in accordance with the directive, mentions that the document has to be handed over to the employee within two months if there is no employment contract signed by the employee and employer. Although the directive requires that any change in the conditions referred to in the written document "must be the subject of a written document to be given by the employer to the employee at the earliest opportunity and not later than one month after the date of entry into effect of the change in question," the new law does not enforce this requirement.

Directive 2002/14, published in the EU's *Official Journal* on March 23, 2002, establishes a general framework for informing and consulting employees in the European Community. The directive requires all undertakings employing at least 50 employees, or all establishments employing at least 20 employees in any one member state, to adopt practical arrangements for exercising the right to information and consultation at the appropriate level. Information and consultation shall cover:

(a) information on the recent and probable development of the undertaking's or the establishment's activities and economic situation;

(b) information and consultation on the situation, structure and probable development of employment within the undertaking or establishment and on any anticipatory measures envisaged, in particular where there is a threat of employment;

(c) information and consultation on decisions likely to lead to substantial changes in work organization or in contractual relations.

Information shall be provided by the employer "at such time, in such fashion and with such content as are appropriate to enable, in particular, employees' representatives to conduct and adequately study and, where necessary, prepare for consultation." A related directive (*Directive 94/45*) on the establishment of a European Works Council sets the rules and procedures to improve the right to information and to consultation of employees specifically in Community-scale undertakings and Community-scale groups of undertakings. The new labor law does not provide any provisions to establish the framework for informing and consulting employees within the context of these directives.

There are also directives on parental leave (96/34),[17] health and safety conditions (89/391 and 91/383), and working conditions in specific sectors (93/104, 99/63, 2000/34, 2000/79, and others). The Turkish labor law is in compliance with most of the provisions of these directives.

European Employment Strategy

The European Council Summits   The treaties establishing the European Community have assigned the responsibility for employment and social protection exclusively to the member states. The role of the European Commission was to promote cooperation between the member states at the EU level. In the early 1990s, persistent European-wide unemployment and structural problems in the labor markets, together with the increased integration of national economies, led to a process of seeking European solutions through closer cooperation and convergence of structural policies, including the employment and social protection policies.

The issuance of the EU's famous "*Delors' White Book*" *on Growth, Competitiveness and Employment* in 1993 set the scene for the development of coordinated employment policies at the EU level. Inspired by the *White Book*, the European Council in Essen in 1994 agreed on five objectives[18] and formulated the Essen Strategy, which was reinforced by successive Council conclusions and resolutions. A permanent Employment and Labour Market Committee was created in 1996. The Essen Strategy declared a political commitment to the issue of employment, but the strategy itself and its implementation were based on nonbinding conclusions of the European Councils. The Treaty of Amsterdam (signed in 1997 and entered into force in 1999) and the new Title on Employment provided the necessary legal framework for implementing a coordinated employment policy.

The European Council in *Luxembourg* (November 1997), which is now known as the Luxembourg Jobs Summit, launched the European Employment Strategy on the basis of the new provisions of the employment title of the Treaty of Amsterdam before it entered into force. The following European Councils have provided additional orientations and targets for the EES and reinforced its links with other EU policies.

The European Council in *Lisbon* (March 2000) set a new strategic goal for the EU for the next decade ("to become the most competitive and dynamic knowledge-based economy in the world, capable of sustainable economic growth with more and better jobs and greater social cohesion") and integrated the EES into a wider framework of policy coordination to achieve this strategic goal. The European Council agreed on the objective of achieving an employment rate as close as possible to 70 percent overall, and exceeding 60 percent for women, on average in the EU by 2010. After the midterm review of the first three years of implementation, the Council proposed strengthening the EES.

The European Council in *Nice* (December 2000) introduced the issue of quality as the guiding thread of the Social Policy Agenda, and in particular quality in work as an important objective of the EES.

Confirming the commitment of the EU and its member states to the goal of full employment, the European Council in *Stockholm* (March 2001) added two intermediate and one additional target: the employment rate should be raised to 67 percent overall by 2005, to 57 percent for women by 2005, and to 50 percent for older workers (aged 55–64) by 2010.

The *Barcelona* European Council (March 2002) underlined that the full employment goal in the EU is at the core of the Lisbon strategy and constitutes an essential goal of economic and social policies. It called for a reinforced EES to underpin the Lisbon strategy in an enlarged EU. After the 2002 evaluation, the Barcelona Council also urged the Council and the Commission to streamline the various policy coordination processes at the EU level.

The *Brussels* European Council (March 2003) reiterated that the EES has the leading role in the implementation of the employment and labor market objectives of the Lisbon strategy, and that it and the Broad Economic Policy Guidelines (BEPG) should operate in a consistent way. The European Council called for the guidelines to be limited in number and for them to be results-oriented in order to allow member states to design the appropriate mix of action.

The 2002 Evaluation of the European Employment Strategy   The EES, from its inception in 1997 to its evaluation in 2002, was based on four "pillars" (employability, entrepreneurship, adaptability, and equal opportunities) together with horizontal objectives. In its fifth year, an extensive evaluation was conducted to give an overview of the objectives of the EES and to strengthen the policy formulation and implementation processes. The study (European Commission 2002d) noted:

> The comprehensive approach of the EES generally strengthened national employment policy coherence and framework. Policies under each pillar were progressively adjusted and employment priorities were mainstreamed into other policy areas like taxation and social security. In addition, the Strategy has brought about a gradual change in priority from managing unemployment to managing employment growth,

and has become gradually embedded in national policy formulation.

> Beyond the clear convergence towards the active labour market principles of the EES in the earlier years of the strategy, the evaluation shows that other policies were also significantly influenced by the EES (notably gender equality and social inclusion policies)... . Over the years, the EES has added momentum to longer term structural reforms in labour markets, not least through the use of recommendations, addressed to individual Member States, adopted by the Council on a proposal from the Commission.

> The EES also fostered political agreement on new common paradigms, such as lifelong learning and quality in work. The need for lifelong learning, and the complementarity between education and training systems, has become generally accepted, and Member States are all in the process of re-designing their education and training policies in a more integrated way. Quality in work appeared as a new priority in the Employment Guidelines for 2000.

Streamlining Policy Processes   After the Barcelona Council, the Commission adopted its communication on streamlining the annual economic and employment policy coordination cycles (European Commission 2002a and 2003a). The main idea is to reorganize existing EU coordination processes around a few key points to make the coordination cycle more transparent and intelligible and to strengthen its visibility and impact. In line with the overall Lisbon strategy, this process is expected to reinforce the focus on the medium term and to improve policy coherence. Within the new approach, the BEPGs are expected to provide the overarching economic policy coordination, and the leading role on employment policy coordination will lie with the Employment Guidelines (EGs) and Recommendations to Member States.

The main building blocks of a better and more clearly articulated policy coordination cycle can be briefly described as follows (European Commission 2003c and 2003d):

(i) *Preparation of the Spring European Council.* The Commission would, in its Spring Report, highlight the main areas where further progress has to be made and the key policy orientations on which general guidance is required from the Spring European Council. The Spring Report would be complemented and presented together with the Implementation Package (including the Implementation Report on the BEPGs, the draft Joint Employment Report, and the implementation report on the Internal Market Strategy). The Commission's various reports and scoreboards (including *inter alia* the Cardiff Report; the state aids, innovation, and enterprise policy scoreboards) will feed into the Implementation Package and the Spring Report. This Commission input would assist different Council formations, as well as any other appropriate actor, in reviewing implementation in their specific policy areas.

(ii) *The Spring European Council.* The Spring European Council is a defining moment in the annual policy coordination cycle. It reviews implementation and, on that basis, gives general political orientations on the main policy priorities.

(iii) *Commission proposals for new guidelines and recommendations.* On the basis of the Spring European Council political orientations, the Commission would present its proposals for further action in the various policy areas together in a Guidelines Package (which would include the Commission drafts for general and country-specific policy recommendations as contained in the BEPGs, the EGs, and the annual employment recommendations to member states). This Package, the first of which would be issued in April 2003, would, in principle, cover a three-year period, i.e., up to 2006. The guidelines would continue to be issued every year to take account of possible major new developments, but should otherwise remain stable until 2006, unless circumstances require otherwise. Consistent with the recommendations of the BEPGs and the outcome and conclusions of the Cardiff process, the Internal Market Strategy—which will accompany the Guidelines Package—would deal with internal market matters at a Community level up to 2006, and would be adjusted in the intervening years only if necessary.

(iv) *Adoption of new guidelines and recommendations.* After, where appropriate, further preparation by the competent Council formations

ahead of the June European Council and following the latter's consideration, the relevant Council formations would adopt the BEPGs, the EGs and the Employment Recommendations to member states and/or endorse action plans (e.g., the Internal Market Strategy) in their competence areas.

(v) *Concentration of implementation review in Quarter 4.* A better streamlined review of implementation requires:

- Systematic information provision by member states on the implementation of policies agreed on at European level. In this context, there may be scope for rationalizing and streamlining current national reporting requirements. Fewer and more comprehensive reports, allowing also for coverage of information on newly identified issues (thus avoiding the need to add new reports and procedures), might help in clarifying and ensuring the coherence of member states' responses to policy recommendations issued by the Community; these reports should ideally be presented together in October at the latest. The National Employment Plans would be sent as a separate document around the same time.

- An implementation assessment by the Commission. On the basis of the available information (through reports, through bilateral contacts, and through the results of various benchmarking exercises), the Commission services would assess implementation in the various relevant policy areas.

The Commission will present the findings of its review in the form of a new Implementation Package together with the Commission's Spring Report in mid-January, marking the start of a new cycle.

The 10 Commandments, Targets, and Indicators

The European Council has identified and confirmed three objectives for the EES:

1. *Full employment.* Employment rate overall, 67 percent in 2005 and 70 percent in 2010 on average; for women, 57 percent in 2005 and 60 percent in 2010; for older workers, 50 percent in 2010.

2. *Quality and productivity at work.* Satisfaction with pay and working conditions, health and safety at the workplace, the availability of flexible work organization, working time arrangements, and balance between flexibility and security. Full attention is given to increasing productivity, in particular through continued investment in human capital, technology, and work organization.

3. *Cohesion and an inclusive labor market.* The reduction of unemployment and of the remaining disparities in access to the labor market, both in socioeconomic and regional terms, is a matter of both the equity and efficiency of the EES.

To support these three objectives, the Commission has identified 10 priorities (10 commandments) for action in the new guidelines:

1. Help unemployed and inactive to find a job, prevent long-term unemployment
2. Encourage entrepreneurship and improve climate for business start-ups
3. Promote adaptability of workers and firms to change
4. Provide more and better investment in human capital
5. Increase labor supply and promote active aging
6. Promote gender equality in employment and pay
7. Combat discrimination against disadvantaged groups
8. Improve financial incentives to make work pay
9. Reduce undeclared work substantially
10. Promote occupational and geographic mobility.

The Commission has also defined specific targets that could be used as a part of an assessment of progress on implementing the guidelines:

- Personalized job search plan for all unemployed before fourth month of unemployment by 2005
- Work experience or training for all unemployed before 12th month of unemployment (before six months for young and vulnerable) by 2005
- Thirty percent of long-term unemployed in work experience or training by 2010
- Reduction of 15 percent in rate of accidents at work and a reduction of 25 percent for high-risk sectors by 2010

- Eighty percent of persons aged 25–64 to have at least upper secondary education by 2010
- Increased rate of participation of adults in education and training, to 15 percent on average in the EU and to at least 10 percent in every member state by 2010
- Increased investment by companies in training of adults from the existing level of the equivalent of 2.3 percent of labor costs up to 5 percent of labor costs on average in the EU by 2010
- An increase in the effective average exit age from the labor market from 60 to 65 years on average in the EU by 2010
- Elimination of gender gaps in employment and halving of gender pay gaps in each member state by 2010
- Child care places available for 33 percent of children aged 0–3 and 90 percent of those from 3 years to mandatory school age in each member state by 2010
- Halving of the school dropout rate in each member state and reduction of EU average dropout rate to 10 percent by 2010
- Reduction by half in each member state in the unemployment gaps for people defined as being at a disadvantage in accordance with national definitions by 2010
- Reduction by half in each member state in the employment gap between non-EU and EU nationals by 2010
- All job vacancies advertised by national employment services accessible and able to be consulted by anyone in the EU by 2005
- National targets to be set for business training, reduced red tape for start-ups, per capita increase in public and private investment in human resources, tax burden on low-paid workers, and undeclared work.

EU Labor Market Policies and Enlargement   In 1999 the European Commission initiated a cooperation process on employment with the candidate countries. The objective of this process is to encourage those countries to define employment policies that prepare them for membership of the EU and progressively adjust their institutions and policies. Moreover, the financial support for accession would be directed toward the employment policy priorities identified in this cooperation process (European Commission 2003b).

It was agreed that as a first step the candidate countries and the Commission would analyze the key challenges for employment policies in Joint Assessment Papers (JAPs). The work was started with background studies funded by the Commission in cooperation with the European Training Foundation. The first JAPs were signed with the Czech Republic, Estonia, Poland, and Slovenia in 2000 and early 2001, followed by Cyprus, Hungary, Lithuania, Malta, and Slovakia in late 2001 and early 2002 and by Bulgaria and Romania in the fall of 2002. The JAP with Latvia was signed in February 2003. Cooperation with Turkey is at an early stage; the background study for the Employment Policy Review was prepared in early 2003 under the auspices of the Turkish Employment Organization (İŞKUR)—see Tunalı and others (2003). This study will form the basis of the JAP to be drawn up with the European Commission.

The candidate countries and the Commission agreed to monitor the implementation of the JAP commitments. After signature of the JAPs, the main commitments were discussed in a series of technical seminars between the Commission and representatives of different institutions in the candidate countries. The Göteborg European Council of June 2001 asked candidate countries to translate the EU economic, social, and environmental objectives underpinning the Lisbon strategy into their national policies and announced that the Synthesis Communication 2003 would include information about the candidate countries on this subject.

Employment Protection and Labor Market Flexibility in Turkey

The growing interest in labor market flexibility has provided an impetus for empirical studies that aim at *measuring* the degree of labor market flexibility, mainly at the national and regional levels. Researchers have developed two sets of measures. The first set of measures, pioneered by the OECD's influential study on employment protection legislation, is based on indicators of labor market regulation that summarize the information on the regulatory environments. The OECD has constructed a database of internationally comparable data on certain economy-wide and industry-specific product market and labor market regulations (for the methodology, the database, and summary

indicators, see Nicoletti, Scarpetta, and Boylaud 2000). Because the OECD database allows researchers to make international comparisons and to analyze the impact of labor market regulations on economic performance in a cross-country setting, it has led to a surge in empirical studies and estimation of similar indicators for other countries. For example, Riboud, Sánchez-Páramo, and Silva-Jáuregui (2002), Cazes and Nesporova (2003), and Heckman and Pagés (2004) have calculated EPL indicators for Latin American, Central and Eastern European (CEE), and transition countries, respectively. In a similar fashion, Betcherman, Luinstra, and Ogawa (2001) present a detailed analysis of labor market regulations in 17 countries, including Turkey. In this section, we will compare the stringency of the EPL in Turkey under the former labor law (which formed the basis of the OECD indicators) and under the new labor law with that in the OECD countries.

The second set of measures, which we define as direct measures, are based on the estimation of various aspects of labor market flexibility using the data on labor market variables. In this study, we use three types of direct measures to assess the labor market flexibility in Turkey: wage differentials, job turnover, and mode-based indicators (employment and wage flexibility).

Employment Protection Legislation

The OECD EPL index, calculated by Nicoletti, Scarpetta, and Boylaud (2000), exploits the raw data published in the *OECD Employment Outlook 1999* (OECD 1999). The data cover two basic elements of the EPL system—restrictions on dismissals of workers with *regular contracts*, and restrictions on the use of *temporary forms of employment contracts*—and refer to the situation in most of the OECD countries in the late 1980s as well as in 1998.

Regulations for regular contracts (permanent employment) cover detailed indicators on

- Procedural requirements (the process that has to be followed from the decision to lay off a worker to the actual termination of the contract)
- Notice and severance pay (for three tenure periods beyond any trial period)
- Prevailing standards and penalties for "unfair" dismissals.

The following elements were considered for regulations for temporary contracts (fixed-term contracts and contracts under temporary work agencies, TWAs):

- "Objective" reasons under which a fixed-term (or a TWA) contract could be offered
- The maximum number of successive renewals
- The maximum cumulated duration of the contract.

Nicoletti, Scarpetta, and Boylaud (2000) assigned a score of 0–5 to each indicator, depending on the degree of stringency of employment protection implied by that indicator, and conducted a factor analysis to aggregate the detailed indicators of each domain (regular employment and temporary employment) into summary indicators of the stringency of regulation by domain. The overall index of stringency of the EPL (EPL index) was obtained by simply averaging the two summary indicators for regular and temporary contracts. The factor analysis was conducted on the 1998 regulatory indicators for 21 OECD countries for which most information was available.

Table 9.4 presents the summary indicators for 25 countries (ranked in descending order by the stringency of the EPL index) for the late 1990s. Turkey has a very high overall score (ranked second), mainly because of its score from the temporary employment domain (index value 4.6, the highest among all countries in the table).

Table 9.5 presents basic indicators—the EPL and EPL index scores—for regular employment for five countries: Germany (a leading country case from the EU, and Turkey's main trade partner), Spain (a latecomer in the EU), Poland (a case for candidate countries), the United States (the extreme case among the OECD countries), and Turkey. The data for Turkey are presented in two columns. The first column refers to the situation prevailing under the former labor law (No. 1475), and the data were taken from Nicoletti, Scarpetta, and Boylaud (2000). The second column refers to the current situation with the new labor law (No. 4857). The values of some indicators are based on our assessment. Table 9.6 presents the same data for temporary employment.

Table 9.5 reveals that the EPL index scores for regular employment for Turkey are higher than those for other countries mainly because of high

severance payments after 4 and 20 years of tenure, a trial period before the eligibility arises, and unfair dismissal compensation (20 years of tenure). Because the new labor law changes these provisions, there is a significant reduction in the EPL index values for regular employment. The EPL index scores for temporary employment are higher than those of the other countries because of the restrictions on fixed-term contracts and the lack of legal framework for TWAs. The draft labor law had special provisions on the TWAs, but these provisions were left out of the law adopted by Parliament. The new labor law allows, with the written consent of the worker, temporary transfer between enterprises belonging to the same holding company, or between different companies if the worker

TABLE 9.4 Employment Protection Legislation Index: OECD Countries, Late 1990s

	EPL Index		
	Average	Regular Contracts	Temporary Contracts
Portugal	3.7	4.3	3.2
Turkey	3.6	2.6	4.6
Greece	3.5	2.6	4.5
Italy	3.3	3.0	3.6
Spain	3.2	2.8	3.7
France	3.1	2.5	3.7
Norway	2.9	2.9	2.8
Germany	2.8	3.0	2.5
Japan	2.6	3.0	2.3
Austria	2.4	2.8	2.0
Netherlands	2.4	3.2	1.5
Sweden	2.4	3.0	1.8
Belgium	2.1	1.6	2.6
Finland	2.1	2.3	1.9
Poland	1.9	2.3	1.4
Czech Rep.	1.7	3.0	0.5
Denmark	1.5	1.7	1.2
Hungary	1.4	2.2	0.6
Switzerland	1.3	1.3	1.2
Australia	1.1	0.9	1.2
Ireland	1.0	1.7	0.3
New Zealand	1.0	1.6	0.5
Canada	0.6	0.9	0.3
United Kingdom	0.5	0.7	0.3
United States	0.2	0.1	0.3

Source: Nicoletti, Scarpetta, and Boylaud 2000.

TABLE 9.5　Employment Protection Legislation for Regular Employment, Selected OECD Countries

		Germany	Poland	Spain	United States	Turkey L. 1475	Turkey L. 4857
		Employment Protection Legislation					
Regular procedural inconveniences							
Procedures	Scale 0–3	2.5	2.0	2.0	0.0	2.0	1.0
Delay to start of notice	Days	17.0	13.0	1.0	1.0	1.0	1.0
Notice and severance pay for no-fault individual dismissals by tenure categories							
Notice period after							
9 months	Months	1.0	1.0	1.0	0.0	1.0	1.0
4 years	Months	1.0	3.0	1.0	0.0	2.0	2.0
20 years	Months	7.0	3.0	1.0	0.0	2.0	2.0
Severance pay after							
9 months	Months	0.0	0.0	0.5	0.0	0.0	0.0
4 years	Months	0.0	0.0	2.6	0.0	4.0	0.0
20 years	Months	0.0	0.0	12.0	0.0	20.0	0.0
Difficulty of dismissals							
Definition of unfair dismissal	Scale 0–3	2.0	0.0	2.0	0.0	0.0	0.0
Trial period before eligibility arises	Months	6.0	1.8	2.5	n.a.	2.0	2.0
Unfair dismissal compensation (20 years)	Months	24.0	3.0	22.0	n.a.	26.0	6.0
Extent of reinstatement	Scale 0–3	1.5	2.0	0.0	0.5	0.0	0.0

Employment Protection Legislation Index Scores

Regular procedural inconveniences						
Procedures	5.0	4.0	4.0	0.0	4.0	2.0
Delay to start of notice	2.0	2.0	0.0	0.0	0.0	0.0
Notice and severance pay for no-fault individual dismissals by tenure categories						
Notice period after						
9 months	3.0	3.0	3.0	0.0	3.0	3.0
4 years	2.0	4.0	2.0	0.0	4.0	4.0
20 years	4.0	2.0	1.0	0.0	1.0	1.0
Severance pay after						
9 months	0.0	0.0	1.0	0.0	0.0	0.0
4 years	0.0	0.0	4.0	0.0	6.0	0.0
20 years	0.0	0.0	4.0	0.0	6.0	0.0
Difficulty of dismissals						
Definition of unfair dismissal	4.0	0.0	4.0	0.0	0.0	0.0
Trial period before eligibility arises	3.0	5.0	5.0	0.0	5.0	5.0
Unfair dismissal compensation (20 years)	4.0	0.0	4.0	0.0	5.0	1.0
Extent of reinstatement	3.0	4.0	0.0	1.0	0.0	0.0

n.a. Not applicable.

Sources: Nicoletti, Scarpetta, and Boylaud 2000; authors' assessment for Law No. 4857.

TABLE 9.6 Employment Protection Legislation for Temporary Employment, Selected OECD Countries

		Germany	Poland	Spain	United States	Turkey L. 1475	Turkey L. 4857
Employment Protection Legislation							
Fixed-term contracts							
Valid cases other than the usual objective reasons	Scale 0–3	2.5	3.0	1.0	3.0	0.0	2.0
Max. number of successive contracts	Number	4.0	2.0	3.0	No limit	1.5	No limit
Max. cumulative duration	Months	24.0	No limit	36.0	No limit	No limit	No limit
Temporary work agencies (TWAs)							
Types of work for which TWA employment is legal	Scale 0–4	3.0	4.0	2.0	4.0	0.0	4.0
Restrictions on number of renewals	Yes/no	Yes	Yes	Yes	No limit	n.a.	n.a.
Max. cumulative duration of temporary work contracts	Months	12.0	No limit	36.0	No limit	n.a.	n.a.
Employment Protection Legislation Index Scores							
Fixed-term contracts							
Valid cases other than the usual objective reasons		1.0	0.0	4.0	0.0	6.0	2.0
Max. number of successive contracts		2.0	4.0	3.0	0.0	5.0	0.0
Max. cumulative duration		3.0	0.0	2.0	0.0	0.0	0.0
Temporary work agencies (TWAs)							
Types of work for which TWA employment is legal		1.5	0.0	3.0	0.0	6.0	4.0
Restrictions on number of renewals		4.0	4.0	4.0	2.0	n.a.	n.a.
Max. cumulative duration of temporary work contracts		4.0	0.0	6.0	0.0	n.a.	n.a.

n.a. Not applicable.

Sources: Nicoletti, Scarpetta, and Boylaud 2000; authors' assessment for Law No. 4857.

FIGURE 9.1   Employment Protection Legislation, Selected OECD Countries

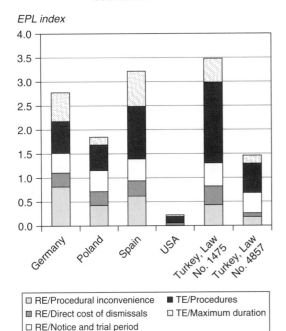

Note: RE = regular employment; TE = temporary employment.

Sources: Nicoletti, Scarpetta and Boylaud 2000; authors' assessment for Law No. 4857.

is employed in a similar position, up to 12 months in total. For fixed-term contracts, the law does not impose any restriction on the maximum cumulative duration or renewal. Thus the new law provides flexibility, under the OECD definition, for temporary employment.

Figure 9.1 shows the EPL index for the same group of countries and the contribution of each main category (factors) on the EPL index. As evident in the figure, the changes introduced by the new labor law (No. 4857) have dramatically reduced the EPL index for Turkey, mainly by making temporary employment easier. The index value would be much smaller had the new law provided the legal basis for TWAs.

Although the EPL measures are used extensively in empirical studies, they have four known shortcomings. First, there are significant *measurement problems*. As Addison and Teixeira (2001) mention, measuring the stringency of employment protection merely from the legal texts may not be a good indicator of the monetary costs to employers,

because the costs to employers depend on various other factors, such as voluntary turnover and the occupational and tenure distributions of the labor force that define the entitlements for severance pay.

Second, the *coverage* of the law and regulations is very important. The OECD EPL index almost completely ignores the coverage issue. The EPL index is a simple average of the indexes for regular and temporary employment, although temporary employment accounts for only 20 percent of wage earners in Turkey. Moreover, the employment protection provisions of the new law do not cover establishments employing fewer than 30 workers, leaving more than 40 percent of workers registered at the Social Insurance Institution (Sosyal Sigortalar Kurumu, SSK) without protection (Household Labour Force Survey 2000 data). The law also excludes certain sectors and activities.

Third, *enforcement and implementation* of the law are a major issue in countries such as Turkey. As Bertola, Boeri, and Cazes (1999) discuss in detail, the EPL is enforced to different degrees, and a simple ranking of countries on the basis of legal provisions may lead to misleading results.

Finally, the existing EPL measures do not reflect the *links and interactions* between the EPL and other labor market institutions, such as unemployment benefit schemes, wage-setting institutions, early retirement, and pensions. Some of these institutions could be substitutes, some others complementary. According to Bertola, Boeri, and Cazes (2000, p. 13),

> Protection against job loss is all the more desirable when only scant unemployment insurance is available, and unemployment insurance is highly appreciated when weak job security provisions increase the risk of job loss. Indeed, in some countries job security—especially case law favourable to employees—does appear to be inversely correlated to the coverage and level of unemployment insurance (suggesting a trade-off between the strictness of EPL and the unemployment benefit system, as in Denmark, Italy or Spain, for example) or other adjustment tools such as early retirement provisions.

Blanchard (2002) observes that there is an inverse relation between the degree of employment protection and the generosity of the state unemployment insurance system in continental Europe.

He explains this inverse relationship by suggesting that these institutions are two different ways of addressing the same failures, each one more appropriate to the circumstances of the country. This is exactly the case in Turkey. Unemployment insurance legislation was enacted in 1999 (Law No. 4447), and it began to provide unemployment benefits for those eligible in 2002. Therefore, severance pay was considered as a kind of protection and insurance against unemployment in the implementation of the former labor law, and it proved to be easier to change the provisions on severance pay in the new labor law after introducing the unemployment insurance system in the country.

There is almost a consensus on the impact of the EPL on flows from and into unemployment (Jackman, Layard, and Nickell 1996; Blanchard 2000). On the one hand, stricter EPL decreases hiring, which, in turn, makes it difficult for the unemployed to find a new job and thus increases long-term unemployment. On the other hand, stricter EPL also decreases firing and decreases (short-term) unemployment. The net effect on unemployment is ambiguous.

Blanchard (2000) discovers a negative correlation between flow into unemployment and the OECD EPL ranking (figure 9.2) and a positive correlation between unemployment duration and the EPL (figure 9.3), but no correlation at all between the unemployment rate and the EPL (figure 9.4), as

predicted by the theory. The Turkish data,[19] not included in Blanchard's study, are also plotted in figures 9.2–9.4. Turkey is an apparent outlier in figure 9.2, and in figure 9.3 to a lesser extent. In other words, the data on flow into unemployment suggest less strict employment protection than is implied by the OECD index. This discrepancy could be regarded as confirmation of the caveats about relying on the EPL as an indicator of flexibility for a country such as Turkey.

Direct Measures of Labor Market Flexibility

Rigidities in labor markets are expected to change the behavior of economic agents and labor market outcomes. In this study, we use three measures that could reflect the extent of labor market rigidities. Because of the lack of internationally comparable data, we focus on the manufacturing industries.[20]

Wage differentials tend to be lower in countries with rigid labor markets, because various labor market institutions, especially labor unions and minimum wage legislation, usually aim at wage compression across sectors and different categories of workers.

Figure 9.5a depicts the data on the evolution of interindustry wage differentials[21] for a selected group of countries for the period 1980–2000. Throughout the period, Turkey had much wider

FIGURE 9.2   Flow into Unemployment and Employment Protection: Selected Countries, 1985–94

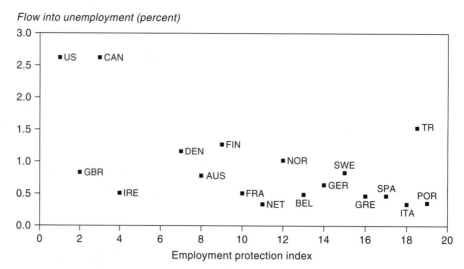

Sources: Blanchard 2000; Turkey for 2000–02, authors' calculations from Turkish State Institute of Statistics, Household Labour Force Survey.

**FIGURE 9.3   Unemployment Duration and Employment Protection: Selected
Countries, 1985–94**

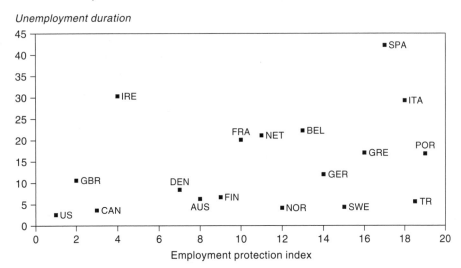

Sources: See figure 9.2.

**FIGURE 9.4   Unemployment Rate and Employment Protection: Selected
Countries, 1985–1994**

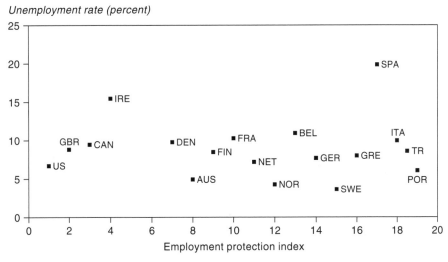

Sources: See figure 9.2.

interindustry wage differentials than the United
States (the benchmark case for flexible labor markets), Greece and Spain (two EU countries), and
Hungary and Poland (two candidate countries). As
might be expected, Poland and Hungary had relatively low wage differentials in the 1980s, but they
have experienced a widening gap in interindustry
wages since the late 1980s because of their transition toward a market economy. Wage differentials
in Turkey increased in the late 1980s when real

wages increased rapidly in the post-military period,
and they declined in the period of wage depressions
in the late 1990s. The same data are presented for
developed EU countries and the United States in
figure 9.5b. Among all the developed countries
depicted in figure 9.5b, the United States has the
highest wage differentials in the manufacturing
industry and the Scandinavian countries have the
lowest. The data in figures 9.5a and 9.5b seem to
confirm the widely held belief that the Scandinavian

FIGURE 9.5a   Interindustry Wage Differentials: Selected Countries, 1980–2000

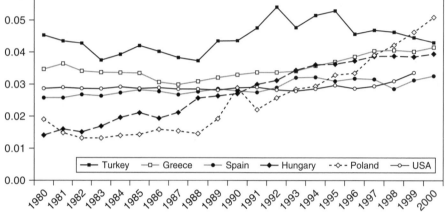

Source: Authors' calculations from UNIDO data.

FIGURE 9.5b   Interindustry Wage Differentials: Selected Countries, 1980–2000

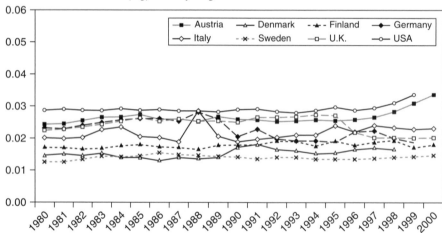

Source: Authors' calculations from UNIDO data.

countries have more equal income and wage distribution as a result of their specific centralized wage-setting institutions.

Rigidities in labor markets make the cost of firing, and the potential cost of hiring, higher. Thus expansion and contraction of firms will be more costly, new firm formation will be limited, and the exit rate will be lower. All those factors will reduce *job turnover*. Table 9.7 presents the data on job turnover for selected countries. The rate of job turnover for Turkey is calculated only for manufacturing establishments employing more than 10 workers. For Chile, Colombia, and the United States, job turnover data are available only for the manufac-

turing industry. For all other countries, the data are available for the whole economy. The U.S. data seem to suggest that the job turnover rate is lower in the manufacturing industry than in other sectors.

The average job turnover rate for the Turkish manufacturing industry for the period 1980–2000 is 21 percent—that is, the proportion of jobs created and abolished in a year is 21 percent of all jobs available. The rate for Turkey is somewhat higher than the one observed in the United States and slightly lower than those in Colombia and Chile. Although cross-country comparisons do present some problems, it could be claimed that the job turnover rate in Turkey is high. Table 9.8 presents

TABLE 9.7 Job Turnover, Selected Countries

	Period	Entry	Expansion	Exit	Contraction	Turnover
Turkey (M)	1980–2000	4.8	6.7	4.1	5.5	21.0
Chile (M)	1980–1995	4.7	9.1	4.7	7.2	25.8
Colombia (M)	1978–1891	5.3	6.6	5.1	6.7	23.8
United States (M)	1984–1988	1.4	6.7	2.7	7.7	18.6
United States	1984–1991	8.4	4.6	7.3	3.1	23.4
Canada	1983–1991	3.2	11.2	3.1	8.8	26.3
France	1984–1991	6.1	6.6	5.5	6.3	24.4
Germany	1983–1990	2.5	6.5	1.9	5.6	16.5
Italy	1987–1992	3.8	7.3	3.8	6.2	21.0
United Kingdom	1985–1991	2.7	6.0	3.9	2.7	15.3

Note: M = manufacturing industries.
Sources: Bertola, Boeri, and Cazes 1999; authors' calculations from Turkish State Institute of Statistics data.

TABLE 9.8 Job Turnover in Turkish Manufacturing Industries
(percent)

	Public	Private			Average
		Small	Medium	Large	
1981–90					
Entry	1.6	14.5	7.1	3.0	4.4
Expansion	2.8	4.7	9.7	8.5	6.8
Contraction	4.5	8.0	6.3	3.4	4.7
Exit	1.3	14.9	5.4	2.7	3.8
Turnover	10.3	42.1	28.4	17.6	19.7
1991–2000					
Entry	0.4	20.2	8.5	3.1	5.2
Expansion	2.1	3.6	8.1	7.7	6.6
Contraction	6.5	10.3	6.8	5.4	6.2
Exit	2.6	17.9	5.7	2.6	4.4
Turnover	11.7	52.1	29.3	18.8	22.3

Source: Authors' calculations from Turkish State Institute of Statistics data.

the same data for the public sector and private sector by size categories for two subperiods, 1980–90, and 1990–2000. The job turnover rate is much higher in the private sector, especially among small establishments, because of high rates of entry and exit. Job turnover stemming from expansion and contraction dominates entry and exit for medium-size and large establishments. There seems to be a slight increase in the job turnover rate in the 1990s.

Model-based indicators are extensively used in empirical studies to assess employment and wage flexibility (see, e.g., Nickell and Layard 1999;

Fabiani and Rodriguez-Palenzuela 2001; Plasmans and others 2002). These indicators are based on the coefficients of adjustment terms or elasticities in employment or wage equations.

Employment flexibility can be defined as the speed of adjustment of employment in a labor demand equation. A simple dynamic conditional labor demand equation can be written as

$$(9.1) \qquad L_{t,i} = \beta_i + \beta_1 L_{t\text{-}1,i} + \beta_2 Q_{t,i} + \beta_3 w_{t,i} + \epsilon_{t,i}$$

where L, Q, and w refer to the number of employed, real output, and real product wage, respectively. All variables are in log form. The subscripts t and i denote time and the cross-sectional unit (industry or firm), respectively; ϵ denotes the usual error terms. The coefficient of the lagged employment, β_1, measures the speed of adjustment, and the coefficient of the wage variable, β_3, the wage elasticity of labor demand.

The wage equation can be defined in a similar way and can be used to estimate the effects of independent variables on wages. In real wage equations, the unemployment rate is usually included in the model to estimate the degree of real wage flexibility, because the coefficient of the unemployment term reflects how sensitive real wages are to the unemployment level. If the rate of unemployment is higher than the NAIRU (nonaccelerating inflation rate of unemployment), then the real wage is expected to decline to clear the market—that is, a statistically significant negative coefficient is expected for the unemployment term. The absolute value of the coefficient will indicate how fast the labor market adjusts.

Because of the lack of data, we estimated only the dynamic labor demand equation for a group of OECD and candidate countries by using panel data at the International Standard Industrial Classification (Rev. 2) three-digit level for the period 1980–2000. The GMM (generalized method of moments) technique is used to estimate the model in difference form. Figure 9.6 plots the adjustment parameter against the wage elasticity. Because a

military government ruled the country in the early 1980s, we reestimated the same equation for Turkey for the 1990s. As is the case of almost all other measures, the United States seems to have a flexible labor market for the manufacturing industries. The adjustment parameter is small, which implies fast adjustment, and the wage elasticity is high. The rate of adjustment is rather slow in Turkey, but it seems to gain speed in the 1990s.

Only a few empirical studies measure wage flexibility for Turkey. Onaran (2002), who estimated a wage equation by using panel data at the industry level, found that real wages are quite flexible in the post-1980 period.[22] The findings by İlkkaracan and Selim (2002) on the basis of a cross-sectional estimation of an individual-level wage equation suggest that there is a statistically significant negative correlation between wages and regional unemployment rates. Separate regressions for men and women, however, show a wage curve to exist only in the male labor market. Unemployment elasticity is higher in the private sector, supporting the anecdotal evidence that the private sector has more flexible employment practices that the public sector.

The evidence presented here suggests that the EPL in Turkey is "rigid," but the legislation excludes a large part of the economy—legally, small businesses and certain sectors, and illegally, the informal sector. There are enforcement problems in the formal sector as well. Some measures studied here show that the labor market for the manufacturing

FIGURE 9.6   Labor Demand Adjustment Speed and Wage Elasticity: Selected Countries, 1980–97

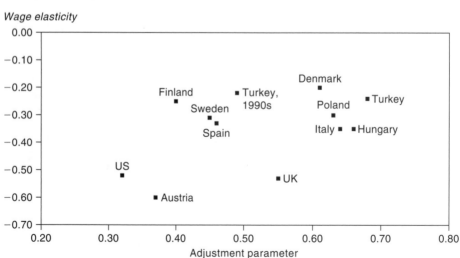

Source: Authors' estimates from UNIDO data.

industry, which is probably the most regulated and unionized sector, is quite flexible. Moreover, the new labor law provides a legal basis for flexible employment practices such as part-time and fixed-term employment.

Problems and Prospects: An Assessment

The labor market institutions in Turkey will confront four major challenges in the next decade[23]:

1. Dealing with the continuing decline in the share of agriculture in total employment by creating more jobs, especially in the services sector.
2. Increasing the employment rate—most important, by increasing the participation rate for urban women. This step will require a substantial increase in employment opportunities for urban women, especially an increase in part-time jobs.
3. Investing in the education and training of the young people in Turkey, whose share of the population will remain quite high compared with the shares in the EU and candidate countries. This demographic window of opportunity for the Turkish economy can turn into an obstacle for development if the educational system fails to raise the skills level of the young people.
4. Eliminating the informal sector that continues to be an important source of low-quality, low-wage jobs. The informal sector is still a source of survival for a huge number of small and medium-size enterprises (SMEs) that enjoy flexible employment practices and are able to avoid paying taxes, SSCs, and so forth. This sector helps to curb the pressures on employment, but at the same time, it hinders the generation of better jobs by the formal sector.

The prospect of EU membership has sparked changes in Turkey's legal framework and labor market institutions so that it can adopt the Community *acquis*. Against the background of these four challenges, the likely effects of adopting and implementing the *acquis* can be discussed at three levels: (1) the impact of the new labor law that has introduced various directives (the short term), (2) the impact of adopting and implementing all employment directives (the medium and long term), and (3) the impact of designing and implementing employment policies in line with the objectives and targets of the EES.

The Impact of the New Labor Law

The new labor law (No. 4857) has introduced changes in accordance with the European Commission directives, but further reform in the labor law and related regulations are needed to comply fully with the *acquis*. The potential effects of the changes introduced by the new labor law can be summarized as follows.

First, the new labor law has provided a legal basis for "atypical" employment relationships—that is, part-time and fixed-term employment. This is the most welcome aspect of the new law for employers. However, as mentioned early in this chapter, part-time employment is not widespread in Turkey (except in the agricultural sector). Moreover, the average work week is quite long, and the lobbying against implementing the directive's provision (93/104) on the maximum average work week (48 hours) has been effective.[24] According to the *Household Labour Force Statistics* of the State Institute of Statistics (SIS 2000b), 41.5 percent of all paid workers work 50 hours or longer a week. Therefore, the law is not expected to have any significant impact on part-time employment. Because of the emphasis on labor market flexibility, one might expect a tendency toward the increasing use of fixed-term and subcontract labor. The directives on part-time and fixed-term employment require "that, in respect of employment conditions, part-time and fixed-term workers shall not be treated in a less favorable manner than comparable full-time and permanent workers," but it could be difficult to enforce these provisions in the Turkish context, at least in the medium term, because the Turkish labor law does not provide sufficient safeguards to protect part-time and fixed-term employees. Moreover, the law does not impose any restriction on the cumulative duration or the number of successive contracts. Thus, employers are expected to lower labor costs by gradually switching to fixed-term contracts and subcontract labor. However, this strategy, if it is thought to be the main strategy for improving competitiveness, could easily turn out to be a "low road" labor flexibility practice that might lead to neglect of investment in human capital.

Second, the new law reduces the cost of layoffs by establishing a special Severance Payment Fund (SPF). Firms are required to pay a certain proportion of the wage bill to the fund, and it then covers all severance payments. Thus the overall effect of the change in the severance pay system is likely to reduce firms' (hiring and firing) costs.

Third, the new labor law has included most of the articles of the law on employment protection (No. 4773), but reduced the coverage of employment protection by excluding those establishments employing fewer than 30 workers (Law No. 4773 excluded only those employing fewer than 10 workers). Therefore, the new labor law has legally provided extensive flexibility to small establishments.

To summarize, the changes introduced by the new labor law address mainly the short-term concerns of employers about achieving labor market flexibility. However, as shown in our earlier analysis, even the labor market for the manufacturing industry seems to be quite flexible. Therefore, excessive emphasis on labor market flexibility may lead to the adoption of a "defensive strategy" by firms that ignores the human capital, entrepreneurship, and innovativeness that the Turkish economy needs to tackle the challenges listed earlier. This process may also delay the restructuring of the corporate sector, because it would tilt the field of competition in favor of less productive firms that reduce their costs by relying on atypical employment relations and avoiding all social expenditures.

The new labor law, by increasing flows from and to unemployment, is likely to change the structure of unemployment. The proportion of short-term unemployment may increase, just as it did, for example, after the labor market reform in Colombia (Kugler 1999; Kugler and Cárdenas 1999).

The Impact of Adopting and Implementing the Employment Acquis

Although the new labor law has made some progress in the field of social policy and employment, it is still far from full alignment with the *acquis*. Therefore, Turkey needs to extensively amend its laws and regulations in order to comply fully with the *acquis*. As the comparison between the new labor law and directives indicates, those provisions that are not yet incorporated into the labor law are exactly those that mean additional costs for firms (e.g., the provisions on the maximum work week and minimum period of

annual leave). These provisions, if implemented, may increase the firms' costs by a few percentage points of the wage bill.

The most important discrepancy between the Turkish labor law (both the former one and the new law) and the EU directives is the complete disregard of any social dialogue, employee participation, and consultation in the Turkish labor law. As Table 9.3 demonstrates, the new law does not refer to the provisions of various directives regarding informing workers, and it does not address at all Directive 2002/14 on consultation and employee representation. Although the draft law prepared by the tripartite Scientific Committee referred to employees' representatives, all these referrals were omitted in the final version of the law adopted by Parliament. Therefore, it is no surprise that the European Commission's report on the progress toward accession by candidate countries points out that "[s]teps have been taken in the field of social policy and employment [in Turkey], but are not always in full conformity with the *acquis*. There is an urgent need to develop and strengthen the conditions for a genuine social dialogue at all levels" (European Commission 2002e). The *Regular Report on Turkey's Progress towards Accession* (European Commission, 2002c) summarizes what needs to be done, as follows:

> As regards social dialogue, despite improvements for trade union rights in free trade zones, further progress needs to be made as a matter of priority to create the conditions for a free and genuine bipartite as well as tripartite social dialogue at all levels in line with the *acquis*. Turkey should make rapid progress towards establishing full trade union rights that includes elimination of restrictive thresholds for forming a trade union branch and requirement of 10% threshold for a trade union to be eligible for collective bargaining at company level. The law on public servants' trade unions, which was adopted in June 2001 and which is not in line with the Community *acquis* and the relevant ILO Conventions ratified by Turkey, has not been amended. The law contains a number of provisions which entail significant constraints on the right to organise in the public sector. Notably, there are restrictive provisions relating to the exclusion of the right to strike and to collective bargaining.

The percentage of the labour force covered by collective agreements is extremely low; it is estimated to be below 15%. No social dialogue exists in most private enterprises, which may limit the proper implementation of the Community *acquis* at enterprise level. . . . Promoting social inclusion and developing a national employment strategy in line with the European Employment Strategy is a matter of priority.

Social dialogue and employee participation are crucial for implementation of the *acquis*, but the current emphasis on short-term solutions makes it difficult to establish cooperative relationships between employers and employees.[25]

The Copenhagen criteria for membership include the *acquis* criterion that highlights the importance not only of incorporating the *acquis* into national legislation, but also of ensuring its effective application through the appropriate administrative and judicial structures.[26] Effective application of the *acquis* by extending the coverage to include the informal sector would be by far the most important impact of the accession process. In other words, firms in the informal sector have to be forced to abide by laws and regulations—that is, they have to bear the costs of taxes and SSCs, together with the firms that had been complying with regulations. This process is likely to eliminate some firms operating in the informal sector and lead to a painful adjustment process in the medium term. With the gradual elimination of the informal sector, the long-run effect is very likely to be positive for productivity, growth, and employment. A simple quantitative analysis is performed later in this chapter to assess the impact of this process.

The Impact of Coordinating Employment Policies

Turkey as a candidate country has committed itself to progressively adjusting its labor market institutions and employment policies and coordinating them with those of the EU. Turkey and the European Commission are expected to analyze the key challenges for employment policies in a Joint Assessment Paper, and the JAP commitments will be monitored systematically. This process of cooperation and coordination is likely to have two crucial effects on policymaking in Turkey.

First, Turkey must establish the institutional framework needed to design and implement employment policies. This step requires making major improvements in the national statistical system, strengthening the Turkish Employment Organization (İŞKUR), and so forth.[27] Second, it is hoped that Turkey will implement, after decades of neglect and disorientation, consistent and systematic employment policies that bring forward long-term objectives. These policies should be in conformity with the three objectives of the EES (full employment, quality and productivity at work, and cohesion and an inclusive labor market) that are also priority issues for Turkey. The "10 commandments" (especially the objectives of more and better investment in human capital, gender equality in employment and pay, the elimination of undeclared work, and the promotion of occupational mobility) are likely to cause an upsurge in the short-term adjustment costs of the corporate sector, although they would be extremely beneficial in the medium and long run. New employment policies are likely to have a significant positive impact on productivity and growth in the long term, if they are accompanied by coherent competition, technology, and innovation policies.

A Simulation Analysis

Because the implementation of laws and regulations that cover the informal sector is likely to lead to the most important effect by far in the accession process, here we conduct a simple simulation exercise to measure the order of magnitude of these effects in the private manufacturing industry.

The first step in any analysis of the informal sector is likely to start with an estimation of its size and characteristics. Because there are almost no data available for the informal sector, we make the following assumptions:

- The SIS's Household Labour Force Survey measures total manufacturing employment. The number of "informal workers" is equal to the number of people employed in microenterprises.
- The SIS's *Annual Survey of Manufacturing Industries* (ASMI) reflects the average characteristics of establishments categorized by size.
- Informal sector firms do not pay any tax (including the income tax for employees) and SSCs.

• Informal sector firms are as productive as "small" formal sector firms that employ 10–24 people.

Figure 9.7 depicts the distribution of employment, value added, and output in the private

FIGURE 9.7   Sectoral Distribution of Employment, Value Added, and Output: Private Manufacturing Industry, Turkey, 2000

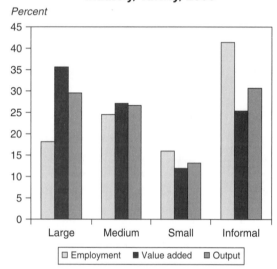

Sources: Authors' calculations and estimates from Turkish State Institute of Statistics data.

manufacturing sector in 2000. Firms are classified into four groups: large (employing 150 or more people), medium (employing 25–49 people), small (employing 10–24 people), and informal (small firms and informal sector firms). Under our assumptions, the share of informal workers is about 41 percent in private manufacturing and 40 percent in all manufacturing.[28] The latter value is comparable with the share of informal workers in Brazilian manufacturing (20.6 percent) and in Colombia (54.0 percent) in the late 1990s (Goldberg and Pavcnik 2003).

The share of the informal sector in total value added (and output) is estimated by assuming that value added per employee in the informal sector is equal to the net value added (value added minus all taxes and social security expenditures) per employee in small formal sector firms (for the composition of output, see table 9.9). Under these assumptions, the informal sector produces only 25 percent of total value added in private manufacturing.

Figure 9.8 shows the structure of value added by four categories of firms. Because cumulative employment is plotted on the horizontal axis, the area under the line defines total value added produced by that category. Large firms are the most productive group. The informal sector firms are

TABLE 9.9   Composition of Output in Private Manufacturing: Turkey, 2000
(percent)

	Large	Medium	Small	Informal
Net wage	5.44	4.35	3.97	4.42
Income tax[a]	1.16	0.78	0.59	0.00
SSC, employees' share[a]	1.16	0.91	0.80	0.00
SSC, employers' share[a]	1.67	1.30	1.15	0.00
Severance payments[b]	1.59	1.53	1.50	0.00
Total labor cost	*11.02*	*8.87*	*8.02*	*4.42*
Interest payments	3.91	2.50	1.37	1.53
Taxes	2.55	1.54	1.46	0.00
Profit	22.50	20.84	19.25	21.47
Materials	53.78	61.07	65.09	72.59
Value added (VA) tax	6.24	5.18	4.82	0.00
Total	*100*	*100*	*100*	*100*
Total VA per employee (millions of Turkish lira)	26,561	14,982	10,149	9,590
Share of VA in output (%)	40.0	33.8	30.1	27.4
VA per employee (large = 1)	1.00	0.56	0.38	0.31

a. Estimated.

b. Includes all compensation payments.

Sources: Large, medium, and small establishments, SIS 2000a; informal sector, authors' estimates.

FIGURE 9.8   Structure of Value Added in Private Manufacturing: Turkey, 2000

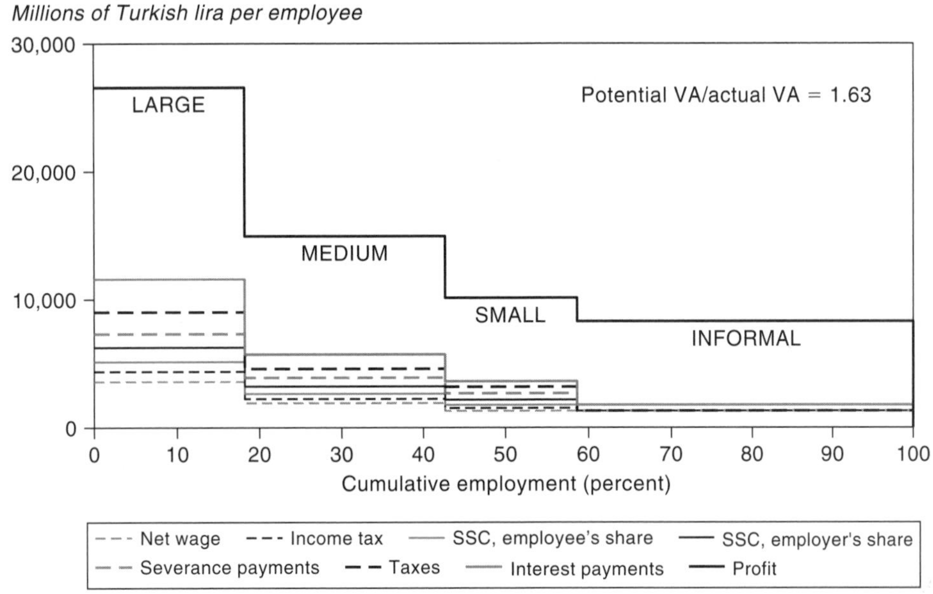

Millions of Turkish lira per employee

Legend:
- Net wage
- Income tax
- SSC, employee's share
- SSC, employer's share
- Severance payments
- Taxes
- Interest payments
- Profit

Source: Large, medium, and small establishments, SIS 2000a; informal sector, authors' estimates.

only 31 percent as productive as the larger firms. The share of labor costs, including severance payments, in value added is 27.6 percent for large firms, 26.3 percent for medium-size firms, and 26.6 percent for small firms. The informal sector firms pay only 16.2 percent of value added as wages to their employees.

If all informal sector firms and workers pay income and corporate taxes and SSCs, their sales prices will increase about 6 percent so that they earn the same amount of profit and pay the same net wage. The value added tax will add another 5 percentage points. In other words, the benefit of operating in the informal sector is somewhat higher than 10 percent of the sales price (including the value added tax).

We conduct five simulations. In the first simulation (*Case 1*), we assume that all informal sector firms pay taxes and SSCs, but that there is no change in the nominal output (size) of the manufacturing industry. Therefore, an increase in prices caused by the increase in the costs of informal sector firms leads to a decline in demand of the same proportion. We also assume that the market shares of four categories of firms do not change.

When the informal sector firms pay taxes and SSCs, the total revenue of the government and social security institutions will increase to a large extent. Therefore, we assume in *Case 2* that the gov-

ernment reduces tax and social security rates so that total tax and social security revenue remain the same. This policy will help formal sector firms by reducing their costs.

Because the assumption on constant market shares is not realistic given the fact that informal sector firms have to increase their prices, in the third simulation (*Case 3*) we assume that the informal sector firms lose half of their market shares. The next case (*Case 4*) adds a reduction in tax and social security rates to the Case 3 simulation.

Finally, in *Case 5* we take into consideration the long-term effects in Case 4 by assuming that total output increases by 10 percent (as a result of productivity increases and other effects).

In all simulations, we assume that the structure and level of output remain the same for the formerly formal sector firms. Nominal net wages and profits for the informal sector firms are assumed to remain constant. Thus our analysis is limited to the effects of reallocation of output between formal and informal sector firms within the same industry.

Table 9.10 summarizes the simulation results. The *Base Case* shows the current situation. When the informal sector firms begin to pay taxes and SSCs (Case 1), the immediate impact will be observed in a reduction in manufacturing employment (4.3 percent; about 150,000 jobs are lost) after the decline in output. Total wage payments will also

TABLE 9.10   Simulation Results

	Base Case	Case 1 Constant Mkt. Share	Case 2 + Tax Reduction	Case 3 50% Lost in Informal	Case 4 + Tax Reduction	Case 5 +10% Growth
		Percentage Change Relative to Base Case				
Employment	3,394,000	−4.3	−1.5	−8.9	−6.0	4.2
Wage bill[a]	6,433,657	−3.0	0.0	−0.9	2.4	13.5
Social security contributions[a]	2,331,012	35.7	0.0	39.2	0.0	0.0
Income tax[a]	2,754,916	31.6	0.0	36.8	0.0	0.0
Value added tax[a]	5,347,145	38.3	0.0	40.7	0.0	0.0
Profit[a]	29,538,664	−3.2	−0.2	−2.0	1.3	12.2
Average net wage[b]	1,896	1.3	1.5	8.7	8.9	9.0
Profit margin	21.3	−3.2	−0.2	−2.0	1.3	2.0
Social sec. contribution rate[c]	5.1	0.0	−28.5	0.0	−30.5	−37.3
Income tax rate[c]	6.0	0.0	−26.4	0.0	−29.4	−36.3
Value added tax rate[c]	11.6	0.0	−29.8	0.0	−31.3	−38.0

a. Billions of Turkish lira.
b. Millions of Turkish lira per employee.
c. Share in value added.
Source: Authors' estimates.

decline (3.0 percent), but the average net wage will increase, because the informal sector will experience the highest employment loss. The share of profits in total output (the profit margin) will decline by 3.2 percent. Meanwhile, there will be a huge increase in tax and social security revenue (about 35 percent). In the second case, the government reduces the SSC rate by 28.5 percent, the income tax rate by 26.4 percent, and the value added tax rate by 29.8 percent, so that total revenue remains at the base level. The reductions in tax and social security rates will help to moderate employment losses (now only 1.5 percent) and the decline in the profit margin (0.2 percent).

If the informal sector firms exit en masse from the market because of their increasing costs (Case 3), the impact on employment will be dramatic: although we assume there is no change in nominal output, the decline in employment will be 8.9 percent because of the lower output-to-labor ratio in the informal sector. Because low-wage jobs will be lost, there will be a substantial increase in the average wage rate (8.7 percent) that will make employees as a group not much worse off. In this case, tax and social security revenue will increase more than in Case 1 because of higher average wages and income in the formal sector. A reduction in tax and social security rates will again moderate employment losses.

If the manufacturing industry succeeds in growing during this period (we assume 10 percent growth), then employment will increase 4.2 percent even if half of the informal sector firms are eliminated, and the average wage rate and the profit margin will increase by 9 percent and 2 percent, respectively. The government, to receive the same amount of revenue that it receives in the Base Case, must cut tax and social security rates substantially (36–38 percent).

This simple simulation exercise shows that there could be significant short-term transitory costs, in terms of a loss in employment opportunities, in eliminating the informal sector. These costs could be reduced if the economy achieves a faster rate of economic growth.

Conclusions and Policy Implications

Turkey has embarked on an effort to change its institutional structure for employment and social affairs. The new labor law has introduced changes in accordance with the European Community directives, mainly the provisions that help to establish flexible employment relationships, but further reform is apparently needed in the labor law and other regulations to fully comply with the EU *acquis.* Adoption of the remaining regulations of the *acquis* on employment and social affairs is likely to raise the costs of adjustment, especially for informal sector firms. Moreover, it also will require a comprehensive change in the mindset of employers if the regulations (such as those on equal treatment of fixed-term and part-time workers and employee participation and consultation) are to be implemented. Because Turkey needs to address all these issues in its employment strategy while heeding the EU's long-term objectives and targets (full employment, quality and productivity at work, and cohesion and an inclusive labor market), it has an opportunity to solve underlying problems that have plagued the processes of economic growth and employment generation for decades. Four areas of action need special consideration:

1. Give priority to strengthening Turkey's institutional capacity (such as the Turkish Employment Organization, İŞKUR) to develop and implement employment strategies. Moreover, develop an institutional framework that guarantees commitment, consistency, and continuity in employment policies.

2. Reduce the costs of adjustment for the successful implementation of new regulations and the gradual elimination of the informal sector. Temporarily reducing tax and social security rates for new firms and hiring new workers could be helpful in this regard.

3. Encourage, support, and even force firms to adopt competitive strategies based on employing a "skilled, trained and adaptable workforce" in the spirit of Article 125 of the Treaty Establishing the European Community. These strategies include various support schemes and initiatives for on-the-job training[29] and technology development, transfer, and diffusion programs especially designed for SMEs.

4. Generate employment and match the demand and supply for skills—steps important to confronting the main challenges summarized earlier in this section. Special attention should be paid to providing part-time jobs (for urban women) by enforcing equal treatment for part-time workers and to strengthening and widening the scope of active labor market policies. The establishment of a national qualification and certification system could help to match the demand and supply for skills.

Notes

1. An earlier version of this paper was presented at the Conference on Turkey: Towards EU Accession, Bilkent University, May 10–12, 2003. The authors would like to thank their discussant, Necdet Kenar, then president of the Turkish Employment Organization, Cem Somel of Middle East Technical University, and three anonymous referees for their valuable comments and suggestions.

2. For a synthesis of views on labor market flexibility, see the OECD's influential *Jobs Study* (OECD 1994a, 1994b). For an overview of the evolution of the concept of labor market flexibility, see Brodsky (1994).

3. Scarpetta and Tressel (2002) claim that "strict regulation may hinder the adoption of existing technologies, possibly because it reduces competitive pressures or technology spillovers."

4. At the time this chapter was written (summer 2003), there were 10 acceding countries (Cyprus, the Czech Republic, Estonia, Hungary, Latvia, Lithuania, Malta, Poland, Slovakia, and Slovenia) and three candidate countries (Bulgaria, Romania, and Turkey).

5. Here, part-time employed in Turkey is defined as those who work less than 25 hours a week. Casual employment (seasonal and temporary employment), as defined by the State Institute of Statistics, is used for fixed-term employment.

6. "Long-term unemployed" refers to those unemployed at least one year.

7. Except in areas where transitional arrangements will have been granted during the accession negotiations.

8. For detailed descriptions of the legal framework in Turkey for the labor market and social protection system, see comprehensive studies by Tunalı and others (2003) and Adaman (2003).

9. Although the first pillar of the EU, the European Community, is analyzed in this study, only the term EU is used for convenience.

10. This section is based on information provided on the Web site of the European Commission DG for Employment and Social Affairs, http://europa.eu.int/comm/dgs/employment_social/index_en.htm.

11. Falkner and others (2002) show how this process works for labor law.

12. For Council directives on employment, see http://europa.eu.int/comm/employment_social/soc-dial/labour/index_en.htm.

13. We also analyzed the draft law prepared by the Scientific Committee formed by nine academicians appointed by the government (the Ministry of Employment and Social Security) and the social partners (the Confederation of Employers' Unions, TİSK, and three confederations of trade unions—Türk-İş, Hak-İş, and DİSK). Because some minor modifications have been made in the draft, we use the one posted on the Web site of the confederation of the Turkish employers' unions, http://www.tisk.org.tr (downloaded on February 22, 2003).

14. The directives usually set the minimum conditions, and the member states may, therefore, introduce laws, regulations, or administrative provisions more favorable for workers.

15. For example, the directive on fixed-term work defines "comparable worker" as a worker with "an employment contract of relationship of indefinite duration, in the same establishment, engaged in the same or similar work/occupation, due regard being given to qualifications/skills. Where there is no comparable permanent worker in the same establishment, the comparison shall be made by reference to the *applicable collective agreement,* or where there is no applicable collective agreement,

in accordance with national law, *collective agreements* or practice" (emphasis added).

16. The draft law prepared by the Scientific Committee envisaged the establishment of a Wage Guarantee Fund (WGF) and required employers to contribute to the fund 0.5 percent of the gross wage. However, the new labor law adopted by Parliament has transferred the financial burden of the WGF to the Unemployment Insurance Fund.

17. Under the parental leave directive (Directive 96/34 of June 3, 1996, on the framework agreement on parental leave concluded by UNICE, CEEP, and the ETUC), fathers and mothers have an individual right to at least three months of parental leave to take care of their (natural or adopted) child. They have the right to return to the same or an equivalent workplace.

18. These included (1) developing human resources through vocational training, (2) promoting productive investments through moderate wage policies, (3) improving the efficiency of labor market institutions, (4) identifying new sources of jobs through local initiatives, and (5) promoting access to the world of work for some specific target groups such as young people, long-term unemployed people, and women.

19. The Turkish data were calculated from the Household Labour Force Survey for the period 2000–02.

20. Unless otherwise stated, the data from the United Nations Industrial Development Organization (UNIDO) Industrial Statistics Database, at the International Standard Industrial Classification (Rev. 2) three-digit level are used throughout this section.

21. Interindustry wage differential is defined as the coefficient of deviation of (log) industry wages.

22. As Agell and Bennmarker (2002) reveal for the Swedish case, it is easier to achieve real wage flexibility in an inflationary environment, even if nominal wages are "rigid."

23. In this study, we focus our attention on the challenges during the accession period. However, after the eventual membership, the conditions in the labor market are expected to be quite different because of the provisions on free movement of people at the EU level. Although it is difficult to predict the extent of migration dynamics under the conditions of stable growth in Turkey, one may expect a limited amount of emigration toward other EU countries that could be mutually beneficial for Turkey and the host countries.

24. In the former labor law, the "weekly working time" was 45 hours, which had to be distributed equally over the week. The new labor law (No. 4857) defines the "*normal* average weekly working time" for which the worker is paid at the "normal" wage rate (the average is calculated over two months) as 45 hours. The law sets the maximum annual limit for overtime work at 270 hours. Thus if a worker works 50 weeks a year, the maximum average weekly working time would be 50.4 hours.

25. In the Laeken Declaration of December 2001 (http://www.europa.eu.int/futurum/documents/contrib/cont071201_en.pdf), the European-level employers' organizations UNICE and CEEP and the trade union confederation ETUC defined the concepts of tripartite concertation, consultation, and social dialogue as follows: *tripartite concertation* designates exchanges between the social partners and European public authorities; *consultation* of the social partners describes the activities of advisory committees and official consultations; *social dialogue* is defined as the bipartite work by the social partners.

The distinction between tripartite concertation and bipartite social dialogue must be emphasized, because the tripartite concertation between the social partners and public authorities (which, in many cases, is dominated by public authorities) is usually confused with genuine bipartite social dialogue in Turkey.

Social dialogue can take place at different levels (company, sectoral, regional, national, and European). Social dialogue at the European level has become more structured and has increased significantly in importance over time, especially since 1991, when the Maastricht Treaty made it possible for the social partners to conclude European-level framework agreements in the area of individual and collective employees' rights. As a result, agreements between the European-level social partners (UNICE, CEEP, and ETUC) on parental leave (1995), part-time work (1997) and fixed-term contracts (1999) have been implemented as European directives. However, the level of social dialogue is far from uniform among the member states. For example, the current U.K. Labour government, which emphasizes the importance of flexibility in labor markets, seems to be uneasy about the way regulations are being implemented at the EU level (for details, see the European Industrial Relations Observatory Web site, http://www.eiro.eurofound.ie). Moreover, as Keller (2003) explains, after the eastern enlargement of the EU, "the already existing degree of diversity [in the EU] could even increase despite the fact that all existing regulations are part of the *acquis communautaire* that has to be adopted by all candidate countries," because the social partners are either weak or do not exist in the accession states (the "social dialogue gap"). For the level of social dialogue in accession countries, see Rychly and Pritzer (2003) and EFILWC (2003).

26. This process may also help to fully implement International Labour Organization (ILO) conventions. For the ILO conventions ratified by Turkey, see Bronstein (2003).

27. The law establishing the Turkish Employment Organization (No. 4904) was enacted by Parliament on June 25, 2003.

28. Because we assume that the number of workers employed in the informal sector is equal to the number of people employed in microenterprises, the share of the informal sector is likely to be overestimated.

29. Recall that the EU aims to increase the investment of companies in the training of adults (on-the-job training) from the existing level of the equivalent of 2.3 percent of labor costs up to 5.0 percent of labor costs on average in the EU by 2010. Although no reliable data on firm-sponsored training in Turkey are available, one could conjecture that the ratio of firm-sponsored training to labor cost is very small in Turkey.

References

Acemoglu, D., and J. Pischke. 1998. "Why Do Firms Train? Theory and Evidence." *Quarterly Journal of Economics* (113): 79–119.

———. 1999. "Beyond Becker: Training in Imperfect Labor Markets." *Economic Journal* (109): 112–42.

Adaman, F. 2003. *Study on the Social Protection Systems in the 13 Applicant Countries: Turkey Country Study.* Study financed by the European Commission DG for Employment and Social Affairs.

Addison, J. T., and P. Teixeira. 2001. "The Economics of Employment Protection." IZA Discussion Paper No. 381, Bonn.

Agell, J. 1999. "On the Benefits from Rigid Labour Markets: Norms, Market Failures, and Social Insurance." *Economic Journal* (109): 143–64.

Agell, J., and H. Bennmarker. 2002. "Wage Policy and Endogenous Wage Rigidity: A Representative View from the Inside." Working Paper No. 2002:12, Institute for Labour Market Evaluation (IFAU), Stockholm.

Algoé Consultans. 2002. *The Construction of an Index of Labour Market Adaptability for EU Member States.* Report of a study funded by the European Commission and directed by Algoé Consultans in conjunction with Alphametrics Limited.

Baker, D., A. Glyn, D. Howell, and J. Schmitt. 2002. "Labor Market Institutions and Unemployment: A Critical Assessment of the Cross-Country Evidence." Working Paper 2002-17, New School University Center for Economic Policy Analysis (CEPA), New York.

Ballot, G., and E. Taymaz. 2001. "Training Policies and Economic Growth in an Evolutionary World." *Structural Change and Economic Dynamics* (12): 311–29.

Bassanini, A., and E. Ernst. 2002. "Labour Market Regulation, Industrial Relations and Technological Regimes: A Tale of Comparative Advantage." *Industrial and Corporate Change* (11): 391–426.

Belot, M. 2002. "Why Is the Employment Protection Stricter in Europe than in the US?" Unpublished paper, CentER, Tilburg University.

Belot, M., J. Boonez, and J. van Ours. 2002. "Welfare Effects of Employment Protection." CentER Discussion Paper No. 2002-48, Tilburg University.

Bertola, G., T. Boeri, and S. Cazes. 1999. "Employment Protection and Labour Market Adjustment in OECD Countries: Evolving Institutions and Variable Enforcement." ILO, Employment and Training Paper No. 48, International Labour Organization, Geneva.

———. 2000. "Employment Protection in Industrialized Countries: The Case for New Indicators." Paper presented at the EC workshop on "Concepts and Measurement of European Labour Markets Flexibility/Adaptability Indices," Brussels, October 26–27.

Betcherman, G., A. Luinstra, and M. Ogawa. 2001. "Labor Market Regulation: International Experience in Promoting Employment and Social Protection." World Bank Social Protection Discussion Paper Series No. 128, Washington, DC.

Blanchard, O. 2000. "Employment Protection, Sclerosis, and the Effect of Shocks on Unemployment." LSE Lionel Robbins Lectures, Lecture 3, London, October.

———. 2002. "Designing Labor Market Institutions." Remarks at the conference Beyond Transition, Warsaw, April.

Brodsky, M. M. 1994. "Labor Market Flexibility: A Changing International Perspective." *Monthly Labor Review* (November): 53–60.

Bronstein, A. 2003. "Labour Law Reform in EU Candidate Countries: Achievements and Challenges." Paper presented at the ILO High-Level Tripartite Conference on Social Dialogue and Labour Law Reform in EU Accession Countries, Malta, February 28–March 1.

Cazes, S., and A. Nesporova. 2003. *Labour Market Flexibility and Employment Security in Transition Countries.* Geneva: International Labour Organization.

EFILWC (European Foundation for the Improvement of Living and Working Conditions. 2003. *Social Dialogue and EMU in the Acceding Countries.* Dublin: European Commission.

European Commission. 2002a. *Communication from the Commission on Streamlining the Annual Economic and Employment Policy Co-Ordination Cycles.* COM (2002) 487 final. Brussels: EC.

———. 2002b. *Draft Joint Employment Report 2002.* COM (2002) 621 final. Brussels: EC.

———. 2002c. *Regular Report on Turkey's Progress Towards Accession.* SEC (2002) 1412. Brussels: EC.

———. 2002d. *Taking Stock of Five Years of the European Employment Strategy.* COM (2002) 416 final. Brussels: EC.

———. 2002e. *Towards the Enlarged Union: Strategy Paper and Report of the European Commission on the Progress towards Accession by Each of the Candidate Countries.* COM(2002) 700 final. Brussels: EC.

———. 2003a. *The Future of the European Employment Strategy (EES): "A Strategy for Full Employment and Better Jobs for All."* COM (2003) 6 final. Brussels: EC.

———. 2003b. *Progress on the Implementation of the Joint Assessment Papers on Employment Policies in Candidate Countries.* COM (2003) 37 final. Brussels: EC.

———. 2003c. *Proposal for a Council Decision on Guidelines for the Employment Policies of the Member States.* COM (2003)176 final. Brussels: EC.

———. 2003d. *Recommendation for a Council Recommendation on the Implementation of Member States Employment Policies.* COM (2003)177 final. Brussels: EC.

European Commission DG for Employment and Social Affairs 2002. 2002. *Employment in Europe 2002: Recent Trends and Prospects.* Brussels: EC.

Fabiani, S., and D. Rodriguez-Palenzuela. 2001. "Model-Based Indicators of Labour Market Rigidity." European Central Bank Working Paper No. 21, European Central Bank, Brussels.

Falkner, G., M. Hartlapp, S. Leiber, and O. Treib. 2002. *Opposition through the Backdoor? The Case of National Non-Compliance with EU Directives.* Political Science Series No. 83. Vienna: Institute for Advanced Studies.

Goldberg, P. K., and N. Pavcnik. 2003. "The Response of the Informal Sector to Trade Liberalization." NBER Working Paper No. 9443, National Bureau of Economic Research, Cambridge, MA.

Heckman, J., and C. Pagés. 2004. "Introduction." In *Law and Employment: Lessons from Latin America and the Caribbean,* ed. J. Heckman and C. Pagés. Chicago: University of Chicago Press.

Hermans, S. 2001. *Avrupa Birliği'nin Sosyal Politikası ve Türkiye'nin Uyumu* [Social Policy in the European Union and Turkey's Adaptation], Turkish translation by H. Cansevdi. Istanbul: İktisadi Kalkınma Vakfı.

İlkkaracan, İ., and R. Selim. 2002. "The Role of Unemployment in Wage Determination: Further Evidence on the Wage Curve from Turkey." Working Paper 2002-11, New School University Center for Economic Policy Analysis (CEPA), New York.

Jackman, R., R. Layard, and S. Nickell. 1996. "Combatting Unemployment: Is Flexibility Enough?" Discussion Paper No. 293, Centre for Economic Performance, London School of Economics.

Keller, B. 2003. "Social Dialogues—The State of the Art a Decade after Maastricht." *Industrial Relations Journal* (34): 411–29.

Kleinknecht, A. 1998. "Is Labour Market Flexibility Harmful to Innovation?" *Cambridge Journal of Eocnomics* (22): 387–96.

Kugler, A. D. 1999. "The Impact of Firing Costs on Turnover and Unemployment: Evidence from the Colombian Labor Market Reform. *International Tax and Public Finance Journal* (6): 389–410.

Kugler, A. D., and M. Cárdenas. 1999. *The Incidence of Job Security Regulations on Labor Market Flexibility and Compliance in Colombia.* Working Paper R-428, Inter-American Development Bank Research Network.

Michie, J., and M. Sheehan. 2003. "Labour Market Deregulation, 'Flexibility' and Innovation." *Cambridge Journal of Economics* (27): 123–43.

Nickell, S., and R. Layard. 1999. "Labor Market Institutions and Economic Performance." In *Handbook of Labor Economics,* Vol. 3, ed. O. Ashenfelter and D. Card. Amsterdam: Elsevier.

Nicoletti, G., S. Scarpetta, and O. Boylaud. 2000. "Summary Indicators of Product Market Regulation with an Extension to Employment Protection Legislation." Economics Department Working Papers No. 226, Organisation for Economic Co-operation and Development, Paris.

OECD (Organisation for Economic Co-operation and Development). 1994a. *OECD Jobs Study, Evidence and Explanations, Part I: Labor Market Trends and Underlying Forces of Change.* Paris: OECD.

———. 1994b. *OECD Jobs Study, Evidence and Explanations, Part II: The Adjustment Potential of the Labor Market.* Paris: OECD.

———. 1999. *OECD Employment Outlook.* Paris: OECD.

———. 2002. *Taxing Wages.* Paris: OECD.

Onaran, Ö. 2002. "Measuring Wage Flexibility: The Case of Turkey before and after Structural Adjustment." *Applied Economics* (34): 767–81.

Plasmans, J., H. Meersman, A. van Poeck, and B. Merlevede. 2002. "The Unemployment Benefit System and Wage Flexibility in EMU: Time-varying Evidence in Five Countries." Department of Economics Working Paper, University of Antwerp.

Riboud, M., C. Sánchez-Páramo, and C. Silva-Jáuregui. 2002. "Does Eurosclerosis Matter? Institutional Reform and Labor Market Performance in Central and Eastern European Countries in the 1990s." World Bank Social Protection Discussion Paper Series No. 0202, Washington, DC.

Rychly, L., and R. Pritzer. 2003. "Social Dialogue at National Level in the EU Accession Countries." Working Paper, International Labour Organization, Geneva.

Salvanes, K. G. 1997. "Market Rigidities and Labour Market Flexibility: An International Comparison." *Scandinavian Journal of Economics* (99): 315–33.

Scarpetta, S., and T. Tressel. 2002. "Productivity and Convergence in a Panel of OECD Industries: Do Regulations and Institutions Matter?" Economics Department Working Paper No. 342, Organisation for Economic Co-operation and Development, Paris.

SIS (State Institute of Statistics). 2000a. *Annual Survey of Manufacturing Industries.* Ankara: SIS.

———. 2000b. *Household Labour Force Statistics.* Ankara: SIS.

Tunalı, İ., H. Ercan, C. Başlevent, and O. Öztürk. 2003. "Background Study on Labor Market and Employment in Turkey." Report prepared for European Training Foundation and presented at the special seminar On the Way to Integration with the EU, Labor Market and Employment in Turkey, İŞKUR, Ankara, February 27. http://www.iskur.gov.tr.

10

TURKEY'S FOREIGN DIRECT INVESTMENT CHALLENGES: COMPETITION, THE RULE OF LAW, AND EU ACCESSION

Mark Dutz, Melek Us, and Kamil Yılmaz

After following inward-oriented development strategies for 50 years, Turkey switched to outward-oriented policies in 1980. The policy of further opening up the economy was pursued with the aim of eventually integrating Turkey into the European Union (EU). The European Council's Helsinki summit, held on December 10–11, 1999, produced a breakthrough in EU-Turkey relations by officially recognizing Turkey as an EU candidate state on an equal footing with other candidate states. With accession, Turkey would become part of the European single market. In joining the EU, Turkey will have to adopt and implement the whole body of EU legislation and standards—the *acquis communautaire*—and also participate eventually in the European Economic and Monetary Union (EMU).

Over the past four years, Turkey has been undergoing a series of serious social, economic, and institutional transformations with the clear political objective of EU membership. The definitive prospect of EU membership should make Turkey very attractive for foreign direct investment (FDI), because, among its other strengths, it has a highly skilled and adaptable labor force, a large domestic market, and geographic proximity both to Europe

and to the Middle East, northern Africa, and Central Asia markets. The recent market–export and domestic market–oriented investments in the automobile industry are a clear indication of Turkey's attractiveness for FDI flows. However, over the last decade, Turkey lost ground to the Central and Eastern European (CEE) countries in attracting foreign investments, especially those from Europe. Although Poland, the Czech Republic, and Hungary together (three countries whose combined population is smaller than that of Turkey) received US$71 billion[1] in FDI flows between 1995 and 2000, Turkey received only $5.1 billion over the same period, almost 14 times less. And it appears from other countries' experiences that, unless there is a major paradigm shift in a country's or its competitors' FDI policies, there is likely to be very little change in FDI inflows.

This chapter explores how Turkey may be different from most CEE countries, and what any differences imply for the appropriate FDI policy in light of EU accession prospects. The chapter begins by outlining the benefits of FDI through an overview of the economic concepts, together with an assessment of the Turkish experience. FDI inflows are not generally considered to be an end goal but rather an instrument to create a globally competitive economy. Through FDI-stimulated increases in productivity, Turkey seeks to be positioned at the higher value added end of the fast-changing worldwide division of labor. In its analysis of obstacles to foreign investment, this chapter will emphasize competition-related and legal and judicial barriers.

After analyzing the benefits from and impediments to FDI, the chapter reviews what steps have been taken to improve the policy and regulatory framework in Turkey and then analyzes what Turkey has yet to do to meet EU requirements and to fully benefit from FDI. In summary, Turkey should benefit significantly from EU accession in terms of a step change in sizable FDI inflows, largely because the accession process would help Turkey to overcome its rule of law and competition-related constraints to foreign direct investment. The EU accession process will encourage more rapid and consistent implementation of the rules and regulations that ensure a level playing field for all companies, which, in turn, would enable Turkey to take full advantage of investment-related benefits.

The Benefits of FDI

As a capital-scarce country, Turkey can benefit substantially from injections of foreign capital that will expand productive capacity and stimulate job creation.

The Role of FDI in Economic Growth

Although foreign direct investment is beneficial, the type of capital inflows matters. Unlike portfolio investments and loans to the private sector, FDI inflows involve direct equity ownership plus significant ownership control, and therefore they are more stable. They do not easily flee in a domestic market downturn. Unlike loans, FDI inflows ensure that business risks are borne by foreign investors.

FDI differs from other forms of capital flows in other crucial aspects. It does not just entail the transfer of financial resources and the creation of new jobs; it is a bundle that involves the transfer of fixed assets, technology, know-how, and international market access. FDI connects the recipient country to international best practices, helps to upgrade the management and work force, and establishes stronger ties between domestic and international markets.

Because FDI entails the transfer of technology and know-how, it usually has both a direct and an indirect impact on the economic growth of a country. And, because FDI involves significant ownership control as well as the transfer of technology, its impact on economic growth takes place through increased productivity, human capital accumulation, research and development activity, and technological and productivity spillovers. Its impact on economic growth could be even greater if the types of FDI that the country receives stimulate—in other words, crowd in—domestic investment activity.

Several studies have established a link between FDI and economic growth. Using data on FDI flows from industrial countries to 69 developing countries over 1970–89 and using a cross-country regression framework, Borensztein, De Gregorio, and Lee (1998) show that FDI flows have a positive impact on economic growth. They also demonstrate that the impact of foreign investment exceeds the impact of domestic investment on growth. Not all countries, however, benefit from FDI. According to Borensztein, De Gregorio, and Lee, countries require a minimum stock of human capital to realize the growth effects of FDI. In other studies, Zhang (1999) shows that FDI inflows helped to stimulate economic growth in several East Asian countries, and Gruben and McLeod (1998) find that in a sample of 18 countries, FDI had a significant impact on economic growth, especially in Latin American countries.

The Role of FDI in Raising Productivity and Stimulating Spillovers

One of the important contributions of FDI companies is to enhance the transfer and diffusion of technology to the host country. A multinational corporation undertaking investment in a country brings to that sector its production technology, its access to global production and distribution networks, and its know-how and experience. Being generally larger corporations, FDI companies have access to large, low-cost investment funds that could be used to finance investment in more advanced technology than is available and accessible in the host country.

The direct technology transfer effect may not be realized in all FDI projects, however. If the FDI is an export-oriented investment, the impact on technology diffusion will generally be more significant than that made by a domestic market–oriented investment. The impact of FDI on technology diffusion was rather limited in the import substitution era, because the main incentive for a foreign company to undertake investment was the heavily protected domestic market. In such an environment, foreign companies preferred to transfer old and outdated technology to their factories in developing countries, creating little technology diffusion.

Today, however, FDI decisions cannot focus only on the domestic market. One result of the push for more liberal trade relations throughout the world is that FDI companies face competition in the domestic markets of the host country through imports. Consequently, FDI decisions, especially in the manufacturing sector, are often made after seriously considering the international competitiveness of the affiliate firm. That firm must have the technological capability and the resulting efficiency that render it flexible enough to target export markets as well as the domestic market. Consequently, one would expect to observe higher productivity in FDI companies when compared with domestic enterprises.

The impact of FDI on the host country economy is not limited to just the direct channels of technology transfer and diffusion; the presence of multinationals also may affect local companies through several channels. One channel is intensified domestic market competition. As the FDI companies become major players in the domestic market, local companies will be forced to adopt newer and more advanced technologies and to use the existing resources of the firm more efficiently in order to survive (see Blomström and Kokko 1998). This channel is similar to the effect of import liberalization, even though the impact on local companies may be more significant than imports. The technology transfer may take embodied (imports of machinery and equipment) or disembodied (know-how, knowledge, licenses) forms. Local enterprises will not find it difficult to organize the transfer of embodied technology, but the transfer of disembodied technology requires absorption capacity. However, the workers and engineers employed by FDI companies will gain experience and accumulate knowledge through their tenure there. In the medium to long run, these employees will have an opportunity to transfer this experience and knowledge to local enterprises.

Other channels through which the presence of FDI companies affects the local companies mostly take the form of spillovers. Productivity spillovers from FDI take place when the entry or presence of multinational corporations increases the productivity of domestic firms in a host country and when the multinationals do not fully internalize the value of these benefits. Spillovers may occur when local firms improve their efficiency by copying technologies of foreign affiliates operating in the local market either by observation or by hiring workers trained by the affiliates. Horizontal spillovers to other firms in the same sector may be accompanied by vertical spillovers—that is, the presence of FDI companies may affect local firms in other sectors of the economy. These vertical spillover effects may take place through backward linkages (purchases of inputs from local suppliers) and forward linkages (supply of outputs to local downstream purchasers).

In line with findings for other countries, in Turkey FDI companies have higher labor productivity than local enterprises.[2] In 1991 the average labor productivity of FDI companies was 35 percent higher than that of all manufacturing plants. Over time, the productivity gap between FDI companies and the sector average was closed slightly, to 30 percent by 1996. The average labor productivity in foreign-owned plants increased from TL (Turkish lira) 4.1 million to TL 4.7 million (from $1,611 to $1,803) in 1990 prices. The average labor productivity in all plants, by contrast, increased from TL 3.1 million to TL 3.6 million (from $1,189 to $1,550). These numbers are a clear indication that the labor productivity gap between foreign- and domestic-owned plants is significant and does not vanish over time.

These annual average values support the case for significant labor productivity differences between FDI and local enterprises, but the possibility cannot be ruled out that these differences stem from plant characteristics other than foreign ownership. Based on regression results using various measures of foreign participation, Yılmaz and Ozler (2004) show that plants with foreign partners have higher total factor productivity even after other plant characteristics and sector and time effects are taken into account.[3] Finally, Yılmaz and Ozler (2004) show that domestic plants tend to have higher total factor productivity (TFP) in sectors with greater FDI involvement than in sectors in which FDI involvement is low. All else being equal, as the foreign ownership–weighted sectoral output share of foreign-affiliated plants increases by 1 percentage point, the total factor productivity of local plants in the same sector increases by 0.82 percentage point. However, horizontal spillovers from all foreign-owned plants are not similar. As the output share of FDI companies with less than 50 percent foreign participation increases by 1 percentage point, the TFP in local firms increases on average by 0.72 percent, and the spillover effect from plants with foreign share ownership greater than or equal to 50 percent but less than full foreign ownership jumps by 1.1 percentage point. Finally, fully foreign-owned plants tend to generate external benefits that would increase the productivity of local plants in the same sector by 0.4 percent.

The Current State of FDI

Foreign direct investment can have strong, positive effects for national economies. The previous section described how FDI in the Turkish manufacturing sector has had both direct and indirect productivity-enhancing benefits. The evidence of these benefits, which is based on plant-level studies, can be viewed as the most reliable evidence available. However, this finding and the results discussed establish only that FDI is desirable for Turkey. The next step in the analysis is to characterize the level and other features of FDI in Turkey relative to those of comparator countries and explore why FDI is so low despite being highly desirable for the country.

FDI in Turkey and in Central and Eastern Europe: A Comparison

The most striking feature of foreign investment flows to Turkey is their low level relative to the flows of the comparator CEE countries' emerging market economies (table 10.1). In terms of population in 2000, Turkey was larger than Poland, the Czech Republic, and Hungary combined. In terms of gross domestic product (GDP) in 2000, Turkey's economy was four times as large as that of the Czech Republic or Hungary and one-quarter larger

than Poland's. And in terms of gross fixed capital formation (GFCF)—the total value of producers' acquisitions of fixed assets—Turkey's investments during 2000 were three to four times as large as those of the Czech Republic and Hungary and roughly a sixth larger than Poland's. As highlighted in table 10.1, however, in terms of average annual inflows of FDI during the 1990s, Turkey's inflows ($800 million) were roughly one-fifth of FDI inflows to Poland ($4.1 billion) and also significantly lower than those of the Czech Republic and Hungary (about $2.1 billion per year).

A second striking feature in comparing Turkey with Poland, the Czech Republic, and Hungary is that the FDI gap did not close throughout the 1990s. To the contrary, with the formal announcement at the December 1997 European Council summit in Luxembourg that EU accession negotiations would open with Poland, the Czech Republic, and Hungary on March 31, 1998, these countries appear to have benefited from a virtuous cycle. The enhanced likelihood of EU accession and further FDI flows improved credit ratings and, in turn, attracted more FDI, thereby increasing the difference between those countries and Turkey. Table 10.1 and figure 10.1 reveal that average annual FDI inflows increased during 1997–2000

FIGURE 10.1   FDI Inflows: Turkey versus Comparator CEE Countries, 1990–2001
(millions of US$)

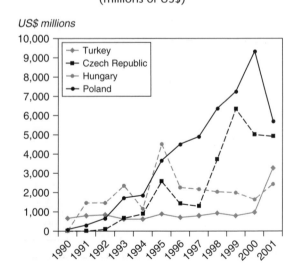

Source: United Nations Conference on Trade and Development (UNCTAD), *World Investment Report*, selected years.

TABLE 10.1　FDI Summary Data: Turkey versus Comparator CEE Countries

	Turkey	Poland	Czech Republic	Hungary
GDP 2000 (US$ millions)	199,267	157,598	51,433	46,604
GFCF 2000 (US$ millions)	44,542	39,212	14,550	11,269
Population, 2000 (millions)	67.4	38.7	10.3	10.0
FDI inflows, 1991–96 (US$ millions, annual average)	751	2,119	939	2,205
FDI inflows, 1997–2000 (US$ millions, annual average)	878	6,971	4,072	1,957
FDI inflows, 2001 (US$ millions)	3,266	5,713	4,924	2,440
FDI inflows/GFCF, 1991–96 (annual average)	1.9%	10.7%	6.4%	26.8%
FDI inflows/GFCF, 1997–2000 (annual average)	1.9%	18.1%	26.5%	17.9%
FDI inflows/GFCF, 2001	12.4%	15.0%	30.6%	20.1%
FDI stocks, 1996 (US$ millions)	5,825	11,463	8,785	14,193
FDI stocks/GDP, 1996	3.2%	8.8%	15.2%	31.4%
FDI stocks, 2000 (US$ millions)	9,335	34,227	21,644	19,804
FDI stocks/GDP, 2000	4.7%	21.7%	42.1%	42.5%
FDI stocks, 2001 (US$ millions)	12,601	42,433	26,764	23,562
FDI stocks/GDP, 2001	8.5%	24.1%	47.1%	45.4%
Exports of affiliates of foreign TNCs,[a] 2000 (US$ millions)	3,684	12,267	10,876[b]	19,558
TNC exports/total exports, 2000	7.2%	26.5%	32.7%[b]	61.1%
Imports of affiliates of foreign TNCs, 2000	12,628	23,554	11,107[b]	22,820
No. of affiliates of foreign TNCs, 2000	5,334	35,840[c]	71,385[d]	26,645

Note: GFCF = gross fixed capital formation; TNC = transnational corporation.

a. An affiliate is an incorporated or unincorporated enterprise in which an investor, who is resident in another country, owns a stake that permits a lasting interest in the management of that enterprise (an equity stake of 10 percent for an incorporated enterprise or its equivalent for an unincorporated enterprise).

b. Foreign trade, 1999.

c. Number of affiliates, 1998 (includes all firms with foreign capital).

d. Number of affiliates, 1999 (includes joint ventures). Of this number, 53,775 are fully owned foreign affiliates.

Sources: International Monetary Fund (IMF), International Financial Statistics (CD-ROM); United Nations Conference on Trade and Development (UNCTAD), World Investment Directory (WID) Country Profiles, 2003; UNCTAD, *World Investment Report*, selected years.

more than threefold in Poland, from $2.1 billion to almost $7 billion, and more than fourfold in the Czech Republic, from $0.9 billion to over $4 billion. Meanwhile, in Turkey they remained completely unchanged relative to gross fixed capital formation. It is remarkable that Turkey's announcement of its EU customs union in 1996 had no discernable effect on aggregate FDI flows.

Anyone comparing FDI inflows across countries should take into account that the FDI definition used by Turkey is much narrower than that of some countries and international institutions, leading to systematic undervaluation of FDI inflows to Turkey.

Turkey adopted the definition of the Organisation for Economic Co-operation and Development (OECD) for FDI in 2001, and that definition was included in the new FDI law of 2003 (see, e.g., OECD 1996, 2003). Table 10.2 compares the elements of Turkey's definition of FDI (in both the 1954 and 2003 FDI laws) with those of the definitions used by other OECD countries, highlighting the omission of preferred stocks traded on the stock exchange, long-term loans, other marketable securities and bonds, and financial derivatives from the previous definition (short-term loans, commercial/retail loans, and leasing are still not included in the new law).

TABLE 10.2 FDI Definition in OECD Countries

	Preferred Stocks Traded on Stock Exchange	Preferred Stocks Not Traded on Stock Exchange	Other Kinds of Nonpreferred Stocks	Reinvested Earnings	Indirectly Owned FDI Enterprises	Capital in Kind	Long-Term Loans	Short-Term Loans	Commerce/Retail Loans	Leasing	Bonds and Marketable Securities	Financial Derivatives
Australia	Yes	Yes	Yes	Yes	Yes	No	Yes	Yes	Yes	—	Yes	Yes
Austria	Yes	Yes	No	—	No	Yes	No	No	No	No	No	No
Belgium	Yes	Yes	Yes	No	No	No	Yes	Yes	No	Yes	No	No
Canada	Yes	Yes	Yes	Yes	Yes	—	Yes	Yes	Yes	Yes	Yes	—
Czech Rep.	Yes	Yes	Yes	Yes	Yes	Yes	Yes	No	No	—	—	No
Denmark	Yes	Yes	Yes	Yes	Yes	Yes	Yes	Yes	No	No	No	No
Finland	No	Yes	Yes	Yes	No	Yes	Yes	Yes	No	Yes	No	No
France	Yes	Yes	Yes	Yes	No	Yes	Yes	Yes	No	No	No	No
Germany	Yes	Yes	Yes	Yes	No	No	Yes	No	No	No	No	No
Greece	Yes	Yes	Yes	Yes	No	No	Yes	Yes	Yes	Yes	Yes	Yes
Hungary	Yes	Yes	Yes	No	Yes	No	Yes	Yes	Yes	Yes	Yes	Yes
Iceland	No	Yes	—	Yes	Yes	—	Yes	Yes	Yes	—	—	—
Ireland	Yes	Yes	Yes	Yes	Yes	Yes	Yes	Yes	Yes	Yes	Yes	No
Japan	Yes	Yes	Yes	Yes	Yes	Yes	Yes	Yes	No	No	Yes	No
Korea, Rep. of	Yes	Yes	Yes	Yes	No	Yes	Yes	Yes	No	No	No	No
Luxembourg	Yes	Yes	Yes	Yes	—	No	Yes	Yes	Yes	Yes	No	No
Mexico	Yes	Yes	Yes	Yes	Yes	Yes	Yes	Yes	Yes	No	No	No
Netherlands	Yes	Yes	Yes	Yes	No	Yes	Yes	Yes	Yes	Yes	No	—
New Zealand	Yes	Yes	Yes	Yes	Yes	No	Yes	Yes	No	No	Yes	No
Norway	Yes	Yes	Yes	Yes	Yes	Yes	Yes	Yes	Yes	Yes	Yes	Yes
Poland	Yes	Yes	Yes	Yes	No	Yes	Yes	Yes	Yes	No	Yes	—
Portugal	Yes	Yes	Yes	Yes	No	Yes	Yes	Yes	Yes	Yes	No	No
Spain	Yes	Yes	Yes	Yes	Yes	Yes	Yes	Yes	Yes	No	Yes	No
Sweden	Yes	Yes	Yes	Yes	Yes	Yes	Yes	Yes	Yes	Yes	Yes	No
Switzerland	Yes	Yes	Yes	Yes	Yes	Yes	Yes	Yes	Yes	Yes	No	Yes
Turkey (6224)	No	Yes	Yes	Yes		Yes	No	No	No	No	Yes[a]	No
Turkey (4875)	Yes	Yes	Yes	Yes	No	Yes	Yes	No	No	No	No	Yes
England	Yes	Yes	Yes	Yes	Yes	Yes	Yes	Yes	Yes	No	No	No
United States	Yes	Yes	Yes	Yes	Yes	Yes	Yes	Yes	Yes	Yes	Yes	Yes

— Not available.

Note: Two sets of entries are given for Turkey: one for the 1954 FDI law (No. 6224) and one for the 2003 FDI law (No. 4875).

a. Excluding state bonds.

Source: OECD 2003.

In addition, even though the new FDI law may allow certain flows to be included, local statistical data collection and recording practices may preclude their inclusion in the official statistics. Capital in-kind is one such example—statistics are generally not calculated and therefore not included. Even though the precise figures are not available, for some big projects Turkey's previous narrower definition and statistical processing can underestimate FDI inflows by significant orders of magnitude. For example, Turkey has traditionally not recorded long-term credits from foreign partners as FDI. It has included such flows only if the foreign partners' receivables are added to the company's capital; otherwise, they are not recorded as an increase in FDI but rather as an increase in external debt. For the first time, however, because of a particularly large intracompany, long-term foreign credit and in response to internal discussions on the matter, in 2001 it was decided to classify such credits as an FDI flow in conformity with international norms. Therefore, the $1.4 billion credit provided by the mobile phone arm of Telecom Italia, the foreign partner of the GSM İş-TIM Telekomunikasyon Hizmetleri A.Ş. company, has been included in 2001 inflows.

In terms of type of investment, most of the growth of FDI companies worldwide in the 1990s was by cross-border mergers and acquisitions (M&As), in particular the acquisitions by foreign investors of privatized state-owned enterprises rather than greenfield investments. Less than 3 percent of the total number of global cross-border M&As during the 1990s are officially classified as mergers; the rest are different types of acquisitions. In terms of ownership, roughly two-thirds of cross-border M&As were full acquisitions, and the remaining one-third were minority acquisitions (10–49 percent control). In terms of value, 70 percent of cross-border M&As are functionally classified as horizontal, between firms in the same industry.[4] Figure 10.2 highlights how this global trend was especially critical in driving FDI in Poland, but also in the Czech Republic and Hungary, in contrast to its significantly lesser influence in Turkey. Figure 10.3 presents evidence suggesting the importance of privatization in fueling M&A-related FDI inflows, and it highlights the much more important role of privatization in the CEE countries throughout the 1990s in

FIGURE 10.2   M&A-Related Inflows: Turkey versus Comparator CEE Countries, 1990–2001
(millions of US$)

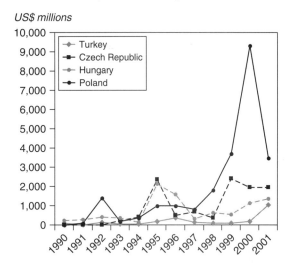

Source: See figure 10.1.

FIGURE 10.3   Privatization Revenues: Turkey versus Comparator CEE Countries, 1990–2000
(millions of US$)

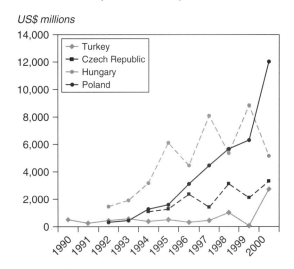

Source: See figure 10.1.

contrast to Turkey. However, although a significant share of FDI in transition economies may have been generated by the privatization process, the privatization process in Poland has, notably, involved a sizable amount of stock market flotation, in which privatization-related capital inflows would be reported as portfolio inflows rather than FDI. The Czech Republic has actively promoted privatization to local investors, which was usually debt financed and thus linked to either domestic or foreign credit rather than FDI.

In terms of industrial subsector allocation, a majority of FDI inflows to Turkey have been directed to the tertiary sector. Table 10.3 illustrates that by the end of 2000 over 57 percent of total FDI stocks in Turkey were dedicated to services, including three of the top five subsectors—transport and communications, banking and other financial services, and trade and repairs—in a pattern similar to that of Poland. The other major recipients of FDI inflows to Turkey have been in the manufacturing sector—the automotive and auto parts subsector and the petroleum, chemicals, rubber, and plastic products subsector. The subsectoral pattern in the smaller countries, the Czech Republic and Hungary, which do not benefit from as large a domestic internal market, is even more concentrated in the tertiary sector, with all five top subsectors dedicated to producing services rather than manufacturing goods. Table 10.4 reports the identity of the largest FDI companies by worldwide sales in each of the four economies, highlighting the important role of the automotive and auto parts subsector and the petroleum, chemicals, and rubber and plastic sector in Turkey. Nine of the

TABLE 10.3   FDI Stocks by Industrial Sector, 2000
(percent)

Sector/Industry	Turkey	Poland	Czech Republic	Hungary
Primary Sector	1.5	0.9	2.0	1.5
Agriculture, hunting, forestry, and fishing	0.8	0.5	0.2	1.1
Mining, quarrying, and petroleum	0.7	0.4	1.9	0.4
Secondary Sector	41.3	38.6	38.1	36.8
Food, beverages, and tobacco	7.3	8.4	4.8	8.9
Textiles, leather, and clothing	1.9	0.7	1.3	1.6
Wood, paper, publishing, and printing	0.3	4.4	3.1	1.9
Petroleum, chemicals, rubber and plastic products	9.5	6.5	6.5	6.8
Nonmetallic mineral products	2.6	—	5.9	2.3
Basic metal and metal products	2.6	2.0	3.6	2.2
Machinery and equipment	0.2	1.3	1.7	1.9
Electrical machinery and apparatus	3.7	1.2	3.3	7.2
Motor vehicles and other transport equipment	12.1	6.4	6.5	3.6
Precision instruments	0.4	—	0.7	—
Other manufacturing	0.7	7.8	0.6	0.4
Unspecified secondary	0.0	—	0.0	—
Tertiary Sector	57.3	60.5	59.8	61.7
Electricity, gas, and water	—	1.2	6.6	9.4
Construction	0.8	6.6	1.5	1.2
Trade and repairs	8.1	16.7	15.0	12.4
Hotels and restaurants	4.4	0.5	0.3	1.8
Transport, storage, and communication	17.0	8.0	11.2	7.7
Finance	16.6	20.0	14.7	11.3
Real estate and business activities	—	7.0	9.2	15.7
Education	0.0	—	—	0.0
Health and social services	7.5	—	—	0.1
Other services	2.8	0.5	1.2	1.9
Total	100	100	100	100

— Not available.

Sources: UNCTAD, World Investment Database (WID) Country Profiles, 2003; Turkey General Directorate of Foreign Investors (GDFI) database.

TABLE 10.4   Largest Affiliates of Foreign Transnational Corporations

Company	Home Country	Industry	Sales (US$ millions)
Turkey, 2001			
1 Tofaş Türk Otomobil Fabrikası A.Ş.	Italy	Motor vehicles	875.5
2 Oyak Renault Otomobil Fabrikaları A.Ş.	France	Motor vehicles	748.4
3 Vestel Elektronik San. ve Tic. A.Ş.	Netherlands	Electronics	690.2
4 Ipragaz A.Ş.	France	Petroleum products	375.5
5 Sasa Dupont Sabancı Polyester Sanayi A.Ş.	Netherlands	Chemicals	333.3
6 Mercedes Benz Türk A.Ş.	Germany	Motor vehicles	284.9
7 Philsa PhilipMorris Sabancı Sigara-Tütün A.Ş.	Netherlands	Tobacco	264.6
8 Bosch Sanayi ve Ticaret A.Ş.	Germany	Auto parts	245.7
9 Siemens Sanayi ve Ticaret A.Ş.	Germany	Electrical machinery	231.3
10 Paşabahçe Cam Sanayi	Saudi Arabia	Glass	223.0
11 Ford Otomotiv Sanayi A.Ş.	United States	Motor vehicles	212.9
12 Goodyear Lastikleri TA.Ş.	United States	Rubber	193.5
13 Trakya Cam Sanayii A.Ş.	United States	Glass	192.0
14 Profilo Telra Elektronik Sanayi ve Tic. A.Ş.	France	Electronics	189.0
15 BSH Profilo Elektrikli Gereçler Sanayii A.Ş.	Germany	Electrical machinery	185.0
16 Alcatel Teletaş Telekomünikasyon End.	Neth./Belgium	Electronics	176.7
17 Türk Pirelli Lastikleri A.Ş.	Italy	Rubber	173.7
18 Korsa Sabancı Dupont End. İplik San. A.Ş.	Netherlands	Textiles	173.2
19 JTI Tütün Ürünleri Sanayi A.Ş.	Japan	Tobacco	168.6
20 İzmir Demir Çelik Sanayi A.Ş.	Saudi Arabia	Iron, steel	161.0
Total			*6,098.0*
Poland, 1999			
1 Fiat Auto Poland SA	Italy	Motor vehicles	1,844.1
2 Makro Cash and Cary Poland	Germany	Distributive trade	1,544.8
3 Centrum Daewoo Sp ZOO	Rep. of Korea	Motor vehicles	916.6
4 Volkswagen Poznan Sp ZOO	Germany	Motor vehicles	661.5
5 Reemtsma Polska SA	Germany	Tobacco	595.7
6 Thompson Polkolor Sp ZOO	France	Electrical equipment	439.3
7 Real Sp ZOO	Germany	Distributive trade	423.7
8 General Motors Poland Sp ZOO	United States	Motor vehicles	411.3
9 Procter and Gamble Polska Sp ZOO	United States	Distributive trade	400.0
10 Geant Polska Sp ZOO	France	Distributive trade	387.9
11 Unilever Polska SA	Netherlands	Distributive trade	383.6
12 International Paper Kwidzyn SA	United States	Paper products	360.7
13 Renault Polska Sp ZOO	France	Motor vehicles	360.7
14 Kulczyk Tradex Sp ZOO	United Kingdom	Distributive trade	304.8
15 Auchan Polska Sp ZOO	France	Distributive trade	297.5
16 Electrocieplownie Warszawkie SA	Sweden	Electricity	293.0
17 Frantschah Swiecie SA	Germany	Paper products	289.9
18 Philips Lighting Poland SA	Netherlands	Electrical equipment	289.4
19 Jeronimo Martins Dystrybucja Sp ZOO	Portugal	Distributive trade	262.0
20 British American Tobacco Polska SA	United Kingdom	Tobacco	282.9
Total			*10,749.4*

TABLE 10.4 (*Continued*)

Company	Home Country	Industry	Sales (US$ millions)
Czech Republic, 1999			
1 Skoda Automobilovi AS	Germany	Motor vehicles	3,292.5
2 Makro Cr Spol SRO	Germany	Distributive trade	736.2
3 Rewe Spol. SRO	Germany	Mach. and equip.	509.2
4 Tabak AS	United States	Tobacco	416.2
5 Philip Morris	United States	Tobacco	402.5
6 Jihomoravska Energetica	Germany	Energy	382.2
7 Tesco Stores Cr AS	United Kingdom	Distributive trade	335.0
8 IPS AS	Finland	Construction	327.6
9 Delvita AS	Netherlands	Distributive trade	318.6
10 Penny Market SRO	Germany	Distributive trade	294.8
11 Severoceska Energetica	Germany	Energy	285.0
12 Julius Meinl AS	Austria	Distributive trade	218.4
13 Siemens Automobilova Technika SRO	Germany	Motor vehicles	208.6
14 Stavby Silnic A Zeleznic AS	France	Construction	207.9
15 Plzensky Prazdroj AS	Netherlands	Beverages	203.9
16 Autopal SRO	United States	Motor vehicles	201.3
17 Glaverbel Czech AS	Belgium/Japan	Nonmetal mineral	196.3
18 Robert Bosch Spol. SRO	Germany	Motor vehicles	162.6
19 Nestle Cokoladovny AS	Switzerland	Food	148.7
20 Siemens Elektromotory SRO	Germany	Mach. and equip.	147.5
Total			*8,995.0*
Hungary, 2000			
1 Audi Hungaria Motor Kft.	Germany	Motor vehicles	3,190.6
2 Philips Magyarorszag Kft.	Netherlands	Electronics	2,266.3
3 IBM Storage Products Kft.	United States	Electronics	2,239.7
4 Matav Rt.	Germany	Telecom.	1,565.3
5 Panrusgaz Magyar-Orosz Gazipari Rt.	Russia	Distributive trade	1,027.6
6 Flextronics International Kft.	United States	Electronics	868.1
7 Metro Holding Kft.	Germany	Distributive trade	715.1
8 GE Hungary Rt.	United States	Electronics	658.1
9 Opel Magyarorszag Jarmugyarto Kft.	United States	Motor vehicles	629.5
10 Kromberg Es Schubert Kabeleket	Austria	Basic metals	628.0
11 Vogel and Noot Mezogepgyar Kft.	Austria	Basic metals	584.4
12 Westel 900 Mobil Rt.	United States	Telecom.	541.9
13 Budapesti Elektromos Muvek Rt.	Germany	Electricity	483.6
14 Elmu Rt.	Germany	Electricity	483.6
15 Tesco Global Rt.	United Kingdom	Distributive trade	447.6
16 Suziki Rt.	Japan	Motor vehicles	446.4
17 Hungarotabak Tobaccoland Rt.	Austria	Trade	442.3
18 Shell Hungary Rt.	Neth./U.K.	Distributive trade	420.5
19 Alcoa Kofem Kft.	United States	Basic metals	395.1
20 BorsodChem	Austria	Chemical	393.5
Total			*18,427.2*

Sources: See table 10.3.

TABLE 10.5 FDI Stocks by Country of Origin, 2000
(percent)

Country of Origin	Turkey	Poland	Czech Republic	Hungary
Austria	0.5	3.2	11.1	12.2
Belgium and Luxembourg	3.4	2.5	5.4	5.3
Denmark	0.5	2.5	1.2	0.5
Finland	0.1	0.6	0.6	1.6
France	7.3	12.2	4.3	6.5
Germany	14.1	18.9	25.5	25.8
Ireland	0.2	1.2	0.0	0.7
Italy	2.0	4.3	0.8	2.7
Netherlands	31.4	24.6	30.1	22.5
Spain	2.2	1.9	0.2	0.4
Sweden	1.0	3.5	1.4	0.9
United Kingdom	6.0	3.3	3.5	1.1
European Union, total	*68.7*	*78.8*	*84.0*	*80.2*
Japan	4.4	0.4	0.5	2.1
Korea, Rep. of	0.7	1.3	0.0	1.0
Switzerland	5.4	2.5	4.0	2.1
United States	8.7	9.5	6.5	8.2
Other OECD countries, total	*19.2*	*13.7*	*11.0*	*13.4*
OECD, total	*87.9*	*92.5*	*95.1*	*93.6*
Other Eastern European countries	0.4	4.3	1.0	0.4
Israel	0.1	0.0	0.0	0.0
Saudi Arabia	1.1	0.0	0.0	0.0
Panama	3.7	0.0	0.0	0.0
Dutch Antilles	1.2	0.0	0.0	0.0
Other countries	5.4	1.8	2.5	5.0
Total	*100*	*100*	*100*	*100*

Sources: See table 10.3.

top 20 Turkish FDI companies are in these two sub-sectors, followed by the electronics and electrical machinery subsector. The absence of service sector companies in the Turkish list is explained by the investment-to-sales profile typical of these subsectors, in which there usually is a lag between the large, lumpy up-front investments required and the subsequent stream of sales revenues generated by the installed infrastructure service networks.

In terms of country of origin, a striking feature of FDI stocks is the significantly greater concentration of investment going from EU countries to the officially recognized EU accession countries than to Turkey (table 10.5). In 2000, Turkey received only 68.7 percent in FDI flows from EU countries, in contrast to Poland, Hungary, and the Czech Republic, which received 79, 80, and 84 percent of their FDI flows, respectively, from EU countries. Turkey has, however, received significantly more FDI inflows from Japan, Saudi Arabia, and offshore locations such as Panama and the Netherlands Antilles than the three CEE countries. Interestingly, in spite of important investments from the United States in the top 20 Turkish FDI companies (motor vehicles, rubber, and glass), the relative share of U.S. investment is not significantly different in Turkey than in the CEE countries.

Determinants of FDI

Investment climate can be defined as the policy, institutional, and behavioral environment, present and expected, that influences the perceived returns and risks associated with investment in terms of both quantity and productivity of investment flows.[5] Investment climate depends on a wide array of factors that can be grouped under three broad headings: macroeconomic and trade policies, infrastructure, and governance and institutions. These factors help to explain both the strong potential attractiveness of Turkey as a global location for FDI and the shortcomings that have led Turkey to fall so far below its potential in this area.

Macro Policies, Infrastructure, and the Automotive Sector

Macroeconomic and Trade Policies. Since the 1980s, Turkey has undergone significant changes in its economic relations with the outside world involving its macroeconomic and trade policies. After the January 24, 1980, decision to open up Turkey's economy, the government put great emphasis on an export orientation. This first step was followed by gradual import liberalization, which began in 1984 and finally culminated in the customs union with the EU in 1996. However, despite the gradual removal of trade barriers and the greater export orientation, Turkey was unable to attract large FDI

inflows. One of the main culprits behind this failure was the uncertain macroeconomic environment. With its heavy dose of patronage relations and rent-seeking activities, domestic politics never allowed the creation of a stable macroeconomic environment. Fiscal imbalances continued throughout the 1990s, and were transformed into rather stark debt dynamics by the end of the decade (table 10.6). Public sector borrowing requirements increased from 5 percent of the gross national product (GNP) in 1995 to as high as 15.5 percent in 1999 and 2001. Chronic budget deficits and the rapidly increasing public debt are at the root of the high and chronic inflation problem that Turkey has suffered over the last 25 years. During that time, the average consumer price inflation rate was 63 percent, and over the last two decades annual inflation has never been lower than 30 percent. Through the second half of 1990s and early 2000s, the real interest rate was quite high. With the exception of 1997 and 2000, the ex post real interest rates on bonds and Treasury bills were above 20 percent, reaching as high as 36 percent. In addition to the high real interest rates that inhibit domestic and foreign investment, the exchange rate devaluation risk created an extra burden on foreign investors who were willing to invest in the country with a long-term perspective.

TABLE 10.6   Macroeconomic Indicators, 1995–2001

	1995	1996	1997	1998	1999	2000	2001
	(percent of GNP)						
Public sector borrowing requirement	5.0	8.6	7.7	9.4	15.6	12.5	15.5
Primary surplus	2.1	1.3	0.0	2.1	−1.9	3.8	6.5
Interest expenditures (consolidated budget)	7.4	10.0	7.7	11.5	13.7	16.3	22.2
Public sector debt stock	37.6	40.3	40.5	41.3	51.8	53.4	97.8
Domestic	14.6	18.5	20.2	21.7	29.3	29.0	66.3
External	23.0	21.8	20.3	19.6	22.5	24.4	31.5
	(percent per year)						
Interest rate on bonds and T-bills (average)	124.2	132.2	107.4	115.5	104.6	38.2	99.6
Inflation (CPI, annual average)	89.0	80.2	85.7	84.6	64.9	54.9	54.4
Ex post real interest rate (CPI-based)	24.4	25.0	12.4	30.7	32.1	−10.5	36.0
GNP growth rate	8.0	7.1	8.3	3.9	−6.1	6.3	−8.5
Real exchange rate (CPI-based index)	100.0	102.7	109.4	118.5	123.1	136.5	112.5
Real exchange rate (WPI-based index)	100.0	101.2	107.0	110.1	107.4	114.3	98.3
Average maturity of borrowings (days)	188.0	186.6	393.5	235.1	502.3	426.8	146.3

Note: CPI = consumer price index; WPI = wholesale price index.
Sources: Yılmaz, Akçay, and Alper 2002; Özatay and Sak 2002.

Because of the uncertainties stemming from domestic politics, the macroeconomic environment, and the ensuing high real interest rates, Turkey experienced very erratic growth performance. After the capital account liberalization in 1989, it was able to attract foreign capital to finance public sector borrowing requirements and generate growth rates of about 5 percent. Yet because of the availability of external funds, successive governments were "unable" to bring budget deficits, and thus inflation, under control. As the country's inability to cope with its economic woes became evident toward the end of the 1990s, the external funds dried up and growth rates declined sharply. The 2001 economic crisis was the final blow that underlined the need for a new economic policy framework in Turkey.

Over the last two decades, Turkey put on hold many decisions that could help foreign investors cope with high inflation. One of the critical measures was an inflation accounting framework. In a country that has lived with an average of 60 percent inflation, it is only now that an inflation accounting framework has been implemented.

Infrastructure-Related Factors. The quantity and quality of Turkey's broadly defined infrastructure, including its geographic and demographic endowments and its physical and financial infrastructure, help to position Turkey as a potentially powerful magnet for FDI inflows. Turkey enjoys a very special location at the crossroads between East and West, overlapping Europe and Asia geographically and culturally. The proximity to the Balkans and the rest of high-income Europe, as well as to the emerging markets in Russia, Caucasia, and Central Asia and the expanding markets of the Middle East and North Africa, offers the potential of over 1 billion consumers.

As highlighted in tables 10.7a and 10.7b, Turkey's demographic endowments present both strengths and weaknesses to foreign investors when compared with those of Poland, the Czech Republic, and Hungary. Turkey's huge and growing domestic market compares favorably with those of the comparator CEE countries. Turkey is projected to continue to have one of the largest populations in the Middle East and Eastern Europe. The domestic market is predominantly urban, and at least 17 major cities have a population in excess of 1 million, led by Istanbul, Ankara, and İzmir. The population is much younger than those of European countries; over 60 percent of the population is below the age of 35. On the negative side, the purchasing power of

TABLE 10.7a Infrastructure-Related Factors—Strengths: Turkey versus Comparator CEE Countries

	Turkey	Poland	Czech Republic	Hungary
Demography and business values				
Population—market size (millions)	67.8	38.7	10.3	10.1
Labor force growth (% change)	2.46	−0.33	−0.04	−0.47
Avg. no. of working hours per year	2,074	1,870	1,976	1,988
Flexibility and adaptability of people (survey)	7.53	4.77	5.83	6.74
Entrepreneurship (survey)	7.03	4.12	6.44	6.74
Availability of competent senior managers (survey)	6.5	5.21	4.92	6.37
Physical and financial infrastructure				
Internet costs for 20 hours (US$)	11.4	39.16	42.92	42.61
Adequacy of communications (survey)	6.66	4.93	7.17	7.19
Quality of air transport (survey)	7.44	4.55	7.00	5.93
Adequacy of distribution infrastructure (survey)	6.06	3.68	5.67	4.89
No. of credit cards issued (per capita)	0.57	0.13	0.21	0.29
Availability of finance skills (survey)	6.88	5.26	4.78	6.52

Note: The survey measures are all reported on a 0–10 scale, with 10 indicating the most positive perception.

Source: All measures are from the Institute of Management Development (IMD) 2002.

TABLE 10.7b   Infrastructure-Related Factors—Weaknesses: Turkey versus Comparator CEE Countries

	Turkey	Poland	Czech Republic	Hungary
Demography and business values				
GDP per capita (US$ at PPP)	6,175.0	9,151.0	14,485.0	12,663.0
Employment (% of population)	29.1	37.1	45.8	37.4
Adult literacy (% of population over 15 years)	84.6	99.0	99.0	99.0
Secondary school enrollment (% of relevant age group)	51.0	87.0	100.0	97.0
Female labor force (% of total labor force)	26.4	45.1	44.7	44.5
Employee training in companies (survey)	4.03	3.74	5.61	5.78
Physical and financial infrastructure				
Electricity costs for industrial clients (US$/kWh)	0.082	0.037	0.043	0.050
Adequacy of energy infrastructure (survey)	3.94	5.57	7.94	6.69
Computers per capita (per 1,000 people)	53.0	122.0	179.0	176.0
Technological cooperation between companies (survey)	4.00	4.03	6.17	5.19
Credit flows from banks to business (survey)	2.84	3.39	3.28	4.52
Venture capital for business development (survey)	1.97	3.42	3.17	3.48

Note: The survey measures are all reported on a 0–10 scale, with 10 indicating the most positive perception. PPP = purchasing power parity.
Source: All measures are from IMD 2002.

the average citizen is still significantly lower than that in the CEE countries, with per capita GDP 30 percent less than Poland's and less than half that of Hungary and the Czech Republic. Yet Turkey's improving consumption patterns and purchasing power, along with its growing middle class, are important positive features of the domestic market. Because Turkey's population growth rate has fallen from over 3 percent to under 2.5 percent, it is on the verge of entering a "golden demographic period" similar to that experienced by East Asia in the 1980s, in which the productive working population is largest relative to children and retirees, providing a critical ingredient for rapid income growth. Only a few emerging markets in the world have the potential to attract investment both for export and for their domestic market. Turkey, however, is in such a privileged position. It has the potential to create a "virtuous investment cycle," in which a more competitive domestic business environment further strengthens the country as a platform for exports, and the exports, in turn, stimulate firms to upgrade and better serve the domestic market.

In addition to geography and demography, another area in which Turkey compares favorably

with its comparator CEE countries is its highly skilled, flexible, and business-oriented labor force. As reported in table 10.7a, Turkey's work force is considered to be significantly more flexible, adaptable, and entrepreneurial than those of its comparator countries.[6] Yet its levels of actual employment, adult literacy, secondary school enrollment, and female labor force participation are low relative to those of the CEE countries, indicating the strong positive role still to be played by more widespread and improved nationwide education services. Although Turkey scores comparatively well in terms of availability of competent senior managers, training of employees is less of a priority in Turkish companies on average than in the CEE countries.

As for the traditional basic infrastructure measures, Turkey is again characterized by areas of strength and weakness (tables 10.7a and 10.7b). In communications and transport, Turkey stands out for its relatively low Internet costs—the cost of Internet access in Turkey for a basket of 20 hours at peak time is the lowest of all countries included in the *World Competitiveness Yearbook 2002* (IMD 2002) and is perceived as providing adequate communications standards. Turkey also is rated highly for both air transport quality and internal distribution infrastructure. Yet Turkey lags behind in its energy infrastructure. Although it recently passed new laws on its electricity and natural gas framework, which are designed to spur significant market-driven improvements in line with Turkey's underlying endowments, effective implementation to yield the expected results will take some time. Turkey also lags behind the CEE countries in computerization and technological cooperation. Finally, in finance, Turkey stands out in the breadth of its private sector–relevant finance skills and access to credit cards. But Turkey performs less well in areas critical to starting new indigenous businesses not connected to existing industrial groups; venture capital for business development is not so easily available, and credit does not flow very easily from banks to businesses.

The Automotive Industry. A natural implication of Turkey's large domestic market is the presence of FDI directed largely toward the internal market. However, the automotive industry is a good example of how an initially protected home market can be transformed into a competitive and increasingly export-oriented industry through FDI inflows. During the debate on the customs union, the automotive industry was expected to be the industry worst affected by lowering protections on EU imports. However, that prediction was proved wrong. Over the last few years, the automotive industry has become the second largest exporter.

By the mid-1990s, four FDI companies had more than 20 years of experience in the Turkish automotive industry (Fiat, Ford, Mercedes, and Renault).[7] In the mid-1990s, with the increasing prospects of a customs union agreement with the EU, Japanese and Korean companies (Honda, Hyundai, Isuzu, and Toyota) began investing in Turkey in joint ventures with Turkish industrialists.[8] Perhaps because of the uncertain business environment in Turkey, these companies did not initially make substantial investments, and they built plants with small production capacity. Once the customs union with the EU went into effect in 1996, the domestic market gradually opened to tough competition from the EU. Actually, in the first couple of years of the customs union, the sector struggled with wild fluctuations in domestic demand as well as with competition from imports.

However, much was at stake. There was already a substantial production capacity, coupled with a competitive parts and accessories industry. In addition, domestic business establishments with years of experience in the automotive industry and low-cost but good quality labor induced FDI companies in the automotive sector to increase their investments in Turkey and build new capacity to produce motor vehicles for the European market. None of the companies just mentioned decided to close shop in Turkey. Only Opel decided to close its small assembly plant near İzmir.

In the meantime, the auto parts industry was also attracting foreign investors. Most of the world leaders in the sector have joint ventures with Turkish partners. Some of them are big suppliers such as Robert Bosch, Valeo, Delphi Packard, and Mannesmann Sachs. Altogether, between 1992 and 2000, the automotive industry realized a total of $3.4 billion in investment. Of this amount, the industry used $750 million for capacity development, $976 million for new model development, $497 million for modernization, $300 million for localization, and $195 million for quality improvement. Moreover, because of the new investment projects directed at the production of new models, in 2000–02 this investment amount increased by almost $1 billion.

The success of the automotive industry in attracting FDI flows, despite the continuing constraints arising from macroeconomic and governance and institutional factors (see next section), is driven largely by the relevance of all the positive aspects of trade and infrastructure for this industry—the reason automobile-related multinational corporations (MNCs) decided to invest in Turkey. If other obstacles were not present, the Turkish auto industry would likely have attracted far more FDI inflows than current levels.

Governance and Institutions: Case Studies   Bottlenecks related to insufficient respect for the rule of law and to weak competition in local markets, reinforced by uneven application of bureaucratic red tape and of competition rules to all economic actors in the market, profoundly damage any country's investment climate. In these critical areas requiring improved governance and more effective institutions, Turkey, unfortunately, compares unfavorably with the comparator CEE countries, as reflected in the perceptions of the global investors and experts who compiled the following rankings. According to the Heritage Foundation's economic freedom index 2003, Turkey ranks 105th (with a score of 3.3), in contrast to Poland, 45th (2.7), and the Czech Republic and Hungary, both tied at 32nd (2.4). In PricewaterhouseCoopers' opacity index 2001, Turkey ranks 74th, compared with the Czech Republic at 71st, Poland at 64th, and Hungary at 50th. Finally, in Transparency International's corruption perception index 2002, Turkey ranks 64th (with a score of 3.2), in contrast to the Czech Republic at 52nd (3.7), Poland at 45th (4.0), and Hungary at 33rd (4.9).

To help illustrate what may be the central underlying factors accounting for Turkey's poor performance in these widely cited indices, the rest of this section presents three case studies that reflect the recent experiences of actual foreign investors. The case studies represent the primary sector (Normandy's experience in gold mining), the secondary manufacturing sector (Cargill's experience in agroprocessing), and tertiary services (İş-TIM's experience in the mobile telecom market). Figure 10.4 summarizes the main facts of the case studies. A discussion of the common elements across the case studies follows.

The Eurogold Investment. Because of its complex geology, Turkey possesses a diverse and rich array of minerals. It is a major world producer of boron minerals (it has two-thirds of the world's borate reserves), marble, copper and chrome ores, feldspar, magnesite, and others. Its total mineral industry revenues (primary and secondary mineral production, including cement, glass, refined petroleum products, steel, and certain inorganic chemicals) are estimated to account for roughly 10 percent of GDP. The mining sector is still overwhelmingly controlled by state-owned companies, although some public companies have been placed in the privatization process. Since enactment of the mining law (No. 3213) in 1985, the peak points in the value of FDI approvals in the sector have occurred with the following major investments: in 1990 in the Omya calcite mine, a joint venture involving the Swiss company of the same name; in 1991 in the Ovacik gold deposit by Eurogold; and in 1995 in an Eskişehir magnesite mine by Magnesit A.Ş., a subsidiary of the Dutch-based Société d'Interets Magnesiens.

Normandy Madencilik A.Ş. (formerly Eurogold, but later purchased by Australia-based Normandy Mining Limited) was registered in 1989 as a 100 percent FDI company. It found total reported gold reserves of 24,000 metric tons (and another 24,000 metric tons of silver) near the village of Ovacik, Bergama, in İzmir province. Under the initial application, the mine was to be operated for eight years, if no more reserves were discovered in the interim. The ore would be mined by both open pit and underground mining methods, followed by cyanide leaching. Gold and silver doré metal were to be the final products. In response to a request by the company in August 1991, the Ministry of Environment issued a letter of no objection in October 1994, indicating no health and environmental drawbacks and allowing the mining and processing facility to operate. The company also secured the required permit for mining activities from the Ministry of Energy and Natural Resources, and related permits, licenses, and investment certificates from relevant government entities. The amount of total investment was $100 million. As part of its application in 1991, Normandy prepared an environmental impact assessment (EIA) report. After enactment of a formal EIA regulation in 1993, Normandy agreed to meet the new discharge limits, even though it was exempt from the EIA because the mining rights were granted before the regulation took effect. Accordingly, the waste material from the facility would be stored in a water retention-type tailings dam, lined with clay and geo-membrane liners, with no discharge to the environment.

The judicial problems facing Normandy began with a court case initiated by the inhabitants of Ovacik and some nongovernmental organizations (NGOs) in 1994, based on a suit to annul the original Ministry of Environment decision authorizing the project. Long-lasting and repeated legal procedures followed. In 1997, after a long judicial process and just as construction of the facility had been completed and the mine was ready to operate, Turkey's highest relevant court, the Council of State (Danıştay), overturned the initial government authorization and ordered the mine and processing plant to be sealed by 1999. The ruling stated that the facility's proposed use of cyanide posed risks for health and environment and thereby violated Article 17 of the constitution, which granted all citizens the right to live in a healthy and balanced environment.

FIGURE 10.4   Case Studies

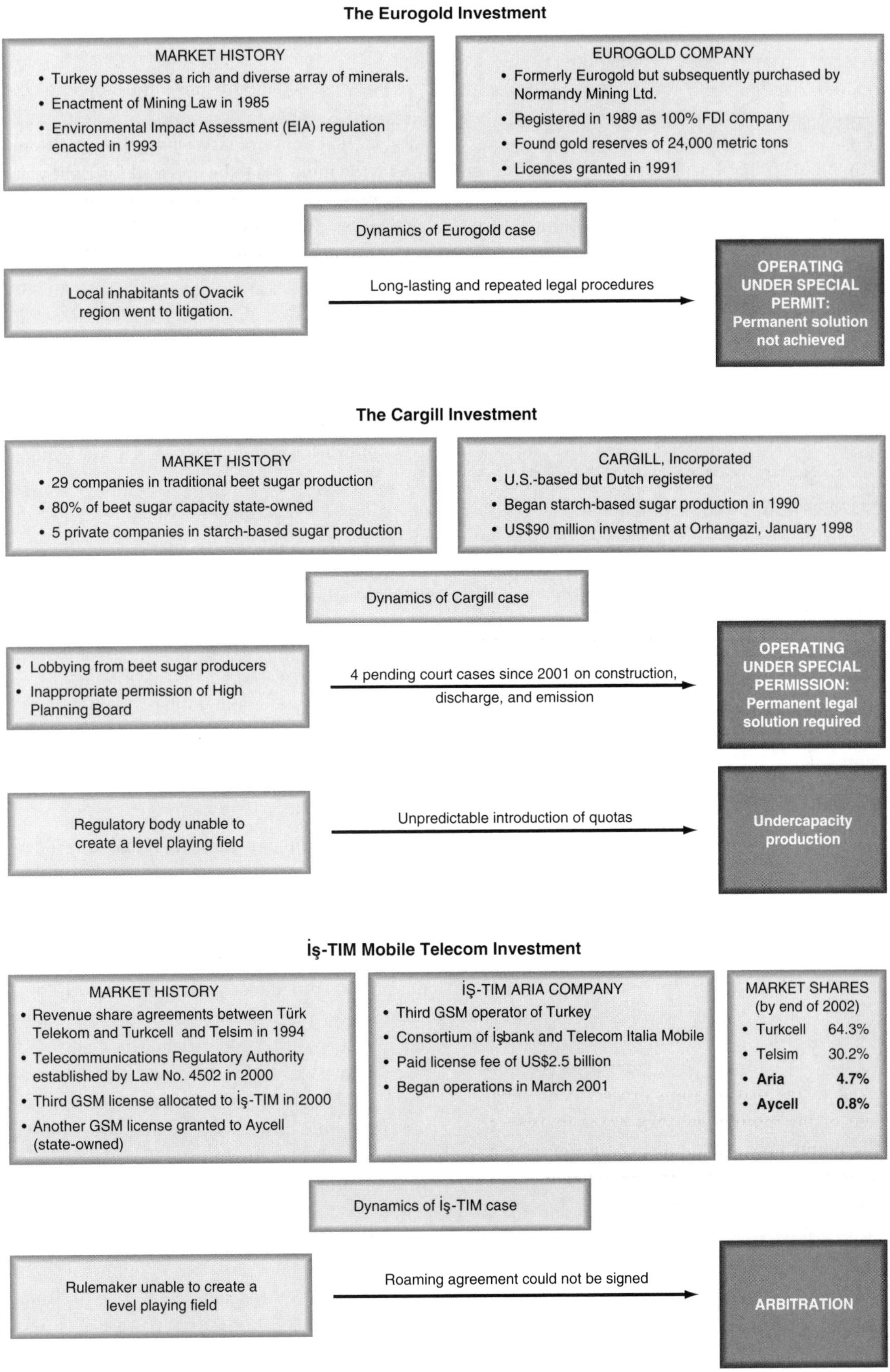

The Eurogold Investment

MARKET HISTORY	EUROGOLD COMPANY
• Turkey possesses a rich and diverse array of minerals. • Enactment of Mining Law in 1985 • Environmental Impact Assessment (EIA) regulation enacted in 1993	• Formerly Eurogold but subsequently purchased by Normandy Mining Ltd. • Registered in 1989 as 100% FDI company • Found gold reserves of 24,000 metric tons • Licences granted in 1991

Dynamics of Eurogold case

Local inhabitants of Ovacik region went to litigation. → Long-lasting and repeated legal procedures → **OPERATING UNDER SPECIAL PERMIT: Permanent solution not achieved**

The Cargill Investment

MARKET HISTORY	CARGILL, Incorporated
• 29 companies in traditional beet sugar production • 80% of beet sugar capacity state-owned • 5 private companies in starch-based sugar production	• U.S.-based but Dutch registered • Began starch-based sugar production in 1990 • US$90 million investment at Orhangazi, January 1998

Dynamics of Cargill case

• Lobbying from beet sugar producers
• Inappropriate permission of High Planning Board → 4 pending court cases since 2001 on construction, discharge, and emission → **OPERATING UNDER SPECIAL PERMISSION: Permanent legal solution required**

Regulatory body unable to create a level playing field → Unpredictable introduction of quotas → **Undercapacity production**

İş-TIM Mobile Telecom Investment

MARKET HISTORY	İŞ-TIM ARIA COMPANY	MARKET SHARES (by end of 2002)
• Revenue share agreements between Türk Telekom and Turkcell and Telsim in 1994 • Telecommunications Regulatory Authority established by Law No. 4502 in 2000 • Third GSM license allocated to İş-TIM in 2000 • Another GSM license granted to Aycell (state-owned)	• Third GSM operator of Turkey • Consortium of İşbank and Telecom Italia Mobile • Paid license fee of US$2.5 billion • Began operations in March 2001	• Turkcell 64.3% • Telsim 30.2% • **Aria 4.7%** • **Aycell 0.8%**

Dynamics of İş-TIM case

Rulemaker unable to create a level playing field → Roaming agreement could not be signed → **ARBITRATION**

Source: The authors.

Some lawyers have criticized Danıştay's decision that the technical method for mining was hazardous to human health. They argue that setting the rules on such a technical issue and prohibiting the use of a technical method are not the responsibility of Danıştay; rather, that responsibility resides with the related ministries or government institutions.

In response to this ruling, Normandy took additional safety measures in 1998 and reapplied to the Ministry of Environment for administrative permission, adding a cyanide destruction system for effluents from the facility, a sealed tailings pond, and a zero discharge system for wastewater. With these measures, the Ovacik facility became known as one of the better examples of environmental protection in the world (see, e.g., Arol 2002). The Ministry of Environment, in turn, consulted with the Prime Ministry. The Prime Ministry appointed a team of scientists under the governance of the Turkish Scientific and Technical Research Institute (TUBITAK) to evaluate the process. Based on a positive report from TUBITAK, the company was allowed to operate the facility for a one-year trial period, and it began operations in June 2001. Normandy has been operating the facility since then and publicizing the results of periodic independent environmental monitoring showing results well within national and international limits.

Project opponents have continued to challenge government decisions in various administrative courts in İzmir, with at least 10 separate court cases filed since August 2000 by local plaintiffs; defendants are the Prime Ministry, Ministry of Environment, Ministry of Health, and Ministry of Forestry. In late February 2002, an administrative court in İzmir ruled that the trial permit was violating the public good and issued an injunction against the facility, ordering it to close on April 2, 2002. However, the government passed a special permit for Normandy to continue operations.

Normandy's involvement in Turkey has benefited the Turkish mining sector in terms of improving environmental standards in the sector, applying state-of-art technology in gold mining and processing, and improving local technical training. Since the start of operations in June 2001, the facility has provided direct employment for 250 persons and indirect employment for an additional 1,200, including through the formation of new businesses in supporting industries. The acquisition of Normandy Mining Limited by U.S.-based Newmont Mining Corporation was completed in February 2002.

This case study highlights the problems for investors arising from the insufficient clarity of and lack of respect for the rule of law in Turkey. In this instance, Normandy followed established rules and procedures. The initial government authorization by the Ministry of Environment based on Normandy's adherence to the prescribed rules did not protect the company from successive legal challenges. After the first order for plant closure, subsequent authorizations based on the company observing newly prescribed rules (the new EIA regulation) by the Ministry of Environment, the Prime Ministry, and TUBITAK again were overturned, and the plant was ordered to be closed for a second time in August 2004. Since the plant shut down, the government has not issued a technical standard on the permitted methods for gold mining and specifically for cyanide leaching. Moreover, the government has adopted new regulations on sectoral licensing authorizing the Ministry of Health and the provincial governors, along with the Ministry of Environment, to issue operating licenses. Faced with insurmountable legal problems and the constantly changing regulations, the parent company, Newmont Mining Corporation, sold Normany Mining to a Turkish company in early February and withdrew from Turkey.

Cargill Starch-Based Sugar Investment. Turkey's sugar production can be divided into traditional beet sugar (sucrose or ordinary table sugar) processed from crushed sugar beets and starch-based sugar (glucose and fructose), a lower-cost alternative processed from maize. Although fructose can be used as a substitute for sucrose (because it is sweeter and metabolizes more slowly, it is often used in food products designed for people with diabetes), glucose cannot be used as a substitute, even though both are used as important sweetener inputs in food processing industries. The more traditional beet sugar is produced by 29 companies in Turkey, with state-owned production capacity accounting for 80 percent of the total. Starch-based sugar is produced by five private companies, of which three are MNCs. In 2001 Turkey produced 2 million metric tons of beet sugar, over five and a half times more than the privately produced 360,000 metric tons of starch-based sugar (235,000 of fructose, 125,000 of glucose). The sugar industry is characterized by substantial excess capacity, with total production capacity of 2.25 million metric tons of beet sugar and 930,000 metric tons of starch-based sugar. However, given the uncompetitively high local production costs of beet sugar, even current levels of beet sugar production are feasible only with extremely high nominal rates of protection of 78.5 percent and effective rates of protection of 1,500 percent. The excess capacity of starch-based sugar is not market based, however. It was artificially created by the new sugar law (No. 4634) announced in April 2001, which imposed a quota limiting starch-based sugar production to 10 percent of total beet sugar production in response to pressure from beet sugar farmers and processors. (This quota can be increased to 15 percent by the Council of Ministers. The actual quota has always been 15 percent.)

U.S.-based but Dutch-registered Cargill Incorporated began starch-based sugar production in Turkey in 1990. It obtained the required investment certificates (10 separate certificates between 1990 and 1997) for a wet corn milling (starch) processing plant in Pendik, Istanbul, with a capacity of 220,000 metric tons. Based on the success of that plant, Cargill obtained an additional investment certificate for a $90 million investment in a second facility at Orhangazi, in Bursa province in January 1998, again with a capacity of 220,000 metric tons. Like the first facility, this plant was constructed in full compliance with all the relevant legislation in force, and it has obtained all the necessary consents, permits, licenses, and authorizations (with a special condition within the foreign investment certificate recognizing the High Planning Board decision transferring the former agricultural area land into industrial area land). Significantly, 800 families and 4,000 people in the region were making their living out of the Orhangazi facility between 1998 and 2002, and 70 percent of the maize processed in the facility in 2002 was purchased from domestic growers.

In response to intense lobbying from the more expensive beet sugar producers, the Orhangazi facility has, since 2001, faced two separate but related problems. First, four court cases, still pending, commenced in 2001 challenging the government's initial granting of construction, discharge,

and emission permits. The plaintiffs, supported by the Bar Association of the city of Bursa, various professional chambers of Bursa, and some national members of Parliament from Bursa, undertook these actions against the Prime Ministry, the Governorship of Bursa, and the Ministry of Public Works and Housing. Although a case in the Sixth Administrative Chamber of the Council of State was decided unanimously in favor of Cargill and the government, it was appealed by the plaintiffs. Eventually, the initial decision was overruled, and the plaintiffs then sought cancellation of the original discharge and emission permits. A separate ruling found that the High Planning Board gave inappropriate permission for facility construction on "first priority agricultural land"— that is, it was claimed that the permission was in contradiction of the constitution. It was, therefore, ruled that the Orhangazi facility must be torn down. For a while, the company operated under special permission by the government. Then, in 2004, the government enacted a new law for the establishment of "industrial zones." The law authorizes the Council of Ministers to designate certain regions or already existing plant locations as industrial zones in which construction, discharge, and emission permits are not obligatory. Cargill has applied to the Industrial Zone Coordination Board for industrial zone status for the Orhangazi facility, and it is likely to be granted. However, no one, including government officials, knows what will happen when the court cases are finalized.

The second problem is related to the unpredictable introduction of quotas on starch-based sugar production in 2001. The initial government policy was to create substantial additional capacity by promoting starch-based production to substitute for higher-cost beet sugar. Although the initial quota for the period 2002–03 was restricted to 234,000 metric tons, it was increased by 50 percent by a subsequent Council of Ministers decision. However, the government's decision to increase the production quota has been ineffective so far, because it has not been implemented by the responsible independent regulatory board (the newly instituted Sugar Board). To add to the already existing chaos, the government abolished some articles of the sugar law at the end of 2004. With this move, the Sugar Administration was abolished. Now the Sugar

Board legally exists, but it does not have an institution to represent. A lawsuit is being prepared for cancellation of the decree on the grounds that the government does not have the authority to change the law unless there are international commitments.

This case highlights problems for investors similar to those encountered in the Eurogold investment, again arising from insufficient clarity of and the lack of respect for the rule of law. Cargill, too, followed the established rules and procedures. The initial government authorization granted in 1998 (supported by a High Planning Board decision) after Cargill followed the prescribed rules again did not protect the company from successive legal challenges, nor did subsequent support by the government (Prime Ministry, Ministry of Public Works and Housing, Governorship of Bursa) protect the company from plaintiffs eager to find legal loopholes to force plant closure (and, again, the legal problems have still not been solved permanently). In addition, this case highlights the negative impact on investments arising from the lack of a level playing field for all firms. In effect, unpredictable and uneven changes in rules with the introduction of highly restrictive quotas on some market players and not on others, together with the biased and anticompetitive decision of the Sugar Board in favor of entrenched local incumbents, have a negative effect on investments not only by efficient companies in the sugar industry but also by efficient companies in all sectors.

İş-TIM Mobile Telecom Investment. The move to liberalize the Turkish telecommunications industry's state-run monopoly began in 1994 with legislation to corporatize (as a state economic enterprise) the sole fixed-line operator, Türk Telekom (TT) and remove telecom services from direct government involvement. Also in 1994, the mobile telecommunications market was opened to limited competition from two private operators, Turkcell and Telsim, which began business under revenue-sharing agreements with Türk Telekom. These duopoly providers were granted 25-year licenses in 1998, although this initial assignment of spectrum was not competitively determined. In January 2000, new legislation (Law No. 4502) established an independent authority, the Telecommunications Authority (TA), and Türk Telekom was granted independence in business operations, but it was to end its monopoly in fixed-voice telephony by December 31, 2003. The third mobile license was allocated on the basis of a competitive tender in April 2000, with the condition that the minimum bid for a fourth license be equal to that paid by the third operator. İş-TIM, a consortium of domestic İşbank and the mobile phone arm of Telecom Italia Mobile (TIM) operating under the Aria brand, won the third tender with an unexpectedly high bid price of $2.525 billion, suspected to have been an attempt to prevent a fourth operator from entering.[9] The tender offer for a fourth license failed, and the fifth license was granted to Türk Telekom (through a newly created subsidiary, Aycell) at the same price paid by İş-TIM. İş-TIM entered the market in March 2001 and Aycell in December 2001. By the end of 2001, the mobile penetration rate had reached 28.7 per 100 inhabitants, surpassing that in the fixed-telephony market. By the end of 2002, Turkcell had a market share of 64.3 percent, Telsim 30.2 percent, İş-TIM 4.7 percent, and Aycell 0.8 percent. Unlike Eurogold and Cargill, which are 100 percent FDI companies, İş-TIM is a joint venture investment in which TIM owns 49 percent and the domestic partner is one of the largest banks and holding companies in Turkey.

The main problem facing İş-TIM since its entry into the Turkish market has arisen from its inability to conclude mutually acceptable roaming agreements with the incumbent competitors, Turkcell and Telsim. After the parties failed to resolve the tariff dispute among themselves, in March 2001 İş-TIM asked the TA to intervene. The regulator determined the terms, conditions, and tariffs for roaming in October 2001, but Turkcell and Telsim obtained preliminary injunction decisions in November 2001 with the aim of suspending implementation of these terms and conditions, and they applied to international arbitration. In March 2002, the TA adopted the Regulation on the Procedures and Merits concerning the Execution of National Roaming Agreements, but Turkcell and Telsim again obtained preliminary injunction decisions and applied to international arbitration for a second time. İş-TIM raised an objection against both injunction decisions as the third party suffering from the decision, but its objections were rejected. İş-TIM sent a letter as a last warning to the TA in February 2003 and filed a lawsuit against the TA with the International Court of Arbitration of the Paris-based International Chamber of Commerce on March 31, 2003, seeking nearly $3 billion in damages as a result of the negative response to its letter (the full value of the paid license fee plus valued added tax, because Turkey did not make available the roaming rights it had purportedly promised). On May 13, after negotiations involving Italian Prime Minister Silvio Berlusconi and Turkish Prime Minister Yılmaz Erdoğan, İş-TIM announced a merger with Aycell (TIM and Türk Telekom each to hold 40 percent of the merged provider, with İşbank holding the remaining 20 percent). With the announcement of the merger, İş-TIM withdrew its lawsuit, because the merger is expected to furnish İş-TIM with national roaming capacity, given Aycell's sizable network of base stations. The Turkish government accepted the merger of the two companies to prevent any further damage to Turkey's already poor reputation with foreign investors. The merger was completed in February 2004. The new company is called TT-TIM and is operating under the Avea brand, with a market share of 16 percent.

In the meantime, on June 9, 2003, Turkey's Competition Board fined Turkcell $15.4 million and Telsim $6.1 million (1 percent of the companies' net sales in 2001) for refusing to allow İş-TIM access to their networks. The Competition Board ruled that Turkcell and Telsim have been deliberately stifling competition in the mobile services market. The Competition Board also urged the TA to provide the requisite remedy by better regulating the market in order to end competition rule violations of this kind.

The request for arbitration arose out of the right that national operators have to national roaming and the presumption by İş-TIM that this right was not adequately guaranteed by the TA. The right of İş-TIM to benefit from national roaming is included in Article 6 of Law No. 4502, which requires mobile operators "to satisfy reasonable, economically proportionate and technically feasible roaming requests of other operators working in the same field" and requires the regulator "to issue regulations setting out the principles of implementation of this provision and the details to which standard reference tariffs, interconnection and roaming agreements are subject." National roaming rights are also presumed to arise out of Article 35 of the concession agreement between İş-TIM and the TA. The article requires the regulator "to provide a necessary, sufficient and fair competitive environment since İş-TIM entered the market," although it also specifies that "the coverage area of the [new] companies should cover 50 percent of the population of the country in three years and 90 percent in five years by investments exclusively made by the operators themselves without any national roaming support." The presumed shortcoming of the TA is that it has been late in coming up with its own regulations on roaming, that standard interconnection tariffs based on the long-run incremental cost accounting methodology have not yet been established, and that no requirement is in place ensuring that regulatory decisions remain in force while court proceedings are undertaken.

The İş-TIM case, like the Cargill case, highlights the negative impact that lack of a level playing field for all firms has on investments. Although the relevant regulatory body in the sugar industry made an anticompetitive decision in favor of entrenched local incumbent enterprises, the anticompetitive impact in this instance arose from the inability of the TA to impose a pro-competitive decision about roaming rights on Turkcell and Telsim in a timely manner. The origins of the problem in this case are related to the too-slow evolution of rules and regulations in the telecommunications sector and the lack of authority of the regulatory body, driven no doubt at least in part by a natural learning process of the TA.

Common Governance- and Institutions-Related Constraints. One of the common features of the three cases examined is the lack of credible industrial policy framework statements that could give investors confidence in the expected rules of the game in each industry. In fact, no such document is available for any industry. Even the changes made in the legislative framework for telecommunications in May 2001 that gave more power to the TA were made without a clearly articulated policy framework. Thus, they hardly form the basis for giving investors confidence about the government's long-term vision for the industry and for the economy as a whole. To help give credibility to such policy framework statements, related legislation, including implementing decrees in line with the policy statements, are essential, as is the subsequent consistent implementation of such legislation.

The case studies highlight two distinct but related classes of constraints that account for Turkey's poor performance in attracting FDI: (a) the legal and judicial constraints related to the insufficient clarity of and lack of respect for the rule of law, and (b) competition constraints related to the absence of a level playing field for all firms. Lack of clarity refers to insufficiently defined, missing, incoherent, or changing rules. Lack of respect for the rule of law refers to the practice of decision making based not on ex ante defined rules but on opportunistic motives irrespective of the prevailing rules. It also refers to both a reluctance to apply rules when they should be applied and a tendency to allow loopholes and ambiguities to persist in the legal framework. Lack of respect for the rule of law creates an environment in which multiple appeals are common and in which successive appeals attempt to overrule the previous court's or public authority's ruling. The ineffectiveness of many of the recently established regulatory boards intensifies the adverse effects of this constraint on foreign investors. In such an environment, it is only natural for investors to lack confidence that established rights will be respected by the courts.

In each of the presented cases, the government as rulemaker has not been able to solve the underlying problems in a timely manner. In those instances in which the government has strived to help the investor, its attempts have been met with judicial challenges. These judicial challenges, when circumvented by the government such as in the Eurogold and Cargill cases, were carried out without addressing the underlying legal bottlenecks. This fundamental problem of unaddressed underlying legal ambiguities appears to be one of the most critical problems. It raises the question of whether lack of clarity in the underlying rule of law is intentional, so that public decision makers have the freedom required to grant special treatment and exemptions whenever politically convenient. Unfortunately, the substantial cost of such unpredictability in the rule of law in terms of forgone current and future investments amplifies the impact of distortions stemming from government allocations based on personal connections.

In the face of competition-related constraints, state-owned, local, joint venture, and fully foreign-owned companies are not able to compete on an equal footing. In both the Cargill and İş-TIM cases, the failure of the relevant regulatory body to rapidly enforce a pro-competitive order has sent negative signals for future investments by existing or new, potentially efficient enterprises. It is, of course, natural for entrenched local incumbents, whether in primary, secondary, or tertiary sectors, to seek to maintain market power and prevent new investors from challenging their local dominance. However, it is the role of properly enforced competition policies, both through the independent regulatory bodies and through the Competition Board, to ensure that incumbent companies only do so by lowering their costs and offering improved products rather than by seeking to dull the competitive market process, either on their own or through alliances with organs of government.

This analysis of governance- and institutions-related constraints in Turkey is consistent with a broader analysis of politics and democracy in Turkey as populist patronage—allowing people greater access to the resources of the state through the help of political parties (see, e.g., Kalaycıoğlu 2001). In a cultural environment in which interpersonal trust is low, regional solidarity ties, blood relations, clientelistic networks, favoritism, and nepotism have deeply influenced and molded the political culture.[10] For patronage to thrive, authorities must distribute favors to their clientele, which is difficult to do if allocation of contracts and contract monitoring, recruitment, promotion, tariff decisions, and expansion of new entrants are conducted purely on meritocratic grounds and through transparent procedures as required by EU standards. Only when rules and laws are applied evenly for all market participants (and not directly modified for politically influential firms) will non-market-based favoritism be overcome and more substantial investments driven by underlying efficiencies be forthcoming.

FDI-Related Policies and Institutions and EU Accession

Turkey scores better than its competitors along many of the dimensions of FDI just described (also see tables 10.7a and 10.7b). A huge and growing domestic market, skilled and cost-effective labor, strong local companies, and access to other expanding markets are all strengths of Turkey. Furthermore, Turkey has had a liberal legal framework for

FDI since 1954 and a convertible currency for almost 15 years, far earlier than its competitors. However, relatively low levels of FDI inflows over past years reveal that Turkey has not been able to translate these competitiveness-related strengths into a sufficiently large number of concrete FDI projects. In comparison with other candidate countries, Turkey's EU candidacy has not positively affected its inflow of FDI, and figures show that even the customs union has had a negligible effect.[11]

The policies Turkey must follow to foster its future competitiveness have to include all the traditional components needed to attract more FDI, such as the further harmonization of trade and industrial policies and the adoption of related legislation and administrative procedures. However, these components are not sufficient conditions for a more competitive economy and will not automatically result in increased inflows of FDI. All EU candidate countries have applied the *acquis,* but each country also has country-specific rules, policies, and institutions to seek FDI. In addition to meeting EU requirements in a broad range of traditional harmonization-related areas, Turkey must attempt to improve its legal/judicial and competition-related environment in order to ensure predictable respect for the rule of law and a level playing field for all firms, not only on paper but also in terms of implementation.

EU Requirements

Turkey's EU candidacy status and obligations as a member of the customs union do not directly impose EU requirements on Turkey's FDI policy. Until 2003, no explicit clause on FDI policy appeared in the accession partnership (AP) report or the "Regular Report on Turkey's Accession," even though Turkey's limits on foreign ownership for certain sectors were criticized in the context of freer movement of capital (European Commission 2003, 2002). However, FDI as well as domestic investments are very much related to the overall business environment and policy decisions on taxes and state aids, intellectual property rights, sectoral licenses, customs, and standards. Furthermore, broader areas of competition policy have a direct impact on how a country performs in attracting FDI. Thus the previous AP documents and the national program of Turkey had included a long list of legislation to be amended, which, in turn, could positively affect the investment climate.

The 2003 accession partnership report for Turkey has, for the first time, clauses related to FDI policy (European Commission 2003). The two requirements, which are explicitly stated in the AP document, both as short-term priorities, are that Turkey should "facilitate and promote the inflow of FDI" (in the Economic Criteria section) and "remove all restrictions affecting FDI [originating from the EU] in all sectors in Turkey" (in the Free Movement of Capital section).

As for broader EU requirements for FDI, the 2002 "Regular Report" contains criticism of the limitations on foreign ownership in some sectors, of the authorization system for investment, and of the obligation to pay $50,000 to establish a company or open a branch in Turkey (European Commission 2002). As for the restrictions on foreign ownership in certain sectors, such as civil aviation, maritime transport, port enterprises, radio and television broadcasting, telecommunications, and mining and energy, the government argues that most of the other candidate countries still have similar restrictions and that Turkey should not remove them until a more definite road map for EU accession is agreed on. However, it is also argued that these restrictions should be removed not only to comply with the EU *acquis,* but also to develop a more competitive investment environment for Turkey.

Reform Efforts to Date

Turkey adopted an ambitious structural reform program in 2001 to lay the foundation for sustainable growth, driven by private investments and supported by a smaller but more effective government. The main pillars of the government's economic program related to development of the private sector include an improved investment climate; a smaller, more transparent, effective public sector; a sound and competitive financial system; accelerated privatization; and a more efficient business infrastructure, with a particular focus on communications and energy. The ongoing reform efforts are closely linked to Turkey's objective to accede to the EU. The government realizes that Turkey has fallen behind many other developing countries in its effective liberalization, enforcement practice, legal, and judicial reforms. Pushing ahead with the ongoing reforms is crucial to the country's economic future.

Currently, Turkey is implementing a major fiscal adjustment program to increase the effectiveness of the public sector while reducing its size. Fiscal and public sector reforms are imperative to ensure a sustainable domestic public debt profile, which is itself critical to establishing macroeconomic stability with low inflation. These actions are essential to allowing lower interest rates, facilitating long-term investment planning, and promoting more robust private sector growth. To complement these reforms and ensure their sustainability, Turkey also is undertaking fundamental reforms of its expenditure and taxation systems. The banks act in 1999 established the Banking Regulation and Supervision Agency (BRSA) as an independent authority to regulate and supervise the banking sector. The BRSA has implemented a comprehensive banking restructuring program to promote more efficient financial intermediation for the enterprise sector. To strengthen the scope for private sector investment in telecoms, Turkey passed an amending law in 2000 to create, as noted earlier, the Telecommunications Authority, an independent regulatory body responsible for licensing, tariffs, spectrum allocation, and other supervisory activities. Similarly, to strengthen the scope for private sector investment in energy, separate electricity and natural gas laws in 2001 established the independent Energy Market Regulatory Authority. In August 1999, Turkey's constitution was amended to establish the legal basis for privatization and to allow public services to be performed under private law. Importantly, the amendments also allow the international arbitration of disputes. A new public procurement law also was enacted in 2002. Although all these policy announcements are desirable and in the right direction, the government must ensure that these policies will be implemented carefully, consistently, and promptly so that business expectations will not be adversely affected.

To address feedback received from international investors about Turkey's troublesome investment climate, the government in 2001 launched a reform process to improve administrative procedures. The idea behind the Reform Program for Improving the Investment Climate was that administrative barriers can make the difference between the perception that a location is an attractive one for investment and the perception that it is not competitive. Indeed, complex and time-consuming administrative procedures appear to be among the most important disincentives to investment, and they can discourage investors, despite other attractive features that a country might have to offer. Taking into account the findings and recommendations of a diagnostic study and a project on administrative barriers to investment, conducted jointly by the government and the Foreign Investment Advisory Service (FIAS, a joint facility of the International Finance Corporation and the World Bank), the government enacted a "Decree on Improving the Investment Climate in Turkey" on December 11, 2001, as part of a national strategy to increase the overall level of income and productivity and to raise the level of competitiveness of firms operating in Turkey (see FIAS 2001).

The challenge facing the government was how to implement this reform vision in a manner that would streamline administrative procedures while incorporating private sector feedback on the measures to be taken. Within this framework, a three-phase strategy was designed and then launched to facilitate the reform process. In the first phase, a clear vision and a consistent direction for the reform were embodied in the December 2001 ministerial decree in order to demonstrate political commitment and consensus behind the reform scheme. The decree established the Coordination Council for the Improvement of the Investment Climate (YOIKK), a coordinating body composed of senior public and private sector decision makers with the mandate to identify and remove regulatory and administrative barriers to private investment. The second phase entailed formulating a clear and precise action plan defining priorities, timing, and responsibilities for attracting more FDI flows. In the third phase, YOIKK was scheduled to hold regular monthly meetings in order to monitor progress made, with quarterly reports submitted to the Council of Ministers.

As shown in figure 10.5, key areas of reform have been identified and grouped under nine technical committees to deal with the following constraints:

- *Company registration.* The goal is to eliminate time-consuming, unnecessary, and duplicative transactions.
- *Employment.* Problems are related to short-term work visas, employment of special groups, and high social contributions by employers.

FIGURE 10.5   Areas for Investment Climate Reform

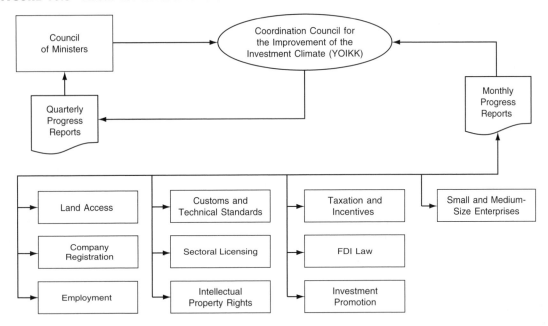

Source: Undersecretariat of the Treasury.

- *Sectoral licenses.* Licensing procedures are unnecessarily complicated in various industries, primarily because of overlapping authorities, highly centralized approval procedures, and little involvement by the private sector.
- *Location.* Access to public lands and site development by the private sector are very time-consuming and subject to some restrictions.
- *Taxes and incentives.* The corporate income tax rate is comparatively high, and the system is complex. Incentives should be aligned with the EU state aids regime, and the process should be simplified and automatic where possible.
- *Customs and standards.* Despite major reform initiatives, customs procedures still cause some delays because of the significant documentation requirements, lengthy testing procedures, delayed valued added tax (VAT) reimbursement, and discretionary decision making with incidences of corruption.
- *Intellectual property rights.* Protection of patents, trademarks, and copyrights is insufficient, mainly because of remaining gaps in the existing legislation, weak implementation and enforcement of laws, and cumbersome procedures.
- *Investment promotion.* No one single entity effectively conducts targeted investment promotion and policy advocacy.

- *FDI legislation.* Legislation on FDI at the time of the formation of YOIKK was based on the 1954 law.

The first YOIKK meeting, held in March 2002, set targets and timelines for these technical committees. One core dimension of the reform process has been private sector involvement in all efforts through disseminating the information and sharing the results obtained over time. This emphasis is in line with the government's conviction that joint evaluation of the needs and identification of appropriate solutions are of utmost importance for the success of the reform initiative.

The reports of the technical committees have been quite positive. The government already has taken several steps in compliance with the recommendations of the committees. Even though there were elections and change in government, the reform program has proved to be effective, and various legislative changes have been made and draft laws prepared. After the November 2002 elections, the new government amended the Council of Minister's decree to include another technical committee on small and medium-size enterprises. To increase the influence of YOIKK, the government decided to head it with a minister. Laws enacted as a direct result of the YOIKK process to date include

(1) a new, up-to-date FDI law that serves as a declaration to foreign investors of their rights and that will enable a shift from an ex ante, control-based "investment permission system" to a "promotion and facilitation approach" with minimal ex post monitoring to continuously improve the investor climate in conformity with international best practices; (2) a law that redesigns the company registration process by diminishing the prior 19 required steps to three and by reducing turnaround from two and a half months to one day; (3) a law on employment of foreign personnel; and (4) a law on the investment allowance system, which enables a shift to an automatic state aids system in line with EU requirements. Among the drafted laws that have been sent either to the Prime Ministry or to Parliament are a law on the duties and responsibilities of the Patent Institute, which will enable the institute to deal with intelllectual property rights issues in a more professional way, and a law on the establishment of an investment promotion agency.

Although some investment promotion initiatives are being undertaken by several public and private institutions, Turkey at present does not have an agency that has a strong and clear mandate, setup, and budget to carry out effective investment promotion, including functions such as investor servicing, investment generation, and policy advocacy, and that is governed jointly by the public and private sectors. Work is still under way on establishing an appropriate institution to carry out these tasks.

YOIKK's efforts also have borne fruit in several other areas, such as recruitment of expatriates, sectoral licensing, customs, and intellectual and industrial property rights. As for customs reform, the Undersecretariat of Customs has been implementing an ambitious reform program to improve its administrative efficiency and effectiveness. The customs automated system has been rolled out to 99 percent of all customs offices and has been further enhanced to assist customs in controlling movement of goods. Important steps taken include modernizing customs laws, regulations, and procedures in line with those of EU legislation and simplifying and harmonizing forms, procedures, and control techniques in line with those internationally recommended by the World Customs Organization. The legislation necessary to strengthen the capacity and infrastructure of the Turkish Patent Institute has been submitted to Parliament. The intent is to ensure effective implementation of the regulations on the protection of intellectual and industrial property rights.

Finally, land acquisition and site development for investment are critical issues for both local and foreign investors. A very useful discussion forum involving public and private sector representatives has led to the creation of a priority list of problems and measures to be taken in this field. The technical committee working on this issue will begin by formulating solutions to the most urgent problems.

Outstanding Priorities

Although current efforts have focused largely on introducing new laws in pre-identified areas to spur administrative reforms, predictable implementation of existing and new legislation is far more important. As for competition-related reforms, it is vital that all investors—existing producers and new entrants, whether local, joint venture, or wholly foreign-owned—face a level playing field in the way that laws, regulations, and administrative procedures are implemented. Certain critical problems still exist for investors in these areas, as highlighted by the case studies.

Legal and Judicial Reforms   Improvements on the legislative front, many of which were achieved in the last few years, were necessary but not sufficient to create an attractive legal framework for foreign investors. Improvements in FDI legislation in the narrow sense fall into this category of the necessary but not sufficient changes required to generate sustainable increases in FDI inflows. One of the critical outstanding impediments to investment is that implementation of the laws in both the executive and judicial branches of government is fraught with problems for investors. The most important, but also probably the most difficult, reforms needed in this area are basic changes in the legal and judicial systems and in the way that administrative procedures more generally are implemented.

The way in which the legal and judicial systems work is a critical determinant of FDI—especially high-value FDI destined for export markets that can go anywhere and that need a reliable, hassle-free environment. Lengthy, nontransparent procedures, combined with unpredictable outcomes, in both the executive branch of government and the courts, are among the main problems in this area. Incomplete reforms and poor implementation of laws and regulations are the overarching issues. Adopted laws are often not implemented on time. All this contributes to the general perception of an unpredictable legal framework. Not only are the administrative procedures time-consuming, but also enforcement procedures for commercial cases in the courts take much longer than in many other countries. The heavy workload of judges is the major reason for these delays. Often, court cases in Turkey consume more than a year. In the survey carried out by FIAS, another point frequently raised by investors was their lack of confidence in the impartiality and quality of the commercial courts (FIAS 2001). Even if the legal issue appears clear, foreign investors routinely state that the judgments are still much more unpredictable than they would be in their home country. Foreign companies and larger companies are very visible, and laws may be applied more strictly to them than to domestic and smaller companies. Although the laws themselves respect the principle of equal treatment stipulated in the 1954 law on foreign capital and the new foreign direct investment law, implementation often has been different.

The government is taking steps to reform the judicial system and enhance its predictability as a component of Turkey's EU accession program. The commitments made in this area, as well as the short- to medium-term plans, are reflected in the national program. These targets will require some years to achieve; however, these reforms should help to improve the perception of Turkey in foreign investors' eyes. One desirable step would be for Turkey to institute a comprehensive legal and judicial review to identify and address important items in existing private sector–related laws that are in contradiction or that are not clearly defined. Furthermore, a specific institution should be entrusted with improved oversight responsibilities to reduce the likelihood of such recurrences in the future. Such a review should also include in its terms of reference the removal of detailed sectoral issues— such as those related to the allocation of land, first-priority agricultural land, privatization, and arbitration—from the constitution and their introduction instead into the appropriate laws. Two related recommendations that could be acted on immediately are to refrain from allowing so much

time to pass between the adoption of laws and their implementing legislation and to seek maximum input from private sector participants, both local and foreign, at the legal preparation phase. Best practice would be to draft implementing regulations in parallel with the law, or at least to have a detailed draft ready at the time the law is adopted on what the implementation will look like. Seeking significant input from business associations before laws and regulations are adopted will result in adequate legislation that reflects the concerns of the private sector. This procedure, common practice in most OECD countries, increases the knowledge base on which legislation is drafted.

Competition-Related Reforms　The general goal of creating a more competitive environment in Turkey has been dealt with as part of the process of meeting basic EU accession requirements. Turkey developed its competition law while negotiating its customs union with the EU. The law was adopted in 1994, taking the EU treaty as its substantive basis. The Competition Board has been actively applying Turkey's competition law since the end of 1997. However, industrial policy, company law, free movement of goods, capital and service provision, taxation, sectoral policies, regional policies, and policy on small and medium-size enterprises (SMEs) are also all related to competition. Progress in all of these areas to comply with the EU *acquis* will help Turkey to achieve a better competitive environment.

As for enforcing the competition law, a few outstanding issues are crucial to effective private sector development. In particular, the current legislation does not allow the Competition Board to apply competition rules to all public undertakings, including those with special or exclusive rights, and to other entities of public administration. It is in Turkey's interest to change this situation and to include the equivalent of Article 86 of the Treaty of Rome (1957), which established the European Community. As privatization progresses and public participation withdraws, care should be given to better aligning the specific sectoral laws with the 1997 Competition Act in order to ensure the efficient enforcement of competition rules. Therefore, it is essential that the government grant the Competition Board enhanced powers to act during the privatization process and in the regulated infrastructure sectors. In this respect, closer coordination should be secured between the Competition Board and special sectoral regulatory authorities. The sectoral regulatory authorities should focus more on ex ante regulation, and the Competition Board should concentrate on ex post regulation. After such "specialization," the current state of competition between these two types of institutions will diminish, laying a stable foundation for cooperation and coordination. This need for improved coordination is evident in the Cargill case, where quotas imposed by the Sugar Board have adversely affected private sector parties by inhibiting competition, and also in the İş-TIM case, where earlier coordination would have helped to address the situation sooner.

A recent study carried out by experts from the Competition Board on legislation not compatible with competition supports the view that the government is not consistent in its application of competition policy principles (Ekdi and others 2002). The study lists various laws and regulations from different sectors that contradict the enacted competition law, and almost all of these sectors are dominated by public enterprises. Although such inconsistencies might be understandable for legislation that dates back to when the government applied an import-substitution strategy and the public sector was the driving force of the economy, there is no economic rationale for such contradictions in legislation adopted after approval of the Competition Act. Such contradictions are most glaring for regulatory bodies. As discussed in the Cargill case, the Sugar Board should not have unilateral authority to impose anticompetitive quotas. More generally, there should be enhanced oversight of competition policy to ensure that the decisions of regulatory boards do not contradict competition principles. A strong case can be made for the desirability of strengthening the traditional competition advocacy responsibilities of the Competition Board, including granting the board the power to introduce or amend new laws to promote competition, the power to modify existing laws that are anticompetitive in their impact, the oversight responsibility to ensure that relevant institutions do not perform an anticompetitive role, and the power to review whether decisions of all regulatory institutions are in the public interest, with the mandate to submit their reports to Parliament and other appropriate public oversight entities.

Another key area of competition policy with an unfinished agenda is state aids. Turkey has been criticized by the EU for not aligning its state aids system with that of the EU, even though such a step has been a commitment of Turkey under the customs union. Progress has been made in this area, but legislative changes and an independent monitoring authority have not yet been established. Moreover, the current attempts to align the state aids rules cover only the aids given to the private sector, whereas public sector incentives also should be covered to ensure a competitive environment.

The broader EU requirements shed light on other issues on which Turkey should focus in seeking a more competitive environment. These include alignment with the *acquis* on intellectual and industrial property rights (company law) and the removal of limitations for foreign ownership in certain sectors (free movement of capital).

The Benefits of Full EU Accession   Turkey's eventual EU membership is very crucial for FDI inflows. Regardless of the many characteristics that render it an attractive place for foreign investment, Turkey cannot attract as much FDI as its competitors in Central and Eastern Europe unless the government takes further steps toward full EU membership. Actually, Turkey would not have to wait very long to start reaping the benefits of an eventual EU accession. With the opening of EU accession negotiations, Turkey is already likely to attract larger sums of FDI, and there are many reasons to expect such a development to take place.

The opening of EU negotiations in October 2005 is expected to act as a strong signal that Turkey will eventually become a full member of the EU, assuming that the government continues on the current path of structural reforms with a clear focus on the sustainability of public debt. Such a decision would assure foreign investors that the Turkish economy will follow a stable growth path for the foreseeable future. Equally important, the opening of EU accession negotiations would provide all investors with enhanced confidence that the legal and judicial environment will improve across all relevant areas of the common *acquis* and that implementation of all required secondary legislation also will improve, because the accession process in Turkey's case requires not only progress in enacting laws but also progress in implementing them. For Turkey, stability, together with institutional reforms that will improve application of the rule of law and enhance competition, would have the benefit of convincing foreign investors to channel more funds to Turkey for domestic as well as export market–oriented projects. Especially with its domestic market potential, Turkey would be very attractive for FDI in nontraded sectors. Because the average size of investments in these sectors is in general larger, it is likely that they would attract significant FDI inflows immediately after the opening of negotiations.

The attractiveness of Turkey for foreign investors will continue to increase as the accession negotiations proceed, allowing it to close the gap with the CEE countries in attracting FDI. Meanwhile, Turkey will continue to take steps toward harmonization with the EU framework. At one step, even before becoming a full member, Turkey will be in a position to accept the authority of EU agencies in the resolution of any problems that may arise between foreign investors and the Turkish government. This step will further ease some of the reservations that foreign investors may still have in relation to Turkey. After all, EU rules and regulations and the ways they are implemented are well known and predictable to foreign investors. It is at this stage that one of the most important benefits from EU accession will be realized by Turkey: the rule of law and competition-related constraints will be eased even further, with concomitant increases in private investment flows.

The Role of Proactive Investment Promotion Policies In each of the anticipated stages in the accession process, a critical question is what shape should the most appropriate set of investment promotion policies, best adapted to the evolving Turkish reality, take? Another question is, in addition to focusing on those elements of the investment climate most critical to moving from one stage to the next in the accession process, what else should Turkey be doing on the policy side?

From these questions emerges one about the desirability of more targeted FDI policies. The experiences of both developed and developing countries demonstrate the potential benefits of specific policies to stimulate investment and of an investment promotion agency (IPA) that will engage in activities such as investment generation, policy advocacy, investor servicing, and image

building (see chapter annex, which describes the functions of an IPA). According to UNCTAD (2000), more than 160 national and over 250 subnational IPAs are in place worldwide. A recent empirical study on the effectiveness of IPAs in 58 countries revealed that FDI inflows are positively correlated with investment promotion activities, and that the quality of the investment climate and the level of development have a significant effect on IPA performance (see Morisset 2003). This finding suggests that countries are well advised to focus on basic improvements in the investment climate first, and then consider introducing an IPA, at a minimum, concurrently with serious efforts to improve the investment climate. Political visibility and participation of the private sector appear to be two elements critical to the success of an IPA. Worldwide experience shows that IPAs are more effective when they are autonomous from the government (though subject to policy oversight by the public sector) and when they are a product of a genuine joint effort by the private and public sectors.[12]

Turkey does not presently have an IPA. The government has been carrying out promotion activities on a negligible budget. Those activities consist mainly of publications, limited advertising, and participation in seminars and trade investment fairs. It is difficult to claim that Turkey has a coherent promotion policy when it is compared with those of many other countries. Nor is it possible to claim that the budget allocated to promotion is sufficient. Under the YOIKK reform program, the Technical Promotion Committee is still working to set up an appropriate institution that could perform the key IPA functions. In addition to the public sector's oversight role in establishing an appropriate institutional framework, a government also has a key role to play in articulating an overall investment policy and specific FDI policy actions. Ideally, a government should first decide on an overall investment and FDI policy and then use incentives where appropriate as tools to achieve the stated objectives. The use of incentives will differ by country, but the World Trade Organization (WTO) has specified some general rules that each country should obey. For Turkey, additional rules stem from the customs union agreement with the EU. As part of cross-national efforts to abolish barriers to investment, bilateral or international agreements are signed between countries to protect mutual investments, with clauses ranging from admission and establishment to standards of treatment and dispute settlement mechanisms.

Attracting more FDI per se should not necessarily be the main target of a country's FDI policy. Just as important are questions of how the country can benefit more from any specific level of FDI and how to prevent any negative effects of FDI. Ideally, FDI policies should provide incentives for investors to act in ways that will contribute most to the country's development process. In order to get the most from FDI, countries can try to build local capabilities, using local suppliers and upgrading local skills, technological capabilities, and infrastructure (UNCTAD 2003). Typically, policymakers attempt to understand the potential and attractiveness of their country before designing a policy accordingly. The sectoral and regional capabilities of the country, the needs of specific investors—be they market seeking or resource seeking—and the development level of specific sectors relative to global trends should all be taken into consideration. Even developed countries apply specific policies to attract FDI, and Germany's use of special incentives to attract investment in information-communication technologies is an example of this practice.

Despite the general shift in attitudes in favor of FDI, significant concerns remain about its possible negative effects. Crowding out of local firms and products, transfers of polluting activities or technologies, and concessions made to investors in special zones that allow them to skirt labor and environmental regulations are examples of these negative effects (UNCTAD 2003: 88).

Given the benefits that could accrue to Turkey from significantly higher levels of FDI, there is indeed more that Turkey could and should do on the policy side—subject to WTO and EU customs union constraints. Indeed, Turkey has negotiated investment agreements with 79 countries and signed 66 of these agreements, and it has signed "double taxation agreements" with 49 countries. It also has taken part in the WTO negotiations for an international investment agreement, and it has participated in FDI-related issues in platforms such as UNCTAD, OECD, WTO, and the European Commission. However, a comparison of Turkey's potential with its actual levels of FDI inflows suggests that the policies implemented to date need

further strengthening. In addition to enhanced legal/judicial implementation and more effective competition across markets, Turkey would benefit from a coherent overall investment and FDI policy that clearly articulates how specific policies and more activist promotion are intended to achieve stated objectives.

Conclusion

This chapter has examined the main challenges currently facing Turkey in attracting foreign direct investment. The setting of the analysis is that FDI can in principle be highly beneficial for a country's growth and development prospects. The available evidence suggests that FDI would indeed highly benefit the Turkish economy as a whole, based on its significant direct and indirect benefits for productivity in the manufacturing sector.

Despite its beneficial effects, however, recorded FDI inflows to Turkey have been extremely low compared with those of the CEE countries. The main FDI challenges facing Turkey, therefore, are determining why FDI inflows have remained so low and how Turkey can increase the inflows to desirable levels. But to what extent do recorded inflows fully reflect actual inflows? This chapter provides preliminary evidence that understatements may be significant in some years, though changes in the new 2003 FDI law, coupled with improved statistical recording, should help to alleviate discrepancies from international common practice.

One of the major culprits behind Turkey's laggard performance in FDI inflows is the country's long-running fiscal problems and the ensuing macroeconomic uncertainty. Turkey's current efforts to implement a major fiscal adjustment, if sustained, should help to achieve lower inflation and macroeconomic stability. The introduction of inflation accounting will no doubt be a welcome interim measure for local and foreign investors alike. Besides macroeconomic uncertainty, specific infrastructure-related weaknesses also continue to diminish Turkey's attractiveness to investors. Although Turkey benefits from its skilled, adaptable, and entrepreneurial work force, and communications and transport do not appear to be major problem areas, it lags behind in its energy infrastructure, its level of computerization, and the availability of credit for the private sector. Turkey's recently passed electricity and natural gas framework laws, to the extent that they are effectively implemented, should spur significant improvements in line with Turkey's underlying endowments in the energy area. Successful implementation of the adjustment program will ensure that more funds will be channeled to the private sector, rather than be used to fund the huge public sector deficit, at low real interest rates.

Perhaps the most important contribution of this chapter is its examination of the standing rule of law and competition-related impediments to investment through three detailed case studies from the primary, secondary (manufacturing), and tertiary (services) sectors. Based on these studies, we argue that the main unaddressed obstacles to increased FDI in Turkey are governance and institutions-related problems related to the rule of law and competition. The most important legal and judicial constraints are the insufficient clarity of and lack of respect for the rule of law. In each of the analyzed cases, the government as rulemaker has failed to address the underlying legal ambiguities in a timely fashion, raising the question of whether lack of clarity in the underlying rule of law is intentional in order to give public decisionmakers the degrees of freedom needed to grant special treatment and exemptions whenever politically convenient. Unfortunately for the country as a whole, the resulting unpredictability has resulted in substantial forgone current and future investments. Competition constraints, in turn, are related to the absence of a level playing field for all companies. In two of the cases examined, the failure of the relevant regulatory body to rapidly enforce a pro-competitive ruling also has sent negative signals for future investments.

As for future policy priorities, we argue that predictable and uniform implementation of existing and new legislation is of utmost importance. In the legal and judicial area, reforms should focus on removing legal ambiguities by addressing all private sector laws and their implementing regulations that are in contradiction or are not sufficiently clearly defined. In the competition area, it is in Turkey's interest to empower the Competition Board to apply competition rules to all public undertakings, aligning its competition law to Article 86 of the Treaty of Rome and its state aids system to that of the EU. Improved coordination between the Competition Board and other independent regulatory

boards should yield more rapid pro-competitive outcomes.

The EU accession process itself should provide Turkey with significant benefits in the way of FDI inflows by helping to ease further the rule of law and competition constraints. The expected EU decision to begin negotiations on full membership for Turkey will be crucial to finally convincing larger numbers of foreign investors to invest in Turkey. Finally, in addition to aligning Turkey's investment climate more closely with that of the EU, Turkey also should follow a more proactive approach by implementing more specific FDI policies and by undertaking active promotion.

Annex: Functions of an Investment Promotion Agency

The groupings of the different functions of an IPA can differ for developed and developing countries or from one country to another. The four-part grouping proposed by Wells and Wint (2001) and used for the studies carried out for the Turkish IPA is described in this annex.

Image building is the function of creating the perception of a country that is an attractive site for international investment. Activities commonly associated with image building include focused advertising, public relations events, and the generation of favorable news stories by cultivating journalists.

Investor servicing and facilitation refer to the range of services provided in a host country that can help an investor to analyze investment decisions, establish a business, and maintain it in good standing. Activities in this area include the provision of information, one-stop shopping services aimed at expediting approval processes, and various forms of assistance in obtaining access to sites and utilities.

Generating investment entails targeting specific sectors and companies with a view toward creating investment leads. Activities include identifying potential sectors and investors and undertaking direct mailings, telephone campaigns, investor forums and seminars, and individual presentations to targeted investors. These activities can be carried out both at home and overseas.

Policy advocacy consists of the activities through which the agency supports initiatives to improve the quality of the investment climate and identifies the views of the private sector on each relevant topic. Activities include surveys of the private sector, participation in task forces, policy and legal proposals, and lobbying.

The emphasis of the IPA facility depends on the purpose of the FDI policy; how much promotion is needed depends on the kind of FDI to be attracted and the basic attractions of the host country. A large and dynamic economy promotes itself less than a small one. The bulk of the massive inflows of FDI to China were not the result of active FDI promotion. And promotion can only go so far. If the economic base is weak and unstable, no amount of persuasion can attract large and sustained FDI flows (UNCTAD 2003).

Of the main investment promotion functions that all countries consider, image building and investor servicing and facilitation are typically the ones best left entirely to the separate public-private IPA.

Notes

1. All dollar amounts are U.S. dollars unless otherwise indicated.

2. This analysis is based on plant-level data collected by the Turkish State Institute of Statistics (SIS) through annual manufacturing surveys. However, the data have limitations. They cover only a small portion of the FDI companies active in the Turkish economy, and so reflect only a subset of manufacturing-related FDI. Although the records of the Undersecretariat of the Treasury indicate that 581 FDI companies were active in the Turkish manufacturing sector in 1991, increasing to 922 by 1996, the SIS manufacturing survey includes only 210 plants, increasing to 273 plants by 1996, as partially or fully owned by foreigners.

3. Variables used to control for other characteristics that could affect productivity include firm size as measured by employment, imported license use, percent share of output exported, imported machinery and equipment use, whether the firm is incorporated, subcontracted input use and subcontracted output sale, measures of agglomeration at the provincial level, and share of skilled production workers.

4. For a detailed description of this trend worldwide, see UNCTAD (2000).

5. For this definition, see Stern (2002).

6. Many of these measures are based on surveys, which in this context are arguably the most appropriate measures, because they reflect the perceptions of actual investors. In 2002, 3,532 executives responded to the World Competitiveness survey, which gauges widespread business knowledge about each country and cross-country international experience.

7. Other producers were, however, active in the domestic market. The four listed had the largest market presence in the automotive industry at the time.

8. Of these four, Honda and Toyota became the sole owners of their production units once they decided to direct their production toward the European rather than the domestic market. This situation is an example of the difficulty that foreign

investors face in entering the domestic market without an insider on board. This argument is strengthened by the fact that the other two multinational corporations (MNCs) retained their local partners, because they continued to target the local market. Anadolu Isuzu focuses on light trucks and midibuses and mainly targets the local market. Hyundai Assan also sells half of its production to the local market.

9. It is known that as part of the final communications prior to the bid, İş-TIM received a verbal promise from the Ministry of Tranport about roaming privileges.

10. Among the 44 countries included in the World Values Survey of 1989–90, Turkey ranks the lowest, with less than 10 percent of its population believing that most fellow human beings are trustworthy. See Kalaycıoğlu (2001).

11. The customs union agreement does not send as strong a signal to investors as the prospects of full EU membership, because it entails only market integration, without ensuring the deeper political, social, and legal transformations that would bring greater comfort to investors.

12. The key functions of a well-designed IPA are summarized in the annex to this chapter.

References

Arol, Ali Ihsan. 2002. "Current Status of FDI and Environmental Issues in Mining in Turkey." Paper presented at the OECD Global Forum on FDI and the Environment, February.

Blomström, Magnus, and Ari Kokko. 1998. "Multinational Corporations and Spillovers." *Journal of Economic Surveys* 12 (2): 1–31.

Borensztein, Eduardo, Jose De Gregorio, and Jong-Wha Lee. 1998. "How Does Foreign Direct Investment Affect Economic Growth?" *Journal of International Economics* 45:115–35.

Ekdi, Barış, Ebru Öztürk, H. Hüseyin Ünlü, Kürşat Ünlüsoy, and Serpil Çınaroğlu. 2002. "Rekabet Kuralları İle Uyumlu Olmayan Mevzuat Listesi" [A List of Regulations Contradicting the Rules of Competition]. *Rekabet Dergisi* [The Competition Journal] 9 (March).

European Commission. 2002. "Regular Report on Turkey's Accession." COM 2002, 700 final, Brussels.

———. 2003. "Council Decision on Accession Partnership with Turkey." COM 2003, Brussels.

FIAS (Foreign Investment Advisory Service). 2001. *Turkey: A Diagnostic Study of the FDI Environment.* Washington, DC: FIAS, February.

Gruben, William C., and Darryl McLeod. 1998. "Capital Flows, Savings, and Growth in the 1990s." *Quarterly Review of Economics and Finance* 38 (fall).

IMD (Institute of Management Development). 2002. *World Competitiveness Yearbook 2002.* Geneva: IMD.

Kalaycıoğlu, Ersin. 2001. "Turkish Democracy: Patronage versus Governance." *Turkish Studies* 2 (spring): 54–70.

Morisset, Jacques. 2003. "Does a Country Need a Promotion Agency to Attract Foreign Direct Investment?" Policy Research Working Paper 3028, World Bank, Washington, D.C., April.

OECD (Organisation for Economic Co-operation and Development). 1996. *OECD Benchmark Definition of FDI*, 3d ed. Paris: OECD.

———. 2003 *Foreign Direct Investment Statistics: How Countries Measure FDI.* Paris: OECD.

Özatay, Fatih, and Guven Sak. 2002. "The 2000–2001 Financial Crisis in Turkey." Central Bank of the Republic of Turkey and Ankara University.

Stern, Nicholas. 2002. "Dynamic Development: Innovation and Inclusion." Munich Lectures in Economics, Ludwig Maximilian University, Munich, November 19.

UNCTAD (United Nations Conference on Trade and Development). 2000. *World Investment Report: Cross-Border Mergers and Acquisitions and Development.* New York: United Nations.

————. 2003. *World Investment Report: FDI Policies for Development: National and International Perspectives.* New York: United Nations.

————. *World Investment Directory: Country Profiles.* Accessible at www.unctad.org.

Wells, Louis T., Jr., and Alvin G. Wint. 2001. "Marketing a Country: Promotion as a Tool for Attracting Foreign Investment." Occasional Paper 13, Foreign Investment Advisory Service (FIAS), Washington, D.C.

Yılmaz, Kamil, and S¸ule Özler. 2004. "Foreign Direct Investment and Productivity Spillovers: Identifying Linkages through Product-based Measures." Koç University, Istanbul, Mimeograph.

Yılmaz, Kamil, Cevdet Akçay, and Emre Alper. 2002. *Enflasyon ve Büyüme Dinamikleri: Gelişmekte Olan Ülke Deneyimleri Işığında Türkiye Analizi [Inflation and Growth Dynamics: An Analysis of Turkey in the Light of Developing Country Experiences].* TUSIAD (Turkish Industrialists' and Businessmen's Association) Publication (December).

Zhang, Kevin H. 1999. "FDI and Economic Growth: Evidence from 10 East Asian Economies." *Economia Internationale* (November).

11

TURKEY ON THE PATH TO EU ACCESSION: THE ENVIRONMENTAL *ACQUIS*

Anil Markandya

In December 1999, the European Council confirmed that Turkey is a candidate state destined to join the European Union (EU) on the basis of the same criteria applied to the other candidate states.[1] A precondition of membership is that candidate countries must align their national laws, rules, and procedures, including those relevant to the environmental sector, with those of the EU in order to give effect to the entire body of law contained in the *acquis communautaire*. In October 2004, the European Commission recommended opening accession talks with Turkey, which gives even more impetus to the alignment process.

This process, also known as the approximation process, requires that (1) all relevant EU requirements be transposed into legal legislation (legal transposition), (2) the appropriate institutional structures with sufficient budgets be established in order to administer the national legislation (practical implementation), and (3) the necessary controls and penalties be put in place to ensure full compliance with the laws (enforcement). Most of these steps have to be undertaken prior to membership in the EU. At the same time, public and private sector entities in Turkey will have to undertake a significant investment program to meet the EU requirements for environmental protection and provision of environmental services. This program typically begins in earnest about three to four years prior to membership, and continues for up to 15 years. Thus, the period of investment to meet the required standards is long, and the fiscal implications of accession depend significantly on the terms of derogation. The fiscal impacts are also sensitive to which parties undertake the investments—the greater the share that can be borne by the private sector, the less the fiscal burden—and to how much funding can be obtained from EU sources.

This chapter looks at the likely costs to Turkey of meeting the environmental *acquis,* with special focus on the costs to the public sector. Fortunately, considerable data are available from the latest group of accession countries, and particularly from large ones such as Poland, which has already met part of the EU's environmental requirements and has prepared detailed plans to 2017 for the rest. These countries' experiences also are good guides to approximating how much support can be obtained from EU funds.

The chapter is structured as follows. The first section reviews the estimates from previous studies of the costs of EU membership for Turkey and other countries, and on this basis some "best guess" estimates of meeting the environmental *acquis* are derived for Turkey. An important factor in making such estimates is that these costs depend on the policies pursued, and the breakdown of the costs between the public and private sectors depends on the extent to which key water and energy services are provided by the private sector.

The second and third sections discuss how the total costs of compliance with the environmental *acquis* can be kept to a minimum and how the burden on the state and local budgets can be reduced.

The fourth section gives a more detailed breakdown of costs based on three scenarios: (1) a base case in which no special reforms are made and the public sector remains much as it is today; (2) a medium reform case in which the private sector's share of the costs of compliance with the *acquis* is increased modestly and in which reforms in pricing reduce the demand for some of the cleanup services; and (3) a high reform, or fast reform, case in which the private sector's role is somewhat greater, and in which the reforms discussed in the first section are implemented more vigorously.

The fifth section compares the cost estimates with some benefit estimates—that is, the possible gains from implementation of the environmental directives in terms of, among other things, reduced health problems, increased recreational use of the natural environment, and less damage to ecosystems. This comparison will reveal where the case for spending is strongest and where a case can be made for delaying the investments on the grounds that the benefits are considerably less than the costs.

The sixth section presents a more detailed, short-term assessment of the three scenarios presented earlier, as well as a time profile of investments by sector that covers the first six years of the program. As noted, the first three to four years of the program to comply with the environmental *acquis* are typically implemented prior to membership. These investment needs are compared with current environmental spending and with the current budgetary resources available. The final section looks at what mechanisms can be developed to mobilize more public sector financing for the environment.

Estimated Costs of the Environmental *Acquis:* Turkey and Other Accession Countries

Estimates of the capital costs of the environmental *acquis* have been made in the following studies:

- Those undertaken as part of the first assessment of the costs for 10 potential candidate countries[2] (Ifo Institute 1994; EDC 1997).

- Further detailed studies undertaken by the 10 countries that joined the EU in 2004. Of these, the estimates for Poland are given in table 11.1.
- Estimates for Turkey undertaken by Carl Bro International as part of the EU-MEDA (Euro-Mediterranean Partnership) funded initiative (Carl Bro International 2002).[3]

The data from these disparate sources are summarized in table 11.1, presented as costs per capita. The following observations are worth noting:

- The range of estimates in the earlier studies (EDC 1997) was quite wide in per capita terms. The highest estimates were five to 10 times higher than the lowest estimates. This situation arises in part from the fact that national programs to comply with the *acquis* have a "fixed-cost" element, so smaller countries tend to have higher costs, and in part from the fact that countries have different gaps to fill in meeting the directives. The average per capita cost is about €1,260, but the range is from €580 to €3,600.
- The estimates from more recent studies are not notably lower than the earlier estimates. For example, the estimate for Poland in the study noted earlier was €988, while the estimate in the national calculations of costs was about €1,170. Part of the reason for the increase is the addition of the Integrated Pollution Prevention and Control (IPPC), nitrate, and other directives, which were not covered in the first round of studies. After these are removed, the estimate for Poland in the national study is €878 versus €988, or a reduction of about 11 percent.
- For Turkey, the figures in the Carl Bro study were considerably lower. This difference reflects in part the different situation in Turkey with respect to some directives. For example, the water supply directive will cost less in Turkey, because it mandates only an increase in quality for those who are already connected to a piped water system; it does not require an increase in connections. Because in Turkey only 35 percent of the population is connected to piped water, the per capita costs of meeting the directive across the whole population are lower. The Carl Bro study did not cover all directives, however. The notes to table 11.1 indicate which directives were not covered by the Carl Bro study. In those

TABLE 11.1 Comparison of Environmental Costs of EU Accession for Turkey and Other Candidate Countries
(euros per capita in 2001 prices)

	Turkey, State Mid-value	Turkey, Nonstate	Turkey, Total Low	Turkey, Total Mid-value	Turkey, Total High	Poland, Mid-value	CEEC10	Range Minimum	Range Maximum
Water supply[a]	12.0	0	9.0	12.0	15.0	41.5	187.4	32.7	385.2
Wastewater[b]	212.1	0	159.1	212.1	265.2	217.1	354.9	117.6	1085.0
Air[c]	83.9	49.4	100.0	133.3	166.6	294.0	508.1	297.2	1240.1
Waste[d]	25.1	74.4	74.6	99.4	124.3	325.4	210.1	132.7	854.9
IPPC[e]	5.8	47.3	39.8	53.1	66.4	184.7	—	—	—
Nitrates[f]	44.1	16.3	45.3	60.5	103.4	103.4	—	—	—
Other[g]	5.1	0.9	4.5	6.0	7.5	7.7	—	—	—
Total	576.4		432.3	576.4	748.2	1173.8	1260.6	580.1	3565.3

— Not available.

Note: Low and high values for Turkey are, respectively, 25 percent lower and 25 percent higher than the mid-values.

a. Water supply estimate is based on Carl Bro study for Turkey. It is lower in per capita terms than those of other countries because only 35 percent of the population is connected to the water supply.

b. Wastewater estimate is based on Carl Bro study for Turkey. Directive 76/464 is excluded. Estimate is taken from data on Poland.

c. Carl Bro estimate is taken for electricity large combustion plants (LCPs). Not included are other LCPs, directive 98/70 on quality of petrol, directive 99/32 on sulfur content of liquid fuels, directive 94/63 on volatile organic compounds (VOCs) from gas stations, and directive 94/67. Estimates for directives not included are minimum estimates from studies of Poland.

d. Caro Bro estimates are not specifically based on assessment of directives but on an earlier World Bank/METAP (Mediterranean Environmental Technical Assistance Program) study that was undertaken in the context of EU directives. Directives 96/59 on PCBs, 94/62 on packaging waste, and 75/439 on oil waste disposal are excluded. Estimates for these are taken from Poland and the Baltic states. Estimate is likely to be at lower end.

e. Carl Bro looked at only a limited number of public enterprises. Most of the expenditure will be in the private sector. Private sector estimates are based on data on Poland.

f. Because no nitrate estimates are available for Turkey, detailed estimates for Poland are used.

g. "Other" includes Directives 97/403 (nuclear safety) and 2000/53 (end of life vehicles).

Sources: Various—see text.

instances, the estimates were based on previous studies (mainly Poland, because that study had the best and most comprehensive data).

- Based on the data from the Carl Bro study, the cost of the environmental directives for Turkey is between €432 and €748 per capita for the 2000 population of 65.3 million. The range is based on a middle value calculated from the estimates provided, a lower value that is 25 percent lower, and a higher value that is 25 percent higher. This range represents the extent to which costs can be reduced, depending on adoption of the appropriate policies, or raised in the absence of a shift to more efficient delivery systems for environmental services. It is based on previous studies that have looked at the scope for reducing costs. Note that the lower end of the cost range is from the studies for the 11 Central and Eastern European (CEE) countries.

What do these per capita figures imply for total costs? The total amount is between €28 billion and €49 billion—an enormous sum. But the outlay is over some 17 years, so the annual amount is more manageable. As noted later in this chapter, annual investments amount to about €2 billion to €3 billion for the high reform, or fast reform, case (i.e., low-cost case) and €3 billion to €5 billion for the base case entailing slow reform (i.e., high-cost case). In the initial years, these investments would amount to 1–1.5 percent of GDP in the low-cost case and 1.5–2.5 percent in the high-cost case. In addition, extra annual operating costs would be incurred, which are difficult to estimate for the early years but would eventually be on the order of €80 billion to €120 billion per capita or €5 billion to €8 billion. To put these figures in perspective, the Organisation for Economic Co-operation and Development (OECD) estimated Turkey's capital spending on the environment in 1999 to be about $US1 billion, or 0.5 percent of its GDP.[4] At the very least, this spending would have to double, or more likely increase by a factor of three or four once the EU accession program was initiated. In addition, a much higher level of current spending would be required.

How to Reduce the Total Investment Costs

The total cost figure is useful only to get some idea of the overall size of the task. What is more important for Turkey is to prepare detailed plans, covering periods of three to six years, that ensure compliance with the agreements arrived at under the environmental chapter and to do so in a way that minimizes the costs and ensures that the underlying financing arrangements are sustainable. Indeed, although the *acquis communautaire* is prescriptive on environmental standards, it leaves considerable latitude on how to meet them. The price of complying varies accordingly.

Savings in investment costs can be achieved in several ways[5]:

- By following a least-cost investment plan, especially in energy-related investments. This plan can, in turn, be promoted by the use of economic instruments such as bubbles and permit trading.
- By increasing the efficiency with which municipalities make investment decisions. Opening up procurement to international tender and undertaking careful project appraisal in evaluating the design of schemes will reduce costs significantly.
- By designing investments to take account of the lower demand for some services when future service charges will have to recover capital and operating costs. The World Bank has had stark experience with such lower demand in the wastewater projects it has funded in the Baltic states. The level of capacity is turning out to be substantially in excess of demand as a result of the large increase in volume-based charges (see box 11.1).
- By allowing for the fact that new investments are likely to reduce *total* operating costs, because the operation and maintenance costs of new equipment will be lower than those of the equipment it replaces. This gain has not been fully accounted for in the current cost figures presented earlier.
- By taking into account that the present value of total costs will fall if the more expensive items are scheduled later in time. This approach would be all the more justifiable when the ensuing benefits are comparatively low.
- By accounting for the fact that environmental mitigation costs may not expand at the same pace as income. With growth and convergence, countries should therefore be better able to meet the *acquis*. The demand for services such as energy and transport and the related costs are likely to rise in tandem, but the demand for

---

BOX 11.1   The Experience of the World Bank with Water Utilities in the Baltic States

The World Bank has provided financing for five water and wastewater projects in the Baltics: one in Estonia, two in Latvia, and two in Lithuania, at a total cost of US$134 million. The upgraded plants are now in operation. The wastewater plants meet Helsinki Commission standards (HELCOM protects the Baltic marine environment as mandated under the Helsinki Convention), and the drinking water plant also meets the highest standards. Although the projects have met many criteria, one of the most serious problems has been the drop in demand for water and in the generation of wastewater. The projects were planned under the assumption that demand would stabilize at a moderate level of consumption similar to that in other comparable countries. Yet such consumption has not materialized, and the actual level has been as much as 50 percent lower than anticipated. This extreme decline in demand has led to:

- Overdimensioning of systems (i.e., making them larger than required)
- Overinvestment in systems
- Higher than optional operations and maintenance costs

- Water quality problems in potable water networks.

The central lesson learned is that, while drafting financial and economic forecasts, the project teams should be conservative in their assumptions of the critical variables that have the greatest impact on revenues and costs. These forecasts tend to be too optimistic, and in the long run the projects are likely to experience lower than anticipated economic and financial rates of return. Project appraisal should ensure that the assumptions are realistic and that contingency plans are drawn for coping with deviations from the most likely outcomes. The range of possible outcomes, with their respective probabilities, although subjective, should be listed in the appraisal document.

Price escalations also tend to be greater than expected (in real terms) because of the elimination of existing market distortions and price disequilibria that were present in the economies during the early transition process. This situation is another important reason for the dramatic reduction in water sales. Tariffs have had to increase more than anticipated.

---

services such as water may not increase proportionately. The resulting increase in total costs may therefore be substantially less than the growth in national income.

- By relaxing statutory standards (particularly for water treatment), if it can be shown (1) that the investment is seriously uneconomical (e.g., if the community served will decline dramatically in the next few years) and (2) that the savings in costs that can be achieved by reducing the attainment level by a small percentage will allow more plants to be built, thereby making a higher overall contribution to meeting the ambient environmental goals.[6]

Reducing the Share of Costs Borne by the Public Sector

Although some CEE countries have now concluded the environmental chapter of the negotiations, it is fair to say that they have not fully established how these investments will be funded. Indeed, the frontline CEE countries have ongoing concerns about the availability of co-financing from the national

budget to match the EU accession funds available under the Pre-Accession Structural Instrument (ISPA), PHARE, and the Special Accession Programme for Agriculture and Rural Development (SAPARD). Indeed, the slow rate of development of projects for such funding can be partly attributed to this factor (as well as to the lack of administrative capacity to implement the *acquis*).

The problem that many countries are having in meeting the local cost share of investments is unlikely to be solved merely by increasing the allocation from the public budget for the environment. Other solutions also must be found.

The scope for moving some items out of the public budget is quite large.[7] As for investment in the manufacturing sector, the more of the sector that is privatized, the less will be the burden of the *acquis* on the public budget. Experience has shown that successful privatization of some of the larger and more polluting industries requires a clear understanding of the liability for past environmental damages through an internationally acceptable audit, accompanied by a legal agreement with the government on the new owner's responsibility for cleanup. If internationally credible investors are to be attracted to bidding for such enterprises, these issues have to be addressed. Furthermore, the state's responsibilities have to be backed by a credible program of investment in remediation. Otherwise, the uncertainty of the private party will result in a failure to bid, or in an offer that reflects the increased risk. This situation illustrates one in which it may pay for the state to undertake investment in remediation with a view toward making the privatization effort more successful and generating higher revenues from the sale of state assets.

The same is true to a large extent of public utilities and infrastructure. A Czech study has shown that as much as half of the big-ticket items could be shifted out of the public budget under certain assumptions (World Bank 1999). To date, however, the detailed national plans for adoption of the *acquis* have paid limited attention to the role of the private sector, and there has been mixed progress on the ground. Hungary has transferred all power generation to the private sector, Poland has moved 9 of its 27 generation stations into private hands, and other countries have moved none.[8]

Privatization is not, however, the only way of sharing the burden of upgrading environmental standards. Another is to commercialize the enterprises even when they are nominally state-owned and to raise the financing for the investment through commercial loans. This strategy is being followed widely in many of the candidate countries. It was successfully adopted, for example, by Poland in the power generation sector. When Poland privatized nine generation stations, the financing for investing in pollution control equipment came from commercial loans, backed by power purchasing agreements between the commercialized generating units and the state electricity authority. The same strategy has been adopted in municipalities dealing with water supply and wastewater in various countries, including the Baltic states. Although it is successful in taking the direct investment cost off the budget, this approach suffers from the problem that the borrowing is invariably guaranteed by the government and therefore forms part of the consolidated national debt. There is also the issue in such cases of subsidies to these enterprises, through working capital and loans from state-owned banks, being given at below commercial rates. To the extent that these

practices prevail (and they are still quite common), the institutional mechanism of commercialization for taking environmental costs off budget will still leave some budgetary burden.

The commercialization of utilities has, however, opened the door to their raising charges for their services to a level that at least recovers the costs of the new investments. The higher charges will result in reduced levels of demand, thus saving the budget the cost of the subsidies the utilities receive for ongoing operations. The same increase in charges will also reduce the size of the investment needed (box 11.1).[9] Another way in which commercialization can save costs is through a rationalization of provision, because many utilities are currently too small to make cost-effective investments or manage operations in an efficient manner.

Breakdown of the Share of Investments by Sector in Turkey

Based on the discussion in the two previous sections, table 11.2 offers a more detailed description of the three scenarios—base case, medium reform, and high reform. The changes in parameter values in the table are only rough estimates, based on judgments about the scope for reform and the potential impacts it would have. Nevertheless, they offer a useful guide to what can be expected if the reforms are made as indicated. The resulting costs for the state and nonstate sectors are shown in table 11.3, which shows state expenditures ranging from €32 billion in the base case to €15 billion in the high reform case, a fall of 52 percent. Of this fall, 42 percent can be attributed to cost savings in general from the reforms and 10 percent to the increased share of the private sector in providing the environmental services. The biggest shift arises for the water supply and wastewater sector, followed by the waste sector. In the base case, the share of state expenditures is 65 percent, and in the high reform case it is 54 percent. In the medium reform case, it is 59 percent.

Comparing the Costs and Benefits of the Environmental Directives

In comparing the costs and benefits of the environmental directives, one can, fortunately, rely on a study undertaken by the European Commission, which made initial estimates of these benefits (ECD 1997).

TABLE 11.2   Scenarios for Implementation of Environmental Investments for the *Acquis*

Policy	Scenario		
	Base Case	Medium Reform	High Reform
Pricing of utilities' services	Slow progress toward cost recovery in water and waste sectors.	Moderate progress toward full-cost recovery and some volume-based pricing.	Rapid progress to full-cost recovery and volume-based pricing.
Use of market-based instruments	Existing charges on effluent continue and new charges on carbon; some products introduced slowly at low rates.	Existing charge levels raised and new charges introduced more rapidly at higher rates.	Existing and new instruments introduced rapidly, with rates that have incentive effects.
Private sector participation in water sector	Virtually no participation of private sector in delivery of services.	Moderate participation, with investment going up to 10% of total.	Substantial participation, with investment going up to 20% of total.
Private sector in waste management	Virtually no participation of private sector in delivery of services.	Moderate participation, with investment going up to 20% of total; some recycling programs effective.	Substantial participation, with investment going up to 30% of total and significant recycling programs.
Reforms in energy sector	Current ownership of energy sector enterprises implies about 37% of all expenditures will be in the nonstate sector; all large plant combustion (LPC) investments in public sector.	Private sector takes over up to 20% of plants needing to respond to LPC; reforms introduce more renewable sources and increase efficiency.	Private sector takes over up to 30% of plants needing to respond to LPC; reforms introduce more renewable sources and increase efficiency faster.
Reforms in industrial sectors	Current estimate is based on 90% of expenditures being undertaken by private sector.	In both of these cases, the share of private sector investment under the Integrated Pollution Prevention and Control (IPPC) goes up to 95%.	

Source: The author.

The study explored the benefits of compliance in three steps:

- *Type of benefits.* What types of benefits arise from implementing the *acquis,* and what are some examples of these benefits in the candidate countries—for example, health impacts or impacts on agriculture, buildings (*also known as "qualitative benefits")?*
- *Extent of benefits.* What is the extent of the benefits—that is, how much are emissions reduced and how many cases of respiratory diseases are avoided (*also known as "quantitative benefits")?*
- *Value of benefits.* What is the economic value of the avoided costs—for example, how much would the reduced emissions and damages avoided by implementing EU directives be worth (*also known as "monetarized benefits" and given in millions of euros)?*

The types of benefits included in the study are summarized in table 11.4.[10] The monetary value of the benefits was estimated using a large body of

TABLE 11.3 Environmental Accession Costs for Turkey
(millions of euros, in 2001 prices)

	State	Nonstate	Total
Base case			
Water supply	976	0	976
Wastewater	17,315	0	17,315
Air	6,848	4,031	10,879
Waste	2,046	6,071	8,117
IPPC	474	3,860	4,334
Nitrates	3,603	1,333	6,749
Other	420	70	490
Total	31,682	15,365	48,860
Medium reform			
Water supply	703	78	781
Wastewater	12,467	1,385	13,852
Air	4,382	4,320	8,703
Waste	1,309	5,184	6,493
IPPC	270	3,197	3,467
Nitrates	2,882	1,066	3,948
Other	336	56	392
Total	22,350	15,287	37,637
High reform			
Water supply	469	117	586
Wastewater	8,311	2,078	10,389
Air	2,876	3,651	6,527
Waste	859	4,011	4,870
IPPC	205	2,395	2,600
Nitrates	2,162	800	2,961
Other	252	42	294
Total	15,134	13,094	28,228

Sources: Author's calculations.

**TABLE 11.4 Types of Benefits of Compliance with Directives, Estimated
for Candidate Countries**

Type of Benefit	Air	Drinking Water	Wastewater	Solid Waste
Health benefits	Avoided respiratory illnesses and premature deaths	Household access to cleaner drinking water	Reduced risk of poisoning and accidents due to methane leakage from landfills	None assessed
Resource benefits	Avoided damage to buildings and crops	Cleaner bathing water and cleaner water for companies	Reduced input of primary material	None assessed
Ecosystems	Avoided global warming from CO_2 emissions	Improved river water quality	Avoided global warming from methane emissions	Protected areas and species

Source: ECOTEC and others 2001.

**TABLE 11.5   Estimated Benefits for Turkey from Compliance
with Environmental Directives**
(millions of 2001 euros)

Directives Relating to	Present Value of Costs	Present Value of Benefits
Water supply	586–976	1,500–26,050
Wastewater	10,400–17,300	7,140
Air	6,500–10,900	> 21,000
Waste	4,900–8,100	800–18,000

Source: ECOTEC and others 2001 and this study. Both benefits and costs are
discounted at 4 percent in real terms.

past and ongoing research on economic valuation. The results of the estimation for Turkey are given in table 11.5, where the benefits are compared with the cost figures in table 11.3. The exercise is only possible for a few areas: air, drinking water, wastewater, and solid waste.

Although the data on benefits are subject to considerable uncertainties, table 11.5 nevertheless reveals some useful findings. First, investments in water supply and reductions in air pollution are amply justified in terms of benefits, even taking the upper end of the costs and the lower end of the benefits. Second, investments in wastewater are not justifiable *given the measurable benefits.* This does not mean that all individual projects for building wastewater treatment have negative net benefits; some almost certainly will be of high priority. But it does mean that *as a program,* with a time profile for investments more or less like the one in the 2004 candidate countries, the net benefits are likely to be negative. Because these results are based on European Commission–supported data, they should prove useful in arguing for derogation for a large part of the wastewater treatment directives. Third, for solid waste the question of whether benefits exceed costs is unresolved; it depends on where the benefits lie in the range that has upper values 20 times the lower values.[11]

The Medium Reform Scenario for EU Accession for Turkey

Those countries that have closed the environmental chapter have committed themselves to complying with the *acquis* by the agreed-on dates. The highest priority in all cases is being given to legal approximation, ensuring that the national legal framework is consistent with the EU legislation. Next in priority is the institutional strengthening of supervisory bodies and environmental agencies. All this is expected to be completed before accession. The investment program necessary for compliance for those joining in 2004 has a completion date of 2015, with interim targets for key directives. For example, Lithuania must comply with the directive on the sulfur content of petrol and diesel by 2005, the large urban wastewater directive by 2010, and so on (Republic of Lithuania 2001). The Baltic states, Poland, and the other 2004 accession candidates commended their investment programs in 1999/2000 (see World Bank 2002, 2003).

Taking the cue from these countries, Turkey would have to start its program in earnest three to four years before entry and negotiate the derogation of the items that have a high cost but that generate have relatively modest benefits, following the analysis presented in the previous section.

The time profile that the present accession countries have negotiated indicates the costs of accession in the first six years of the program. Table 11.6 was derived from this profile (giving the share of total costs in the first six years and the share of the six-year total by year) and from the total estimated costs for Turkey. The table also includes estimates of the external funding agreed to for this period. It is reported separately and is assumed to reduce the part of state expenditure that has to be financed from domestic sources.

The table reveals an important point, that funds such as ISPA and SAPARD will provide only between 25 percent and 30 percent of the "state" spending— that is, the "state from domestic" plus the "state from

TABLE 11.6   Costs of Accession for Turkey in First Six Years
(millions of 2001 euros)

	Year 1	Year 2	Year 3	Year 4	Year 5	Year 6	Total
Base case							
State	1,253	1,636	2,422	2,546	2,703	2,773	13,334
Domestic nonstate	1,215	1,317	1,560	1,656	1,728	1,712	9,187
External	474	617	822	853	910	938	4,613
Total	2,942	3,571	4,804	5,054	5,340	5,423	27,134
Medium reform							
State	807	1,055	1,561	1,641	1,742	1,787	8,593
Domestic nonstate	1,148	1,245	1,474	1,565	1,633	1,618	8,683
External	332	433	576	598	638	658	3,235
Total	2,288	2,732	3,611	3,804	4,013	4,063	20,511
High reform							
State	560	731	1,082	1,138	1,208	1,239	5,958
Domestic nonstate	962	1,043	1,235	1,311	1,368	1,355	7,275
External	221	288	383	397	424	437	2,150
Total	1,743	2,062	2,700	2,846	3,000	3,032	15,383

Source: Author's calculations.

external." Thus the domestic state sources will have to undertake a significant expenditure; in table 11.6 this expenditure increases from €1.2 billion in year 1 to €2.8 billion in year 6 under the base case and €0.6 billion in year 1 to €1.2 billion in year 6 under the high reform case.

The differences between the base case and the other cases depend on how much of the reform actions can be undertaken prior to the actual start of the formal program. Without prejudging the date of accession for Turkey, it is possible to say that a rapid program of reform over the next five years would place it in a position in which the estimated state expenditures in table 11.6 could be considered realistic. If, however, reforms do not take place prior to the accession period, which starts three to four years before the date of accession, then the estimates under the reform scenarios will be too low.

How do these estimates of environmental spending compare with current spending on the environment? Unfortunately, data are available only for the period 1997–99 and then, except for 1997, not for all the categories—see table 11.7. The table shows that

- Spending by government organizations was about €480 million in 1997, of which three-quarters was for investment. By 1999 the total had fallen to €420 million, of which only 55 percent

was for investment. Total spending was about 1 percent of government expenditure in 1997, but it had fallen to 0.6 percent in 1999.

- Spending by municipalities amounted to €1,200 million in 1997 and €1,500 million in 1998. Of this, about 30–34 percent was for investment.

- Manufacturing sector environmental investments (available only for 1997) were only €52 million.

- Investment by thermal power plants amounted to €294 million in 1997, €61 million in 1998, and €104 million in 1999.

- The total investment in all sectors amounted to €2.2 billion or 1.4 percent of GDP.

If municipalities and thermal power plants are included as part of public sector spending, the total amount of investment by the state sector amounted to about €1 billion in 1997 and in 1998. The comparison in table 11.6 of this figure with the required investment by the state sector reveals that, in fact, the amounts needed in state investments are not very different from the actual levels in 1997–98. State investment, after accounting for EU funds, ranges from €0.6 billion to €1.3 billion in year 1, but rises sharply in the next six years (table 11.6).

Although this comparison does not establish firmly that the actual investments in the environment were of the right amount to meet the first year

TABLE 11.7 Environmental Expenditures in Turkey, 1997–99

	1997	1998 (TL billions)	1999	1997	1998 (€ millions)	1999
Government organizations						
Current	20,898	35,941	85,401	121.3	123.1	191.2
Investment	62,602	115,342	105,989	363.5	395.0	237.2
As % of budget	1.0%	0.9%	0.6%	1.0%	0.9%	0.6%
Municipalities						
Current	147,576	287,864	—	856.9	985.8	—
Investment	62,542	148,269	—	363.1	507.8	—
Manufacturing						
Current	11,499	—	—	66.8	—	—
Investment	8,871	—	—	51.5	—	—
Thermal power plants						
Current	26,913	4,455	—	156.3	15.3	—
Investment	50,605	17,747	46,502	293.8	60.8	104.1
Total						
Current	206,886	—	—	1201.2	—	—
Investment	184,620	—	—	1071.9	—	—
As % of GDP	1.4%	—	—	1.4%	—	—

— Not available.

Note: Data for 1998 are not confirmed.

Sources: Turkish State Institute of Statistics and International Monetary Fund.

TABLE 11. 8 Estimated Annual Spending on Monitoring and Enforcement, Turkey

Directive	Expenses of Regulator (€ millions)	Comments
Integrated Pollution Prevention and Control IPPC	2.2	Recoverable from industry on a purchasing power parity (PPP) basis
Air quality	19.6	Monitoring in 287 towns with more than 25,000 inhabitants
Water quality	14.2	26 teams in each of 26 water basins
Nitrates	2.2	4 teams, one for each affected catchment
Conservation of habitats	0.9	Monitoring of habitats of wild birds and protection of animals used in experiments
Total	39.1	

Source: Carl Bro International 2001.

of the EU accession investment program (the coverage and priorities may not have been the same), it does suggest that *if state investment spending could be maintained at 1997–98 levels and if the external funds are forthcoming, the amount will at least be enough to start the accession program. The big gap appears to be in private sector spending, which is very much below what would be required.* Table 11.6 gives a figure of €1 billion to €1.2 billion for the first year, whereas actual spending for the one year for which data are available (1997) was €52 million.

Finally, an allowance also must be made for an increase in the budgets needed for monitoring and compliance enforcement. Table 11.8 provides the figures estimated by Carl Bro International for this purpose, which amount to about €39 million a year. This figure does not include an increase in the analytical and management capacity of the Ministry of Environment, which has not been estimated but requires an increase in the ministerial staff of about 20 percent.

Conclusions

This chapter has looked at the environmental dimension of EU accession for Turkey. As a country now in accession talks with the EU, Turkey has actively begun to prepare for the approximation process, and the environmental component is a major part of the process. The time period required for most of the approximation process is about three to four years before accession and 15 years after accession. Based on estimates of the investment costs of accession made for other candidate countries and (partly) for Turkey, the total cost comes out between €28 billion and €49 billion. This range looks frightening, but, spread over 18–19 years, it amounts annually to 1–2.5 percent of GDP for Turkey. This amount is more than the country has been investing in the environmental sector, which is about 0.5 percent of GDP. The investment must come from various sources: the state, municipalities, state enterprises, and the private sector. The analysis shows that, whereas the first three (which are consolidated into the state sector) have current investment at a level similar to that required by the approximation, private sector spending is woefully short. *This situation implies that the appropriate regulations will have to be put in place to ensure compliance by the private sector in accordance with the agreement on investment reached with the EU.*

The costs of the environmental *acquis* are not predetermined and depend on policy choices and reforms. This chapter has identified those actions that can, first, reduce the costs and, second, shift the costs from the state sectors to the private sector. Reducing costs will require a more careful assessment of the least-cost options, better procurement in public spending, and better assessment of future demand as prices increase. The whole process of commercialization and privatization has a major role to play in shifting costs from the state sectors to the private sector. This chapter has provided three

scenarios that reflect different rates of reform and different rates of increase in the involvement of the private sector in the provision of environmental services. The resulting costs for the state sector range from €32 billion in the base case to €15 billion in the high reform case, a drop of 52 percent. This drop is made up of 42 percent from cost savings from the reforms and 10 percent from the increased share of the private sector in providing the environmental services.

The costs of accession can also be compared with its potential benefits by drawing on a major European Commission study that included Turkey. Although the data on the benefits of the water supply, wastewater, air, and solid waste directives are subject to considerable uncertainties, the results reveal the following:

- Investments in water supply and a reduction in air pollution are amply justified in terms of benefits, even taking the upper end of the costs and the lower end of the benefits.
- Investments in wastewater are not justifiable *given the measurable benefits.* This finding does not mean that all individual projects for building wastewater treatment have negative net benefits; some almost certainly will be of high priority. But it does mean that *as a program,* with a time profile for investments more or less like that in the 2004 candidate countries, the net benefits are likely to be negative. Because these results are based on European Commission–supported data, they should prove useful in arguing for derogation for a large part of the wastewater treatment directives.
- For solid waste, the issue of the program is unresolved; it depends on where the benefits lie in a range in which the upper values are 20 times the lower values.

This chapter has described a possible medium-term accession program for Turkey (i.e., covering the first six years). Based on the time profiles for investment in the candidate countries, external funds such as ISPA and SAPARD will provide only between 25 and 30 percent of the "state" spending. Thus domestic state sources will have to provide a significant amount of the expenditure, which increases from €1.2 billion in year 1 to €2.8 billion in year 6 under the base case and from €0.6 billion in year 1 to €1.2 billion in year 6 under the high reform case. There is also an urgent need to increase the budget and resources available to the Ministry of Environment if the program is to be realized. An EU study has estimated this amount to be about €39 million annually.

In summary, Turkey faces an enormous challenge in meeting the environmental *acquis*, but not one that is beyond its capabilities. By adhering to a vigorous reform program and adopting increased incentives for the private sector to make the necessary investments, it should be able to achieve the goals in much the same way as the other candidate countries—by a combination of good management, good luck, and a little help from its friends.

Notes

1. The views in this paper are those of the author and do not necessarily reflect the official position of the World Bank.

2. The countries are Bulgaria, the Czech Republic, Hungary, Poland, Romania, the Slovak Republic, Slovenia, Estonia, Latvia, and Lithuania.

3. The estimates by Carl Bro International are undiscounted costs over the period of up to 18 years. In the figures presented here, a real rate of 4 percent has been applied to a typical profile of costs. For Turkey, this approach would imply a nominal rate today of about 35 percent.

4. Details of the OECD estimate were not obtainable, but earlier data confirm a similar figure for 1997 (see the final section of this chapter).

5. Total costs may also fall over time as manufacturers drop their prices for capital equipment in response to the larger level of production (Hager 2000).

6. The marginal costs of standards rise with the standards themselves, and this observation holds true particularly in the area of wastewater treatment.

7. The increased level of private sector activity implies a greater effort by the state to ensure compliance. This effort, in turn, requires investment in capital equipment for monitoring and testing, among other things. Funding for this can be obtained from ISPA, if the demands can be bundled to meet the €5 million threshold.

8. A comprehensive status of privatization in the energy and utility sectors for the CEE countries does not appear to be available and is being prepared by the World Bank.

9. The constraints on raising charges, however, are real and raise issues of affordability for the poorer customers. Most countries adopt some lifeline rates to get around such a situation, although adoption of the rates tends to be done in an ad hoc fashion and is not based on a careful assessment of a structure that meets specified targets at least cost.

10. The results from the exercise are reported as the net present value of benefits, discounted at a real rate of 4 percent. In actual practice, countries may use higher discount rates, if only to ensure that they give priority to those investments that will yield earlier benefits for the populations.

11. Benefits from the waste directives arise largely from the landfill directive, which reduces methane emissions as well as amounts of waste subject to disposal. The benefit range is so wide because the benefits depend on how much recycling takes place and how much incineration is carried out. The higher the recycling and the less the amount incinerated, the greater are the benefits.

References

Adler, A., and others. 1994. *Economic Costs and Legislation in Western and Eastern Europe*, Munich: Ifo Institute.

Carl Bro International. 2002. *Analysis of Environmental Legislation in Turkey.* Project Number LOHAN-23-MEDA/TUR/ENLARG/D4-01. European Commission: DG Enlargement, Brussels.

ECOTEC, IEEP, Metroeconomica, TME, and Candidate Counter Experts. 2001. *The Benefits of Compliance with the Environmental Acquis for the CEECs.* Brussels: European Commission.

EDC (Environmental Development Consultants). 1997. *Compliance Costing for Approximation of EU Legislation in the CEEC.* European Commission: DG Environment, Brussels.

Hager, W. 2000. "Environmental Investment in the CEEC Preparing for Accession." World Bank, Washington, DC. (Ifo Institute 1994; EDC 1997).

Republic of Lithuania. 2001. "National ISPA Strategy: Environment Sector." Ministry of Environment, Vilnius.

World Bank. 1999. "Czech Republic: Towards EU Accession: Summary Report." World Bank Country Study, Washington, DC.

———. 2002. "Expenditure Policies toward EU Accession." Technical Paper No. 533, Washington, DC.

———. 2003. "Poland: Toward a Fiscal Framework for Growth." Report No. 25033-POL, Washington, DC.

PART IV

IMPLICATIONS OF EU ACCESSION FOR TURKEY AND THE EU

12

ECONOMIC IMPLICATIONS OF EU ACCESSION FOR TURKEY

Sübidey Togan

With accession to the European Union (EU), Turkey will complete the harmonization of its technical regulations, liberalize entry and exit into various sectors of its economy, impose hard budget constraints on all of its public and private enterprises, adopt the EU's Common Agricultural Policy (CAP), liberalize its trade with the EU in services, and join the European single market. Furthermore, joining the EU will require Turkey to adopt and implement the whole body of EU legislation and standards—the *acquis communautaire*. According to the EU membership criteria, new members must be able to demonstrate the "ability to take on the obligations of membership including adherence to the aims of political, economic and monetary union." Thus Turkey is expected to adopt the euro when it is ready to do so, but not immediately upon accession.

Welfare Effects of Integration

Any study of the effects of integration on the Turkish economy must keep in mind that the customs union in industrial goods between the EU and Turkey was established in 1996 and that a period of perhaps 10 years or more will precede full membership and Turkish participation in the internal market. Harrison, Rutherford, and Tarr (1997), who have calculated the impact of the customs union in industrial goods on Turkish welfare, estimate that

the gains to Turkey will amount to 1.1 percent of its gross domestic product (GDP) per year. If liberalizing trade in industrial goods can affect the GDP, then there should be comparable gains from liberalizing agriculture and also services.

Agriculture

Because Togan, Bayener, and Nash thoroughly study in chapter 2 of this volume the impact of EU enlargement to Turkey on Turkey's agricultural markets and incomes, this section only briefly summarizes the main points presented by the authors. According to Togan and his colleagues, adoption of the CAP will lead to substantial changes in the agricultural incomes of producers, the welfare levels of consumers, and the budget revenues of the government. Because the prices for many major agricultural products in Turkey will have to be reduced at some point between now and accession, consumers will derive great benefits. The authors estimate that, in the medium to long term, EU-like policies will lead to a 1.87 percent increase in real household incomes in Turkey, which is equivalent to about €2.92 billion. Lower-income households (rural households) will experience an even more significant increase in real income.

Yet adoption of the CAP will require substantial adjustments on the part of Turkish farmers, and the effect on farmers' incomes will be driven mainly by

TABLE 12.1 Impact of Agenda 2000 Policies
(millions of euros)

Effect on real income	2,916
Effect on agricultural value added	
Direct payments equal to those applied in the EU	2,145
Direct payments at 35 percent of payments granted in EU countries	341
Effect on government budget	−2,998

Source: Chapter 2 of this volume.

the amount of CAP-like compensation payments granted to farmers. Farmers' incomes will decrease considerably under Agenda 2000 policies without direct payments and will increase under Agenda 2000 policies with direct payments. Table 12.1 shows that agricultural value added will increase by €2.15 billion under Agenda 2000 policies with direct payments equal to those applied in the EU and by €0.34 billion under Agenda 2000 policies with direct payments equal to 35 percent of payments granted in the EU member countries.

The budgetary costs to Turkey of adopting EU-like agricultural policies will depend on whether Turkey receives compensation from the EU budget for introducing these policies. If Turkey does not receive any compensation from the EU budget, the cost will amount to €3 billion under Agenda 2000 policies with direct payments equal to those applied in the EU and to €1.2 billion under Agenda 2000 policies with direct payments equal to 35 percent of payments granted in the EU member countries.

Services and Network Industries

To join the EU, Turkey must liberalize its services and network industries. This section considers the banking, telecommunications, transportation, electricity, and natural gas sectors as representative of those making up Turkey's services and network industries.

Banking Sector Before 1999, Turkey lacked the crucial components of financial markets: competent supervisory authorities, a regulatory framework, and a legal and institutional infrastructure. In addition, regulations in Turkey were lax and poorly enforced. In February 2001, Turkey faced a

currency crisis. The cost of this crisis in terms of its effect on the banking sector has been estimated at US$46 billion,[1] or about 27–30 percent of the Turkish GDP (the crisis and its effects are described in more detail by Pazarbaşıoğlu in chapter 6). After the crisis, Turkey changed its legislative, regulatory, and institutional framework. As of 2004, Turkish prudential requirements related to capital adequacy standards, loan classification and provisioning requirements, limits on large exposures, limits on connected lending, and requirements for liquidity and market risk management were generally in conformity with those of the EU.

The welfare effects of policies followed by Turkey in the banking sector are illuminated by comparing a base case—the Turkish economy operating under the rules and regulations that prevailed in the banking sector during the latter half of the 1990s—with a case in which Turkey adopts and implements in the banking sector all of the rules and regulations of the EU.

The effects of the adoption of EU rules and regulations in the banking sector on the price of banking services are illuminated by a study by McGuire and Schuele (2000) in which they develop index values of restrictiveness in financial services for several countries. McGuire and Schuele, in extending the work of McGuire (1998), base their analysis on 1997 data and distinguish between prudential and nonprudential requirements. The authors note that prudential requirements aimed at ensuring the stability of the banking system by preserving solvency, limiting risks, and protecting bank deposits are, in general, similar across economies. Therefore, they abstract from consideration of prudential requirements and concentrate on nonprudential requirements. The index values of the nonprudential variables considered by McGuire and Schuele (2000) are shown in table 12.2; scores range from 0 (least restrictive) to 1 (most restrictive). In the table, the restrictions have been divided into two groups: those affecting "commercial presence" and "restrictions on ongoing operations." The first group indicates the restrictions on the movement of capital, and the second group is modeled as restrictions on trade in banking services. The commercial presence restrictions group covers restrictions on licensing, direct investment, joint venture arrangements, and the permanent movement of people. The other group covers restrictions on raising funds, lending

TABLE 12.2   Restrictiveness Index Scores and Price Effects for Banking Services, EU and Turkey

	Restrictiveness Index		Price Effect (%)	
	EU	Turkey	EU	Turkey
Licensing of banks	0.0100	0.2000	0.7515	16.8479
Direct investment	0.0100	0.0100	0.7515	0.8424
Joint venture arrangements	0.0050	0.0525	0.3758	4.4226
Permanent movement of people	0.0085	0.0119	0.6403	1.0025
Restrictions on establishment total	0.0335	0.2744	2.5191	23.1154
Raising funds by banks	0.0075	0.0075	0.5636	0.6318
Lending funds by banks	0.0075	0.0075	0.5636	0.6318
Other business of banks—insurance and securities services	0.0050	0.0525	0.3758	4.4226
Expanding the number of banking outlets	0.0025	0.0131	0.1879	1.1056
Composition of board of directors	0.0119	0.0120	0.8973	1.0126
Temporary movement of people	0.0028	0.0074	0.2131	0.6213
Restrictions on ongoing operations total	0.0373	0.1000	2.8013	8.4257
Index value	0.0708	0.3744	5.3203	31.5410

Source: Australian Productivity Commission (http://www.pc.gov.au).

funds, providing other lines of business, expanding banking outlets, composition of the board of directors, and the temporary movement of people. Based on the scores shown in table 12.2 for each variable considered, the authors assign weights to the variables and obtain first restrictiveness index values for the two groups and then the overall restrictiveness index values for the economies considered.

Table 12.2 reveals that the Turkish banking system is more restrictive than the banking system in the EU. Kalirajan and others (2000) use this information to study the effects of restrictions in the banking sector on performance indicators. The authors note that banks provide a wide range of financial services, including deposit taking, lending, insurance, and securities. But they emphasize that, although banks are diversified entities, their core business remains matching depositors and lenders. Thus the price of banking services can be measured by the net interest margin—that is, the difference between the interest rate banks charge on their loans and the rate they pay on their deposits. Restrictions on trade in banking services is expected to increase the interest margin. The effect of these restrictions in the banking sector on the net interest margin is shown in the third and fourth

columns of table 12.2 for the EU countries and Turkey. The table reveals that, as a result of restrictions in the banking sector, the net interest margin in the EU increases relative to the free trade net interest margin by 5.32 percent, and that the increase amounts to 31.54 percent for Turkey. One could thus infer that the net interest margin in Turkey will decrease by 26.22 percent when Turkey adopts and implements the EU rules and regulations on banking services.

Telecommunications   The telecommunications industry in Turkey has been dominated by Türk Telekom, a national monopoly with exclusive rights to all fixed-line voice operations. It also provides cable services, and so also has been responsible for the radio and television transmitters. Türk Telekom has a monopoly on the provision of international calls, and prices for local calls through fixed lines were cross-subsidized by national long-distance and international calls. Reforms since the early 1990s have led to the introduction of four new mobile telephone companies and a series of private companies that provide value added services such as Internet access and cable television.

Akdemir, Başçı, and Locksley note in chapter 5 of this volume that the Turkish Parliament approved legislation to reform the telecommunications sector in 2000 and that the legislation was amended in May 2001. The reform program was quite successful in transforming the Turkish telecommunications system into a modern one. The objective of the legislative and regulatory reform was to bring the regulatory and supervisory regime for the Turkish telecommunications sector up to the level of international practice in line with EU standards. The objective has been achieved partially by opening the mobile telecom market to competition. With accession to the EU, Turkey will have to introduce full competition in telecommunications, and it will have to adopt and implement the EU legislative measures centering on liberalization of all telecommunications services and infrastructures, adoption of open network provision measures to the future competitive environment, maintenance and development of a minimum supply of services, and definition of common principles for financing the universal service.

The welfare effects of policies followed by Turkey in the telecommunications sector are studied here by comparing the situation of the Turkish economy in the base case—the Turkish economy operating under the rules and regulations that prevailed in the telecommunications sector during the latter half of the 1990s—with the case in which Turkey adopts and implements in the telecommunications sector all of the rules and regulations of the EU. The effects of adoption of EU rules and regulations in the telecommunications sector on the price of telecommunications services are examined as well. The telecommunications sector is a heterogeneous service industry just like the banking sector, and its services include fixed-line voice services (e.g., local, domestic, and international long-distance telephony), mobile services (mobile access, calls, and messaging services), Internet services (e.g., dial-up and Web hosting), data services (e.g., leased lines, asynchronous transfer mode [ATM] services, and public data network services), and content services (e.g., pay TV and online information and entertainment). Thus the price of telecommunications will be an index of all these prices.

Warren (2000a) considers four types of impediments to trade in telecommunications services: restrictions on cross-border trade, restrictions on establishment, restrictions on direct investment in fixed and mobile network services, and restrictions on ongoing operations. For each type, Warren derives index values, for which the higher values indicate greater restrictions. The index of restrictions on cross-border trade captures policies that discriminate against all potential entrants (domestic and foreign) seeking to supply cross-border telecommunications services, and the index of restrictions on establishment captures policies that discriminate against all potential entrants (domestic and foreign) seeking to supply telecommunications services via investment in the country. The index of restrictions on direct investment is designed to capture policies that discriminate against potential foreign entrants seeking to supply telecommunications services via investment in the country. Finally, the index of restrictions on ongoing operations captures policies that discriminate against potential foreign entrants seeking to supply cross-border telecommunications services. Based on the index values derived from an international survey undertaken by the International Telecommunications Union (1998) for 136 countries, Warren (2000b) estimates first the impact of impediments to trade and investment in telecommunications services on the penetration of fixed and mobile telecommunications network and thereafter the price impact.

The results are shown in table 12.3. The table reveals that Finland and the United Kingdom follow liberal trade and investment policies in telecommunications and that, as a result of restrictions in the trade of telecommunications services, Turkish telecommunications prices are 33.53 percent higher than the prices in Finland and the United Kingdom.

Transportation   In the transportation sector, one can distinguish broadly between three different modes of transport: land transport (including rail and road transport), maritime transport, and air transport. In Turkey, road transport constitutes the significant portion of transport services. Roads carry an estimated 90 percent of domestic freight volumes and 40 percent of international freight values. The sector is competitive domestically; there are many competing firms; and access to the roads is relatively simple. Conditions in the international segment of the market are very different from those in the domestic freight segment, however.

TABLE 12.3   Restrictiveness Index Scores for Telecommunications Services

| | Restrictiveness Index | | | | | Price Effect (%) | | | | |
| | Restrictions on Establishment | | Restrictions on Ongoing Operations | | | Restrictions on Establishment | | Restrictions on Ongoing Operations | | |
	Restrictions on Direct Investment in Fixed and Mobile Network Services	Restrictions on Establishment Total	Restrictions on Cross-Border Trade	Restrictions on Ongoing Operations Total	Index Value	Restrictions on Direct Investment in Fixed and Mobile Network Services	Restrictions on Establishment Total	Restrictions on Cross-Border Trade	Restrictions on Ongoing Operations Total	Price Effect
Austria	0.1333	0.1333	0.0000	0.0000	0.1333	0.8480	0.8480	0.0000	0.0000	0.8480
Belgium	0.1334	0.1334	0.0667	0.0667	0.2001	0.8710	0.8710	0.4353	0.4353	1.3063
Denmark	0.0333	0.0333	0.0000	0.0000	0.0333	0.1985	0.1985	0.0000	0.0000	0.1985
Finland	0.0000	0.0000	0.0000	0.0000	0.0000	0.0000	0.0000	0.0000	0.0000	0.0000
France	0.2100	0.2100	0.0000	0.0000	0.2100	1.4298	1.4298	0.0000	0.0000	1.4298
Germany	0.0493	0.0493	0.0000	0.0000	0.0493	0.3195	0.3195	0.0000	0.0000	0.3195
Greece	0.1609	0.1609	0.3000	0.3000	0.4609	1.5778	1.5778	2.9424	2.9424	4.5202
Ireland	0.3533	0.3533	0.0000	0.0000	0.3533	2.6655	2.6655	0.0000	0.0000	2.6655
Italy	0.1369	0.1369	0.0000	0.0000	0.1369	1.0019	1.0019	0.0000	0.0000	1.0019
Luxembourg	0.1667	0.1667	0.0000	0.0000	0.1667	1.0458	1.0458	0.0000	0.0000	1.0458
Netherlands	0.0300	0.0300	0.0000	0.0000	0.0300	0.2025	0.2025	0.0000	0.0000	0.2025
Portugal	0.1100	0.1100	0.4000	0.4000	0.5100	1.3473	1.3473	4.8992	4.8992	6.2465
Spain	0.1793	0.1793	0.2333	0.2333	0.4127	1.7099	1.7099	2.2247	2.2247	3.9346
Sweden	0.1000	0.1000	0.0000	0.0000	0.1000	0.6530	0.6530	0.0000	0.0000	0.6530
U.K.	0.0000	0.0000	0.0000	0.0000	0.0000	0.0000	0.0000	0.0000	0.0000	0.0000
Turkey	0.3987	0.3987	0.4000	0.4000	0.7987	16.7384	16.7384	16.7944	16.7944	33.5328

Note: The restrictiveness index scores range from 0 to 1. The higher the score, the greater are the restrictions for an economy.

Source: Australian Productivity Commission (http://www.pc.gov.au).

Operations between countries are regulated by a web of bilateral and multilateral agreements that restrict quantity and capacity by limiting the number of permits available for a truck to make a journey between jurisdictions. Bilateral agreements generally prohibit cabotage.[2] Thus the domestic Turkish market is reserved for Turkish firms. By contrast, the road freight market within the EU for EU national firms is highly liberalized, including cabotage freight. Effectively, it is a single market in which the only entrance requirement is a national license from an EU country that permits unrestricted international and domestic carriage within the EU irrespective of the country of origin of the carrier within the EU. Ultimate access to the EU would largely solve the access problems of the Turkish industry, but it would also lead to increased competition from abroad.

As for rail transport, Turkish Railways is a national monopoly with exclusive rights to the transport of passengers and freight by rail in Turkey. By contrast, the EU *acquis* in the rail transport sector has been designed to improve the competitiveness of the rail transport sector and to liberalize rail transport markets. Harmonization of the current rules in the rail transport sector with the EU *acquis* requires that access rights be extended and that different organizational entities be set up for rail operations and infrastructure management in the rail transport sector. Functions such as rail capacity allocation, infrastructure charging, and licensing will have to be separated from rail operators. In addition, the financial relations between different parties and activities must be clearly defined by separation of accounts to enable the cost of operations to be accurately established and to avoid cross-subsidization.

Maritime transport is another area in which compliance with the EU *acquis* requires major changes in the sector. The EU *acquis* covers freedom to supply services, the requirements for competition, pricing practices, and the conditions to be applied to vessels carrying dangerous or polluting goods. As in road transportation, access to the Turkish maritime transportation market is restricted. With accession, access problems will be solved, and the sector will face increased competition from abroad.

Finally, in the air transport sector Turkey has taken major steps toward liberalizing air transport services. Major reforms were introduced during the 1980s. In this sector, Turkey will need to harmonize its regulations with those of the EU on civil aviation licenses, civil aviation rules and procedures, air carrier liability in the event of accidents, allocation of slots, ground handling at airports, aviation safety, and traffic management. But, overall, the existing structure will satisfy the requirements of the *acquis* on air transport services with relatively little alignment.

Francois's study in chapter 6 of this volume is helpful in determining the tariff equivalent of trade barriers in transportation services. Francois asserts that the tariff equivalent is roughly 8.9 percent.

Electricity   The Turkish electricity sector is dominated by state-owned enterprises. The two largest firms are the Turkish Electricity and Transmission Company (TEAŞ) and the Turkish Electricity Distribution Company (TEDAŞ). Recently, TEAS was separated into three companies covering generation, trading, and transmission activities. Some privately owned firms have entered the industry through build-operate-transfer (BOT), build-operate-own (BOO), or auto-generator schemes. Today, these firms account for more than 21 percent of electricity generation. Under the regulations prevailing in Turkey, the private operators signed long-term power purchase agreements with the state-owned generation enterprise in which the enterprise committed itself to buying the output of the plants for a period of, say, 20 years at a fixed price in foreign currency. In these contracts, the price has been on average between $.08 and $.09 per kilowatt-hour for the first 5–10 years of operation. These contracts, guaranteed by the Treasury, assured investors that the projects would be profitable irrespective of the demand for power.

Recently, the government of Turkey passed, as noted by Atiyas and Dutz in chapter 7 of this volume, a new electricity law. The law provides for the establishment of a new independent Energy Market Regulatory Authority. With this law, the government is introducing a market model, like the one in the EU, that will transfer most of the task of supplying and distributing electricity and the associated market risks to the private sector, eliminate the need for additional state-guaranteed power purchase agreements, and minimize costs through competitive pressures on producers and distributors along the EU model.

The welfare effects of policies followed by Turkey in the electricity sector are studied here by comparing the situation of the Turkish economy in the base case—the Turkish economy operating under the rules and regulations that prevailed in the electricity sector during the latter half of the 1990s—with the case in which Turkey adopts and implements in the electricity sector all of the rules and regulations of the EU. The effects of regulation on the price of electricity are examined by means of table 12.4, which summarizes the status of the regulatory environment and market structure in the electricity sector in selected EU countries and Turkey as of 1998. In the electricity markets, competition can be secured as long as the principle of third party access (TPA) is observed. This principle is based on the idea that the owner of the network is obliged to give access to all delivery requests through the network by production and sales operators. The table shows that by 1998 Finland, Germany, and the United Kingdom had liberalized access to transmission and distribution networks, and that access liberalization in Finland and Britain had taken the form of regulated TPA, which is a legal obligation to provide network access under nondiscriminatory conditions. Germany has chosen the negotiated TPA arrangement, in which consumers and producers contract directly with each other and then negotiate with the transmission and distribution companies for access to the network. Turkey, by contrast, had not observed the principle of TPA by 1998, and it introduced this principle only in 2001 under the regulated TPA regime.

But TPA alone will not secure competition in the electricity sector. The owner of the network could charge high access prices, which would put the competitors in the final market at a disadvantage. The achievement of competition requires that the access charge be nondiscriminatory and cost-reflective and that it give the network owner the appropriate incentives to maintain and develop the infrastructure so that the system avoids bottleneck problems. The two dominant models for this approach are cost-based (rate of return) pricing and loosely regulated prices (the model more prevalent in countries with a decentralized electricity supply industry and a tradition of regulation and control on a more local level). Under rate of return regulation, the government sets the transmission prices so that they effectively guarantee a

firm and "fair" rate of return. By contrast, under price cap regulation, prices are indexed to a moving indicator, such as the producer price index, less a portion that provides incentive for innovation and improved efficiency. Under this type of regulation, firms could realize negative returns in the short run if they are operating inefficiently. Table 12.4 reveals that Finland and Germany have introduced cost-based pricing and that the United Kingdom favors price cap regulation, but that Turkey did not have an explicit transmission pricing regulation during 1998.

The separation of generation and transmission, in tandem with expanded TPA, is crucial to encourage competition. Without separation, the network owner has very high incentives to preclude, or at least limit, the access of competitors in the downstream market, thereby eliminating liberalization. If the network owner does not participate in the downstream markets, it is neutral toward the applicants. Thus "unbundling" is important. The allocation of transmission rights must be separated from transactions between upstream and downstream firms. Where generation and transmission have been unbundled, there may be either an accounting separation, a legal separation, or a propriety separation into different companies. Accounting separation is the weakest form of separation, and legal separation is achieved through the creation of different companies under a common holding. Propriety separation is the preferred alternative.

Table 12.4 shows the degree of overall integration—from generation through transmission and distribution to supply—as well as the presence and type of separation of generation from transmission in each of the countries considered. Finland and the United Kingdom have separated generation and transmission into legally distinct firms, whereas Germany has introduced accounting separation. The table also shows that, distinct from liberalization, countries vary as well in the degree of private ownership that has developed over time, as well as in the decision made about privatization at the time of liberalization. Indeed, it reveals the current status of ownership in the generation segment of the electricity sector, and it provides details about privatization in electricity generation at the firm level for the countries selected. The decision to privatize does not necessarily correlate with the degree of liberalization. Germany has mixed ownership in

TABLE 12.4 Country Data on European and Turkish Electricity Sectors, 1998

	Finland	Germany	United Kingdom	Turkey
Regulatory reform				
Third party access (TPA)	Regulated TPA	Negotiated TPA	Regulated TPA	None
Electricity market	Finnish Electricity Exchange (1995)	None	English and Wales market (1990)	None
Transmission price regulation	Cost-based	Cost-based	Price cap	n.a.
Consumer choice thresholds	1995, 500 kW; 1997, 0 kW	1998, 0 kW	1990, 1 MW; 1994, 100 kW; 1998, 0 kW	No choice
Vertical integration in the industry				
Degree of vertical integration	Unbundled	Unbundled	Unbundled	Integrated
Generation separate from transmission	Separate companies	Accounting separation	Separate companies	Integrated
Ownership in the industry	Mostly public	Mixed	Private	Mostly public
Privatization in electricity generation	2/1/1997, Komijoki Oy, 25%	7/5/1994, Rhein-Main Donau, 75.5% 12/31/1995, Neckar, 99%	3/6/1991, National Power, 60% 3/6/1991, Power Gen, 60% 3/1/1995, National Power, 40% 3/1/1995, Power Gen, 40% 7/19/1996, British Energy, 87.73%	Private participation

n.a. Not applicable.

Sources: Steiner 2000 and the author.

the industry; the United Kingdom has made privatization a central feature of reform.

A further requirement for liberalization of electricity markets is the "opening of the demand side." This principle promotes the idea that eligible customers have the right to seek the most convenient supplier. The table reveals that Finland and the United Kingdom introduced consumer choice initially for large consumers and then gradually phased in full consumer choice, that Germany introduced full consumer choice immediately in 1998, and that Turkey had not opened the demand side by 1998.

Finally, competition requires the existence of exchange markets, which should yield prices in line with marginal costs covering fixed costs. By 1998 Finland and the United Kingdom had introduced such markets for electricity and allowed the prices and quantities traded to be determined by the equivalence of supply and demand. Germany and Turkey did not have such a market by 1998.

Steiner (2000), basically using the information provided in table 12.4, extends it to 19 Organisation for Economic Co-operation and Development (OECD) economies over the period 1986–96 and develops indexes of regulatory indicators, which he then uses to investigate empirically the linkages among regulatory regimes, market environments, and performance in electricity supply. Using the productive efficiency of generation plants and retail electricity prices as indicators of performance, Steiner concludes that unbundling of generation and transmission, expansion of the TPA, and introduction of electricity markets reduce the industrial end user prices. The results obtained by Steiner (2000) were later extended by Doove and others (2001) by increasing the number of countries considered from 19 to 50. The results are shown in table 12.5. As a result of restrictions, Turkish electricity prices are 20.7 percent higher than the prices in Finland and the United Kingdom, which follow liberal policies in the electricity sector.

Natural Gas The natural gas sector in Turkey is dominated by government-owned entities. The Petroleum Pipeline Corporation (BOTAŞ) owns the pipeline infrastructure for oil and gas transmission, liquefied natural gas (LNG) terminals, and the gas distribution network. BOTAŞ had monopoly rights for gas imports and exports and wholesale

TABLE 12.5 Price Impact of Regulation in Electricity Supply, EU and Turkey
(percent)

	Impact on Price
Austria	13.2
Belgium	15.4
Denmark	8.5
Finland	0.0
France	16.0
Germany	8.3
Greece	16.6
Ireland	13.9
Italy	17.1
Luxembourg	13.8
Netherlands	15.5
Portugal	17.9
Spain	9.5
Sweden	0.0
U.K.	0.0
Turkey	20.7

Source: Doove and others 2001.

trading. In 2000, domestic consumption was 14.6 billion cubic meters, with imports accounting for 96 percent of consumption. Demand growth was about 17 percent a year between 1990 and 1999. The distribution of natural gas is carried out by local companies that are owned either by the municipalities or by BOTAŞ. Pricing was determined by BOTAŞ, with indirect influence by the government. In May 2001, the Turkish government passed, as described by Mazzanti and Biancardi in chapter 8 of this volume, a new gas law. With this law, the government plans to establish a competitive market like the one in the EU and encourage private sector participation through a phased policy. The Energy Market Regulatory Authority, which regulates both the gas industry and the electricity industry, determines the transmission and distribution access rules and tariffs and the method for regulating retail prices.

Competition in the electricity sector can be achieved as long as the competition upstream is sufficiently developed and network access is open, but the situation is quite different in the natural gas industry, where firms are burdened with long-term investments in the upstream phase (gas contracts and infrastructures). They buy the gas from producers under long-term contracts with take-or-pay clauses. Under these obligations, gas purchasers must pay 70–90 percent of the contracted capacity whether they receive the natural gas or not. Thus firms have to sink huge investments in extraction fields and international pipelines, where they face huge fixed costs and almost zero marginal costs. In those cases, the extractor needs coverage from the market risk. It is often claimed that vertical integration is needed to cover firms' take-or-pay obligations. Table 12.6 describes the main features of the natural gas industry in EU countries for three main areas of interest: access to the network, the unbundling of monopolized activities from the competitive ones, and the opening of the demand side.

According to Polo and Scarpa (2003), three main issues must be determined for implementation of the TPA principle: (1) the technical and commercial conditions to be set for access (access price setting), (2) how disputes about access will be solved, and (3) the kind of regulatory regime to be used. According to the authors, a key aspect of the TPA is the institution that deals with disputes and acts as an arbitrator. In most of the EU countries, the regulatory authority intervenes in disputes in the natural

gas sector (table 12.6). In Ireland, Luxembourg, and Spain, the Ministry of Industry is in charge of dispute resolution in this sector, but the authority is unspecified for France, Greece, and Portugal.[3] Finally, the national liberalization plans also differ in the kind of regulation that is adopted on the TPA. The majority of countries have chosen ex ante regulation in which the regulator sets the price and technical conditions in advance, rather than an ex post regime in which the regulator intervenes ex post on the tariffs communicated by firms.[4] Table 12.6 shows that demand opening, the third element to create a level playing field in the natural gas sector, has been treated rather differently across countries. Germany and the United Kingdom had already completed their process by 2000, and in most other countries the complete opening will be reached by 2007 at the latest. However, in some important countries—Denmark, France, Greece, and Portugal—a final date for the process has not been set. In Turkey, the process of liberalization began only in 2001 with the new gas law.

To weigh the overall effectiveness of the liberalization plans of the EU countries for the natural gas sector, Polo and Scarpa (2003) use a scoring procedure in which higher scores correspond to a more advanced solution. The authors find that the more

TABLE 12.6   EU Country Data on European Natural Gas Sectors

	Third Party Access				Demand Opening		
	Access Price Setting	Dispute Solution	Type of Regulation	Unbundling	Percent Eligible	Complete Opening	Score
Austria	Negotiated	Regulator	Ex post	Accounting	49	2001	10
Belgium	Regulator	Regulator	Ex ante	Legal	59	2005	16
Denmark	Regulator	Regulator	Ex post	Legal	30	Unspecified	11
Finland	Regulator	Regulator	Ex post	Proprietary	90	2003	21
France	Unspecified	Unspecified	Ex ante	Accounting	20	Unspecified	4
Germany	Negotiated	Antitrust	Ex post	Accounting	100	2000	12
Greece	Unspecified	Unspecified	Ex ante	Unspecified	Unspecified	Unspecified	2
Ireland	Ministry	Ministry	Ex ante	Legal	75	2005	14
Italy	Regulator	Regulator	Ex ante	Legal	65	2003	17
Luxembourg	Ministry	Ministry	Ex ante	Accounting	51	2007	11
Netherlands	Negotiated	Regulator	Ex ante	Accounting	45	2004	10
Portugal	Unspecified	Unspecified	Ex ante	Unspecified	Unspecified	Unspecified	2
Spain	Ministry	Ministry	Ex ante	Legal	72	2003	15
Sweden	Regulator	Regulator	Ex post	Accounting	47	2006	11
U.K.	Regulator	Regulator	Ex ante	Proprietary	100	1998	23

Source: Polo and Scarpa 2003.

advanced solutions have been adopted by Finland, Sweden, and the United Kingdom.

Welfare Effects

This section examines the welfare effects of Turkish accession to the EU by considering the 1996 input-output table of the Turkish economy. The table has 97 sectors. Of these, banking is sector 84; telecommunications, sector 83; transport via railways, sector 78; land transport, sector 79; water transport, sector 80; air transport, sector 81; electricity production, transmission, and distribution, sector 69; and natural gas, sector 70.

Consider the case in which Turkey adopts and implements the EU rules and regulations in the banking sector. A denotes the 97×97 matrix of input coefficients. Given A, the 96×96 input matrix B is formed by deleting the 84th column and 84th row referring to the banking sector. The 84th row where the 84th column element has been deleted is denoted by e; p denotes the 1×96 price vector of the 96 commodities, excluding the banking sector; and va denotes the corresponding 1×96 unit gross value added vector. The price equation can then be written as

$$(12.1) \qquad p = pB + p_b e + va$$

where p_b denotes the price of the banking services. From this equation follows

$$(12.2) \qquad p = p_b e(I - B)^{-1} + va(I - B)^{-1}$$

Thus, given the price of banking services that will prevail in Turkey after it adopts and implements the EU rules and regulations, p_b, the equilibrium prices of the other 96 commodities can be determined from equation 12.2, assuming that there is no change in the unit gross value added vector va. Given the equilibrium price vector p, the 1×97 price vector can be formed as $\pi = (p\ p_b)$. If CON denotes the 96×1 consumption expenditure vector obtained from the 1996 input-output table by deleting the value of consumption of the banking sector and if con_b denotes the value of consumption of banking services, the 97×1 consumption vector can be formed as

$$(12.3) \qquad CONS = \begin{bmatrix} CON \\ con_b \end{bmatrix}$$

Initially, all base year prices equal unity. The value of the total consumption expenditure evaluated at the base prices of 1996 can be expressed as

$$(12.4) \qquad C = u\ CONS$$

where u denotes the 1×97 unit vector. The value of the total consumption expenditure evaluated at the prices that will prevail after Turkey adopts and implements the EU rules and regulations in the banking sector is then given by

$$(12.5) \qquad C^* = \pi\ CONS$$

The effect on consumer welfare[5] can now be calculated as

$$(12.6) \qquad (C - C^*) \times 100/C^*$$

By construction, the prices of all commodities in the base year equal unity. The previous section revealed that adoption of the EU rules and regulations by the banking sector will decrease the net interest margin by 26.22 percent. If the value of the 26.22 percent decrease is taken as the percentage change in the price of banking services stemming from adoption of the EU rules and regulations by the banking sector, it is possible to conclude that the welfare of society will increase by 1.36 percent after adoption of the EU rules and regulations by the banking sector. The change in consumer welfare will amount to about €2.12 billion.[6]

Assuming that with the adoption of EU rules and regulations by the telecommunications, transportation, and electricity sectors prices will decline by 33.5 percent in the telecommunications sector, 8.9 percent in transport services, and 20.7 percent in the electricity sectors, a study similar to that in the banking sector reveals that adoption of the EU rules and regulations by the telecommunications, transportation, and electricity sectors will cause the welfare of society to increase in those sectors by 0.59 percent, 1.01 percent, and 0.53 percent, respectively. The effect of the adoption of EU rules and regulations by the telecommunications, transportation, and electricity sectors thus amounts, respectively, to increases of €915 million, €1.57 billion, and €822 million in the real incomes of consumers.

Table 12.7 reveals that the natural gas prices in Turkey are considerably higher than those in some EU countries, which, as was determined earlier, have adopted more advanced regulatory solutions in the sector. A weighted average of natural gas prices for the industry in Finland and the

TABLE 12.7   Retail Prices of Natural Gas and Electricity, 2000

	Natural Gas for Industry (US$/10^7 kcal, GCV basis)	Natural Gas for Households (US$/10^7 kcal, GCV basis)	Electricity for Industry (US¢/kWh)	Electricity for Households (US¢/kWh)
Austria	..	348.40	3.80	11.80
Finland	130.70	159.50	3.90	7.80
France	167.80	347.50	3.60	10.20
Germany	187.90	373.40	4.10	12.10
Greece	216.10	287.20	4.20	7.10
Ireland	145.00	345.80	4.90	10.10
Spain	175.40	491.40	4.30	11.70
U.K.	104.60	292.80	5.50	10.70
Turkey	175.20	259.60	8.00	8.50

.. Negligible.
Note: GCV = gross calorific value.
Source: International Energy Agency 2003.

United Kingdom demonstrates that Turkish natural gas prices are 48.9 percent higher than the average price in those countries. Calculation then shows that with the adoption of EU rules and regulations by the natural gas sector, the welfare of society will increase by 0.08 percent. This change amounts to a €128 million increase in the real income of consumers.

The findings described in this section therefore reveal that Turkey will benefit from adopting EU rules and regulations in the banking, telecommunications, transportation, electricity, and natural gas sectors, and that liberalization within the context of EU integration in those sectors will lead to a 3.56 percent increase in real household incomes. This increase is equivalent to a change in consumers' welfare of €5.56 billion. During 1996, consumption was 72.95 percent of GDP, and thus the percentage change in the welfare of the society is equivalent to a 2.6 percent increase in real GDP.

Because the estimates of the price wedges caused by service barriers are the key parameters determining the welfare effects of services liberalization and liberalization in the calculations just presented, the estimates made here of tariff equivalents are compared with estimates from other sources. Figures 12.1 and 12.2 show, respectively, the telecommunications prices for business and residential customers in selected countries. By contrast, table 12.8 presents the OECD basket of international telephone charges during November 2001. The figures

and the table reveal that the price wedge implicit in these figures is much larger than the figure of 33.5 percent used in the calculations made here.[7] Thus the estimates presented of the price wedge in the telecommunications sector are rather conservative, and the estimate of the effects of liberalization in telecommunications services gives the lower bound of the welfare gains derived in the sector.

A look at the nominal prices for electricity over the period 1990–2000 in Turkey reveals that electricity prices for industrial customers have fluctuated between $.075 and $.095 per kilowatt-hour and prices for residential customers between $.045 and $.10 per kilowatt-hour. The prices for industrial consumers are almost exactly as high as those for residential consumers. Because the cost of supplying residential consumers is much higher than that of supplying industry, there seems to be cross-subsidization in favor of residential consumers. According to TEAS, the state-owned generation and transmission company, the sales prices per kilowatt-hour at the end of 1999 for industrial customers was $.0687 for high-voltage customers, $.0715 for intermediate and low-voltage customers, and in the range of $.04 per kilowatt-hour for distributors. However, the cost of producing electricity, as noted by OECD (2002), is much larger than is suggested by these data. The cost of purchasing additional electricity from BOT, BOO, and transfer of operating rights (TOOR) contract generators reaches $.11–$.12 per kilowatt-hour. Atiyas and

FIGURE 12.1 **OECD Composite Telecommunications Business Basket, November 2001**
(US$ PPP)

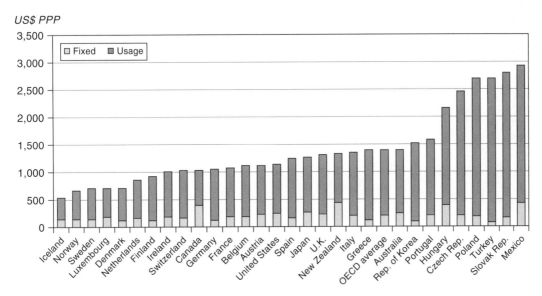

Note: VAT is excluded; calls to mobile networks and international calls are included; PPP = purchasing power parity.
Source: OECD.

FIGURE 12.2 **OECD Composite Telecommunications Residential Basket, November 2001**
(US$ PPP)

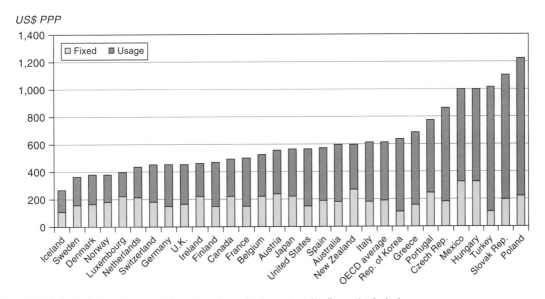

Note: VAT is included; calls to mobile networks and international calls are included.
Source: OECD.

Dutz point out in chapter 7 of this volume that the average cost of producing electricity will further increase over time as new BOT, BOO, and TOOR plants begin to produce electricity. Table 12.7, which presents the electricity prices in EU coun- tries and Turkey, reveals that the electricity prices in Turkey are considerably higher than those in the EU countries where prices are the least expensive. Thus the price wedge implicit in these figures is much larger than the figure of 20.7 percent used

TABLE 12.8   OECD Basket of International Telephone Charges, November 2001

	Business, Excluding Tax		Residential, Including Tax	
	(US$)	(US$ PPP)	(US$)	(US$ PPP)
Austria	0.77	0.83	1.06	1.15
Belgium	0.49	0.56	0.57	0.66
Denmark	0.50	0.46	0.80	0.73
Finland	0.78	0.74	1.00	0.95
France	0.34	0.37	0.66	0.73
Germany	0.42	0.45	0.62	0.67
Greece	0.77	1.12	1.17	1.69
Ireland	0.51	0.55	0.70	0.76
Italy	0.90	1.16	1.32	1.69
Luxembourg	0.37	0.41	0.49	0.55
Netherlands	0.30	0.35	0.46	0.53
Portugal	0.71	1.08	0.96	1.46
Spain	0.78	1.01	1.12	1.46
Sweden	0.34	0.34	0.53	0.54
U.K.	1.18	1.16	1.61	1.58
Turkey	1.51	3.98	1.89	4.98

Note: PPP = purchasing power parity.
Source: OECD 2002.

TABLE 12.9   Estimated Tariff Equivalents in Traded Services and Network Industries

	Current Study	Hoekman (1996)	Francois (1999) and Hoekman (2000)
Financial services		9.2	46.3
Banking	31.54		
Telecommunications	33.53		
Basic telecommunications		92.9	
Value added telecommunications		42.9	

Source: The author.

here in calculations, and the estimate made here of the price wedge in the electricity sector is thus rather conservative.

Table 12.9 shows the tariff equivalents of trade barriers in traded services and network industries estimated by different authors for Turkey. Research into the measurement of services trade barriers is fairly recent, and very few studies cover Turkey. One such study was conducted by Hoekman (1996), who used information from the country schedules of the General Agreement on Trade in Services (GATS). Hoekman's estimates for Turkey are shown in the second column of table 12.9. According to the figures, the tariff equivalent in the banking sector is 9.2 percent, in the basic telecommunications sector 92.9 percent, and in the value added telecommunications sector 42.9 percent. But these estimates have, as Hoekman notes, certain drawbacks.[8] First, the method assumes that the absence of positive country commitments in the GATS schedules can be interpreted as indicating the presence of restrictions. Second, the different types of restrictions are given equal weight and are not distinguished according to their economic impact. Finally, the method assumes that market access restrictions are the only type of barriers to trade in services.

Francois (1999) fits a gravity model to bilateral trade in services between the United States and its major trading partners, taking Hong Kong (China) and Singapore as free trade benchmarks. The independent variables are per capita income, gross domestic product, and a Western Hemisphere dummy variable. He interprets the differences between actual and predicted imports as indicative of the size of barriers to trade. These differences between actual and predicted imports are then normalized relative to the free trade benchmarks. These quantity measures also are converted into tariff equivalents by assuming a specific value of demand elasticity. Francois's estimate for Turkey, reported in Hoekman (2000) and shown in the third column of table 12.9, is 46.3 percent in financial services. Finally, a comparison of the tariff equivalents for Tunisian financial services and telecommunications sectors used by Konan and Maskus (2002) with the estimates made here of tariff equivalents reveals that the estimates used in this study are rather reasonable.

Economic Challenges

This section considers issues related to Turkey's membership in the European Economic and Monetary Union (EMU), labor markets, compliance with EU environmental directives, and state aids.

Membership in the European Economic and Monetary Union

Participation in the European Economic and Monetary Union is a must for Turkey, because the *acquis* is expected to be adopted in full, including EMU participation, as well as, in due time, all the requisite "Maastricht criteria" for Euro Area integration. Turkey is not expected to adopt the euro immediately upon accession. According to Article 122 of the Treaty Establishing the European Community, upon accession Turkey will be treated as a "country with a derogation" until it fulfills the convergence criteria, which involve conditions on price stability, interest rate convergence, the budget deficit, the government debt, and exchange rate stability.

As emphasized by the European Commission (2003), during the preaccession period Turkey must adopt the required EMU legislation in order to acquire the status of "Member State with a derogation" for adoption of the euro. In particular, Turkey needs to take the relevant steps to liberalize capital movements completely, prohibit the privileged access of financial institutions to the public sector, and attain the political and economic independence of the monetary authorities. Upon accession, the common macroeconomic policy framework will become more constraining, with strong reinforcement of fiscal discipline and the integration of other economic policies. Budgetary policy and outcomes will become subject to the excessive deficit procedure and the nonpunitive parts of the Stability and Growth Pact (SGP). The Maastricht Treaty specifies that the country will have to progress toward fulfillment of the Maastricht criteria, and under the conditions of the SGP it will have to endeavor to avoid excessive deficits. Furthermore, exchange rate policy will become a matter of common interest. Finally, adoption of the euro will require Turkey to become part of the single, stability-oriented monetary policy and of the ensuing single exchange rate policy. Furthermore, Turkey will become subject to the sanction parts of the SGP. Once Turkey adopts the euro, it will replace its domestic currency with the euro at an irrevocably fixed exchange rate, transfer the bulk of its reserves to the European Central Bank, and agree to be bound by the SGP.

In addition to the legislative changes just described and thorough implementation of this legislation, Turkey will face the problem of attaining over time sustainable development while simultaneously satisfying the Maastricht criteria. The country realizes that, in the long run, price stability and fiscal discipline create the best conditions for sustained, robust economic growth. But the current situation is problematic. Turkey is not satisfying the Maastricht conditions. In 2003 the inflation rate was 25.3 percent compared with 2.7 percent, the reference value for inflation in the EU; public sector borrowing requirements as a percentage of GDP were 8.8 percent compared with 3 percent, the reference value of the budget deficit in the EU; the debt-to-GDP ratio was 80.3 percent compared with 60 percent, the reference value of the debt-to-GDP ratio in the EU; and the average interest rate was 28.5 percent compared with 6.2 percent, the reference value of long-term interest rates in the EU. But as of the end of 2004, the annual inflation rate had been reduced to 9.2 percent, and the average interest rate on government debt during December 2004 to 19.8 percent. During 2004, the growth rate of GDP is expected to be more than 8 percent, and the unemployment rate as of the second quarter of 2004 had been reduced to 9.3 percent. Although these are all positive developments, the annual current account deficit during 2004 amounted to $15.6 billion, and the annual current account deficit-to-GDP ratio for 2004 is expected to exceed 5 percent.

The challenge facing Turkey is how to move from the current state of affairs to a state in which the Maastricht criteria are satisfied. According to Togan and Ersel in chapter 1 of this volume, the following issues are facing Turkey:

- Although the country has reduced the inflation rate considerably through strict implementation of the International Monetary Fund (IMF) economic program, the reduction was achieved partially through decreases in the cost of imported goods stemming from real appreciation of the Turkish lira. But reducing the inflation rate through real appreciation of the currency is not sustainable in the long run, because such a measure will lead to problems of sustainability of the current account.
- Although the country has reduced the debt-to-GDP ratio substantially during the last few years by running primary surpluses amounting to 6.3 percent, such as during 2003, the reduction was achieved partially through real appreciation of the currency. However, reducing the debt-to-GDP ratio by this means is not sustainable in the long run.
- Because the debt-to-GDP ratio can be reduced over time by achieving surpluses of government revenues over noninterest expenditures amounting to at least 6.5 percent of GDP, the government will be constrained in its use of fiscal policy to decrease the unemployment rate in the economy, which in 2004 was still 9.3 percent. The constraint may have political implications.
- A close look at the issues related to the sustainability of the current account reveals that the choice of exchange rate policy during the preaccession period will be of prime importance for Turkey. The policy of real exchange rate appreciation pursued during the last two years is not sustainable in the long run under rather realistic

values of foreign real interest rates. Sustainability of the current account requires depreciation of the real exchange rate over time to its long-run equilibrium value.

Labor Markets

In chapter 9 of this volume, Taymaz and Özler describe the flexibility of the Turkish labor market, which stems primarily from the fact that the labor market is not homogeneous. It has different wage-setting mechanisms in its formal and informal sectors. The informal sector is largely free from most types of labor regulation and pays few taxes and related charges. Activities in this sector rely mostly on the provision of labor services without formal employment contracts. Job insecurity is pervasive, and workers receive very few benefits from their employers. By contrast, the formal sector observes labor regulations and pays all taxes and related charges such as social security contributions and payments to various funds. According to various studies, the share of the informal sector of total employment is about 60 percent.[9] The reasons for the relatively high share of the informal sector in total employment are (1) the very high tax rates on wage income, the high tax-related charges, and the substantial payments to various funds that must be paid by those working in the formal sector to comply with the social security law and the laws regulating the taxation of personal incomes; (2) the relatively high firing costs imposed by the labor law and the stringency of the various clauses of the labor law; and (3) the lack of enforcement mechanisms for the respective laws in the economy.

The population of Turkey increases on average at a rate of 1 million persons per year, and thus the country must continually create new jobs to accommodate this growth. In addition, Turkey must create jobs for those unemployed and must increase the labor force participation rate from its low level of 48.3 percent. In the past, Turkey successfully managed the unemployment problem through its large, flexible informal sector where wages are free to equilibrate demand and supply and through labor migration from Turkey.

With its accession to the EU, Turkey will have to enforce the rule of law uniformly in the country. It can no longer tolerate the lack of enforcement mechanisms for different laws and regulations in the economy. Yet such a shift will have to occur without increasing Turkey's unemployment rate. Taymaz and Özler estimate that when all manufacturing firms in the informal sector begin to pay taxes and social security contributions at the same rates as in the formal sector and when informal sector firms lose half of their market shares because of the change, employment in the manufacturing sector will decline by 8.9 percent. Thus about 300,000 jobs will be lost. But the effect of the policy change on employment—when all informal sector firms in all sectors of the economy begin to pay taxes and social security contributions at the same rates as in the formal sector—will actually be much more drastic, because the effects on employment in the agricultural and services sectors must be considered as well. In the end, the number of jobs lost will far exceed the 300,000 estimated by Taymaz and Özler. Thus to avoid an increase in unemployment the country must introduce comprehensive labor market reform. Such a reform will probably entail substantial decreases in the tax rates on wage income, tax-related charges and payments to various funds, decreases in the firing costs, and changes in various clauses of the labor law so they are less stringent.

Complying with EU Environmental Legislation

To join the EU, Turkey must adopt and implement the entire body of EU legislation and standards on environmental protection. Bringing its environmental protection system, infrastructure, and standards up to Western European levels will require, in turn, substantial investments by the public and private sectors as well as changes in regulations and supporting institutions.

Within the EU regulations on wastewater collection and treatment, the urban wastewater directive (91/271/EEC) requires all urban areas with a total wastewater discharge of 2,000 population equivalent to be connected to the sewer system, and the discharges of sewers must receive at least secondary treatment. The directive allows exceptions for towns with a population of less than 10,000 when sewers would produce no environmental benefit or would involve excessive cost.

In 1997 the population of Turkey was 62.87 million. Of this number, 13.75 million were living in areas with a population of 2,000 or less, 49.12 million in areas with more than 2,000, 22.57 million in areas with 10,000 and less, and 40.3 million in areas

with more than 10,000. In 1997 there were 2,835 municipalities with a total population of 48.2 million; 7.3 million people were living in rural municipalities. According to the State Planning Organization, 72 percent of the people living in municipalities were not connected to sewage treatment. For an additional 23 percent of population, sewer systems were under construction. Upon the completion of these systems, 51 percent of the population living in municipalities (24.5 million out of 48.2 million) will be connected to sewer systems, leaving 23.7 million with no connection. Two percent of municipalities have wastewater treatment facilities and 14 percent of people living in villages have a sewer connection with septic tanks, but 11.8 million people have no sewer connection.

The costs of meeting sewer needs will depend on three parameters: (1) the proportion of the rural population living in towns that would be classified as agglomerations with a population of more than 2,000 population equivalent; (2) the proportion of towns with between 2,000 and 10,000 population that will be exempted from constructing sewer systems on the grounds of no environmental benefit or excessive costs; and (3) the proportion of rural population that must have sewers. Once the European Commission and Turkey agree on these parameters during the negotiations, the cost of compliance with the EU directive would be determined. The investment cost of complying with the directive has been roughly estimated at more than $10 billion. Adding the additional operations, maintenance, and replacement costs would increase this cost even further.

Environmental protection will therefore present challenges for Turkey. The costs will be substantial when, in addition to the costs of complying with EU regulations on wastewater collection and treatment, the costs of complying with those on drinking water, industrial pollution, dangerous chemicals, fuel standards, air quality, and waste management are considered. In chapter 11 of this volume, Markandya estimates that the total cost would be between €28 billion and €49 billion. But he notes that because the outlay will be over a long period (about 17 years), the annual amount will be more manageable. Furthermore, he finds that annual investments would amount to around €2 billion to €3 billion in the "fast reform" (low-cost) case and €3 billion to €5 billion in the slow reform (high-cost) case. In the initial years, this investment would amount to 1–1.5 percent of GDP in the low-cost case and 1.5–2.5 percent of GDP in the high-cost case. The extra annual operating costs also incurred would range from €5 to €8 billion. Markandya reports that OECD has estimated Turkey's capital spending on the environment at about 0.5 percent of GDP. Thus with accession, this spending would have to double, or more likely increase by a factor of three or four. In addition, a much higher level of current spending would be required. These costs, although substantial by any standards, could be considered the price for joining the EU. One could also argue that these investments would have been made in any case by Turkey. Only the timing of the investments would be different, because EU directives may not correspond to Turkey's priorities at this stage of its development.

State Aid

During the 1980s, Turkey used three tools of industrial policy intensively: investment incentives, export incentives, and policy on state-owned enterprises. In each case, the government tried to obtain a preferred allocation of resources through the use of subsidies. The investment incentives, regulated by laws and decrees, have been directed toward reducing the cost of investment, reducing the need for external financing, and increasing profitability. On the export side, the government's use of various types of export incentives during the 1980s increased the profitability of export activities. As for the policy on state-owned enterprises in Turkey, the Turkish public enterprise sector has been and still is very large. The state-owned enterprises have in general exhibited poor economic performance because of the soft-budget constraints they have faced. Public enterprises are not subject to commercial code and, as such, they escape bankruptcy laws. Moreover, they receive subsidies from the government in the form of direct transfers, equity injections, and debt consolidation.

Recently, Turkey eliminated most of the investment and export incentives. Within this context, General Agreement on Tariffs and Trade (GATT) legal subsidies (e.g., research and development subsidies and subsidies to facilitate the adaptation of plants to new environmental regulations) have been introduced. Export subsidies in Turkey are restricted to those given to research and develop-

ment activities and environmental projects and to export promotion activities. Although considerable progress has been achieved in the fields of investment and export incentives, similar progress has not been possible for public enterprises. Privatization has become a prominent part of the Turkish structural adjustment program since 1983, but it did not gain momentum until very recently. Turkey recognizes that it will have to stop subsidizing its public enterprises at the prevailing rates and that it will have to take steps to align its state aid policies with those of the EU, to apply the same competition policies to all firms whether private or public, and to privatize public enterprises.[10]

Growth Effects

The preceding discussion of the welfare effects of accession reveals that Turkey's integration within the EU will remove the distortions in the country's price system, which, in turn, will boost allocative efficiency within the economy. The heightened efficiency also will make the country a better place in which to invest. Investment will therefore increase, as will foreign direct investment. Thus the allocative efficiency gains from integration will be boosted by induced capital formation. When investment rises above its normal level, the Turkish economy will experience a growth effect. All this means improved material well-being for the Turkish people in the long term.

The growth effects of accession will be studied here by first forecasting the volume of trade between Turkey and the EU15, under the assumption that it will reach the same level of intensity as the present trade between the EU member states. The forecast is then used to study the growth effects of accession.

The forecast of the volume of trade between Turkey and the EU is based on estimation of a gravity function for trade within the EU15. The gravity function, which has been used to explain the volume of bilateral international trade since the 1960s, has proved remarkably successful. It postulates that the volume of trade between a pair of countries is a function of (1) the size of the trading partners, measured by GDP, population, or geographic area; (2) their income level or capital abundance, measured by GDP per capita; and (3) trade costs, measured by a variety of factors such as tariffs and other administratively imposed trade barriers,

TABLE 12.10 Gravity Estimates for Intra-EU15 Trade

	Estimate
Constant	−3.884133
	(−3.193833)
ln real product GDP	0.815026
	52.1816
ln real product GDP per capita	−0.145238
	(−2.705978)
ln distance	−0.901144
	(−21.50092)
R-squared	0.622767

Source: The author.

geographic distance, common borders, common language, or common legal systems. The following standard version of the gravity function was estimated:

(12.7) $\ln [(\text{exports from country } i \text{ to country } j + \text{exports from country } j \text{ to country } i)/2]$
$= \text{constant} + \beta_1 \ln (\text{GDP of country } i \times \text{GDP of country } j) + \beta_2 \ln (\text{GDP per capita of country } i \times \text{GDP per capita of country } j) + \beta_3 \ln (\text{geographic distance}) + \text{error term}.$

The dependent variable in the gravity equation is the logarithmic average of bilateral exports. It is explained by the logarithmic product of GDP; the volume of trade is simply assumed to rise in proportion to the combined economic size of the trade partners. GDP per capita can be thought of as a measure of product differentiation and specialization. The higher the per capita income, the more differentiated are taste and production and the larger is the volume of trade based on product differentiation and increasing returns to scale. A high per capita income is also an indication of abundant physical and human capital relative to manual labor. Thus the per capita variable should serve to capture both the intraindustry trade produced by product differentiation and the increasing returns to scale and interindustry trade produced by differences in factor endowments. Trade costs are controlled by the inclusion of geographic distance, which is an indicator of transportation costs, but

also of the costs of cultural differences, which tend to increase with geographic distance.

The estimates of the gravity equation are presented in table 12.10. The equation explains more than 90 percent of the variation in the data. All coefficients are estimated with a very high level of statistical significance (less than 1 percent) and have the expected sign, with one exception. The product of real per capita GDP is found to have an unexpected *negative* effect on the volume of trade. The estimate of the gravity equation is then used to make forecasts of bilateral trade for Turkey with the EU15. The forecasted value of Turkish–EU15 trade for 2000 is $25.75 billion, which is almost 25.2 percent higher than the actual average value of $18.55 billion for the period 1999–2001. For that period, the average of Turkish exports to the EU was $14.99 billion and of imports from the EU $22.1 billion.

Next, it is assumed that Turkey eventually will have a share of EU trade to total trade that is equal to that of the four largest EU countries—58 percent. Then, the total trade of Turkey will increase to $44.4 billion. When this value is divided by the average value of GDP for the period 1999–2001, it produces a ratio between the average of exports and imports to GDP of 25.2 percent. The actual value of total trade to GDP over the 1999–2001 period is, by contrast, 20.67 percent. Noting the assertion by Frankel and Rose (2002) that every percent increase in the country's overall trade relative to GDP raises income per capita by at least one-third of a percent, one then finds that, with EU accession, per capita income in Turkey will increase by about 1.5 percent.

Conclusion

To join the EU, Turkey must attain macroeconomic stability, adopt the EU's Common Agricultural Policy, and liberalize its services and also its network industries. Integration will be beneficial for Turkey, because it will remove the distortions in the price system, thereby boosting allocative efficiency within the economy, which, in turn, will make the country a better place to invest. Furthermore, with accession Turkey will be eligible for EU structural funds. The increase in infrastructural investments will contribute to economic growth in Turkey. Turkey will also reap benefits from monetary integration.

The welfare gains derived by Turkey from integration will, however, have a price. The price will be the adjustment costs associated with the attainment of macroeconomic stability, adoption of the CAP, adoption of the EU's labor market rules and regulations, and compliance with EU environmental directives.

Notes

1. All dollar amounts are U.S. dollars unless otherwise indicated.

2. Cabotage refers to the carriage of freight within a country or between two countries by a carrier that is from neither country.

3. Polo and Scarpa (2003) consider it more appropriate that an independent regulatory authority devoted to the liberalization of the industry fill the delicate role of arbitrator rather than a ministry, which is typically responsible for a broader range of political objectives.

4. Although in both cases the regulator has the final word on the access conditions, Polo and Scarpa (2003) argue that the ex ante regime, requiring the regulator to act as a first mover, forces it to reach a better solution.

5. This approach determines the equivalent variation in consumer income.

6. When considering the welfare effects of integration, I abstract from explicit consideration of problems of implementation and assume that once the *acquis* is adopted liberalization of the sector will be achieved. This is a simplification introduced in the analysis.

7. The implicit price wedge is derived from the relation $p = p^* (1 + t)$, where p refers to the Turkish price p^*, the best practice price in the EU, and t is the price wedge parameter.

8. See Stern (2002) and Whalley (2004) for further discussion of the state of knowledge on barriers to trade in services and the robustness of existing empirical research in this area.

9. Taymaz and Özler report that the share of the informal sector in manufacturing is 40 percent. Its share is much higher, however, in the agricultural and services sectors.

10. Turkish competition law is silent on the subject of public undertakings. It does not contain a clause like Article 86 (ex Article 90) of the Treaty Establishing the European Community, which explicitly brings public undertakings within the scope of competition policy. Recently, state aid in Turkey has taken the form of injections to private banks under the management of Savings Deposit Insurance Fund (SDIF). These banks are largely those hit by capital losses during the November 2000 and February 2001 crises. The capital losses stemmed from the sharp decline in the market value of government securities holdings and the sharp increase in the foreign exchange rate. According to EU regulations, state aid to the banking sector is subject to the same conditions as any other state aid and as such it should be avoided.

References

Doove, S., O. Gabbitas, D. Nguyen-Hong, and J. Owen. 2001. "Price Effects of Regulation: International Air Passenger Transport, Telecommunications and Electricity Supply." Productivity Commission Staff Research Paper, Productivity Commission, Canberra.

European Commission. 2003. *2003 Regular Report on Turkey's Progress towards Accession.* Brussels: EC.

Francois, J. 1999. "Estimates to Barriers to Trade in Services." Erasmus University, Rotterdam.

Frankel, J., and A. Rose. 2002. "An Estimate of the Effect of Common Currencies on Trade and Income." *Quarterly Journal of Economics* 117: 437–66.

Harrison, G. W., T. F. Rutherford, and D. G. Tarr. 1997. "Economic Implications for Turkey of a Customs Union with the European Union." *European Economic Review* 41: 861–70.

Hoekman, B. 1996. "Assessing the General Agreement on Trade in Services." In *The Uruguay Round and the Developing Economies,* ed. W. Martin and L. A. Winters. Cambridge: Cambridge University Press.

————. 2000. "The Next Round of Services Negotiations: Identifying Priorities and Options." *Federal Reserve Bank of St. Louis Review* 82: 31–47.

International Energy Agency. 2003. *Energy Prices & Taxes: Quarterly Statistics Fourth Quarter 2002.* Paris: IEA.

International Telecommunications Union. 1998. *Telecommunications Reform.* Geneva: ITU.

Kalirajan, K., G. McGuire, D. Nguyen-Hong, and M. Schuele. 2000. "The Price Impact of Restrictions on Banking Services." In *Impediments to Trade in Services: Measurement and Policy Implications,* ed. C. Findlay and T. Warren. London: Routledge.

Konan, D. E., and K. E. Maskus. 2004. "Quantifying the Impact of Services Liberalization in a Developing Country." Working Paper No. 3193, World Bank, Washington, DC.

McGuire, G. 1998. "Australia's Restrictions on Trade in Financial Services." Productivity Commission Staff Research Paper, Australian Productivity Commission, Melbourne.

McGuire, G., and M. Schuele. 2000. "Restrictiveness of International Trade in Banking Services." In *Impediments to Trade in Services: Measurement and Policy Implications,* ed. C. Findlay and T. Warren. London: Routledge.

OECD (Organisation for Economic Co-operation and Development). 2002. *Turkey: Crucial Support for Economic Recovery.* OECD Reviews of Regulatory Reform. Paris: OECD.

Polo, M., and C. Scarpa. 2003. "The Liberalization of Energy Markets in Europe and Italy." Paper presented at the 4th Mediterranean Social and Political Research Meeting, Florence, March 19–23.

Steiner, F. 2000. "Regulation, Industry Structure and Performance in the Electricity Supply Industry." Economics Department Working Paper No. 238, Organisation for Economic Co-operation and Development, Paris.

Stern, Robert. 2002. "Quantifying Barriers to Trade in Services." In *Development, Trade and the WTO: A Handbook,* ed. B. Hoekman, A. Mattoo, and P. English. Washington, DC: World Bank.

Warren, T. 2000a. "The Identification of Impediments to Trade and Investment in Telecommunications Services." In *Impediments to Trade in Services: Measurement and Policy Implications,* ed. C. Findlay and T. Warren. London: Routledge.

————. 2000b. "The Impact on Output of Impediments to Trade and Investment in Telecommunications Services." In *Impediments to Trade in Services: Measurement and Policy Implications,* ed. C. Findlay and T. Warren. London: Routledge.

Whalley, John. 2004. "Assessing the Benefits to Developing Countries of Liberalisation in Services Trade." *World Economy* 27: 1223–53.

13

THE IMPACT OF TURKEY'S MEMBERSHIP ON EU VOTING

Richard Baldwin and Mika Widgrén

The Treaty of Nice in 2001 and the Constitutional Treaty in 2004 radically reformed the voting rules of the Council of the European Union (also known as the Council of Ministers).[1] The Constitutional Treaty rules were accepted politically at the Brussels summit in June 2004. The Nice rules went into effect in November 2004. Implementation of the changes was postponed by five years and made conditional on ratification of the constitution by all 25 member states of the European Union (EU). The next EU enlargement (Bulgaria and Romania) is tentatively scheduled for 2007. Thus Bulgaria and Romania will enter under the current Nice Treaty rules, but future new members are likely to join under the rules of the Constitutional Treaty.

This chapter evaluates the impact of Turkey's membership on EU voting—specifically, decision-making efficiency and the distribution of power in the EU's leading decision-making body, the Council of Ministers. The chapter compares two alternative Council voting rules: those accepted in the Treaty of Nice and implemented by the Accession Treaty for the 10 entrants in 2004 and the rules laid down in the Constitutional Treaty.[2]

Council of Ministers Voting Reforms

The Constitutional Treaty explicitly sets out two sets of voting procedures for the Council of Ministers and implicitly recognizes the current system implemented by the Accession Treaty (Article 24).

Up to October 31, 2004, the pre–Treaty of Nice rules apply—that is, qualified majority voting with weighted votes and the old majority threshold of 71 percent to win. The number of votes for the incumbent 15 are unchanged; those for the 10 newcomers are a simple interpolation of EU15[3] votes as specified in the Accession Treaty.

From November 1, 2004, to October 31, 2009, the Nice Treaty rules apply (as per the "Draft Council Decision relating to the implementation of Article I-24"). The Nice Treaty rules maintain the basic "qualified majority voting" framework, but add two extra criteria for the number of yes voters and the population they represent. Specifically, the vote threshold is 72.2 percent of Council votes (232 of 321 votes); the member threshold is 50 percent of members (13 members); and the population threshold is 62 percent of the EU population.[4]

As of November 1, 2009, the Constitutional Treaty rules apply, and thus weighted voting is out and a double majority is in. A winning coalition must represent at least 55 percent of EU members and 65 percent of the EU population. A last-minute summit compromise inserted the requirement that at least 15 members vote yes, but this compromise was irrelevant; 15 of 25 members is 60 percent and thus greater than 55 percent. By the time these rules take effect, however, the EU should have 27 members, and 55 percent of 27 is 15 (Bulgaria and Romania are tentatively slated for membership in 2007). The 15-member rule will therefore be redundant when it takes effect. Turkey's and

Croatia's membership will, in any case, materialize after that date.

To enter into force, the Constitutional Treaty rules must be ratified by all member states. The fallback position is the Nice Treaty rules, which means that Turkey and Croatia may enter the EU under those rules. Therefore, what follows is an evaluation of these two rules for the EU25 and EU29. It compares especially the impact of Turkey's membership on the countries of the EU25 that have the most substantial say in the ratification process of the constitution.

Tools of Assessment

"Capacity to act" and "decision-making efficiency" are slippery concepts. However, one quantitative tool in voting game theory will help to achieve precision. Passage probability gauges how likely it is that the Council would approve a randomly selected issue—random in the sense that each EU member would be equally likely to vote for or against it. The best way to describe this measure is to explain how it is calculated.

First, the researcher, with the help of a computer, calculates all possible coalitions among EU members—that is, every possible combination of yes and no votes by EU members (134 million coalitions are possible in the EU27). Second, each coalition is evaluated to determine whether it is a winning coalition under the Nice Treaty voting system. This process is carried out using each member's actual weight for three criteria (votes, members, and population) and the three thresholds. Passage probability is, then, the likelihood that a random proposal would attract a winning coalition, assuming all coalitions are equally likely (random in the sense that member states do not know what their stance would be). Admittedly, passage probability is a crude measure, but it is objective and precise, and its strengths and shortcomings are clear.

Even if the exact passage probability is meaningless (the European Commission does not put forth random proposals), figure 13.1 reveals that the Nice Treaty fails on efficiency grounds, because it implies a level of efficiency that is far, far below that of the EU15. Indeed, the Nice Treaty reforms actually make matters worse. Admitting 12 new

FIGURE 13.1 **Passage Probabilities: European Council, 1957–2004, and after Entry of Bulgaria, Romania, Croatia, and Turkey**

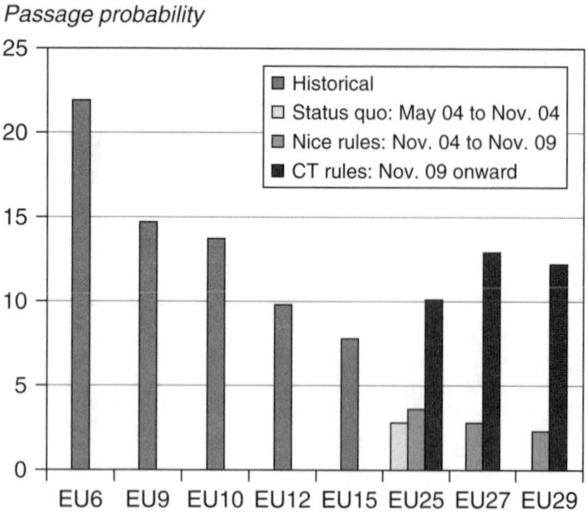

Passage probability

Legend:
- Historical
- Status quo: May 04 to Nov. 04
- Nice rules: Nov. 04 to Nov. 09
- CT rules: Nov. 09 onward

Categories: EU6 EU9 EU10 EU12 EU15 EU25 EU27 EU29

Note: Passage probability measures the likelihood that a randomly selected issue would pass in the Council of Ministers.
Source: Authors' calculations.

members without any reforms would cut the passage probability to 2.5 percent—a third of its already low level. With the Nice Treaty reforms, the figure drops even further, to 2.1 percent. The main source of the lower efficiency is the high threshold of the Nice Treaty rules for Council votes. An even cruder but more transparent efficiency-measuring tool—blocking-minority analysis—confirms these efficiency findings.

No perfect measure of power exists, but even imperfect measures are useful when considering complex voting rules, because a voting scheme's political acceptability turns almost completely on its power implications. The measures used here— the normalized Banzhaf index (NBI) and the Shapley-Shubik index (SSI)—gauge how likely it is that a nation finds itself in a position to "break" a winning coalition on a randomly selected issue.[5] The NBI assumes that each possible coalition has the same probability of occurrence. Thus all coalitions are equally likely to be winning ones, and power is measured simply by calculating the score of breaking positions for each player. A relative measure of power is then obtained by dividing this score by the total of all of scores. On particular issues, some countries may be much more powerful or much less powerful than others, especially if they are part of a like-minded group (see Baldwin and others 2001 for details and simple numerical examples), but the NBI has recently proved its worth, especially as an unbribable tool in assessing and designing voting rules.

What follows is a simple example of how the NBI works. Consider a three-person voting body, such as the Council of Ministers, in which the voters are labeled A, B, and C. Suppose that A has four votes, B has two votes, and C has one vote, for a total of seven votes. It is assumed that five votes are needed to pass proposals. The three winning coalitions are then

$$\underline{A}B \quad \underline{A}C \quad \underline{A}BC$$

where underlining indicates the actors able to "break" a winning coalition. In this situation, A has three breaking positions, B has two, and C only one, for a total of six breaking positions. Thus the NBI of A is 1/2, whereas the NBIs of B and C are 1/3 and 1/6, respectively.

The SSI tries to capture a different abstract voting model. It assumes that voters have different intensities in terms of accepting or rejecting a proposal. Suppose that these intensities can be expressed as a continuum that extends between the extremes of more spending and less spending. For example, when the issue is the support for hillside farmers, A may be the most reluctant to increase spending, and B may be the second most reluctant, leaving C as the most favorably disposed toward increasing support for this purpose. On another day, the issue might be the inclusion of reindeer meat in the price support mechanism of the Common Agricultural Policy (CAP). This time, a different order of preferences might emerge.

In general, given a large enough number of issues, all preference orders of A, B, and C are equally likely. In the example used earlier, six orderings are possible:

$$A\underline{B}C \quad A\underline{C}B \quad B\underline{A}C \quad BCA \quad C\underline{A}B \quad CB\underline{A}$$

where the critical voter is underlined. A critical voter exerts the power of being able to break a winning coalition. In the first order of ABC, B can break the winning coalition AB. Voter A favors spending more on this issue than does B. Therefore,

A is not critical. Should voter A try to break the winning coalition AB by voting against spending, voter B would have already broken that coalition because B is less eagerly in favor of spending. In the example, voter A has four pivotal positions, and voters B and C have one each. In relative terms, winning probabilities ("power") of 2/3 are obtained for A and 1/6 for both B and C. If SSI is a meaningful estimate of power and if power politics is able to explain EU budget, then these fractions should represent the budget shares of A, B, and C, respectively.

Clearly, these measures of power do not provide a detailed description of real-world voting procedures. For example, they lack all the strategic aspects, such as who makes the proposal to be voted on or the sequence of moves. They both contain, however, some information on voters' preferences, understood as the intensities of holding a favorable position. The measures also consider all possible orderings of intensities (SSI) or presume the equal likelihood of all coalitions (NBI), and so they represent a very long-term concept. For a general evaluation of voting rules, this is a desirable property.

The example just described demonstrates that the NBI and SSI can have very different values. Which one should then be chosen to assess decision-making power? The answer is not clear, but a rough distinction can be made between the two measures. If one is interested in voting rules as such, the NBI is more advantageous. If one is more interested in decision making and bargaining under certain rules, knowing that actors communicate, then the SSI is a far more suitable tool.[6]

Impact of Turkey's Membership on EU Voting

Turkey's accession to the EU would have implications for EU decision making. As a large country, Turkey would play a relatively bigger role in the EU than many other entrants. To what extent will accession change the balance of power?

Implications of Turkey's Membership for EU's Capacity to Act

Turkey's membership would have only moderate implications for the passage probabilities—see figure 13.1. This finding is not surprising, because moving from 27 members to 29 members does not change much. Although the addition of Croatia increases the number of small nations in the EU, Turkey's large population means that efficiency suffers little. (Efficiency, if not legitimacy, tends to be higher when a large share of power is in the hands of just a few nations.) The vote thresholds used in calculations of passage probabilities are extrapolations of the current Nice Treaty/Accession Treaty threshold. In EU29, it is 276 out of a total of 381 votes, plus the two additional criteria: at least 15 member states and 62 percent of population. In EU27, it is 250 out of a total of 345 votes, plus the two additional

criteria—at least 14 member states and 62 percent of population.

The Nice Treaty rules—which are essentially unworkable in an EU27—become even less viable in an EU29. The same does not hold for the Constitutional Treaty voting rules. The passage probability jumps drastically from the low levels of the Nice Treaty rules up to the level of the EU12 and even higher. Surprisingly, under the Constitutional Treaty rules the EU's ability to act improves when its membership expands from 25 to 27 or 29. There is only a slight drop from EU27 to EU29 from 12.9 to 12.2 percent.[7]

In summary, the passage probability calculations demonstrate that Turkey's membership in the

FIGURE 13.2   Change in Power for EU25, Nice Treaty to Constitutional Treaty Rules
(percentage points)

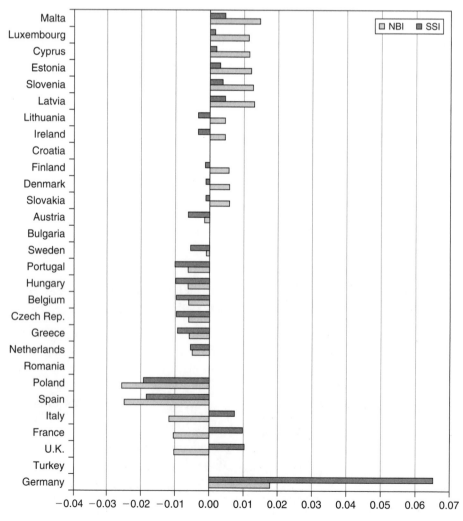

Source: Authors' calculations.

EU does not erode the EU's ability to act. Under the Constitutional Treaty rules, the effect of Croatia and Turkey together is significantly smaller—one percentage point—than Turkey's alone. The most important impact on the EU's capacity to act stems from the switch from the Nice Treaty rules to the Constitutional Treaty rules.

Impact of Turkey's Membership on the Distribution of Power

The Constitutional Treaty and the Nice Treaty rules also differ substantially in power evaluation. Figure 13.2 shows the difference between these rules in terms of the NBI and SSI for the EU25,

and figure 13.3 reveals the same numbers for the EU29. The difference is measured in percentage points.

According to figure 13.2, before Turkey's entry the Constitutional Treaty rules favor the four biggest nations and the six smallest—that is, Latvia and smaller—if the comparison is made using the SSI. Based on the NBI, the conclusion is somewhat different: Germany and Slovakia and smaller countries would gain from the Constitutional Treaty rules compared with the Nice Treaty rules. This result differs from that obtained by Baldwin and Widgrén (2004b) for EU27, in which the NBI produced exactly the same pattern as the SSI here.

FIGURE 13.3 **Power Difference between Nice Treaty and Constitutional Treaty Rules for EU29**
(percentage points)

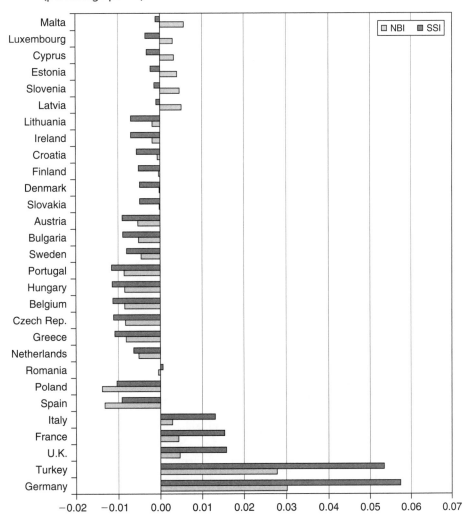

Source: Authors' calculations.

FIGURE 13.4   NBI Values under Nice Treaty and Constitutional Treaty Voting Rules for EU29

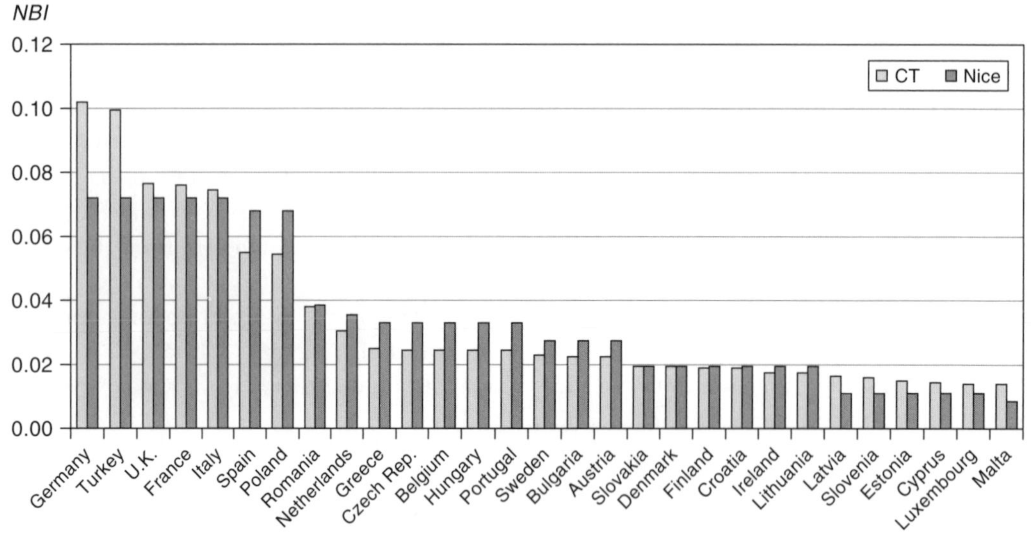

Source: Authors' calculations.

After Turkey's entry into the EU, the biggest nations gain more from the Constitutional Treaty rules than was the case for the EU25. This finding holds true for both power measures. For the smallest countries, the effect is ambiguous: the NBI shows gains for Latvia and smaller nations, whereas the SSI shows small losses. Otherwise, both indices show consistent results.

Figure 13.4 explicitly compares the Nice Treaty and Constitutional Treaty rules by showing the NBI values under both rules. The message of the figure is very clear. The countries that gain the most from the Constitutional Treaty rules are the biggest nations, Germany and Turkey. The biggest losers are Spain and Poland, as well as the medium-size countries, from the Netherlands to Austria. This finding could affect these countries' attitudes toward either the ratification of the Constitutional Treaty or Turkey's membership. (The index values for both the EU25 and EU29 are found in the annex to this chapter.)

Impact of EU Enlargement on Incumbent's Power   Figures 13.5 and 13.6 evaluate the impact of the EU25 to EU29 enlargement in terms of both power indices. Under the Nice Treaty rules, the countries' power losses are proportional to their sizes. Thus Germany, the biggest country, loses the

most power, while the smaller nations lose less. The relative losses are of the same magnitude. This finding reflects the fact that in weighted voting power, the indices tend to converge to voting weights if the number of actors increases and if the voting weights have relatively small variance.

In figure 13.6, the result is more interesting. When evaluated by the NBI, the enlargement from EU25 to EU29 benefits France and the United Kingdom.[8] The losses of the other large countries (the Netherlands and larger nations) are very small. For the countries smaller than Romania, the losses increase slightly as the nations become smaller. The SSI, however, gives a somewhat different picture. The most notable exceptions are the biggest countries, especially Germany. The power loss of the Netherlands remains small.

Conclusions

This chapter investigates the decision-making impact of expanding the EU from 25 members to 29 members with the addition of Bulgaria, Romania, Turkey, and Croatia. The chapter focuses on a measure of the EU's capacity to act—passage probability—and the power distribution among members.

FIGURE 13.5   Impact of Enlargement on EU25 Power, Nice Treaty Rules
(percentage points)

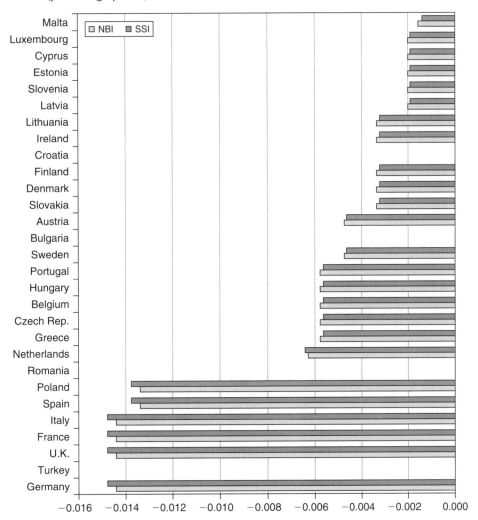

Source: Authors' calculations.

As for the capacity to act, the enlargement is projected to have relatively little impact if the Constitutional Treaty voting rules take effect. In particular, Turkey's membership would have only a negligible effect on the EU's capacity to act. The answer is quite different, however, if the Constitutional Treaty is rejected and the Nice Treaty rules remain in place. Under the Nice Treaty voting rules, the EU25 to EU29 enlargement would substantially lower the ability of the EU25 to act. Thus our findings confirm that the enlarged EU cannot function well under the Nice Treaty rules. It also suggests that if the Constitutional Treaty is rejected, the Nice Treaty voting rules must be reformed before further enlargement.

As for power, Turkey's membership in the EU will have a big impact. Under either the Nice Treaty or Constitutional Treaty rules, Turkey would be the second most powerful member of the EU29. Under the Constitutional Treaty rules, Turkey would be substantially more powerful than France, Italy, and Britain, while under the Nice Treaty rules the power differences among the members with more than 50 million population would be small. Plainly, this situation might decrease the acceptability of the Constitutional Treaty or Turkey's membership.

The impact of the enlargement from EU25 to EU29 on the voting power of EU incumbents depends heavily on the rules. Under the

FIGURE 13.6   Impact of Enlargement on EU25 Power, Constitutional Treaty Rules
(percentage points)

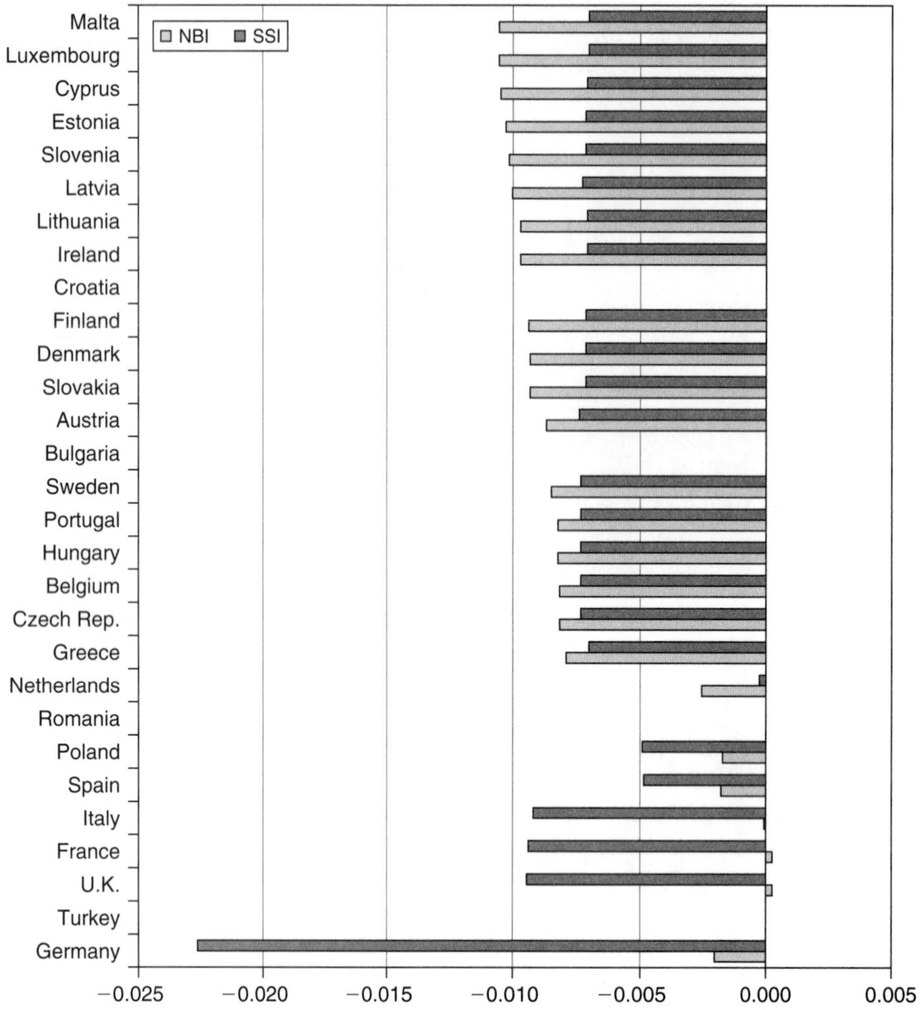

Source: Authors' calculations.

Constitutional Treaty rules, the enlargement lowers the power of all incumbents on a fairly even basis, with the marked exception of Germany; Germany loses more than twice as much power as any other member. Under the Nice Treaty rules, the power loss is more heavily skewed toward the big incumbents. Again, all incumbents are projected to lose power, but the power loss increases progressively with member size. For example, the power loss to France under the Nice Treaty rules is about seven times larger than the power loss to Malta.

Annex: Power Indices under the Constitutional Treaty Rules and Nice Treaty Rules

TABLE 13.1   Power Indices under Constitutional Treaty Rules

Member State	NBI_EU29	NBI_EU25	SSI_EU29	SSI_EU25
Germany	0.10203	0.10407	0.13556	0.15816
Turkey	0.09960	n.a.	0.13152	n.a.
U.K.	0.07644	0.07614	0.09389	0.10332
France	0.07611	0.07587	0.09339	0.10278
Italy	0.07469	0.07475	0.09121	0.10041
Spain	0.05491	0.05670	0.06313	0.06798
Poland	0.05429	0.05602	0.06203	0.06694
Romania	0.03786	n.a.	0.03664	n.a.
Netherlands	0.03052	0.03715	0.02701	0.03440
Greece	0.02495	0.03304	0.01991	0.02721
Czech Rep.	0.02474	0.03287	0.01964	0.02693
Belgium	0.02463	0.03279	0.01950	0.02680
Hungary	0.02453	0.03271	0.01936	0.02666
Portugal	0.02442	0.03262	0.01922	0.02651
Sweden	0.02314	0.03162	0.01758	0.02489
Bulgaria	0.02250	n.a.	0.01676	n.a.
Austria	0.02239	0.03103	0.01663	0.02403
Slovakia	0.01940	0.02870	0.01288	0.02000
Denmark	0.01940	0.02870	0.01288	0.02000
Finland	0.01918	0.02854	0.01261	0.01975
Croatia	0.01886	n.a.	0.01221	n.a.
Ireland	0.01768	0.02737	0.01077	0.01785
Lithuania	0.01768	0.02737	0.01077	0.01785
Latvia	0.01628	0.02630	0.00905	0.01631
Slovenia	0.01585	0.02598	0.00853	0.01568
Estonia	0.01521	0.02547	0.00774	0.01487
Cyprus	0.01445	0.02490	0.00680	0.01384
Luxembourg	0.01413	0.02465	0.00641	0.01342
Malta	0.01413	0.02465	0.00641	0.01342

n.a. Not applicable.
Source: Authors' calculations.

TABLE 13.2   Power Indices under Nice Treaty Rules

Member State	NBI_EU29	NBI_EU25	SSI_EU29	SSI_EU25
Germany	0.07189	0.08630	0.07814	0.09292
Turkey	0.07189	n.a.	0.07814	n.a.
U.K.	0.07189	0.08630	0.07814	0.09292
France	0.07189	0.08630	0.07814	0.09292
Italy	0.07189	0.08630	0.07814	0.09292
Spain	0.06821	0.08159	0.07237	0.08613
Poland	0.06821	0.08159	0.07237	0.08613
Romania	0.03832	n.a.	0.03615	n.a.
Netherlands	0.03565	0.04195	0.03340	0.03983
Greece	0.03305	0.03881	0.03082	0.03648
Czech Rep.	0.03305	0.03881	0.03082	0.03648

TABLE 13.2   (Continued)

Member State	NBI_EU29	NBI_EU25	SSI_EU29	SSI_EU25
Belgium	0.03305	0.03881	0.03082	0.03648
Hungary	0.03305	0.03881	0.03082	0.03648
Portugal	0.03305	0.03881	0.03082	0.03648
Sweden	0.02771	0.03246	0.02560	0.03024
Bulgaria	0.02771	n.a.	0.02560	n.a.
Austria	0.02771	0.03246	0.02560	0.03024
Slovakia	0.01954	0.02291	0.01777	0.02099
Denmark	0.01954	0.02291	0.01777	0.02099
Finland	0.01954	0.02291	0.01777	0.02099
Croatia	0.01954	n.a.	0.01777	n.a.
Ireland	0.01954	0.02291	0.01777	0.02099
Lithuania	0.01954	0.02291	0.01777	0.02099
Latvia	0.01124	0.01324	0.00999	0.01190
Slovenia	0.01124	0.01324	0.00999	0.01190
Estonia	0.01124	0.01324	0.00999	0.01190
Cyprus	0.01124	0.01324	0.00999	0.01190
Luxembourg	0.01124	0.01324	0.00999	0.01190
Malta	0.00841	0.00998	0.00755	0.00895

n.a. Not applicable.
Source: Authors' calculations.

Notes

1. Legally, the Accession Treaty for the 10 new member states in 2004 implemented the voting system agreed on politically in the Treaty of Nice. The voting rules of the Constitutional Treaty will come into force on November 1, 2009, if it is ratified by all member states.

2. This chapter draws on the methodology and results described in Baldwin and Widgrén (2003a, 2004a, 2004b).

3. EU15 refers to the 15 members of the EU prior to the 2004 enlargement in which 10 more countries joined the EU. The 15 countries are Austria, Belgium, Denmark, Finland, France, Germany, Greece, Ireland, Italy, Luxembourg, the Netherlands, Portugal, Spain, Sweden, and the United Kingdom.

4. The rules that took effect in November 2004 were not those agreed on at the Nice summit in December 2000. The deal struck at 4 a.m. at the end of the longest EU summit in history was a political commitment. The legally binding changes are in the Accession Treaty. Because EU leaders eventually realized how inefficient the Nice rules were, they improved efficiency by lowering the vote threshold from the 74 percent mentioned in the Nice Treaty.

5. In the literature, the term *swing* is quite often used instead of *break*.

6. See, for example, Widgrén (1994), Laruelle and Widgrén (1998), and Laruelle and Valenciano (2004). A recent empirical application of the SSI can be found in Kauppi and Widgrén (2004).

7. Note that in EU28 (EU27 + Turkey), the passage probability is 11.2 percent, which is lower than it is in EU29 (see Baldwin and Widgrén 2003b). The reason is that the membership quota—55 percent of membership—is 16 in both EU28 and EU29. It is thus closer to 55 percent in EU29 than in EU28—the exact numbers are 55.2 percent and 57.1 percent, respectively.

8. This phenomenon is often referred to as the paradox of new members.

References

Baldwin, R., and M. Widgrén. 2003a. "Decision-Making and the Constitutional Treaty: Will the IGC Discard Giscard?" CEPS Policy Brief No. 37, Center for European Policy Studies, Brussels.

———. 2003b. "The Draft Constitutional Treaty's Voting Reform Dilemma?" CEPS Policy Brief No. 44, Center for European Policy Studies, Brussels.

———. 2004a. "Winners and Losers under Various Dual Majority Rules for the EU Council of Ministers." In *Reasoned Choices—Essays in Honor of Academy Professor Hannu Nurmi on the Occasion of His 60th Birthday*, ed. M. Wiberg. Helsinki: Finnish Political Science Association.

———. 2004b. "Council Voting in the Constitutional Treaty: Devil in the Details." CEPS Policy Brief No. 53, Center for European Policy Studies, Brussels.

Baldwin, Richard, Erik Berglöf, Francesco Giavazzi, and Mika Widgrén. 2001. "Nice Try: Should the Treaty of Nice Be Ratified?" *Monitoring European Integration 11.* London: Centre for Economic Policy Research.

Kauppi, H., and M. Widgrén. 2004. "What Determines EU Decision-Making: Needs, Power or Both. *Economic Policy* 39: 221–66.

Laruelle, A., and F. Valenciano. 2004. "Bargaining in Committees of Representatives: The Optimal Voting Rule." Discussion Paper 45/2004, Departamento de Economía Aplicada IV, Basque Country University, Bilbao, Spain.

Laruelle, A., and M. Widgrén. 1998. "Is the Allocation of Voting Power among EU States Fair?" *Public Choice* 94: 3–4, 317–39.

Widgrén, M. 1994. "Voting Power in the EU and the Consequences of Two Different Enlargements." *European Economic Review* 38: 1153–70.

14

ECONOMIC EFFECTS OF TURKEY'S MEMBERSHIP ON THE EUROPEAN UNION

Harry Flam

From the perspective of the European Union (EU), which is considering the economic consequences of accepting Turkey as a member, the most important facts about Turkey are its size and its low per capita income.[1]

With a population of almost 70 million, Turkey would, in terms of today's population figures, become the second largest member of the EU. However, the population of Turkey is relatively young, and it is likely to exceed Germany's 82 million by 2020, if not earlier.

By comparison with the European countries, Turkey is poor. It has a PPP (purchasing power parity)-adjusted per capita income of roughly US$7,000,[2] which is equal to those of Bulgaria and Romania, countries slated to join the EU in 2007. The income disparities across Turkey are great; the population in the southeast has less than half the national average income, and the large rural population is generally much poorer than the urban population. Turkey's relatively low level of development is evident in the share of the labor force in agriculture and in the sector's share in value added. Only Bulgaria and Romania have a similar dependence on agriculture.

The descriptive statistics suggest that the important economic effects of Turkey's accession to the EU should be related to its size, per capita income, and dependence on agriculture. For the EU, these three factors combine to create a huge immigration potential if migration is let free. Moreover, these factors indicate that Turkey may become the largest recipient of transfers from the EU budget, at least under the present rules and policies.

As for trade, Turkey's accession is not likely to have any significant trade effects, and consequently any significant effects for EU industry, for two reasons. First, Turkey is not an important trading partner of the EU countries, with the exception of Greece. (The EU is, however, Turkey's most important trading partner.) Second, Turkey has free commodity trade with the EU under a customs union, except for agricultural commodities. By the time Turkey becomes a member of the EU, the customs union will have been in effect for more than a decade.

Migration

The PPP-adjusted per capita income of the EU15[3] is four times higher than that of Turkey. Because Turkey has had about the same per capita growth rate as the EU15 since 1990, the probability that Turkey will catch up in the foreseeable future seems very low. The income differential will therefore continue to be a strong incentive for migration from Turkey to the EU. Turkish migration to Western Europe was particularly high in the 1960s, but it continues to be steady flow, particularly to Germany and, to a lesser extent, the Netherlands. In the 1950s and 1960s, many of the present EU countries actively recruited foreign labor, but that recruitment ended after the first oil crisis in 1973–74. Since then, immigration policies have become successively more restrictive, and immigrants have mostly consisted of relatives of former immigrants, refugees, and asylum seekers. Most migrants from Turkey have ended up in Germany, which has a population of Turkish origin of 2.1 million. The second largest recipient has been the Netherlands, which has 250,000 immigrants and their descendants from Turkey.

The prospect of large-scale immigration from Turkey is a source of considerable concern among the EU15; they fear immigrants will depress wages, boost unemployment, and cause social frictions and political upheavals. Free migration will surely not be allowed immediately upon full membership. After the enlargement in the 1980s and the latest enlargement in 2004, old member countries were allowed to restrict immigration from new member countries for a period of seven years. It can therefore be safely assumed that immigration from Turkey will be subject to restrictions for several years.

Migration Theory

The effects of migration from Turkey to any of the EU15 member states are illustrated in figure 14.1. The horizontal axis measures the total supply of labor in Turkey and, say, Germany. The simplified approach used here first assumes that labor is a homogeneous factor of production. Later, labor is

FIGURE 14.1 Effects of Migration

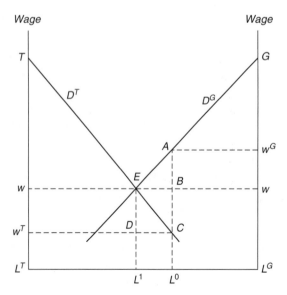

Source: The author.

differentiated by education, training and experience. The demand for labor by employers in Turkey is shown by the demand curve D^T. Likewise, the demand for labor in Germany is shown by the demand curve D^G. The total supply of labor in Germany and Turkey is assumed to be fixed. Initially, the total supply is divided so that the supply of labor in Turkey is measured by the length of the line segment $L^T L^0$ and the supply of labor in Germany by the length of the line segment $L^G L^0$. The supply of labor in each country is assumed to be inelastic. Before migration is allowed, the equilibrium wage in Germany is w^G, which is much higher than the equilibrium wage in Turkey, w^T.

When free migration is allowed, labor will move from Turkey to Germany to earn the higher wage. Migration stops when the wage is equalized between the two countries, at w, and when $L^1 L^0$ of the labor force has moved from Turkey to Germany. Thus one effect of migration is that it raises the wage in the sending country and reduces the wage in the receiving country. Migrants as well as those remaining in Turkey gain, while German workers lose. The effects for capital owners are the opposite; Turkish capital owners now earn the surplus TwE instead of $Tw^T C$, and German capital owners earn $Gw^G A$. (It is assumed that capital does not migrate in response to earnings differences.) The fact that part of the labor force has moved from Turkey to Germany also means a decline in the Turkish gross domestic product (GDP) and a rise in the German GDP. All these changes amount to an increase in the combined social surplus or welfare. The increase is given by the area ACE, and it is captured by German capital owners and Turkish migrants. The welfare increase stems from a more efficient allocation of labor; Turkish laborers become more efficient when moved to Germany, and the optimal allocation is achieved when the marginal productivity of labor in Germany and that in Turkey are equalized.

Figure 14.1 provides a simplistic but powerful analysis of the income, redistribution, output, and welfare effects of migration. It builds on the assumption that migration is entirely driven by a wage differential and that no unemployment exists. Unemployment can be easily added to the model. Assume that before migration is allowed, $L^1 L^0$ of the Turkish labor force is unemployed. Those employed now earn a higher wage—w instead of w^T.

Assume also that employment is decided periodically by a lottery. Thus the expected wage (the actual wage w times the probability of winning employment) is lower than the actual wage and lies somewhere between w and w^T. The expected wage in Turkey is still below the certain wage w^G in Germany. Consequently, labor will migrate to Germany once migration is allowed. Assume that all the unemployed in Turkey migrate to Germany, that those who remain are employed, and that some fraction of the larger labor force in Germany cannot be employed because of a lack of new investment. Employment in Germany is also decided periodically by a lottery, in which German and Turkish workers have equal probabilities of winning. The expected wage therefore falls below w^G, but not all the way to w. Thus in the new equilibrium, both the actual and the expected wage are higher in Germany than the actual wage in Turkey. The expected wage can be higher in Germany because workers attach a negative value to the risk of becoming unemployed and demand a higher expected wage to compensate for the risk. The analysis here captures an idea first expressed in a model by Harris and Todaro (1970) of rural to urban migration in a developing country.

Turkish migration can, then, serve both to depress wages in the receiving country and to raise unemployment. Changes in the assumptions made, such as allowing employment to increase in Germany or letting immigrant Turkish workers have a higher risk of becoming unemployed than native German workers, would not change the basic conclusions. One assumption in the analysis is questionable, however—that labor is homogeneous. In reality, labor is highly differentiated by education, training, experience, and many other characteristics. Thus there are not just two factors of production—labor and capital; there are many types of labor and many types of capital. As soon as three factors or more are allowed for, the effects of migration on income distribution and social welfare become less clear-cut (see Borjas 1995). In general, its effects on native labor and capital become more favorable when immigrants are complements to rather than substitutes for the native factors. For example, if German workers are skilled and Turkish immigrants are unskilled, then immigrants tend to increase the productivity and wages of German workers. Likewise, the increase in social surplus

from migration tends to rise the more complementary migrants and native workers are. In terms of figure 14.1, a smaller substitutability between labor and capital means that the demand curves become steeper and the size of the surplus triangles becomes greater (up to a point).

The decision to migrate depends not only on relative wages and unemployment, but also on many other factors. The early theoretical research (e.g., Berry and Soligo 1969) focused on income differentials and individual decisions. Recent research stresses that migration is a household decision and that social networks, culture, language, geographical distance, and other factors are also important. For example, the adjustment cost for a migrant depends on the size of the migrant population from the same source country in the receiving country and on language and cultural differences. Turks are attracted to Germany in part because of the large Turkish immigrant population there, and Algerians are attracted to France partly because of their knowledge of French and familiarity with French culture (for a survey, see Ghatak, Levine, and Wheatley Price 1996).

Empirical Research Findings

Empirical research on immigration has focused largely on two questions (Borjas 1994). First, how do immigrants perform in the host country? Second, what is the impact of immigration on the wages and employment of natives? Most of the research has been carried out on the United States, and it is therefore not fully relevant for Europe. In the past, immigration to the United States has been more permanent in nature than immigration in Europe, and permanence has an impact on the performance of immigrants. Furthermore, European labor markets are generally considered to be more rigid than those in the United States because of their stronger labor unions, more regulation, and immigration policies.

The recent wave of immigration in the United States differs from past waves by the markedly lower level of education of immigrants compared with that of natives. Whereas earlier immigrants reached the income and employment levels of natives fairly soon, later immigrants do not. Moreover, there is a high correlation between first- and second-generation immigrants in terms of educational attainment, and therefore a high probability that the second generation, too, will fall behind (Borjas 1994). These findings for the United States may be applicable to Europe and, in particular, to immigration from Turkey, which mostly consists of people from rural areas with low levels of education.

There is little evidence that immigration has a significant negative effect on the employment opportunities of natives, either in the United States or in Europe. There is, however, some evidence of small negative effects on the wage of unskilled labor in both. A positive effect on the wage of skilled labor has been found in Germany, which can be expected when unskilled immigrants are complements to skilled native workers.[4]

A third question that has been the subject of some research and has received much attention from policymakers and the general public is whether immigrants are net recipients of or net contributors to the public coffer. The problem with earlier studies is that they focus on a single year, neglecting the cost and expenditures for an immigrant later in life, such as pensions, and they do not consider some general equilibrium interactions, such as that between immigrants and an aging population. The studies by Auerbach and Oreopoulos (1999) and Storesletten (2000) for the United States take a dynamic, life-cycle approach with partial or general equilibrium interactions. They find negative, but relatively small, fiscal effects for low-skilled immigration. Storesletten estimates the average net present value of a representative low-skilled legal immigrant to be −$36,000. A high-skilled immigrant, by contrast, contributes $96,000 over his or her lifetime. A study of Germany by Bonin (2001) finds a significant positive effect for the average immigrant over his or her life cycle; net immigration of 200,000 persons to Germany is estimated to yield natives €200 per capita per year. The positive effect stems from the fact that the average immigrant has a younger working age and thus is obliged to participate in the repayment of the existing government debt. The fiscal impact of immigration is bound to differ among European countries, depending on the structure and level of taxes and benefits.

The relatively scant empirical research on the economic effects of immigration to Germany, host to the largest immigrant population among the EU15 and the largest population of Turkish immi-

grants by far, seems to indicate fairly small and mixed effects: employment opportunities are not much affected; the wage of low-skilled labor is somewhat depressed but that of skilled labor is raised; and the net present value of public transfers is positive. It is more difficult to evaluate the social costs and benefits of immigration. Immigrant ghettos with high unemployment, crime rates, and social problems loom large in the minds of the native population in many countries, although the immediate costs are mostly borne by the immigrants themselves.

Estimated Model of Migration to Germany from Southern Europe

The forecast of free Turkish migration to Germany presented in this section is based on an estimated model of immigration to Germany from the EU15, Norway, Turkey, the United States, and former Yugoslavia by Boeri and Brücker (2000) in a report to the European Commission. The choice of Germany is dictated by the facts: first, Germany is home to the largest population of Turkish immigrants among the EU15 countries by far, and it can therefore be expected to attract the largest numbers of future immigrants; and second, there is a paucity of data on migration flows and stocks before the 1990s for most of the EU15 countries.

Boeri and Brücker estimated how the flow of migration depends on the wage differential, employment rates in the home and host countries, the stock of migrants from the home country, restrictions on migration, and country specifics, such as language differences, distance, and institutions. The migration decision is assumed to be dependent on expectations about the following factors: the future wage differential, based on present and past values of the differential, conditioned by the individual probability of finding employment in the host country relative to the home country, which is assumed to be based on present and past average employment rates; the ease of adjustment, proxied by the number of migrants in the host country; the difference in development between the home and host country and language differences; and the agreements regulating migration, such as guest worker agreements. Migration flows are viewed as short-run adjustments to a long-run equilibrium in which migration has ceased and the migrant population relative to the source country population has attained an equilibrium level dependent on the wage differential, the employment rate differential, restrictions on migration, and country-specific factors. The long-run equilibrium is also estimated, thereby producing long-run relations between the ratio of migrants to the source country population and the explanatory variables.[5] The existence of a long-run equilibrium builds on the assumption that the propensity to migrate has a certain distribution over individuals in the home country; the equilibrium is reached when those with the highest propensity have emigrated for the given long-run values of the explanatory variables and those remaining do not find emigration worthwhile.[6]

As expected, the migrant population as a proportion of the source country population is in the long run positively related to the income differential between the receiving and the source country, the employment rate in the receiving country, and free migration and guest worker agreements, and is negatively related to the employment rate in the source country.

Forecast of Migration from Turkey to Germany

Boeri and Brücker's estimates are used here to forecast free migration from Turkey to Germany from 2000 to 2030. Making such a forecast requires assumptions about population and GDP growth rates and employment rates for the whole period. Population growth is based on forecasts by the World Bank in its World Development Indicators database. It is assumed that the employment rates in 2000 remain constant during the period under consideration. German GDP growth is assumed to be the average for 1990–2000. The GDP and population growth rates yield a GDP per capita growth rate of 1.7 percent. For Turkey, a higher GDP growth rate is assumed. The forecasts are based on the admittedly optimistic assumption that, alternatively, 1, 2, or 3 percent of the per capita income gap is closed every year. This assumption means, in turn, that GDP per capita in Turkey is assumed to grow at (a very high) 9, 12, or 15 percent at the beginning of the period and at about 3 percent at the end. The assumption of a 2 percent yearly reduction of the per capita income gap implies an average GDP per capita growth rate of 5.5 percent.

FIGURE 14.2 Forecast of Turkish Immigrant Population in Germany, 2000–30

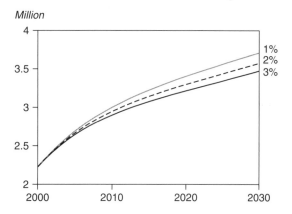

Note: Figure shows forecasts for a 1, 2, and 3 percent convergence rate of per capita income between Germany and Turkey.

Source: Author's calculations based on Boeri and Brücker 2000.

This rate can be compared with the average GDP per capita growth rate of about 3 percent over the last five decades.

The results of the forecast are shown in figure 14.2. In the figure, the Turkish immigrant population starts out at about 2.2 million in 2000 and reaches about 3.5 million in 2030 under the assumption that no restrictions are placed on migration. This forecast, however, is highly uncertain. It depends on the specification of the migration model, the precision of the estimates, and heroic assumptions about GDP and population growth rates. Furthermore, it is assumed that estimates made for a group of countries can be applied to a different country pair and a different time period. If anything, the assumed rates of convergence may be overly optimistic, considering the fact that no convergence has taken place since 1990. The rate of migration is about 80,000 per year in the beginning of the forecast period, when little convergence has taken place. This finding implies that in the extreme case of no convergence, about 2.5 million Turks would migrate to Germany over a 30-year period compared with about 1.3 million in the case in which 2 percent of the income gap is closed every year.

Although forecasts of Turkish migration to all EU15 countries are desirable, lack of data makes it impossible to estimate the flow of migration along the lines of Boeri and Brücker for more than one or two countries. However, Germany is by far the most important target country of migration from Turkey, and it would dominate any estimate of immigration to the whole of the EU.

The EU Budgetary Effects of Turkey's Membership

The structure of the present system of EU revenue and expenditure is such that rich member states transfer resources to poor members, but the relation between income per capita and net transfer is far from straightforward.[7] Some rich countries give proportionately more than others, and some poor countries receive a disproportionate share of the transfer. The countries that joined the EU in 2004 and Turkey are all poor relative to the EU15. Much attention has therefore been given to the effects of EU enlargement on the EU budget, assuming that enlargement will be very costly for the EU15. The present net recipients from the EU budget fear that they will be the ones to bear a disproportionate share of the cost, and the net contributors fear that they will be required to raise their contributions.

The major items on the revenue and expenditure sides of the budget in 2002 are shown in table 14.1. Revenues are collected from three sources: member states' valued added tax (VAT) revenues, customs duties collected by member states, and a tax related to member states' gross national product (GNP).

The total contribution by a member state to the EU budget is, by decision, capped at an annual amount equal to 1.27 percent of GNP until 2006, when the present budget ends.

Expenditures have two main destinations: the Common Agricultural Policy (CAP) and Structural Operations, aimed at disadvantaged countries and regions. Until recently, the CAP focused on price supports. The prices of many agricultural products were kept above world market prices by purchasing excess supplies at administratively determined minimum prices and by protecting EU markets from low world market prices by imposing duties on imports. Excess supplies were disposed of at a loss in the EU and on the world market. Since 1993, the CAP has gradually shifted away from price support to income support. Prices in the EU have been reduced so that they are more in line with world market prices, and farmers are increasingly receiving support payments based on their holdings of land and animals. The CAP favors farmers and the main agricultural products—grains, sugar beet, dairy products, and beef—of the original EU6 (Belgium, Federal Republic of Germany, France, Italy, Luxembourg, and the Netherlands). Fruits, vegetables, poultry, and pork, important products of the newer, southern members, receive less or no support.

Structural Operations are based on criteria of underdevelopment and the structural disadvantages of particular regions and countries. Regional support is furnished through the EU's Structural

TABLE 14.1   EU Budget, 2002

	Revenues			Expenditures	
	Amount (€ millions)	Share (%)		Amount (€ millions)	Share (%)
Duties and levies	15,267	17.3	Agriculture	40,506	48.6
Value added tax	35,193	40.0	Structural operations	27,591	33.1
GNP	37,580	42.7	Internal policies	5,361	6.4
Correction[a]	−71		External expenditure	5,231	6.3
Total	87,969	100.0	Administrative		
Other revenue[b]	4,755		expenditure	4,643	5.6
Total	92,724		Total	83,331	100.0

a. Does not add up to zero because of exchange rate differences.
b. Consists of interest, surplus from previous years, fines, taxes on salaries of employees of European institutions, and so forth.
Source: European Commission 2001.

Funds. For example, to be eligible for support under the classification of Objective 1, a region must have a per capita income that is less than 75 percent of the EU average. About 55 percent of the Structural Operations expenditure falls under this classification. By construction, the Cohesion Fund is exclusively directed at Greece, Ireland, Portugal, and Spain. The Cohesion Fund expenditure is modest, or about 2 percent of the total budget, but it is important for the recipient countries.

Turkey's contributions to and receipts from the EU budget can be calculated by estimating the "tax base"—that is, VAT and tariff revenue and GNP—and the extent to which Turkish agriculture and regions are eligible for support from the CAP, Structural Funds, and Cohesion Fund. Such a calculation is likely to produce a large net transfer to Turkey, both because of the size of the agricultural sector and because Turkey is relatively poor. It is unlikely that the EU will accept Turkey as a member if this transfer proves to be very costly. Moreover, the enlargement in 2004 included countries with relatively large agricultural sectors that will put a heavy demand on the EU budget once the present transition period has come to an end. Negotiations are presently under way on the EU budget for 2007–13. It is expected that the EU15, which is a large net contributor to the budget, will try to modify the rules for contributions to and receipts from the budget in order to reduce the amount of redistribution from rich to poor member states.

Under past enlargements, rules were changed if an acceding country became a disproportionately large net contributor or was a disadvantaged recipient of CAP or Structural Funds support under the existing rules. For example, the United Kingdom has a relatively small agricultural sector and receives modest CAP support. After a long struggle, it won a permanent rebate—a "correction of budgetary imbalances"—on its contribution. Portugal and Spain also receive modest CAP funding, because their agriculture produces relatively little grain. After Portugal and Spain acceded to the EU, the member states decided to limit the aggregate CAP spending in favor of Structural Funds spending, which benefited both countries. The Cohesion Fund, established in 1993 ostensibly to help the poor members cope with the European Economic and Monetary Union (EMU), can be viewed as well as a form of compensation to Greece, Ireland, Portugal, and Spain. Austria, Finland, and Sweden do not have poor regions eligible for much support from the Structural Funds. Objective 6 of those funds (later included in Objective 1) was tailored for support to the northernmost parts of Finland and Sweden and the mountainous areas of Austria as compensation.

The present rules for contributions to and receipts from the EU budget favor poor countries, because contributions are more or less proportional to income per capita. Meanwhile, Structural Operations are targeted at poor countries and regions to raise their incomes relative to those of the richer countries and regions. The CAP has a bias toward temperate climates and therefore the richer members, but not enough to overturn the redistributive effects of Structural Operations. In the final instance, the rules in a future EU29 (i.e., an EU that includes Bulgaria, Croatia, Romania, and Turkey) will depend on whether the decision rules under the new Constitutional Treaty will come into force in 2009 and what strategy the countries that entered in 2004 and the four candidate countries are going to follow.

The old pre–Nice Treaty rules gave small countries much more voting power per capita than large countries (see chapter 13). This situation produced these extremes: Germany, with a population of 82 million, had 10 votes in the Council of Ministers, while Luxembourg, with a population of 400,000, had two, giving voters in Luxembourg 42 times the voting power of voters in Germany. The Nice Treaty rules modified the inequality, giving Luxembourg voters 22 times more weight than German voters. The Constitutional Treaty rules, which are supposed to take effect in 2009, do away with weighted voting and introduce a double majority rule: for a decision to pass, it has to be supported by 55 percent of EU members and 65 percent of the EU population. A coalition of the 14 countries that entered the EU in 2004 or will enter later would comprise 48 percent of EU members and 28 percent of the population. Thus such a coalition could be powerful and even decisive in a future EU that includes Turkey.[8]

The present redistribution of funds between member countries through the EU budget reflects the pre–Nice Treaty distribution of votes in the Council of Ministers. Calculation of the transfers to the countries that entered the EU in 2004 and to Turkey if these rules were unchanged would indicate what incentive the EU15 has to alter the rules in order to reduce the transfer of funds to the new members.

The contribution per capita to the EU budget is explained by regressing contribution per capita on GDP per capita, and the receipts per capita are explained by regressing receipts per capita on the number of Council votes per capita plus the level of development as defined by eligibility for Cohesion Fund status.[9] The results are shown in table 14.2.

The table reveals that GDP per capita alone can explain 78 percent of the variation in contributions per capita among the EU15. The estimated coefficient is highly significant. As for receipts per capita, the number of votes per capita and Cohesion Fund status can explain as much as 86 percent of the variation in the data. The effect of voting power is borderline significant (it is significant at the 10 percent confidence level, but not at the 5 percent confidence level), whereas the effect of Cohesion Fund status is highly significant.

The estimates in table 14.2 were then used to estimate the contributions and receipts of each new member country, plus Bulgaria, Romania, and Turkey, on the assumption that each country would receive a number of votes consistent with pre–Nice Treaty rules (table 14.3). The exact number of votes

that each country will have is, of course, somewhat uncertain, but it is known that each country will receive a number of votes equal to that of an EU15 country with a population of similar size. Whether a country will have Cohesion Fund status is also uncertain. The assumption is that all countries except Cyprus have such status.

TABLE 14.2   Estimates of EU Budget Contributions/Receipts Equations

	Receipts per Capita	Contributions per Capita
GNP per capita		0.008 (0.00)
Votes per capita	19.3 (0.067)	
Cohesion dummy[a]	629.9 (0.00)	
Adjusted R^2	0.86	0.78
No. of observations	30	15

Note: P values appear in parentheses. Receipts per capita are based on for 1999 and 2000 data, and contributions per capita are based on 2000 data.

a. Interacted with votes per capita.

Source: European Commission 2001.

TABLE 14.3   Estimated EU Budget Contributions and Receipts

	Population (millions)	GDP (€ billions)	Assumed Number of Votes	Cohesion Fund Status	Contribution per Capita (euros)	Total Contribution (€ millions)	Receipts per Capita (euros)	Total Receipts (€ millions)
Poland	38.7	174	8	1	90	3,472	297	11,505
Romania	22.4	39	6	1	67	1,499	337	7,544
Czech Rep.	10.3	55	5	1	96	992	477	4,917
Hungary	10.0	49	5	1	93	930	487	4,868
Bulgaria	8.2	13	4	1	65	536	479	3,927
Slovak Rep.	5.4	21	3	1	84	453	523	2,823
Lithuania	3.7	12	3	1	79	293	688	2,544
Latvia	2.4	8	3	1	79	190	971	2,331
Slovenia	2.0	19	3	1	133	266	1,133	2,266
Estonia	1.4	5	3	1	84	118	1,548	2,168
Cyprus	0.8	10	2	0	159	128	212	170
Malta	0.4	4	2	1	133	53	3,394	1,358
Turkey	65.3	215	10	1	80	5,200	263	17,152
Total						14,130		63,572

Source: World Bank 2001 and author's estimates.

The total net transfer to the 13 countries is quite large, €49 billion, which is more than half of the present budget of the EU15. Turkey would receive a net transfer of about €12 billion and Poland a net of about €8 billion. The smaller countries receive net transfers that are much larger per capita than those of the larger countries because of their greater voting power. The extreme cases are Malta and Turkey, with net transfers of €3,400 and €263 per capita, respectively.

It is clear that balancing the EU budget will require changes in the EU budget rules and in the CAP. The calculations in table 14.3 assume full CAP subsidies to the new members, but, at present, the countries that entered in 2004 receive 25 percent of CAP subsidies. Such changes must take effect before the new members are eligible for full CAP and Structural Operations support. (The latter are more redistributive than the CAP.)

Trade

Commodity trade between Turkey and the EU has been practically free since the late 1990s, except for agricultural commodities. The pattern of trade is not expected to change substantially as a result of full EU membership for Turkey, but the *volume* of trade could increase considerably. The 2004 entrants have experienced substantial increases in trade volumes as a result of large investments by firms from Western Europe and elsewhere, which combine their technical, managerial, and marketing assets with a generally well-educated and skilled labor force at low wages. Turkey has a long way to go before it can hope to attract the same level of foreign direct investment (FDI) as some of the more successful countries in Central and Eastern Europe. For example, Turkey attracted $15 in foreign direct investment per capita in 2000 compared with Poland's $256 per capita. FDI in Turkey is hampered by political and economic uncertainty, bureaucracy, detailed regulation, and—by rumor—corruption. Indeed, according to UNCTAD (2002), Turkey has one of the lowest rankings in terms of FDI potential and performance. EU membership and adoption of the *acquis communautaire* will go some way toward establishing a better investment climate, which, in turn, should lead to higher volumes of trade.

What follows is a forecast of the volume of trade between Turkey and the EU15 under the assumption that trade will reach the same level of intensity as trade between the EU member states at present. The forecast is based on estimation of a gravity equation for trade within the EU15.[10] In the gravity equation, the trade between a pair of countries is explained by the size of their GDP and their GDP per capita, as well as the geographical distance between them and whether they share a common land border. GDP captures the effect of country size; a large country typically has more trade than a smaller country. GDP per capita is a measure of product differentiation and specialization. The higher the per capita income, the more differentiated are taste and production, and the larger is the volume of trade based on product differentiation and increasing returns to scale. A high per capita income is also an indication of abundance of physical and human capital relative to manual labor. Thus the per capita variable should serve to capture both intraindustry trade caused by product differentiation and increasing returns to scale and interindustry trade caused by differences in factor endowments. Trade costs are controlled for by the inclusion of geographical distance and a common land border. Geographical distance is an indicator of transportation costs, but also of the costs of cultural differences, which tend to increase with geographical distance. Finally, a common land border is considered to have a level effect on the volume of trade. The ordinary least squares (OLS) estimates of the gravity equation are presented in table 14.4.

In the column OLS (1), the estimated coefficient on GDP per capita has an unexpected negative sign. Leaving out distance as an explanatory variable in the specification OLS (2) yields the expected positive sign. Apparently, the effects of GDP per capita and distance are confounded in the original specification because of a high positive correlation between distance and differences in GDP per capita; the poorest countries are on the periphery of Europe. (The correlation between distance and the log of the product of GDP per capita is –0.51.)

The OLS (1) estimates were then used to forecast the bilateral trade of each of the 2004 entrants and Turkey with the EU15, notwithstanding the negative sign on GDP per capita. For one thing, distance is a more important factor between the candidate countries and the EU15 than between the EU15 countries and should therefore be included. Second, both

TABLE 14.4 Pooled Panel Gravity Estimates for Intra-EU15 Trade

	OLS (1)	OLS (2)
Log real product GDP	0.8577	0.8818
	(0.0098)	(0.0120)
Log real product GDP per capita	−0.2802	0.2439
	(0.0362)	(0.0384)
Log distance	−0.8819	
	(0.0326)	
Common border	0.4000	1.2557
	(0.0516)	(0.0673)
R^2-adjusted	0.9249	0.8797

Note: Estimates are based on 1,155 observations, annual data for 15 countries, 1990–2000. Intercept and year controls are not recorded. Standard errors are in parentheses. All estimates are significant at less than 1 percent.

Sources: GDP and population: OECD 2001; trade: OECD Monthly Statistics of International Trade, CD-ROM, June 2001; great circle distances between capitals: U.S. Department of Agriculture, http://www.wcrl.ars.usda.gov/cec/java/lat-long.htm.

specifications have about the same explanatory power. The results are presented in table 14.5. In the table, the forecast value of Turkish–EU15 trade is $26.3 billion in 2000, which is much higher than the actual value of $18 billion. Most of the 2004

entrants are also projected to increase their trade with the EU15, some of them considerably more than Turkey, and two countries—Estonia and Hungary—actually have higher actual trade than projected trade. However, the point estimates obtained with this forecast method are highly uncertain, as shown by the 95 percent confidence intervals for the point estimates.

Conclusion

Turkey's membership in the EU is not expected to have significant economic effects on the present EU members, with the possible exception of immigration and EU budget transfers. Turkey has a large population, a low level of income, and a large agricultural sector. These facts could stimulate substantial migration from Turkey to Germany and other West European countries and make Turkey a recipient of large transfers from the richer EU members.

Provided that migration from Turkey to the EU is free, it is estimated that about 1.3 million people would migrate to Germany—the country with the largest Turkish immigrant population—over a 30-year period and thus increase its population by 1.5 percent. However, this estimate is highly uncertain; it rests on heroic assumptions about relative growth rates and parameters in the estimating equation, among other things.

TABLE 14.5 Forecast of Trade with EU15

Country	Forecast, 2000 (€ billions)	95% Confidence Interval		Forecast/Actual Trade, 2000
		Lower Bound	Upper Bound	
Bulgaria	4.4	1.6	12.3	1.82
Czech Rep.	24.4	9.0	65.3	1.29
Estonia	1.8	0.7	5.1	0.69
Hungary	15.0	5.5	40.4	0.80
Lithuania	3.5	1.3	9.4	1.82
Latvia	2.5	1.0	6.7	1.59
Poland	42.0	15.6	112.8	1.75
Romania	10.4	3.9	28.4	1.63
Slovak Rep.	11.1	4.1	30.4	2.02
Slovenia	7.3	2.7	19.5	1.26
Turkey	26.3	10.5	76.3	1.46

Sources: GDP and population data: World Bank, World Development Indicators; trade: OECD Monthly Statistics of International Trade, CD-ROM, June 2001; great circle distances between capitals: U.S. Department of Agriculture, http://www.wcrl.ars.usda.gov/cec/java/lat-long.htm.

If present rules for contributions to and receipts from the EU budget were unchanged—including the Common Agricultural Policy—it is estimated that Turkey would receive a net transfer of €12 billion, which corresponds to about 14 percent of the present EU budget. The overall net contribution to the 2004 entrants and Turkey was projected to correspond to about 60 percent of the present budget. The EU budget for 2006–13 is now under negotiation. It is unlikely that present rules will not change in the face of such large increases in net transfers from richer to poorer countries.

Turkey has had free trade with the EU since the late 1990s, except in agricultural products. The pattern of trade should therefore not change as a result of membership, but there is the potential for a higher volume of trade should Turkey become more attractive for foreign direct investment. If the volume of trade between Turkey and the EU were to reach the same level as that of trade among the EU15—controlling for differences in income levels, geographical distance, and the absence of common land borders—it would be about 50 percent higher than at present, according to the estimates presented in this chapter.

Notes

1. The author is grateful for comments on earlier versions of this chapter by Refik Erzan and Sübidey Togan, for research assistance by José Mauricio Prado Jr., and for editorial work by Christina Lönnblad.

2. All dollar amounts are U.S. dollars unless otherwise indicated.

3. EU15 refers to the 15 members of the EU prior to the 2004 enlargement in which 10 more countries joined the EU. The 15 countries are Austria, Belgium, Denmark, Finland, France, Germany, Greece, Ireland, Italy, Luxembourg, the Netherlands, Portugal, Spain, Sweden, and the United Kingdom.

4. For the United States, see Friedberg and Hunt (1995); for Europe, see Zimmerman (1995); for Germany, see Haisken-De New and Zimmerman (1996); and for Germany and Austria, see Winter-Ebner and Zimmerman (1998).

5. Boeri and Brücker estimate an error-correction model. The assumptions and the model are described in detail in Boeri and Brücker (2000).

6. A common approach to explaining migration is to estimate a gravity equation. Yearly migration is explained by wage and employment rate differentials, distance, language, regulation, and the stock of earlier migrants in the host country—that is, much the same variables as in the present error-correction model. A problem with this approach is the long-run implication that the entire population will leave for a sufficiently large income differential. The error-correction model tests for the existence of a long-run equilibrium in which only a (small) part of the population has emigrated. Technically, it tests for co-integration between the variables. I estimated a gravity equation

of migration between Germany as the host country and Greece, Portugal, and Spain as the home countries with disappointing results—most of the coefficients were insignificant or very small. An examination of the time-series data makes it clear that other factors not accounted for, such as political developments, played a major role.

7. This section draws on the corresponding discussion in Baldwin, Francois, and Portes (1997).

8. In chapter 13 of this volume, Baldwin and Widgrén analyze various aspects of the different sets of rules for decision making in the EU.

9. This approach was taken in Baldwin, Francois, and Portes (1997).

10. A fixed-effects estimation is preferable, but it cannot be used to make out of sample forecasts. Standard versions of the gravity equation can be derived from all three basic trade models—that is, the Ricardian, Heckscher-Ohlin, and increasing returns to scale models, as well as from other models, as demonstrated by Anderson (1979), Bergstrand (1990), Deardorff (1998), and Helpman (1998). Recent research has sought to ascertain to what extent the various models contribute to the empirical success of the gravity equation and thereby to evaluate their empirical relevance—see Feenstra, Markusen, and Rose (2001) and Evenett and Keller (2002). A tentative conclusion is that models based on increasing returns and product differentiation are more successful in explaining intraindustry trade, whereas trade in homogeneous goods is better explained by differences in factor endowment or differentiation of goods by country of origin (Armington assumption).

References

Anderson, J. 1979. "A Theoretical Foundation for the Gravity Equation." *American Economic Review* 69: 106–16.

Auerbach, A., and P. Oreopoulos. 1999. "Analyzing the Fiscal Impact of U.S. Immigration." *AER Papers and Proceedings* 89: 176–80.

Baldwin, R., J. Francois, and R. Portes. 1997. "The Costs and Benefits of Eastern Enlargement: The Impact on the EU and Central Europe." *Economic Policy* 24: 127–76.

Bergstrand, J. 1990. "The Heckscher-Ohlin-Samuelson Model, the Linder Hypothesis and the Determinants of Bilateral Intra-industry Trade." *Economic Journal* 100: 1216–29.

Berry, R. A., and R. Soligo. 1969. "Some Welfare Effects of International Migration." *Journal of Political Economy* 77: 778–94.

Boeri, T., and H. Brücker. 2000. "The Impact of Eastern Enlargement on Employment and Labour Markets in the EU Member States." European Integration Consortium 2000, Berlin.

Bonin, H. 2001. "Fiskalische Effekte der Zuwanderung nach Deutschland: Eine Generationenbilanz." IZA Discussion Paper No. 305, Institute for the Study of Labor, Bonn.

Borjas, G. 1994. "The Economics of Immigration." *Journal of Economic Literature* 32: 1667–17.

———. 1995. "The Economic Benefits from Immigration." *Journal of Economic Perspectives* 9: 3–22.

Deardorff, A. 1998. "Determinants of Bilateral Trade: Does Gravity Work in a Neoclassical World?" In *The Regionalization of the World Economy*, ed. J. A. Frankel. Chicago: University of Chicago Press.

European Commission. 2001. "Allocation of 2000 EU Operating Expenditure by Member State." European Commission, Brussels.

Evenett, S. J., and W. Keller. 2002. "On Theories Explaining the Success of the Gravity Equation." *Journal of Political Economy* 110: 281–316.

Feenstra, R. C., J. A. Markusen, and A. K. Rose. 2001. "Using the Gravity Equation to Differentiate among Alternative Theories of Trade." *Canadian Journal of Economics* 34: 430–47.

Friedberg, R. M., and J. Hunt. 1995. "The Impact of Immigrants on Host Country Wages, Employment and Growth." *Journal of Economic Perspectives* 9: 23–44.

Ghatak, S., P. Levine, and S. Wheatley Price. 1996. "Migration Theories and Evidence: An Assessment." *Journal of Economic Surveys* 10: 159–98.

Haisken-De New, J., and K. F. Zimmerman. 1996. "Wage and Mobility Effects of Trade and Migration." CEPR Discussion Paper No. 1318, Centre for Economic Policy Research, London.

Harris, J., and M. Todaro. 1970. "Migration, Unemployment and Development: A Two-Sector Analysis." *American Economic Review* 60: 126–77.

Helpman, E. 1998. "The Structure of Foreign Trade." NBER Working Paper No. 6752, National Bureau of Economic Research, Cambridge, MA.

OECD (Organisation for Economic Co-operation and Development). 2001. *Economic Outlook No. 70.* Paris: OECD, December.

Storesletten, K. 2000. "Sustaining Fiscal Policy through Immigration." *Journal of Political Economy* 108: 300–23.

UNCTAD (United Nations Conference on Trade and Development). 2002. *World Investment Report 2002.* Geneva: UNCTAD.

Winter-Ebner, R., and K. F. Zimmerman. 1998. "East-West Trade and Migration: The Austro-German Case." IZA Discussion Paper No. 2, Institute for the Study of Labor, Bonn.

World Bank. 2001. *World Development Report 2000/2001: Attacking Poverty.* Washington, DC: Oxford University Press.

Zimmerman, Klaus. 1995. "Tackling the European Migration Problem." *Journal of Economic Perspectives* 9: 45–62.

INDEX

References to boxes, figures, tables, and notes are denoted respectively by b, f, n, and t.